FORENSIC ACCOUNTING

Robert J. Rufus
Rufus & Rufus Accounting Corporation, Huntington, WV
University of Charleston, WV

Laura Savory Miller
Rufus & Rufus Accounting Corporation, Huntington, WV
University of Charleston, WV

William Hahn
Southeastern University, Lakeland, FL

PEARSON

Boston Columbus Indianapolis New York San Francisco Upper Saddle River
Amsterdam Cape Town Dubai London Madrid Milan Munich Paris Montréal Toronto
Delhi Mexico City São Paulo Sydney Hong Kong Seoul Singapore Taipei Tokyo

Editor in Chief: Donna Battista
Acquisitions Editor: Lacey Vitetta
Sponsoring Editor: Nicole Sam
Editorial Project Managers: Christina Rumbaugh and Karen Kirincich
Editorial Assistants: Jane Avery and Lauren Zanedis
Director of Marketing: Maggie Moylan Leen
Marketing Manager: Alison Haskins
Managing Editor, Production: Jeff Holcomb
Production Project Manager: Carla Thompson
Procurement Specialist: Carol Melville
Senior Art Director: Anthony Gemmellaro
Cover Design: PreMediaGlobal
Interior Design: Anthony Gemmellaro
Cover Photos: pen, Yanas/Shutterstock; shredded paper, Tom Biegalski/Shutterstock
Full-Service Project Management/Composition: S4Carlisle Publishing Services
Printer/Binder: Courier Kendallville
Cover Printer: Lehigh-Phoenix Color/Hagerstown
Text Font: 10/12 Times

Credits and acknowledgments of material borrowed from other sources and reproduced, with permission, in this textbook appear on appropriate page within text or on page 418.

Cataloging-in-Publication Data is on file at the Library of Congress.

10 9 8 7 6 5 4 3 2 1

PEARSON

ISBN 13: 978-0-13-305047-9
ISBN 10: 0-13-305047-5

About the Authors

Dr. Robert J. Rufus is the Managing Principal of Rufus & Rufus Accounting Corporation located in Huntington, West Virginia, a boutique CPA firm with a concentrated practice in forensic accounting, tax, and litigation support. Dr. Rufus has more than thirty years of field experience as a forensic expert and investigative accountant in both civil and criminal matters. He started his professional career with the Treasury Department, where he worked as an IRS agent for five years. Dr. Rufus is currently the Program Director for the Master of Forensic Accounting program at the University of Charleston, West Virginia. He has also held instructor positions at Ohio University and Marshall University. Dr. Rufus has contributed to the science of forensic accounting through numerous journal publications and conference presentations. He received his B.S. from Concord College, his M.B.A. from Marshall University, and his D.B.A. from Nova Southeastern University, all with concentrations in Accounting. Dr. Rufus is a Certified Public Accountant, a Certified Valuation Analyst, Certified in Financial Forensics, and a licensed private investigator.

Laura Savory Miller is a forensic analyst at Rufus & Rufus Accounting Corporation in Huntington, West Virginia. Her areas of specialization include business valuations, quantitative methods, and calculations of economic damages. In her ten years with the firm, Ms. Miller has authored or coauthored hundreds of expert reports and has testified in several jurisdictions. Ms. Miller is also a lead instructor in the University of Charleston's Master of Forensic Accounting program and provides investment advisory services through Advanced Investment Strategies, Inc. Ms. Miller is a doctoral candidate (D.B.A. in Finance) at Nova Southeastern University in Fort Lauderdale, Florida, with an anticipated graduation date of May 2014. She received her B.S. in Finance from Marshall University and her M.A. in Economics from Ohio University. Her professional designations include Chartered Financial Analyst and Certified Valuation Analyst.

Dr. William Hahn is a professor of accounting at Southeastern University in Lakeland, Florida. Dr. Hahn has published frequently in refereed and banking journals and has presented at both academic conferences and CPA continuing education programs. Before entering the education profession, Dr. Hahn spent twenty years in the banking industry as both a CFO and COO for NASDAQ-traded companies. In his banking career, he managed accounting, investments, loan and deposit operations, computer operations, legal, facilities, and human resources. Prior to his banking career, he spent four years as an auditor with what is now Ernst & Young, CPAs. Dr. Hahn received his B.S. in Accounting from Ball State University, his M.B.A. in Finance from the University of Toledo, and his D.B.A. in Management and Accounting from Nova Southeastern University. He is a Certified Public Accountant licensed in Ohio.

Brief Contents

Contents

Preface

This text is the first to provide a comprehensive view of what forensic accountants actually do and how they do it. With experience as both practitioners and educators, we offer a unique perspective that bridges the gap between theory and practice. Our objective is to introduce students to the knowledge and skills required in the practice of forensic accounting. As emphasized throughout the text, the scope of forensic accounting services extends far beyond the realm of fraud investigation, which is commonly emphasized in academic settings. Despite the engagement-specific nature of the work, forensic accounting engagements share common elements such as gathering and analyzing evidence, interpreting and communicating findings, and applying specialized knowledge. The building-block structure of this text is designed to guide students through each component, in the context of real-world situations.

Although intended primarily for use in upper-level undergraduate or graduate courses, this text is also a valuable resource for new practitioners or even seasoned practitioners seeking a review of critical concepts.

FORENSIC ACCOUNTING KNOWLEDGE AND SKILLS

Consistent with the AICPA curriculum for the Certified in Financial Forensics (CFF) credential, this text highlights a three-layer skill set for forensic accountants:

1. core skills,
2. fundamental forensic knowledge, and
3. specialized forensic knowledge.

As illustrated, the center of the CFF Wheel is core skills. These skills, which are considered prerequisites for this text, include functional competencies in accounting, economics, and finance. Armed with core skills, students can use this text as a springboard for developing both fundamental and specialized forensic knowledge.

Focus of the CFF

CFF Holder

Bankruptcy, Insolvency, and Reorganization

Computer Forensic Analysis

Fundamental Forensic Knowledge

- Professional responsibilities and practice management
- Laws, courts, and dispute resolution
- Planning and preparation
- Information gathering and preservation (documents, interviews/interrogations, electronic data)
- Discovery
- Reporting, experts, and testimony (Durkin and Ueltzen, 2009)

Economic Damages Calculations

Family Law

CPA Core Skills

Financial Statement Misrepresentation

Valuation

Specialized Forensic Knowledge

Fraud Prevention, Detection, & Response

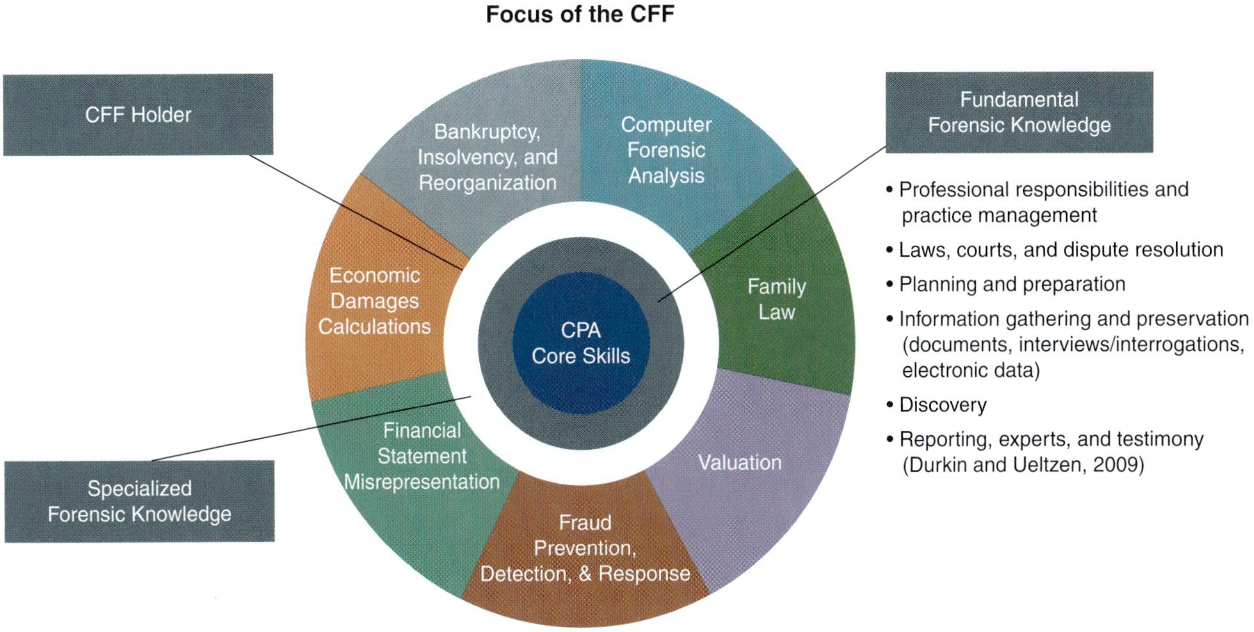

Source: From the *International Glossary of Business Valuation Terms*. Reprinted by permission of the American Institute of CPA's.

Areas of fundamental forensic knowledge include the legal environment, engagement planning, methods of analysis, report writing, and professional responsibilities. Specialized knowledge, in contrast, pertains to specific practice niches such as fraud, business valuation, family law, economic damages, bankruptcy, and computer forensics.

Fundamental Forensic Knowledge

Students begin the development of fundamental forensic knowledge in **Chapter 2**, with a comprehensive discussion of the legal environment of forensic accounting. This discussion includes a description of the anatomy of a trial, along with explanations of the key concepts of discovery, evidence, expert methodology, expert opinions, and attorney-client privilege.

Chapter 3 highlights the importance of screening and staging engagements, primary factors to consider before accepting an engagement, necessary elements of engagement letters, and considerations involved in framing a case. This chapter also explores a scientific approach to forensic accounting engagements and demonstrates the value of different forms of research.

Chapter 4 introduces students to interactive evidence, specifically evidence gathered through interviews and observations. Key learning objectives include an understanding of the communication process, the ability to implement the concept of active listening, and an appreciation of the significance of body language. Students also learn the different types of interviews, interview questions, and stages of an interview.

Chapter 5 discusses financial statements analysis in a forensic accounting context. This chapter is designed to challenge the assumed reliability of the financial reporting process. Part of this challenge involves looking beyond the numbers to the context of financial statements. In addition to basic analytical techniques, students learn the value of nonfinancial measures and the footnotes to financial statements.

In **Chapters 8 and 9**, the text transitions from gathering evidence to analyzing evidence. Analysis, along with interpretation, is necessary for the development of meaningful conclusions. **Chapter 8** explains how to frame the data analysis task and introduces various tools and techniques commonly used by forensic accountants. In **Chapter 9**, students learn analytic methods appropriate for large volumes of quantitative data. The operative focus, which extends to all areas of forensic accounting, is sufficient relevant data.

Although highlighted throughout the text, **Chapter 10** provides a focused discussion of the forensic accountant's specific professional responsibilities—to the client, the court, the profession, and the public.

Development of fundamental forensic knowledge concludes with **Chapter 12**. Section 12.1 introduces the concept of method of proof, highlighting the differences between direct and indirect methods of proof. Students learn about specific indirect methods of proof used by forensic accountants, circumstances in which they are used, and the respective strengths and weaknesses of each method. Section 12.4 addresses the report writing task, which is arguably the most critical element of the engagement process, representing the culmination of all preceding efforts. Although the form and content of any report is determined by the nature, scope, purpose, and terms of the specific engagement, students learn that forensic accountants must adhere to applicable judicial mandates and professional guidelines.

Specialized Forensic Knowledge

This text presents discussions of four areas of specialized knowledge: fraud (**Chapters 6 and 7**), business valuation (**Chapter 11**), economic damages (**Chapter 12**), and computer forensics (**Chapter 12**). Although limited in scope, these discussions equip students with a working knowledge of key issues in each specific area. According to recent AICPA surveys, and consistent with our professional experience, these areas comprise the vast majority of actual forensic accounting engagements.

UNIQUE FEATURES

A Case-Based Instructional Design

A unique feature of this text is its case-based instructional design, in which each chapter is accompanied by a case that highlights key issues addressed in the chapter. The cases are sometimes presented in their entirety at the beginning of the chapter and sometimes split into a prologue and epilogue. We make the cases an integral part of the text by including references throughout the body of each chapter and revisiting the cases in the end-of-chapter exercises. Also included in some of the end-of-chapter exercises are smaller cases that highlight specific applications.

Case-based instruction provides situational context that increases student understanding and facilitates the integration and application of diverse concepts. Moreover, the use of cases promotes critical thinking and active learning, providing students with the opportunity to recognize problems, make assessments, and define solutions. Such an approach is essential in the instruction of forensic accounting, given its context-specific nature. Unlike other sciences, forensic accounting does not address abstract problems. Rather, each engagement involves a unique purpose, situation, and cast of characters.

Because most of the cases used in this text are products of our professional experiences, they represent authentic scenarios that students can expect to encounter in their careers. Unlike hypothetical cases found in many texts, we present real narratives involving real people and consequences. The cases are comprehensive, providing the levels of breadth and depth necessary to facilitate meaningful analysis and discussion. Several of the case narratives include detailed accounts of trial proceedings, offering students an up-close perspective of forensic accounting in action. Moreover, records of some cases are available in the public domain, allowing students to exercise their research skills in gathering additional information.

The Scientific Approach

Another unique feature of this text is its emphasis on the scientific approach. The text advocates the scientific process as the most effective and efficient approach for gathering, synthesizing, and summarizing evidence—the basic functions of a forensic accounting engagement. Our experience as practitioners confirms the value of the scientific approach in bringing order and reasoning to forensic accounting engagements. Moreover, the approach enhances the credibility of a forensic accountant's analysis and conclusions, which is critical for expert witness testimony.

Using scientific methods introduced in **Chapter 3** and advocated throughout the text, students employ the scientific approach step by step in **Chapter 7** to complete their first forensic accounting assignment—a fraud investigation involving Mountain State Sporting Goods.

Special Elements

We incorporate a variety of special elements throughout the text, including:

- *Special notes* that provide greater detail or clarification
- *Working examples* that facilitate application and discussion
- Opportunities for students to *dig deeper* through independent exploration
- Challenges in which students apply reasoning skills to *think about it*
- *Cautions* that every forensic practitioner should consider
- *Practitioner's perspectives* through which the authors share insights gained through their experiences

Also included as exhibits and appendices to various chapters are examples of documents that forensic accountants commonly encounter in practice, such as a legal complaint, an engagement letter, interview transcripts, and financial statements. As with the cases, these are drawn from our professional experiences in actual cases.

End-of-Chapter Exercises

The end-of-chapter exercises provide several different types of learning opportunities for students. Short-answer **Chapter Questions** and **Multiple-Choice Questions** focus attention on key chapter concepts and terminology. **Workplace Application** projects are more abstract in nature, challenging students to apply key concepts and exercise critical thinking. Consistent with the scientific approach, **Chapter Problems** require students to independently explore the chapter content in more depth, thereby practicing a required skill of forensic accountants. Finally, each chapter includes (in the chapter interior or the end-of-chapter exercises) one or more **Cases** that require students to integrate several chapter learning objectives to analyze a problem and arrive at a solution. The **Workplace Applications**, **Chapter Problems**, and **Cases** also provide opportunities for students to enhance their skills in business writing, online research, and use of spreadsheet software.

SUPPLEMENTS FOR INSTRUCTORS AND STUDENTS

Instructor's Solutions Manual

Comprehensive solutions, prepared by the authors, are provided for all end-of-chapter material. The manual includes a chapter-by-chapter listing of problems correlated to each learning objective.

Test Item File

This is a ready-to-use bank of testing material that contains, for each chapter, a variety of types of questions. For ease of use, each question is linked to chapter objectives and also provides a suggested difficulty level.

TestGen

This testing software is designed to aid in creating custom tests in minutes. Features include question randomization, a point-and-drag interface, and extensive customizable settings.

PowerPoint Presentation

Complete PowerPoint presentations are provided for each chapter. Instructors may download and use each presentation as is or customize the slides. Each chapter's set of PowerPoints allows instructors to offer an interactive presentation using colorful graphics, outlines of chapter material, and graphical explanations of difficult topics. This supplement is available online at www.pearsonhighered.com/rufus.

Course Companion Web Site

This web site, www.pearsonhighered.com/rufus, provides additional resources for students and faculty, including links to articles cited in the text.

ACKNOWLEDGMENTS

We wish to thank the following reviewers whose feedback was helpful in developing this edition:

Richard G. Brody, University of New Mexico
Brent S. Daulton, West Virginia University
William Green, CFE
Jacquelyne L. Lewis, North Carolina Wesleyan College
Mike Seda, Pfeiffer University
Robert L. Taylor, Lees-McRae College
Tim Weiss, University of Northwestern Ohio

Dr. Robert J. Rufus
Laura Savory Miller
Dr. William Hahn

1 Introduction to the World of Forensic Accounting

INTRODUCTION

On April 23, 1930, the Chicago Crime Commission issued its first Public Enemies List. At the top of the list was Alphonse Capone (also known as "Big Al," "Scarface," and "Big Shot"), one of the most notorious gangsters in U.S. history. Unable to convict Capone of murder,* the U.S. Attorney's Office aggressively pursued criminal prosecution against him in an effort to "restore respect for federal laws" that had been eroded by the gangster class.[1] On March 13, 1931, a secret federal grand jury issued an indictment against Capone charging him with tax evasion for year 1924. Similar indictments for years 1925 through 1928 followed shortly thereafter. The Internal Revenue Service (IRS)† estimated Capone's annual gross earnings (from gambling, prostitution, and bootlegging) at more than $100 million.[2] *The government's challenge, however, was proving it.*

Capone maintained no bank accounts, kept no activity records, bought no property in his own name, conducted all his financial transactions in cash, and *never filed a tax return*. Moreover, Capone's reputation for violence created a strong disincentive for any potential informants. In the eyes of most, Capone was bigger than the government . . . and certainly more deadly.

Development of the case against Al Capone was assigned to IRS Special Agent Frank J. Wilson. Wilson's assignment was to find evidence that would persuade a jury *beyond a reasonable doubt* (the standard of proof for conviction in a criminal case) of Capone's guilt. The investigation included hundreds of witness

Learning Objectives

After completing this chapter, you should be able to:

LO1. Explain what forensic accounting is.

LO2. Identify common types of forensic accounting engagements.

LO3. Compare and contrast the role of the forensic accountant with the roles of transactional accountants and auditors.

LO4. Identify the necessary skills of forensic accountants.

LO5. Recognize major providers of forensic accounting certification and continuing education.

LO6. Identify potential careers in forensic accounting.

Al Capone

Source: www.fbi.gov

* The St. Valentine's Day Massacre of February 14, 1929, was ascribed to Capone, although Capone himself was in Florida on that date. Capone was also suspected of murdering Assistant State's Attorney W.H. McSwiggin on April 26, 1926.

† Then called the Bureau of Internal Revenue.

IRS Special Agent Frank Wilson

Source: www.life.com

interviews, wiretaps, and search raids, which failed to produce sufficient evidence. Near a point of hopelessness, Wilson took a second look at the evidence and discovered his first key witness—Leslie A. Shuway. Shuway, one of Capone's former gaming parlor cashiers, was a waterfall of information. He identified Capone as the principal owner of a gambling syndicate and confirmed amounts paid to Capone. He also identified other individuals (leads) who could provide additional evidence against Capone.

The testimonial evidence gathered by Wilson was compelling, but not convincing beyond a reasonable doubt. The government's challenge was to explain to the jury the complexities of accounting and tax in a manner that was not only persuasive, but could also withstand the test of cross-examination. Meeting this challenge head on, Wilson developed and presented to the jury a calculation of Capone's unreported taxable income using what he called the "net worth method."[‡] The underlying theory of this method is quite simple—you can't spend what you don't have. Wilson's analysis is summarized in Table 1-1.

Special Note

The net worth method, which is fully explained in Chapter 12, is an application of deductive reasoning. As discussed later in this chapter, deductive reasoning reaches a conclusion (unreported income) through underlying propositions (cash spent versus cash available). The advantages of deductive reasoning (and the net worth method) are its intuitive appeal—it "makes good sense"—and its ease of application in certain situations.

On October 18, 1931, Al Capone was convicted of tax evasion for years 1925 through 1927 and failure to file income tax returns for years 1928 and 1929. Shortly thereafter, he was sentenced to 11 years in federal prison, fined \$50,000, and charged \$7,692 for court costs, in addition to a tax loss of \$215,000 plus interest. On November 16, 1939, Capone was released after serving seven years, six months, and fifteen days. Capone lived the balance of his life in seclusion, never returning to gangland politics. He died on January 25, 1947.

Table 1-1 | Net Worth Calculation

Step	Action	Example Calculation*
1	Determine ending net worth.	$2.250m
2	Determine beginning net worth.	$1.125m
3	Calculate the change in net worth during the period.	$1.125m
4	Determine expenditures (consumption) during the period.	$ .500m
5	Calculate the sum of funds used for asset acquisitions and consumption.	$1.625m
6	Calculate the sum of reported income and other legitimate sources of funds. (Remember, Capone never filed tax returns.)	-0-
7	Calculate the difference between legitimate sources and uses of funds, which indicates unreported income.	$1.625m

* Numbers are for illustration purposes only.

‡ Also known as the net worth plus expenditures method.

Dig Deeper

In February 2008, the IRS released for public view records related to Al Capone's criminal investigation. Such a release is highly unusual because all federal tax records are confidential by law. The records were released due to their historical significance and interest to the public. Students are encouraged to the visit the IRS web site[§] to review copies of reports and letters that summarize the events and activities of the three-year investigation of Al Capone. Another information source is the FBI's Reading Room,[**] which provides historical documents related to famous cases such as Capone's.

Frank J. Wilson, who was rightfully credited[3] with bringing down Al Capone, is commonly recognized as the first forensic accountant. His net worth method was the first indirect method[††] to receive judicial approval,[4] and it continues to be used by IRS and FBI agents, as well as forensic accountants. Like Wilson, modern-day forensic accountants are often called upon to reconstruct missing or destroyed information, develop leads, interview witnesses, assist counsel in advancing (or challenging) the theory of a case, and communicate complex concepts to a jury. In addition to financial analysis, these diverse tasks require intellectual tools such as logic, reasoning, and intuition.

WHAT IS FORENSIC ACCOUNTING?

The term *forensic* is defined in *Black's Law Dictionary* as "used in or suitable to courts of law or public debate."[5] Extending this concept, we can define ***forensic accounting*** as the use of accounting theories, principles, or analyses in a legal action, often through expert witness testimony.

Other common definitions include the following:

- A discipline that deals with the relationship and application of financial facts to business problems, conducted in a legal setting.[6]
- A discipline that is focused on: (1) the prevention, detection, and investigation of both occupational fraud and financial statement fraud; and (2) the rendering of other litigation-support services.[7]
- The application of financial facts to legal situations.[8]

As will be explored throughout this text, forensic accounting involves the application of accounting, finance, economics, statistics, law, research, and investigative methods in the collection, analyses, and communication of findings. Given the adversarial nature of litigation, the role of a testifying forensic accountant is not suitable for everyone. Nonetheless, the unique skills of forensic accounting are valuable competencies that can easily be transferred to activities outside the courtroom.

The term *forensic accountant* was first used by Maurice Peloubet in 1946 in the *Journal of Accountancy*[9] to recognize and celebrate IRS Special Agent Frank J. Wilson as the man who brought down Capone. Peloubet identified Wilson's "mindset" as the difference between accountants and forensic accountants. What is a mindset? More importantly, what is the mindset of a forensic accountant?

The Mindset of the Forensic Accountant

Broadly speaking, a person's ***mindset*** is his or her mental state, which evolves from education, experience, prejudices, and so on.[10] Specifically, your mindset incorporates mental processes that dictate how you respond to situations or challenges. Activating one mindset instead of another may change your observations—what you see and how you see it,

---

[§] Can be accessed at http://www.irs.gov/foia/article/0,,id=179352,00.html

[**] Can be accessed at http://www.fbi.gov/foia/

[††] Indirect methods are necessary when, for whatever reason, books and records are inadequate to determine taxable income. As with Al Capone, indirect methods are often used against suspected recipients of illegal income. Other indirect methods include the bank deposits method, the expenditures method, and the reverse net worth method.

questions you ask, judgments you form, and decisions you make.[11] For example, auditors are prone to have a "same as last year" (or SALY) mindset, wherein they expect and accept findings consistent with prior years. A different mindset might start with the premise that something has changed, which requires a new assessment of risk and management.

Forensic accountants are both researchers and problem solvers. As such, they need to be intellectually curious. An intellectually curious individual possesses a restless mind—one that is never satisfied with his or her understanding of an issue, regardless of experience and expertise. Moreover, forensic accountants must have the instinct to explore problems that challenge conventional wisdom. Perhaps most importantly, they must be willing to question their own preexisting judgments and conclusions.

In addition to a curious mindset, forensic accountants must also embrace systemic thinking. For example, forensic accountants recognize that problems are not always attributable to negligence or misconduct. Instead, these problems may be indicators of broader systemic failures within an organization. Forensic accountants do not rush to judgment; they take a second look—and they look *beyond the numbers*!

Finally, forensic accountants must exercise a healthy dose of professional skepticism. This reflects a proactive, questioning mindset, where nothing is as it seems and "trust, but verify" is the general rule.

FORENSIC ACCOUNTING SERVICES

Forensic accountants are in major part defined by the nature of their work. Although most people equate forensic accounting with fraud, the scope of forensic accounting work is actually much broader. According to *Accounting Today's* survey of the top 100 CPA firms, the most common forensic services are business valuations, fraud investigations, and litigation support.[12] For the past sixteen years, these service categories have been offered by a majority of the respondent firms. The results of a 2011 American Institute of Certified Public Accountants survey, illustrated in Figure 1-1, indicate that business valuations are by far the most significant practice component.[13]

A distinctive feature of this text is its comprehensive view of the forensic accounting profession, providing a more accurate picture of what forensic accountants actually do. The largest practice components, as identified in Figure 1-1 (fraud, business valuations, and economic damages) are discussed in detail in Chapters 6, 7, 11, and 12.

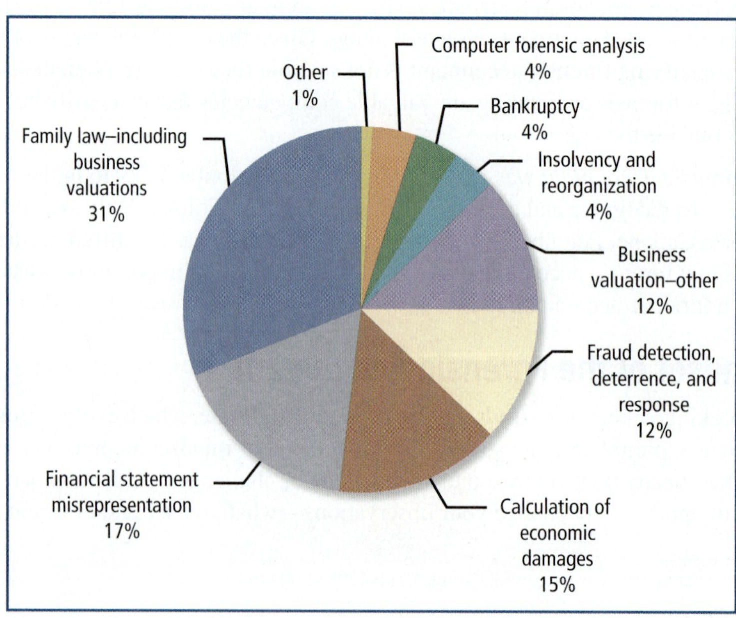

Figure 1-1
Forensic Accounting Practice Components

Source: AICPA 2011 Forensic and Valuation Services Trend Survey

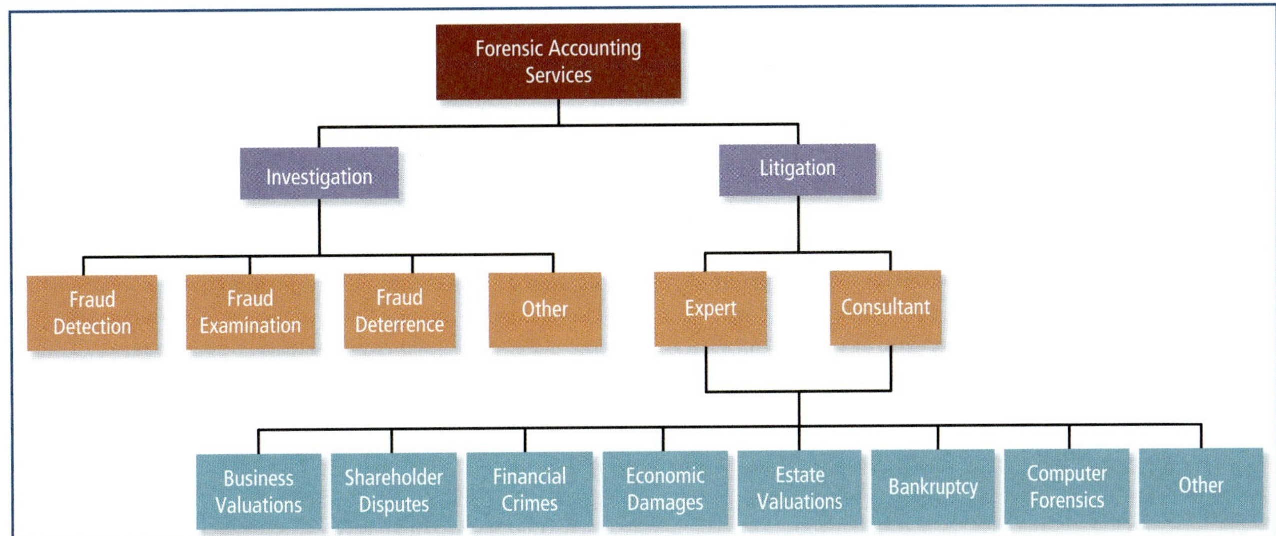

Figure 1-2
Categories of Forensic Accounting Services

As illustrated in Figure 1-2, forensic accounting services are commonly divided into two major components: investigative services and litigation services.

Special Note

The framework depicted in Figure 1-2 is advocated by the AICPA's Code of Professional Conduct (hereinafter the "Code"). In the context of the Code, this framework is intended to address independence in the performance of nonattest services (ET §101.05).[14] Although qualified in the Code as being limited in use (p. 1728, footnote 25), these categories have been embraced in practice.

As will be emphasized throughout this text, forensic accounting services are engagement-specific. Even so, all forensic accounting engagements share four common phases:

1. Defining the engagement—the "why"
2. Discovery—gathering evidence
3. Analysis—interpreting evidence
4. Communication—presenting evidence (opinions) orally or in writing

The remaining chapters of this text guide you through each of these phases within the context of investigative services and litigation services.

Investigative Services

As defined by the Code (ET §101.05, p. 1730), forensic accounting ***investigative services*** include all forensic accounting engagements that do not (at least at the outset) involve actual or threatened litigation. An investigation is defined as a systematic inquiry, search, or research to obtain facts regarding a specific or general concern or concerns.[15] Investigative services provided by forensic accountants are generally related to corporate investigations, which are initiated for the purpose of protecting the organization and its assets from internal or external threats (for example, employee fraud, misappropriation of assets, financial statement fraud, or corruption). Specific types of forensic accounting investigations include fraud detection, fraud examination, and fraud deterrence.

Fraud Detection

As the name implies, ***fraud detection*** is simply the discovery of fraud. Fraud detection includes a variety of strategies, such as internal control procedures, statistical analysis, financial statements analysis, and anonymous reporting channels (such as hotlines). Importantly, detective procedures are designed to identify an error or irregularity *after* it has occurred, whereas preventive procedures (discussed in a later section) are designed to discourage such occurrences *before* they happen. But *how* are frauds actually detected?

Fraud studies consistently identify tips as the most common source of fraud detection, thus highlighting the need for reporting channels. For example, a 2012 study by the Association of Certified Fraud Examiners (ACFE) reports that 43.3% of occupational frauds are detected by tips.[16] According to this same study, more than half of all tips (50.9%) come from employees, followed by customers (22.1%), anonymous sources (12.4%), and vendors (9%). A distant second source of fraud detection is management review (14.6%), followed by internal auditors (14.4%), and detection by accident (7%). Interestingly, the ACFE study reports that only 3.3% of occupational frauds are detected by external auditors. Thus, although auditors play an important role in fraud deterrence (discussed in the "Fraud Deterrence" section), they cannot be relied on to detect fraud.

Fraud Examination

A ***fraud examination*** is conducted *after* the fact, that is, in response to some indication of a crime. Its purpose is to investigate specific allegations or suspicions of fraud. The primary focus of a fraud examination is to determine the following elements of the fraud: *who* committed the fraud, *how* they committed it (the fraud scheme), *when* it was committed (time frame and duration), *how much* was taken, and *who else* was involved. The *why* (need or motive), although important to our overall understanding of fraud, is not the immediate challenge.

The forensic accountant employs a systematic and scientific approach in the discovery, analysis, and determination of alleged fraudulent activity. As highlighted throughout this text, a fraud examination is an evolutionary process that adjusts as new evidence is gathered and evaluated.

A forensic accountant may conduct the entire investigation from start to finish or may be retained to investigate only a specific component. In either situation, the forensic accountant commonly works together with other interested parties, including legal counsel, corporate security, internal and external auditors, and management representatives.

Special Note

An operative first step in a fraud investigation is to confirm the existence of an investigation policy and, if one exists, secure a copy to ensure compliance. An investigation policy identifies the process and interested parties and establishes investigative and reporting protocols. Such policies are designed to ensure that investigations are carried out promptly and in a fair and equitable manner to the individuals involved, allowing them an opportunity to respond to the matter under investigation. Moreover, investigation policies establish thresholds for identifying significant issues worth pursuing.

Fraud Deterrence

Fraud deterrence differs from fraud detection and fraud examination in that it describes *proactive* (rather than *reactive*) strategies. Such deterrence strategies include both short-term and long-term initiatives. Examples of short-term (or procedural) strategies include evaluation of hiring practices, internal controls, and performance monitoring. Because fraud requires individual actors (the offenders), a reasonable starting point for fraud deterrence is employee relations. Long-term strategies are more abstract in nature, addressing issues such as organizational culture and the tone set by top management (that is, "tone at the top").

Proactive employee strategies include preemployment screening, employee training, employee monitoring, perception of detection (through internal controls and external audits), and organizational culture. Aside from a policy of not hiring criminals, we contend that the most effective means of fraud deterrence is promoting the expectation (perception) among employees that wrongdoers will be caught and that punishment will be swift and appropriate for the offense.

Working Analogy

A simple analogy for explaining the distinction between detection, investigation, and deterrence is unhealthy weight gain.[17]

- Detection = identification of the specific health concern (that is, unhealthy weight gain)
    - In its early stages, weight gain can be detected by scales; as the problem progresses, it becomes more visibly noticeable.
- Investigation = identification of the factors that caused the weight gain
    - Potential explanations include changes in diet, alcohol consumption, sleeping patterns, stress, work, family, or exercise.
- Deterrence = addressing the causal factors
    - Mitigating strategies include improved diet (both food selection and consumption) and increased physical activity.

Other Investigations

In addition to the fraud-related investigations previously discussed, forensic accountants are commonly engaged to conduct investigations unrelated to fraud. Examples of such investigations include whistleblower complaints and financial viability concerns. A ***whistleblower complaint*** is a disclosure by a person (usually an employee) of wrongdoing or misconduct within the organization.[18] Usually, a forensic accountant is utilized when the allegation is considered serious (for example, involving senior management) or when the appearance of independence is important. ***Financial viability investigations*** include short- or long-term assessments of financial and managerial sustainability (related to concerns of customers, vendors, or investors) or the reasonableness of insurance claims (such as lost profits or business interruption).

Litigation Services

As defined by the Code (ET §101.05, pp. 1728–29), forensic accounting ***litigation services*** are provided in connection with actual, pending, or potential legal or regulatory proceedings—criminal or civil. These services are segregated into expert witness (testifying) services and consulting (nontestifying) services.

Expert Witness Services

All evidence in a trial is presented by witnesses. A witness, as defined by *Black's Law Dictionary*, is "one who gives testimony in a cause before a court."[19] There are two types of witnesses: *fact witnesses* and *expert witnesses*. As the name implies, a ***fact witness*** testifies about the facts—his or her firsthand knowledge about a fact in issue or person involved in the litigation. An ***expert witness***, on the other hand, is an individual with scientific, technical, or other specialized knowledge who is engaged to assist the "trier of fact" (a judge or jury) to understand the evidence or to determine a fact in issue. Importantly, expert witnesses differ from fact witnesses in that they can express *opinions*. As will be discussed in Chapter 2, an expert's opinion must be based on sufficient facts or data, be the product of reliable methodology, and be case-specific.

As emphasized throughout this text, forensic accountants providing expert witness services have a duty to the court, the public, and the profession to offer *objective* and *independent* opinions that will assist the trier of fact. This is no small task, given the adversary–advocacy nature of the field. These challenges and the forensic accountant's professional responsibilities are discussed in detail in Chapter 10.

Consulting Services

A forensic accountant may also be engaged by an attorney as a ***consulting expert***. In this role, unlike the role of a testifying expert, the consultant assists an attorney in advocating for the client. Consulting experts perform many of the same tasks as testifying experts, with the exception of offering expert testimony. Depending on the circumstances of the specific engagement, a consulting expert may serve only a peripheral role or may participate in several aspects of the case, including the development of key arguments.

FORENSIC ACCOUNTANTS VS. TRANSACTIONAL ACCOUNTANTS AND AUDITORS

Forensic accountants differ in many respects from transactional accountants and auditors. These differences flow primarily from their respective objectives. To enhance your understanding of forensic accounting, let's compare these roles.

Transactional Accountant

Accountants working for an organization employ generally accepted accounting principles (GAAP) to process information useful in decision making. The accounting process has three basic steps: recording, classifying, and summarizing. To facilitate this process, transactional accountants require core accounting skills. Most have undergraduate degrees in accounting, and many have one or more professional certifications, such as Certified Public Accountant (CPA), Certified Management Accountant (CMA), or Certified Internal Auditor (CIA).

Internal Auditor

Aside from management, the first line of defense against accounting failures within an organization is the internal auditor, whose responsibilities extend beyond the processing functions of a transactional accountant. The internal auditor's function is to report on the adequacy of internal controls, the accuracy and propriety of transactions, the extent to which assets are accounted for and safeguarded, and the level of compliance with a company's internal policies as well as external laws and regulations. This function exists to support the other three representatives of an organization: the board of directors (BOD), executive management, and the external auditor. In addition to core accounting skills, internal auditors must possess critical thinking, problem-solving, and communication skills.

External Auditor

External auditors, who work for CPA firms, are hired by organizations to evaluate their internal control systems and test their transactions and accounts to ensure that all economic events are recorded and reported in the proper accounting period. The purpose of the external auditor is to form and express an opinion as to whether the organization's financial statements, taken as a whole, reflect its financial position on a given date and the results of its operations for a given period. An unqualified (clean) opinion from the external auditor adds credibility to the organization and its financial statements. Skills required by external auditors are similar to those for internal auditors.

As summarized in Table 1-2, the objectives and processes of forensic accountants vary significantly from those of transactional accountants, internal auditors, and external auditors.

FORENSIC ACCOUNTING SKILLS

In 2009, Davis, Farrell, and Ogilby surveyed a mix of attorneys, CPAs, and academics to gain a better understanding of the dominant skills and characteristics of effective forensic accountants.[20] The diversity of the survey respondents is significant because it provides information from different points of view: attorneys (consumers of forensic accounting services), CPAs (providers of forensic accounting services), and academics (initial educators of forensic accountants). Three essential characteristics or skills identified in the study (and consistent with our experience) are critical thinking, reasoning, and communication.

Table 1-2 Comparative Analysis: Accountant, Auditors, and Forensic Accountant

	Transactional Accountant	Internal Auditor	External Auditor	Forensic Accountant
Timing	Day-to-day and month-to-month	Conducted according to a plan or because a deficiency has been identified	Conducted on a recurring basis	Conducted on an as-needed (nonrecurring) basis
Scope	Manage the organization's accounting and internal control system	Validate effectiveness of controls in various processes or areas of the organization	Examination of the financial data	Defined by the specific engagement
Objective	Capture and record all economic transactions of the organization	Ensure compliance with policy and procedures; offer recommendations for improvement of internal controls	Form an opinion on the overall financial statements taken as a whole	Address a specific question/issue
Purpose	Prepare financial statements for decision makers	Required by the BOD based on overall corporate risk assessment	Usually required by third-party users of financial statements	Defined by the specific engagement
Value	Information useful for decision-making purposes	Provides assurance that management is adequately identifying and mitigating risks	Adds credibility to reported financial information	Completion of stated engagement objective
Source of Evidence / Methodology	Original transactions for the acquisition and employment of assets, liabilities, equity, revenue, and expense in the conduct of business	Inquiry, observation, examination, and testing of processes	Inquiry, observation, examination, and reconstruction of accounting transactions to support financial statement representations	Review detailed financial and nonfinancial data, search public records, conduct interviews, and make observations
Sufficiency of Evidence	Reasonable assurance	Reasonable assurance	Reasonable assurance	Establish facts to support the conclusion/opinion
Audience	Management at all levels and the BOD	Executive management and the BOD	Serves the public interest, specifically investors and other stakeholders	Engaging party

Critical Thinking

As previously discussed, forensic accountants provide services in a variety of engagements. Most (if not all) involve ***critical thinking***. Commonly identified attributes of critical thinkers include:[21]

- Rational—Considers all known evidence in an unbiased manner
- Skeptical—Suspends judgment to allow proper consideration of evidence, context, and methodologies
- Reasonable—Measures behaviors and conclusions with sound judgment and common sense
- Well-informed—Possesses adequate and reliable information
- Open-minded—Free of bias and receptive to new information and ideas from others

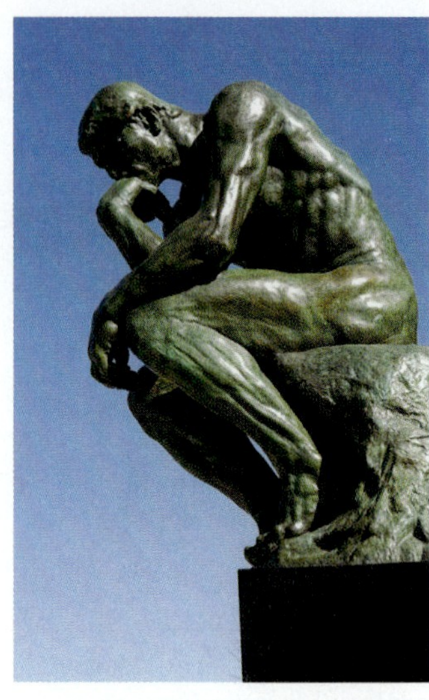

- Self-aware—Cognizant of one's own emotions and biases and how they impact decisions
- Persistent—Resists jumping to conclusions

What Is Critical Thinking?

John Dewey (1933), who is widely recognized as the father of modern critical thinking, defined it as "active, persistent, and careful consideration of a belief or supposed form of knowledge in the light of the grounds which support it and the further conclusions to which it tends."[22] Several other definitions are presented in the following list, in chronological order, to illustrate key (recurring) themes and demonstrate the development of the concept over time.

- McPeck (1981) defined critical thinking as "the propensity and skill to engage in an activity with reflective skepticism."[23]
- Brookfield (1987) defined it as a process in which individuals recognize and research assumptions that challenge their thoughts and actions.[24] Brookfield identified five activities and processes that take place when individuals are thinking critically:
    - Critical thinking is a productive and positive activity that requires active engagement with life.
    - Critical thinkers continuously question assumptions; therefore, critical thinking is a process and not an outcome.
    - The thinking processes of critical thinkers vary enormously according to the contexts in which it occurs.
    - Critical thinking results from individuals experiencing positive and negative events that can initiate the process of questioning previously trusted assumptions.
    - Critical thinkers find emotions central to the critical thinking process, allowing them to be emotive and rational with their assumptions.
- Lipman (1988) defined critical thinking as an activity involving "skillful, responsible thinking that facilitates good judgment because it: (a) relies upon criteria, (b) is self-correcting, and (c) is sensitive to context."[25]
- Ennis (1996) perceived critical thinking as "a process, the goal of which is to make reasonable decisions about what to believe and what to do."[26]
- The AICPA (1999) defined critical thinking as the "ability to link data, knowledge, and insight together from various disciplines to provide information for decision making."[27]
- Banning (2006) characterized it as a process of evaluating and reflecting on information gathered from multiple sources to make judgments that lead to the development of a thought or action.[28]

A common theme among these definitions is the idea of questioning assumptions, particularly with respect to cause–effect relationships. A critical thinker exercises judgment, using criteria developed from past observations and experiences. This process is flexible and highly sensitive to the context in which it occurs. Finally, critical thinking should ultimately influence decision making and thus lead to action.

The Value of Critical Thinking

Critical thinking is a necessary skill for any type of investigation, research, or scientific inquiry. As will be emphasized throughout this text, the analytical processes employed by forensic accountants are based on a scientific approach. This involves (1) identifying a question, (2) gathering sufficient relevant data, (3) analyzing the data, (4) drawing conclusions, and (5) communicating results. In this context, critical thinking serves as a guiding frame to preserve the integrity of the scientific process. Various threats to the integrity of this process are manifested in the concept of "blind spots." Blind spots are caused by mistakes in reasoning, human irrationality, biases, distortions, and self-interest. As humans, we all have blind spots. However, by exercising critical thinking, we can more easily detect our own blinds spots as well as those of others.

Dig Deeper

The concept of blind spots can be further examined via a "poles apart" assignment. This exercise requires you to choose an issue you feel strongly about, research it, and present arguments supporting both sides of the debate. The objective, of course, is to develop your critical thinking skills—from "what" to think to "how" to think.

Reasoning

Reasoning is a problem-solving skill that involves drawing inferences or conclusions from known or assumed facts.[29] Reasoning is closely associated with critical thinking in that it is a rational process of attempting to understand an event or behavior. Just like the iconic Sherlock Holmes, forensic accountants use both deductive and inductive reasoning to identify clues and patterns of behavior, gather and evaluate evidence, question arguments, and develop conclusions.

Deductive Reasoning

Let's first consider ***deductive reasoning***, which is defined as "reasoning from the general to the specific, or from the premises to a logically valid conclusion."[30] In other words, you first identify two or more general premises (either known or assumed to be true) and then apply these accepted truths to a specific situation. Importantly, deductive conclusions are statements of certainty that imply 100% confidence.

Consider this classic example of deductive reasoning:

Major Premise	All men are mortal.
Minor Premise	Socrates is a man.
Conclusion	Socrates is mortal.

Let's now consider the case of *U.S. v. Capone* and the net worth method:

Major Premise	You can't spend what you don't have.
Minor Premise	Capone spent more than he reported (which was nothing).
Conclusion	Capone underreported his income (indicating tax evasion).

These examples illustrate the basic idea of deductive reasoning: The conclusion is arrived at through the underlying premises. Importantly, no new information is provided. If something is true in general (all men are mortal), then it is true for a class of things (Socrates is a man), and that truth applies to all members of the class (Socrates is mortal). The certainty of deductive reasoning is tied to the truth of the underlying premises. If either of the premises is false, then the line of reasoning fails and the conclusion is unreliable.

Inductive Reasoning

In contrast to deductive reasoning, ***inductive reasoning*** draws conclusions from patterns. The inductive reasoning process flows from a set of specific observations, facts, or data to a working hypothesis and then a general conclusion (that is, bottom up).

Inductively developed arguments extend beyond their underlying observations, thus facilitating learning from experience. In other words, inductive reasoning allows us to predict future results based on past observations. Due to this predictive aspect, inductive conclusions cannot be 100% certain.

Consider this simple example of inductive reasoning:

Observation: Every time a ball is kicked into the air, it comes back down.

Conclusion: The next time the ball is kicked into the air, it will come back down.

The work of a forensic accountant is *evidence-based*: gathering evidence, analyzing the evidence, and then drawing conclusions. This, in essence, is a process of inductive reasoning.

As such, forensic accountants deal with *probabilities*, not *certainties*. This proposition is central to the legal concepts of "standard of proof" and "reasonable degree of professional certainty," which are introduced in Chapter 2.

Special Note

Forensic accountants also use ***intuitive reasoning***, a subject matter of importance in psychology.[31] Intuitions are judgments that arise through rapid, nonconscious, and holistic associations.[32] Thus, intuitive reasoning can be described as a feeling (or sense) based on how something *seems* rather than facts or data. Forensic accountants are encouraged to embrace intuitive reasoning as a good starting point for inductive reasoning. However, caution must be exercised because intuitions are easily distorted by personal biases and misconceptions.

Communication

As previously noted, the final step of the scientific method is communicating results. In forensic accounting, where there is often a wide knowledge gap between the expert and the audience, this may be the most challenging component of the process. Thus, forensic accountants are expected to have strong communication skills, both written and oral. As will be discussed in Chapter 2, one of the primary responsibilities of a testifying expert is to render an opinion that will assist the trier of fact (judge or jury) in understanding the evidence. To that end, an expert's opinion must be stated in a legally sufficient manner and must be based on reliable facts, data, and methodology.

Forensic accountants expect their reports, and every word contained therein, to be closely examined and challenged. Thus, all written reports must be clear, concise but comprehensive, and grammatically correct, with a professional tone. As a rule, expert reports prepared in the course of litigation are exempt from professional report writing standards. However, reports prepared outside litigation may be subject to such standards (discussed in Chapter 12), which contain specific requirements for both form and content.

A forensic accountant must also be skilled in oral communication. Whether the communication is with an attorney, a client, a law enforcement officer, or a judge/jury, the ability to relate findings in a simple, professional, and convincing manner is a critical success factor. Because effective communication is a *shared* meaning and understanding, your message must be tailored to the recipient.

Communication failure is often caused by a misunderstanding of the relative importance of the three components of oral communication: (1) body language, which accounts for roughly 55% of the message; (2) voice tone, which accounts for roughly 35% of the message; and (3) words, which account for only 10% of the message.[33] Thus, nonverbal cues are critical: *How* you say it is more important than *what* you say. While delivery can (and should) be practiced, the key to exuding confidence in your message is to actually *be* confident in the quality of your analysis. No amount of "window dressing" can hide an unfounded opinion, especially under challenge such as cross-examination.

Special Note

Forensic accountants are commonly called upon to present evidence to a judge or jury. A recent phenomenon, called the "CSI effect," describes the enhanced level of expectation among jurors with regard to forensic evidence. Exposure to television portrayals of criminal trials, which often exaggerate the role of forensic evidence, may cause jurors to expect an abundance of such evidence in every trial. If valid, this effect has implications for the findings and presentations of expert witnesses, including forensic accountants. "Jazzing up" a presentation can be an especially difficult task for the forensic accountant, given the tedious and data-intensive nature of many engagements.

In summary, the Davis et al. (2009) study supports our experience that the work of forensic accounting demands different skills from those employed by a traditional accountant. In

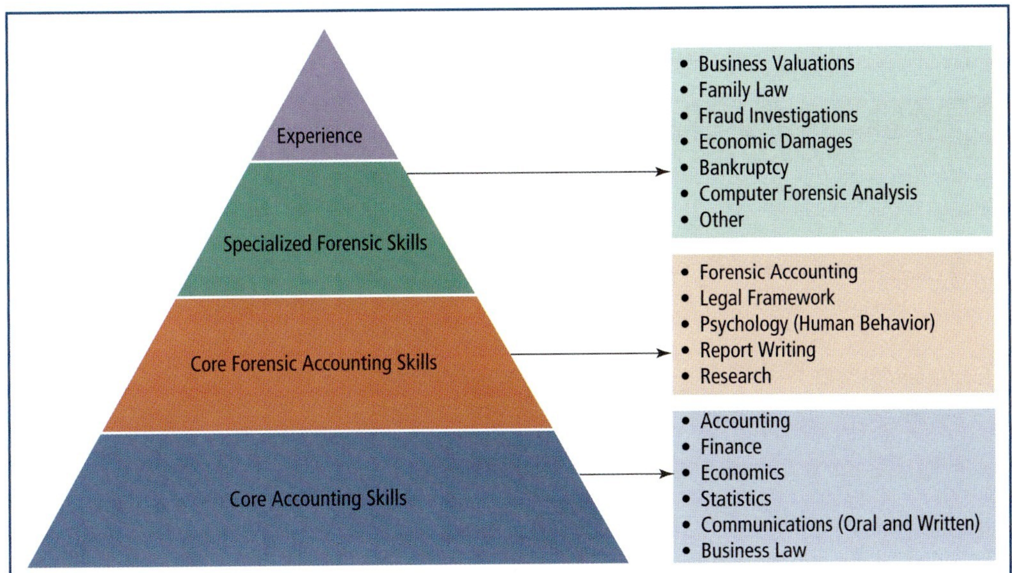

Figure 1-3
Pyramid of Forensic Accounting Skills

addition to core accounting skills, forensic accountants must have a working knowledge of the judicial process (the legal environment) and the underlying concepts of evidence, discovery, and legally sufficient opinions. Moreover, successful forensic accountants must have specialized knowledge in a variety of practice areas, such as business valuation and fraud investigation. Our pyramid of forensic accounting skills (illustrated in Figure 1-3) is consistent with the AICPA's CFF Core Focus Wheel, an illustrative tool used to identify the requisite skills required to become certified in financial forensics (discussed in the following section).

FORENSIC ACCOUNTING CERTIFICATIONS AND SUPPORTING ORGANIZATIONS

The AICPA estimates that 25,000 CPAs currently provide forensic accounting services.[34] This group of specialized practitioners is expected to increase in size, as demand for these services continues to grow. In a 2011 AICPA member survey, the vast majority of respondents (79%) expect a greater demand for forensic accounting services in the next two to five years. Of these respondents, 67% attributed this growth to economic damages calculations, 56% to marital disputes, and 54% to fraud investigations.[35] Moreover, the survey confirmed that CPAs represent the vast majority (94%) of forensic experts hired.

Strong demand for forensic accounting services implies a need for practitioners with specialized education and training. Recognizing this need, the American Accounting Association (AAA) has recently created the Forensic and Investigative Accounting (FIA) Section, which is dedicated to the continued improvement of forensic accounting research and education. A number of professional associations offer specialized forensic certifications, continuing education, and networking opportunities. The three most prominent of these associations are identified in Table 1-3.

The Davis et al. (2009) study supports our experience that specialty credentials (see Table 1-3) provide a competitive advantage. To address this need, the AICPA's Forensic and Valuation Services (FVS) Section offers two forensic accounting credentials: the Certified in Financial Forensics (CFF) credential and the Accredited in Business Valuation (ABV) credential. To become a CFF or ABV credential holder, candidates (CPAs)

Table 1-3 Forensic Accounting Credentials

Association	Specialized Certifications	Web Address
American Institute of Certified Public Accountants (AICPA)	Accredited in Business Valuation (ABV) Certified in Financial Forensics (CFF)	www.aicpa.org
National Association of Certified Valuators and Analysts (NACVA)	Certified Valuation Analyst (CVA) Certified Forensic Financial Analyst (CFFA)	www.nacva.com
Association of Certified Fraud Examiners (ACFE)	Certified Fraud Examiner (CFE)	www.acfe.com

must successfully pass the CFF Exam or ABV Exam and meet minimum experience and education requirements.

Following are the major areas of the body of knowledge covered in the CFF exam and the ABV exam, along with the location of this subject matter in our text:

CFF Exam

- Professional responsibilities and practice management—Chapter 10
- Fundamental forensic knowledge—Chapter 2
- Specialized forensic knowledge, such as fraud, business valuations, computer forensics, and economic damages calculations—Chapters 6, 7, 11, and 12

ABV Exam

- Qualitative and quantitative analysis—Chapters 8 and 9
- Valuation analysis—Chapter 11
- Related topics, such as defining the engagement and professional standards—Chapters 3–5

Aside from the AICPA's offerings, the National Association of Certified Valuators and Analysts (NACVA) is currently the industry leader in forensic accounting training. Although NACVA is best known for its business valuation credential—Certified Valuation Analyst (CVA)—its portfolio of offerings is much broader. As of the date of this writing, NACVA has trained more than 18,000 CPAs and other consulting professionals in the fields of business valuation, financial forensics, and various related specialty services. Due to NACVA's quality reputation and diversity of offerings, the AICPA has engaged NACVA to develop a course to help CPAs prepare for the qualifying exam for the CFF credential.

CAREERS IN FORENSIC ACCOUNTING

As previously highlighted, professionals with forensic accounting qualifications are in high demand. Table 1-4 lists examples of the many career opportunities for forensic accountants in both the private and public sectors. The salary range for an entry-level position is $30,000 to $60,000 per year, depending on the location and the size of the firm. For practitioners with specialized credentials, salaries begin around $60,000 and can reach six digits with greater experience. Those at the top of this profession earn between $250,000 and $500,000 per year.

The forensic accounting profession offers great variety, including roles for individuals with different skills and talents. Of course, not everyone is cut out for expert witness testimony. Some may prefer to work "behind the scenes," focusing more on analytical tasks. As you work through this text, you will get a better idea of where you may fit into the world of

Table 1-4 | Careers in Forensic Accounting

Employer	Position
Various companies / organizations	Internal Auditor Compliance Officer
CPA / consulting firms	External Auditor Valuation Analyst Expert Witness Consulting Expert Fraud Investigator
Insurance companies	Claims Examiner Fraud Investigator
Law enforcement (state and federal)	Documents Examiner Digital Analyst Forensic Analyst (FBI) Special Agent (FBI)
Regulatory agencies (for example, Federal Reserve or SEC)	Financial Analyst Examiner
Internal Revenue Service	Tax Examiner Tax Specialist Tax Compliance Officer Internal Revenue Agent Criminal Investigator
Government Accountability Office	Financial Analyst Financial Auditor Criminal Investigator

forensic accounting. Moreover, the foundational knowledge it offers is widely applicable in many other professions.

SUMMARY

Forensic accounting is a dynamic field that continues to grow in both size and significance in the United States and around the world. Although forensic accounting services are engagement-specific, all forensic accounting engagements share four common phases: (1) defining the engagement, (2) collecting evidence, (3) analyzing evidence, and (4) communicating results.

Forensic accounting students (and practicing forensic accountants) are frequently asked to explain what forensic accounting is and what makes it different from traditional accounting. Forensic accountants receive specialized training in investigations and the legal environment, including discovery, evidence, methodology, judicial process, burden and standard of proof, and formation and expression of expert opinions. Forensic accountants are thus uniquely qualified to assist counsel in civil or criminal litigation, as a testifying or consulting expert. Moreover, forensic accounting assignments are "engagement-specific," with each having a different purpose, a unique set of challenges, and its own cast of characters.

Successful forensic accountants are differentiated by their abstract skills, including critical thinking, reasoning, and communication. To develop these competencies, a mix of formal education, practical experience, and specialized training is necessary.

Key Terms

Consulting expert
Critical thinking
Deductive reasoning
Expert witness
Fact witness
Financial viability investigation
Forensic accounting
Fraud detection
Fraud deterrence
Fraud examination
Inductive reasoning
Intuitive reasoning
Investigative services
Litigation services
Mindset
Reasoning
Whistleblower complaint

Chapter Questions

1-1. For what crime was Al Capone convicted and sent to prison?

1-2. Frank J. Wilson is considered to be the first forensic accountant in the United States. What method did he use to determine Al Capone's unreported taxable income? Explain how this method works.

1-3. Define forensic accounting.

1-4. What is meant by a forensic accountant's mindset?

1-5. What are the four phases of a forensic accounting engagement?

1-6. Discuss the types of investigative services provided by forensic accountants.

1-7. Discuss the types of litigation services provided by forensic accountants.

1-8. Compare and contrast the roles of a testifying expert (expert witness) and a nontestifying (consulting) expert.

1-9. Identify and describe two types of nonfraud engagements a forensic accountant might perform.

1-10. How does the role of a forensic accountant differ from the role of a transactional accountant?

1-11. How does the role of a forensic accountant differ from the role of an external auditor?

1-12. How does the role of a forensic accountant differ from the role of an internal auditor?

1-13. What are the three essential characteristics/skills possessed by a forensic accountant?

1-14. What is meant by critical thinking, and what are the key attributes of this thinking process?

1-15. Define and provide an example of both inductive and deductive reasoning.

1-16. Does a forensic accountant use inductive or deductive reasoning when conducting an engagement? Explain.

1-17. Why are both written and oral communication skills important to a forensic accountant?

1-18. Identify several characteristics of a good written report. Why is the quality of a written report important?

1-19. Discuss the CSI effect as it relates to forensic accounting.

1-20. Identify two associations that provide forensic accounting certifications. How can a certification enhance the career of a forensic accountant?

1-21. What types of organizations hire forensic accountants? How much can forensic accountants expect to earn?

Multiple-Choice Questions

1-22. Who is widely recognized as the first forensic accountant?

a. Al Capone
b. Elliot Ness
c. Frank J. Wilson
d. J. Edgar Hoover

1-23. Which statement best describes the mindset of a forensic accountant?

a. A stubborn attitude based on life lessons
b. An instinct to explore problems that challenge conventional wisdom
c. A preconceived idea about how a fraud was conducted
d. A conservative approach to conducting an investigation

1-24. Which of the following is NOT a service provided by forensic accountants?

a. Business valuations
b. Fraud detection
c. Fraud examination
d. Financial statement reporting

1-25. Which of the following is NOT a significant practice area of forensic accounting?

a. Family law
b. Fraud detection
c. Tax and merger business valuations
d. Independent audits of financial statements

1-26. What is the objective of a fraud examination?

a. Add credibility to reported financial statements
b. Investigate suspicions and accusations of fraud
c. Fulfill a regulatory requirement
d. Provide financial statements to stakeholders

1-27. Which of the following is NOT a critical skill of forensic accountants?

a. Critical thinking ability
b. Reasoning ability
c. Prosecution ability
d. Communication ability

1-28. If all dogs eat meat, and Sheldon eats meat, what can we conclude using deductive reasoning?

a. Sheldon is a dog.
b. Meat eats Sheldon.
c. Sheldon enjoys meat.
d. It is not possible to conclude that Sheldon is a dog.

1-29. You eat an apple and get cramps. You eat a pear and get cramps. You eat a cherry and get cramps. You conclude that eating fruit gives you cramps. This is an example of what type of reasoning?

a. Deductive reasoning
b. Reciprocal reasoning
c. Inductive reasoning
d. Linear reasoning

1-30. When preparing a written report, a forensic accountant should do which of the following?

a. Write clearly.
b. Eliminate all grammatical errors.
c. Be concise, but cover the material in a comprehensive manner.
d. All of the above are correct.

1-31. Forensic accounting organizations, such as ACFE, NACVA, and the AICPA, provide valuable services to their members. Which of the following is not a service provided by these organizations?

a. Networking opportunities
b. Continuing education opportunities
c. Certifications
d. Assurance of a successful forensic accounting practice

1-32. Fraud deterrence includes the following proactive strategies to prevent fraud *except*:

a. Whistleblower rewards
b. Preemployment screening
c. Employee training
d. Code of conduct

Workplace Applications

1-33. Describe the education, training, and experience a forensic accountant needs in order to develop a successful career.

1-34. Using the Internet, explore job opportunities in the forensic accounting field. Identify two jobs you would like to apply for and prepare a memo to your professor identifying the employer, job title, job description, required qualifications and experience, and salary.

1-35. Prepare a ten-year professional development plan that will prepare you for a career in forensic accounting.

Chapter Problems

1-36. Critical thinking ability is a necessary skill of forensic accountants as well as a key component of the scientific method. Find three published articles on the scientific method. Based on your research, prepare a memo to your professor explaining how critical thinking can be utilized in each step of the scientific method.

1-37. Forensic accountants require strong reasoning skills. Find one published article on inductive reasoning and one on deductive reasoning. Prepare a memo to your professor comparing and contrasting these two types of reasoning.

1-38. Forensic accountants must have the ability to communicate effectively in writing. Research the topic of how to write a business memo, and then prepare a memo to your professor summarizing what you learned from your research.

1-39. Using the Internet, research two organizations that offer certifications in forensic accounting. Visit each organization's web site and explore the nature of the certification and how it is obtained (e.g., requirements for education, experience, and testing methodology).

---

1 IRS. Letter dated July 8, 1931, from Internal Revenue Agents W. C. Hodgins, Jacque L. Westrich, and H.N. Clagett to the Internal Revenue Agent in Charge, Chicago, IL. Can be accessed at http://www.irs.gov/pub/irs-utl/file-1-letter-dated-07081931-in-re-alphonse-capone.pdf

2 IRS. Summary Report dated December 21, 1933, prepared by Special Agent Frank J. Wilson at the request of the Chief, Intelligence Unit, Bureau of Internal Revenue, Washington, D.C. Can be accessed at http://www.irs.gov/pub/irs-utl/file-2-report-dated-12211933-in-re-alphonse-capone-by-sa-frank-wilson.pdf

3 Ward, P. (Mar. 20, 1932). The man who got Al Capone. *Baltimore Sun.*

4 *Holland v. U.S.* (1954). 348 US 121.

5 *Black's Law Dictionary*. (2009). 9th Ed., 721.

6 Bologna, J., Lindquist, R., & Wells, J. (1992). *The Accountant's Handbook of Fraud and Commercial Crime.* John Wiley & Sons.

7 Buckhoff, T., & Shrader, R. (2000). The teaching of forensic accounting in the United States. *Journal of Forensic Accounting, 1*, 135–46.

8 Michaelson, W. (1996). Divorce: A game of hide and seek? *Journal of Accountancy, 181*(3), 67–69.

9 Peloubet, M. E. (Jun. 1946). Forensic accounting: Its place in today's economy. *Journal of Accountancy*, 458–62.

10 *Websters' New World College Dictionary.* (1999). 4th Ed., 916.

11 Freitas, A. L., Gollwitzer, P., & Trope, Y. (2004). The influence of abstract and concrete mindsets on anticipating and guiding others' self-regulatory efforts. *Journal of Experimental Social Psychology, 407*, 39–75.

12 *Accounting Today*. (2012). 2012 Top 100 Firms. Go to www.pearsonhighered.com/rufus for a link to this article.

13 AICPA. The 2011 Forensic and Valuation Services (FVS) Trend Survey. Go to www.pearsonhighered.com/rufus for a link to this survey.

14 AICPA. (2011). Code of Professional Conduct. ET §101.05, 1728.

15 *Webster's' New World College Dictionary.* (1999). 4th Ed., 751.

16 ACFE. (2012). Report to the Nation on Occupational Fraud and Abuse. Go to www.pearsonhighered.com/rufus for a link to this report.

17 Cendrowski, J., Martin, J., & Petro, L. (2007). *The Handbook of Fraud Deterrence.* John Wiley & Sons.

18 *Black's Law Dictionary.* (2009). 9th Ed., 1734.

19 *Black's Law Dictionary.* (2009). 9th Ed., 1740.

20 Davis, C., Farrell, R., & Ogilby, S. (2010). Characteristics and skills of the forensic accountant. American Institute of Certified Public Accountants, FVS Section. Go to www.pearsonhighered.com/rufus for a link to this white paper.

21 Facione, P. A. (1990). Critical thinking: A statement of expert consensus for purposes of educational assessment and instruction. American Philosophical Association Delphi Research Report. California Academic Press.

22 Halpern, D. F. (2003). *Thought and Knowledge: An Introduction to Critical Thinking* (4th Ed.). Lawrence Erlbaum Associates.

23 McPeck, J. (1981). *Critical Thinking and Education.* St. Martins.

24 Brookfield, S. D. (1987). *Developing Critical Thinkers: Challenging Adults to Explore Alternative Ways of Thinking and Acting.* Jossey-Bass.

25 Lipman, M. (1988). Critical thinking: What can it be? In L. S. Behar-Horenstein & A. C. Ornstein (Eds.), *Contemporary Issues in Curriculum* (pp. 145–53). Allyn and Bacon.

26 Ennis, R. H. (1996). *Critical Thinking.* Prentice Hall.

27 AICPA (1999). Broad business perspective competencies. Go to www.pearsonhighered.com/rufus for a link to this article.

28 Banning, M. (2006). Measures that can be used to instill critical thinking in nurse prescribers. *Nurse Education in Practice, 6*(2), 98–105.

29 *Websters' New World College Dictionary.* (1999). 4th Ed., 1194.

30 *Websters' New World College Dictionary.* (1999). 4th Ed., 377.

31 Gore, J., & Sadler-Smith, E. (2011). Unpacking intuition: A process and outcome framework. *Review of General Psychology, 15*(4), 304–16.

32 Dane, E., & Pratt, M. G. (2009). Exploring intuition and its role in managerial decision making. *Academy of Management Review, 32*, 33–54.

33 Harmeyer, J., Golden, S., & Summers, G. (1984). *Conducting Audit Interviews.* Institute of Internal Auditors.

34 AICPA Press Release. (Aug. 31, 2010). AICPA contracts NACVA to develop course for CPA forensic credential exam. Go to www.pearsonhighered.com/rufus for a link to this press release.

35 AICPA. The 2011 Forensic and Valuation Services (FVS) Trend Survey. Go to www.pearsonhighered.com/rufus for a link to this survey

2 The Legal Environment of Forensic Accounting

INTRODUCTION

A unique feature of forensic accounting is the *legal context* in which it occurs. Working in a legal environment obligates the forensic accountant to be knowledgeable about the judicial process and procedures and the controlling rules of evidence. The purpose of this chapter is to introduce key concepts that shape the legal environment of forensic accounting. Much of this information is likely to be unfamiliar, since it extends beyond the scope of commercial law courses generally required for business students. Moreover, our discussion is presented through the lens of a forensic accountant, not an attorney. We do not (and, frankly, could not) address all elements of the various legal actions in which a forensic accountant might be engaged. Rather, we employ a targeted approach, highlighting the specific issues and challenges relevant to the forensic accountant's limited role as either a *testifying* or *consulting* expert, as introduced in Chapter 1.

Caution

This narrative is intended for educational purposes only and should not be construed as legal advice.

We begin with a synopsis of a real criminal case, *United States v. Bonnie J. Bain*, which provides context for many of the legal concepts discussed in this chapter.

Special Note

All information contained in this case synopsis is available in the public domain.

UNITED STATES V. BONNIE J. BAIN

Background

On October 2, 2007, while assembling data for a presentation on effective cash management, a regional Cash Manager with BB&T noticed unusual activity at a small branch bank (West Side Branch) located in Charleston, West Virginia. The activity included abnormal levels of currency orders and nearly ten times the number of "cash-in" and "cash-out" tickets* expected for the subject branch. The Cash Manager flagged the activity as "suspicious" and forwarded his observations to an analyst for further investigation.

The analyst proceeded with a "transactions investigation," during which he questioned West Side's Branch Manager regarding the suspicious activity. Dissatisfied with the Branch Manager's responses, the analyst contacted the Area Operations Manager on October 4, 2007, to request an audit of the entire branch, including its tellers, vaults, ATMs, and all cash end-points. The following day, the auditors arrived at West Side Branch to perform the audit. In the audit process, it was

* Cash-in and cash-out tickets are used to validate customer banking transactions. If the customer makes a deposit, the corresponding document is a cash-in ticket; if the customer cashes a check, the corresponding document is a cash-out ticket. These documents (for example, the cashed check and the cash-out ticket) are submitted to the Proof Department on a daily basis for reconciliation.

Learning Objectives

After completing this chapter, you should be able to:

LO1. Explain why it is necessary for a forensic accountant to have a working knowledge of the legal environment.

LO2. Describe the classification (categories) of law and the basic structure (three stages) of a civil trial.

LO3. Explain the concepts of burden of proof and standard of proof.

LO4. Describe the court's gatekeeping role in determining the admissibility of evidence.

LO5. Identify the rules of evidence that address expert testimony and the specific criteria for the admissibility of expert testimony.

LO6. Describe the purpose and process of a *Daubert* challenge, and identify the factors that should be considered when evaluating expert testimony.

LO7. Identify the requisite elements for establishing attorney-client privilege.

determined that the teller drawer of Ms. Bonnie Bain (Teller #5) was short by $1 million. In addition to the drawer shortage, the auditors discovered bogus cash-out tickets totaling $973,715, indicating a total cash shortage of $1,973,715. Ms. Bain was immediately placed on administrative leave (with pay) pending further investigation.

The matter was then transferred to BB&T's corporate investigation (CI) division to identify the "who, what, when, how, who else, and how much" of the fraudulent activity. Based on information contained in the referral, CI hypothesized that Ms. Bain's embezzlement extended from 2000 through October 2005 and was concealed via exploitation of co-workers and manipulation of bank records.

The Bank's Investigation

The heart of BB&T's CI investigation included the collection and analysis of paper documents, digital evidence, employee interviews, and personal observations. Due to missing records, CI's analysis was limited to the period May 27, 2004, to October 5, 2007. Working backward from October 5, 2007, CI employed a methodology known as the transactions analysis method. This methodology involved compiling internal transactions (day-by-day) that occurred within the bank, specifically among employees, departments, and branches. Examples include transactions between the line tellers and the vault teller (buying and selling cash) and transactions between the tellers and the Proof Department. CI tracked all transactions that were identified as being processed by Teller #5 (Ms. Bain). For the specified time period, CI's transactions analysis determined an embezzlement loss of $640,923.

In November 2007, CI issued its investigation summary, concluding that Ms. Bain had acted alone in the embezzlement. CI determined that Ms. Bain concealed her crime by "force balancing" her teller drawer and manipulating her co-workers and the audit process. For example, if Ms. Bain needed $1.2 million to balance the vault at the end of the day, she simply processed a cash-out ticket for $1.2 million. The bogus cash-out ticket would be flagged in the Proof Department (as out-of-balance) and then sent back to Ms. Bain (the Head Teller) for investigation. CI concluded that Ms. Bain would "float" the increasing shortage with misdirection and manipulation of records, akin to a shell game. In addition to Ms. Bain's embezzlement, CI's report also identified several "problems" in the branch's internal controls, such as missing records (including audit reports), failed audits, and various supervisory and policy violations.

The Government's Investigation

BB&T presented its investigative findings to federal authorities, who conducted their own criminal investigation.[†] Investigative efforts employed by the Secret Service and the FBI included witness interviews (such as family members), analysis of Ms. Bain's financial dealings (such as bank records and tax returns), and consideration of her lifestyle and other patterns of behavior (such as gambling, drugs, and gifts). Through these efforts, federal authorities were attempting to track the use of the embezzled funds and thereby validate the amount that Ms. Bain embezzled.

Plea Agreement

On June 6, 2011, Ms. Bain entered into a plea agreement with the U.S. Attorney's Office, summarized in the following Department of Justice (DOJ) press release.[1]

> **Former Branch Banking and Trust Employee Pleads Guilty to Making a False Bank Entry**
>
> CHARLESTON, W.Va. – A former Branch Banking and Trust Company (BB&T) employee pleaded guilty today in federal court before United States District Judge John T. Copenhaver, Jr. for making a false bank entry. Bonnie J. Bain, 60, of Belle, Kanawha County, West Virginia, was an employee of BB&T and its predecessors from 1977 to November 2007. From 2004 until October 2007, Bain was a teller supervisor at the Westside Branch of BB&T in Charleston, West Virginia. She also held positions of head teller and primary vault teller during her employment with the banking company.

† The purpose of a criminal investigation is to gather evidence to identify a suspect and support an indictment/conviction.

> Bain admitted that from at least May 2004 to October 2007, she embezzled at least $200,000 in cash from the Westside Branch of BB&T. In order to conceal the embezzlement scheme and the resulting cash shortage, Bain admitted to making false entries in the company's books and records to make it appear as if the cash total reconciled when in fact it did not. Bain "floated" the outage among her teller drawer and general ledger accounts using various methods. To further her embezzlement scheme, Bain admitted to recording fictitious cash dollar amounts in her teller/vault drawer by force balancing. Bain also admitted that, on other occasions, she would reduce the cash shown in her teller/vault drawer by creating fictitious cash-out tickets. Bain faces up to 30 years in prison and a $1 million fine.

Although Ms. Bain entered a guilty plea, she did not agree with the U.S. Attorney's Office regarding the amount embezzled. The plea agreement established a floor for this amount (>$200,000), but not a ceiling. The government argued that Ms. Bain embezzled $640,923 as determined by BB&T's investigation. Ms. Bain's attorney, Ms. Mary Lou Newberger, argued that the correct amount was $293,376, as determined by the forensic accountant she had engaged. The amount of the embezzlement is important because it determines sentencing (jail time) and restitution. This determination would be made by the court following oral arguments and expert testimony at the sentencing hearing.

Special Note

The epilogue for this case is presented at the conclusion of the chapter. It describes the analysis employed by Ms. Bain's forensic accountant to determine the amount of the embezzlement and relays the ultimate findings of the court.

UNDERSTANDING THE LEGAL ENVIRONMENT

What level of "legal knowledge" is expected of the forensic accountant?

- By attorneys—consumers of forensic accounting services?
- By the courts—gatekeepers of expert evidence?
- By jurors—evaluators of forensic accounting testimony?
- By the profession—promoters and regulators of forensic accounting services?

The short answer is the *highest level*. As will be discussed in this chapter (and emphasized throughout this text), testifying forensic accountants should expect their qualifications (education, training, and experience), their work on the subject engagement (what they did, why they did it, and who/what they relied on), and their resulting opinions to be thoroughly challenged by opposing counsel. They should also expect their knowledge of the judicial process and applicable professional standards to be tested. Why this high level of scrutiny? Simply stated, expert witness testimony can be the tipping point between winning and losing at trial. Given this critical role, opposing counsel will seize any weakness or misstep to challenge an expert's competence, credibility, and opinions.

Special Note

The court is obligated to serve as a gatekeeper when an expert opinion is proffered (or submitted) as evidence. A motion by opposing counsel to exclude an expert is known as a *Daubert* challenge. As explained later in this chapter, a *Daubert* challenge is a special hearing (absent the jury) conducted before the trial judge to determine: (1) whether an expert witness is qualified and (2) whether the expert's opinion is founded on reliable facts, data, and methodology rather than mere speculation or conjecture. Being excluded by a court can have a long-term negative impact on a forensic accountant's career. Past exclusions are often revealed in future engagements and are publicly available in online databases (such as Daubert Tracker). Such exclusions can have a cumulative effect, as courts can refuse to admit an expert based solely on past exclusions.[2]

As discussed in Chapter 1, the AICPA has identified specific areas of competency for practice as a forensic accountant: core accounting skills, fundamental forensic knowledge, and specialized forensic knowledge. Included in fundamental forensic knowledge is an understanding of the legal environment. Consistent with the topics proposed by the AICPA and the CFF credentialing program,[3] this chapter introduces the key concepts required for a working knowledge. We begin our discussion at "ground zero."

Definition and Functions of Law (Ground Zero)

In the United States, we advocate a rule of law doctrine, which proposes that governance via a cumulative body of legal principles is superior to the rule of any human leader (for example, a dictator, king, or president) and that all people stand equal in the eyes of the law—that is, no person is above the law.[4]

Black's Law Dictionary defines law as the "legal order, system, or regime that orders human activities and relations through systematic application of the force of politically organized society, backed by force."[5] According to this definition, the law serves to influence, protect, regulate, and maintain our society. Moreover, it suggests that the law is fluid, forever evolving in response to social, economic, and political forces.

Law has three basic functions: (1) dispute resolution (criminal and civil actions), (2) protection of property (such as use and contract rights), and (3) preservation of the state.[6] The law is enforced with the use of ***sanctions***. In criminal cases, sanctions include imprisonment, home confinement, probation, day reporting, fines, or even capital punishment. In civil cases, sanctions generally involve compensation for loss or wrongs suffered (for example, economic damages).

Law and Justice

U.S. citizens enjoy the constitutional promise of ***justice***, which appears in the Preamble to the United States Constitution:

> We the people of the United States, in order to form a more perfect union, establish justice, insure domestic tranquility, provide for the common defense, promote the general welfare, and secure the blessing of liberty to ourselves and our posterity, do ordain and establish this Constitution for the United States of America.[7]

Justice is a profound concept generally defined by its context. For example, *Black's Law Dictionary* defines multiple forms of justice:[8]

- *Civil justice.* Justice concerned with the private affairs of citizens and their respective rights, including certain freedoms of speech and action and equal treatment, protection, and opportunities regardless of race, sex, or religion.
- *Criminal justice.* A system directly involved in the apprehension, prosecution, defense, sentencing, incarceration, and supervision of those suspected of or charged with criminal offenses.
- *Personal justice.* Justice between parties to a dispute, regardless of any larger principles that might be involved.
- *Social justice.* Justice that conforms to a moral principle (for example, all people are equal).
- *Substantial justice.* Justice fairly administered according to the rules of substantive law (such as a fair trial).

Although *law* and *justice* are different concepts, most of us look to the law for justice. In a legal setting, justice is viewed as both a process and an outcome. As a process, justice implies fair and equal treatment (rights and protections) within the judicial system. The judicial process is administered and managed by the court, acting as the *trier of law*. Two components of the judicial process that are important to forensic accountants include *procedures* and *evidence,* both of which are discussed in later sections of this chapter. Outcomes (or verdicts) are determined by the *trier of fact*, which is the jury in a jury trial or the judge in a bench trial. *Verdicts* are (or are expected to be) decided based on the evidence presented during the trial.

> **Special Note**
>
> Courts across the country face the challenge of managing jurors' use of technology (such as smartphones, Facebook, Twitter, and Google) to gather and share information about cases and ongoing deliberations. As noted previously, jurors are supposed to reach a verdict based *only* on the evidence presented at trial (that is, allowed by the court). Consideration of outside information, which has not been subjected to challenge, violates the rules of evidence. If identified, such violations can result in removal of the juror/s, mistrials, or appeals. As one might expect, attorneys in high-profile cases have begun to monitor jurors' blogs and web sites.

Classification of Law

As illustrated in Figure 2-1, law can be classified into two categories: public and private. Public law regulates the relationships of citizens with the state and serves to protect the public's interest. The three major divisions of public law are criminal law, constitutional law, and administrative law. Sub-divisions that commonly involve forensic accountants include tax law, labor law, bankruptcy law, environmental law, banking law, and securities law.

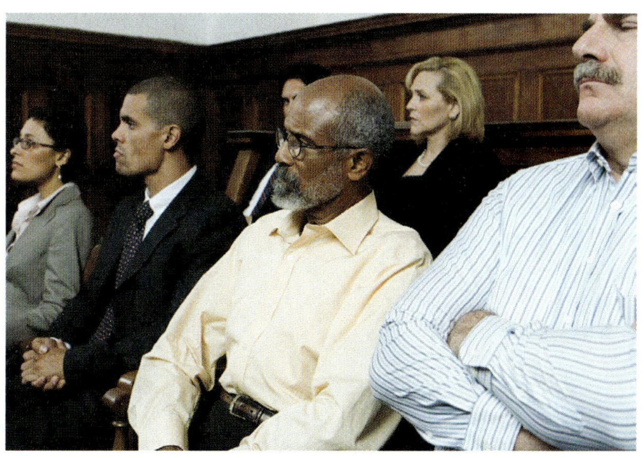

Private (or civil) law, on the other hand, regulates the relationships between individuals or entities within a state and serves to protect (or determine) their rights and liabilities. Divisions of private law that commonly involve forensic accountants include divorce law, contract law, tort law, property law, agency law, partnership law, corporate law, and sales law.

Throughout this chapter, we will highlight similarities and differences between civil law and criminal law. As noted

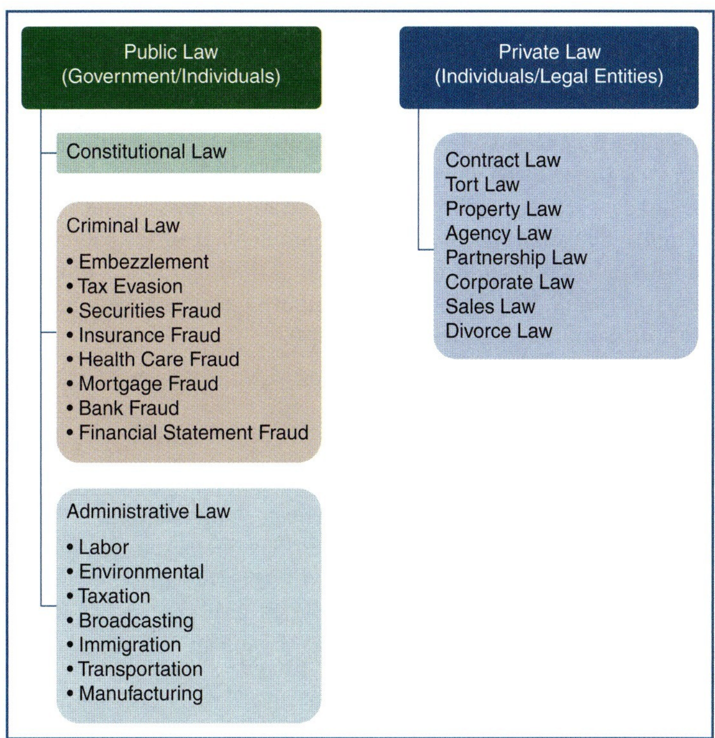

Figure 2-1
Classification of Law

previously, civil (private) law defines and protects individual rights. In contrast, criminal law defines conduct prohibited by legislative bodies (that is, state or federal statutes) and thus serves to protect the authority and welfare of the state.

Special Note

A complete discussion of the sources and hierarchy of law is beyond the scope and purpose of our discussion. However, an illustrative diagram is provided at the end of the chapter (Appendix 2-A). For additional information in this regard, students are encouraged to revisit their business law texts.

PROCEDURE: THE ANATOMY OF A TRIAL

What most of us know (or think we know) about our justice system comes primarily from television shows or the movies. Such portrayals, however entertaining, do not represent reality. Our experience suggests at least five key differences:

- The law is not fast. There is no one- or two-hour litigation. Rather, civil trials commonly last two days, following a year (or more) of pleadings.[‡]
- There is rarely (if ever) a "gotcha" moment (such as "You can't handle the truth!"[§]). The discovery process (discussed in a later section) serves to eliminate such surprises at trial. Moreover, witnesses are generally well prepared by counsel.
- TV shows are about drama. Given the extended discovery process, real trials (aside from the verdict) rarely provide much drama— that is, unless you are the plaintiff or defendant.
- Jury selection and opening statements are the most important parts of a trial—not cross-examination and closing arguments, as often represented on TV. Selecting who is responsible for rendering the verdict is, of course, paramount. Opening statements provide the first chance for the parties to connect with jurors and tell their sides of the story.
- The role of the jury is not passive. Because jurors serve as the trier of fact, they must actively evaluate the evidence and decide who and what to believe.

To operationalize these concepts, let's consider the anatomy (or structure) of a civil trial, which includes three basic stages: pleading stage, discovery stage, and trial stage. As previously noted, a civil action is a non-criminal complaint involving private property rights.

Pleading Stage

A civil proceeding starts with the filing of a complaint (or lawsuit), which identifies the parties, outlines the alleged facts and one or more violations, and presents a demand for relief. Once a defendant has been served with the complaint, the individual or entity has a limited amount of time (20 days) to respond by filing an answer. The answer addresses each paragraph of the complaint by admitting, denying, or claiming lack of sufficient knowledge to respond. The answer also asserts affirmative defenses.[**] Failing to file a timely response can result in a ***default judgment***, which is a binding judgment against a party based on some failure to take action (similar to a forfeiture in sports).

A sample complaint and answer/counterclaim are provided in Appendices 2-B and 2-C.

Discovery Stage

The second stage of the process is ***discovery***. As the name implies, the discovery process allows for the gathering of information from the opposing party as well as third-party witnesses. Information is typically gathered (discovered) via interrogatories, requests for production of documents, subpoenas, and depositions. In federal courts, the discovery process is governed by the ***Federal Rules of Civil Procedure*** (FRCP), specifically Rules 26–37.[9] Although states may determine their own rules, most have adopted rules that are modeled after the FRCP.

[‡] The pleading stage of a trial is discussed in the following section.

[§] Famous line from the film *A Few Good Men* (2005).

[**] An assertion that, even if the facts alleged are true, there is no merit to the plaintiff's claim.

Rules of special interest to the forensic accountant include Rules 26(a)(2), 26(b)(1), 26(b)(4), and 26(e)(2).

Rule 26(a)(2)

This rule requires the disclosure of all experts (such as forensic accountants) expected to testify at trial. The disclosure is generally accompanied by the expert's written report, which must contain the following elements:

- A complete statement of all opinions the witness will express, along with the basis and reasons for them
- The facts or data considered by the witness in forming the opinions
- Any exhibits that will be used to summarize or support the opinions
- The witness's qualifications, including a list of all publications authored in the preceding ten years
- A list of all other cases in which the witness has testified as an expert (either at trial or by deposition) during the preceding four years
- A statement of the compensation to be paid for the study and testimony in the case

Rule 26(b)(1)

This rule limits discovery to "non-privileged" information, thus excluding any privileged information.[††]

Rule 26(b)(4)

This rule limits discovery of an expert's communications with engaging counsel and any report drafts that may be prepared. It also limits discovery of facts and opinions held by an expert who is engaged to assist counsel in trial preparation (a consulting expert) but not expected to be called as a witness.

Rule 26(e)(2)

This rule requires a testifying expert to supplement his or her report to include any changes or additional information that has not been previously presented but is expected to be offered at trial.

As explained previously, the rules of discovery not only identify the various methods by which certain information *must be disclosed*, but also prescribe means by which other information can be *protected from disclosure*. This may include information protected under the attorney-client privilege or work product doctrine, expert report drafts, and communications with engaging counsel. Given these complexities, the forensic accountant (whether a consulting or testifying expert) *must* have a working knowledge of the discovery process. This is necessary both to assist counsel in complying with the disclosure requirements and to avoid interfering with the protection of any privileged information.

The rules also frame the testifying expert's reporting duties and responsibilities. Violations or failures in this regard can damage the client's case and possibly even result in court sanctions or malpractice allegations against the expert.

Trial Stage

Following completion of discovery, the proceeding advances to the trial stage. In the case of a jury trial, this stage begins with the selection of a jury. Prospective jurors include residents from the local county who are randomly selected and summoned to the court. The jury is selected through a process known as ***voir dire***, wherein the judge and the attorneys question prospective jurors about their backgrounds and beliefs. As previously emphasized, the selection of the jury is a critical part of the trial. Generally, there are twelve jurors in a criminal case and six in a civil case. These individuals collectively serve as the trier of fact, with the responsibility of rendering the verdict.[‡‡]

[††] See discussion of the attorney-client privilege and work product doctrine presented later in this chapter.

[‡‡] This refers to a jury trial only. In a bench trial, the judge is the trier of fact.

Following jury selection, the attorneys for both parties make their opening arguments (statements). The first to present is the plaintiff, whose opening statement serves to outline its theory of the case and any supporting evidence. The plaintiff is followed by the defendant, who may choose to defer its opening statement until the conclusion of the plaintiff's case. Opening arguments are important because they provide the first opportunity for the parties to connect with the jury and tell their respective sides of the story.

After opening arguments, the plaintiff presents its witnesses, which the defendant may cross-examine. Importantly, all evidence is presented to the jury through witnesses (such as a forensic accountant). The plaintiff continues the presentation of its case (known as the "case in chief") until complete. A similar process is then followed by the defendant. After the defendant completes its presentation, the plaintiff is afforded an opportunity for rebuttal witnesses, which is then followed by the defendant's opportunity for sub-rebuttal witnesses.

After all the witnesses have testified and the evidence has been admitted by the court, the parties present their closing arguments. Closing arguments are the last opportunity for the parties to summarize the testimony and highlight key points.

Following closing arguments and instructions by the judge, the case proceeds to jury deliberation. During this time, the jurors collectively evaluate the evidence to render a verdict. Although it varies in state courts, verdicts in federal cases must be unanimous. An important component of the jury instructions is a description of the requisite standard of proof, which is discussed in detail in a later section.

Is the Structure of a Criminal Case Different?

The answer is yes and no. The basic structure of a criminal case is similar to that of a civil case, with the addition of a fourth stage—sentencing. However, the pleading stage of a criminal case is very different. Criminal cases are initiated with a criminal complaint accompanied by an investigator's affidavit that summarizes the evidence against the defendant. During the first appearance (arraignment), the defendant is informed of the charges and advised of his or her rights. At this time, the defendant also enters a plea to the charge or charges—guilty or not guilty. This is followed by the discovery stage[§§] and the trial stage, as discussed previously. If the defendant is found not guilty, the case is over; if found guilty, the case then moves to the sentencing stage. The verdict in a criminal case (guilty or not guilty) differs from the verdict in a civil case, wherein the defendant is found either liable or not liable (for damages).

Prior to sentencing by the court, the case is evaluated by the probation department, which prepares a pre-sentence report (PSR). The PSR summarizes the case (including the crime, the case facts, and the offender's profile) and offers a recommendation for sentencing. Forensic accountants are frequently engaged to assist counsel in white collar criminal cases (as illustrated in *U.S. v. Bonnie Bain*), because sentencing and restitution are driven, in major part, by an economic factor (for example, tax loss or amount embezzled).

A comparison of the key elements of civil and criminal actions is provided in Table 2-1.

Burden and Standards of Proof

The ***burden of proof*** is the obligation of the plaintiff or prosecution to prove liability (in a civil case) or guilt (in a criminal case). The defendant is not required to prove his or her innocence—it is presumed.

[§§] In criminal cases, only the prosecution is required to disclose.

Table 2-1 Comparison of Civil and Criminal Actions

	Civil Law	Criminal Law
Category	Private	Public
Purpose	Resolve disputes between individuals or entities	Convict and punish offenders
Objective	Compensation Deterrence	Punishment Deterrence Rehabilitation Protection of the welfare of the state
Commencement of Action	Plaintiff (may be individuals or entities, including government)	Government (Prosecution)
Responding Party	Defendant	Defendant
Burden of Proof	Plaintiff	Government
Standard of Proof	Generally a "preponderance" (that is, more likely than not). In certain cases, the standard is "clear and convincing," which is greater than preponderance.	"Beyond a reasonable doubt" (that is, no significant or fair doubt based on reason and common sense)
Verdict	States vary; federal courts require unanimous verdict	Must be unanimous
Decision	Plaintiff or defendant may be found liable, not liable, or partially liable	Defendant is found either guilty or not guilty
Sanctions	Compensation (damage awards); cannot be imprisoned	Imprisonment, fines, penalties, etc.
Judicial Rules	Rules of civil procedure	Rules of criminal procedure
Appeal	Either party	Only defendant

The ***presumption of innocence*** must be overcome by a certain ***standard of proof***, which describes the amount of evidence the plaintiff must present to prove its case. In a civil case, the requisite standard is a ***preponderance of the evidence***—more likely than not (>50% probability). Some civil cases (such as civil fraud) must be proven by ***clear and convincing evidence***. Clear and convincing is greater than a preponderance, but no specific percentage can be assigned. In a criminal case, the prosecution has a legal obligation to prove all elements of an alleged offense (such as fraud, tax evasion, or murder) ***beyond a reasonable doubt***.[***] Again, no percentage can be assigned. The applicable burden and standard of proof are explained to the jury by the judge and included in the jury instructions.[†††]

Figure 2-2 illustrates the ascending levels (or standards) of proof.

The forensic accountant *must* understand the requisite standard of proof for any litigation engagement and articulate his or her opinion accordingly. For example, in a civil case with a preponderance standard, the expert's opinion must be stated within a ***reasonable degree of professional certainty***, meaning more probable than not (>50%). This is critical, since expert testimony that does not meet the necessary threshold will be rejected by the court. In

[***] For sentencing, the standard of proof is reduced to a preponderance of the evidence.

[†††] Another standard of proof that may be encountered by forensic accountants is *probable cause*, which is commonly used by grand juries to determine whether to issue a criminal indictment. It is also used in civil cases when plaintiffs seek a prejudgment remedy.

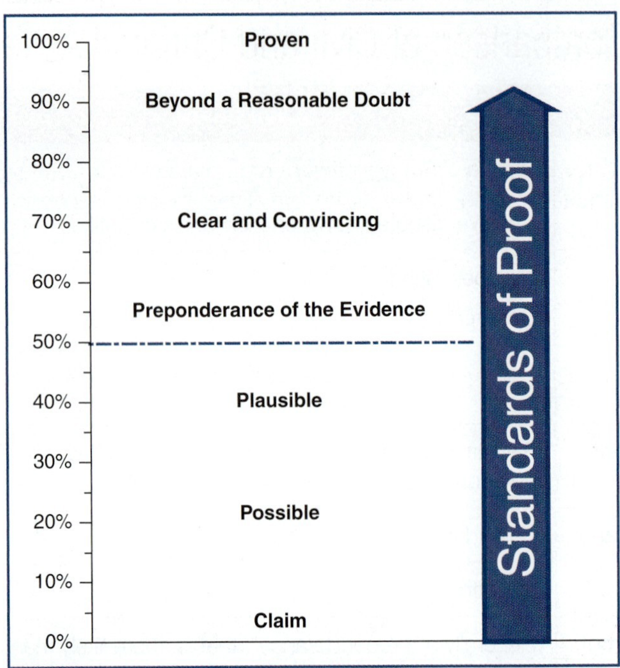

Figure 2-2
Ascending Levels (Standards) of Proof

this situation, the client will be left without an expert, and the court will have no choice but to accept the opinion of the opposing expert.

Alternative Dispute Resolution

Litigation is not the only means for settling disputes between parties. Forensic accountants may also participate in alternative dispute resolution (ADR), the most common forms of which are mediation and arbitration. ***Mediation*** is a non-binding informal process wherein a mediator (mutually selected by the parties) evaluates the arguments of both sides and helps the parties reach common ground. If mediation fails, the parties may proceed with litigation. ***Arbitration***, on the other hand, is a "mini trial" wherein each party presents its case to one or more arbitrators, who render a binding decision that generally cannot be appealed. Arbitration is often voluntary but can also be mandatory (required by a statute or a contract between the parties).

ADR may be preferred over litigation because it is less expensive, is generally faster, and allows for greater privacy. Moreover, ADR is often used in disputes regarding complex or technical issues, since mediators or arbitrators with the necessary expertise can be selected.

EVIDENCE AND THE EXPERT

Armed with a basic understanding of procedure, let's now turn our attention to the other component of the judicial process that is important to forensic accountants—evidence.

The Court's Gatekeeping Role

The trial judge runs the courtroom and makes all legal rulings, including those regarding the admissibility of evidence. In general, the rules of evidence (discussed in the following section) put a premium on first-hand observations. Opinion testimony is discouraged except under certain circumstances (expert testimony), and hearsay evidence is generally excluded.

The court's role as a gatekeeper for evidence is paramount, especially in the world of forensic accounting. The rules of evidence allow expert witnesses greater latitude than other witnesses to testify based on evidence (such as hearsay evidence) that would not otherwise be admissible. Moreover, a higher level of credibility is generally attached to an expert's testimony. As explored in the following section, the trial judge is challenged to carefully qualify both the expert and his or her testimony.

Rules of Evidence

The rules of evidence may vary from jurisdiction to jurisdiction and even from court to court (such as criminal, civil, or family court). However, most state rules of evidence are based on the ***Federal Rules of Evidence*** (FRE),[10] which will serve as the basis for our discussion. These rules govern *if, when, how,* and *for what purpose* evidence is allowed to be presented to the trier of fact for consideration. The purpose of the FRE is stated in Rule 102, which reads as follows:

> These rules should be construed so as to administer every proceeding fairly, eliminate unjustifiable expense and delay, and promote the development of evidence law, to the end of ascertaining the truth and securing a just determination.

Simply stated, the purpose of the FRE is to seek justice and truth in a fair and reasonable manner.

What Is Evidence?

Evidence, as defined by *Black's Law Dictionary*, is "something (including testimony, documents, and tangible objects) that tends to prove or disprove the existence of an alleged fact."[11] In other words, evidence is presented to persuade the fact finder (judge or jury) of the probability of the truth of some fact asserted in the case. As previously discussed, the FRE establish guidelines for the admissibility of evidence. According to FRE 401, ***relevant evidence*** must have the "tendency to make a fact more or less probable than it would be without the evidence," and the fact must be "of consequence in determining the action."

As a general principle, all relevant evidence is admissible unless it is inadmissible due to another rule of evidence or law. FRE 403 allows relevant evidence to be excluded if its ***probative value*** is substantially outweighed by danger of unfair prejudice, of confusing or misleading the jury, or of wasting the court's time. For example, evidence that the victim of a car accident was apparently a "liar, cheater, womanizer, and a man of low morals" was deemed unduly prejudicial and irrelevant to whether he had a valid product liability claim against the manufacturer of the tires on his van (which had rolled over, resulting in severe brain damage).[12] The presentation of evidence is subject to objection by the opposing party ("Your Honor, I object!"). The basis of an objection must be stated (for example, prejudice or hearsay) and will be ruled on by the court—overruled or sustained.

In addition to probative value exclusions, many social policies operate to exclude relevant evidence. For example, there are limitations on the use of evidence of liability insurance, subsequent remedial measures, settlement offers, and plea negotiations. Why? Because the use of such evidence discourages parties from carrying insurance, fixing hazardous conditions, offering to settle, and pleading guilty to crimes.

Table 2-2 lists several types of evidence.[13] Some of these concepts are more relevant to forensic accounting than others, but practitioners should at least be familiar with all of them.

Evidence Rules Dealing Specifically with Experts

Several evidence rules specifically address expert witness testimony and thus are of special interest to the forensic accountant: Rules 702, 703, 704, and 705.

Rule 702

Rule 702 allows the testimony of an expert witness if it will assist the trier of fact (judge or jury) through the maze of "scientific, technical, or other specialized knowledge." Under this rule, expert testimony is admissible *only* if it meets three specific criteria:

- The testimony is based on *sufficient facts or data.*
- The testimony is the product of *reliable principles and methods.*
- The principles and methods have been *applied reliably* to the facts of the case.

Table 2-2 Types of Evidence

Type of Evidence	Description
Legal evidence	All admissible evidence, both oral and documentary, that reasonably and substantially proves the point rather than merely raising suspicion or conjecture
Admissible evidence	Evidence that is relevant and is of such a character (for example, not unfairly prejudicial or based on hearsay) that the court should receive it
Relevant evidence	Evidence that is both probative (tends to make a fact more or less probable) and material; admissible unless excluded
Material evidence	Evidence having some logical connection with the consequential facts or issues
Direct evidence	Evidence that is based on personal knowledge or observation and that, if true, proves a fact without inference or presumption
Circumstantial evidence	Evidence based on inference and not on personal knowledge or observation; also known as indirect evidence. Examples include fingerprints and DNA samples or, in a financial crime, evidence of the defendant's lifestyle
Character evidence	Evidence regarding someone's personality traits or moral standing in a community; based on reputation or opinion
Demonstrative evidence	Physical evidence that one can see and inspect
Documentary evidence	Evidence supplied by writing or other document, which must be authenticated before it is admissible
Hearsay evidence	Testimony given by a witness who relates not what he/she knows personally, but rather what others have said; depends on the credibility of someone other than the witness; generally inadmissible
Privileged evidence	Evidence that is exempt from production to an opposing party because it is covered by one or more statutory and common-law protections (such as attorney-client privilege)
Expert evidence	Evidence about a scientific, technical, or professional issue given by a person qualified to testify because of familiarity with the subject or special training in the field; also called expert testimony

Expert witnesses are usually qualified at the beginning of direct examination. Qualification is based on the expert's specialized knowledge, skill, experience, training, or education. Importantly, all five are not required.

Rule 703

Rule 703 allows an expert witness a considerable degree of latitude regarding the facts or data upon which his or her opinions are based. These facts or data need not be admissible as evidence themselves (such as hearsay), as long as they are of a type that is reasonably relied upon by experts in that field.

Rule 704

Rule 704 allows an expert to testify on areas that embrace an ultimate issue to be decided by the fact finder (for example, valuation of a business in a divorce action).

Rule 705

Rule 705 allows an expert to state an opinion without first testifying to the underlying facts or data, with the understanding that the opinion is subject to cross-examination. This cross-examination is important because an expert's opinion is only as good as the facts, assumptions, data, and methodology upon which it is based.

Expert Methodology

As previously discussed, an expert can expect his or her opinions, and the underlying foundation (facts, data, and methodology), to be thoroughly challenged by opposing counsel. An expert's methodology may be challenged in two ways:

- As unreliable "junk science." Because this type of challenge is a matter of law, it requires a *Daubert* ruling by the judge (discussed in the following section).
- As a legitimate area for cross-examination. Even if the judge allows an expert to testify, his or her testimony is still subject to cross-examination.

Daubert Challenge

As previously introduced, a ***Daubert challenge*** is a special hearing conducted before the trial judge to determine the relevance and reliability of an expert's opinion—that is, to rule on its admissibility. For an expert's opinion to satisfy the reliability requirement, the expert must be qualified in the relevant field, and the expert's opinion must be the product of sufficient relevant facts and data, reliable methodology, and the reasonable application of the methodology to the case facts. The term *Daubert challenge* comes from the 1993 U.S. Supreme Court Case, *Daubert v. Merrell Dow Pharmaceuticals.*[14]

Daubert established that a trial court judge has the duty to act as a "gatekeeper" under the FRE to ensure the scientific validity of the expert's testimony. Moreover, it set forth several factors that should be considered when evaluating expert testimony:

- Whether the methodology employed has been tested
- Whether the theory has been peer-reviewed
- What the known or potential error rate of the method is
- How well accepted the methodology is within the professional community
- Whether the expert's methodology existed before the subject litigation began

As provided in *Daubert*, the "court must focus on the methodology, not on the conclusions generated by the methodology." In other words, a *Daubert* hearing is not to decide whether the expert is correct. Opposing evidence (including opposing expert opinions) and cross-examination are traditional and appropriate means of attacking dubious but admissible expert testimony.

Prior to *Daubert*, the governing standard for determining the admissibility of scientific evidence was the *Frye* test.[‡‡‡] Under this test, expert opinion based on scientific methodology was admissible only if the methodology was "generally accepted" in the relevant scientific community. Critics of the *Frye* test argue that it is not flexible enough to address new scientific issues where general acceptance has not yet been established. In *Daubert*, the Supreme Court ruled that the FRE supersede the *Frye* test as the standard for admissibility of expert testimony in federal courts. Many, but not all, states have also adopted the *Daubert* standard in place of the *Frye* test.

The *Daubert* Trilogy

Four years after *Daubert*, in *G.E. v. Joiner* (1997),[15] the Supreme Court limited appellate review of the trial court's decision to admit or exclude expert testimony. Later, in *Kumho Tire v. Carmichael* (1999),[16] the Supreme Court directed that the *Daubert* factors be applied to *all* expert testimony, including testimony of a non-scientific nature (such as forensic accounting). In this ruling, the Supreme Court also granted trial courts freedom to consider other factors. Together, these three cases, known as the "*Daubert* trilogy," serve to interpret Rule 702.

Special Note

The rejection of expert testimony is the exception rather than the rule. The courts have displayed a tendency to favor the admission of weak expert evidence, if a minimum threshold of reliability is met, to let the adversarial system test it.[17]

---

‡‡‡ Based on *Frye v. United States*, 293 F. 1013 (1923).

PRIVILEGED COMMUNICATION

Privileged communication is a legal principle that protects communications taking place within a *protected relationship*. Commonly recognized protected relationships include attorney-client, husband-wife, doctor-patient, and clergyman-penitent. The privilege is a legal right of the source (for example, the client or patient rather than the lawyer or doctor). The underlying theory of privileged communication, articulated by the U.S. Supreme Court in *Upjohn Co. v. United States* (1981),[18] is that in certain instances, society is best served by the suppression (protection from disclosure) of information.

Suppression of information, however, is inconsistent with the general duty to disclose and is thus closely guarded by the courts. As previously discussed, in the discovery phase of civil litigation, each party is obligated to disclose to the opposing party all relevant and non-privileged evidence it proposes to use at trial, whether favorable or unfavorable.

Attorney-Client Privilege

Attorney-client privilege, the oldest of the protected privileges in law, is defined as the "client's right to refuse to disclose and to prevent any other person from disclosing confidential communications between the client and the attorney."[19] The requisite elements for establishing privilege include a *communication* that:[§§§]

- Relates to the rendering of legal services,
- Is made in confidence, and
- Is made to a person the client reasonably believed was an attorney.

The attorney-client privilege is intended to encourage individuals involved in legal disputes to be candid with their attorneys, thus enabling the attorneys to give sound legal advice. Once the attorney-client privilege has been established, it may be extended to non-attorneys (such as subordinates and consulting experts) who assist attorneys in rendering legal advice or services.

Work Product Doctrine

The ***work product doctrine***, recognized by the U.S. Supreme Court in *Hickman v. Taylor* (1947),[20] provides protection from discovery of documents, interviews, statements, and other items prepared by an attorney in anticipation of trial. The work product doctrine allows lawyers to prepare for litigation without risk that their work will be revealed to court adversaries.[****] Consistent with the rules governing attorney-client privilege, the work product doctrine can be extended to items prepared by non-attorneys who assist in rendering legal services.[21]

Courts have applied different tests to interpret the phrase "in anticipation of litigation." A minority of courts apply a stringent test under which documents are protected only if they were created for the "primary purpose" of assisting in litigation. In contrast, the majority view employs the "because of" standard.[22] Under this standard, work product protection applies if the document can fairly be said to have been created "because of" the prospect of litigation.

As a general rule, however, work product protection does not attach to documents that are prepared to satisfy legal or regulatory obligations in the ordinary course of business, or that would have been created in essentially the same form regardless of the litigation.[23]

Extending Attorney-Client Privilege and the Work Product Doctrine

An accountant-client privilege and accountant work product protection *do not exist* under federal (and most state) law.[††††] Any protection is by virtue of an engagement relationship

[§§§] For a full discussion of the foundation of attorney-client privilege and the classic test, see *U.S. v. United Shoe Mach. Corp.* (110 F. Supp. 295, 1953).

[****] Unlike attorney-client privilege, the work product doctrine is a right of the attorney rather than the client.

[††††] An exception is federally authorized tax preparers (FATP), who may have some limited "tax advice" privilege in civil matters under IRC 7525; 17 states protect (by statute) accountant-client communications to varying degrees.

with an attorney, through attorney-client privilege and attorney work product protection. These privileges *can* be extended to forensic accountants, but only under certain circumstances. Of particular significance is the nature of the engagement—that is, whether the forensic accountant serves as a consulting or testifying expert.

Communications between attorneys and *consulting* experts are generally protected under the attorney-client privilege and/or work product doctrine. Until recently, no such protection was afforded to communications with a *testifying* expert. This changed in December 2010, when FRCP 26(b)(4) was amended to allow the extension of work product protection to most attorney-expert communications and to all draft expert reports. This was a highly practical change, which served to reduce the cost of litigation and make the process more efficient.

Dig Deeper

For an extended discussion of these concepts, we recommend that students read "Attorney-Client Privilege and the Forensic Accountant" by Rufus and Miller (2007), published in *The Value Examiner*.

WORKING WITH ATTORNEYS

In addition to the rules and principles previously discussed, another key element of the legal framework is working with attorneys. An effective forensic accountant must have an open and honest working relationship with engaging counsel. There are, of course, many keys to maintaining such a relationship. Our top five include the following:

- *Communication.* There must be a clear understanding of what the forensic accountant has been engaged to do, the timeline in which the work is expected to be completed, the nature and venue of the case (federal vs. state or civil vs. criminal), and the payment of fees. This understanding should be clearly articulated in an engagement letter executed by both parties.
- *Respect.* There must be mutual respect between the parties in their specific roles. It is understood that lawyers advocate for their clients—with the intent of winning. In contrast, a testifying expert advocates for his or her opinion. The forensic accountant, when serving as an expert witness, must remain neutral and objective—that is, outside the influence of engaging counsel.
- *Responsiveness.* The forensic accountant must be responsive throughout the engagement, from the gathering and analysis of data to the timely development and presentation of the final report. The attorney must also be responsive in providing the expert with any requested information and promptly advising of schedule changes.
- *Responsibility.* The forensic accountant has a responsibility to the engaging attorney to exercise competence and due professional care in the development and presentation of his or her opinions. Moreover, the forensic accountant has a responsibility to the court to develop and present opinions honestly and objectively.
- *Ethical obligations.* In almost every case, some "gray area" will arise that must be resolved in a fair and ethical manner. To avoid a claim of "adversarial bias," a common practice is to resolve such issues in favor of the opposing party. Because there is often no clear answer, these concerns must be openly discussed with engaging counsel.

Dig Deeper

Over the years, many films have been created that provide illustrations of the judicial process. Although somewhat dated, we encourage students to consider the following selections: *Twelve Angry Men* (1957), *Anatomy of a Murder* (1959), *Inherit the Wind* (1960), *To Kill a Mockingbird* (1962), and *Presumed Innocent* (1990).

EPILOGUE: *U.S. V. BONNIE BAIN*

The Forensic Accountant's Analysis

In preparation for the sentencing hearing, Ms. Bain's attorney hired a forensic accountant to offer expert testimony regarding the amount of the embezzlement. The expert determined this amount, within a reasonable degree of professional certainty (the standard of proof in a sentencing hearing) by employing the net worth method. Because no increase in Ms. Bain's net worth could be identified, the expert's working hypothesis was narrowed to the simple proposition that the amount embezzled could be calculated as the excess of Ms. Bain's consumption (for example, living expenses and discretionary spending) over her legitimate income sources (for example, wages, gifts, and loans). Similar to the FBI's investigation, the expert's efforts included witness interviews, analysis of Ms. Bain's financial history, and consideration of her lifestyle and other patterns of behavior. The primary difference was that the expert had the opportunity to interview Ms. Bain. Interestingly, the expert's findings were nearly identical to those of the FBI.

Ms. Bain's forensic accountant was also asked to review the investigation report prepared by BB&T's CI division. Although she agreed with the report's conclusion that Ms. Bain had manipulated the bank's internal controls (for which she pled guilty), the forensic accountant identified several CI observations that questioned the probability (certainty) of the bank's findings. Examples include the following statements:

- "The policy violations make it difficult to determine if the differences (shortages) are due to theft or just a lack of supervision or proper management."
- "We still do not have concrete proof of how or when . . . the money was taken."
- "Extensive research has helped determine that Teller #5 (Ms. Bain) is *connected* (emphasis added) with the disappearance."
- "It's possible that BB&T purchased the embezzlement when it acquired the Bank."

The expert's report also identified certain investigative failures that challenged BB&T's working proposition that Ms. Bain acted alone in the embezzlement and was fully responsible. Examples of these failures include the following:

1. There was no investigation of "access" by others to the vault.
2. There was no investigation of access by others to identifying controls (for example, Teller numbers and passwords).
3. There was no investigation or consideration of possible co-conspirators.
4. CI's report demonstrated a false understanding of the legal concept of "proof."
5. BB&T's methodology provides an *indication* of supervisory and internal control failures, but not *proof* of the amount of money taken by Ms. Bain.
6. BB&T's findings are speculative and not presented within a reasonable degree of professional certainty.

Sentencing Hearing

To advance their respective arguments, both parties submitted copies of their expert reports for the court's consideration. On January 12, 2012, the sentencing hearing began with the court immediately challenging the expert report proffered by the government (BB&T's report), stating that it was not properly articulated or thoroughly supported. Moreover, the court expressed disapproval with the expert's opinion that something "could" have happened—that Ms. Bain could have walked out of the bank with more than $1 million. Due to these deficiencies, the court refused the expert's testimony.

The court then addressed the written report of Ms. Bain's forensic accountant, acknowledging the methodology employed (the net worth method) and the rationale presented in support of specific opinions. The court also acknowledged the similar analysis and findings of the FBI. At the court's encouragement, the matter was resolved (without further litigation) with the acceptance of the expert's findings ($293,376 as the amount embezzled) for the purposes of both sentencing and restitution.

As noted in the following DOJ press release, Ms. Bain was sentenced on February 6, 2012.[24]

Former Branch Banking and Trust Employee Sentenced to 30 Months in Prison for Making a False Bank Entry

> CHARLESTON, W.Va. – A former Branch Banking and Trust Company (BB&T) employee was sentenced today to 30 months in prison by United States District Judge John T. Copenhaver, Jr. for making a false bank entry.
>
> Bain admitted that from at least May 2004 to October 2007, she embezzled between $200,000 and $400,000 in cash from the West Side of Charleston's branch of BB&T. In order to conceal the embezzlement scheme and the resulting cash shortage, Bain admitted to making false entries in the company's books and records to make it appear as if the cash total reconciled when in fact it did not. Bain "floated" the outage among her teller drawer and general ledger accounts using various methods. To further her embezzlement scheme, Bain admitted to recording fictitious cash dollar amounts in her teller/vault drawer by force balancing. Bain also admitted that, on other occasions, she would reduce the cash shown in her teller/vault drawer by creating fictitious cash-out tickets.
>
> "Bank employees enjoy a special position of trust," said U.S. Attorney Booth Goodwin. "To abuse that trust is unconscionable," Goodwin continued. "It's a crime not only against the bank, but against everyone who counted on this defendant to keep their money safe and sound. I'm pleased we were able to bring her to justice, and I hope her sentence sends a powerful message."

The court ordered Ms. Bain to pay restitution of $293,376, payable in $250 monthly installments. Ms. Bain was ordered to report on March 16, 2012 to begin serving her sentence.

Special Note

U.S. v. Bonnie Bain highlights the difference between the work (purpose, objectives, and responsibilities) of a testifying expert and a fraud investigator. More importantly, it demonstrates the necessity, in either role, of understanding the legal environment.

APPENDIX 2-A
Hierarchy of Law

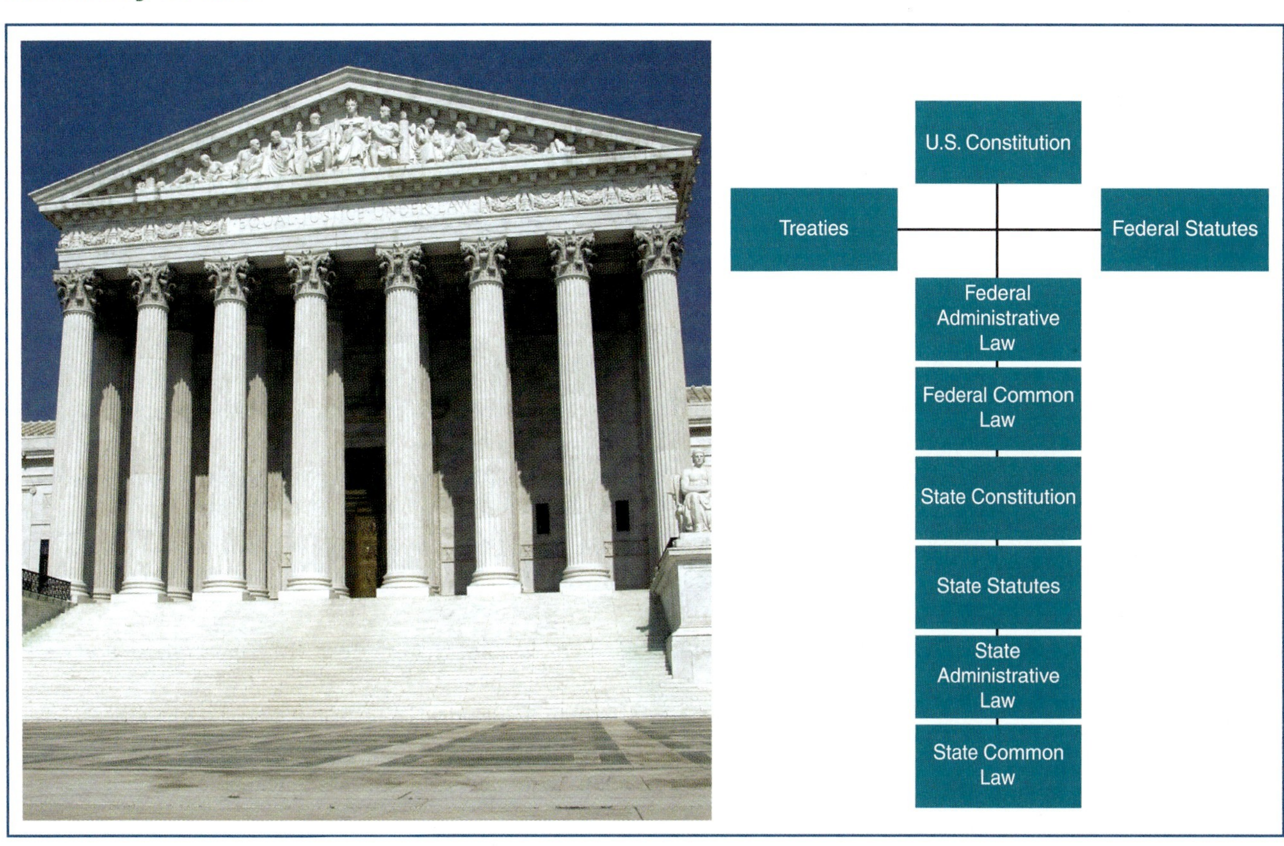

APPENDIX 2-B
Sample Complaint

IN THE CIRCUIT COURT OF KANAWHA COUNTY,
WEST VIRGINIA

John and Jane Doe,
Plaintiffs,
v. Civil Action No. ________

Robert J. Fellow,
Defendant.

TO: ROBERT J. FELLOW Service—Personal
111 Alphabet Street
Huntington, WV 25701

Summons
To the above-named Defendant:

IN THE NAME OF THE STATE OF WEST VIRGINIA, you are hereby summoned and required to serve upon **Joseph D. Jones,** Esquire, P.O. Box 1111, Charleston, West Virginia 25301, an Answer, along with any counterclaim you may have, to the Complaint filed against you in the above styled civil action, a true copy of which is herewith delivered to you. You are required to serve your answer within twenty **(20)** days of service of this Summons upon you, exclusive of the day of service. If you fail to do so, judgment by default will be taken against you for the relief demanded in the Complaint and you will be thereafter barred from asserting in another action any claim you may have which must be asserted by counterclaim in the above styled civil action.

Dated: December 1, 2012

CLERK OF COURT: ________

IN THE CIRCUIT COURT OF KANAWHA COUNTY,
WEST VIRGINIA

John and Jane Doe,
Plaintiffs,
v. Civil Action No. ________

Robert J. Fellow,
Defendant.

Complaint

1. Plaintiffs, John and Jane Doe (hereinafter referred to as "plaintiffs"), are residents of Charleston, Kanawha County, West Virginia.
2. Defendant, Robert J. Fellow (hereinafter referred to as "defendant") is a resident of Huntington, Cabell County, West Virginia.
3. On or about April 1, 2012, defendant was operating a 1962 Volkswagen Beetle on the campus of the University of Charleston in Charleston, Kanawha County, West Virginia.
4. On said date, the plaintiffs were walking on the University grounds in front of the Student Union.
5. The defendant, Robert J. Fellow, lost control of his vehicle because he was traveling at a high rate of speed while talking on his cell phone and negligently struck the plaintiffs, causing great bodily injury, pain and suffering, and emotional distress.

6. As a direct and proximate result of the negligence of defendant Robert J. Fellow, the plaintiffs suffered various serious and permanent injuries and incurred multiple medical expenses and are reasonably expected to incur future medical expenses.
7. As a direct and proximate result of the negligence of defendant Robert J. Fellow, the plaintiffs have endured pain, suffering, mental anguish, and emotional distress.
8. As a direct and proximate result of the negligence of defendant Robert J. Fellow, plaintiffs have in the past and will in the future suffer a diminished capacity to enjoy life.

WHEREFORE, the plaintiffs, John and Jane Doe, pray for judgment against defendant, Robert J. Fellow, in such amount as justified by the evidence.

Plaintiffs demand a trial by jury on all issues so triable.

John and Jane Doe,
By Counsel,

Joseph D. Jones, Esquire (WVSB #1111)
P. O. Box 1111
Charleston, West Virginia 25301
(304) 555-1111
(304) 555-1112 (telefax)

APPENDIX 2-C
Sample Answer

IN THE CIRCUIT COURT OF KANAWHA COUNTY, WEST VIRGINIA

John and Jane Doe,
Plaintiffs,
v. Civil Action No. _________

Robert J. Fellow,
Defendant.

Answer and Counterclaim of Defendant, Robert J. Fellow

NOW COMES the defendant, Robert J. Fellow, by counsel, Zachary M. Gallagher, and responds to the plaintiffs' Complaint as follows:

First Defense

Plaintiffs' Complaint fails to state a cause of action upon which relief can be granted and, accordingly, should be dismissed pursuant to Rule 12(b)(6) of the West Virginia Rules of Civil Procedure.

Second Defense

1. The defendant is without sufficient knowledge or information to either admit or deny the allegations contained in paragraph 1 of plaintiffs' Complaint and therefore demands strict proof thereof.
2. The defendant admits the allegations contained in paragraph 2 of plaintiffs' Complaint.
3. The defendant denies that he was operating a 1962 Volkswagen Beetle but admits the remaining allegations contained in paragraph 3 of plaintiffs' Complaint.
4. The defendant is without sufficient knowledge to admit or deny the allegations contained in paragraph 4 of plaintiffs' Complaint and demands strict proof thereof.

5. The defendant admits that he was talking on his cell phone but denies that he was driving at a high rate of speed. The defendant denies the remaining allegations contained in paragraph 5 of plaintiffs' Complaint.
6. The defendant is without sufficient knowledge to admit or deny the allegations contained in paragraph 6 of plaintiffs' Complaint and demands strict proof thereof.
7. The defendant is without sufficient knowledge to admit or deny the allegations contained in paragraph 7 of plaintiffs' Complaint and demands strict proof thereof.
8. The defendant is without sufficient knowledge to admit or deny the allegations contained in paragraph 8 of plaintiffs' Complaint and demands strict proof thereof.
9. The defendant denies that the plaintiffs are entitled to the recovery demanded in their Complaint.

Third Defense

The defendant further denies each and every other allegation asserted in the plaintiffs' Complaint not specifically and expressly admitted herein.

Fourth Defense

The defendant denies that he is liable to the plaintiffs in any amount or that the plaintiffs are otherwise entitled to the recovery and/or relief sought in the plaintiffs' Complaint.

Fifth Defense

Plaintiffs are guilty of acts of negligence which proximately caused or proximately contributed to the alleged injuries and damages, if any.

Sixth Defense

The defendant invokes the defenses of contributory negligence, assumption of risk, and comparative negligence.

Seventh Defense

The defendant asserts all of the affirmative defenses contained within Rule 8(c) of the West Virginia Rules of Civil Procedure as if fully set forth herein, including statute of limitations.

Eighth Defense

The defendant reserves unto himself any and all defenses disclosed by discovery herein.

WHEREFORE, the defendant demands that the plaintiffs' Complaint filed herein against him be dismissed and that he be awarded his costs in defending this action.

Counterclaim

COMES NOW, the counterclaimant, Robert J. Fellow, by way of Counterclaim, and states as follows:

1. Robert J. Fellow is an individual who lives in Huntington, Cabell County, West Virginia.
2. On April 1, 2012, Robert J. Fellow was the owner and operator of a 1964 Volkswagen Beetle.
3. That on the date aforesaid, plaintiffs attempted to cross the street outside a designated crosswalk and carelessly stepped into the path of defendant's vehicle.
4. As a result of the plaintiffs' careless actions, the alleged injuries sustained by the plaintiffs, if any, were the result of their own misconduct and negligence.
5. The sole and proximate cause of the plaintiffs' injuries, if any, was the result of said misconduct and negligence.

WHEREFORE, Robert J. Fellow demands judgment as follows:

1. Judgment in favor of Robert J. Fellow for defamation of character in the amount of $1,000,000.00 (One Million Dollars).
2. Judgment in favor of Robert J. Fellow for his annoyance, inconvenience, embarrassment, humiliation, and loss of control of his life, all in excess of $2,000,000.00 (Two Million Dollars).

WHEREFORE, the Counterclaim of Robert J. Fellow demands judgment of and against John and Jane Doe in the amount $3,000,000.00 (Three Million Dollars), or such other amount as a jury may award, together with prejudgment interest, costs and attorney fees.

Robert J. Fellow,
By Counsel, _________

Zachary M. Gallagher, Esquire (WVSB #2222)
P. O. Box 2222
Charleston, West Virginia 25301
(304) 555-2222
(304) 555-2223 (telefax)

IN THE CIRCUIT COURT OF KANAWHA COUNTY, WEST VIRGINIA

John and Jane Doe,
Plaintiffs,
v. Civil Action No. _________

Robert J. Fellow,
Defendant.

Certificate of Service

I, Zachary M. Gallagher, counsel for defendants, do hereby certify that I have served the foregoing **Answer And Counterclaim Of Defendant, Robert J. Fellow** upon the following by placing a true and correct copy thereof in a properly addressed, postage-paid envelope and depositing same in the United States mail this 15th day of December, 2012.

Joseph D. Jones, Esquire
P. O. Box 1111
Charleston, West Virginia 25301

____

Zachary M. Gallagher

Key Terms

Arbitration
Attorney-client privilege
Beyond a reasonable doubt
Burden of proof
Clear and convincing evidence
Daubert challenge
Default judgment
Discovery
Evidence
Federal Rules of Civil Procedure
Federal Rules of Evidence
Justice
Mediation
Preponderance of the evidence
Presumption of innocence
Privileged communication
Probative value
Reasonable degree of professional certainty

Relevant evidence

Sanctions

Standard of proof

Verdict

Voir dire

Work product doctrine

Chapter Questions

2-1. Explain the "rule of law doctrine" as used in the United States.

2-2. Describe the three basic functions of law, and explain the importance of each to the U.S. judicial system.

2-3. What are the subdivisions of public law in which a forensic accountant might be engaged? Provide a short explanation of each.

2-4. What are the categories of private law in which a forensic accountant might be engaged? Provide a short explanation of each.

2-5. Identify five key differences between the actual process of the U.S. judicial system and its portrayal in popular television programs such as *Law & Order* and *CSI.*

2-6. What are the three stages of a civil trial? Discuss each stage.

2-7. Who files a complaint, and what type of information does it contain?

2-8. What is an answer? Who files an answer, and how is it presented?

2-9. What is the purpose of the discovery process? What types of activity occur during this process?

2-10. As set forth in the Federal Rules of Civil Procedure, what specific items must an expert report contain?

2-11. What is meant by *voir dire*? What types of personal information do attorneys seek to obtain from prospective jurors in the *voir dire* process?

2-12. Identify the key stages of a civil trial, and describe what occurs during each stage.

2-13. Describe the significant differences between the structure of a civil trial and the structure of a criminal trial.

2-14. Who bears the burden of proof in a legal action? Explain.

2-15. Identify the two standards of proof that may be applicable to a civil case. Describe each in terms of probability.

2-16. What standard of proof is required for a prosecutor to obtain a guilty verdict in a criminal case? What level of probability is assigned to this standard?

2-17. Explain why a testifying expert can provide an opinion in a civil or criminal case, but other witnesses cannot do so.

2-18. What purpose do the Federal Rules of Evidence serve in the U.S. judicial system?

2-19. What constitutes evidence in the U.S. judicial system?

2-20. Define relevant evidence. When is relevant evidence admissible?

2-21. What is meant by probative value? Provide examples of when a court may exclude evidence from being admitted because it lacks probative value.

2-22. Identify and discuss the three necessary criteria for expert witness testimony under FRE 702.

2-23. What are the two ways in which an expert's testimony can be challenged during a trial?

2-24. What is a *Daubert* challenge? Who initiates this challenge and why?

2-25. Under the *Daubert* standard, what five factors should a judge, as gatekeeper, consider in determining the admissibility of expert witness testimony?

2-26. What is privileged communication? Explain and provide examples.

2-27. What are the three criteria that must be met to establish attorney-client privilege?

2-28. Describe the work product doctrine. What is its primary purpose?

2-29. Identify five key elements of a forensic accountant's relationship with engaging counsel.

Multiple-Choice Questions

2-30. According to the AICPA, a working knowledge of the legal environment is a core forensic accounting skill.

a. True

b. False

2-31. Each of the following is a function of law *except*:

a. Preservation of the state

b. Ensuring fairness is achieved in all trials

c. Protection of property

d. Dispute resolution

2-32. The judicial process is administered and managed by the trial attorneys.

a. True

b. False

2-33. A juror is permitted to conduct personal research in an effort to obtain additional information regarding a case.

a. True

b. False

2-34. Each of the following is a division of public law *except*:

a. Contract law

b. Criminal law

c. Administrative law

d. Constitutional law

2-35. Divisions of private law that commonly involve the services of forensic accountants include all of the following *except*:

a. Partnership law

b. Tort law

c. Sales law

d. Contract law

e. All of the above are divisions of private law

2-36. Television programs and movies present realistic portrayals of how the U.S. judicial system works.

a. True

b. False

2-37. Which of the following is a specific stage in a civil trial?

a. Opening remarks stage

b. Juror testimony stage

c. Pleading stage

d. None of the above is a stage in a civil trial

2-38. The Federal Rules of Civil Procedure govern the way in which information is gathered in a civil action. These rules are applicable to which stage of a civil case?

a. Jury deliberations

b. Sentencing

c. Juror selection

d. Discovery

2-39. Rule 26(a)(2) requires that all expert opinions, such as those of a forensic accountant, be disclosed to the opposing party during the discovery stage.

a. True

b. False

2-40. In the trial stage of a legal proceeding, *voir dire* refers to the process during which the judge and participating attorneys question prospective jurors about their backgrounds and beliefs.

a. True

b. False

2-41. "A preponderance of the evidence" describes a higher standard of proof than "clear and convincing."

a. True

b. False

2-42. In a criminal trial, witnesses are never permitted to offer their opinions as evidence.

a. True

b. False

2-43. In most states, the admissibility of evidence is governed by:

a. Federal Rules of Civil Procedure

b. Evidence Admission Procedures

c. Common Law Provisions

d. Federal Rules of Evidence

2-44. A primary purpose of expert testimony is to:

a. Ensure that testimony by other witnesses is relevant

b. Assist the trier of fact in understanding complex issues

c. Help an attorney present opening and closing arguments

d. None of the above are purposes of expert testimony

2-45. Which of the following is a *Daubert* criterion that a trial judge should consider when evaluating expert testimony?

a. The degree of acceptance of a method within a professional community
b. Whether a theory has been peer-reviewed
c. Whether a methodology has been tested
d. The known or potential rate of error of a method
e. All of the above should be considered

2-46. Communications between attorneys and testifying experts have always been protected under the work product doctrine.

a. True
b. False

2-47. Each of the following is a requisite element for establishing a communication that is protected under the attorney-client privilege *except*:

a. Is made to a person reasonably believed to be an attorney
b. Is made to the arresting police officer
c. Relates to the rendering of legal services
d. Is made in confidence

2-48. The work product doctrine is intended to:

a. Allow attorneys to prepare for litigation without risk that their work will be revealed to court adversaries
b. Ensure that all court documents are prepared and presented in a timely manner
c. Verify that all witnesses disclose their intended testimony during discovery
d. Ensure that all documents presented at trial are filed in a manner prescribed by the court

Workplace Applications

2-49. For the case *U.S. v. Bonnie Bain*, address the following:

1. Why was the investigation conducted by BB&T limited in scope to its internal documents and interviews of its employees?
2. Why did the BB&T investigators make observations and present information favorable to Ms. Bain's defense?
3. Why was Ms. Bain put on paid administrative leave?
4. What is the difference between a "preponderance of the evidence" and "beyond a reasonable doubt"?
5. Did the BB&T investigators expect to have their report submitted to the court, and thus subject to FRCP 26 provisions?
6. What constitutes the presentation of an expert opinion in a *legally sufficient manner*?
7. How certain must an expert's opinion be? What is the difference between plausible, possible, and probable?
8. What is meant by *sufficient* facts or data?
9. What is *reliable* methodology?
10. Did the forensic accountant expect to have his report submitted to the court?

2-50. Considering the case *U.S. v. Bonnie Bain*, develop a list of items the defense might seek to obtain through the discovery process.

2-51. Go to a state or federal courthouse and observe part of a trial. If jurors are being selected, try to determine the basis on which the attorneys for the defendant and the plaintiff are accepting or rejecting potential jurors. If the trial is in progress, observe the process by which testimony is offered and evidence is presented. Which of the Federal Rules of Evidence discussed in this chapter are reflected in your observations? If an expert testifies, observe how the expert's professional credentials are established and how his/her opinion is presented to the court. Describe how the direct examination of the expert witness differs from cross-examination.

Prepare a memo to your instructor setting forth what you observed and how it relates to the concepts you learned in this chapter.

Chapter Problems

2-52. Go to the AICPA web site and review the document entitled *Characteristics and Skills of the Forensic Accountant.* Identify the top five characteristics or skills as identified by attorneys, and compare those to the top five as identified by CPAs. Write a memo to your instructor that:

a. Identifies the characteristics by ranking

b. Discusses the specific nature of each characteristic or skill

c. Discusses the differences in ranking between attorneys and CPAs

2-53. Review Rule 26(a) of the Federal Rules of Civil Procedure. Prepare a memo to your instructor outlining the specific information an expert's written report must contain to satisfy the requirements of this rule.

2-54. Review Rule 26(b) of the Federal Rules of Civil Procedure. Prepare a memo to your instructor outlining the rules of discovery for:

a. Materials

b. Experts

c. Those claiming privilege

2-55. Review Rule 26(e)(2) of the Federal Rules of Civil Procedure. Prepare a memo to your instructor outlining the requirements for a testifying expert to provide additional information, not previously presented, that is expected to be offered at trial.

2-56. Review the Federal Rules of Evidence, specifically Rules 101, 102, 103, and 104. Identify the key requirements set forth in each rule, and prepare a memo to your instructor discussing how each rule impacts the presentation of evidence in a civil and criminal trial.

2-57. Review the Federal Rules of Evidence, specifically Rules 401 and 402. Prepare a memo to your instructor that explains relevant evidence, including what makes it admissible in a court of law.

2-58. Investigate Rule 702 of the Federal Rules of Evidence. What qualifies a witness as an expert? Under what conditions may an expert testify in a court of law? Prepare a memo to your instructor describing the requirements for expert witness testimony.

2-59. Find a summary of the *Daubert v. Merrell Dow Pharmaceuticals* court case. Identify five criteria a trial judge should consider when evaluating expert testimony. Prepare a memo to your instructor discussing each of the five criteria.

2-60. Obtain a copy of Rufus and Miller's 2007 article, "Attorney-Client Privilege and the Forensic Accountant" published in *The Value Examiner.* (A link to this article is available at www.pearsonhighered.com/rufus.) Study this article and prepare a memo to your instructor outlining the key court cases that determine how privilege can be extended to a consulting forensic accountant as well as to his/her work product.

2-61. Watch a clip from the film *My Cousin Vinny* (available via a link at www.pearsonhighered.com/rufus) that provides a humorous example of how the qualifications of an expert witness can be challenged.

After viewing this clip, prepare a memo to your instructor identifying the factors used to establish the witness as an expert. Also, explain how the testimony of the expert might influence the jury's consideration of the evidence.

---

1 Go to www.pearsonhighered.com/rufus for a link to this press release.

2 *Nunez v. Allstate Ins. Co.*, 604 F.3d 840, 847 (5th Cir. 2010).

3 AICPA. (2012). CFF Content Specification Outline. Go to www.pearsonhighered.com/rufus for a link to this document.

4 *Black's Law Dictionary.* (2009). 9th ed., 1448.

5 Ibid., 942.

6 Cravens, S. M. (2007). In pursuit of actual justice. *Alabama Law Review, 59.* University of Akron Legal Studies Research Paper No. 07-09.

7 U.S. Constitution, Preamble.

8 *Black's Law Dictionary.* (2009). 9th Ed., 942–43.

9 Go to www.pearsonhighered.com/rufus for a link to this document.

10 Go to www.pearsonhighered.com/rufus for a link to this document.

11 *Black's Law Dictionary.* (2009). 9th Ed., 635.

12 *Winfred D. v. Michelin North America, Inc.* (2008). 165 Cal. App. 4th 1011.

13 *Black's Law Dictionary.* (2009). 9th Ed., 635–40.

14 *Daubert v. Merrell Dow Pharmaceuticals*, 509 U.S. 579 (1993).

15 *G.E. v. Joiner*, 118 S. Ct. 512. (1997).

16 *Kumho Tire Co. v. Carmichael*, 119 S. Ct. 1167 (1999).

17 Stern, A. J. (2011). *Federal Civil Practice Update 2011: A Practical Guide to New Developments, Procedures & Strategies*. Practising Law Institute.

18 *Upjohn Co. v. United States*, 449 U.S. 383 (1981).

19 *Black's Law Dictionary.* (2009). 9th Ed., 1317.

20 *Hickman v. Taylor*, 329 U.S. 495 (1947).

21 *U.S. v. Nobles* (422 U.S. 225, 238, 1975).

22 *Maine v. United States Dept. of Interior*, 298 F.3d 60 (1st Cir. 2002).

23 Russell, R. (2009, Oct. 18). Case exposes tax work papers to IRS. *Accounting Today*.

24 Go to www.pearsonhighered.com/rufus for a link to this press release.

3 Screening and Staging Engagements

INTRODUCTION

In the world of forensic accounting, screening and staging engagements are paramount to success. Screening, as the name implies, is a vetting process to avoid undesirable clients and cases, especially where the threats (risks) exceed the rewards. We liken preengagement screening to preemployment screening, where the objective is to hire the right applicant—or accept the right engagement. Staging, simply stated, means to plan and coordinate the engagement in terms of scheduling the work to be completed and compiling the necessary resources.

As will be illustrated in this chapter, these foundational functions require careful consideration and cannot be overemphasized. First, we identify the primary factors to consider *before* accepting an engagement. Second, we introduce and encourage the use of engagement letters, which serve as the contract for service. Third, we discuss framing a case in the context of specific control factors. Finally, we review the usefulness of the scientific approach and the value of research. Throughout our discussion, we offer recommendations for best practices and identify potential pitfalls to be avoided. In short, the purpose of this chapter is to familiarize you with the efforts involved in *preparing* for an engagement—before the actual work begins.

Learning Objectives

After completing this chapter, you should be able to:

LO1. Identify five primary factors that should be considered when screening an engagement.

LO2. Define a conflict of interest in the context of a forensic accounting engagement, and explain the importance of identifying and disclosing any potential conflicts.

LO3. Describe the purpose and content of an engagement letter.

LO4. Identify the factors involved in "framing" a case, and explain how each impacts case development.

LO5. Explain how a scientific approach can be used in forensic accounting engagements.

LO6. Describe the value and role of research in forensic accounting.

Mattco Forge, Inc. v. Arthur Young & Company

As a preface to our discussion, let's consider the landmark case of *Mattco Forge, Inc. v. Arthur Young & Company*, which is an extreme illustration of failed screening and staging that resulted in twelve years of convoluted and costly litigation.

Special Note

This is a significant case for the accounting profession for three reasons: (1) it was the first successful case against a major CPA firm for negligence in litigation support services; (2) it was the first appellate case that adopted the "trial-within-a-trial" approach for determining accounting malpractice; and (3) it created an important precedent for limits on expert witness immunity.

Background

Mattco Forge, Inc. (Mattco) is a manufacturing company located in Paramount, California, that supplies forged metal parts to various businesses, including General Electric (GE). In September 1985, Mattco filed a federal civil rights action against GE alleging that its removal (delisting) as an approved subcontractor was racially motivated. To prevail in its claim, Mattco needed to prove damages (lost profits) with reasonable certainty *and* prove that the proximate cause of the damages was the wrongful act/s of GE.

To help develop its case, Mattco engaged the services of Arthur Young & Company (EY) as a damages consultant and expert witness. EY's challenge was to determine Mattco's "lost profits" attributable to its wrongful delisting by GE. Importantly, EY was engaged (selected) based on representations by Richard E. Lamping, EY's managing partner, regarding the firm's specialized (forensic accounting) training and litigation support expertise.

Special Note

In 1989, Arthur Young & Company merged with Ernst & Whitney to create Ernst & Young (EY), one of the largest professional service firms in the world and one of the current "Big Four" accounting firms.

The Engagement

As an expert witness, EY was expected to develop its opinion through the consideration of sufficient relevant facts/data and the employment of accepted methodology. Thus, EY was expected to consider reliable factors without undue speculation. EY was also expected to identify and consider "other factors" that may have contributed to Mattco's lost profits, adjusting its damage calculations accordingly.

EY assigned the Mattco engagement to Thomas W. Blumer. Although Blumer was a CPA and a member of EY's litigation support group, he had no forensic accounting training or experience in litigation matters.

Special Note

As discussed in Chapters 1 and 2, a unique feature of forensic accounting is the legal context in which it occurs. For this reason, forensic accountants receive specialized training in investigations and the legal environment, including discovery, evidence, methodology, judicial process, and forming and expressing expert opinions. You should recall FRE 702 (Chapter 2), which provides for expert witness testimony (scientific, technical, or other specialized knowledge) that will assist the trier of fact *only* if it is based on sufficient facts or data and is the product of reliable and case-appropriate methodology.

Calculation of Mattco's Lost Profits

A calculation of lost profits commonly includes: (a) determination of lost gross revenues, (b) determination of avoided costs,* and (c) determination of "net" lost profits, computed by subtracting *b* from *a*. In other words, only "net" lost profits are considered damages.

To calculate Mattco's lost profits, Blumer focused on prior competitively bid contracts with GE, specifically sixty job folders. The folders purported to contain (among other job-specific items) original estimate sheets used by Mattco to approximate its costs. During his review of the available records, Blumer discovered that twenty-six of the estimate sheets were missing. At Blumer's request, Mattco prepared new estimate sheets. Blumer placed these sheets in the twenty-six job folders and proceeded to use them in his calculation of Mattco's net lost profits.

Following submission of EY's expert report, GE requested copies of all documents that EY relied on in forming its opinion. In response, Blumer assembled packets of information on each of the sixty jobs, commingling the new estimate sheets and the original records without qualification. He delivered the packets to Mattco's attorneys, who then delivered them to GE.

GE's Counterclaim

In August 1987, after examining the records provided by EY and other evidence obtained through discovery, GE filed a motion to dismiss and counterclaim against Mattco alleging fraud in the production of evidence "in an attempt to fraudulently increase the damages." Specifically, GE alleged that Mattco, with the assistance of its forensic accountant EY, altered and fabricated estimate sheets that were used by EY to calculate damages.

Mattco argued that the new estimate sheets were prepared at the request of EY (Blumer) and were presented to EY as "rough" or "best recollections." Moreover, Mattco claimed that EY knew the records were not exact replications of the missing estimate sheets. Finally, citing the deposition testimony of Richard Lamping, Mattco argued that the productions (new estimate sheets) were not relevant because EY had not relied on them in calculating damages.

* Incremental costs that were not incurred because of the lost revenues.

The Court's Ruling

In March 1989, following an exhaustive review of the evidence, Federal Judge Richard Gadbois granted GE's motion to dismiss with the following findings:

- Mattco knowingly altered, fabricated, and produced estimate sheets used to help calculate damages, thereby perpetrating a fraud upon GE, the court, and the judicial process.
- EY relied on the fabricated estimate sheets in calculating damages.
- The actions of Mattco tainted all the evidence produced.
- Due to EY's intimate involvement in producing the fabricated evidence, EY was prohibited from involvement in any future production of evidence in this action.
- No work papers, files, or other materials used by EY to calculate Mattco's damages could be used in any future production of evidence on that subject.

Judge Gadbois also issued an Order of Sanctions against Mattco for $1.4 million, directly related to the fabrication of evidence issue. Mattco did not appeal the federal court's rulings.

Special Note

The epilogue for this case, which describes Mattco's subsequent claims against EY, is presented at the conclusion of the chapter.

SCREENING ENGAGEMENTS

As illustrated in the *Mattco* case, deciding whether to accept or reject an engagement is a critical decision that requires careful evaluation of the engagement's proposed risks and rewards. Risks include, but are not limited to, threats to compliance, threats to competence, consumption of resources, missed deadlines, logistics, suitability of the specific engagement, litigation (malpractice claims), court sanctions, and damage to the practitioner's (and firm's) professional reputation. Rewards, on the other hand, include compensation, recognition, enhanced professional reputation, sense of accomplishment, and employee or firm morale.

An economic assessment of an engagement's risks and rewards can be stated in terms of its risk-reward ratio. In practice, the determination of this ratio differs widely among practitioners, due primarily to their subjective perceptions of the definition and importance of each of the two components (risks and rewards). In other words, no two individuals will have the same perception of what constitutes a risk or reward and how much positive or negative value it provides. It is our experience that practitioners (especially new forensic accountants) focus too heavily on the rewards and grossly understate the threats associated with a potential assignment.

Special Note

In Chapter 10, we discuss engagement threats and safeguards and the challenge of making good decisions. The AICPA's *A Guide for Complying with Rules 102–505* (2008) is introduced as a meaningful practice aid.

Preengagement Considerations

As part of the screening process, several preengagement factors should be considered.

1. *The engaging attorney (that is, the client).* Attorneys are "in it to win it." Because their purpose is to advocate for their clients, attorneys look for experts who can assist them in this effort. As with all experts, forensic accountants must be aware that some attorneys are quite willing to sacrifice an expert's reputation to advance their clients' cause (and thus their own). A few red flags of such "bad" clients are identified as follows:

- Reputation for unethical practices and poor/marginal work
- Reputation for expert abuse, such as:
    - Demanding rush assignments
    - Pirating an expert's name and reputation[†]

[†] Occurs when an attorney settles or attempts to settle a case based on the expert's name and reputation, without actually engaging the expert.

    - Failing to provide material evidence
    - Manipulating the expert's evaluation of the evidence
    - Pushing the expert outside his/her areas of expertise
    - Failing to sign and return an engagement letter
- Reputation for being slow or nonresponsive to information/data requests
- Reputation for slow (or no) payment

A "good" client, in contrast, displays the following characteristics:

- Direct, timely, and proper communication (keeps you "in the loop")
- An understanding and respect for the role of the expert witness (little or no pushing)
- Responsive to data requests (provides on a timely basis and does not hide adverse information)
- Prompt payment of invoices

2. *Conflicts of interest.* Any potential conflicts of interest must be identified before accepting an engagement. Why? What is a conflict of interest? Moreover, how do you identify a conflict of interest?

Let's first address the concept of a conflict of interest. In the context of forensic accounting, a ***conflict of interest*** is defined as a real or perceived incompatibility between the interests of two clients or between the interests of the client and the forensic accountant (or firm).[1] Key considerations in this regard are impaired objectivity and independence. ***Objectivity*** requires the forensic accountant to be neutral (unbiased) and intellectually honest, while ***independence*** precludes the acceptance of any engagement that impairs the forensic accountant's objectivity. If a potential conflict of interest is identified, it must be fully disclosed to the client before the engagement is accepted. Moreover, written ***consents*** must be obtained, by which the affected parties explicitly acknowledge the conflict and waive any objections related thereto.

Let's now consider the "why." In addition to specialized knowledge and skills, a forensic accountant's calling cards are independence, integrity, and objectivity. An allegation of a conflict, whether real or perceived, may serve to undermine an expert's credibility. Thus, regardless of consents, we recommend the rejection of all engagements in which a potential conflict has been identified.

Conflicts of interest can be identified by reviewing the subject complaint, which specifies the parties (plaintiffs and defendants), the case facts, and the respective attorneys. The expert should consider whether a past or present relationship with any of the named parties could be perceived as a conflict.

Caution

A forensic accountant may be engaged as a "joint expert," or an expert for both parties, which most commonly occurs in domestic (divorce) litigation. The rationale is that hiring one expert reduces fees and saves time. Moreover, by eliminating the bias that may result from working for either of two adverse parties, a joint expert's expert opinion is thought to be more objective. Despite these proposed benefits, we strongly advise against this practice because the risk for the expert is simply too great. Our experience suggests that one (or both) of the parties will be dissatisfied with the results—that is, the expert's opinion.

A joint expert is in the precarious position of being subject to suit by both parties, which essentially doubles the risk without any increase in reward. However, this risk may be mitigated if an expert is appointed by the court (the court's expert), rather than being agreed upon by the attorneys (a joint expert). A court-appointed expert is generally granted quasi-judicial immunity, which limits exposure to malpractice claims. Still, we caution that joint expert engagements should generally be avoided.

3. *Competence and due care.* Before accepting an engagement, the forensic accountant should always compare the required competencies against his or her portfolio of skills and resources. The diversity of forensic accounting engagements makes this a critical consideration. For example, one who is skilled in performing business valuations is not necessarily skilled (professionally competent) to conduct a fraud investigation or determine economic damages. In firms with multiple associates, those with less experience must be properly supervised and managed. (Remember Tom Blumer!)

All forensic accounting engagements are conducted within a set of time constraints, established by deadlines. These deadlines are often set by the court and are outside the control of the attorney or the expert. Missing a report deadline can result in serious consequences, including court sanctions, legal claims from the client, and damage to one's reputation. Thus, before accepting an engagement, a forensic accountant must confirm the case timeline (applicable deadlines) and balance these demands with competing obligations. Our experience suggests that rushed engagements are destined for disaster—like a speeding car in a school zone. Rarely (if ever) does the reward justify the risk.

4. *Nature and scope of the assignment.* Another preengagement consideration is the specific nature and scope of the proposed assignment, or, exactly what the expert is being engaged to do. In addition to the expert's competence to complete the task, the conditions surrounding the engagement must be evaluated. Examples of key factors include the availability and condition of data, accessibility of witnesses, unusual risks, travel requirements, scope limitations, and other special circumstances. Evaluating the nature and scope of a proposed assignment allows the expert to effectively assess its risk and make appropriate strategic decisions (for example, acceptance, planning, staffing, and pricing).

5. *Compensation.* The final consideration before accepting an engagement is compensation. How much are you going to be paid? When? Who is responsible for payment? How are fee disputes resolved?

We consider only one compensation arrangement to be safe: an hourly fee with a retainer. Hourly fees vary based on the education and experience of the practitioner, as well as market factors (supply and demand). The advantages of an hourly fee include its self-explanatory nature, ease of measurement, and ease of communication—work is billed as it is performed. A retainer is an advance payment for services, against which hourly fees are charged. Retainers should be collected before work begins and should be replenished when depleted. In so doing, the expert avoids establishing a creditor relationship with clients, which can create various pressures that may undermine independence and objectivity. The amount of the retainer should be based on the scope of anticipated services.

Given the many unknowns of a forensic accounting engagement, we discourage fixed or flat-fee payment arrangements. Moreover, under no circumstances can an expert witness provide services under a contingent fee, successful efforts, or outcome-based arrangement. Again, independence and objectivity would certainly be undermined in such a situation.

The Engagement Letter

After deciding to accept a proposed engagement, the next step is to secure an engagement letter. This can also be considered a screening procedure, because it identifies clients who are unwilling to accept the forensic accountant's conditions for the engagement.

Purpose of an Engagement Letter

An ***engagement letter*** identifies the responsible parties, defines the nature (or purpose) of the relationship, identifies limitations on the scope of the work to be performed, and outlines specific terms (such as fee schedule and terms of payment). In essence, engagement letters are contracts that define the legal relationship and demonstrate clients' understanding and acceptance of their responsibilities. To ensure a meeting of the minds, we suggest that engagement letters be signed by both parties—that is, the engaging attorney and/or client and the expert.

Engagement letters are generally addressed to the engaging attorney, to establish the expert's relationship as the attorney's agent. As discussed in Chapter 2, this agency relationship has critical implications for protecting communications under the attorney-client privilege and work product doctrine. Even when engaged as a testifying (rather than consulting) expert, which implies very limited protection, the expert is still considered an agent of the attorney.

Practitioner's Perspective

Some attorneys are hesitant to sign engagement letters, because they do not want to accept personal responsibility for payment of the expert's fees. In such cases, the client can sign the engagement letter, although it should still be addressed to the attorney. This is a reasonable compromise only for attorneys with whom the expert has an established relationship. Unfamiliar attorneys who immediately posture themselves to avoid payment of the expert's fees should be managed with caution.

As an engagement evolves, it is common to amend or supplement the engagement letter. Of course, since the engagement letter is a contract, any such modifications must be approved by both parties.

Are engagement letters required when providing litigation services? Yes and no. As previously discussed, forensic accountants work in a legal environment with specific responsibilities as either consulting or testifying experts. A critical function of the engagement letter is to establish the nature of an engagement and any protections attached therewith (attorney-client privilege and work product protection).

Special Note

The 1961 landmark decision *U.S. v. Kovel* established guidelines for determining when communications involving an accountant who works for an attorney may be protected under the attorney-client privilege. Referring to this decision, an engagement letter that establishes an agency relationship between the attorney and the expert is commonly referred to as a "Kovel letter." Specifically, a Kovel letter should confirm that the expert is being retained to assist the attorney in providing legal services. For an extended discussion of the historical development and significance of the Kovel letter, as well as the perils of not securing one, see "Attorney-Client Privilege and the Forensic Accountant" by Rufus and Miller (2007), published in *The Value Examiner*.

Despite their many benefits, engagement letters for providing litigation services are currently not required under the AICPA's professional standards. (They are encouraged, but not required.) Regardless, an engagement (Kovel) letter is absolutely necessary to protect both the practitioner and the client and reduce the opportunities for misunderstandings.

Content of an Engagement Letter

The specific content of an engagement letter depends on the nature of the engagement. As a general rule, however, an engagement letter should address the following issues:[‡]

- Identification of responsible parties
- Purpose of the engagement (services to be performed)
- Nature of the relationship (consulting or testifying expert)
- Limitations on the scope of the work
- Issues of independence, conflicts of interest, and confidentiality
- Ownership, use of materials, and attorney work product
- Fees, invoicing procedures, and retainers
- Right to terminate
- Dispute resolution provisions

‡ See Engagement Letters for Litigation Services—Forensic and Valuation Services (FVS) Practice Aid 04-1 (AICPA, 2004).

When drafting an engagement letter, it is important to consider that engagement letters of testifying experts are discoverable. In such cases, opposing counsel may use an expert's engagement letter as a valuable source of insight into the litigation strategy of the client. Moreover, opposing counsel can use the engagement letter to challenge the expert's work process and conclusions. If the expert did not do exactly what he or she was engaged to do, this discrepancy will be a likely target for challenge. We caution that, although certain content is necessary in engagement letters, too much information provides fodder for cross-examination.

Clients frequently request estimates of both when an assignment will be completed and how much it will cost. Because these determinations are difficult to make at the outset of an engagement, we advise the avoidance of such commitments. However, if provided, the expert must ensure the client's understanding that estimates are *estimates*— not *guarantees*. Moreover, we caution against including such estimates in the engagement letter, due to the binding nature of this document.

Special Note

You are encouraged to review and discuss the various components of this chapter's appendix, a typical forensic accounting engagement letter.

STAGING AN ENGAGEMENT

After accepting an engagement and executing an engagement letter, the forensic accountant begins to stage the engagement. Staging, as previously noted, involves planning and coordinating an assignment. Relevant to this effort are framing, the scientific approach, and the value of research.

Special Note

Your understanding of the framing factors discussed in this section will evolve as you continue reading this text. Our immediate objective is to guide you to begin thinking like a forensic accountant.

Framing a Case

Framing a case involves "boxing" it by specific control factors including, but not limited to, the following:

- *Type of case.* As previously discussed, the type of case (criminal or civil) determines the requisite standard of proof (preponderance of the evidence vs. beyond a reasonable doubt). The standard of proof may drive the evidence-gathering process (such as accessibility and significance) and thus the scope of the engagement. The standard of proof also impacts the manner in which an expert opinion must be expressed.

- *Jurisdiction.* A court's ***jurisdiction*** is the domain over which it exercises judicial authority. Different jurisdictions (federal vs. state, one state vs. another, family court vs. circuit court) have unique characteristics that significantly impact how a case is developed and how evidence, including an expert's report, is presented. For example, federal cases are formal (a "black tie affair"). Moreover, most federal courtrooms have extensive technological resources, thus facilitating more flexibility in the presentation of visual evidence such as photographs, videos, and slide presentations. State courts tend to be less formal and sophisticated and family courts even less so.

More importantly, different jurisdictions often have different laws and use different rules of procedure and evidence. For example, domestic law varies from state to state, which will impact a business valuation engagement for the purpose of divorce. As discussed in Chapter 2, although most states have embraced the federal rules of procedure and evidence, there are certain exceptions. Thus, before accepting an engagement, practitioners should address any potential jurisdictional issues with engaging counsel. Moreover, practitioners must familiarize themselves with the relevant statutes and case law and be prepared to conduct any additional research necessary for the specific engagement.

- *Professional standards.* A forensic accountant must adhere to all applicable ***professional standards***, such as AICPA or NACVA, when performing an engagement. In the world of forensic accounting, the highest (most rigorous) level of professional standards always applies. Professional standards commonly include:
    - General/ethical standards, including issues such as integrity and objectivity, professional competence, and due professional care
    - Development standards, which address the development of the expert's opinion (including sufficiency and reliability of the data, scope limitations, and methodology)
    - Reporting standards, which address the form and content of the expert's report

Experts must have a working knowledge of the applicable professional standards, since they are often a key component of questioning in depositions and cross-examinations. More importantly, failure to adhere to the requisite standards undermines the validity of the expert's opinion in the specific case and may damage his or her professional reputation going forward.

- *Nature of the engagement.* The nature of the engagement (such as fraud investigation, business valuation, or economic damages calculation) is the most obvious distinguishing characteristic of a case. It drives the type of evidence to be gathered, the ways in which the evidence is analyzed, and the substance of the conclusion.

Although certain basic competencies are required of all forensic accountants, the different types of engagements involve specialized knowledge and skills. Moreover, within any given type of engagement, certain specific knowledge may be necessary. For example, practitioners that perform business valuations may specialize in certain industries, such as oil/gas or health care. As previously noted, practitioners may not be qualified to perform every type of engagement.

- *Purpose of the engagement.* The different types of forensic accounting engagements clearly have different purposes. However, even engagements of the same type may have different purposes. For example, a fraud investigation may stem from an internal suspicion or a formal criminal charge. Similarly, a business valuation can be performed for a variety of purposes, such as divorce, estate/gift tax, or a shareholder dispute.

Just as the type of engagement drives the development of a case, so too does its purpose. For example, a business valuation performed for estate or gift tax purposes is substantially more comprehensive than one prepared for a divorce case, specifically because of compliance mandates (IRS Revenue Ruling 59-60). Valuations for the purpose of divorce, on the other hand, may require the bifurcation of goodwill in jurisdictions where enterprise goodwill is considered marital (and thus subject to division) and personal goodwill is considered non-marital (and thus not subject to division).

- *Scope.* Engagements may be limited with regard to their ***scope***, which defines the extent of the analysis. Scope limitations often take the form of assumptions on which the expert relies. Some assumptions are common to most engagements, such as reliance on the client's representations or other third-party data without independent verification.

In a fraud investigation, for example, the scope of analysis may be limited to a particular individual, time frame, location, or activity. For business valuations, the lack of available data (financial data, organizational records, management interviews, or industry/economic data) may require scope limitations. Economic damages calculations, which often involve projections many years into the future, require many assumptions. Because the future cannot be known with certainty, factors such as the injured party's expected future earnings, duration of employment, and life expectancy must be assumed. It is important, however, that all assumptions be identified and qualified as such.

- *Relevant dates.* Most forensic accounting engagements involve a pre-determined date or time period, which acts as a scope limitation. A fraud investigation may cover a specific time period (for example, January through September 2012), based on some preliminary indication of the duration of the suspected activity. Similarly, a business valuation has a specific valuation date (for example, June 30, 2012). Although the applicable date/s may appear to be a relatively straightforward determination, this critical factor must be carefully considered. If the time period for a fraud investigation is wrong, the investigation will find no evidence of the activity and incorrectly conclude the absence of fraud. Dates are also critical in business valuations, since the value conclusion may be very different for different valuation dates.

As illustrated in Figure 3-1, the elements comprising the framework of a case demonstrate the fusion of law and accounting—forensic accounting. The framing process enables the forensic accountant to view the case through the right lens—in other words, its proper context. This contextualization facilitates efficient and effective planning and execution of the assignment, from defining the engagement to communicating results.

As we explore throughout this text, these framing factors are integrated (linked). Because a change in one factor may drive changes in another factor, they must be considered together, not in isolation. Finally, and perhaps most importantly, framing a case identifies the requisite, or legally sufficient, manner in which an expert's opinions must be communicated. Failing to properly frame a case early in the engagement can result in serious consequences, such as court sanctions or malpractice claims.

Special Note

This framework may be difficult to conceptualize without a specific case scenario to which it can be applied. Thus, you are encouraged to revisit this discussion during the case development challenges presented in subsequent chapters.

A Scientific Approach

Forensic accountants are commonly challenged with gathering, synthesizing, and summarizing evidence. Filtering and assimilating large amounts of evidence can be a daunting task. Our experience suggests that the most effective and efficient approach is to employ a ***scientific process***. The five steps of the scientific process (discussed below) provide order, reasoning, and direction to the assignment. Moreover, the use of a scientific approach enhances the credibility of the expert's opinions and the ease of communicating those opinions.

1. *Define the purpose (or problem).* This seemingly easy first step is more than just a re-statement of the purpose specified in the engagement letter. Rather, the problem must be considered in its entire context. Exactly what have you been engaged to do? What type of

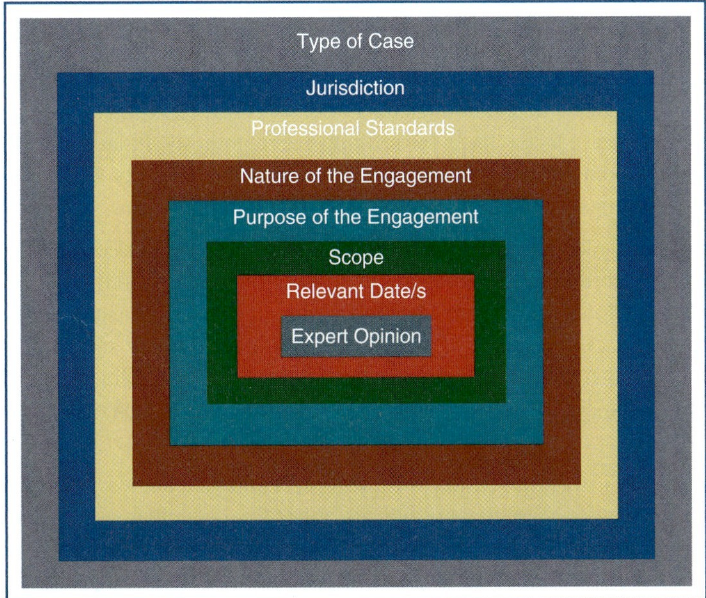

Figure 3-1
The Framework of a Case

conclusion will your analysis produce? Will this conclusion offer a solution to the problem? A properly stated problem serves as the guiding force for subsequent case development. In determining the relevance of potential data or methodologies, one must always consider how the results will shed light on the problem of interest.

2. *Form a hypothesis.* Forming a working hypothesis is generally the most difficult task in the scientific process for both students and practitioners. A hypothesis is not a statement of fact; it is simply a tentative explanation based on preliminary observations (case facts or suspicions) that must be tested. Preliminary observations can be provided by the engaging party or generated through the expert's independent research.

At this point in the engagement, the goal is not to identify the single "right answer," but rather to identify a reasonable explanation or solution for the stated problem that can be adequately tested with the available data. Identification of potential explanations is accomplished through the application of abstract reasoning, not some systematic procedure. Due to the ambiguity inherent in this reasoning process, it is a skill that grows with application and experience.

3. *Gather evidence.* The purpose of gathering evidence is to test the validity of the hypothesis. In other words, does the evidence support the hypothesis? Can the facts of the case be explained in terms of the hypothesis? The evidence-gathering process should be iterative in nature. This means that the forensic accountant must constantly re-evaluate and refine his or her working hypothesis as new evidence is collected and evaluated.

Evidence-gathering techniques commonly used by forensic accountants and explored in this text include the following:

- Direct observations
- Interviews
- Structured activities, such as surveys and focus groups
- Financial statements analysis
- Statistical analysis
- Benchmarking
- Case studies

4. *Interpret data and refine the hypothesis.* Interpreting data involves an evaluation of *all* the evidence to determine the probability that the hypothesis is true. Although certain statistical techniques can produce specific probabilities, such instances are rare in the world of forensic accounting. Thus, for most engagements, the concept of probability must be considered more generally.

When evaluating evidence, the forensic accountant cannot ignore negative facts, inconsistencies, or discrepancies that challenge his or her working hypothesis. Instead, these observations should serve as the basis for refining the hypothesis. Finally, applying critical thinking skills, the forensic accountant should not immediately accept all evidence at face value. Remember, things (and people) are not always what they seem.

When evaluating evidence, the forensic accountant should make an effort to document and date all items considered. Such a record will help keep the process on track and avoid duplication of efforts. Moreover, it can be used at a later stage to demonstrate to the court the fairness of the process, thus enhancing the validity of the final conclusions. Because this data log, like an engagement letter, may be used by opposing counsel as a resource for challenging the expert witness, it should be limited to facts and direct observations only, without speculation.

5. *Draw conclusions.* After gathering sufficient facts and data and employing reliable methodology, the forensic accountant draws his or her final conclusions (opinions). This last step requires a mix of both deductive and inductive reasoning. If the previous steps in the scientific process have been properly executed, the conclusion should flow logically from the data analysis. Likewise, any weaknesses in the underlying framework will undermine the validity of the conclusion.

Specific report writing strategies (for example, mandates of FRCP Rule 26) will be discussed in Chapter 12. For now, it is sufficient to know that an expert's report generally identifies the purpose and nature of the assignment, provides a detailed discussion of the specific steps followed, identifies the information considered and relied upon, identifies limiting conditions, provides conclusions (opinions), and discloses any other pertinent information.

We acknowledge that practitioners develop their own methods and techniques, which are modified to fit the unique circumstances of a given engagement. Even so, we argue that general adherence to a scientific approach, as illustrated in Figure 3-2, is a best practice. Specific benefits of the scientific approach include the following:

- Ensures a systematic process that can be duplicated to confirm results
- Reflects professionalism and due care
- Decreases liability by reducing the potential for missed steps
- Facilitates communication of the process and results (in both report form and deposition/trial testimony)
- Enhances the credibility of conclusions and opinions (because the process is commonly accepted in the professional community)

The Value of Research

How does anyone know anything? Can people gain knowledge through education, training, observation, common sense, experience, advice from others, or media exposure? Let's consider this operative question in the context of forensic accounting.

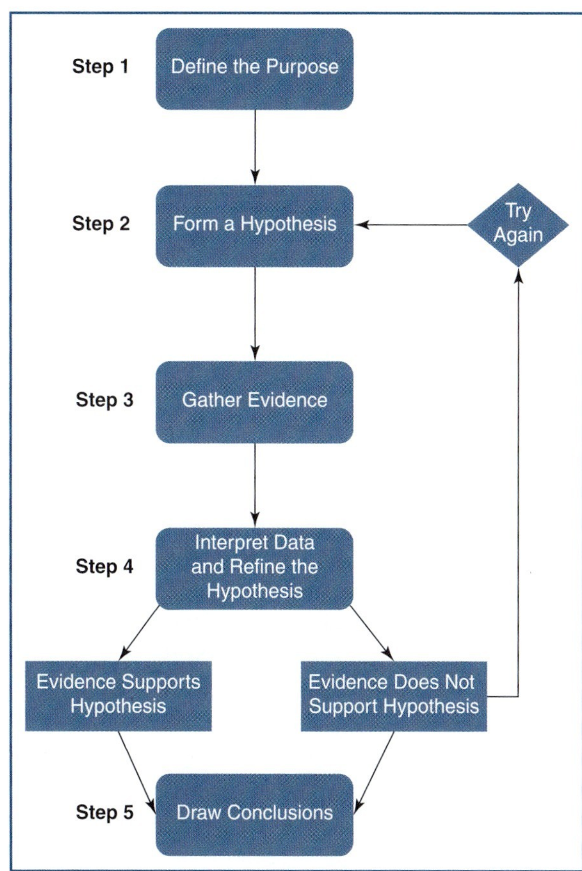

Figure 3-2
Scientific Approach to an Engagement

Forensic accountants are engaged to complete a specific assignment, within a specific context, employing professionally accepted processes, theories, and/or methodologies. As previously discussed, this requires the collection of sufficient relevant facts and data, along with the application of appropriate methodologies to develop and support conclusions. To that end, forensic accounting work involves substantial research.

What Is Research?

For the purposes of our discussion, ***research*** is defined as a systematic investigative process that starts with a question or problem (purpose of the engagement) and involves the collection, analysis, and interpretation of information to answer the question, solve the problem, or simply provide a greater understanding of the situation.[2] Research enhances critical thinking and reasoning skills and, by extension, results in fewer mistakes and better decisions—in other words, a more fully developed, reasoned, and defensible opinion.

Primary Research

Forensic accountants perform both primary and secondary research. ***Primary research*** is engagement-specific and involves the collection, analysis, and interpretation of primary (original) data. Examples of primary sources of information regularly considered by forensic accountants include:

- Witness interviews
- On-site observations
- Financial data (tax returns, general ledgers, financial statements, payroll records, projections/forecasts, audit reports, and asset schedules)
- Bank records (bank statements, cancelled checks, and loan documents)
- Asset protection data (insurance policies and appraisals)
- Organizational data (stock certificates, corporate minutes, and shareholder/operating agreements)
- Communications data (phone records and email histories)
- Personnel data (personnel policies, employee personnel files, and organizational charts)

Because forensic accounting engagements are frequently data intensive, primary research can be time-consuming and expensive. It is rarely possible for a forensic accountant to analyze the entire universe of relevant data. Rather, a sample is usually selected, which may be determined externally (by the client or by availability/access restrictions) or independently by the forensic accountant. In either case, this represents a scope limitation that must be disclosed.

Another implication of the data intensive nature of forensic accounting engagements is the necessity of a detailed research plan. This plan is developed at the outset of the engagement and continuously refined thereafter. A key function of a research plan is to specifically identify the data to be collected and analyzed. This determination is necessary to establish: (a) whether the data is available and (b) whether it can be processed within the time frame of the engagement. Moreover, the research plan is a useful tool in case development, serving as a roadmap for the data analysis stage. The plan should be clearly linked to the purpose of the engagement, to ensure that the results shed light on the subject research question/problem.

Secondary Research

In contrast to primary research, ***secondary research*** involves the collection, analysis, and interpretation of data (information) that has been compiled and published by others. Secondary sources of information are rarely case-specific, but rather relate more generally to the subject matter of the research question or problem. Secondary research is commonly used by forensic accountants in refining a hypothesis, developing critical assumptions, and selecting methodologies. Secondary research may also serve as a springboard for primary research, helping to identify relevant data and select an appropriate sample. Examples of secondary sources of information considered by forensic accountants include:

- Published statistics (tax, employment, income, education, life expectancy, and historical economic data)
- Published economic forecasts (trends and projections)
- Academic publications (theory development, methodology development, and the existing body of primary research)
- Professional publications (best practices, trends, application of theory and methodology, and case studies)
- Law review articles (legal arguments, summaries of case law, and defense or prosecution strategies)
- Published court cases
- Media (newspapers, magazines, and television)

Online Research

The Internet can be a valuable resource for the forensic accountant. Many of the data sources utilized in secondary research are now available online. In addition to information published by independent third parties, the Internet also contains "unpublished" content regarding entities or individuals, such as company web sites, web logs, social networks, and chat rooms. Such unpublished content might also provide important evidence in an engagement.

Although online research clearly has a place in the forensic accountant's tool box, it is a double-edged sword. The Internet has a number of research benefits, including breadth and depth of subject matter, quick access, and ease of use. However, it also contains much false and/or misleading information, which is clearly inconsistent with the *Daubert* standard. Moreover, the sheer volume of available information can be easily overwhelming and difficult to navigate, leading the researcher off track. Thus, you are encouraged to view Internet sources with caution and skepticism and, whenever possible, use academic search engines (such as ProQuest and LexisNexis).

Characteristics of Good Research

Only quality research should be used to support an expert opinion, whether it is the practitioner's own primary research or references collected through secondary research. As highlighted previously, an online search will produce sources of varying quality. Although the tendency is to focus on studies that are highly relevant to the subject matter of the engagement or that support the practitioner's working hypothesis, care must be taken to determine whether they reflect a sound research process. "Bad" research is not always easy to identify, because low-quality studies are often published, sometimes even in highly reputable publications. To assist in evaluating the work of others, as well as the practitioner's own research efforts, several characteristics of "good research" provide guidance:

- Research starts with a clearly stated problem or question.
- Research follows a specific plan of procedures that is designed to gather sufficient, relevant, and reliable data. Reliable data must have an authoritative source, such as academic or peer-reviewed journals.
- Research is guided by the specific problem and a working hypothesis. As previously discussed, a working hypothesis is a tentative explanation based on preliminary observations. Ultimately, hypotheses are never proved or disproved—they are either supported or rejected.
- Research accepts certain critical assumptions that provide a foundation or framework for the analysis.
- Research requires reliable methodology that facilitates the collection, analysis, and interpretation of the data.

EPILOGUE: *MATTCO FORGE, INC. V. ARTHUR YOUNG & COMPANY*

Following the dismissal of its case against GE, Mattco pursued a series of claims against EY.

Mattco v. EY—Part I

In July 1989, Mattco sued EY in the Los Angeles Superior Court alleging eight counts of professional misconduct, including negligence, fraudulent misrepresentation, and fraudulent concealment.

Before trial, EY filed a motion for summary judgment citing expert litigation privilege. EY's argument was based on the doctrine of witness immunity, a longstanding protection that encourages witnesses to be forthright and candid in their testimony without fearing legal retaliation. Generally, the privilege applies to any communication (1) made in judicial proceedings, (2) by litigants or other authorized participants, (3) to achieve the objects of the litigation, and (4) that had some logical relation to the action.[3] The motion was granted, and Mattco appealed.

Mattco v. EY—Part II

On appeal, Mattco argued that the expert litigation privilege should not apply to EY because the firm was engaged as a voluntary (friendly) expert and was compensated for its services. Mattco further argued that a testifying expert must be accountable for negligence and held to professional standards, specifically the duties of competence and due professional care.[4] Finally, Mattco argued that it was fraudulently induced to engage EY based on the firm's false representations of specialized training in forensic accounting and litigation support expertise.

The court ruled that the expert litigation privilege does not shield a party's own witness (EY) from an action by the party (Mattco) arising from the expert's negligence and breach of contract. The appeal was granted, and the case was remanded for trial.

Mattco v. EY—Part III

The trial against EY started in February 1994. Mattco's case-in-chief was that its claim against GE had "value" that was not realized because of EY's negligence and fraud. Mattco argued that, in addition to the lost value of its claim against GE, it also incurred significant out-of-pocket expenses (including accounting and legal fees) in defending the numerous discovery and dismissal motions in GE's counterclaim.

Mattco's position was that, if not for EY's "inept process of calculating damages," the twenty-six new estimate sheets would never have been created and Mattco would not have been placed in the position of defending the damage calculation based on the estimate sheets. Mattco argued that EY's promotional literature advertised the firm as having the ability to assist attorneys and clients having a "real or apparent lack of data." Moreover, Mattco argued that the new estimate sheets were not necessary because the actual costs were available and could have been used in calculating lost profits. Finally, Mattco argued that EY had fraudulently misrepresented its training and experience in litigation support. Key evidence included the firm's "glossy promotional brochure," Blumer's lack of qualifications, and EY's failure to comply with the AICPA professional standards.

Special Note

As previously discussed, the forensic accountant must *always* comply with the requisite professional standards. The specific standard of interest in the *Mattco* case is Rule 201 (General Standard) of the AICPA's Code of Professional Conduct, which mandates that its members have *professional competence,* exercise *due professional care,* adequately *plan and supervise* the services being performed, and secure *sufficient relevant data* to provide a basis for the opinions offered.

Although the AICPA's professional standards will be discussed in Chapter 10, you are encouraged to review Rule 201 in the context of *Mattco.*

Throughout the proceeding, EY maintained that Mattco *would not* have prevailed in its claim against GE and thus had suffered no damages from EY's negligence (if so found). In support of its argument, EY offered the findings of Federal Judge Richard Gadbois. EY also attempted to offer expert legal testimony that Mattco's case against GE was "doomed" and would have been dismissed. However, the trial court refused EY's expert testimony, finding it to be "speculative."

The trial lasted four months (February to June), during which 40 witnesses and 880 marked exhibits were presented to the jury. The case was given to the jury with the following instructions:

- If you find that Mattco *has not* sustained its burden of proof (preponderance of the evidence), the verdict must be for EY.
- If you find that Mattco *has* sustained its burden of proof, the verdict must be for Mattco.
- If you find that Mattco is entitled to recover for damages proximately caused by EY, you must consider the following elements:
    - The value of Mattco's case against GE
    - Mattco's out-of-pocket expenses
    - Interest on the out-of-pocket expenses
    - Punitive damages by "clear and convincing evidence" that EY was guilty of fraud

In June 1994, the jury rendered its verdict in favor of Mattco, with a total award of $42 million, including $14.2 million in compensatory damages and approximately $28 million in punitive damages. EY was found responsible for professional malpractice, fraudulent misrepresentation, and fraudulent concealment. EY appealed the verdict, arguing that the trial court erred in ruling that Mattco was not required to establish that, absent EY's negligence, Mattco would have prevailed in its claim against GE. In summary, EY argued that the lack of a proper causation instruction allowed Mattco to avoid its burden of proving that EY's negligence caused Mattco to lose its lawsuit against GE.

Mattco v. EY—Part IV

In February 1997, the California Court of Appeals[5] ruled that the trial court's fundamental instructional ruling was erroneous and prejudicial and thus reversed the judgment for Mattco's award of damages, except for the portion related to Mattco's out-of-pocket expenses ($1 million, including $45,000 paid to EY) and interest thereon. The case was remanded for a new trial.

On April 30, 1997, Mattco's appeal to the Supreme Court of California was denied. The parties subsequently settled, and the lawsuit was mutually dismissed.

Think About It

The *Mattco* case illustrates the importance of properly screening and staging an engagement. Consider the findings of the jury: professional malpractice, fraudulent misrepresentation, and fraudulent concealment. Also consider the condemning evidence against EY: twenty-six falsely represented estimate sheets, a failed and "inept process of calculating damages," EY's promotional literature, and EY's failure to comply with the AICPA professional standards. What did you learn?

APPENDIX 3-A

Sample Engagement Letter

February 29, 2012

Zachary M. Gallagher, Esq.
P. O. Box 2222
Charleston, West Virginia 25301

Re: Imperial Concrete Company v. Myers Trucking et al.
Civil Action No. _____

Dear Mr. Gallagher:

This letter serves to establish the terms of our engagement in the above matter.

1. ***Assignment***

   We will assist you in evaluating any economic damages related to the subject claim.

2. ***Conflicts of Interest***

   We have undertaken a reasonable review of our records to determine our professional relationships with the persons or entities you identified. We are not aware of any conflicts of interest or relationships that would, in our sole discretion, preclude us from performing the above work.

3. ***Fees***

   Our work will be conducted on a time and materials basis and will be charged at the following hourly rates:
   - Richard Thacker: $275/hr ($350/hr for trial or deposition);
   - Shelley Johnson: $200/hr ($250/hr for trial or deposition); and
   - Administrative support: $45/hr.

   Our hourly rates are subject to change from time to time due to increased experience of our staff and changing market conditions. We will advise you immediately if rates are being adjusted. You will be responsible for fees at the increased rates.
   We charge a minimum two-hour deposition fee, which must be paid in advance by the deposing attorney. This fee is non-refundable in the event of cancellation within 48 hours of the scheduled deposition.

4. ***Payment for Services***

   All invoices are due on presentation. Invoices for which payment is not received within 30 days of invoice date shall accrue a late charge of 1.5 percent (or the highest rate allowable by law) compounded monthly.

   We reserve the right to halt further services until payment is received on past-due invoices. You will be notified if/when it becomes necessary to exercise this right.

   If you have any questions regarding an invoice, or dispute any time charges or costs contained therein, you agree to contact us in writing within 30 days of receipt of the invoice. We will promptly respond to explain the charges or correct any errors.

5. ***Retainer***

Given the nature of this engagement, a refundable retainer of $5,000 is herewith requested. Invoices will be charged against this retainer until it is depleted. Depending upon the anticipated scope of services required, an additional retainer may then be requested.

6. ***Documents Review***

Due diligence requires that we review all documents you send to us. Time spent in such review will be billed at our regular hourly rates.

7. ***Confidentiality***

We understand that all communications between us and your firm, either oral or written, as well as any materials or information developed or received by us during this engagement, are protected by applicable legal privileges and, therefore, will be treated by us as confidential. Accordingly, we agree, subject to applicable law or court order, not to disclose any of our communications, or any of the information we receive or develop in the course of our work for you, to any person or entity apart from your office, or such other persons or entities as your office may designate.

8. ***Work Product***

Any written reports or other documents that we prepare are the property of Thacker & Johnson, AC. They are to be used only for the purpose of this litigation and may not be published or used for any other purpose without our express written consent.

9. ***Documents Retention***

At the end of the engagement, you will have two options related to the documents or copies of documents that we do not need to retain in our files: (a) have us return all such documents to you; or (b) authorize us to destroy them. At the end of the engagement, please contact us regarding your desired disposition of documents. We reserve the right to destroy the documents if there are no instructions from you within ninety (90) days of the completion of our assignment.

10. ***Dispute Resolution***

In the event of a dispute over fees for our engagement, we mutually agree to try in good faith to resolve the dispute through mediation by selecting a third party to help us reach an agreement. If we are unable to resolve the fee dispute through mediation, we agree to submit to resolution by arbitration in accordance with the rules of the American Arbitration Association. Such arbitration shall be binding and final.

If the above fairly sets forth your understanding of our services, please sign below and return this letter as soon as possible.

Respectfully,

Thacker & Johnson, AC

____

Accepted by:

Key Terms

Conflict of interest

Consent

Engagement letter

Independence

Jurisdiction

Objectivity

Primary research

Professional standards

Research

Scientific process

Secondary research

Chapter Questions

3-1. What are the five primary factors a forensic accountant should consider before deciding to accept an engagement?

3-2. When determining whether to accept an engagement with an attorney, what negative indicators suggest the possibility of an undesirable professional relationship?

3-3. When determining whether to accept an engagement with an attorney, what positive factors suggest that a favorable professional relationship will exist?

3-4. Describe a conflict of interest. Why should forensic accountants seek to avoid conflicts of interest?

3-5. How are the concepts of objectivity and independence related to the consideration of a possible conflict of interest?

3-6. Assume that a forensic accountant cannot identify a specific conflict of interest related to a potential engagement, but there is a chance that the engagement might create the perception of a conflict of interest in the professional community. Should this engagement be accepted? Explain why or why not.

3-7. How might a forensic accountant use a complaint to assess the potential for a conflict of interest?

3-8. What is meant by the term *joint expert*? If you are asked to serve in this capacity, what factors should you consider before accepting the engagement?

3-9. What is professional competence? How does ensuring consistency between a forensic accountant's skills and the skills required by a specific engagement relate to professional competence?

3-10. How was a lack of professional competence exhibited by Tom Blumer in the *Mattco* case?

3-11. How might a case deadline imposed by the court impact a forensic accountant's consideration of due professional care?

3-12. What is meant by "determining the nature and scope" of a forensic accounting engagement?

3-13. What factors should a forensic accountant consider when determining the compensation structure for an engagement?

3-14. A common compensation structure in forensic accounting engagements is an hourly fee with a replenished retainer. Define and discuss this arrangement.

3-15. Should a forensic accountant accept an engagement on a contingent-fee basis? Why or why not?

3-16. What is the purpose of an engagement letter?

3-17. Assume that an attorney asks you to provide services as a consulting expert but refuses to sign an engagement letter. What is an appropriate response?

3-18. What is a Kovel letter? Discuss its significance in a forensic accounting engagement.

3-19. Do the AICPA professional standards require an engagement letter?

3-20. Identify the nine components commonly included in an engagement letter. Briefly discuss each.

3-21. Why is it important that a forensic accountant's actual execution of an engagement be consistent with the assignment specified in the engagement letter?

3-22. What is meant by *framing* a case?

3-23. What is the purpose of framing a case? What general categories are considered in the framing process?

3-24. Why is the type of case (criminal or civil) significant?

3-25. Define *jurisdiction* in terms of a forensic accounting engagement.

3-26. Does the jurisdiction of a case impact the manner in which evidence is presented? Explain.

3-27. How should a forensic accountant respond when more than one set of professional standards is applicable to an engagement?

3-28. Which of the framing factors is the most obvious distinguishing characteristic of a case? Why?

3-29. How does the purpose of an engagement impact the work product of a forensic accountant?

3-30. Define the scope of a forensic accounting engagement and provide examples of common scope limitations.

3-31. Explain why a clear understanding of relevant dates is critical to a forensic accounting engagement.

3-32. What is a scientific process? What are the primary steps in such a process? Briefly discuss each step.

3-33. What is a hypothesis?

3-34. Why does a forensic accountant gather evidence?

3-35. Identify three evidence-gathering techniques and provide a brief explanation of each.

3-36. What does a forensic accountant consider during the data interpretation step of a scientific process?

3-37. Discuss the skills a forensic accountant draws on when reaching a conclusion in a scientific process.

3-38. What are the advantages of applying a scientific process to a forensic accounting engagement?

3-39. Define *research*. How is it valuable to a forensic accountant?

3-40. What is primary research? Identify and discuss two examples of information sources for primary research.

3-41. Describe a research plan. How is it employed by a forensic accountant?

3-42. What is secondary research? Identify and discuss two examples of information sources for secondary research.

3-43. Define online research. What should a forensic accountant consider when using this research tool?

3-44. Discuss five characteristics of good research.

3-45. What is the primary lesson a forensic accountant should learn from the *Mattco* case presented in this chapter?

Multiple-Choice Questions

Select the best response to the following questions related to the engagement acceptance decision:

3-46. Deciding to accept or reject an engagement requires careful consideration of the case's risks and rewards.

- **a.** True
- **b.** False

3-47. Which of the following is *not* a primary factor in determining whether an engagement should be accepted or rejected?

- **a.** The engaging attorney's reputation
- **b.** Professional circumstances
- **c.** Compensation
- **d.** Competence and due care
- **e.** Conflicts of interest

3-48. A "bad" client will exhibit one, and possibly more, of the following attributes *except*:

- **a.** Slow payment
- **b.** Rush assignments
- **c.** Failing to provide material evidence
- **d.** Pirating an expert's name/reputation
- **e.** All of the above are attributes of a bad client.

3-49. A "good" client will exhibit all of the following attributes *except*:

- **a.** Prompt payment
- **b.** Timely communication
- **c.** Respect for the role of an expert
- **d.** Reluctance to share information
- e. All of the above are attributes of a good client.

3-50. Performing a conflicts of interest check is a must before accepting an engagement.

- **a.** True
- **b.** False

3-51. If a forensic accountant's objectivity and independence are impaired, there is a high likelihood that a conflict of interest exists.

- **a.** True
- **b.** False

3-52. Which of the following is an attribute of objectivity?

- **a.** Involved
- **b.** Unbiased
- **c.** Participating
- **d.** Engaged

3-53. Independence means that objectivity is not impaired.

- **a.** True
- **b.** False

3-54. If a potential conflict exists, it must be identified, written consents must be secured, and the matter must be fully disclosed after an engagement has been completed.

- **a.** True
- **b.** False

3-55. Where there is no real conflict of interest, but a perception of a conflict exists, the best practice is to reject the engagement.

- **a.** True
- **b.** False

Select the best response to the following questions related to engagement acceptance:

3-56. The best source of information for identifying conflicts of interest is:

- **a.** The engaging attorney
- **b.** The presiding judge
- **c.** Reading the complaint
- **d.** Talking to the plaintiff

3-57. If all members of a firm have passed the CPA exam, they have the appropriate competencies for any type of forensic accounting engagement.

- **a.** True
- **b.** False

3-58. Determining the nature and scope of a proposed engagement allows a forensic accountant to do which of the following?

- **a.** Assess the engagement's risk
- **b.** Plan the engagement
- **c.** Develop a supervision plan
- **d.** Price the engagement
- **e.** All of the above are benefits of scope qualification.

3-59. A retainer is an advance payment for services that is earned as services are completed.

- **a.** True
- **b.** False

3-60. The preferred compensation arrangement for a forensic accountant is:

- **a.** Percentage of the damage award
- **b.** Contingent fee based on the final outcome of an engagement
- **c.** Hourly fee with a replenished retainer
- **d.** All of the above are acceptable compensation arrangements.

3-61. An engagement letter identifies all of the following aspects of an engagement *except*:

- **a.** The party who will cross-examine witnesses in a trial
- **b.** Responsible parties
- **c.** Compensation arrangement
- **d.** Scope limitations
- **e.** Nature of the relationship

3-62. An engagement letter is a contract that defines the legal relationship, as well as the obligations, of each party to an engagement.

- **a.** True
- **b.** False

3-63. It is not possible to modify an engagement letter once it is signed by all parties.

- **a.** True
- **b.** False

3-64. A Kovel letter provides a basis for protecting the communications of a forensic accountant under the attorney-client privilege.

- **a.** True
- **b.** False

3-65. The AICPA requires an engagement letter for all litigation services provided by a forensic accountant.

- **a.** True
- **b.** False

Select the best response to the following questions related to framing a case:

3-66. Framing a case involves identifying the key parameters that drive case development.

- **a.** True
- **b.** False

3-67. Which of the following is *not* a factor considered by a forensic accountant in framing a case?

- **a.** Date of the engagement letter
- **b.** Jurisdiction
- **c.** Nature of the engagement
- **d.** Professional standards
- **e.** All of the above are relevant factors.

3-68. If a case is framed properly, it will help a forensic accountant identify the legally sufficient manner in which to communicate an opinion.

- **a.** True
- **b.** False

3-69. Understanding the type of case (civil or criminal) is useful to a forensic accountant in each of the following areas *except*:

- **a.** Determining the requisite burden of proof
- **b.** Evidence-gathering considerations
- **c.** Communications between a forensic accountant and an attorney
- **d.** Scope of the engagement
- **e.** Manner in which an expert opinion is expressed

3-70. The jurisdiction of a case impacts how the case is developed and how evidence is presented.

- **a.** True
- **b.** False

Select the best response to the following questions related to the scientific approach:

3-71. The best approach for gathering, synthesizing, and summarizing large amounts of evidence is:

- **a.** The forensic approach
- **b.** The GAAP approach
- **c.** The scientific approach
- **d.** The legal evidence approach

3-72. Which of the following is *not* a step in the scientific approach?

- **a.** Draw conclusions
- **b.** Gather evidence
- **c.** Define the purpose
- **d.** Testify under oath

3-73. A hypothesis is a tentative explanation resulting from preliminary observations.

- **a.** True
- **b.** False

3-74. In order to test a hypothesis, a forensic accountant does which of the following?

- **a.** Performs a certified audit
- **b.** Gathers evidence
- **c.** Watches how other forensic accountants do it
- **d.** Follows GAAP

3-75. When interpreting data, a forensic accountant is trying to determine the probability that the hypothesis is true. In this process, the accountant must be careful not to ignore:

- **a.** Negative facts
- **b.** Inconsistencies in the data
- **c.** Discrepancies that challenge the theory of the case
- **d.** None of the above should be ignored.

3-76. When collecting evidence, it is recommended that a forensic accountant:

a. Number and date all evidence considered
b. Put the evidence in alphabetic order
c. Put the evidence in chronological order
d. Compile similar items in separate binders

3-77. When arriving at a conclusion, a forensic accountant uses both inductive and deductive reasoning based on the evidence gathered.

a. True
b. False

3-78. There is one specific way in which the scientific process can be applied to a forensic accounting engagement.

a. True
b. False

Select the best response to the following questions related to the value of research:

3-79. Research is the collection of sufficient relevant facts and data in order to develop and support a conclusion.

a. True
b. False

3-80. Research enhances critical thinking and reasoning skills and thus results in better decisions.

a. True
b. False

3-81. Each of the following is an example of primary research *except*:

a. Interviewing witnesses
b. Examination of email histories
c. Analysis of bank records
d. Collection of published economic data
e. All of the above are primary sources.

3-82. A forensic accountant always analyzes all possible data that can be collected.

a. True
b. False

3-83. A key function of a research plan is to identify the data that need to be collected and analyzed.

a. True
b. False

3-84. Secondary research is helpful to a forensic accountant in refining hypotheses, arriving at critical assumptions, and selecting analysis methods.

a. True
b. False

3-85. Each of the following is an example of an information source for secondary research *except*:

a. Published court cases
b. A market value appraisal prepared for the engaging organization
c. Academic publications
d. Databases with historical market transactions
e. All of the above are information sources for secondary research.

3-86. Internet sources such as personal web sites and chat rooms always provide reliable data that is consistent with the *Daubert* standard.

a. True
b. False

3-87. Which of the following is a useful and reliable Internet source?

a. LexisNexis
b. William Hellemn, CPA web site
c. Southern College's web site
d. Wikipedia
e. All of the above are useful and reliable sources.

3-88. Characteristics of "good" research include all of the following *except*:

a. Is guided by a working hypothesis
b. Employs a reliable methodology
c. Has a clear problem statement
d. Is based entirely on secondary data

Workplace Applications

3-89. Refer to the *Mattco* case summary presented in this chapter. Identify and discuss the operational problems/issues the case illustrates for forensic accountants. Frame your analysis in the context of Rules 102 and 201 of the AICPA professional standards. Using what you have discovered in your analysis, prepare a memo to your instructor highlighting areas where key members of the EY staff failed to comply with AICPA guidance.

3-90. Using the *Mattco* case study and the chapter content related to engagement letters, draft an engagement letter assuming that you are a CPA employed by Ernst and Young. If sufficient information is not available for any of the engagement letter components, use the standard language suggested by the AICPA in Business Valuation and Forensic and Litigation Services Practice Aid 04-01 entitled *Engagement Letters for Litigation Services*.

3-91. Frame the *Mattco* case using the factors set forth in this chapter. Specific areas that should be addressed in this exercise include:

- **a.** Type of case
- **b.** Jurisdiction
- **c.** Professional standards
- **d.** Nature of the engagement
- **e.** Purpose of the engagement
- **f.** Scope (limitations) of the engagement
- **g.** Relevant dates

Using the guidance presented in this chapter, prepare a memo to your instructor summarizing the framing components and presenting your analysis of the risks related to this engagement.

Chapter Problems

3-92. Obtain a copy of the following article: "Expert Witness Malpractice Actions: Emerging Trend or Aberration?" published in *The Practical Litigator* in March 2004. Prepare a summary of the article that addresses the following questions:

- **a.** What is the thesis of the article?
- **b.** What is meant by a friendly expert?
- **c.** How do the cases summarized in the article illustrate expert negligence?
- **d.** Does the *Mattco case* support the author's thesis?
- **e.** What is the final conclusion of this article?
- **f.** How might the preengagement considerations discussed in this chapter help prevent a friendly expert negligence action?

3-93. Obtain a copy of *In re. Oneida Ltd. et al.* [Case No. 06-10489 (ALG)] adjudicated in the United States Bankruptcy Court, Southern District of New York. This case involves a dispute over the provisions included in an engagement letter between Oneida and Peter J. Solomon Company, L.P. After reading the case, prepare a memo to your instructor that identifies:

- **a.** The engagement letter provision being contested
- **b.** The position taken by each party relative to the engagement letter provision
- **c.** The court's decision and supporting rationale
- **d.** Your opinion as to how well the engagement letter served the parties involved

3-94. Prepare a research paper on the scientific approach/method. Your study should reference at least five academic articles and address the following key areas:

- **a.** Steps in the process
- **b.** Advantages
- **c.** Disadvantages
- **d.** Value in terms of credibility of the concept being studied

Case

3-95. Attorney Barney Fifield specializes in embezzlement cases. He is dedicated and determined to win every case he takes on, which he usually does. In his efforts to defend clients, he pushes his team hard. While he is slow to provide information, he expects quick turnaround from his staff as well as consultants and experts hired to assist the defense team. Fifield's clients are wealthy and pay premium fees to obtain his services. Fifield demands up-front payment from his clients, but his normal practice is to pay consultants and experts more than 90 days after a case is completed. He defends this decision by stating, "Experts who work with me win cases. This provides them with an excellent reference and reputation for attracting additional clients." Fifield has approached you to provide expert witness services for a new case.

- **a.** What factors should you consider in deciding whether to accept this engagement?
- **b.** Will you take the case? Explain why or why not.

---

1 *Black's Law Dictionary.* (2009). 9th ed., 341.

2 *Webster's New World College Dictionary.* (1999). 4th Ed., 1219.

3 *Mattco Forge, Inc. v. Arthur Young & Co.*, 6 Cal. Rptr. 2d 781, 787 (Cal. Ct. App. 1992).

4 *Mattco Forge, Inc. v. Arthur Young & Co.*, 60 Cal. Rptr. 2d 780, 788 (Cal. Ct. App. 1997).

5 No. B087488. Second Dist., Div. Three. Feb. 7, 1997.

4 Gathering Evidence—Interviews and Observations

INTRODUCTION

Following the acceptance and framing of an engagement, the forensic accountant gathers evidence to develop, test, and refine his or her working hypothesis. As discussed in Chapter 2, evidence encompasses testimony, documents, and tangible objects that tend to prove or disprove the existence of an alleged fact.[1] The types of evidence collected, the methods and timing of collection, the chain of custody,[*] and the analysis of evidence are logically determined by the nature and scope of the engagement. Moreover, the role of the forensic accountant—whether an agent of law enforcement or an expert engaged by an attorney—determines specific procedures to be followed. For example, law enforcement (such as the FBI, IRS, or State Police) must adhere to specific evidence-gathering rules, generally starting with obtaining a search warrant. An attorney, on the other hand, gathers evidence through the discovery process.

The types of evidence considered by forensic accountants generally fall into one of two categories: documentary or interactive. Examples of documentary evidence include financial records (for example, general ledger, financial statements, and tax returns), organizational documents, communication logs (for example, phone and email), and photographs. Various analytical techniques for documentary evidence will be discussed in later chapters. The purpose of this chapter is to introduce interactive evidence. As the name implies, interactive evidence is information gathered through dynamic relational processes—interviews and observations. A unique feature of interactive evidence is its interpersonal nature. In other words, the forensic accountant plays an active role in both collecting and interpreting the evidence. A specialized set of skills is required of the interviewer/observer, skills that fall far outside the realm of traditional accounting education. Although this chapter provides a useful introduction, such skills are developed over time with application and experience.

Learning Objectives

After completing this chapter, you should be able to:

LO1. Describe the use of interviewing in a forensic accounting engagement.

LO2. Describe the role of body language in communication.

LO3. Describe the types of interviews and interview questions commonly employed by forensic accountants.

LO4. Identify the three fundamental stages of the interview process.

LO5. Explain the value of observations in a forensic accounting engagement.

LO6. Explain how forensic accountants can use public records to gather evidence.

Caution

Although forensic accounting engagements are often adversarial in nature—that is, they involve opposing parties—most are nonthreatening. Even so, because interviews and observations are interactive experiences, practitioners must always be cognizant of their surroundings and careful to avoid compromising situations. In other words, always think safety.

U.S. v. Ronda Nixon (2009) is a criminal case in which the interviews and observations of a testifying forensic accountant were used as evidence. This case demonstrates how an expert can be challenged on such evidence in court, stressing the importance of proper collection and documentation techniques. This case also highlights the fluid and uncertain nature of forensic accounting engagements and the need to understand the legal environment.

United States v. Ronda Nixon

Background

In July 2007, Garis Pruitt, the managing partner of Pruitt & Thorner, L.C., a two-partner law firm located in Catlettsburg, Kentucky, was contacted by Community

[*] Identifies the individuals who have access to the evidence.

Trust Bank regarding the overdue status of the firm's operating line of credit. Believing the loan had been previously paid off, Mr. Pruitt immediately contacted his partner and the firm's CPA to investigate the issue.

A preliminary review of the firm's accounting records confirmed a balance due and also identified a number of unauthorized draws on the loan by one of the firm's former employees, Ronda Nixon. Ms. Nixon, who worked as the firm's bookkeeper for approximately four years, had recently resigned to enroll in law school. Mr. Pruitt proceeded to contact his insurance company and local law enforcement regarding his suspicions of fraud.

Analysis and Findings of the Forensic Accountant

On August 9, 2007, Mr. Pruitt engaged the services of a forensic accountant to assist in evaluating the suspected fraudulent activity. The forensic accountant was challenged with determining the amount embezzled (if any), the responsible parties, and the schemes employed. Based on his preliminary observations, Mr. Pruitt limited the scope of the analysis to the period from June 1, 2006, to May 31, 2007 (one year).

Following a detailed interview of Mr. Pruitt, the forensic accountant developed and implemented an investigative plan. The plan included a comprehensive analysis of the firm's general ledger (G/L), bank records, digital data (including emails, G/L audit logs, and phone records), partner and employee interviews, a tour of the firm's facility (including individual workstations), and third-party interviews (bank employees and the firm's CPA). On October 16, 2007, the forensic accountant met with Mr. Pruitt to review the preliminary findings of the investigation and confirm the validity of suspicious transactions.

On October 31, 2007, the forensic accountant attempted to contact Ms. Nixon by phone. She left a message with a brief introduction, contact information, and a request for an interview. At 8:05 a.m. the following morning (November 1, 2007), the forensic accountant received a return call from Ms. Nixon. At the outset of the phone conversation, the forensic accountant advised Ms. Nixon of the nature of the investigation and the purpose of the requested interview, specifically to gather information (that is, a response) regarding the alleged embezzlement activity while she was employed at Pruitt & Thorner. Ms. Nixon refused to schedule an interview, citing her school schedule and family obligations. Following an appeal by the forensic accountant, Ms. Nixon agreed to an immediate 20-minute interview. At that time, the forensic accountant placed Ms. Nixon on hold to pull the file and get a corroborating witness.

Special Note

After reading this chapter, you will understand that the situation described here was far from ideal. Given the early hour, the forensic accountant was not completely prepared. Moreover, the phone interview prevented the forensic accountant from evaluating Ms. Nixon's body language and the effects of stress (discussed later in the chapter). Finally, the limited time frame (20 minutes) actually created stress for the forensic accountant to address the many issues in question. Conscious of the perils, the forensic accountant chose to proceed with the phone interview, fearing it might be her only opportunity to question Ms. Nixon.

During the next 20 minutes, Ms. Nixon provided the following summary responses:

- She had just recently become aware of the allegations.
- She was not currently being represented by an attorney.
- She understood the seriousness of the allegations; however, she was convinced that something could be worked out, which would be "best for all parties."
- She admitted to using the firm's credit card for unauthorized purchases, explaining that the charges were funded by draws against the firm's line of credit.
- She admitted to issuing unauthorized checks, including payments on the line of credit and checks with altered payees.
- She advised that no one else was involved in the embezzlement.

- She disputed the estimated amount of the embezzlement ($125,000), claiming that she kept a record of the unauthorized transactions on her home computer.
- She offered no defenses for her actions (such as financial hardship or drug use).
- She advised that her husband had previously contacted Mr. Pruitt to "work something out."

Think About It

The forensic accountant was immediately suspicious of Ms. Nixon's openness and "confession." The fact that Ms. Nixon was a law student with previous work experience in a law firm provided pause for concern. Why was she seemingly cavalier about the situation? Why was she confessing? Was she trying to protect other parties? Did she have an "ace in the hole"?

The forensic accountant transcribed her interview notes and forwarded a copy to Mr. Pruitt for his consideration. Prior to finalizing her report, the forensic accountant contacted Mr. Pruitt regarding the interview and Ms. Nixon's confession. The final report concluded that the evidence, including Ms. Nixon's admissions, indicated that Ms. Nixon had willfully converted to her own personal use the law firm's property in the total amount of $79,998. Not included in this amount were suspicious transactions without reasonable certainty, specifically bonuses and reimbursements for travel and supplies.

Mr. Pruitt subsequently submitted the forensic accountant's report to the firm's insurance company in support of its claim. The report was also submitted to the FBI and the U.S. Attorney's office for use in the criminal prosecution of Ms. Nixon.

Special Note

The U.S. Attorney's office is authorized to decline prosecution of any case unless required by statute. Reasons for declining to prosecute include, but are not limited to, lack of resources, lack of evidence, political appeal, jury appeal, complexity, monetary loss, and perceived importance. In other words, crimes are prioritized. It is believed that Ronda Nixon's case was selected for prosecution because of the evidence (documentary and interactive, including Ms. Nixon's confession) and the perceived significance of the identity theft charge. As a final note, prosecution policies are generally not made public. Can you think of any reasons why?

Not Guilty Plea

Following a federal grand jury indictment, Ms. Nixon pleaded *not guilty* to federal fraud charges on July 28, 2008.[2] She was arraigned in U.S. District Court in Ashland, Kentucky, on eighteen counts of wire fraud, one count of bank fraud, and one count of identity theft. If convicted on all charges, Ms. Nixon faced a fifty-year prison sentence and fines up to $1.5 million.

Special Note

The epilogue of this case is presented at the conclusion of the chapter. It describes Ms. Nixon's trial, including the direct and cross-examination of the forensic accountant and the ultimate jury verdict.

THE INTERVIEW: A PRIMARY EVIDENCE-GATHERING TOOL

The ***interview*** is a favored evidence-gathering tool of forensic accountants for two primary reasons: it is a direct means of obtaining information (straight to the source), and it provides immediate results. As illustrated in the preceding case discussion, an interview is a purposeful dialogue between two or more people (interviewer and interviewee) that involves an exchange of questions and answers.[3] However, effective interviewing is much more than just asking questions. It is a systematic process that requires planning, staging, execution, and active listening.

During the course of an interview, the interviewer must be attentive to changes in the interviewee's behavior that might indicate stress, discomfort, or deception. Our experience suggests that people are more likely to omit part of a story than to actually lie during an interview. Thus, interviewers should be on the lookout for indicators of concealment as well as deception.

The Communication Process

As a foundation for our discussion on interviewing, let's first consider the basic ***communication process***. The six primary components of this process include:[4]

- ***Communicators***—Communication is a coinciding, dynamic, and fluid process in which both the sender and receiver are communicators.
- ***Message***—The message is the information (or understanding) to be shared.
- ***Channel***—The channel is the means of communicating (for example, face-to-face, telephone, or email).
- ***Decoding***—The ability to decode the message is necessary for understanding to occur. Thus, communication requires that the codes (or languages) of the communicators have some commonality.
- ***Noise***—Noise is comprised of secondary signals that obscure or confuse the message. Noise, which might appear at any point in the communication process, can be either internal or external. Internal noise is attributable to the communicators themselves, while external noise is attributable to the physical setting. Examples of internal noise are fatigue, poor listening, attitude, lack of interest, fear, mistrust, lack of common experience, and emotions. External noise can be manifested as distractions, bad phone connections, Internet problems, or the time of day.
- ***Environment***—Aspects of the communication environment include both physical factors, such as the location, and personal factors, such as the individual experiences and cultural backgrounds of the communicators.

Given this diverse set of components, communication is not a skill in and of itself. Rather, it involves several skills, such as active listening, encoding and decoding messages, observing nonverbal communication (body language), and recognizing and managing stress and emotion, both your own and that of others.

Active Listening

Effective interviewing requires ***active listening***. As the name implies, active listening involves an individual's undivided attention, with both eyes and ears. Active listening on the part of the interviewer not only facilitates accurate collection of information, but also demonstrates an interest in what the interviewee is saying. Interest is demonstrated by letting the speaker finish his or her response without interruption and accepting the response without judgment. Then, the interviewer can confirm an understanding by repeating in his or her own words the interviewee's responses. In addition to confirmation, this repeat strategy also enables the interviewer to test for emotion (such as anger, stress, or frustration) and helps establish rapport. In sum, active listeners look for a balance between the interviewee's words and body language.

Special Note

Another communication strategy used by seasoned forensic accountants is discriminative listening.[5] A discriminative listener is sensitive to changes in the interviewee's rate of speech, volume, tone, pauses, and other vocal and nonverbal cues. This is a valuable skill, given the magnitude of communication that occurs through the tone of a person's voice, estimated at 35%.[6]

Dig Deeper

Most of us are lazy, passive, and/or selective listeners. Active listening is an experiential skill that requires continuous development. To this end, we encourage you to search for video clips on the Web that demonstrate listening skills, active versus reflective listening, and role-playing exercises.

Body Language

Body language is what you are saying—without actually saying a word. It involves communicating with the movement or position of the human body, both consciously and unconsciously. Research indicates that roughly 55% of all communication is done through body language, 35% through voice tone, and only 10% through the content of words.[7] Thus, the importance of understanding body language cannot be overemphasized.

Our discussion of body language is framed with the following cautions:

- Because body language varies among cultures (there is no "universal" body language), cultural context is a critical consideration.
- Evaluating body language requires some baseline for comparison: Abnormal behavior cannot be identified until normal behavior is established. Thus, it is necessary for an interviewer to "norm" the body language of the interviewee before making assessments.
- Body language is a two-way form of communication. In other words, the interviewee is also reading the interviewer's body language.

Several examples of body language commonly associated with different body regions are provided in Table 4-1.

Dig Deeper

Given its inherently visual element, videos can be effective tools for illustrating the analysis of body language. One such example is the "Secrets of Body Language" video series produced by *History* (available at www.history.com; links to selected clips available at www.pearsonhighered/rufus).

Effects of Stress on the Communication Process

Stress is generally defined as emotional and/or physical strain suffered by a person in response to pressure from the outside world, such as an interview.[8] From a physiological perspective, its purpose is to act as a stimulus (alarm) to an unusual or unexpected situation that threatens a person's normal state. Stress inhibits effective communication because it creates internal noise that negatively impacts our ability to listen and think clearly. To mitigate this negative impact, interviewers must be sensitive to an interviewee's signals of stress.

Reactions or adaptations to stress can be manifested in a number of physical and emotional symptoms. Examples of physical symptoms include an increase in blood flow and adrenaline, skin irritations (such as blotchy face and/or neck), breathing difficulties, and nervous gestures (such as self-touching). Common emotional symptoms of stress are anger and frustration, which tend to be displayed in aggressive or defensive behaviors.

Remember, the objective of an interview is to gather information. Although we cannot manage an interviewee's stress level, we can adapt the questioning process to diffuse tension at specific points in the interview. For example, challenging questions can be introduced intermittently throughout the interview or delayed until the end. Rather than attempting to alleviate stress after it appears, the interviewer can take preventive measures that create a more relaxed environment at the outset. One such strategy is to establish rapport with the interviewee, as discussed in the following section.

The Value of Rapport

Rapport is a connection between the interviewer and interviewee that serves as a foundation for building trust and confidence. Rapport has the opposite effect of stress on the communication process: Whereas stress is a negative factor, rapport is positive. It allows the interview to evolve without hostility, fostering the perception that "it's safe to talk."[9] Research also suggests that rapport increases the quality of witness remembrance by decreasing the amount of misinformation, especially in response to open-ended questions.[10]

Table 4-1 Examples of Body Language

Body Region	Position or Gesture	Common Indication
Hands	Palms up	Inviting, open
	Palms down	Dominating, hostile
	Fists	Anger, frustration
	Pointing fingers	Hostile, aggressive
	Hidden	Deception
	Self-touching (such as rubbing face or arms, clasping or clenching hands, touching hair)	A calming motion to assure oneself, may indicate deception or uncertainty
Head	Nodding	Agreement
	Shaking	Disagreement or denial
	Leveling	Confidence
	Angling up	Superiority
	Angling left or right	Interest
Face	Flushed	Anxiety or deception
Eyes	Raising eyebrows	Doubt
	Looking up	Boredom or frustration
	Looking down	Submission
	Avoiding eye contact	Deception
	Rolling eyes	Disbelief, frustration
	Excess blinking	Deception
Arms	Crossed arms	Fear or defensiveness
	Hands on hips	Anger or aggression
Posture	Slouching	Insecurity, boredom, or indifference
	Angling toward someone	Interest
	Angling away from someone	Lack of interest or deception
Legs and Feet	Crossing legs while sitting	Usually for comfort
	Crossing legs while standing	Nervousness
	Exaggerated movement	Deception
	Jiggling feet	A comforting gesture to soothe anxiety

Based on Hagen, H. (2008). The Everything Body Language Book. *Avon, MA: Adams Media; and Walters, S. (2000).* The Truth about Lying: How to Spot a Lie and Protect Yourself from Deception. *Naperville, IL: Sourcebooks, Inc.*

During the planning stage of the interview (discussed later in the chapter), forensic accountants consider ways to establish rapport. A starting point is to select an interview setting that provides a comfortable atmosphere, in both a physical and psychological sense. During the course of an interview, interviewers should "calibrate" their techniques to build rapport. This can be accomplished by adjusting their breathing, rate of speech, and tonality to match that of the interviewee.

Understanding Personal Space (Proximity)

Rapport building requires an understanding of, and respect for, the interviewee's ***personal space***. Four conceptualized "zones" are commonly used to define personal space:[11]

- Intimate zone—6 to 18 inches from the individual; reserved for intimate relationships.
- Personal zone—18 inches to 4 feet from the individual; reserved for friends and co-workers.
- Social zone—4 to 10 feet from the individual; an individual pays little or no attention to people in this zone.
- Public zone—10 feet and beyond; an individual pays little or no attention to anything or anyone in this zone.

Violation of an interviewee's personal space can quickly destroy rapport and create stress. The proper position for an interviewer is approximately two feet from the interviewee (in the personal zone). If necessary, the interviewer can adjust proximity as the interview progresses.

CONDUCTING INTERVIEWS

Armed with an understanding of the communication process and the primary factors that impact the effectiveness of communication, we now focus our discussion on guidelines for conducting effective interviews.

Types of Interviews

Forensic accountants can conduct either formal or informal interviews. A ***formal interview*** is *systematic* in nature, with a blend of open-ended and structured questions. ***Open-ended questions***, which do not call for a yes or no response, are designed to stimulate conversation. They allow interviewees to tell their own stories, using their own terms, and offering information they consider important. In contrast, ***structured questions*** are short-answer (for example, age, marital status, and education) or closed-ended (yes or no). Most formal interviews begin with structured (introductory) questions and progress to open-ended (informational) questions.

An ***informal interview*** is *unsystematic* in nature in that it is not controlled by a specific set of detailed questions. Although the interviewer may have some key questions prepared in advance, an informal interview relies on the spontaneous generation of questions in the natural flow of an interaction. To facilitate this natural flow, informal interviews are generally conducted in a friendly, nonthreatening tone. They tend to be used in the early stages of a forensic accounting engagement, when there is insufficient information to develop a formal interview.

Special Note

Forensic accountants (aside from those working in law enforcement) rarely conduct interrogation-type interviews. As previously noted, the purpose of an interview is to gather information. An ***interrogation***, on the other hand, is an admission-seeking exercise that generally involves the employment of aggressive strategies. Interrogations are conducted in the context of criminal investigations, only after sufficient evidence has been gathered to establish a likelihood of guilt. This evidence can be used in the interrogation as leverage to elicit a confession.

Three Types of Questions

As emphasized throughout this chapter, an interview is a conversation with a purpose—that is, to gather information. The type of information gathered logically flows from the questions being proposed. Thus, careful consideration should be paid to the type, placement, and wording of each question. Although the content of interview questions is driven by the facts and circumstances of the specific engagement, forensic accountants commonly employ three types of questions:

1. **Introductory questions**
   - **a.** Personal information (name, address, and so on)
   - **b.** Used to establish rapport (create comfort and a connection)
   - **c.** Generally structured questions (short answer or yes/no)
   - **d.** Should be nonconfrontational and nonthreatening
   - **e.** Can be used to norm the interviewee (observe body language, tone of voice, and attitude)
2. **Informational questions**
   - **a.** Purpose is to gather information
   - **b.** Questions may include a mix of:
     - Open-ended questions (require a monologue response)
     - Closed-ended questions (limit responses to yes or no)
     - Leading questions (contain the answer as part of the question)
     - Direct questions (address specific facts and events)
     - Cross questions (the same question asked different ways and at different times to confirm consistency)
     - Review (repeat) questions (used to summarize and confirm understanding)
   - **c.** Question sequence should proceed from general to specific
3. **Closing questions**
   - **a.** Purpose is to summarize and gather any additional information the interviewee wants to share
   - **b.** Often includes leading questions, based on previous responses
   - **c.** Concludes the interview

Special Note

Two additional types of aggressive questioning—assessment and admission-seeking—are identified by some professional organizations. Assessment questions are used to establish the credibility of a respondent, while admission-seeking questions seek to obtain a confession. Although no single approach is appropriate in all interview situations, our experience suggests that aggressive questioning is usually counterproductive. For this reason, it is rarely used outside law enforcement. Recall that our objective is limited to *gathering information*.

Stages of the Interview

The interview process includes three fundamental stages: planning, doing, and memorializing. Each of the stages is described in this section in the context of a forensic accounting engagement.

In the ***planning stage***, the forensic accountant completes three basic tasks:

- Identify the role of the witness relative to the specific engagement and to other witnesses. Examples of relevant considerations include the following:
  - What information is the witness expected to provide?
  - How close was the witness to the people or activities of interest?
  - Can the witness corroborate or refute representations of other witnesses?

- Develop a question bank or outline based on the working hypothesis and any preliminary information that may be available. Each question should have a purpose related to the ultimate goal of gathering relevant evidence.
- Develop an interview schedule (that is, who, when, and where).

The ***doing stage*** is the implementation of the interview plan. This plan provides a valuable reference point, but some element of flexibility must be maintained to allow for any necessary improvisation. Because each interview is unique, we cannot offer detailed instructions or a checklist. However, the following guidelines are generally applicable.

1. Create the desired setting (comfortable or intense). Safety must always be considered when selecting an interview site and arrangement. We strongly recommend a team approach whenever possible.
2. Begin with introductory questions, and then progress to informational questions.
3. Norm the interviewee—that is, establish a standard of normal body language.
4. Be an active listener.
   a. Repeat responses to confirm understanding.
   b. Evaluate the consistency between words and body language.
   c. Look (and listen) for both verbal and nonverbal indicators of deception.
   d. Use follow-up questions.
5. Encourage the interviewee to do most (80%–85%) of the talking.
6. Terminate the interview immediately if you feel threatened or lose control of the situation.
7. Take notes.
8. Close the interview by giving the interviewee an opportunity to offer any additional information he or she feels is relevant.

The final stage of an interview is ***memorializing*** (transcribing) your notes. As previously stated, we recommend taking notes during the course of an interview. Although note taking can slow down the process, it communicates to interviewees the importance of their responses. More importantly, it provides documentation of what was said (or not said). To minimize the disruption of note taking, we recommend two interviewers—one to initiate questions and another to take notes.

Hand-written interview notes should be transcribed into a ***memorandum of interview*** as soon as possible. This enhances readability and reliability and also allows for organization by topic and highlighting of key points. In the transcription process, the interviewer should make an effort to use the interviewee's word choices and grammar, indicating direct quotes with quotation marks. When possible, the memorandum should be reviewed with the interviewee to ensure accuracy and completeness. Although facts should always be presented without bias, the memorandum may also include findings, observations, recommendations, and opinions as appropriate. Of course, any content attributable to the interviewer should be clearly identified as such.

Special Note

The forensic accountant's memorandum of interview in the case *U.S. v. Ronda Nixon* is provided in Appendix 4-A.

Finally, practitioners should be aware that interview notes (like engagement letters) may be subject to third-party examination. For this reason, some interviewers (excluding law enforcement) choose to discard their handwritten notes after they are transcribed. This avoids file clutter and the possibility of challenge by opposing counsel regarding any transcription errors, deletions, or embellishments.

Special Note

Should interviews be recorded? It may be appropriate to record an interview in some situations. For example, we recommend recording an interview when a large magnitude of detailed information is involved. However, because it requires practice and quality equipment, recording should not be the interviewer's only means of documenting the content of the interview. *Important:* To avoid potential violations of state or federal laws, the interviewee should be advised of the recording. In practice, a recorded interview begins with the interviewer identifying the date, time, and participating parties. At this time, the interviewee should acknowledge his or her understanding that the interview is being recorded and confirm approval.

Establishing the Order of Witnesses

As emphasized throughout this text, the investigative process generally proceeds from the general to the specific. When multiple individuals are identified as potential sources of information, a similar approach should be used to establish the order in which they are interviewed. We recommend that the interview order track the proximity of the individual to the subject of interest, beginning with peripheral players, then moving to the insiders.

For example, in the context of a criminal investigation, the order of witnesses often proceeds as follows:

- ***Neutral third-parties***—Those having some knowledge but no involvement.
- ***Corroborative witnesses***—Those not directly involved but able to corroborate specific facts related to the offense.
- ***Suspected co-conspirators*** in the alleged offense—Beginning with least culpable and proceeding to most culpable.
- ***Target***—The suspect.

Scheduling witness interviews in the order of probable culpability allows the forensic accountant to gather as much information as possible before the target is interviewed. In many cases—especially criminal cases—you only get one opportunity to interview key witnesses. Thus, maximum preparation is essential.

Legal and Professional Considerations

Forensic accountants, aside from law enforcement, must work within rules governing professional conduct. Moreover, they must be aware of the potential legal challenges associated with interviews. The key proposition is that only legally obtained evidence can be presented in court or used as the foundation of an expert's opinion. Given the complexities involved, preparation for sensitive interviews should include consultation with the engaging attorney.

Employee Interviews

As a general rule, employees have a duty to cooperate with internal (fraud) investigations as long as the information requested is *reasonable*. Moreover, they do not have the right to be represented by counsel during an interview. An employee's constitutional rights under the Fifth and Sixth Amendments are triggered when he or she is confronted with a state action. Thus, private employers cannot be sued for Fifth or Sixth Amendment violations.

Public employees may, without administrative penalty, refuse to answer questions from a forensic accountant if they have exposure to criminal liability. If unsure of any such exposure, the employee is allowed to contact an attorney before being interviewed. However, an employee, whether public or private, can be fired for refusing to answer questions or to be interviewed during an administrative or civil proceeding.

Working Example

Evidence collected through employee interviews may become a contested issue, as illustrated in the 2013 case *The State of Georgia v. Beverly Hall, et al.* In March 2013, Ms. Hall and other former educators were indicted on charges of conspiracy, false statements and writings, false swearing, theft by taking, and influencing witnesses. A key argument of the defense was that statements from some of the former educators were collected through coercive means, specifically under threat of job loss. Such action would constitute a violation of the Constitution's Fifth Amendment, which protects citizens from self-incrimination. Citing the U.S. Supreme Court case *Garrity v. New Jersey* (1967), the defense attorneys argued that public employees cannot be fired for refusing to talk if they have exposure to criminal liability.

In June 2013, Fulton County Judge Jerry Baxter ruled against the defendants, finding they were not explicitly threatened with firing. As of the date of this writing, Ms. Hall has denied any wrongdoing or knowledge of the alleged cheating conspiracy. The case is ongoing.

Special consideration is required if an interviewee is a union employee. Following the Supreme Court's 1975 decision in *NLRB v. Weingarten* (420 U.S. 251), union employees have the right to union representation during an investigative interview, provided the employee "reasonably believes" he or she has exposure to disciplinary action.

Special Note

In a civil case, a forensic accountant may ask the engaging attorney to request interviews of various individuals during the discovery process. If they decline to cooperate, the attorney may schedule depositions, through which witnesses provide oral testimony (under oath) outside of court.

Depositions are conducted by attorneys, but it is common for forensic accountants to assist in preparing questions. Although a deposition occurs in a more structured setting, most of the issues previously addressed for interviewing generally are still applicable. For example, it is still possible to create some level of comfort and build rapport. Observing body language is still an important consideration, especially if the deposition is not being video-recorded.

Tips for Conducting Effective Interviews

As with most abstract skills, interviewing skills are developed over time through trial and error. Moreover, each interview situation presents its own unique opportunities and challenges that cannot be anticipated. Even so, we offer the following "top ten" tips based on our own experiences.

1. Choose the right setting, both time and place. Again, think safety!
2. Be prepared. Review the facts of the case and all available records and data before the interview. In other words, know who you are talking to and what you are talking about.
3. Avoid interviewing multiple people together.
4. Control the interview. Do not allow the interviewee to direct the line of questioning.
5. Select the best combination of strategies and mix of questions.
6. Do not automatically discredit information that is unfavorable to your position.
7. Save sensitive or difficult questions (stress triggers) for later in the interview.
8. Be an active listener.
9. Memorialize the interview as soon as possible after its conclusion.
10. Remember your objective is simply to gather information, not to challenge or influence the interviewee.

Special Note

Students often inquire about the use of lie detector tests (polygraphs) and their admissibility in court. First used in the 1920s, modern-day polygraph machines measure certain objective physiological indicators of stress or deception: heart rate, blood pressure, rate of breathing, and perspiration. Although the measures themselves are objective, there remain many uncertainties about the technique (for example, types of questions, order of questions, wording of questions, and tonality) and results (meaning). In other words, polygraph tests are not considered scientifically valid and thus are not admitted as reliable evidence.

THE VALUE OF OBSERVATIONS

Because forensic accountants are generally engaged after an event has occurred (such as embezzlement, dispute, death, or divorce filing), our observations generally flow from gathering and analyzing data. Nonetheless, it is common for a forensic accountant to visit the scene of a crime or a business being valued. Why? Why would the forensic accountant in the Ronda Nixon case want to visit the office site?

Observations are visual in nature. Site visits facilitate observations because they allow the opportunity to see the physical setting, such as the condition of the facilities, the layout, locations of individual workstations, and security infrastructure. Perhaps even more valuable are observations about people in these settings, including how they communicate, how specific tasks are performed, what accounting processes are employed, which internal controls are observed, how work flows, and what the overall mood and tone are.

Creating a visual context for the various items of information gathered in the investigation allows the forensic accountant to "connect the dots" and further refine the working hypothesis. Thus, observations may produce evidence in and of themselves, or they may shed light on existing evidence or identify additional evidence to be obtained. Finally, observation is important because it is the means through which body language messages are received.

Practitioner's Perspective

In practice, forensic accountants commonly employ a "four corners" view of a scene. For example, in the Ronda Nixon case, the forensic accountant viewed and filmed Nixon's workspace from each corner of her office. Viewing objects from multiple perspectives helps to maximize the information obtained from an observation. Moreover, creating a record of the observation, such as a photo or video, allows for further examination at a later time. It is physically impossible for a person to immediately absorb every sensory detail of an environment, and certain objects in that environment may not immediately be recognized as significant. Following her site visit, the forensic accountant diagrammed the entire office layout and created flowcharts of the accounting process. What do you think was the value of these graphical depictions? What might Ms. Nixon's workspace say about her?

Legal Observations

Forensic accountants must exercise caution when making observations, to ensure that the information is legally obtained and can be used as a reliable basis for forming an expert opinion. ***Legal observations*** are made in situations where there is *no expectation of privacy*. They may include visual observations (what we see) and auditory observations (what we hear). Legal *visual* observations (obtained through drive-bys or surveillance) involve things that can be seen in plain view, such as:

- A car in the driveway
- License plate numbers
- Location of a residence or business

- Times and locations of meetings
- A person's routine or schedule
- Lifestyle observations

Legal *auditory* observations involve things we hear where there is no expectation of privacy, such as a conversation in a restaurant or movie theater. Compared to visual observations, auditory observations are more limited because they require closer proximity to the subject of interest. In contrast to a legal auditory observation, an example of an illegal auditory observation is the use of a recording device in a location where the observer is not present. Recording conversations, even with one-way consent, may be illegal. Thus, legal counsel should always be sought with regard to such activity.

What about abandoned property, such as trash? As a rule, there is no expectation of privacy for abandoned property. Thus, "one man's trash is another man's treasure."

Public Records

Forensic accountants commonly access public records to gather evidence. Such records can be used to support or refine the working hypothesis or to identify relationships and potential interview subjects. Many records are available in the public domain through individual government agencies. Examples include addresses, deeds, liens, Uniform Commercial Code (UCC) filings, business organization data, and bankruptcy filings, to name only a few. Because the process of collecting such information takes time, as well as knowledge regarding the appropriate resources, various commercial databases offer consolidated data for a fee.

In addition to records in the public domain, legal observations can be considered a type of public record. Another recent addition to this category is the multitude of information that is available on the Internet through personal or business web sites and social networking sites. While promotional web sites are clearly intended to be public, social networking sites (which have access limitations) claim some level of privacy. As of the writing of this text, there are more than 100 social networking sites in existence, the most popular of which are Facebook, Twitter, and LinkedIn. Because the access limitations of such sites can be easily manipulated, any information contained therein can be considered a public record.

Searching public records has four primary advantages in a forensic accounting engagement:

1. The information is public, so anyone can access it.
2. Access is fast and cheap, especially when the information is available on the Internet.
3. The search is discreet compared to other methods of investigation.
4. Results are tangible and can be replicated.

What About Pretexts?

A ***pretext*** is the use of deception by one party, such as posing as someone else, or using an individual's personal identifiers to obtain information from another party who would not otherwise disclose such information. While there are some circumstances in which pretexts can justifiably be used, we caution that pretexts are often inappropriate and may even be illegal. For example, accessing records that fall outside open or authorized access—such as bank records, phone records, or email records—is illegal.

Working Example

As an example of pretexts, consider the Hewlett-Packard scandal of 2006. Patricia Dunn, HP's Chairman at the time, engaged outside investigators to evaluate her concerns that certain members of its board of directors were leaking confidential and strategic information to various news outlets. The investigators obtained "unauthorized access" to phone records by impersonating the people whose information they were after. The fallout included, among other things, the resignation of various HP board members and officers (including Dunn), an SEC inquiry, and criminal charges. Although all criminal charges against HP executives and employees were dropped, three investigators pled guilty to identity theft and conspiracy. In December 2012, Bryan Wagner, one of the three investigators, was sentenced to three months of incarceration and two years of supervisory release. Investigators Joseph and Mathew DePente (father and son) were sentenced to three years probation.

Under the ***Fair Credit Reporting Act***, consent is required to obtain credit information on individuals. Specifically, this law prohibits the following actions:

- Using false, fictitious, or fraudulent statements or documents to get customer information from a financial institution or directly from a customer of a financial institution.
- Using forged, counterfeit, lost, or stolen documents to get customer information from a financial institution or directly from a customer of a financial institution.
- Asking someone to get another person's customer information using false, fictitious, or fraudulent statements or using forged, counterfeit, lost, or stolen documents.

Questioned Documents

During the course of an engagement, a forensic accountant commonly views a substantial number of source documents. Although rarely trained in questioned document examination (QDE), forensic accountants should be attentive to any concerns raised by the working hypothesis, such as forgery, fake checks, and fabricated or altered invoices.

A questioned document is a document that, either in its entirety or in part, is subject to question regarding its authenticity and/or origin. Questioned documents are often a component of illegal activities, such as forgery and embezzlement, and become trial evidence. Examples of questioned documents commonly encountered by forensic accountants include checks, tax returns, invoices, and contracts. In the review of such documents, any signature, handwriting, typewriting, or other questionable marks should be flagged for QDE by a trained expert.

Dig Deeper

Visit the FBI's web site to learn about the various types of forensic examinations conducted by its Questioned Documents Unit, such as signatures, inks, paper, typewriter, handwriting, hand printing, photocopier comparison, identification, and writing sequence.

EPILOGUE: *U.S. V. RONDA NIXON*

The Trial

On February 9, 2009, Ms. Nixon's trial began. The government's case-in-chief included testimony from Mr. Pruitt; various bank and credit card representatives; Ms. Nixon's extended family members, friends, and travel companions; the forensic accountant; and the FBI. The forensic accountant's expert opinion was considered critical to the government's case, specifically Ms. Nixon's admissions and efforts to conceal.

On *direct examination*, the forensic accountant was questioned by the prosecutor regarding the nature and scope of the engagement, data and facts considered, methodologies employed, and concluding opinions. Her memorandum of interview with Ms. Nixon was enlarged for the jury's viewing and marked as an exhibit. Prompted by questions from the prosecutor, the forensic accountant discussed her analysis, highlighting the following key points.

- An objective, systematic, and scientific process had been employed to arrive at the report conclusions.
- Each suspicious transaction was scrutinized to confirm its proper inclusion (or exclusion).
- Ms. Nixon confessed to the allegations, specifically unauthorized credit card charges, false deposits, and check alterations.

- Ms. Nixon offered no defenses or evidence to support an absence of intent.
- Ms. Nixon did not dispute the acts committed, only the amount.
- Ms. Nixon claimed she maintained a file evidencing the amounts taken.

The *cross-examination* of the forensic accountant was largely focused on two areas: the limitations of the engagement and the memorandum of interview with Ms. Nixon. Upon questioning by Ms. Nixon's counsel, the forensic accountant acknowledged the following:

- She had never met Ms. Nixon.
- Mr. Pruitt identified Ms. Nixon as the suspected embezzler and provided a copy of her personnel file.
- Mr. Pruitt outlined his suspicions of fraud, including the alleged schemes.
- Mr. Pruitt limited the scope of the analysis.
- An ideal interview would be face to face, not via telephone.
- Her interview of Ms. Nixon was not ideal.
- She could not be absolutely certain that the person she interviewed via telephone was indeed Ms. Nixon.
- She had no knowledge as to the caller's surroundings or who else may have been present.
- Telephone interviews can be complicated by both internal and external barriers, such as poor listening, noise, time of day, and bad phone connections.
- Words are only one component of the communication process.
- She could not assess the caller's physical or mental state.
- She had not defined the word "intent" for the caller.
- Ms. Nixon had been forthright in her responses and seemingly cooperative.
- She had concerns about Ms. Nixon's confessions, sensing that "something seems off."
- She had questioned Mr. Pruitt about other evidence following the interview with Ms. Nixon.
- She was not aware that Mr. Pruitt intended to present her report to the FBI.

Upon *redirect* by the prosecutor, the forensic accountant responded as follows:

- She was virtually certain that the caller was Ms. Nixon because of her responses to qualifying questions, specifically her social security number, date of birth, and work experience with the law firm.
- Ms. Nixon admitted to the specific acts but disputed the amount.
- The phone connection had been clear.
- The interview was immediately transcribed (that is, the same day).
- It was her opinion, within a reasonable degree of professional certainty, that Ms. Nixon had embezzled at least $79,998.

There was no *re-cross* by Ms. Nixon's attorney.

The forensic accountant's testimony was followed by the summary testimony of FBI Special Agent Timothy Cox. Agent Cox testified that he too had interviewed Ms. Nixon, wherein she acknowledged much (if not all) of the information contained in the forensic accountant's memorandum of interview. Agent Cox also testified that he had independently confirmed Ms. Nixon's unauthorized use of the law firm's funds and false representations.

Conviction & Sentencing

On February 12, 2009, following four days of trial, the federal jury convicted Ronda Nixon of 17 charges related to the theft of nearly $100,000 from her ex-employer, Pruitt & Thorner.[12] Specifically, she was found guilty of eleven wire fraud counts, two bank fraud counts, three aggravated identity theft counts, and one count of using an unauthorized access device.

In August of 2009, Ms. Nixon was sentenced to fifty-four months in federal prison, with a scheduled release date of August 31, 2013.

APPENDIX 4-A

U.S. v. Ronda Nixon: Memorandum of Interview

MEMO TO FILE

Date: November 1, 2007

Re: Pruitt & Thorner, L.C.

Subj: Phone interview of Ronda Nixon by XXXXX (Also present was XXXXXX, witness)

Received call at 8:05 a.m. from RN re. phone message and request for interview

1. Introduction
   - **a.** Expressed appreciation for the return call
   - **b.** Intro. as follows:
      - **i.** Engaged by Garis Pruitt
      - **ii.** Purpose: to investigate allegations of embezzlement by her while employed at Pruitt & Thorner
      - **iii.** Want to get her side of the story – response to allegations
   - **c.** RN asked how I got her phone number
      - **i.** Advised by XXXXX

2. Request for interview
   - **a.** RN stated that she just recently became aware of the allegations
   - **b.** RN advised she was not interested in meeting – too busy with school and family obligations
      - **i.** I advised it was in her best interest to review our analysis and offer her side of the story
   - **c.** RN stated her husband had contacted GP yesterday to get an amount and "work out an arrangement for repayment outside the courts"
   - **d.** RN stated she was pressed for time (class) but would give me 20 min.

[Requested break to get file; joined by associate XXXXX via speaker phone at 8:10 a.m.]

3. Confirmation / qualifications
   - **a.** SSN
   - **b.** DOB
   - **c.** Confirm notes from personnel file (hire / termination / office specifics)
   - **d.** Education / any specialized training in accounting – none
   - **e.** Inquired about her motivation to go to law school
      - **i.** RN response – "To change my life"

4. RN freely responded as follows:
   - **a.** That she was not represented by an attorney
      - **i.** She "hoped to work it out"
   - **b.** Acknowledged exchange of emails on Aug. 9 with GP regarding loan and credit card transactions – "was expecting a call"
   - **c.** Confirmed understanding of seriousness of allegations
   - **d.** Believed it would be "best for everyone to stay out of court"
   - **e.** Wanted to put the matter behind her – GP overreacting
   - **f.** Acknowledged that while employed by GP she had used the firm's credit card for personal spending
      - **i.** RN knew personal use was not authorized although they all did it
      - **ii.** "The only real issue is how much"

- **iii.** I advised that our current determination was between $75k and $125k, that it was in her best interest to sit down and discuss
- **iv.** I advised that some items have not been confirmed
- **v.** I advised that we were missing some credit card and bank statements

g. RN stated $125k amount was too much

- **i.** RN advised that most personal items were run through the credit card – very few checks

h. RN stated she had maintained a record on her computer that would verify exactly how much she took

i. RN stated she may have some of the missing records

j. RN stated she used only one credit card – AMEX

k. "Situation simply got out of control"

l. She "accepts responsibility for using the firm's credit card for personal use"

5. Inquired about RN's record – why maintain?

- **a.** 3 credit cards were issued – only one to her
- **b.** She always tracked her usage
- **c.** Identified personal use, intended to repay (with bonuses)
- **d.** Maintained record in case she needed to explain the transactions
  - **i.** Explain how? RN response – "Like today" (?)
- **e.** I requested copy of her file; RN response – "Should not be a problem"

6. Reasoning for credit card use

- **a.** Card was issued to her – "I was authorized to use it"
- **b.** Understood it was primarily for business use
  - **i.** Explain primarily? RN response – "Others, including GP, used for personal use"
- **c.** Tried to keep the balance paid down
  - **i.** How?
    - 1. RN response – "Through firm funds and bonuses not taken"
  - **ii.** Asked for explanation;
    - 1. RN response – Percentage of collections (10%) not taken
  - **iii.** RN stated she saved the firm money – not classified as payroll

7. Inquired about relationship with GP

- **a.** Small office, but not close
- **b.** Did not socialize outside office
- **c.** No personal relationship outside office

8. Inquired about internal accounting – who did what

- **a.** RN stated she was paralegal and did all the in-house accounting
- **b.** Duties included the general ledger (Quick Books)
- **c.** Also received and paid bills and payroll
- **d.** RN stated she had the authority to sign checks
- **e.** Commonly talked with bank personnel / made deposits
- **f.** RN stated she generally talked with CPA
- **g.** The "lawyers practiced law," and she ran the office

9. Inquired about specific methods

- **a.** Credit card for personal use
  - **i.** RN acknowledged
  - **ii.** I advised that amount was approximately $45k, including 247 transactions from Sept. '06 through Jun. '07
    - 1. RN stated she can't remember – would like to compare with her records

- **iii.** I advised that we were missing credit card statements from Mar. 5, 2007 through May 18, 2007
    1. RN again advised that she had some credit card records
- **iv.** I requested confirmation of when she first used the firm's credit card
    1. RN responded she was not sure
- **v.** I inquired why she kept the credit card records
    1. RN stated she kept them in case she needed them – "Like today"
    2. RN stated that many purchases were legit
- **vi.** I advised that we had sorted the credit card transactions into various categories, e.g., clothing, fuel
    1. RN advised that some of the fuel charges and WalMart charges were legit; she needed to see detail to confirm
    2. I offered to meet and review, but she requested they be emailed
        - **a.** I agreed to exchange for copy of her file
- **vii.** I inquired about transaction related to law school ($11k)
    1. RN stated this must be a mistake – cannot be $11k
    2. I agreed to review

b. Altered payees
- **i.** RN acknowledged there may be a few
- **ii.** I inquired about specifics of Nov. 20, 2006 check for $7,229.40, coded in G/L as trust payment to XXXXX, later voided in the G/L, but actually cleared as payment to herself and deposited into her account
    1. RN acknowledged a vague remembrance
    2. RN stated she would have to see transaction; XXXXX had been a client of the firm
- **iii.** I inquired about her knowledge of QB audit log, which allows tracking of changes in G/L
    1. RN stated that her knowledge limited – not aware

c. Unauthorized checks for bonuses, loans, and reimbursement for travel
- **i.** RN stated she did receive legit bonuses and reimbursement for travel
    1. Bonuses based on collections – 10%
- **ii.** Can't recall unauthorized checks or checks for cash
- **iii.** RN acknowledged that bonuses should have been posted through the payroll account
- **iv.** RN does not recall checks coded as loans
- **v.** I inquired about a check to XXXXX dated Sept. 21, 2006 in the amount of $1,060; appears to have been endorsed by XXXXX
    1. RN stated that XXXXX was not involved – knew nothing
    2. RN stated that she vaguely recalled the transaction – remembers that XXXXX cashed the check and gave her some cash back
    3. RN believes a large portion of the check was monthly payment for cleaning services – $60 per week
    4. I advised RN that we had confirmed $60 weekly payments to XXXXX before and after the subject transaction
    5. RN stated she could not remember – was not sure
    6. RN again stated that XXXXX was not involved

d. Unauthorized loans
- **i.** RN stated she had the authority to draw on the firm's line of credit to pay bills
- **ii.** Acknowledged that "additional" draws were needed to cover her credit card transactions and checks
- **iii.** Does not recall discussing with GP

10. Others involved
    a. RN stated that no one else was involved
    b. Husband did not know
11. Inquired about defenses
    a. RN offered none
    b. I specifically inquired about duress, use of medications, gambling problems, drugs – RN stated none
    c. Requested explanation as to why – intent to commit a crime?
        i. RN acknowledged she was wrong but never had intent to harm; meant to pay back
12. Closing
    a. Asked if there was anything she wanted to add or wanted us to consider
        i. RN stated she had nothing to add
        ii. RN stated she doesn't challenge the allegations – the question is how much
        iii. RN stated she "wanted to work it out"
        iv. She requested that we call back when we had a final number or if we had additional questions
            1. I advised that reviewing her file would help answer questions
            2. Provided my email address
        v. RN stated she would be available at 3:30 p.m. I advised that I would review her materials, update my analysis and review with GP. Would try to call back around at 3:45 p.m.

<u>*Action Notes:*</u>

- Discuss with GP
    - Confirm his communications with RN and spouse (promises?)
    - Discuss intent – what about the loans argument?
    - Concerns about quick confession – why?
        - Any additional evidence?
        - Cover up for someone else?
            - Husband / sister-in-law / others
    - Credit card use – "everyone did it"
    - What about – "best for everyone to stay out of court"
    - Something seems off

Key Terms

Active listening
Communication process
Corroborative witnesses
Doing stage
Fair Credit Reporting Act
Formal interview
Informal interview
Interrogation
Interview
Legal observations
Memorandum of interview
Memorializing
Neutral third parties
Open-ended questions
Personal space
Planning stage
Pretext
Rapport
Stress
Structured questions
Suspected co-conspirators
Target

Chapter Questions

4-1. What is the purpose of an interview?

4-2. What are four requirements of an effective interview?

4-3. What are the six primary components of the interview process? Briefly discuss each.

4-4. Define active listening.

4-5. What attributes are demonstrated by active listeners?

4-6. What is discriminative listening, and how is it useful to a forensic accountant?

4-7. Define body language and discuss its importance in communication.

4-8. When observing an interviewee's body language, what cautions should a forensic accountant keep in mind?

4-9. Identify five ways that a person's hands can send a message. Briefly discuss each.

4-10. Identify and discuss five head movements that provide communication cues.

4-11. How do a person's eyes provide insight into his or her emotional state?

4-12. Can the placement of a person's arms provide communication cues? Explain.

4-13. How does a person's posture reflect his or her interest in a topic being discussed?

4-14. How is anxiety exhibited by the placement of a person's legs and feet? Explain.

4-15. Define stress. How does stress impact communication?

4-16. What are the physical and emotional symptoms manifested by a person under stress?

4-17. What is rapport, and how is it useful in the communication process?

4-18. How might a forensic accountant use rapport to enhance the effectiveness of an interview?

4-19. How is the concept of personal space relevant to establishing rapport in an interview?

4-20. Identify two types of interviews a forensic accountant might conduct.

4-21. What is a formal interview? How are questions normally structured in this type of interview? Provide examples.

4-22. Define an informal interview. How are questions formed in this type of interview?

4-23. What is the difference between an information-gathering interview and an interrogation?

4-24. What are the three types of questions forensic accountants commonly employ during interviews? Provide two examples of each.

4-25. Discuss the three fundamental stages of the interview process.

4-26. What are three things a forensic accountant should consider in the planning stage of the interview process?

4-27. Identify the key steps in conducting an interview. Discuss each.

4-28. Why is transcribing notes important to the success of the interview process?

4-29. Should an interview be taped? Discuss why or why not.

4-30. Discuss the order in which witnesses should be interviewed.

4-31. Identify and discuss the legal considerations that impact an employee's right to have an attorney present at an interview, depending on whether the employer is a public or private entity.

4-32. Identify and discuss ten tips for conducting a successful interview.

4-33. Define observations. How are visual and auditory observations useful to a forensic accountant? Provide an example of each.

4-34. Discuss four advantages of searching public records.

4-35. What must a forensic accountant do to legally obtain a credit report under the Fair Credit Reporting Act? What specific actions are prohibited by this Act?

Multiple-Choice Questions

Select the best response to the following questions related to the communication process:

4-36. In the communication process, the sender is the only communicator.

- **a.** True
- **b.** False

4-37. Each of the following is a channel of communication *except*:

- **a.** Face-to-face
- **b.** Email
- **c.** Voice tonal quality
- **d.** Telephone

4-38. For a communication to be understood, it must be properly:

a. Employed
b. Decoded
c. Deployed
d. Referenced

4-39. Noise is a communication constraint. Each of the following is a type of noise *except*:

a. Bad phone connection
b. Fear
c. The nature of the allegation
d. Attitude of the sender

4-40. An active listener demonstrates each of the following attributes *except*:

a. Anticipates questions while the speaker is talking
b. Allows the speaker to finish his or her statement
c. Repeats the interviewee's statement by paraphrasing the message
d. Searches for a balance between an interviewee's words and his or her body language

4-41. Most experts believe that the hands display more emotion than any other part of the body.

a. True
b. False

4-42. Which of the following might be considered an indication of hostility?

a. Palms extended upward
b. Rubbing one's face
c. Pointing a figure
d. Shaking one's head

4-43. You are sitting at a table talking to your instructor, and he or she is leaning toward you. This may be an indication of what?

a. Hostility
b. Domination
c. Interest
d. Indifference

4-44. Stress is defined as an emotional and physical strain caused by one's response to pressure from the outside world.

a. True
b. False

4-45. Stress can manifest itself through either physical or emotional symptoms.

a. True
b. False

4-46. Which of the following should a forensic accountant seek to establish in an interview?

a. A dominant position
b. Rapport
c. Friendship
d. None of the above

4-47. All of the following are conceptualized zones related to an individual's personal space *except*:

a. Public zone
b. Personal zone
c. Intimate zone
d. Preferential zone

4-48. Stress is often created when the interviewer respects and honors an interviewee's personal space.

a. True
b. False

Select the best response to the following questions related to conducting interviews:

4-49. Effective interviewing requires each of the following *except*:

a. Active listening
b. Planning
c. Staging
d. Execution
e. Each of the above is required in an effective interview

4-50. An interview is a purposeful dialogue through which information is sought and exchanged.

a. True
b. False

4-51. A formal interview is an unsystematic method in which the interviewer decides on questions as the interview progresses.

a. True
b. False

4-52. Which of the following statements describing formal and informal interview methods is *not* correct?

	Formal	Informal
a. Primarily uses open-ended questions	Y	N
b. Primarily uses closed-ended questions	Y	N
c. Relies on the spontaneous generation of questions	Y	Y
d. Controlled by a specific set of detailed questions	Y	N

4-53. Interrogation is an interview technique commonly employed by a forensic accountant in a fraud investigation.

a. True
b. False

4-54. Which of the following is *not* a fundamental component of the planning stage of an interview?

- **a.** Determining how to establish rapport with the interviewee
- **b.** Developing a question bank
- **c.** Considering how to intimidate a witness
- **d.** Developing an interview schedule

4-55. In the actual conduct of an interview, forensic accountants generally start with introductory questions and move to informational questions.

- **a.** True
- **b.** False

4-56. Memorializing an interview involves which of the following actions?

- **a.** Asking detailed questions
- **b.** Tape recording the interview discreetly
- **c.** Transcribing notes into a memorandum of interview
- **d.** All of the above are aspects of memorializing an interview

4-57. The covert taping of interviews is considered the most effective means of obtaining honest answers from an interviewee.

- **a.** True
- **b.** False

4-58. It is always best to start a series of interviews by talking to the target first.

- **a.** True
- **b.** False

4-59. Which of the following is *not* a type of question normally employed in an interview process?

- **a.** Informational questions
- **b.** Closing questions
- **c.** Introductory questions
- **d.** Transitional questions

4-60. Employees always have the right to counsel when being interviewed about company matters.

- **a.** True
- **b.** False

4-61. If an interviewee is a public employee, he or she is entitled to have an attorney present at an interview if there is a possibility of exposure to criminal liability.

- **a.** True
- **b.** False

Select the best response to the following questions related to the value of observations:

4-62. Forensic accountants must exercise caution when making engagement-related observations to ensure they are legal and can thus be used as a reliable basis for forming an expert opinion.

- **a.** True
- **b.** False

4-63. A legal visual observation includes each of the following *except*:

- **a.** Searching a suspect's trash can for evidence
- **b.** Observing the condition of a residence
- **c.** Assessing the location of a business enterprise
- **d.** Reading a suspect's personal diary

4-64. A legal auditory observation includes which of the following?

- **a.** Secretly recording a conversation in a meeting room
- **b.** Listening to a conversation in a restaurant
- **c.** Recording a telephone conversation without informing the person with whom you are talking
- **d.** All of the above are legal auditory observations

4-65. Public records can be used by a forensic accountant to support or refine a fraud hypothesis.

- **a.** True
- **b.** False

4-66. Each of the following is an advantage of searching public records *except*:

- **a.** The search can be done in secret
- **b.** It is a legal source of information
- **c.** Results cannot be replicated by others
- **d.** Gaining access is fast and inexpensive

4-67. Social networking web sites are resources a forensic accountant might use to obtain information about an individual's family and other personal matters.

- **a.** True
- **b.** False

4-68. A pretext is the use of deception to obtain information about someone from another party who might not otherwise disclose such information.

- **a.** True
- **b.** False

4-69. The Fair Credit Reporting Act requires that consent be acquired prior to obtaining an individual's credit information.

- **a.** True
- **b.** False

Workplace Applications

4-70. Review the interview notes memorialized by the forensic accountant in the *U.S. v. Ronda Nixon* case (provided in Appendix 4-A) and respond to the following questions:

- **a.** Do the notes provide evidence that the interview was planned?
- **b.** How was the interview structured?
- **c.** What were some strengths of the interview?
- **d.** Can you identify any weaknesses of the interview?

4-71. Revisit the *U.S. v. Bonnie Bain* case presented in Chapter 2. Assume that you have been engaged by Ms. Bain's counsel to assist in her defense. Considering this chapter's discussion on the value of observations, what might be relevant about:

- **a.** The layout of the bank?
- **b.** The location of Ms. Bain's workstation?
- **c.** The location of the bank's vault?
- **d.** The manner in which passwords and other control information are used?
- **e.** Ms. Bain's home?
- **f.** Ms. Bain's automobile?

4-72. Review the following body language lessons at history.com (links available at www.pearsonhighered.com/rufus):

- **a.** Secrets of Body Language Part 1
- **b.** Secrets of Body Language Part 2

Identify several body language messages in these video clips. Were you able to detect them prior to the expert pointing them out?

4-73. Tom Golden discusses the discovery of fraud in the workplace in a video entitled: "My First Fraud Investigation." Find a link to this video at www.pearsonhighered.com/rufus.

After viewing the video, respond to the following questions:

- **a.** How did Tom Golden detect the fraud?
- **b.** Did he violate ethical standards in his investigation?
- **c.** If he was to develop a preliminary hypothesis, what might it be?
- **d.** Are any concepts from this chapter highlighted in this video? If so, explain.

4-74. Body language is a key factor in the interviewing process. View a video entitled "Forensic Accounting Experiment" on YouTube (a link to this video is available at www.pearsonhighered.com/rufus).

Using the guidance on interviewing and body language presented in this chapter, answer the following questions:

- **a.** How was the interview structured?
- **b.** What body language messages did the interviewer send to the interviewee?
- **c.** How do you interpret the interviewee's body language?
- **d.** After the interviewee had counted the cash, do you believe she was lying or not lying? Identify any verbal and visual clues that support your conclusion.

4-75. Assume that you are preparing to interview yourself regarding how you made the decision to attend college. Create a list of interview questions that address personal information you are willing to share with the class. Using these questions, the instructor will conduct a mock interview of each student.

Applying the mindset of a forensic accountant, plan your questions to move from the general to the specific. After each question, indicate whether you will answer it truthfully or untruthfully as the mock interview progresses.

The class will monitor both the verbal and nonverbal communication of the student interviewee in an effort to determine if his or her responses are truthful. The instructor will compile the observations and perceptions of the class and conduct a discussion regarding both the effectiveness of the interview (what worked and what did not) and what the interviewee's body language disclosed about the truthfulness of the responses.

Chapter Problems

4-76. Go to www.bing.com/videos and search for body language videos using key words such as lying, how to tell, and FBI. Select a body language video and answer the following questions. In addition, be prepared to present your video and question responses in class.

- **a.** What is the thesis of this video?
- **b.** Which body language indicators from this chapter were demonstrated in the video?
- **c.** What did you learn about body language that will help you in your forensic accounting career?

4-77. Retired FBI agent Bill Brown discusses how body language can indicate lying in a video clip entitled "FBI Agent Explains How to Spot Liars" on YouTube (a link to this video is available at www.pearsonhighered.com/rufus). Based on this video, discuss several body language mannerisms that may indicate lying.

4-78. Prepare a research paper on one aspect of body language presented in this chapter. Your paper should have a minimum of five authoritative references and should include the following elements: how a specific body language mannerism manifests, how to interpret that mannerism, and how it might be useful in a forensic investigation.

4-79. Using resources available on the Internet, select an individual approved by your instructor and perform a search with the objective of discovering information about the person's job, education, and personal matters. Compile a list of which sites you used and what information you discovered on each site. Be prepared to present your findings in class.

Case

4-80. The Columbia River Crossing (CRC) project is intended to improve traffic flow in the I-5 corridor in the greater Vancouver, Washington, and Portland, Oregon, region. The proposed project is estimated to cost between $3.1 billion and $3.5 billion plus interest on loans needed to fund the project. These estimates are based on construction beginning in 2013 with completion over an estimated seven- to nine-year period.

Proponents of the CRC project claim that traffic congestion will be reduced by 70% and commuter time reduced by twenty minutes per day. Also, there will be fewer traffic accidents, the quality of life in the metropolitan area will be enhanced, and the local economy will benefit from jobs related to the ongoing construction.

As the nature of this project was disclosed, a coalition of individuals and local organizations began to publicly challenge it, attacking both the cost projections and claimed benefits. These opponents argue that the proposed solution is too costly and will undermine the funding of necessary construction work in other parts of Oregon and Washington. Opponents also claim that, because projects of this type normally run over budget, the ultimate cost of the CRC project will likely exceed the initial projection. Finally, opponents claim that the proposal violates the National Environmental Protection Act and will fail to significantly relieve traffic congestion.

The nature and scope of the project are described in a YouTube video titled "The Columbia River Crossing: A Boatload of Questions 1.3," which was created by an opponent of the project. (A link to this video is available at www.pearsonhighered.com/rufus.)

As the CRC project progressed, spending began to exceed initial estimates. Because there was inadequate financial reporting to allow monitoring of the project's financial management, a local Vancouver businessman provided the funding to hire a forensic accountant to perform a review of documentation and spending.

The forensic accountant's preliminary findings were presented at a 2010 meeting and can be viewed in the following two video clips entitled:

- "Forensic Accountant Tiffany Couch shares her findings at 'Bridging the Gaps' event Part 1" (go to www.pearsonhighered.com/rufus for a link to this clip).
- "Forensic Accountant Tiffany Couch shares her findings at 'Bridging the Gaps' event Part 2" (go to www.pearsonhighered.com/rufus for a link to this clip).

Following a review of many of the documents discussed in these videos, Ms. Couch prepared a comprehensive report that was presented to Washington State Representative Ann Rivers (18th District, R-LaCenter). The report (called "Tiffany Couch's CRC White Paper") can be obtained via a link at www.pearsonhighered.com/rufus.

A. After viewing these video clips, answer the following questions:

1. What types of information is Ms. Couch attempting to gather?
2. What are her preliminary findings?
3. What body language cues do you detect as you watch Ms. Couch present her preliminary findings?
4. What body language cues do you detect from Mr. Paul Guppy seated immediately behind Ms. Couch as she presents her findings?
5. Develop a preliminary hypothesis about the CRC finances based on your observations from Ms. Couch's presentation.

B. After reading the first ten pages of Ms. Couch's letter to Rep. Rivers, respond to the following questions related to gathering evidence:

1. What was the purpose of the engagement?
2. How was the requested material delivered to Ms. Couch?
3. What was accomplished in the meeting/interview involving Ms. Couch and representatives of CRC and WSDOT?
4. What do you think Ms. Couch needed to do in order to convert the information provided by WSDOT into a usable format?
5. What were Ms. Couch's three most significant findings related to financial matters at CRC?
6. Based on Exhibit P from Ms. Couch's letter, what did she conclude about financial matters at CRC?
7. Revise the preliminary hypothesis you developed in A-5 above.

---

1 *Black's Law Dictionary.* (2009). 9th Ed., 635.

2 Hart, K. (2008, July 28). Former law firm worker pleads not guilty. *The Independent* (Ashland, KY).

3 Vessel, D. (1998, October). Conducting successful interrogations. *FBI Law Enforcement Bulletin.*

4 Foulger, D. (2004). Models of the communication process. *Evolutionary Media.*

5 Kline, J. (1996). *Listening effectively.* Maxwell Airforce Base, AL: Air University Press.

6 Harmeyer, W. J., Golen, S., & Sumners, G. (1984). *Conducting audit interviews.* Institute of Internal Auditors.

7 Ibid.

8 Cotetiu, A., & Toader, R. (2007, May). Considerations on stress and its consequences regarding the communication process. Paper presented at the 7th International Multidisciplinary Conference, Baia Mare, Romania.

9 Walsh, D., & Bull, R. (2010). Interviewing suspects of fraud: An in-depth analysis of interviewing skills. *Journal of Psychiatry & Law, 38(12),* 99–135.

10 Vallano, J., & Compo, N. S. (2011). A comfortable witness is a good witness: Rapport-building and susceptibility to misinformation in an investigative mock-crime interview. *Applied Cognitive Psychology, 25*(6), 960–70.

11 Evans, G., & Wener, R. (2007). Crowding and personal space invasion on the train: Please don't make me sit in the middle. *Journal of Environmental Psychology*, *27*(1), 90–94.

12 Catlettsburg bookkeeper convicted for defrauding law firm. (2009, August). FBI Press Release. Go to www.pearsonhighered.com/rufus for a link to this press release.

5 Financial Statements Analysis—Reading Between the Lines

ZZZZ Best Carpet Cleaning Service

In October 1982, 16-year-old Barry Minkow started a carpet cleaning business in his parents' garage. That company, headquartered in Los Angeles, was named ZZZZ Best Carpet Cleaning Service (ZZZZ Best). By 1986, ZZZZ Best was a Wall Street favorite with a stock market valuation of more than $175 million. Two years later, the company was bankrupt, and Minkow was headed to prison.[1] In a 2004 interview with the *Los Angeles Daily News*, Minkow explained that the company's instant success created cash flow problems he solved by committing fraudulent acts. Such acts included forged money orders, false insurance claims, overbilling, and check kiting—whatever it took to stay afloat.[2]

During the development of a training video for auditors, Minkow admitted to former FBI agent Joseph Wells that ZZZZ Best was built entirely on lies. Wells reports that the company's initial public offering was based on fabricated financial statements, including fictitious revenues (insurance restoration contracts) and accounts receivable supported by fraudulent documents.[3] To legitimize these fictitious numbers, Minkow obtained audited financial statements from a local CPA firm. Following the public offering, the company's stock price soared. Minkow's plan was to wait out the two-year period imposed by the U.S. Securities and Exchange Commission (SEC), during which insiders of the company were not allowed to sell the newly issued stock. He then planned to sell enough stock to clean up his fraudulent activities and begin operating the business in a legal, legitimate manner.

However, as is the case with most frauds, Minkow's luck ran out when one of his employees (Norman Rothberg) tipped off the auditors that a certain $7 million restoration contract was fictitious and that the building to be restored did not even exist. On May 29, 1987, the auditors (Ernst & Whinney) advised Minkow and ZZZZ Best's audit committee of the fraud tip and recommended the engagement of fraud investigators. Minkow denied the allegations and denied even knowing

Barry Minkow

Learning Objectives

After completing this chapter, you should be able to:

LO1. Explain the importance of the context in which financial reporting occurs.

LO2. Explain the concept of earnings management and its role in financial statement manipulation schemes.

LO3. Explain the purpose and process of various methods of financial statements analysis, including horizontal (trend) analysis, vertical (common-size) analysis, ratio analysis, cash flow analysis, and journal entry testing.

LO4. Discuss how content analysis is useful in a forensic examination.

LO5. Identify the differences between personal and business financial statements.

Rothberg. Rothberg immediately recanted his story. The auditors subsequently discovered a check (dated May 29, 1987) from Minkow to Rothberg (the payoff), which heightened their suspicions of fraud. Ernst & Whinney resigned on June 2, 1987, before completing the audit of ZZZZ Best.[4]

On June 17, 1987, ZZZZ Best filed its quarterly report with the SEC advising that Ernst & Whinney had resigned without material disagreements. On July 3, ZZZZ Best announced that Minkow had resigned because of a "severe medical problem." Less than a week later (July 8), the company filed for Chapter 11 bankruptcy protection. On July 16, Ernst & Whinney responded to ZZZZ Best's latest SEC filing, explaining its withdrawal from the audit engagement and its suspicions of fraud.

In January 1988, Minkow and 12 associates, including Norman Rothberg, were named in a fifty-four-count indictment alleging racketeering, money laundering, and securities fraud. The indictment alleged that Minkow and his associates operated ZZZZ Best as a giant Ponzi scheme in which funds from new investors were used to pay older ones, money was laundered from criminal activities, and millions of dollars were skimmed for personal use. Losses to investors were estimated to exceed $100 million.[5]

The trial against Minkow opened on August 24, 1988. Prosecutors described Minkow as a con artist and swindler who lived in a $1 million house and drove a Ferrari. They accused him of fooling bankers, accountants, and brokerage firms alike while amassing a fortune built on lies, specifically fake insurance contracts to restore damaged buildings. Minkow's attorney, David Kenner, argued that Minkow was forced to stage the elaborate fraud scheme by organized crime figures, who took control of ZZZZ Best and silenced him with threats. Minkow, who testified at trial, confessed to stock manipulation while under duress, claiming that he was a "hostage of mobsters and loan sharks."[6]

On December 14, 1988, following four months of trial and five days of jury deliberations, Minkow was convicted on all counts. He was sentenced on March 28, 1989, to twenty-five years in prison and was ordered to pay $26 million in restitution for his fraud. After serving less than eight years, Minkow was released from prison.

Wells contends that basic ratio analysis might have uncovered the ZZZZ Best fraud well before the company went public and investors lost over $100 million in value. Three ratios that should have alerted analysts to the possibility of fraud include the current ratio, the debt-to-equity ratio, and the return-on-equity ratio. Wells calculated these ratios for 1985 and 1986, as illustrated in Table 5-1.

As highlighted by Wells, "The current ratio shows a company with no cash in 1986 despite record 'revenues.' The 1986 debt-to-equity ratio is up 8600% from the prior year; return on equity has dropped by more than 75%. These are not indicators of a legitimate business."[7]

Special Note

Following his release from prison in 1995, Minkow operated Fraud Discovery Institute (FDI), a for-profit white-collar crime investigation firm. Six years later, in March 2011, Minkow entered into a plea agreement with the U.S. Attorney for the Southern District

Table 5-1 ZZZZ Best Ratios

Ratio	1985	1986
Current	36.552	0.977
Debt to equity	0.017	1.486
Return on equity	183.75%	46.59%

of Florida to one count of conspiracy to commit securities fraud for his participation in a scheme to manipulate the stock price of a publicly traded company (Lennar). Based on fraudulent information advanced by Minkow, Lennar suffered a 20% drop in its stock price within a two-day period in January 2009, equivalent to more than $500 million in value. In July 2011, Minkow was sentenced to five years in prison, followed by three years of supervised release. He was also ordered to pay $583,573 in restitution.[8]

INTRODUCTION

Forensic accountants use a variety of information-gathering techniques. One of the most common—and critical—is financial statements analysis. As you have previously learned, financial statements serve to organize and summarize a company's financial activities. Each of the three primary statements (income statement, cash flow statement, and balance sheet) presents a different perspective of a company's financial activity. Because the information contained in the statements is interrelated, they must be considered together. This is the essence of financial statements analysis—to compare and contrast information and identify relationships.

This chapter aims to challenge your belief in the reliability of financial statements, the good faith of corporate managers, and the basic nature of financial reporting. Armed with a working knowledge of finance, economics, and accounting fundamentals, you will learn to "read between the lines." As you progress through this chapter, keep in mind that financial statements analysis is simply an information-gathering technique—a means rather than an end. Moreover, do not forget that forensic accounting engagements are situation-specific; thus, your analysis will *always* be driven by the unique nature and scope of the assignment.

This chapter will also push you beyond the standard measurements of traditional financial statements analysis (for example, horizontal/vertical analysis and ratios). To that end, our working hypothesis is that financial statements rarely (if ever) reflect economic reality and often conceal more than they reveal. From a forensic accountant's perspective, ***economic reality*** means an accurate and comprehensive financial profile—the true essence of a company's financial condition and earning potential.

Consistent with the theme of the entire text, this chapter displays application of the scientific method in both the collection and analysis of financial data. Hallmarks of the scientific method include a systematic approach, objective and accurate observations, an understanding of context, and, of course, a strong dose of professional skepticism.

CONTEXT OF FINANCIAL REPORTING

The importance of understanding the context in which financial reporting occurs cannot be overstated. What is context, and why is it relevant to financial statements analysis? Simply stated, ***context*** is the information surrounding an event. Context provides an enhanced level of meaning and understanding through perspective, frame, background, or history. Although context itself does not have a specific meaning, the meaning of a communication (such as a financial statement) is always driven by its context. Context allows us to make the comparisons and contrasts that are necessary for effective financial statements analysis.

Important elements of the context of financial statements include the following:

- They are prepared primarily for users *outside* the business.
- They are representations of management.
- They are prepared for a specific period of time.
- They reflect *historical* information.
- They include the activity of the entire organization.
- Preparation standards allow for substantial reporting flexibility.
- They rarely, if ever, represent economic reality.
- They never tell the complete story.

Financial Reporting

A key consideration when analyzing financial statements is the understanding that they are *representations of management*. Thus, we begin with the critical questions of *why* financial statements are prepared and *to whom* they are presented. Generally, financial statements are prepared to meet external reporting obligations and to aid in internal decision making. For example, all publicly traded companies in the United States are required by the SEC to file annual reports (Form 10-K) that include audited financial statements. Private companies may also be required to present annual reports (audited or not) by virtue of creditor or investor agreements.

Special Note

The Securities Exchange Act of 1934 empowered the SEC to require periodic reporting of information by companies with publicly traded securities. Companies with more than $10 million in assets whose securities are held by more than 500 owners must file annual and other periodic reports. Form 10-K provides a comprehensive overview of the company's business and financial condition and includes audited financial statements. Generally, Form 10-K must be filed with the SEC within 90 days following a company's fiscal year-end.

Aside from compliance with legal requirements, financial statements are useful for a variety of purposes. For example, financial statements are used by:[9]

- Management to make business decisions, such as operations, resources, and capital
- Existing owners (investors) to assess management performance
- The board of directors to assess management performance
- Prospective investors to assess the viability of investing
- Creditors and vendors to assess creditworthiness
- Employees to assess bargaining positions
- Existing competitors for benchmarking
- Potential competitors to evaluate the industry
- Rating agencies (for example, Standard & Poor's and Moody's) to assign credit ratings
- Investment analysts to make buy/sell recommendations
- Government agencies to assess taxes
- Special interest groups, such as politicians and the media, to explore public issues

As discussed in the "Reporting Standards" section later in this chapter, companies are required to disclose to users of financial statements all *material* information that would likely affect their decision making. It is important to note that evaluations of materiality are made from the company's perspective, not the user's. Different users will likely have different levels of financial sophistication and different goals. Reporting companies cannot be expected to predict the information needs of all users or how they will use this information.[10]

Types of Financial Statements

Forensic accountants must have a working knowledge of the differences between commonly issued financial statements (***audit***, ***review***, and ***compilation***), specifically, an awareness of their suggested credibility and reliability. As illustrated in Table 5-2, each type has a different objective and a different "implied" level of assurance that the financial statements are not materially misstated. We say this assurance is implied because it is *obtained by* the issuing accountant but not *provided to* users.

Audit

Audited financial statements provide users with the auditor's opinion about whether the financial statements are presented fairly and, in all material respects, in conformity with generally accepted accounting principles (GAAP). The auditor has a responsibility to plan

Table 5-2 | Types of Financial Statements

	Compilation	Review	Audit
Accountant/ Auditor's Objective	To assist management in presenting financial information *without obtaining any level of assurance* that there are no material modifications that should be made to the financial statements	To obtain *limited assurance* that there are no material modifications that should be made to the financial statements	To obtain *reasonable assurance* that the financial statements as a whole are free of material misstatements
Level of assurance provided to users	None As provided by the AICPA's Statements on Standards for Accounting and Review Services (SSARs), the issuing accountant is required to read the financial statements and consider whether they appear to be free from obvious material errors.	None The report contains a statement that the accountant is not aware of any material modifications that should be made to the financial statements.	None The auditor provides an opinion of whether the financial statements present fairly, in all material respects, the company's financial position, results of operations, and cash flows.
Requirement to understand the entity's internal controls and assess fraud risk	No	No	Yes
Requirement to perform inquiry and analytical procedures	No	Yes	Yes
Requirement to perform verification and substantiation procedures	No	No	Yes

Source: Adapted from AICPA (2010). What Is the Comparative Difference Between a Compilation, a Review and an Audit? Comparative Overview.

and perform the audit to obtain *reasonable assurance* that the financial statements are free of *material misstatement*. Reasonable assurance is, of course, not absolute assurance. Rather, it is a high level of assurance (or relatively low level of risk) of a material misstatement. As previously noted, assurance is *obtained by* the auditor but not *provided to* the user of the financial statements. Thus, reasonable assurance is implied, but not actually provided.

Review

Reviewed financial statements have a limited implication of assurance. In other words, based on the accountant's review, he or she is unaware of any material modifications that should be made to the financial statements to be in conformity with GAAP. Compared to an audit, a review is narrower in scope, consisting primarily of inquiries of company personnel and analytical procedures applied to financial data. Analytical procedures generally include a review of the company's historical trends, financial ratios, and industry comparisons. The issuing accountant focuses more on the relationships among accounting data than on the verification of the data presented. Again, no assurance is actually provided to the user of the financial statements. Limited assurance is implied, but not actually provided.

Compilation

The last type of financial statement—the compilation—represents the most basic level of financial statements. The objective of a compilation is to assist management in presenting financial information in the form of financial statements, with *no implied assurance*. In other words, the issuing accountant has obtained no assurances regarding conformity with GAAP. Still, the issuing accountant must comply with Statements on Standards for Accounting and Review Services (SSARS), which requires specific industry knowledge and consideration of whether the financial statements appear appropriate and free from obvious material errors (for example, that the balance sheet balances).

Reporting Standards

Financial statements are normally prepared and presented in accordance with GAAP. Mandated for publicly held companies, GAAP encompasses the conceptual framework determined by the American financial community, a framework that is both accepted and expected. The fundamental accounting principles (concepts that drive the rules) are listed below.

- ***Cost principle***. The cost principle highlights the proposition that *value* is not the focus of accounting and is not represented in financial statements. To avoid the subjectivity of value assessments, the cost principle is used to measure, record, and report transactions. In applying the cost principle, costs are measured objectively on a cash or cash-equivalent basis. In other words, amounts shown on financial statements reflect *historical costs*, not *current values*.
- ***Matching principle.*** A major objective of accounting is the determination of periodic net income, specifically by matching appropriate costs with revenues (the accrual method of accounting). Because revenues continuously flow into a business, the matching principle requires that:
    - A specific reporting period be selected (month, quarter, or year)
    - Revenues be measured within the specific reporting period (earned regardless of receipt)
    - Costs incurred be matched with the reported revenues
    - Costs be deducted from the reported revenues to determine the period's net income
- ***Objectivity principle.*** The objectivity principle requires that accounting transactions be supported by objective (arm's-length transaction) evidence. Thus, opinions of management are always suspect.
- ***Consistency principle.*** The consistency principle, while recognizing the validity of different accounting methods (such as inventory and depreciation), requires the consistent application of a selected method, period after period, to allow for comparability.
- ***Full-disclosure principle.*** The full-disclosure principle requires that financial statements and accompanying notes fully disclose all material and relevant data for the reporting period. Significant accounting policies are generally listed as the first note to the financial statements.
- ***Conservatism principle.*** The conservatism principle requires that financial reporting be conservative, neither disproportionately overstating nor understating a situation. While conservatism is no longer listed as a constraint in the conceptual framework, many accountants continue to view conservatism as a practical way to justify accounting choices.
- ***Materiality principle.*** The materiality principle holds that strict adherence to accounting principles is not required for items of little significance. Although there is no clear distinction between material and immaterial (because each situation is unique), an item is generally considered material if it would influence one's judgment of a situation.

The reporting rules of GAAP are complex and have evolved over an extended period of time. GAAP mandates use of the accrual method (as opposed to the cash method) of accounting. As noted previously, the objective of accrual accounting is to relate (match) revenues, expenses, gains, and losses to specific periods of time in order to measure a company's performance.

Regulatory Framework

Currently, the Financial Accounting Standards Board (FASB) is the highest authority in establishing GAAP for public and private companies, as well as nonprofit organizations.* For local and state governments, GAAP is determined by the Governmental Accounting Standards Board (GASB). Financial reporting for federal government entities is regulated by the Federal Accounting Standards Advisory Board (FASAB).

Recent Developments

In June 2009, the FASB issued Statement No. 168—Accounting Standards Codification (ASC). Although not intended to change GAAP or any requirements of the SEC, ASC achieved a major restructuring of accounting and reporting standards in GAAP through disassembling and reassembling thousands of nongovernmental accounting pronouncements. Moreover, since 2002, the FASB and the International Accounting Standards Board (IASB) have been working to merge U.S. GAAP with international financial reporting standards (IFRS), a process known as *convergence*.

Since May 2008, privately held companies have been permitted to prepare their financial statements in accordance with IFRS. However, as of the date of this writing, domestic public companies cannot use IFRS for their filings with the SEC. In July 2012, the SEC released its work plan (Staff Report) regarding implications of incorporating IFRS into the financial reporting system for U.S. issuers. The Staff Report did not recommend adoption. Still, given the global context of finance, an SEC mandate to adopt IFRS seems inevitable.

Standards for Private Companies

Fewer than 15,000 companies are registered with the SEC, compared to an estimated 29 million private businesses and nonprofit organizations.[11] In early 2010, a Blue Ribbon Panel was formed jointly by the AICPA, the Financial Accounting Foundation (FAF),† and the GASB, with support from the National Association of State Boards of Accountancy (NASBA), to provide recommendations on the future of standard setting for private companies. The panel's position was that, because much of what is included in current financial statements (as mandated by GAAP) is not useful and is too costly for private company owners, a different set of accounting standards was warranted.

In May 2012, the FAF announced its final decision to create a Private Company Council (PCC) to improve the standards-setting process for private companies. The PCC will determine the need for GAAP exceptions or modifications required by users of private company financial statements. Recommendations of the PCC are subject to FASB approval (endorsement). In June 2012, the AICPA announced its support of the initiative and commitment to making the process work. The AICPA also announced an initiative to develop a self-contained financial reporting framework for owner-managed entities that do not use GAAP.[12]

Earnings Management

By design, GAAP sanctions a wide range of both operational and reporting freedoms (managerial judgments) in financial statements.[13] ***Operational freedom*** involves making operational choices at year-end to enhance the appearance of certain accounts, while ***reporting freedom*** involves the use of judgment in determining the amounts reported. Under GAAP, these freedoms are, at least theoretically, held in check by the principle of conservatism, which directs management to select methods and estimates that avoid overstating assets, revenue, and income.

---

* Section 101 of the Sarbanes-Oxley Act of 2002 established the Public Company Accounting Oversight Board (PCAOB), which is required to establish or adopt auditing, quality control, ethics, independence, and other standards relating to the preparation of audit reports for public companies. The PCAOB has delegated its responsibility in this regard to the FASB.

† The oversight body of the FASB.

As evidenced repeatedly over the last three decades, reporting flexibility provides opportunity that, when coupled with the right motivation, can result in ***earnings management***. Earnings management, as defined by Schipper (1989), is the "purposeful intervention in the external financial reporting process, with the intent of obtaining some private gain."[14] According to Healy and Wahlen (1999), "earnings management occurs when managers use judgment in financial reporting and in structuring transactions to alter financial reports to either mislead some stakeholders about the underlying economic performance of the company, or to influence contractual outcomes (management incentive contracts, debt covenants, and so forth) that depend on reported accounting numbers."[15]

In practice, earnings management encompasses a wide variety of legitimate and illegitimate actions by management that impact reported earnings.[16] Legitimate earnings management includes reasonable and proper practices that are part of operating a well-managed business and delivering value to shareholders. In contrast, illegitimate earnings management is intervening to hide real operating performance by creating artificial accounting entries or stretching estimates beyond a point of reasonableness.[17]

As outlined in Table 5-3, earnings management decisions may include conservative, neutral, aggressive, and even fraudulent schemes.

In-Class Exercise

For the purposes of illustration, let's consider the reporting methods identified in Table 5-4 and the related classification as conservative, neutral, aggressive, or fraudulent. Do you agree with these classifications? Why or why not? What is the consequence of each method—understating or overstating income? When do they cross the line of conservatism?

Aggressive and fraudulent earnings management involves one or more of three basic schemes: (1) overstating revenues, (2) understating expenses, and (3) overstating financial condition and/or liquidity. Why would a manager or a team of managers (senior, mid, or lower level) manipulate financial statements? To conceal true performance? Yes, but why? Why would managers risk their reputations, livelihoods, and perhaps even their freedom? Table 5-5 highlights some well-publicized financial statement failures (manipulations) for discussion.

Table 5-3 | Earnings Management Decision Grid

Classification	Accounting Choices Within GAAP
Conservative	Overly aggressive recognition of provisions or reserves Overvaluation of acquired in-process R&D in purchase acquisitions Overstatement of restructuring charges and asset write-offs
Neutral	Earnings that result from a neutral operation of the process
Aggressive	Understatement of the provisions for bad debts Drawing down provisions or reserves in an overly aggressive manner
	Accounting Choices That Violate GAAP
Fraudulent	Recording sales before they are realized Recording fictitious sales Backdating sales invoices Overstating inventory by recording fictitious inventory

Source: Adapted from Dechow, P. M., & Skinner, D. J. (2000). Earnings Management: Reconciling the Views of Accounting Academics, Practitioners, and Regulators. *Accounting Horizons,* 14(2), 235–50.

Table 5-4 Assessment of Reporting Strategy

Approach	Classification
Accelerated depreciation (for financial and tax reporting) of new equipment pursuant to Internal Revenue Code Sec. 179	Conservative
Failure to fully write down impaired nonoperating assets	Fraudulent
Understatement of loan losses by a bank	Fraudulent
Reduced estimate of the useful lives of intangibles recorded as a result of business combination	Conservative
Capitalization of ordinary period expenses	Fraudulent
Capitalization of internally developed software costs	Neutral
Reducing the actuarially determined discount rate to compute the pension liability	Conservative

Source: Compiled from Nelson, M., Elliott, J., & Tarpley, R. (2003). How Are Earnings Managed? Examples from Auditors. *Accounting Horizons,* 17, 17–35.

Table 5-5 Financial Statement Failures

Company	Year	Scheme	Notes
Micro Strategy	2000	Revenue recognition	$66 million revenue overstatement through management manipulation of customer contracts to manage quarterly earnings
Xerox	2000	Revenue overstatement	$6 billion overstatement by "storing" revenue to record in down periods and accelerating revenue by classifying operating leases as capital leases
Enron	2001	Revenue recognition, mark-to-market accounting, and special entity manipulation	Enron failed, leaving about $67 billion in outstanding debt; investors lost everything, and Arthur Andersen went out of business
AOL	2002	Revenue recognition	Executives gave advertisers cash from stock issues; this was done so that advertisers could buy advertisement coverage from AOL, which boosted advertising revenue
Freddie Mac	2002	Income smoothing	Understated earnings by about $5 billion from 2000 to 2002 to meet analyst expectations
Qwest Communications	2002	Revenue recognition, expense understatement	$4 billion overstatement of revenue by reporting one-time sales as ongoing revenue; recognized gains on asset swaps as current revenue and understated expenses by recording capacity purchases as assets rather than expenses
WorldCom	2002	Expense manipulation	Recorded many types of period costs as capital expenses; total fraud about $4 billion
HealthSouth	2003	Revenue recognition, expense manipulation	Reported fictitious sales; timing of sales between accounting periods; capitalization of expenses; total fraud about $1.5 billion
Madoff Investment Securities	2008	Ponzi scheme, phantom assets	Reported false trades and returns to investors; monies from newer investors used to satisfy cash flow needs of older investors; total fraud about $18 billion
Lehman Brothers	2008	Balance sheet manipulation	Entered into repurchase agreements with offshore financial institutions and recorded them as sales rather than liabilities; total fraud about $50 billion

Special Note

Why does earnings management occur? Academic research highlights the ***agency problem*** as a root cause. The agency problem arises when a company's management is separate from its owners, and the owners (principals) delegate decision-making authority to managers (agents). Because principals and agents have different objectives, this situation creates the potential for conflicts of interest. An understanding of agency theory adds important context when analyzing a company's financial statements.

Private Companies and Non-GAAP Reporting

Many privately held companies issue non-GAAP financial statements, employing either income tax or cash basis representations. Statements prepared with the ***income tax basis*** use accounting regulations determined by the IRS. Statements prepared with the ***cash basis*** report income as it is received and expenses as they are paid, thus ignoring the matching principle of GAAP (that is, matching expenses with revenue). Many small businesses use the cash basis because it is easier to understand, easier to perform, less rigorous, and less expensive. Authoritative guidance on cash- and tax-basis financial statements is vague and leaves much room for professional judgment.

Nonfinancial Measures

Given the dubious nature of financial reporting, forensic accountants commonly consider nonfinancial measures (NFM) in their analysis of financial statements.[18] What are NFMs? Common examples include the number of employees, employee turnover, number of locations, investment in new equipment, investment in research and development (R&D), customer satisfaction surveys, and the size and condition of production facilities. One would expect a reasonable correlation between NFMs and financial measures. For example, increased revenue would suggest growth, which is often accompanied by increased employment or increased investment in technology. Consideration of extra measures does not diminish the importance of financial data, but rather serves to enhance the analyst's understanding of the company's operating environment.

Consideration of NFMs should also include an assessment of a company's competitive advantages and disadvantages within its industry and target market. Research suggests that susceptibility to financial distress (and related accounting deceptions) can be identified using industrial organizational theory, as illustrated in Michael Porter's five competitive forces model.[19] Porter's five forces include:

- The threat of new competitors
- The threat of substitute products or services
- The bargaining power of customers
- The bargaining power of suppliers
- The intensity of competitive rivalry

NFMs add an important layer of context to the forensic accountant's analysis. Many NFMs can be located in a company's ***annual report***, which is filed with the SEC via Form 10-K. In addition to financial statements, the annual report contains other valuable financial and nonfinancial information. Although the format varies, annual reports generally include the following components:

- Description of the subject business and industry
- Financial statements
- Legal proceedings
- Management discussion and analysis (MD&A) of operations
- Executive compensation
- Non-GAAP financial measures
- Information regarding the company's directors and executive management team
- Market price of the company's stock and history of dividends

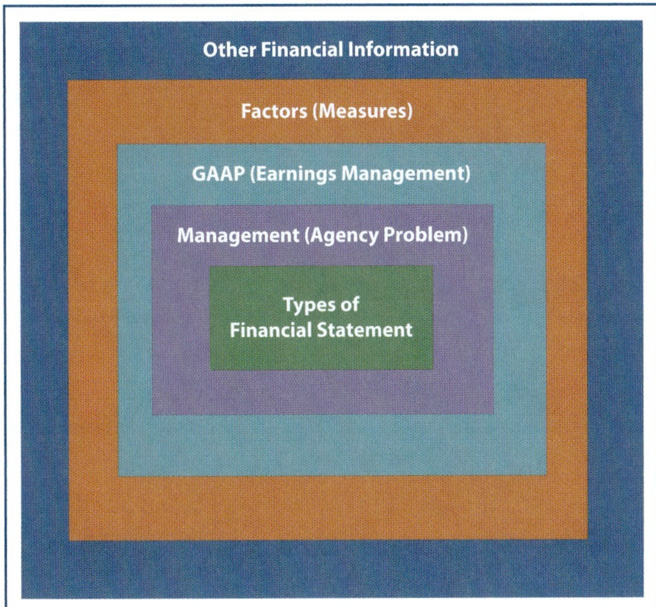

Figure 5-1
Financial Statements Context

Context Summary

Forensic accountants do not analyze financial statements in a vacuum. Financial statements analysis requires context—an understanding of the subject company, its management, its accounting policies and processes, and the environment in which it operates. Context brings clarity, perspective, and focus to the analysis. As illustrated in Figure 5-1, context provides the proper framework within which a meaningful understanding can be established.

FOUNDATIONS OF FINANCIAL STATEMENTS ANALYSIS

Financial statements analysis is the examination of financial statements for the purpose of *acquiring additional information* (questions or concerns) about the activities of a business. As previously discussed, this analysis is not conducted in a vacuum. The financial data must be viewed in context (market, industry, accounting policies, key employees, and historical trends).

Various analytical review methods commonly employed by forensic accountants include:

- Trend (horizontal) analysis
- Common-size analysis (vertical analysis or component percentages)
- Ratio analysis
- Budgetary comparisons
- Industry benchmark comparisons
- Examination of footnotes
- Review of the general ledger and adjusting entries

Internal and External Comparisons

Financial statements analysis requires both internal and external comparisons, which can reveal unexpected relationships or the absence of expected relationships. An internal comparison involves comparing the subject company's current performance and financial condition with its past experience. Such comparisons allow us to examine changes within a company over time. In contrast, external comparisons involve comparing the subject company with similar companies or with the industry as a whole (industry averages). Such comparisons

Table 5-6 | Sources of Industry Data

Name	Scope	Content
Dunn & Bradstreet *Industry Norms and Key Business Ratios*	Data compiled from credit reports of more than 1 million public and private companies in all size ranges. Includes more than 800 industries classified by SIC Code.	14 key financial ratios, including liquidity, profitability, and efficiency ratios
The Risk Management Association (RMA) *Annual Statement Studies*	Data compiled from more than 250,000 financial statements of small- and medium-size companies submitted to RMA member institutions. Includes more than 750 industries classified by NAICS Code.	Common-size income statement and balance sheet data, as well as 19 ratios
Troy's Almanac of Business and Industrial Financial Ratios	Derived from IRS data on almost 5 million U.S. and international companies. Includes 199 industries.	50 performance indicators
Financial Research Associates *Financial Studies of the Small Business*	Data compiled from financial statements of more than 30,000 small companies (capitalization less than $2 million) provided by 1,500 independent CPA firms nationwide.	16 key financial ratios, including liquidity, profitability, and efficiency ratios
Schonfield & Associates, Inc. *IRS Corporate Financial Ratios*	Data compiled from more than 3.7 million corporate tax returns in 250 industry groups.	76 ratios, including common-size income statement and balance sheet data

reveal the company's *relative* performance and financial standing. Sources of industry data commonly used by forensic accountants are identified in Table 5-6.

Forensic Engagements and Financial Statements Analysis

Forensic accounting engagements commonly require the analysis of financial statements. Examples of such engagements include the following:

- Business valuations (divorce, merger/acquisition, liquidation, and estate/gift tax)
- Management assessments
- Contract negotiations (management, employee collective bargaining, and banks)
- Reorganizations
- Buy-sell agreements
- Shareholder disputes
- Damage claims (product liability, business interruption, and punitive damages)
- Financing arrangements
- Bankruptcy
- Incentive stock options
- Government actions
- Fraud

The forensic accountant uses the same tools as a financial analyst, but with a different mindset. In a forensic engagement, the analysis is conducted with an attitude of professional skepticism. The purpose is to identify not just the expected results, but also the *unexpected* results—inconsistencies that may highlight areas for further investigation. Moreover, the forensic accountant commonly works backward, using incomplete information, whereas an accountant or auditor typically works forward from the source of an economic event to its representation in the financial records.

Review of Financial Statements

Before addressing specific strategies, we provide a review of the accounting process and the basic financial statements.

The Accounting Cycle

The ***accounting cycle*** starts with a transaction or an event. The process involves: (a) identifying, (b) classifying, (c) quantifying, and (d) recording the transaction. This process is performed throughout the accounting period as transactions occur. At the end of an accounting period, a trial balance is generated (debits = credits), corrections are made (adjusting entries), and financial statements are prepared.

Basic Financial Statements

Financial statements are used to convey a concise picture of a company's operating activity (and related profitability) over a period of time and its financial position on a specific date. The three basic statements include:

- ***Balance sheet.*** The purpose of the balance sheet is to show the financial position of an organization on a specific date. It reports major classes and amounts of assets (resources owned or controlled by the business), liabilities (external claims on those assets), and equity (owners' or investors' contributions or other sources of capital).

  Assets are either purchased or generated through operations. They are, directly or indirectly, financed by the creditors or investors. As previously discussed, accounting principles (cost and objectivity) demand that assets be recorded at their historical cost.
- ***Income statement.*** The purpose of the income statement is to summarize the performance of the organization over a specific period of time (accounting period, such as a quarter or year). It explains some (but not all) changes in the assets, liabilities, and equity of a company between two consecutive balance sheet dates.

  If prepared using GAAP, the income statement is governed by the matching principle, which provides that performance can be measured only if revenues and related costs are accounted for during the same time period.
- ***Statement of cash flows***. The cash flow statement covers the reporting period and serves to reconcile sources and uses of cash, which are classified as operating, investing, or financing activities. This statement helps explain changes in consecutive balance sheets and serves to supplement information provided by the income statement.

Because these three statements depict different components of a company's financial activity, we must consider each in relation to the others.

Special Note

The fourth financial statement is the Statement of Changes in Owners' Equity, which is not commonly prepared for private companies.

METHODS OF FINANCIAL STATEMENTS ANALYSIS

The primary methods of financial statements analysis employed by forensic accountants include horizontal (trend) analysis, vertical (common size) analysis, ratio analysis, and cash flow analysis. Just as each financial statement offers a different perspective of a company's financial activities, so do the various methods for analyzing the statements. Due to their complementary nature, these methods are most effectively applied together in a reiterative (rather than sequential) process.

In this section, we consider the methods that are directly applied to income statement and balance sheet items—horizontal, vertical, and ratio analysis. Cash flow analysis, which takes a more indirect approach, is addressed later in a separate section.

Horizontal (Trend) Analysis

Horizontal analysis compares key financial statement items over time (from one accounting period to the next) to identify changes that may warrant further investigation. This analysis can be performed in two ways:

- *Absolute dollar amounts.* Comparing changes in absolute dollar amounts can assist in identifying the effects of outside influences on a company (such as changes in input prices and various fixed costs).
- *Percentages.* Tracing percentage changes is useful when comparing companies of different size.

The most important revelation of horizontal analysis is a significant *trend.* Trends in direction, speed, and magnitude can be compared within a company over time, with similar companies, or with industry averages.

Trend analysis commonly includes comparison of the growth rates of key accounts. One valuable growth measure is the ***compound annual growth rate*** (CAGR), which reflects average annual growth over a period of multiple years.

Working Example

$\text{CAGR}\ (t_0, t_n) = V(t_n)/V(t_0)^{1/(t_n - t_0)} - 1$

Suppose that a company reported the following revenues:

2006: $435,321

2007: $468,942

2008: $502,778

2009: $487,581

2010: $519,113

The CAGR of revenues over the four-year period from the *end* of 2006 to the *end* of 2010 is:

$\text{CAGR}\ (0,4) = (519{,}113/435{,}321)^{(1/4)} - 1$

An advantage of the CAGR is that it smoothes the year-to-year volatility of annual growth rates, thereby reducing noise in the analysis. By comparing the CAGRs of key accounts, the analyst can identify potentially significant changes in relationships. For example, if revenue growth substantially exceeds or lags growth in related expenses, further investigation is likely warranted.

Another application of trend analysis is the comparison of a company's reported growth to its ***sustainable growth rate*** (SGR). The SGR is the maximum growth rate a company can sustain without obtaining additional financing (debt and/or equity). It is calculated as the product of the retention ratio and return on equity:

$$\text{SGR} = \text{R} * \text{ROE}$$
$$\text{R} = \text{Retention Ratio} = (\text{Net Income} - \text{Dividends}) / \text{Net Income}$$
$$\text{ROE} = \text{Return on Equity} = \text{Net Income} / \text{Shareholders' Equity}$$

Although the SGR makes several assumptions (for example, a stable profit margin and stable proportion of assets to sales), it provides a useful reference point for evaluating the reasonableness of reported past growth or projected future growth. Moreover, it has implications for valuation models that require estimation of a growth rate that can be sustained for many years into the future.

Special Note

Appendix 5-A, located at the end of this chapter, illustrates how a trend analysis is prepared from income statement data.

Vertical Analysis

Vertical, or common-size, analysis compares the relative size of key accounts by converting all income statement items to a percentage of revenue and all balance sheet items to a percentage of total assets. The primary advantage of vertical analysis is that it allows the comparison of financial statements regardless of firm size. As with horizontal analysis, common-size financial statements can be compared within a company over time, with similar companies, or with industry averages.

Special Note

Illustrations of common-size income statements and balance sheets are provided in Appendix 5-A.

Ratio Analysis

In a formal setting such as a deposition or trial, the forensic accountant might describe financial ratios as quantitative indicators of a firm's financial strengths and weaknesses.[20] In basic terms, a ***financial ratio*** is simply a ratio expressing the relationship between two items reported in the financial statements. Ratios can be expressed as fractions, decimals, percentages, or relationships. For example, a ratio of 2/1 can be expressed as 2.00, 2x, 200%, 2 to 1, or 2:1.

Ratio analysis is made possible by the structure of the accounting equation: assets must equal liabilities plus equity. In a system with good internal control, all accounting transactions are recorded in a manner that keeps this equation in balance. While the equation is simple in terms of mathematical construction, there is genius in its simplicity. Maintaining equality of the accounting equation causes the income statement, balance sheet, and statement of cash flows to be interrelated. It is difficult for a financial statement manipulator to maintain this symmetry, and financial ratios often reveal the dissymmetry caused by false reporting.

Financial ratio analysis allows for a large number of items in the financial statements to be reduced to a limited number of ratios. No single ratio provides enough information to develop a complete understanding of the financial condition or performance of a business. However, each ratio can be used to identify specific strengths and weaknesses that contribute to a company's overall financial viability. Two conditions must exist for ratios to be useful in financial statements analysis:

- The ratio must be meaningful—a significant comparison.
- There must be a standard of comparison—is the ratio good or bad?

Financial ratios are generally grouped into five categories, as summarized in Table 5-7. The usefulness of this categorization is to describe the information provided by the different ratios. For example, leverage ratios describe the organization's debt position, while liquidity ratios describe its ability to meet short-term obligations.

Special Note

Appendix 5-A presents ratios calculated from the income statement and balance sheet data used for illustrations throughout this chapter.

Dupont Model

Return on equity (ROE) is the most widely recognized profitability ratio. In the ***DuPont Model***, which was developed by financial executives at the DuPont Corporation in 1919, ROE is broken down into three component ratios: net profit margin, total asset turnover, and the equity multiplier:

$$\text{ROE} = \frac{\text{Net income}}{\text{Sales}} \times \frac{\text{Sales}}{\text{Total assests}} \times \frac{\text{Total assets}}{\text{Total shareholders' equity}}$$

The purpose of this breakdown is to identify the source of an inferior or superior ROE—profitability, operating efficiency, or financial leverage. The DuPont Model highlights the

Table 5-7 Financial Ratio Calculations and Presentation

Ratio Type	Ratio Name	Calculation Formula	Reported
Profitability	1. Gross margin percent	Gross margin / Sales	%
	2. Return on sales	Net income / Sales	%
	3. Return on assets	Net income / Total assets	%
	4. Return on equity	Net income / Total shareholders' equity	%
Efficiency (Utilization)	1. Total asset turnover	Sales / Total assets	Decimal
	2. Accounts receivable turnover	Sales / Accounts receivable	Decimal
	3. Average accounts receivable days	365 / Accounts receivable turnover	Days
	4. Inventory turnover	Cost of goods sold / Inventory	Decimal
	5. Average inventory days	365 / Inventory turnover	Days
	6. Operating cycle	Accounts receivable days + Inventory days	Days
Leverage	1. Debt to assets	Total liabilities / Total assets	%
	2. Equity to assets	Total shareholders' equity / Total assets	%
	3. Debt to equity	Total liabilities / Total shareholders' equity	Decimal
	4. Equity multiplier	Total assets / Total shareholders' equity	Decimal
Liquidity	1. Current ratio	Current assets / Current liabilities	Decimal
	2. Quick (acid test) ratio	(Current assets – Inventory) / Current liabilities	Decimal
	3. Net working capital	Current assets – Current liabilities	$
	4. Times interest earned	EBIT / Interest expense	Decimal
Equity	1. Book value per share	(Common equity – Preferred equity) / Common shares outstanding	$
	2. Earnings per share	Net income to common equity /Common shares outstanding	$
	3. Price to earnings	Market value per share / Earnings per share	Decimal
	4. Dividend payout ratio	Dividends paid / Net income	%
	5. Dividend yield	Dividends per share / Market value per share	%

fact that two companies with the same ROE may not be of equal quality. For example, a company with poor profitability and efficiency could artificially boost its ROE by taking on excessive debt.

Altman's Z-Score

Developed in 1968, Altman's predictive model, known as ***Altman's Z-score***, enhances the usefulness of financial ratio analysis in assessing the performance of a business, specifically its probability of experiencing financial distress.[21] Altman hypothesized that a predictive model could be created by selecting and weighting significant financial ratios. Employing the statistical technique of multiple discriminant analysis, Altman evaluated 22 different financial ratios using a database of 66 publicly traded manufacturing firms. His research concluded that the combination of five financial ratios, with different weights to account for their relative importance, produces a reliable indicator of financial distress. Altman's conventional Z-score model for publicly traded manufacturing firms follows:

$$Z = 1.2(X1) + 1.4(X2) + 3.3(X3) + 0.6(X4) + 0.999(X5)$$

X1 = Net working capital / Total assets

X2 = Retained earnings / Total assets

X3 = Earnings before interest & taxes / Total assets

X4 = Market value of equity / Book value of total debt

X5 = Sales / Total assets

The conventional model has been modified as follows for use by privately held firms and non-manufacturing firms:

Altman's Z-score for privately held firms:

$$Z = 0.717(X1) + 0.847(X2) + 3.107(X3) + 0.420(X4) + 0.998(X5)$$

Altman's Z-score for publicly traded nonmanufacturing firms:

$$Z = 6.65(X1) + 3.26(X2) + 6.72(X3) + 1.05(X4)$$

For privately held firms, X4 (market value of equity/book value of total debt) cannot be calculated. Thus, Altman modified the conventional model, replacing market value of equity with book value of equity. Because X5 (total asset turnover) can vary significantly among firms in nonmanufacturing industries, Altman removed this factor from his modified model for nonmanufacturing firms.

To facilitate interpretation of the Z-score, Altman established boundary points that provide a prediction of bankruptcy. The boundary points are presented in Table 5-8. For example, Altman found that publicly traded manufacturing firms with Z-scores below 1.81 always went bankrupt, while healthy firms displayed Z-scores above 2.99. Firms with scores between these boundary points were sometimes misclassified, so this zone is labeled a "zone of ignorance."

Decades after its introduction, Altman's Z-score continues to enjoy widespread recognition and use in the financial community. Its value lies in its comprehensive nature, simultaneously addressing several critical indicators of performance, combined with its simplicity of application and interpretation. Moreover, statistical models like the Z-score are more precise, lead to clearer conclusions, and avoid judgment bias.[22]

Table 5-8 | Altman's Z-Score Boundaries

Prediction	Publicly Traded Manufacturing	Privately Held Manufacturing	Publicly Traded Non-Manufacturing
Bankrupt	< 1.81	< 1.23	< 1.10
Zone of Ignorance	1.81 to 2.99	1.23 to 2.90	1.10 to 2.60
Non-Bankrupt	> 2.99	> 2.90	> 2.60

Application of Ratio Analysis

When applying financial ratios, the inputs to these ratios (the balance sheet and income statement items that act as numerators and denominators) must be examined for validity. After all, the results of financial statements analysis (or any type of analysis) are only as reliable as the source data—"garbage in, garbage out." Forensic accountants work with a variety of data, ranging in quality from "shoebox data" to audited financial statements. Furthermore, it is important to recognize that financial ratios represent *effects*, not *causes*. Looking beyond the mechanical application of a ratio to its root cause is a critical component of financial statements analysis. By identifying the reasons behind financial ratios, whether strong or weak, the forensic accountant can obtain a better picture of a company's financial condition.

Although financial ratios provide useful information, caution should be exercised in their interpretation. Analysts should avoid using simple rules of thumb, because valid judgments can only be made in comparison to relevant benchmarks, such as similar firms or industry averages. However, even industry averages can be misleading, especially if the sample size is small or the industry is not homogenous. Another important consideration is the standardization of the accounting data used for the comparisons, to ensure that you are comparing apples to apples. Finally, the presence of accounting estimates in the data, such as depreciation or allowance for bad debts, may introduce distortion.

Don't Forget the Footnotes!

An old adage is "always read the fine print." This certainly rings true when analyzing financial statements. As we've discussed, financial statements are rarely clear and easy to follow. Moreover, many disclosures are contained—or hidden—in the footnotes.

Footnotes provide details about long-term debt, such as maturity dates and interest rates, that can provide a better picture of a company's liquidity and future cash flow challenges. Footnotes may also disclose errors in previous accounting statements or pending legal actions. In reviewing the footnotes, the forensic accountant seeks to identify what might have been omitted from the financial statements. Consider a classic example: In 2001, Dell transferred $2.5 billion in customer financing to a joint venture with Tyco, thus removing a large liability from its balance sheet. This made Dell's liquidity position and capital structure seem better when, in fact, little had changed. However, this information did not disappear from the financial statements entirely: A conscientious analyst could have found it in the footnotes.

Caution! Although footnotes are a required component of financial statements, there are no standards for clarity or conciseness. Another problem with the footnotes is that companies may attempt to confuse investors by filling the notes with legal jargon and technical accounting terms.

CASH FLOW ANALYSIS

Financial statements analysis has traditionally focused on data in the income statement and balance sheet. Although the income statement discloses the results of a company's operations for a specific period of time, it does not report the results of other activities (such as financing and investing). Similarly, although comparative balance sheets illustrate changes in assets, liabilities, and equity, they do not explain the causes of these changes. The only financial statement that provides information about a company's operating, investing, and financing activities is the cash flow statement.[23]

The Statement of Cash Flows

As its name implies, the purpose of the cash flow statement is to provide information about a company's sources of cash inflows and outflows during the reporting period, which may be attributable to operating, investing, or financing activities. The net cash flow from these activities should equal the overall change in the reported cash balance during the period.

The cash flow statement represents a powerful, yet underused, data source for the forensic accountant. Its value is attributable to the fact that it is the most difficult financial statement to manipulate. Despite this value, the forensic application of cash flow analysis is not widely recognized. One explanation for this unfamiliarity is that the concepts underlying the balance sheet and income statement date back several hundred years, whereas the cash flow statement (SAS No. 95, November 1987) is relatively new.[24] Another hindrance is that, because most closely held businesses do not prepare a statement of cash flows, it is often necessary for the forensic accountant to do so independently.

A common method for preparing the cash flow statement is the indirect method, which requires reconciliation between the accrual- and cash-basis accounting methods. Specifically, to reconcile net income to net cash flow, one must: (1) remove the effects of accrual-basis transactions that have no cash effect and (2) include effects of cash-basis transactions that have no effect on net income. Preparing a cash flow statement using the indirect method is an excellent test of one's basic understanding of the income statement and balance sheet and how they relate to each other. Without this understanding, a forensic accountant cannot effectively analyze a set of financial statements.

Special Note

Appendix 5-A provides an example of cash flow statements prepared using the indirect method.

Cash Flow Analysis Techniques

Given the breadth of information contained in the cash flow statement, several cash flow analysis techniques are available to the forensic accountant.

Reconciling Cash

The starting point for cash flow analysis is ensuring that the net cash flow for a given year matches the change in the reported cash balance from the beginning of the year to the end. A discrepancy in this regard indicates that either: (a) the cash flow statement has not been prepared correctly, or (b) all cash transactions are not accurately reflected in the income statement and balance sheet.

Cash Flow Comparisons

Another useful tool is to compare various measures of cash flow, such as operating cash flow and free cash flow,[‡] to each other and to net income.[25] Due to the accrual nature of GAAP, net income is expected to deviate from operating cash flow. However, manipulated financial statements often exhibit unexpected relationships and trends. For example, Figure 5-2 compares Enron's key cash flows over the period 1991 to 2000. Notice the divergence between operating cash flow and free cash flow beginning in 1997, which was an

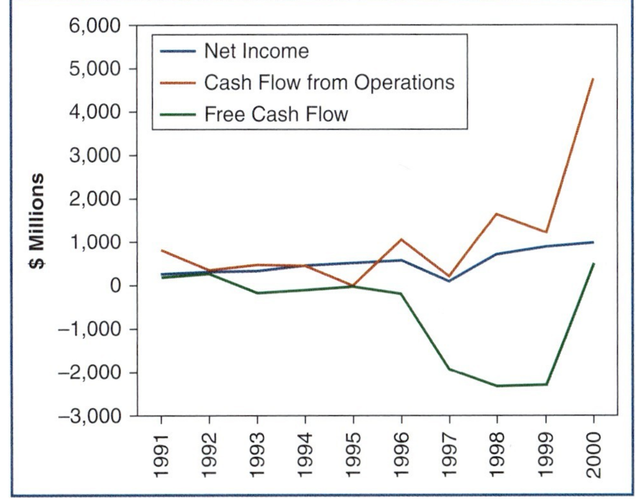

Figure 5-2
Enron Corp. Cash Flows

Source: Form 10-K

‡ Operating cash flow minus capital expenditures.

early warning sign of manipulated reporting. Although cash flow measures can diverge for legitimate reasons, differences of this magnitude and variation are certainly suspect.

Trend Analysis

As with the income statement and balance sheet, horizontal (trend) analysis can be applied to the cash flow statement. Cash flow trends can provide an indication of the company's future direction.[26] For example, investments in fixed assets may signal plans for future expansion.

The analyst must also consider changes over time in the composition of cash inflows and the quality of these inflows.[27] Whether cash inflows are generated by operations, borrowing, or investment is critical to the assessment of a company's financial condition. A healthy company normally generates much of its cash through operations. In contrast, a company that generates most of its cash through borrowing may be approaching insolvency.

Cash Flow Manipulations

Following the numerous accounting scandals of recent years, financial statement users became more skeptical of earnings-based metrics of financial performance. This has resulted in an increased focus on the cash flow statement, which is more difficult to manipulate than the income statement or balance sheet. However, manipulations that serve to artificially boost reported cash flows are still possible. Examples of such techniques, which may not constitute GAAP violations, include:[28]

- *Stretching Out Payables.* Perhaps the simplest means for a company to improve its operating cash flow is to slow down its payment to vendors. Although delaying vendor payments has traditionally been interpreted as a sign of cash flow strain, companies are now spinning this practice as a prudent cash-management strategy.
- *Financing of Payables.* A more complex variation of stretching out payables is the financing of payables. This involves a company borrowing from a third-party financial institution to pay its vendors in the current period, with the intent of paying off the loan in the subsequent period. Of course, the effect is to delay the timing of cash outflows.
- *Securitization of Receivables.* To accelerate cash inflows, a company can package its accounts receivable and transfer them to a financial institution. Under certain circumstances, GAAP allows the company to report the sale proceeds as an operating cash inflow.

As the investment community shifts its focus toward the cash flow statement, accounting regulations need to adapt. SAS No. 95, which addresses the cash flow statement, includes only fifteen paragraphs that discuss the appropriate categorization of cash expenses. In contrast, there is an abundance of guidance regarding the calculation and presentation of earnings on the income statement.

JOURNAL ENTRY TESTING

Given the ability of journal entries (JE) to alter financial statement credibility, forensic accountants must have a working knowledge of the JE process and the training to recognize inappropriate or unusual activity. As guidance, we encourage consideration of the JE testing prescribed by SAS No. 99, which identifies several common characteristics of fraudulent entries. Such characteristics may include entries:[29]

- Made to unrelated, unusual, or seldom-used accounts.
- Made by individuals who do not normally make journal entries.
- Recorded at the end of the period or as post-closing entries with no explanation.
- Having no account number.
- Containing round numbers or consistent ending numbers.
- Applied to accounts that contain complex transactions, contain significant estimates or end-of-period adjustments, have been prone to errors in the past, have not been

timely reconciled, contain intercompany transactions, or are otherwise associated with an identified fraud risk.

Dig Deeper

You are encouraged to consider AICPA Practice Alert 2003-02, which provides guidance on procedures for journal entry testing and the use of computer-assisted audit tools.

Given the scope of the relevant data, it is often impractical for the forensic accountant to manually review a company's general ledger. In fact, research indicates that financial statement fraud occurs in less than 1% of digital transactions.[30] Furthermore, journal entries often exist only in electronic form, requiring extraction of the data before any analysis can be performed. Computer-assisted audit tools (CAATs) provide an alternative to manual review for identifying journal entries to be tested and detecting unusual ledger activity.

There are several benefits of automated journal entry testing. First and foremost, it addresses a primary method of financial statement fraud—the top-side journal entry (an adjusting entry made at the management level). Moreover, it provides a better chance of fraud detection, because 100% of the data (rather than a sample) can be analyzed. Finally, it supports conclusions with substantial quantitative data.[31] Despite these benefits, CAATs, like any tool, have their limitations. They do not replace skilled forensic accountants, but rather allow them to focus their efforts on the highest-risk journal entries.

Special Note

CAATs can cost anywhere from hundreds to thousands of dollars. Examples of specific software packages are discussed in Chapter 9.

CONTENT ANALYSIS

Financial statements represent *historical data*. Thus, in many cases the damage (such as fraud) has already been done. As such, researchers are constantly evaluating strategies to detect accounting failures earlier and thus reduce the related damage. One such strategy is content analysis.

Content analysis is a systematic technique for categorizing words into content categories using special coding rules. Simply stated, it's a *qualitative* method of determining characteristics of interest based on grammatical structure, word content, and other fundamental characteristics of communication. The method tests for multiple indicators and statistically analyzes them to determine characteristic patterns reflecting deception.

Research conducted by Churyk and Clinton (2008) identified certain "tells" or communication characteristics in the context of the MD&A section of annual reports, related to financial statement deception.[32] Such characteristics include:

- Significantly fewer colons
- Fewer words per sentence
- Fewer optimistic words
- More words related to downward direction
- Fewer words describing certainty
- Fewer instances of the words *note* and *see*
- Fewer self-references
- More past-tense words
- Fewer present-tense words

In this study, the researchers used a software program called *Linguistic Inquiry and Word Count* (LIWC), which parses and identifies parts of speech and syntax and then tallies the frequencies of the word occurrences (for example, "we" or "I"). LIWC also analyzes individual text files and computes the percentage of words in each text file that fall into each of more than 70 linguistic categories of detail. These groupings of word occurrences reflect themes that are categorized and statistically analyzed by the software.

PERSONAL FINANCIAL STATEMENTS

In addition to business financial statements, forensic accounting engagements commonly require the consideration and analysis of *personal* financial statements. What are personal financial statements? Why are they issued? How do they differ from business financial statements? ***Personal financial statements***, like business financial statements, serve to provide information about an individual's financial condition, income profile, and cash flow. They are commonly required by banks and other creditors to support loan applications or other requests for financing.

Generally, a personal financial statement consists of a single form that reports an individual's personal assets and liabilities, as well as personal sources of income and expenses. The nature and extent of the form is determined by the organization (bank or vendor) supplying the credit. However, personal financial statements compiled or reviewed by an accountant should be accompanied by a written report. This written report serves to qualify or limit the accountant's level of assurance and responsibility for the financial statement.

Personal Balance Sheet

Similar to a company's balance sheet, a personal balance sheet provides a snapshot of an individual's financial condition at a *specific point in time*. Recall that a balance sheet is a summary of assets (resources), liabilities (obligations), and net worth (assets minus liabilities).

Contrary to rules employed in the preparation of business financial statements (specifically, the GAAP cost principle), personal financial statements should present assets at their estimated current values[§] and liabilities at their estimated current amounts.[**] In determining the estimated current values of assets and liabilities, the following items should be considered:

- Has cash on hand been disclosed? Does it include funds in a safe deposit box?
- Have bank account balances been reconciled?
- Is there evidence of recent transactions involving similar assets and liabilities in similar circumstances?
- Have the valuation methods employed been followed consistently from period to period?
- Are marketable securities valued at quoted market prices?
- Are investments in life insurance shown at the cash value of the policy less the amount of any loans against it? Is the face amount also disclosed?
- Are investments in closely held businesses presented at current value (rather than book value)?
    - Is there evidence that the reported value is the amount at which the investment could be exchanged between an informed buyer and seller, neither of whom is compelled to buy or sell?
    - Has goodwill been considered?
- Have investments in collectibles (for example, stamps, coins, guns, and art) been considered?
- Is there evidence supporting real estate values (such as appraisals)?
- Are all nonforfeitable rights to receive future sums presented as assets at their discounted amounts? How was the discount rate determined?
- Are accounts payable, including credit cards, and other liabilities presented at the discounted amounts of cash to be paid?

---

§ Defined as the amount at which the item could be exchanged between a buyer and seller, each of whom is well informed and willing to buy and sell. See FASB Accounting Standards Codification (ASC) glossary term *estimated current value*.

** The methods used to determine the estimated current values of assets and estimated current amount of liabilities are detailed in Paragraphs 4–15 of FASB ASC 274-10-35.

- Are noncancellable commitments presented as liabilities at their discounted amounts?
- Are there any contingent liabilities? For example, is the individual a guarantor of another's debt obligation (e.g., credit cards, business loan, or car loan)?
- Is there pending litigation?
- Is a liability for income taxes presented?
    - Is a provision made for estimated income taxes on the differences between the estimated current values of assets and the estimated current amounts of liabilities and their tax bases?
    - Was a marginal or effective tax rate used? How was it determined?

Personal Income (Cash Flow) Statement

Similar to a company's income statement, a personal income statement prepared on the cash basis serves to provide information regarding an individual's cash inflows and outflows over a period of time. Cash inflows include salaries, dividends, interest, capital gains, rental income, and so forth. Cash outflows include all living expenses, such as rent or mortgage payments, car payments, utility bills, food, clothing, and entertainment.

A personal income statement discloses an individual's net cash flow (cash inflows minus cash outflows). Banks and other third parties use this information to measure capacity to manage current and/or proposed debt.

Special Note

Examples of a personal balance sheet and income statement are provided in Appendix 5-B.

Personal Financial Statement Disclosures

Like business financial statements, personal financial statements prepared in accordance with GAAP require sufficient disclosures to make them adequately informative.[††] The following items are commonly disclosed:[33]

- Clear identification of the effective (as of) date of the financial statements
- Proper identification of the individuals covered by the financial statements
- Statement that the assets are presented at their estimated current values and liabilities are presented at their estimated current amounts
- Identification of the methods used in determining the estimated current values of major assets and the estimated current amounts of major liabilities
- Statement that the valuation methods used in determining the major categories of assets and liabilities have been employed consistently from one period to the next
- Statement (qualification) regarding any assets held jointly with another person and the nature of the joint ownership

Personal Financial Statements and Forensic Accounting Engagements

Personal financial statements represent affirmative statements made by the submitting party and, as such, provide evidence for consideration (analysis) by the forensic accountant. Three common forensic accounting engagements that commonly require the analysis of personal financial statements include:

1. *Domestic Relations.* In domestic relations (divorce) cases, the analysis of personal financial statements provides significant context for the forensic accountant. These statements measure an individual's net worth, or wealth, as of a specific date. Moreover, a comparative analysis (for example, the last three years) allows the measurement of changes in specific assets and liabilities. Such an analysis might identify missing assets

[††] Examples of personal financial statements are provided in FASB ASC 274.

(cash), unexplained changes in reported values, or increased debt. The personal financial statement might also establish one's ability to pay child support or alimony.

2. *Embezzlement/Fraud.* In an embezzlement or fraud allegation, the analysis of one's personal financial statement may provide support (or lack thereof) for alternative theories explaining the acquisition or expenditures of cash. For example, a beginning cash balance on hand of $100,000 might explain a bank deposit of $10,000 or the cash purchase of an automobile for $7,500.
3. *Arson.* Motive is a critical element in an arson (insurance fraud) case. A common motive alleged by insurance companies in denials of claims is financial distress on the part of the claimant. To support or refute this allegation, forensic accounting experts for both sides will analyze personal financial statements to identify indicators of financial distress.

Other forensic accounting engagements requiring the analysis of personal financial statements include mortgage fraud, tax fraud, risk management audits, and employment/background checks.

SUMMARY

This chapter discusses concepts and techniques useful for analyzing financial information as part of a forensic examination. With a foundational understanding of accounting principles, especially the relationships among the financial statements, a forensic accountant is equipped to use the various tools of financial statements analysis. Such analysis provides a basis for identifying significant patterns, trends, or inconsistencies that may warrant further investigation. Using these findings, preliminary hypotheses can be developed and additional tests, such as journal entry testing and content analysis, can be employed to test these hypotheses.

APPENDIX 5-A

Illustration of Financial Statements Analysis

Table 5A-1 Summary Income Statement

Green Mountain Coffee Roasters, Inc.
Income Statement ($ Thousands)
Fiscal Year Ending Sept. 30

	2007	2008	2009	2010	2011
Net Sales	341,651	492,517	786,135	1,356,775	2,650,899
Cost of Sales	210,530	318,477	540,744	931,017	1,746,274
Gross Profit	131,121	174,040	245,391	425,758	904,625
Selling & Operating Expenses	72,641	90,882	121,350	186,418	348,696
General & Admin. Expenses	30,781	41,759	30,655	100,568	187,016
Operating Income	27,699	41,399	93,386	138,772	368,913
Other Income	54	(235)	(662)	(269)	(8,509)
Interest Expense	(6,176)	(5,705)	(4,693)	(5,294)	(57,657)
Income Before Taxes	21,577	35,459	88,031	133,209	302,747
Income Tax Expense	(8,734)	(13,790)	(33,592)	(53,703)	(101,699)
Net Income	**12,843**	**21,669**	**54,439**	**79,506**	**201,048**

Table 5A-2 | Income Trend Analysis

Green Mountain Coffee Roasters, Inc. Income Statement Trend Analysis Fiscal Year Ending Sept. 30				
	2007–2008	2008–2009	2009–2010	2010–2011
Net Sales	44.16%	59.62%	72.59%	95.38%
Cost of Sales	51.27%	69.79%	72.17%	87.57%
Gross Profit	32.73%	41.00%	73.50%	112.47%
Selling & Operating Expenses	25.11%	33.52%	53.62%	87.05%
General & Admin. Expenses	35.66%	–26.59%	228.06%	85.96%
Operating Income	49.46%	125.58%	48.60%	165.84%
Other Income	–535.19%	181.70%	–59.37%	3063.20%
Interest Expense	–7.63%	–17.74%	12.81%	989.10%
Income Before Taxes	64.34%	148.26%	51.32%	127.27%
Income Tax Expense	57.89%	143.60%	59.87%	89.37%
Net Income	**68.72%**	**151.23%**	**46.05%**	**152.87%**

Table 5A-3 | Common-Size Income Statement

Green Mountain Coffee Roasters, Inc. Common-Size Income Statement Fiscal Year Ending Sept. 30					
	2007	2008	2009	2010	2011
Net Sales	100.00%	100.00%	100.00%	100.00%	100.00%
Cost of Sales	61.62%	64.66%	68.79%	68.62%	65.87%
Gross Profit	38.38%	35.34%	31.21%	31.38%	34.13%
Selling & Operating Expenses	21.26%	18.45%	15.44%	13.74%	13.15%
General & Admin. Expenses	9.01%	8.48%	3.90%	7.41%	7.05%
Operating Income	8.11%	8.41%	11.88%	10.23%	13.92%
Other Income	0.02%	–0.05%	–0.08%	–0.02%	–0.32%
Interest Expense	–1.81%	–1.16%	–0.60%	–0.39%	–2.17%
Income Before Taxes	6.32%	7.20%	11.20%	9.82%	11.42%
Income Tax Expense	–2.56%	–2.80%	–4.27%	–3.96%	–3.84%
Net Income	**3.76%**	**4.40%**	**6.92%**	**5.86%**	**7.58%**

Table 5A-4 Balance Sheet

Green Mountain Coffee Roasters, Inc. Balance Sheet ($ Thousands) Fiscal Year Ending Sept. 30					
	2007	**2008**	**2009**	**2010**	**2011**
Assets					
Current Assets					
Cash & Cash Equivalents	3,172	965	242,091	4,756	40,512
Short-Term Investments			50,000		
Receivables	39,373	54,782	91,559	172,200	310,321
Inventories	38,909	85,311	132,182	262,478	672,248
Other Current Assets	6,369	11,032	21,535	55,835	108,446
Total Current Assets	87,823	152,090	537,367	495,269	1,131,527
Fixed Assets (Net)	65,692	97,678	135,981	258,923	579,219
Intangibles (Net)	34,208	29,396	36,478	220,005	529,494
Goodwill	73,840	73,953	99,600	386,416	789,305
Other Long-Term Assets	2,964	4,531	3,979	9,961	168,342
Total Assets	**264,527**	**357,648**	**813,405**	**1,370,574**	**3,197,887**
Liabilities & Shareholders' Equity					
Current Liabilities					
Current Portion of Long-Term Debt	63	33	5,030	19,009	6,669
Accounts Payable	37,778	43,821	79,772	139,220	265,511
Accrued Expenses	16,893	26,314	37,159	73,515	135,380
Income Taxes Payable	1,443	2,079	1,225	1,934	9,617
Other Short-Term Liabilities	871	673	3,257	4,377	54,197
Total Current Liabilities	57,048	72,920	126,443	238,055	471,374
Long-Term Debt	90050	123517	73,013	335,504	575,969
Deferred Income Taxes	18,330	21,691	26,599	92,579	189,637
Other Long-Term Liabilities				5,191	48,692
Total Liabilities	165,428	218,128	226,055	671,329	1,285,672
Shareholders' Equity					
Common Stock	2,470	2,549	13,081	13,282	15,447
Additional Paid-In Capital	45,704	63,607	441,875	473,749	1,499,616
Retained Earnings	58,981	81,280	134,338	213,844	411,727
Other Comprehensive Income (Loss)	(512)	(419)	(1,870)	(1,630)	(14,575)
ESOP Unallocated Shares	(208)	(161)	(74)		
Treasury Stock	(7,336)	(7,336)			
Total Shareholders' Equity	99,099	139,520	587,350	699,245	1,912,215
Total Liabilities & Shareholders' Equity	**264,527**	**357,648**	**813,405**	**1,370,574**	**3,197,887**

Table 5A-5 Common-Size Balance Sheet

Green Mountain Coffee Roasters, Inc. Common-Size Balance Sheet Fiscal Year Ending Sept. 30	2007	2008	2009	2010	2011
Assets					
Current Assets					
Cash & Cash Equivalents	1.20%	0.27%	29.76%	0.35%	1.27%
Short-Term Investments	0.00%	0.00%	6.15%	0.00%	0.00%
Receivables	14.88%	15.32%	11.26%	12.56%	9.70%
Inventories	14.71%	23.85%	16.25%	19.15%	21.02%
Other Current Assets	2.41%	3.08%	2.65%	4.07%	3.39%
Total Current Assets	33.20%	42.53%	66.06%	36.14%	35.38%
Fixed Assets (Net)	24.83%	27.31%	16.72%	18.89%	18.11%
Intangibles (Net)	12.93%	8.22%	4.48%	16.05%	16.56%
Goodwill	27.91%	20.68%	12.24%	28.19%	24.68%
Other Long-Term Assets	1.12%	1.27%	0.49%	0.73%	5.26%
Total Assets	**100.00%**	**100.00%**	**100.00%**	**100.00%**	**100.00%**
Liabilities & Shareholders' Equity					
Current Liabilities					
Current Portion of Long-Term Debt	0.02%	0.01%	0.62%	1.39%	0.21%
Accounts Payable	14.28%	12.25%	9.81%	10.16%	8.30%
Accrued Expenses	6.39%	7.36%	4.57%	5.36%	4.23%
Income Taxes Payable	0.55%	0.58%	0.15%	0.14%	0.30%
Other Short-Term Liabilities	0.33%	0.19%	0.40%	0.32%	1.69%
Total Current Liabilities	21.57%	20.39%	15.54%	17.37%	14.74%
Long-Term Debt	34.04%	34.54%	8.98%	24.48%	18.01%
Deferred Income Taxes	6.93%	6.06%	3.27%	6.75%	5.93%
Other Long-Term Liabilities	0.00%	0.00%	0.00%	0.38%	1.52%
Total Liabilities	62.54%	60.99%	27.79%	48.98%	40.20%
Shareholders' Equity					
Common Stock	0.93%	0.71%	1.61%	0.97%	0.48%
Additional Paid-In Capital	17.28%	17.78%	54.32%	34.57%	46.89%
Retained Earnings	22.30%	22.73%	16.52%	15.60%	12.87%
Other Comprehensive Income (Loss)	–0.19%	–0.12%	–0.23%	–0.12%	–0.46%
ESOP Unallocated Shares	–0.08%	–0.05%	–0.01%	0.00%	0.00%
Treasury Stock	–2.77%	–2.05%	0.00%	0.00%	0.00%
Total Shareholders' Equity	37.46%	39.01%	72.21%	51.02%	59.80%
Total Liabilities & Shareholders' Equity	**100.00%**	**100.00%**	**100.00%**	**100.00%**	**100.00%**

Table 5A-6 Financial Ratio Analysis

Green Mountain Coffee Roasters, Inc. Financial Ratio Analysis					
	2007	2008	2009	2010	2011
Profitability					
Gross Margin Percent	38.38%	35.34%	31.21%	31.38%	34.13%
Return on Sales	3.76%	4.40%	6.92%	5.86%	7.58%
Return on Assets	4.86%	6.06%	6.69%	5.80%	6.29%
Return on Equity	12.96%	15.53%	9.27%	11.37%	10.51%
Efficiency					
Total Asset Turnover	1.29	1.38	0.97	0.99	0.83
Accounts Receivable Turnover	8.68	8.99	8.59	7.88	8.54
Average Accounts Receivable Days	42.06	40.60	42.51	46.33	42.73
Inventory Turnover	5.41	3.73	4.09	3.55	2.60
Average Inventory Days	67.46	97.77	89.22	102.90	140.51
Operating Cycle	109.52	138.37	131.73	149.23	183.24
Leverage					
Debt to Assets	63%	61%	28%	49%	40%
Equity to Assets	37%	39%	72%	51%	60%
Debt to Equity	1.67	1.56	0.38	0.96	0.67
Equity Multiplier	2.67	2.56	1.38	1.96	1.67
Liquidity					
Current Ratio	1.54	2.09	4.25	2.08	2.40
Quick (Acid Test) Ratio	0.86	0.92	3.20	0.98	0.97
Net Working Capital	30,775	79,170	410,924	257,214	660,153
Times Interest Earned	4.49	7.22	19.76	26.16	6.25

Table 5A-7 Cash Flow Analysis

Green Mountain Coffee Roasters, Inc. Cash Flow Analysis ($ Thousands) Fiscal Year Ending Sept. 30					
	2007	**2008**	**2009**	**2010**	**2011**
Operating Activities					
Net Income	12,843	21,669	54,439	79,506	201,048
Non-Cash Expenses	15,759	27,722	39,491	85,206	186,835
Non-Cash Losses	159	207	943	385	24,949
Tax Benefits	46	(6,615)	(11,163)	(15,303)	(73,955)
Deferred Expenses	4,748	7,004	8,502	1,179	1,747
ESOP Contributions	200	200	1,000	1,376	
Changes in Operating Accounts	(3,921)	(48,241)	(54,714)	(162,884)	(339,839)
Cash Flow from Operations	29,834	1,946	38,498	(10,535)	785
Investing Activities					
Purchases of Fixed Assets	(21,844)	(48,718)	(48,298)	(118,042)	(283,444)
Purchases of Short-Term Investments			(50,000)		
Proceeds from Sales of Fixed Assets	187	407	162	526	1,192
Proceeds from Sales of Short-Term Investments				50,000	
Proceeds from Notes Receivable				1,788	499
Acquisitions			(41,361)	(459,469)	(907,835)
Other Investing Activities					1,916
Cash Flow from Investing Activities	(21,657)	(48,311)	(139,497)	(525,197)	(1,187,672)
Financing Activities					
Change in Line of Credit	(12,800)	33,500	(95,500)	145,000	333,835
Proceeds from Issuing Common Stock	3,123	5,653	378,046	8,788	955,787
Tax Benefits	3,307	6,168	10,761	14,590	67,813
Capital Lease Obligations				(217)	(8)
Proceeds from Issuing Long-Term Debt	45		50,000	140,000	796,375
Repayment of Long-Term Debt	(100)	(63)	(217)	(8,500)	(906,885)
Other Financing Activities		(907)	(1,084)	(1,339)	(47,072)
Cash Flow from Financing Activities	(6,425)	44,351	342,006	298,322	1,199,845
Other Change in Cash Balance					(5,160)
Effect of Exchange Rate Changes					790
Net Cash Flow	**1,752**	**(2,014)**	**241,007**	**(237,410)**	**8,588**
Beginning Cash Balance	1,066	2,818	804	241,811	4,401
Ending Cash Balance	**2,818**	**804**	**241,811**	**4,401**	**12,989**

APPENDIX 5-B

Sample Personal Financial Statement

OMB APPROVAL NO. 3245-0188
EXPIRATION DATE: 8/31/2011

U.S. SMALL BUSINESS ADMINISTRATION

PERSONAL FINANCIAL STATEMENT

As of June 30, 2012

Complete this form for: (1) each proprietor, or (2) each limited partner who owns 20% or more interest and each general partner, or (3) each stockholder owning 20% or more of voting stock, or (4) any person or entity providing a guaranty on the loan.

Name John and Mary Jones — Business Phone 304-552-4862

Residence Address 111 Meadow Lane — Residence Phone 304-795-4685

City, State, & Zip Code Huntington, WV 25701

Business Name of Applicant/Borrower

ASSETS	(Omit Cents)	LIABILITIES	(Omit Cents)
Cash on hand & in Banks	$ 35,000	Accounts Payable	$ 4,000
Savings Accounts	$ 15,000	Notes Payable to Banks and Others (Describe in Section 2)	$
IRA or Other Retirement Account	$ 525,000	Installment Account (Auto)	$
Accounts & Notes Receivable	$	Mo. Payments $	
Life Insurance-Cash Surrender Value Only (Complete Section 8)	$	Installment Account (Other)	$
Stocks and Bonds (Describe in Section 3)	$ 500,000	Mo. Payments $	
Real Estate (Describe in Section 4)	$ 775,000	Loan on Life Insurance	$
Automobile-Present Value	$ 35,000	Mortgages on Real Estate (Describe in Section 4)	$ 296,000
Other Personal Property (Describe in Section 5)	$ 10,000	Unpaid Taxes (Describe in Section 6)	$
Other Assets (Describe in Section 5)	$	Other Liabilities (Describe in Section 7)	$
		Total Liabilities	$ 300,000
		Net Worth	$ 1,595,000
Total	$ 1,895,000	Total	$ 1,895,000

Section 1. Source of Income		Contingent Liabilities	
Salary	$ 250,000	As Endorser or Co-Maker	$
Net Investment Income	$	Legal Claims & Judgments	$
Real Estate Income	$ 25,000	Provision for Federal Income Tax	$
Other Income (Describe below)*	$	Other Special Debt	$

Description of Other Income in Section 1.

*Alimony or child support payments need not be disclosed in "Other Income" unless it is desired to have such payments counted toward total income.

Section 2. Notes Payable to Banks and Others. (Use attachments if necessary. Each attachment must be identified as a part of this statement and signed.)

Name and Address of Noteholder(s)	Original Balance	Current Balance	Payment Amount	Frequency (monthly,etc.)	How Secured or Endorsed Type of Collateral

SBA Form 413 (10-08) **Previous Editions Obsolete** (tumble)

This form was electronically produced by Elite Federal Forms, Inc.

Federal Recycling Program Printed on Recycled Paper

Section 3. Stocks and Bonds. (Use attachments if necessary. Each attachment must be identified as a part of this statement and signed).

Number of Shares	Name of Securities	Cost	Market Value Quotation/Exchange	Date of Quotation/Exchange	Total Value
1,000	ABC, Inc.	1,000			$500,000

Section 4. Real Estate Owned. (List each parcel separately. Use attachment if necessary. Each attachment must be identified as a part of this statement and signed.)

	Property A	Property B	Property C
Type of Property	Residential	Rental	
Address	111 Meadow Lane Huntington, WV	1068 6th Ave Huntington, WV	
Date Purchased	12/12/1996	5/5/2010	
Original Cost	465,000	$215,000	
Present Market Value	550,000	$225,000	
Name & Address of Mortgage Holder	BB&T Huntington, WV	N/A	
Mortgage Account Number	32568136		
Mortgage Balance	$296,000		
Amount of Payment per Month/Year	$1,136		
Status of Mortgage	Current		

Section 5. Other Personal Property and Other Assets. (Describe, and if any is pledged as security, state name and address of lien holder, amount of lien, terms of payment and if delinquent, describe delinquency)

Section 6. Unpaid Taxes. (Describe in detail, as to type, to whom payable, when due, amount, and to what property, if any, a tax lien attaches.)

Section 7. Other Liabilities. (Describe in detail.)

Section 8. Life Insurance Held. (Give face amount and cash surrender value of policies - name of insurance company and beneficiaries)

I authorize SBA/Lender to make inquiries as necessary to verify the accuracy of the statements made and to determine my creditworthiness. I certify the above and the statements contained in the attachments are true and accurate as of the stated date(s). These statements are made for the purpose of either obtaining a loan or guaranteeing a loan. I understand FALSE statements may result in forfeiture of benefits and possible prosecution by the U.S. Attorney General (Reference 18 U.S.C. 1001).

Signature: Date: Social Security Number:

Signature: Date: Social Security Number:

PLEASE NOTE: The estimated average burden hours for the completion of this form is 1.5 hours per response. If you have questions or comments concerning this estimate or any other aspect of this information, please contact Chief, Administrative Branch, U.S. Small Business Administration, Washington, D.C. 20416, and Clearance Officer, Paper Reduction Project (3245-0188), Office of Management and Budget, Washington, D.C. 20503. **PLEASE DO NOT SEND FORMS TO OMB.**

SBA Form 413 (10-08) **Previous Editions Obsolete**

APPENDIX 5-C

Case Study: A Closer Look at ZZZZ Best

Let's use ZZZZ Best, the company highlighted in the opening case, to illustrate some of the techniques presented in this chapter. The data contained in the balance sheet and income statement are modified from statements appearing in a prospectus filed with the SEC on December 9, 1986, in which the company stated its intent to offer 1,100,000 common shares at a price of $12 per share (a total potential issue of $13,200,000).

The 1986 financial statements were audited by Greenspan & Company of Englewood Cliffs, New Jersey, while the 1985 and 1984 financial statements were audited by Larry G. Baker, CPA of Bakersfield, California. Unaudited financial statements for the three months ended July 31, 1986, were also presented in the prospectus but are not included in this illustrative case. A review report was prepared by Ernst & Whinney of Los Angeles, California, for this interim period.

The income statements and balance sheets for years 1984 through 1986, including a common-size analysis and trend analysis, are provided in Tables 5C-1 and 5C-2.

As illustrated in Table 5C-1, net income increased significantly from 1985 to 1986, driven primarily by a 291% increase in revenues with only 256% growth in cost of revenue. The company attributed the slower growth rate in cost of revenue to efficiencies realized in the residential cleaning segment. This trend is represented by an increase in gross profit margin from 53.5% in 1985 to 57.7% in 1986. Notice that the common-size statement, in isolation, does not highlight any other questionable relationships. However, the trend analysis raises a question as to how the company could generate such operating efficiencies while experiencing rapid growth in business.

The trend analysis in Table 5C-2 shows rapid growth in many of the asset, liability, and equity accounts, and the common-size analysis highlights changes in the relationships of these accounts to total assets. For example, property and equipment increased from 32.3% of assets in 1985 to 60.6% in 1986. This is consistent with the rapid growth in sales.

Interestingly, cash decreased from 17.0% of total assets in 1985 to 1.7% of assets in 1986, and accounts receivable increased from 0% in 1985 to 13.7% in 1986. While rapid growth

Table 5C-1

ZZZZ Best Co., Inc.
Income Statement
Fiscal Year Ending Apr. 30

	1984		1985		1986		Trend	
	$	%	$	%	$	%	1984–1985	1985–1986
Total Revenue	575,117	100.0%	1,240,524	100.0%	4,845,347	100.0%	116%	291%
Cost of Revenue	284,058	49.4%	576,694	46.5%	2,050,779	42.3%	103%	256%
Gross Profit	291,059	50.6%	663,830	53.5%	2,794,568	57.7%	128%	321%
Operating Expenses	138,867	24.1%	306,016	24.7%	1,125,541	23.2%	120%	268%
Operating Income	152,192	26.5%	357,814	28.8%	1,669,027	34.4%	135%	366%
Other Income/Expense (Net)*	-	0.0%	-	0.0%	143,659	3.0%	n/a	n/a
Income Before Income Tax	152,192	26.5%	357,814	28.8%	1,812,686	37.4%	135%	407%
Provision for Income Tax	-	0.0%	36,053	2.9%	867,041	17.9%	n/a	2305%
Net Income	**152,192**	**26.5%**	**321,761**	**25.9%**	**945,645**	**19.5%**	**111%**	**194%**

*Includes joint venture revenue of $186,679

Table 5C-2

ZZZZ Best Co., Inc. Balance Sheet Fiscal Year Ending Apr. 30	1985		1986		Trend
	$	%	$	%	1985–1986
Assets					
Current Assets					
Cash & Cash Equivalents	30,321	17.0%	87,014	1.7%	187%
Receivables (Net)		0.0%	693,773	13.7%	n/a
Unbilled Charges on Restoration Contracts		0.0%	413,231	8.2%	n/a
Other Current Assets	76,775	43.1%	533,955	10.6%	595%
Total Current Assets	107,096	60.2%	1,727,973	34.2%	1513%
Property and Equipment (Net)	57,490	32.3%	3,059,455	60.6%	5222%
Goodwill		0.0%	22,249	0.4%	n/a
Other Assets	13,450	7.6%	235,994	4.7%	1655%
Total Assets	**178,036**	**100.0%**	**5,045,671**	**100.0%**	**2734%**
Liabilities & Shareholders' Equity					
Current Liabilities					
Trade Accounts Payable and Accrued Expenses	2,930	1.6%	265,367	5.3%	8957%
Equipment Purchase Payable		0.0%	575,000	11.4%	n/a
Short-Term Debt and Current Portion of Long-Term Debt		0.0%	928,068	18.4%	n/a
Total Current Liabilities	2,930	1.6%	1,768,435	35.0%	60256%
Obligation Under Capital Leases		0.0%	428,471	8.5%	n/a
Deferred Federal Income Taxes		0.0%	819,014	16.2%	n/a
Total Liabilities	2,930	1.6%	3,015,920	59.8%	102832%
Shareholders' Equity					
Common Stock	55,000	30.9%	76,675	1.5%	39%
Additional Paid in Capital	55,000	30.9%	942,325	18.7%	1613%
Retained Earnings	65,106	36.6%	1,010,751	20.0%	1452%
Total Shareholders' Equity	175,106	98.4%	2,029,751	40.2%	1059%
Total Liabilities & Shareholders' Equity	**178,036**	**100.0%**	**5,045,671**	**100.0%**	**2734%**

can create a cash flow crunch, pertinent questions include: Why were there no accounts receivable shown in 1985, and what changed to significantly increase their balance in 1986? Further, is this an indication that the recognition of sales may have been delayed from 1985 to 1986? If so, does this contribute to the rapid revenue growth? A forensic accountant would use these observations to develop tentative hypotheses, which would then be further investigated.

As noted in the introductory case, a ratio analysis shows dramatic deterioration in key ratios from 1985 to 1986, as illustrated in Table 5C-3. A potential explanation (as opposed to fraud, which was ultimately discovered) is that management was unable to effectively manage the company's rapid growth. However, a forensic accountant would investigate these inconsistencies further to assess the possibility of fraud.

Table 5C-3

ZZZZ Best Co., Inc. Financial Ratio Analysis	1985	1986
Profitability		
Gross Margin Percent	53.5%	57.7%
Return on Sales	25.9%	19.5%
Return on Assets	180.7%	18.7%
Return on Equity	183.8%	46.6%
Efficiency		
Total Asset Turnover	6.97	0.96
Accounts Receivable Turnover	n/a	6.98
Average Accounts Receivable Days	n/a	52.3
Leverage		
Debt to Assets	1.6%	59.8%
Equity to Assets	98.4%	40.2%
Debt to Equity	0.02	1.49
Equity Multiplier	1.02	2.49
Liquidity		
Current Ratio	36.55	0.98
Net Working Capital	104,166	(40,462)

Finally, the development of a cash flow analysis provides additional insights. While the cash flow statement provided in Table 5C-4 highlights the inflow and outflow of cash from various activities, the most interesting observation is the relationship of net income to accruals.

Net income of $945,645 for year 1986 was driven primarily by increases in receivables ($693,773), unbilled charges on restoration contracts ($413,231), and other current assets, including supplies ($115,477), prepaid expenses ($125,307), and advance on material purchases ($156,000). Professional skepticism requires a forensic accountant to determine the reasons for these changes during the year, as well as the authenticity of the year-end balances.

Possible questions raised by the cash flow analysis include: Have accounts payable been extended or financed using short-term debt? Does the dramatic increase in receivables and other current assets represent actual work completed by ZZZZ Best?

Table 5C-4

ZZZZ Best Co., Inc. Cash Flow Analysis Fiscal Year Ending Apr. 30	1986
Operating Activities	
Net Income	$ 945,645
Add Noncash Items:	
Depreciation	97,588
Deferred Income Taxes	819,014
Changes in Operating Accounts:	
Increase in Receivables	(693,773)
Increase in Unbilled Charges	(413,231)
Increase in Other Current Assets	(457,180)
Increase in Accounts Payable	262,437
Cash Flow from Operations	560,500
Investing Activities	
Purchase of Property, Plant & Equipment	(3,099,553)
Acquisition of Goodwill	(22,249)
Acquisition of Other Assets	(222,544)
Cash Flow from Investing Activities	(3,344,346)
Financing Activities	
Proceeds from Short-Term Borrowing	928,068
Proceeds from Borrowing on Capital Lease	428,471
Proceeds from Issuance of Common Stock	909,000
Proceeds from Equipment Purchase Borrowing	575,000
Cash Flow from Financing Activities	2,840,539
Net Cash Flow	**56,693**
Beginning Cash Balance	30,321
Ending Cash Balance	**87,014**

Key Terms

Accounting cycle
Agency problem
Altman's Z-score
Annual report
Audit
Balance sheet
Cash basis
Compilation
Compound annual growth rate
Conservatism principle
Consistency principle
Content analysis
Context
Cost principle
DuPont Model
Earnings management
Economic reality
Financial ratio
Full-disclosure principle
Income statement

Income tax basis
Matching principle
Materiality principle
Objectivity principle
Operational freedom
Personal financial statements
Reporting freedom
Review
Statement of cash flows
Sustainable growth rate

Chapter Questions

5-1. What is meant by the context of financial reporting?

5-2. Who is responsible for the structure and content of financial statements?

5-3. Identify five potential users of financial statements and discuss how the statements may be used by each.

5-4. Compare and contrast the differences in assurance levels for a compilation, review, and audit.

5-5. What are reasonable assurance and limited assurance? Compare and contrast these two concepts.

5-6. Why are accounting principles important to financial statement integrity?

5-7. Identify and discuss seven fundamental accounting principles that are important to the presentation and analysis of financial statements.

5-8. Do public and private companies follow the same set of accounting rules? Explain.

5-9. How does operational and reporting freedom impact financial reporting?

5-10. What is meant by the term *earnings management*?

5-11. Define *conservative*, *neutral*, *aggressive*, and *fraudulent accounting choices* made by managers of firms.

5-12. What are the three most common financial statement manipulation schemes?

5-13. What is the agency problem?

5-14. Discuss two types of non-GAAP financial statements that private companies commonly employ.

5-15. What are nonfinancial measures, and how does a forensic accountant use them?

5-16. How can Porter's five competitive forces model be used in a forensic investigation?

5-17. Where in an annual report might a forensic accountant find important nonfinancial information?

5-18. Identify seven analytical review methods commonly employed by forensic accountants.

5-19. Why is it important for a forensic accountant to employ both internal and external comparisons in financial statements analysis?

5-20. What is professional skepticism, and how is it used by the forensic accountant?

5-21. Identify five examples of forensic accounting engagements that commonly require the analysis of financial statements and discuss how mindset might impact this type of analysis.

5-22. What three basic financial statements are commonly involved in financial statements analysis?

5-23. What is horizontal analysis? How does it offer insight to financial statements analysis?

5-24. What is a compound annual growth rate? How is it useful to a forensic accountant?

5-25. What is a sustainable growth rate? How is it useful to a forensic accountant?

5-26. What are common-size financial statements? How are they calculated? Why are they a valuable analysis tool?

5-27. Define *financial ratio*. What two conditions must exist for a ratio to be useful in financial statements analysis?

5-28. Identify five common categories of financial ratios. How are ratios in each category normally expressed in terms of decimal, percentage, or dollar?

5-29. What is the DuPont Model? How is it useful in financial statements analysis?

5-30. What is Altman's Z-score? What makes it valuable to a forensic accountant?

5-31. Compare and contrast Altman's Z-score models for publicly traded manufacturing firms and privately held firms.

5-32. What must a forensic accountant consider when applying and interpreting financial ratios?

5-33. Why should a forensic accountant consider footnotes in financial statements?

5-34. Why is the cash flow statement considered to be a powerful analysis tool?

5-35. Identify and discuss three cash flow analysis techniques.

5-36. What are three common methods of cash flow manipulation?

5-37. What is the purpose of journal entry testing?

5-38. What are the advantages of using a computer-assisted audit tool?

5-39. SAS No. 99 identifies six characteristics of journal entries. Discuss the nature of each.

5-40. What is content analysis, and why is it useful to a forensic accountant?

5-41. What are common "tells" or communication characteristics that appear in Management's Discussion and Analysis that might alert a forensic accountant to financial statement deception?

5-42. What is the purpose of personal financial statements, and how do they differ from those presented by an audited organization?

5-43. Explain the basis of presentation of a personal balance sheet and how it differs from GAAP.

5-44. Explain the basis of presentation of a personal income statement and how it differs from GAAP.

5-45. Do personal financial statements prepared in accordance with GAAP require sufficient disclosures to make them adequately informative? Explain.

5-46. Identify three types of engagements in which forensic accountants often use personal financial statements. Briefly discuss each.

Multiple-Choice Questions

Select the best response to the following questions related to the context of financial reporting, Part One:

5-47. The information surrounding an event is called:

- **a.** Noise
- **b.** Context
- **c.** Contribution
- **d.** Calibration

5-48. A key consideration when analyzing financial statements is understanding that they are:

- **a.** Representations of management
- **b.** Representations of the external auditor
- **c.** Representations of the internal auditor
- **d.** Always accurate and complete

5-49. A financial statement fraud most often violates which of the following accounting principles?

- **a.** Matching
- **b.** Conservatism
- **c.** Materiality
- **d.** All of the above are often violated

5-50. Which of the following is not a user of financial statements?

- **a.** Management
- **b.** Creditors
- **c.** Government agencies
- **d.** All of the above are users of financial statements

5-51. Which of the following implies the highest level of assurance?

- **a.** Review
- **b.** Compilation
- **c.** Audit
- **d.** None of the above implies assurance

5-52. An auditor has the responsibility to plan and perform an audit to obtain _____ that the financial statements are free of material misstatement.

- **a.** Certainty
- **b.** Reasonable certainty
- **c.** Absolute certainty
- **d.** Reasonable assurance

5-53. Each of the following is a fundamental accounting principle *except*:

- **a.** Continuality
- **b.** Matching
- **c.** Materiality
- **d.** Full disclosure

5-54. Since May 2008, privately held companies have been permitted to prepare their financial statements in accordance with IFRS.

- **a.** True
- **b.** False

5-55. The purposeful intervention in the external financial reporting process with the intent of obtaining some private gain is known as:

- **a.** Earnings regulation
- **b.** Earnings management
- **c.** Earnings deployment
- **d.** Earnings extrapolation

5-56. The ability to make operational choices at year-end to enhance the appearance of a certain account is known as:

- **a.** Operational freedom
- **b.** Reporting freedom
- **c.** Management freedom
- **d.** Accounting freedom

Select the best response to the following questions related to the context of financial reporting, Part Two:

5-57. The use of judgment in determining the amounts reported in financial statements is known as:

- **a.** Operational freedom
- **b.** Reporting freedom
- **c.** Timing freedom
- **d.** None of the above

5-58. The accounting principle that directs management to select methods and estimates that avoid overstating assets, revenue, and income is called:

a. Ethnicity
b. Confluence
c. Collectivism
d. Conservatism

5-59. Earnings management actions can be classified as each of the following *except*:

a. Aggressive
b. Conservative
c. Active
d. Neutral

5-60. Which of the following is not a financial statement fraud scheme?

a. Overstating dividends
b. Overstating financial condition or liquidity
c. Understating expenses
d. Overstating revenue

5-61. Privately held companies may present financial statements using which of the following non-GAAP alternatives?

a. Direct and indirect basis
b. Income tax and cash basis
c. Conservation and accumulation
d. Current and deferred

5-62. Which of the following statements does not accurately reflect the agency problem?

a. Managers always protect the collective interest of shareholders
b. Managers control the operations of an organization
c. Shareholders delegate decision making to managers
d. Managers can make decisions that benefit their personal interests

5-63. Forensic accountants consider both financial data and nonfinancial data in financial statements analysis.

a. True
b. False

5-64. Porter's five forces model includes each of the following *except*:

a. Threat of new competitors
b. Primary and support activities
c. Bargaining power of customers
d. The intensity of competitive rivalry

5-65. Nonfinancial material can be found in a public company's:

a. 10-K annual report
b. Bank loan application
c. Accreditation report
d. Disclosure report

5-66. Context brings clarity, perspective, and focus to financial statements analysis.

a. True
b. False

Select the best response to the following questions related to the financial statements analysis, Part One:

5-67. Financial statements analysis is the examination of financial statements for the purpose of acquiring additional information.

a. True
b. False

5-68. To discern unexpected relationships, or the absence of expected relationships, financial statements analysis requires:

a. Insightful and useful comparisons
b. GAAP and non-GAAP material
c. Applied and theoretical calculations
d. Internal and external comparisons

5-69. What is the mindset employed by a forensic accountant in financial statements analysis?

a. Professional certainty
b. Professional skepticism
c. Reasonable probability
d. Counter-intuitiveness

5-70. A forensic accountant always works forward, starting at point A and progressing toward point B.

a. True
b. False

5-71. Which of the following is not a basic financial statement?

a. Statement of cash flows
b. Balance sheet
c. Income statement
d. Schedule M reconciliation

5-72. A horizontal analysis is conducted by a forensic accountant to identify:

a. Scale
b. Trends
c. Affluence
d. Structure

5-73. A measure that expresses the average annual growth rate over a multiple-year period is called:

a. Simple interest growth rate
b. Log-linear growth rate
c. Progressive growth rate
d. Compound growth rate

5-74. The maximum growth rate a company can sustain without obtaining additional financing is called:

a. Compound growth rate
b. Progressive growth rate
c. Sustainable growth rate
d. Measurable growth rate

5-75. A type of analysis that allows comparison of financial statements for companies of different sizes is called:

a. Comparable financial statement
b. Horizontal financial statement
c. Common-size statement
d. Dependable financial statement

5-76. In preparing a common-size income statement, the denominator in all calculations is:

a. Net income
b. Total assets
c. Operating income
d. Total revenue

Select the best response to the following questions related to financial statements analysis, Part Two:

5-77. Which of the following describes the result of calculating a financial ratio?

a. An asset as a percent of revenue
b. The numerator expressed in terms of one unit of the denominator
c. Net income as a percent of cash flow
d. Absolute dollar amounts

5-78. To be useful in financial statements analysis, a ratio must meet what two conditions?

a. Robustness and fruitfulness
b. Calculated and interpreted
c. Meaningful and have a standard of comparison
d. Expressed and interpreted

5-79. Each of the following is a primary ratio category *except*:

a. Efficiency
b. Leverage
c. Liquidity
d. Precipitous

5-80. Each of the following is a component of the DuPont expansion of the ROE equation *except*:

a. Efficiency
b. Liquidity
c. Leverage
d. Profitability

5-81. Altman's Z-score is used for what purpose?

a. Discern liquidity
b. Predict bankruptcy
c. Calculate profitability
d. Determine liquidity

5-82. Although useful in the 1970s and 1980s, due to the increase in computer processing capability in the 1990s and 2000s, Altman's Z-score is no longer considered a reliable indicator.

a. True
b. False

5-83. It doesn't matter if all the inputs to a ratio calculation are valid, as the forensic accountant is still capable of pinpointing areas of concern.

a. True
b. False

5-84. Financial ratios offer insight into how a company is achieving its performance.

a. True
b. False

5-85. Footnotes are not useful to the analysis of financial statements.

a. True
b. False

5-86. Footnotes may provide details that alert a forensic accountant to information that has been omitted from a company's financial statements.

a. True
b. False

Select the best response to the following questions related to cash flow analysis, journal entry testing, content analysis, and personal financial statements:

5-87. What is the value of the statement of cash flows?

a. Easy to structure
b. Difficult to manipulate
c. Regimented in its layout
d. Interpreted by CPAs

5-88. Preparing a statement of cash flows is an excellent test of a forensic accountant's understanding of the income statement and balance sheet and how they _____ to each other.

- **a.** Reverse
- **b.** Develop
- **c.** Relate
- **d.** Contrast

5-89. Each of the following is a cash flow analysis technique *except*:

- **a.** Reconciling cash
- **b.** Conjoint analysis
- **c.** Cash flow comparisons
- **d.** Trend analysis

5-90. Which of the following is not a common cash flow manipulation scheme?

- **a.** Stretching out payables
- **b.** Financing of payables
- **c.** Securitization of receivables
- **d.** Compromising property, plant, and equipment

5-91. As prescribed in SAS No. 99, journal entry testing is a way to identify:

- **a.** Possible fraudulent entries
- **b.** Internal control consequences
- **c.** Management prerogatives
- **d.** Employee sanctions

5-92. Computer-assisted audit tools help identify journal entries that should be manually investigated by a forensic accountant.

- **a.** True
- **b.** False

5-93. _____ is a systematic technique for categorizing words into content categories using special coding rules.

- **a.** Operations analysis
- **b.** Content analysis
- **c.** Journal entry testing
- **d.** Data parsing

5-94. A personal financial statement often consists of a single form that reports an individual's personal assets and liabilities as well as personal sources of income and expenses.

- **a.** True
- **b.** False

5-95. Personal balance sheets are usually stated at:

- **a.** Historical cost
- **b.** Purchase price
- **c.** Market value
- **d.** Amortized value

5-96. Each of the following is a type of forensic accounting engagement that may involve the analysis of personal financial statements *except*:

- **a.** Embezzlement fraud
- **b.** Conscription fraud
- **c.** Arson
- **d.** Domestic relations

Workplace Applications

Using Spreadsheets

5-97. Using a spreadsheet program and the ZZZZ Best financial statements provided in Appendix C, calculate the common-size statements and ratios presented in Tables 5C-1, 5C-2, and 5C-3. Which calculations did you have difficulty reproducing? Can you explain the meaning of each calculation? What did you learn about the relationship between the income statement and balance sheet?

5-98. Using a spreadsheet program and the ZZZZ Best financial statements provided in Tables 5C-1 and 5C-2, reproduce, using formulas, the cash flow analysis set forth in Table 5C-4. Depreciation for 1986 was $97,588, and no assets were disposed of during the year. Which items on the cash flow analysis would you investigate further? Why?

Writing a Business Memo

5-99. As you may recall from the introductory case study, the 1985 and 1986 financial statements of ZZZZ Best were audited by CPA firms. After reviewing the case study, along with the sections of the chapter related to the types of financial statements and their implied assurances, prepare a memo to your professor discussing the following:

- The nature of the implied assurances
- The accounting principles that may have been violated by ZZZZ Best
- The context of the financial statement presentation

Chapter Problems

5-100. Locate Tootsie Roll's annual report at www.tootsie.com. Using the 2010 annual report:

a. Prepare a common-size balance sheet and income statement.

b. Compute the following financial ratios:

Profitability
- Gross margin percent
- Return on sales
- Return on assets
- Return on equity

Efficiency
- Total asset turnover
- Accounts receivable turnover
- Accounts receivable days
- Inventory turnover
- Inventory days
- Operating cycle

Leverage
- Debt to assets
- Equity to assets
- Debt to equity
- Equity multiplier

Liquidity
- Current ratio
- Acid test (quick) ratio
- Net working capital

Equity
- Book value per share
- Earnings per share
- Price to earnings
- Dividend payout ratio
- Dividend yield

c. Prepare a memo to your professor discussing five key findings revealed by your analysis.

5-101. Using the following financial statements for ZZZZ Best:

a. Prepare a common-size balance sheet and income statement for the three-month interim period ending July 31, 1986.

b. Compute the following financial ratios for the three-month interim period ending July 31, 1986:

Profitability
- Gross margin percent
- Return on sales
- Return on assets
- Return on equity

Efficiency
- Total asset turnover
- Accounts receivable turnover
- Accounts receivable days

Leverage
- Debt to assets
- Equity to assets
- Debt to equity
- Equity multiplier

Liquidity
- Current ratio
- Acid test (quick) ratio
- Net working capital

5-102. Using the ratio analysis developed in problem 5-101, identify areas where further analysis might be warranted. Write a memo to your professor detailing your findings. Include two preliminary hypotheses regarding potential fraudulent activity.

5-103. Using the data provided in problem 5-101, prepare a cash flow analysis for the interim period ending July 31, 1986. Additional information required for this analysis includes the following:
- Depreciation for the period is $105,651.
- Amortization of goodwill for the period is $618.
- All deferred tax adjustments are noncash in nature.

Problem 5-101 Financial Statements

ZZZZ Best Co, Inc. Income Statement ($)				
	Fiscal Yr. Ending Apr. 30		3 Mos. Ending Jul. 31	
	1985	1986	1985	1986
Total Revenue	1,240,524	4,845,347	638,408	5,395,754
Cost of Revenue	576,694	2,050,779	320,460	2,976,205
Gross Profit	663,830	2,794,568	317,948	2,419,549
Operating Expenses	306,016	1,125,541	91,346	622,811
Operating Income	357,814	1,669,027	226,602	1,796,738
Other Income/Expense (Net)	-	143,659	-	37,969
Income Before Income Tax	357,814	1,812,686	226,602	1,834,707
Provision for Income Tax	36,053	867,041	95,734	938,754
Net Income	**321,761**	**945,645**	**130,868**	**895,953**

ZZZZ Best Co., Inc. Balance Sheet ($)			
	As of Apr. 30		As of Jul. 31
	1985	1986	1986
Assets			
Current Assets			
Cash & Cash Equivalents	30,321	87,014	9,907
Receivables (Net)	-	693,773	2,461,098
Unbilled Charges on Restoration Contracts	-	413,231	-
Advances on Material Purchases	-	136,000	1,330,000
Other Current Assets	76,775	533,955	441,984
Total Current Assets	107,096	1,863,973	4,242,989
Property and Equipment (Net)	57,490	3,059,455	3,698,282
Goodwill	-	22,249	21,631
Other Assets	13,450	99,994	237,189
Total Assets	**178,036**	**5,045,671**	**8,200,091**

(table continued on next page)

ZZZZ Best Co., Inc. Balance Sheet ($)			
	As of Apr. 30		As of Jul. 31
	1985	1986	1986
Liabilities & Shareholders' Equity			
Current Liabilities			
Trade Accounts Payable and Accrued Expenses	2,930	265,367	428,076
Equipment Purchase Payable	-	575,000	-
Billings in Excess of Cost	-	-	107,301
Deferred Income Taxes	-	-	1,400,139
Short-Term Debt and Current Portion of Long-Term Debt	-	928,068	2,169,180
Total Current Liabilities	2,930	1,768,435	4,104,696
Obligation Under Capital Leases	-	428,471	418,195
Deferred Federal Income Taxes	-	819,014	236,496
Other Long-Term Debt	-	-	515,000
Total Liabilities	2,930	3,015,920	5,274,387
Shareholders' Equity			
Common Stock	55,000	76,675	76,675
Additional Paid-in Capital	55,000	942,325	942,325
Retained Earnings	65,106	1,010,751	1,906,704
Total Shareholders' Equity	175,106	2,029,751	2,925,704
Total Liabilities & Shareholders' Equity	**178,036**	**5,045,671**	**8,200,091**

5-104. What level of assurance was implied for ZZZZ Best's financial statements for 1985? For 1986? For the interim period ending July 31, 1986? Would the level of assurance impact a forensic accountant's mindset? Explain.

5-105. Go to www.sec.gov and obtain WorldCom's Form 10-K405 for 2001. Using the income statement found on page F-2 and the balance sheet found on page F-3 of the 10-K405 form:

a. Prepare a common-size balance sheet and income statement for years 2000 and 2001.

b. Compute the following financial ratios for years 2000 and 2001:

Profitability

- Gross margin percent
- Return on sales
- Return on assets
- Return on equity

Efficiency

- Total asset turnover
- Accounts receivable turnover
- Accounts receivable days

Leverage

- Debt to assets (including minority interest and preferred)
- Equity to assets
- Debt to equity
- Equity multiplier

Liquidity

- Current ratio
- Acid test (quick) ratio
- Net working capital

Equity

- Book value per share
- Earnings per share
- Price to earnings

c. Does your analysis raise any questions that might lead to a fraud hypothesis? Explain.

5-106. Go to www.sec.gov and obtain WorldCom's Form 10-K for year 2002. Using the restatement information presented on pages 42–48 of the form, identify any inappropriate adjusting entries (or failure to make appropriate adjusting entries) in the following areas:

a. Impairment

b. Inappropriate reduction of access costs

c. Purchase accounting

i. Goodwill and intangible assets

d. Long-lived assets

e. Revenue-related adjustments for:

i. Deferral of customer activation, installation, and provisioning revenue and cost

ii. Accounts receivable adjustments

iii. Revenue recognition adjustments

Example: *Impairment* on page 43. WorldCom overstated net income by failing to perform impairment tests on goodwill and other long-lived assets. This failure to write down assets resulted in a pre-tax understatement of expenses of $12,592 in 2001 and $47,180 in 2000, which overstated operating income by the same amounts.

5-107. Using the WorldCom 2001 Form 10-K405 and the Tootsie Roll 2010 10-K, perform a content analysis using the following as search terms:

a. Fraud

b. Restatement

c. Inappropriate

d. Bankruptcy

e. Forensic

f. Investigation

g. Audit

h. Internal control

5-108. Go to www.sec.gov and find the section entitled Accounting and Auditing Enforcement Releases (AAERs). For the most recent full year, review the releases and select one that relates to financial statement fraud. Write a memo to your professor containing the following:

a. Identify and discuss the issue the SEC is pursuing.

b. Summarize the SEC's findings.

c. Discuss the company's reaction to the investigation.

d. Outline how the issue will be corrected.

5-109. For one of the companies listed in Table 5-5 in this chapter, find five published articles in either academic journals or practitioner magazines. Prepare a report that discusses the following:

a. When and how the fraud was conducted

b. Who was harmed and in what amount

c. How the issue was resolved

d. What the firm's present status is

5-110. The 1986 prospectus for ZZZZ Best included the following:

- April 30, 1984 and 1985, financial statements audited by Larry G. Baker, CPA of Bakersfield, California
- April 30, 1986, financial statements audited by Greenspan & Company of Englewood Cliffs, NJ
- July 31, 1986, three-month interim financial statements reviewed by Ernst & Whinney of Los Angeles

Consider how the ZZZZ Best fraud might have impacted each of these CPA firms, then conduct an Internet search to determine their actual experiences. Are the facts consistent with your initial expectations? Prepare a memo to your professor discussing your findings and conclusions.

5-111. As disclosed in the introductory case study, Barry Minkow served time in prison for his fraud. Using the Internet, research Mr. Minkow's career following his release. In your research, explore the concept of "behavioral consistency theory" as it relates to Mr. Minkow. Prepare a memo to your professor discussing your findings and conclusions.

5-112. The ZZZZ Best fraud resulted in the Treadway Commission report on Fraudulent Financial Reporting (1987) as an attempt to reform areas that fostered frauds of the type perpetrated by Minkow. Go to www.pearsonhighered/rufus for a link to this report. Prepare a memo to your professor outlining the major recommendations made by this Commission.

5-113. As a result of the WorldCom fraud, the AICPA issued SAS No. 99—Consideration of Fraud in a Financial Statement Audit (2003). Go to www.pearsonhighered/rufus for a link to this document and review the auditing guidance. Prepare a memo to your professor summarizing the primary requirements of this guidance as it relates to fraud.

1 Elmer-Dewit, P., & Brown, S. (Jul. 20, 1987). ZZZZ Best May be ZZZZ. *Time*. Go to www.pearsonhighered/rufus for a link to this article.

2 Anonymous. (Jul. 22, 2011). 'I am a 45-year-old loser' Ex-Valley whiz kid heads back to prison. *Los Angeles Daily Times*, A1.

3 Wells, J. T. (Aug. 2001). Irrational ratios: The numbers raise a red flag. *Journal of Accountancy*. Go to www.pearsonhighered/rufus for a link to this article.

4 Gaines, S. (Feb. 2, 1988). ZZZZ Best auditors have say. *Chicago Tribune*. Go to www.pearsonhighered/rufus for a link to this article.

5 Akst, D. (Jan. 18, 1988). ZZZZ Best Founder indicted on racketeering and fraud charges. *Wall Street Journal*. Go to www.pearsonhighered/rufus for a link to this article.

6 Adelson, A. (Dec. 15, 1988). Founder of ZZZZ Best is convicted. *The New York Times*. Go to www.pearsonhighered/rufus for a link to this article.

7 Wells, J. T. (Aug. 2001). Irrational ratios: The numbers raise a red flag. *Journal of Accountancy*. Go to www.pearsonhighered/rufus for a link to this article.

8 See press releases from the United States Attorney's Office for the Southern District of Florida (link available at www.pearsonhighered/rufus). Related court documents and information may be found on the web site of the District Court for the Southern District of Florida (link available at www.pearsonhighered/rufus).

9 Conceptual Framework for Financial Reporting 2010. International Accounting Standards Board. Go to www.pearsonhighered/rufus for a link to this document.

10 Ross, D. (2005). What every ratio user should know about assets. *Commercial Lending Review, 20, 19–47.*

11 Elifoglu, H., Fitzsimons, A., & Sillman, B. (2012). Separate financial reporting standards and standard setting for private companies. *Review of Business, 32*(2), 23–32.

12 Lynch, N. (Jul. 2012). The controversy over private company reporting standards. *The CPA Journal, 82(7)*, 46–53.

13 Ross, D. (2005). What every ratio user should know about assets. *Commercial Lending Review, 20*, 19–47.

14 Schipper, K. (1989). Commentary on Earnings Management. *Accounting Horizons, 3*, 91–102.

15 Healy, P., & Wahlen, J. (1999). A review of earnings management literature and its implications for standard setting. *Accounting Horizons, 13*(4), 365–83.

16 Rufus, R. J. (Jan./Feb. 2003). The challenge of earnings management: A valuator's perspective. *The Valuation Examiner*, 18–20.

17 Parfet, W. (2000). Accounting subjectivity and earnings management: A preparer perspective. *Accounting Horizons, 14*(4), 481–88.

18 Brazel, J. F., Jones, K., & Zimbelman, M. F. (2009). Using nonfinancial measures to assess fraud risk. *Journal of Accounting Research, 47*, 1135–66.

19 Porter, M. E. (1980). *Competitive Strategy*. New York: Free Press.

20 Rufus, R. J. (May/Jun. 2003). Financial ratios: Use, predictive power and the Z-score. *The Valuation Examiner*, 14–17.

21 Altman, E. I. (1968). Financial ratios, discriminate analysis, and the prediction of corporate bankruptcy. *Journal of Finance, 23*, 589–609.

22 Rufus, R. J. (May/Jun. 2003). Financial ratios: Use, predictive power and the Z-score. *The Valuation Examiner*, 14–17.

23 Grossman, S. D., & Pearl, D. (1988). Financial analysis of the statement of cash flows. Ohio CPA Journal, 47, 11–14.

24 Dorrell, D., Gadawski, G., & Brown, T. (2007). Is the moneyed spouse lying about the money? *American Journal of Family Law, 21*(1), 298–327.

25 Ibid.

26 Grossman, S. D., & Pearl, D. (1988). Financial analysis of the statement of cash flows. *Ohio CPA Journal, 47*, 11–14.

27 Ibid.

28 Siegel, M. A. (2006). Accounting shenanigans on the cash flow statement. *The CPA Journal, 76*, 38–43.

29 Lanza, R., Gilbert, S., & Lamoreaux, M. (2007). A risk-based approach to journal entry testing. *Journal of Accountancy, 204*, 32–35.

30 Ibid.

31 Ibid.

32 Churyk, N., Lee, C., & Clinton, D. (2008). Can we detect fraud earlier? *Strategic Finance, 90*(4), 51–54.

33 FASB ASC 274-10-50-2.

6 Fraud and White-Collar Crime

INTRODUCTION

Forensic accounting has become affixed to the terms *fraud* and *white-collar crime*. Why? Fraud is not an accounting problem, is it? A primary consequence of fraud and white-collar crime is, of course, economic loss. Accounting professionals, especially auditors, continue to be viewed as the principal guardians of the public's interest, acting as "defenders" against financial crime. The numerous financial failures of the past two decades have highlighted the gap between what auditors *actually* do and what the public *thinks* they do. This expectation gap is especially relevant in the consideration of fraud.

The pervasiveness of fraud—and the public outcry in response to it—has moved forensic accounting to center stage. As emphasized throughout this text, forensic accountants are uniquely skilled in fraud deterrence, fraud detection, and fraud investigation. Moreover, forensic accountants have an understanding of the judicial process, including the rules of evidence and the requisite burden and standards of proof.

The purpose of this chapter is to operationalize the concepts of fraud and white-collar crime. To that end, we discuss what fraud and white-collar crime are, the different types of fraud, the conditions generally present when fraud occurs (the "fraud triangle"), and several fraud theories. We also introduce the "calculus of fraud," which frames fraud as an economic decision based on specific variables. Finally, we review research that offers insight into the human element of fraud—*who* commits fraud and *why*?

Special Note

Before reading this chapter, you are encouraged to review the provisions of SAS No. 99, which represents the cornerstone of the AICPA's anti-fraud program. This auditing standard emphasizes professional skepticism and mandates that certain fraud evaluation procedures be integrated into the overall audit process. Relevant to our immediate discussion are paragraphs AU §316.05 and 316.07, which define fraud and identify the three conditions generally present when fraud occurs (incentive, opportunity, and rationalization).

This chapter offers a unique perspective of financial crimes, highlighting five key points:

- *Financial crimes are criminal offenses.* As such, the standard of proof is beyond a reasonable doubt. Moreover, the burden of proof is on the prosecution.
- *Financial crimes are crimes of intent.* Absent an admission, circumstantial evidence (including expert witness testimony) is used to establish or infer fraudulent intent.
- *Financial crimes are not victimless.* In addition to economic loss, financial crimes can result in emotional and physical harm to individuals.
- *Financial crimes may involve violent acts.* Although white-collar crime is generally considered a nonviolent activity, the possibility of violence cannot be ignored.

Learning Objectives

After completing this chapter, you should be able to:

LO1. Define fraud and describe white-collar crime.

LO2. Explain the development of fraud theory, beginning with the fraud triangle.

LO3. Explain various theories for why people commit fraud.

LO4. Identify the characteristics of a typical fraudster.

LO5. Describe the impact of white-collar crime on victims.

LO6. Describe the government's role in prosecuting white-collar crime.

- *The government (prosecution) is not always right.* A criminal indictment is not proof of a crime. It is simply an assertion that a crime has been committed. Importantly, the law presumes that every defendant is innocent until proven guilty.

State of West Virginia v. Keith O. Peoples

To provide some context for our discussion, let's consider the case *State of West Virginia v. Keith O. Peoples.*

Special Note

This case provides an example of the reality and significance of what forensic accountants do, highlighting the importance of mindset, critical thinking, and the scientific approach. It also illustrates the anatomy (and drama) of a criminal trial. While the subject fraud (double-dipping) is atypical, the investigative and judicial processes described are not.

Although a case summary is presented below, you are encouraged to consider the comprehensive narrative (including opening statements, witness testimony, closing arguments, and jury instructions) presented in Appendix 6-A.

Charleston Police Officer Indicted on Fraud Charges

On May 16, 2008, a grand jury in Kanawha County, West Virginia, charged Corporal Keith O. Peoples with obtaining money by fraudulent schemes. The indictment alleged that Cpl. Peoples was feloniously,[*] willfully, and unlawfully compensated as a security officer by a private employer, the Charleston Town Center Mall (TCM), while on duty with the Charleston Police Department (CPD)—a scheme commonly known as "double-dipping."

Following his arraignment, Cpl. Peoples, an 18-year veteran of the CPD and a past recipient of the Officer of the Year award, entered a "not guilty" plea. Cpl. Peoples was immediately placed on administrative leave pending the outcome of the criminal proceeding. If convicted, Peoples faced imprisonment for a period up to two years and a maximum fine of $2,500.

Think About It

As discussed in Chapter 2, the prosecution always has the burden of proof. Remember, Cpl. Peoples is presumed to be innocent! The presumption of innocence in a criminal case can only be overcome by proof *beyond a reasonable doubt*. Absent a confession (that is, direct evidence), the prosecution was challenged with proving Cpl. Peoples's guilt through circumstantial evidence. Circumstantial evidence *infers*[†] intent from objective evidence (facts and data) of what actually happened. Although circumstantial evidence may provide a reasonable basis for inferring intent, it does not provide "proof certain" of the actual subjective intent of the suspect.

The Case of the Prosecution

Peoples's trial began on May 18, 2009, one year after his indictment. The state's case was presented by Assistant Prosecutor Scott Reynolds as "a violation of public trust and a case of common sense . . . you simply can't be in two places at the same time." The foundation of the state's case was the testimony of its lead investigator, Captain John Tabaretti.

Following testimonial evidence by the City Auditor and TCM representatives regarding the authenticity of their respective payroll records, Capt. Tabaretti testified that he had analyzed Cpl. Peoples's payroll records from both employers (CPD and TCM) for the period Jan. 1, 2001, through Aug. 31, 2004, and determined that Cpl. Peoples had 478 hours of overlapping time. In other words, "he was on the clock of both employers at the same time." Capt. Tabaretti also testified that TCM had a mandatory "off duty" policy for all CPD officers

[*] Criminal offenses are classified as either misdemeanors or felonies. A felony is the more serious of the two and exposes the accused to more severe punishments (e.g., extended incarceration and higher fines/penalties). Each state has its own laws governing what constitutes a felony crime and the corresponding punishment.

[†] An inference is a deduction of fact that may be logically and reasonably drawn from another fact or group of facts.

providing security services and that Cpl. Peoples was aware of the policy. Finally, he testified that the statistical evidence of overlapping was undisputed.

In closing, the state challenged the jury to question whether Peoples knew his actions were wrong. "Sure he did," stated Reynolds. Did we prove it? "Absolutely, remember the evidence." Reynolds concluded by stating, "The statistical evidence compiled by Capt. Tabaretti is undisputed and provides absolute proof, proof beyond a reasonable doubt, the actions and intent of Cpl. Keith Peoples."

The Case of the Defense

People's defense attorney, Dwane Tinsley, cautioned the jury that the state's case, including Tabaretti's investigation, was "ripe with investigative error and completely void of reasoning." Tinsley argued that the state had refused to consider several alternative explanations for its calculations of overlapping and had absolutely no evidence of intent. The defense first offered the testimony of various CPD officers, including Cpl. Peoples's former supervisors, regarding the culture of the department, specifically overtime slips, early releases, and the imprecise nature of timesheets. As best described by retired Cpt. Brad Rinehart, "Timesheets are not time clocks. . . . Overlapping is expected and unavoidable."

The defense then presented the analysis of its forensic accounting expert, who identified numerous breakdowns in the state's evidence, specifically Tabaretti's investigation. Investigative failures identified by the forensic accountant included Tabaretti's failure to interview key witnesses and his refusal to consider evidence that did not support the state's case. The forensic accountant opined that, while Tabaretti had properly calculated overlapping events (time), he had failed to refine and confirm the data or to consider alternative explanations—both of which are mandates for a meaningful assessment. The forensic accountant provided a mix of alternative explanations, supported by the preceding testimony of CPD officers regarding payroll errors, overtime slips, and early releases. He refused to assign any value to Tabaretti's analysis, describing it as "ripe with failure and bias."

In closing, Tinsley challenged the jury to question Tabaretti's analysis. "We don't challenge his ability to build an Excel spreadsheet that mathematically identifies overlapping hours—a simple task," Tinsley stated. "However, you must challenge his failure to consider and investigate alternative explanations," including overtime slips, early releases, authorized exits from the mall, and payroll errors. Tinsley exclaimed, "How dare the state and its investigator fail to properly investigate this case!" He continued, "Ask yourself why, even when confronted with reliable testimony from Cpl. Peoples's immediate supervisors and co-workers, does Tabaretti refuse to consider these explanations? I'll tell you why—it kills their case. These are false allegations, and they know it."

The Court's Instructions

On May 22, 2009, after five days of trial, fifteen witnesses, and more than fifty exhibits, both sides rested. The judge then presented the jury's instructions, including legal definitions addressing the concepts of evidence, intent, burden of proof, presumption of innocence, and standard of proof. Highlights include the following:

- You are to consider only the evidence presented, and you may not guess or speculate as to the existence of other facts.
- The burden is always on the state to prove guilt beyond a reasonable doubt.
- If the jury has a reasonable doubt that the defendant is guilty of the charge, it must acquit.
- Proof beyond a reasonable doubt is proof of such a convincing character that a reasonable person would not hesitate to rely and act upon it.
- The jury will remember that the defendant is never to be convicted on suspicion, conjecture, or speculation.
- Expert testimony was admitted in this case. That does not mean that you must accept the expert witness's opinion. As with any other witness, you must decide the extent to which, if any, to rely upon the opinion offered.

- You, as the jurors, are the sole judges of the credibility of a witness and the weight of the evidence.
- You must determine whether the state proved its case against the defendant based solely on the testimony of the witnesses and the exhibits.

The Jury Is In

After more than eight hours of deliberation, the jury found Cpl. Peoples not guilty of fraudulent schemes.

Special Note

Three days after the trial, Mr. Tinsley conducted a post-trial survey of the jurors regarding their views on the trial strategy, witness testimony, case arguments, and trial exhibits. This survey was motivated by the extended duration of the deliberation process. Key results of the survey include the following:

- After two hours of deliberation, the vote was eleven (of twelve) to acquit.
- The holdout, a CPA, demanded that the jury review the Excel worksheets prepared by the respective experts, arguing that "the truth is in the numbers."
- The jury foreman, a middle-school science teacher, identified the meaning and significance of alternative explanations.
- The case boiled down to dueling experts.
- The question of intent, the most critical issue in the case, was never specifically addressed by the jury.

FRAUD AND WHITE-COLLAR CRIME

There are two methods of *illegally* obtaining property from others: robbery and fraud. Robbery, of course, is the use of force to persuade someone to surrender his or her property. Fraud, on the other hand, uses deception.

Special Note

Although this chapter specifically addresses the concept of "white-collar crime," we view it as a subset of fraud. Thus, for our purposes, the terms *fraud*, *white-collar crime*, and *financial crime* are used interchangeably.

It is important to keep in mind that fraud is a criminal offense. As discussed in Chapter 2, a criminal offense is a violation of local, state, or federal law that prohibits certain conduct. The seriousness of a criminal offense (and related sanctions) increases the standard of proof to the highest level—beyond a reasonable doubt. A person[‡] convicted of felony fraud may be subject to imprisonment, fines, penalties, restitution, probation, and community service. Additional consequences of a felony fraud conviction can include loss of professional license and certain civil liberties (for example, the right to vote, run for public office, or own firearms).

What Is Fraud?

Simply defined, ***fraud*** is the unlawful taking of another's property by deception. Under common law,[§] fraud has four basic elements:

- A material false statement or omission.[**]
- The suspect had knowledge that the statement or omission was false.

[‡] Entities (corporations, partnerships, and so on) can also be charged with fraud.

[§] Also known as case law, common law has no statutory basis. It is derived from judicial opinions that are binding on future decisions of lower courts in the same jurisdiction. The United States is a common law country and, except for Louisiana (which is based on the French civil code), the common law of England was adopted as the general law of the state.

[**] In this context, *material* refers to a statement that would induce a reasonable person to assent or that the maker knows is likely to induce a reasonable person to assent.

- The suspect intended to induce the victim to rely on the false statement or omission.
- The victim relied on the false statement or omission and suffered injury or damage as a result thereof.

These elements can be identified in the following definitions of fraud:

- An "intentional perversion of truth in order to induce another to part with something of value or to surrender a legal right."[1]
- A knowing misrepresentation of the truth or concealment of a material fact to induce another to act to his or her detriment.[2]
- "Any intentional act or omission designed to deceive others, resulting in the victim suffering a loss and/or the perpetrator achieving a gain."[3]
- "An intentional act that results in a material misstatement in financial statements that are the subject of an audit."[4]
- "A generic term, embracing all multifarious (assorted) means which human ingenuity can devise, and which are resorted to by one individual to get advantage over another by false suggestions or by suppression of truth, and includes all surprise, trick, cunning, dissembling, and any unfair way by which another is cheated."[5]

A common thread among these definitions is that *fraud is a crime of intent*. What exactly do we mean by "intent," and how do we, as forensic accountants, help establish or corroborate intent? *Black's Law Dictionary* defines intent as a "state of mind accompanying an act. While motive is the inducement to do some act, intent is the mental resolution or determination to do it. When the intent to do an act that violates the law exists, motive (such as good intentions) becomes immaterial."[6]

An intentional act is a product of free will—you *meant* to do it (that is, you have a guilty mind). In other words, the act itself does not create guilt (criminal intent) unless the mind is also guilty. The challenge of establishing criminal intent is why we do not prosecute children or the mentally impaired. These individuals are incapable of deciding to commit their crimes with a true understanding of the significance of their actions. Even so, the law is unmoved by "yes, but" defenses: Yes, but I had a bad childhood. Yes, but I was under financial duress. Yes, but I was drunk, on drugs, and so on.

In the world of fraud and white-collar crime, a suspected offense may be morally reprehensible, unethical, and irresponsible but, absent evidence of intent (the guilty mind), it is not necessarily criminal. A timely example is the limited number of criminal indictments related to the financial crisis of 2008–2009.[7] While it may be possible to prove that the actions of certain individuals contributed to the crisis, prosecutors have failed to identify sufficient evidence of intent in many cases.

Evidence of Fraudulent Intent

Absent a confession—that is, direct evidence—circumstantial evidence is used to establish fraudulent intent. To that end, forensic accountants are commonly engaged to gather and analyze objective evidence (facts and data) of what actually happened. The reliability of circumstantial evidence for the purpose of establishing intent depends on two key factors: (1) alternative explanations, and (2) degree of impact. In other words, if there are no alternative explanations for specific observations (such as the overlapping hours in *State v. Peoples*) and the degree of impact (the significance of the observations relative to the issue in question) is high, the reliability of the circumstantial evidence is established and assigned probative value. In contrast, if alternative explanations do exist and the degree of impact is low, the reliability of the circumstantial evidence is not established and is deemed to have little, if any, probative value.[8]

In addition to data analysis, forensic accountants also consider the environment and actions surrounding an activity, such as opportunity, efforts to conceal, patterns of behavior, false statements, and indications of motive. Although such factors may seem insignificant when viewed in isolation, they may be compelling when viewed collectively. This is the essence of circumstantial evidence, a collection of fragmented evidence that supports one inference over another. Students are cautioned that, while a forensic accountant's analysis may provide a reasonable basis for inferring intent, it does not provide "proof certain" of the actual subjective intent of the suspect.

Working Example

Let's operationalize this discussion (that is, the distinction between direct and circumstantial evidence and the question of intent) by further developing the state's case in *State v. Peoples*. The state hypothesized that Peoples was "willfully and unlawfully" on the clock of two employers (Charleston Police Department and Town Center Mall) at the same time—hence, double dipping. Without a confession, the state was challenged to prove its case beyond a reasonable doubt by circumstantial evidence. The state's investigation proceeded as follows:

1. Tabaretti tested the state's hypothesis by first compiling the payroll records of both employers. This initial step confirmed the existence of overlapping hours.
2. To refine the hypothesis and confirm his observation of overlapping hours, Tabaretti searched for alternative explanations (reasons for the overlapping other than a double-dipping scheme). According to Tabaretti, none were identified.
3. The next challenge was proving knowledge—that Cpl. Peoples knew his actions were wrong and proceeded regardless. To address this challenge, Tabaretti gathered evidence from TCM's representatives, specifically with regard to its policy that all security officers be "off duty" from CPD before clocking in. Moreover, TCM representatives confirmed this policy was communicated to and understood by Cpl. Peoples.

Armed with cumulative circumstantial evidence (statistical evidence of overlapping and knowledge of TCM's policy), the state framed its case as a matter of common sense: "You can't be in two places at the same time."

Consider the preceding investigative process and identify any failures or weaknesses in the state's position. Assuming that you've been engaged by People's defense attorney, where would you start? What does the evidence prove (or infer)? Does it prove beyond a reasonable doubt that Cpl. Peoples intentionally violated the law?

White-Collar Crime

White-collar crime is a major subcategory of fraud. The term *white-collar crime* was coined by Edwin Sunderland, a prominent criminologist, in 1939.[††] Sunderland defined ***white-collar crime*** as "a crime committed by a person of respectability and high social status in the course of his occupation."[9] Sunderland's research focused on antisocial behavior related to occupations considered legitimate, such as professionals, business and industry leaders, and corporate officers.

For nearly 75 years, criminologists have labored to comprehensively define white-collar crime, drawing distinctions between the actions of a *corporation*, the actions of the corporation's *management* acting on behalf of the corporation, and the actions of *employees* acting in self-interest. The U.S. government has also offered definitions:

- In 1979, the U.S. Congressional Subcommittee on Crime presented the following operational definition of white-collar crime: "an illegal act or series of illegal acts committed by nonphysical means and by concealment or guile to obtain money or property, to avoid the payment or loss of money or property, or to obtain personal or business advantage."[10]
- In 1989, the FBI defined white-collar crime as "illegal acts which are characterized by deceit, concealment, or violation of trust and which are not dependent upon the application or threat of physical force or violence. Individuals and corporations commit these acts to obtain money, property, or services; to avoid the payment or loss of money or services; or to secure personal advantage."[11]

[††] At this time, established Wall Street law firms were called "white-shoe" firms, a reference to the white bucks commonly worn by the Ivy League elites.

Consistent with these definitions, the literature identifies six attributes of white-collar crime:[12]

- *Deceit* – Offenders misrepresent and conceal the truth.
- *Intent* – Fraud does not happen by accident.
- *Breach of trust* – Offenders are generally in a position of trust that is manipulated or breached to facilitate the fraudulent action.
- *Losses* – White-collar crime is the unlawful taking of another's property.
- *Concealment* – White-collar crime can continue for years or might never be discovered.
- *Outward respectability* – As the name implies, white-collar crime is commonly perpetrated by individuals (for example, professionals and executives) who are seemingly beyond reproach.

The Commerce Clause of the U.S. Constitution gives the federal government the authority to police white-collar crime.[13] A number of federal agencies, including the FBI, IRS, Secret Service, SEC, EPA, and U.S. Customs, participate in the enforcement of federal white-collar crime legislation. In addition, most states employ their own agencies to enforce white-collar crime laws at the state level.

Types of White-Collar Crime

Although there is some debate as to what qualifies as white-collar crime, the term generally encompasses a variety of frauds committed by professionals, corporate leaders, businesses, and public officials for unlawful financial gain. As illustrated in Table 6-1, the FBI has identified and categorized eight major types of financial crime.[14]

Table 6-1 | Major Types of White-Collar Crime

Type	Act / Activity
Securities and Commodities Fraud	• Securities market manipulation • Investment fund (such as Ponzi) schemes • Broker embezzlements
Corporate Fraud	• Financial statement fraud • Self-dealing by corporate insiders • Obstructive conduct
Health Care Fraud	• Billing schemes • False or exaggerated medical disability • Excessive or unnecessary treatment
Mortgage Fraud	• A material misstatement, misrepresentation, or omission relating to a real estate transaction that is relied on by one or more parties to the transaction • Subcategories include fraud for profit and fraud for housing
Financial Institution Fraud	• Insider fraud (for example, embezzlement or misapplication) • Check fraud • Counterfeit negotiable instruments • Check kiting
Insurance Fraud	• Insurance agents or brokers diverting policyholder premiums for their own benefit • Unauthorized and unregistered entities engaging in the sale of insurance
Mass Marketing Fraud	• Exploitation through telemarketing, mass mailings, and the Internet • Examples include advance fee fraud, overpayment fraud, and foreign lottery fraud
Money Laundering	• Efforts by criminals to infuse illegal money into the stream of commerce

Other major categories of white-collar crime that are outside the primary jurisdiction of the FBI include tax fraud, mail fraud, Social Security fraud, food stamp fraud, immigration fraud, and bank fraud. These frauds are investigated by other federal agencies such as the IRS, U.S. Postal Service, Secret Service, Social Security Administration, Department of Agriculture, and U.S. Immigration.

Special Note

A comprehensive discussion of each of the many types of fraud is beyond the scope of this text. You can visit the web site of the FBI (or other agencies) for additional information such as characteristics of fraud types, significant cases, and enforcement statistics.

A Leap to Violence

As discussed previously, there are many types of white-collar crime involving many segments of our society. Although such crimes are commonly characterized as nonviolent, the circumstances of each financial crime engagement must be evaluated with caution. Consider the pressure that drives an individual to commit fraud. Now, multiply that pressure by a factor of five (or more) to determine the extreme measures a white-collar criminal might use to avoid detection or punishment.

The link between violence and white-collar crime is a growing concern among practitioners and researchers alike. Perri and Lichtenwald (2007)[15] suggest that behavioral data linking white-collar crime and homicides support a sub-classification—"red-collar criminals." Their findings suggest that, within this subgroup, the threat of fraud detection is a motive to kill. Brody and Kiehl (2010)[16] explain the leap from nonviolent white-collar crime to red-collar crime using the fraud triangle (discussed later). Specifically, they propose that every criminal has a breaking point challenged by pressure; as the pressure (real or perceived) intensifies, so too does the propensity for violence.

In practice, financial crimes such as money laundering, food stamp fraud, prescription fraud, insurance fraud, and identity theft are often linked to organized and street crime. Our experience supports the preceding propositions—that white-collar crime is more complex than it might first appear, with a very real potential for violence. As emphasized throughout this text, you must always think safety.

Armed with an understanding of what fraud is, let's now consider the conditions generally present when fraud occurs.

FRAUD THEORY

Fraud theory is founded in the seminal research of Donald Cressey, a student of Edwin Sunderland, who in 1949 interviewed 209 inmates at three prisons in the Midwest for the purpose of studying embezzlement behavior. Cressey presented his research findings in the 1953 book *Other People's Money*, in which he theorized that fraud results from the convergence of three factors: pressure, opportunity, and rationalization.

Pressure

Cressey described ***pressure*** (which was identified in every inmate interview) as a need or nonshareable problem that precedes the criminal violation of financial trust. Many different situations constitute nonshareable problems, such as status seeking, status maintenance, or a pressing financial concern. Cressey concluded that nonshareable problems, whether real or perceived, provide the necessary stimulus or motive for a violation of trust.

Opportunity

Cressey theorized that a nonshareable problem is a stimulus to a violation only when the person's position of trust is perceived as offering a solution. Thus, motivation alone does not induce a crime; even the most motivated offenders must have opportunity. ***Opportunity*** is often attributable to the fact that individuals trained in the routine duties of a position of trust have essentially been trained in the skills necessary to violate that trust. In other words, individuals who play a role in control functions are in a position to manipulate or circumvent those controls.

Rationalization

Cressey theorized that rationalization enables the violator to "adjust" or reconcile two sets of conflicting values and behavior patterns. Thus, ***rationalization*** is a process by which a person attempts to make his or her actual or intended behavior more logical or justified. This justification allows individuals to perceive violations of trust as a legitimate means for solving their nonshareable problems. Violators generally engage in rationalization before (or at the same time) the act takes place. Cressey explained that violations of trust are often rationalized as essentially noncriminal, part of some general irresponsibility for which the individual is not completely accountable. Examples of common rationalizations include the following:

- "It was a loan."
- "Everyone does it."
- "I'm underappreciated and underpaid."
- "I did it to help other people."
- "It's covered by insurance."

The Fraud Triangle

In sum, Cressey's research suggests that violations of trust (fraud) occur when the position of trust (opportunity) is viewed by the trusted person as a rational means (solution) to solve a nonshareable problem (pressure). This research is the foundation for the ***fraud triangle***, which proposes that three factors—pressure (or need), opportunity, and rationalization—constitute the conditions under which fraud occurs (see Figure 6-1). The implication, of course, is that *influencing any one of these conditions can impact the likelihood that fraud will occur*.

Fraud Characteristic "Red Flags"

Forensic accountants must be familiar with the indicators (or conditions) that are commonly present when fraud occurs. Research consistently identifies certain red flags that are related to the incidence of fraud. In Table 6-2 we list our "top five" indicators, segregated into two categories—personal characteristics and organizational characteristics.

Figure 6-1
The Fraud Triangle

Table 6-2 | Top Five Fraud Characteristics

	Personal Characteristics	Organizational Characteristics
1	Living beyond one's means	Placing too much trust in key employees
2	Abuse of drugs or alcohol	No segregation of duties/responsibilities
3	Feeling of being underpaid	Lack of complete and timely reconciliations
4	Excessive gambling habits	Lack of independent checks on performance
5	Undue family or peer pressure	Lack of clear lines of authority and responsibility

Special Note

Consider these fraud characteristics in the context of the fraud triangle, noting that personal characteristics relate to pressure (need/motive) and rationalization, while organizational characteristics relate to opportunity. For example, living beyond one's means might suggest pressure; placing too much trust in key employees provides opportunity; and a feeling of being underpaid could be a rationalization.

Research conducted by Skousen and Wright (2008)[17] examined the effectiveness of Cressey's fraud theory framework (1953).[18] The results of the study[‡‡] offer supporting evidence, indicating that rapid asset growth, increased cash needs, and external financing are positively related to the likelihood of fraud. The study also concluded that control of the board of directors (which provides opportunity) suggests a greater incidence of financial statement fraud.

Finally, Dechow, Larson, and Sloan (2008)[19] observed a strong correlation between both market pressure and financing needs and financial statement fraud. Consistent with previous research, they found that the most common type of financial statement fraud is overstatement of revenues. Almost all major corporate scandals (such as Enron, Worldcom, and HealthSouth) involved this scheme.

Recent Developments in Fraud Theory

There have been numerous attempts to extend (or modify) Cressey's fraud triangle in an effort to enhance our understanding of why individuals commit fraud. Although these discussions may have little, if any, immediate practitioner value, they do add to our critical thinking and reasoning skills regarding fraud. Two of the many contributions are discussed in the following sections.

The Fraud Diamond

The "fraud diamond," shown in Figure 6-2, was proposed in 2004 by Wolfe and Hermanson.[20] The underlying proposition is that, in addition to pressure, opportunity, and rationalization (the fraud triangle), offenders also need the "capability" to commit the act. Wolfe and Hermanson assert that opportunity opens the door, incentive and rationalization draw offenders toward the door, and capability pushes them through.

Although no empirical research supports this additional condition, a suspect's capacity (ability, know-how, or competency) should certainly be considered by the forensic accountant. Moreover, a suspect's *incapacity* is often used as an argument by defense attorneys because of its proximity to the question of intent. Under the "knucklehead defense," an attorney

‡‡ Comparative analysis of 92 fraud firms (SEC Accounting and Auditing Enforcement Releases) and nonfraud firms from 1992 to 2001.

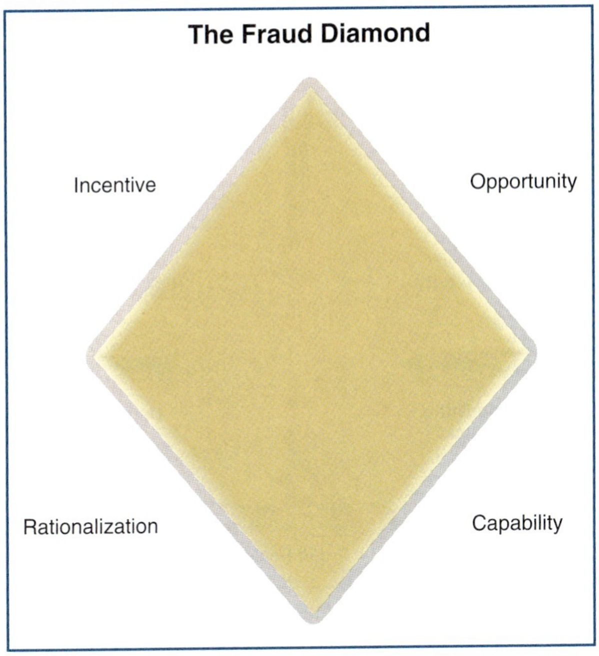

The Fraud Diamond

Incentive

Opportunity

Rationalization

Capability

Figure 6-2
The Fraud Diamond
Source: Reprinted from *The CPA Journal,* December 2004, Copyright © 2004, with permission from the New York State Society of Certified Public Accountants.

argues that, even if the client was motivated to commit the crime and had the opportunity, he or she did not have the ability to carry it out.

The Fraud Scale

A byproduct of Albrecht et al.'s 1984 study is the "fraud scale." Their study proposes replacing the rationalization component of the fraud triangle with integrity. The underlying proposition is that integrity (reflected in one's decisions) influences deviant behavior. As illustrated in Figure 6-3, fraud is more (less) likely to occur when there is high (low) pressure, greater (less) opportunity, and low (high) personal integrity. All else equal, the scales are in balance.

Meta Model of White-Collar Crime

Dorminey, Fleming, Kranacher, and Riley (2012)[21] propose a meta model of white-collar crime (see Figure 6-4). As the name implies, the model represents a collection of concepts, anchored by Cressey's fraud triangle. The purpose of the model is to strengthen relationships between the concepts, specifically the conditions that create the impetus for fraud (that is, pressure, opportunity, and rationalization), efforts to prevent and deter fraud (internal control and probability of detection), and aspects of the fraud action. Specifically designed as a "framework for instruction" in the classroom, the meta model is the latest contribution to the exploration and discussion of why people commit fraud.

Fraud Studies

This chapter introduces several theoretical concepts that attempt to explain and predict fraudulent behavior. At this point, you may be wondering what the facts are or what fraud actually looks like. Table 6-3 summarizes the findings of three empirical fraud studies, each providing a different perspective—data from actual incidences of occupational fraud, a survey of fraud examiners, and results of law enforcement efforts.

WHY DO PEOPLE COMMIT FRAUD?

Why do smart, talented, well-educated, and seemingly respectable people commit fraud? Traditional economic theory suggests that such individuals are motivated by self-interest.

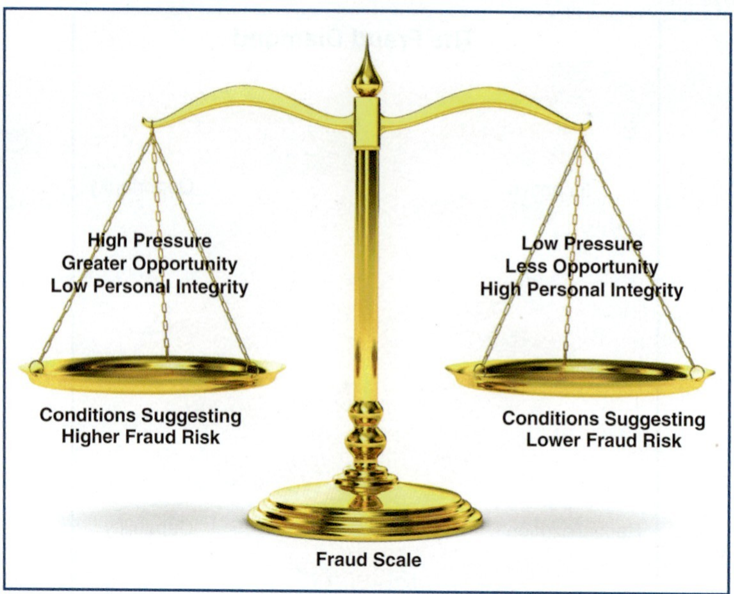

Figure 6-3
The Fraud Scale

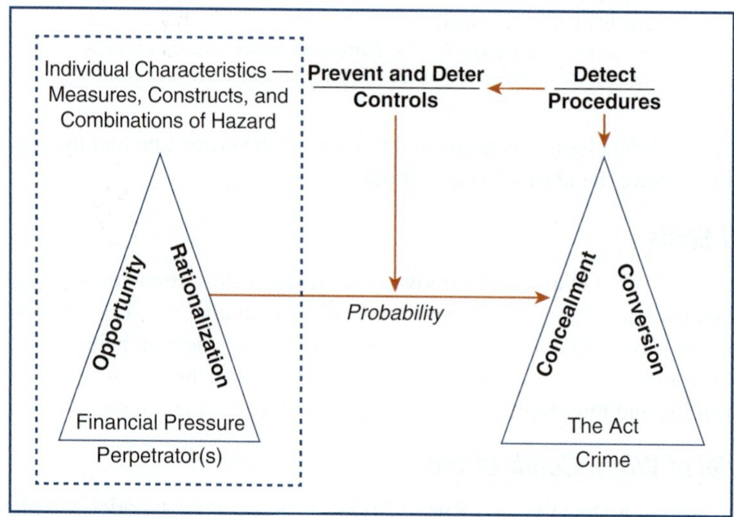

Figure 6-4
Meta Model of White-Collar Crime
Source: Dorminey, J., Fleming, A. S., Kranacher, M., & Riley, R. (2012). The evolution of fraud theory. *Issues in Accounting Education,* 27(2), 555-579. Reprinted with permission of the American Accounting Association.

Thus, we can reason that people are more likely to commit fraud when it is in their self-interest to do so. Consistent with this line of reasoning, we propose the calculus of fraud.

Calculus of Fraud

The ***calculus of fraud*** reflects the simple proposition that individuals will commit fraud when the reward (R) is greater than the product of the probability of getting caught (P) and the perceived gravity of the loss (L).[§§] This relationship is formalized as follows:

$$R > PL$$

[§§] The calculus of fraud is an extension of the calculus of negligence theory, which proposes that individuals balance decisions using risk vs. reward variables. The calculus of negligence was first opined in the 1947 case *United States v. Carroll Towing Co.* (159 F.2d 169).

Table 6-3 Fraud Study Highlights

2012 ACFE Report to the Nations Global Fraud Study	2007 Oversight Systems Report on Corporate Fraud	2010–2011 FBI Financial Crimes Report to the Public
• Data compiled from 1,388 cases of occupational fraud	• National survey of 86 fraud examiners during late 2006	• Based on field office crime surveys; establishes national priorities
• Participants estimated (median estimate) that organizations lose 5% of annual revenues (approx. $3.5 trillion) to fraud	• 66% indicated increasing prevalence of fraud as compared to preceding five years	• Priorities include public corruption, corporate fraud, securities fraud, health care fraud, financial institution fraud, insurance fraud, money laundering, and mass marketing fraud
• Median length of fraud schemes was 18 months from start until detection	• Expense and reimbursement schemes were a major risk	• FBI employs multi-agency investigative approach (for example, DOJ, SEC, NASD, and IRS)
• Frauds most commonly detected through tips (estimated at 43.3%), more than double the rate for internal (14.4%) and external (3.3%) auditors	• 56% of respondents had personally observed fraud	• Majority of corporate fraud cases involve accounting schemes to deceive investors, auditors, and analysts
• Most common small-business frauds involved check tampering, skimming, and fraudulent billing	• Checklist approach was not considered an effective tool	• During FY 2011, corporate fraud cases pursued by the FBI resulted in 242 indictments and 241 convictions; $2.4 billion in restitution and $16.1 million in fines were ordered
• Roughly 26% of frauds in the study were committed by accounting personnel; 15% by executives	• 43% perceived corporate interest and vigilance in fraud as starting to fade	• As of the end of FY 2011, the FBI was investigating 1,846 cases of securities and commodities fraud and recorded 520 indictments and 394 convictions ($8.8 billion in restitution orders and $751 million in forfeitures)
• In 81% of cases, the fraudster displayed one or more behavioral red flags commonly associated with fraud; most frequent "red flags" were living beyond one's means and experiencing financial difficulties	• 81% indicated pressure to meet goals as a major reason for executive fraud	• During FY 2011, the FBI investigated 2,690 cases of health care fraud, resulting in 1,676 informations or indictments and 736 convictions ($1.2 billion in restitution orders, $1 billion in fines, and $96 million in seizures)
• Lack of internal controls was cited as the major factor allowing fraud	• 40% indicated failure to perceive wrongness of actions as a reason for executive fraud	• Estimates that health care frauds account for 3–10% of total health care expenditures
• Most common anti-fraud measures in the U.S. were a Code of Conduct and external auditors	• Leadership from the top is the most effective means to prevent fraud	• Certain geographical areas and ethnic groups employ similar health care fraud schemes

This proposition frames the decision-making circumstance as a *calculated* choice. Consider the situation where an executive's compensation is based on firm performance. If the firm has failed to perform, a bonus is not awarded. However, by tweaking the numbers to give the appearance of strong performance (that is, earnings management), the executive can ensure receipt of the bonus. Facing this decision, the executive compares the rewards (the spouse's smiling face, the new car, business accolades, and so on) with the potential losses (loss of job, loss of reputation, criminal/civil proceedings) weighted by the likelihood of detection. The calculus of fraud suggests that when the rewards exceed the probable loss, the executive is more likely to commit fraud.

Of course, the previous example of a rational calculation (a risk-adjusted, cost-benefit analysis) is only a crude approximation of reality. Human behavior is far too complex and uncertain to be accurately described in such simple terms. Behavioral research indicates that, in some situations, an executive may engage in fraudulent activity even when a purely rational calculation would suggest otherwise.[22] This can occur when behavioral factors such as overconfidence, self-serving bias, confirmation bias, and suppression of negative information influence the decision-making process.

Criminal Decision Making—A Rational Choice?

Theories of the criminal decision-making process (the reasoning behind the action) continue to evolve. Much of the recent research is based on ***rational choice theory***.[23] Rooted in economic theory, rational choice suggests that offenders are "rational calculators" who choose courses of action such as fraud that produce optimal rewards with limited effort.[24]

The decision to commit crime is generally based on a number of factors, such as temperament, upbringing, self-perception, and previous experience with crime.[25] Once a person has decided to commit a crime, the specific crime (for example, embezzlement) is chosen through an analysis of opportunities and the cost-benefit trade-off. Perceived benefits of a crime that increase its likelihood include low effort, little skill, available targets, high expected yield, confrontation or lack thereof with a victim, and low risk of apprehension. Costs, on the other hand, include high effort, high skill, high risk of getting caught, and so on.

Rational choice is considered a crime-specific theory because different crimes meet different needs for the offender and because the context in which the rational choice occurs (the cost-benefit analysis) is unique to each offense. In other words, cost-benefit assessments are subjective and fluid. Under the right circumstances, risks that once deterred a crime may become acceptable or rewards that were previously overlooked become powerful incentives.

The subjectivity of the decision process allows criminal behavior to be considered rational. A decision that seems irrational to one person may be entirely rational to someone else, because each individual defines the decision differently in terms of factors to be considered (costs and benefits) and how those factors are weighted (which is more important). Offenders use such an analytical process, whether consciously or not, when they attempt to rationalize their crimes.

Techniques of Rationalization (Neutralization)

Fraudsters can rationalize their behavior to themselves, and to the world, in a variety of ways. A principal theory of rationalization is ***neutralization***, which proposes denial, condemnation, and higher loyalty as means by which offenders neutralize their role in a crime.[26] There are three common denial techniques:

- *Denial of responsibility.* When offenders deny responsibility, they view their behavior as a result of circumstances beyond their control.
- *Denial of injury.* When offenders deny injury, they feel as though their behavior did not hurt anyone, even though it is against the law.
- *Denial of the victim.* When offenders deny the victim, they conclude that the victim was deserving of the injuries.

Condemnation is an effort to neutralize one's actions by shifting blame to those who condemn the behavior (such as co-workers, employers, prosecutors, and law enforcement). For example, condemnation is commonly used by student cheaters, who claim that instructors are unfair, unethical, or uncaring.

A final technique of neutralization is loyalty to a group with which the offender associates. Offenders may feel their crime is legitimized because a bond dictates greater relevance to this group than to conventional society. For example, the HealthSouth fraud was facilitated by a number of staff-level employees who were motivated not by personal gain, but by a strong commitment to the organization.

The above techniques of neutralization may be employed singly or in combination. Moreover, they may be employed before the commission of a crime, afterward, or at both times.

General Theory of Crime

We continue our discussion of fraud theory with the ***general theory of crime***, which explains crime as a natural consequence of uncontrolled human desire to seek pleasure and avoid pain. Crime is an attractive means of pursuing self-interest because it provides "immediate, easy, and short-term pleasure."[27] The general theory of crime is applicable to all types of crime, including white-collar crime.[28]

As proposed by Gottfredson and Hirschi (1990), a criminal act requires low self-control and opportunity. Self-control, simply defined, is one's ability to control his or her emotions and desires.[***] Gottfredson and Hirschi describe high self-control as the "tendency to avoid acts whose long-term costs exceed their momentary advantages."[29] In other words, individuals with high self-control consider the long-term consequences of their behavior, whereas those with low self-control do not. Research on self-control suggests that it is learned, usually early in life, and once learned is highly resistant to change.

Of course, criminal motivation in and of itself does not produce a crime. Even the most motivated criminals must have opportunity. Opportunities are, in major part, determined by the activities of one's daily life—"work, leisure, and the ways by which humans acquire food, shelter, and other basic needs or desires."[30] Thus, routine activities often provide means for offenders to act out their motivations.

Organizational Misconduct

Although fraud theory applies to individuals, an extension to organizational misconduct is intuitive. After all, the misconduct of an organization is perpetrated by its agents or employees. For purposes of our discussion, we define ***organizational misconduct*** as misconduct performed by individuals on behalf of an organization. Research on organizational misconduct has historically focused on the *why* (why fraud occurs). The dominant working theory proposes that misconduct occurs when an individual in an organization encounters the right combination of *pressure* and *opportunity*, without the fear of detection.[31] At the extreme, this proposition, like fraud theory, assumes that organizational agents are amoral rational thinkers, weighing costs against benefits.

For example, we accept that financial statement fraud ("cooking the books") is driven by a company's pressure to conceal true financial performance. Given this pressure, what would drive its management, especially lower-level management, to commit fraud on the company's behalf? Self-interest? Peer pressure? Or perhaps it is something less sinister, such as unreflective reliance or acceptance? Again, because each organization is unique, as are the individuals within the organization, there can be no single right answer. Moreover, it is likely that a combination of motives is at play.

In large organizations, where financial pressures are often present and opportunities for misconduct are more difficult to control, the leadership of top management is especially critical in building an ethical culture that discourages misconduct. This is sometimes referred to as "tone at the top." Consistent with our experience, research suggests that tone at the top is most influential on individuals with lower positions in the company hierarchy.

*** Two types of self-control measures are common: (1) attitudinal measures, which have respondents rate themselves on indicators of self-control, and (2) behavioral measures, which assess involvement in noncriminal acts thought to be manifestations of low self-control.

WHO COMMITS FRAUD?

It is estimated that 85% of the population would commit fraud given the right stimulus or tipping point, and 5% would do so regardless of the conditions.[32] This leaves only 10% who would not commit fraud under any circumstances. Does this statistic surprise you? Where do you see yourself in the mix?

Alongside the development of fraud theory, research has examined the questions of whether certain individuals are more likely than others to commit fraud and, if so, whether they can be identified. In other words, is there a typical fraudster? According to a 2011 KPMG study, which examined 348 fraud investigations in 69 countries, a typical white-collar fraudster has the following characteristics:[33]

- Above-average intelligence
- Relatively well-educated
- 36–45 years old
- Male
- White
- Inclined to take risk
- Commits fraud against own employer
- Works in collusion with another offender
- Employed by the company for more than ten years
- Holds a senior management position
- Works in finance or accounting
- Lacks feelings of anxiety and empathy
- Feels a lack of control over circumstances (external locus of control)

In-Class Exercise

Are the previous characteristics of the typical fraudster consistent with the various propositions of fraud theory introduced in this chapter? Can you match each characteristic with a specific theoretical concept (fraud triangle, fraud diamond, general theory of crime, and so on)?

VICTIMS OF WHITE-COLLAR CRIME

White-collar crimes are often a low priority for law enforcement. Furthermore, victims frequently encounter skepticism, suspicion, and contempt when they seek to report an offense. Even when law enforcement does pursue a case, financial crimes are often difficult and expensive to prove. This is due to the data-intensive nature of such cases and the challenge of using circumstantial evidence to infer intent. Finally, most law enforcement agencies are often ill-prepared to properly investigate and prosecute such crimes.

Even when tried and convicted, offenders commonly receive light or no detention and rarely make full restitution (remember Bonnie Bain!). Offenders generally consume available resources, including fruits of the fraud, before being identified or in their defense. Moreover, being a convicted felon reduces one's earnings capacity and thus the ability to pay restitution. Common post-conviction strategies include bankruptcy, living via cash (no bank accounts), and no accumulation of assets. Of course, the goal of such strategies is to make oneself "judgment-proof."

Given these realities of the justice system, fraud victims are often left with no closure, which may impede their financial and psychological recovery. Moreover, fraud victims often lack support from family and friends, who blame them or ridicule them for their gullibility.

The point of this discussion is that financial crimes are not victimless acts. Real people are damaged—not only financially, but psychologically as well.

THE GOVERNMENT IS NOT ALWAYS RIGHT

The government, like any organization, is made up of individuals. As discussed in Chapter 2, the government generally advances a financial crimes case following the filing and investigation of a criminal complaint, accompanied by an investigator's affidavit that summarizes the evidence against a suspect. Which financial crimes are prosecuted is determined by the local prosecuting attorney (federal or state) and generally selected based on probability of conviction, operating plan, budget, notoriety, and public impact. Keep in mind that an indictment is not a statement of fact—it is simply an accusation.

Although the majority of criminal indictments are based on good-faith evidence and belief of wrongdoing, misconduct on the part of prosecutors is not uncommon. ***Prosecutorial misconduct*** is an "act (or failure to act), especially involving an attempt to avoid required disclosure or to persuade the jury to wrongly convict a defendant or assess an unjustified punishment."[34] Examples of prosecutorial misconduct include hiding, destroying, or tampering with evidence; failing to disclose evidence that might exonerate the defendant (exculpatory evidence); and threatening witnesses.

Dig Deeper

Consider conditions that might contribute to prosecutorial misconduct. Can these include the same elements as the fraud triangle (pressure, opportunity, and rationalization)? A classic example of prosecutorial misconduct is *United States v. Senator Ted Stevens.* Research this case and identify lessons learned.

WHY YOU NEED TO KNOW

After reading this chapter, it should be clear that *fraud is not an accounting problem*—it is a social phenomenon. Thus, an understanding of the offender's perceptions, opportunities, and risk-assessment processes ("criminal calculus") is critical in fraud engagements.

All organizations are exposed to fraud risks, and no organization—no matter how vigilant—can eliminate fraud with complete certainty. Accepting this proposition, the challenge of a forensic accountant might be to investigate, detect, or deter (but not eliminate) fraud. Although we are not criminologists, forensic accountants must have some understanding of why criminals do what they do. The better prepared you are, the more efficient and effective you will be.

APPENDIX 6-A

State of West Virginia v. Keith O. Peoples

Indictment: Obtaining Money by Fraudulent Schemes (Felony)

Filed May 15, 2008

Charleston Police Officer Indicted on Fraud Charges*

On May 16, 2008, a Kanawha County grand jury charged 44-year-old Corporal Keith O. Peoples with obtaining money by fraudulent schemes. The indictment alleged that, from January 19, 2001, through August 24, 2004, Peoples unlawfully, feloniously, and willfully engaged in a scheme to defraud Forest City Enterprises (d/b/a Charleston Town Center Mall, hereinafter "TCM") and the Charleston Police Department, City of Charleston, West Virginia (hereinafter "CPD") of money, goods, and services by means of fraudulent pretenses.

---

*Go to www.pearsonhighered.com/rufus for a link to this article.

The felony fraud indictment alleged that Peoples, CPD's former Officer of the Year, was unlawfully being compensated as a security officer by a private employer (TCM) while on duty with CPD, a scheme commonly known as "double-dipping." Elements of the offense[†] include: (1) the intent to defraud, (2) an actual fraud, (3) the use of false pretense to accomplish the fraud, and (4) the false pretense induced the owner to part with his property. If convicted, Peoples faced imprisonment for a period up to two years and a maximum fine of $2,500.

Following his arraignment, in which he entered a "not guilty" plea, Cpl. Peoples was immediately placed on administrative leave[‡] pending the outcome of the criminal proceeding.

Opening Statements in Case of Double-Dipping

Peoples's trial began on May 18, 2009, one year after his indictment. In opening arguments, Kanawha County Assistant Prosecutor Scott Reynolds stated, "While there is nothing unusual about someone having two jobs . . . it is unusual, in fact impossible, to be in two places at the same time." Reynolds told the jury that, through an internal investigation conducted by CPD, it was determined that Peoples was "charging two employers (CPD and TCM) for the same time," a fraudulent scheme known as double-dipping.

Reynolds promised the jury documentary and testimonial evidence regarding the process and results of the investigation, which proved Peoples's intent to defraud beyond a reasonable doubt. Reynolds advised that the lead investigator, Captain Tabaretti, would "explain what he did and why he did it" in investigating the fraudulent scheme. Finally, Reynolds described the alleged crime as "a violation of public trust and a case of common sense . . . you simply can't be in two places at the same time."

Peoples's attorney, Dwane Tinsley, cautioned the jury, "This is a high stakes case—Keith Peoples's life, career, and civil liberties are at stake." Tinsley advised that, through the entirety of the proceeding, "There are two terms you must keep in mind—intent and burden of proof." He instructed the jury that the state was required to prove every element of the crime beyond a reasonable doubt, specifically that Keith Peoples "knowingly committed a crime."

Tinsley encouraged the jury to question Cpt. Tabaretti's investigation, which he characterized as "ripe with investigative error and completely void of reasoning." Tinsley argued that, although the state had refused to consider alternative explanations for its calculations of overlapping hours, it was the jury's duty to do so. He proffered, "Having two jobs is not a crime . . . going to your second job after you've been released is not a crime." Finally, Tinsley urged the jurors to "actively listen" to all the testimony being presented by the state and to ask themselves "Why are we here, and does this make sense?"

Following opening arguments by both attorneys, the state introduced its first two witnesses: a payroll clerk and the City Auditor. Both testified that the payroll records given to Cpt. Tabaretti were "complete and accurate copies." During cross-examination, both acknowledged that the term "accurate" meant "accurate copies . . . not accurate data." The City Auditor also acknowledged that her office did not "audit" the payroll submissions from the various departments and would only question something (for example, overtime) if it "jumped off the page."

Day 2: When Is a Police Officer "Off Duty"?

On the second day of trial (May 19, 2009), the state introduced its third witness, Dennis Lewis, the Security Director at TCM. During direct examination, Lewis testified as follows:

- He is a retired CPD officer.
- TCM commonly hires "off-duty" police officers as security guards because "presence is very important."

[†] WV Code §61-3-24 (2008).

[‡] Leave from active duty with pay and benefits.

- TCM pays the officers "to perform their normal duties, but on our property, during mall hours."
- They are "not supposed to be on the clock at CPD while they're working at the mall."
- TCM policy mandates that they be "off duty."
- A computerized time clock with "swipe cards" is used to record time (in and out) and is very accurate.
- The computer payroll records were provided to Cpt. Tabaretti.

During cross-examination, Lewis testified as follows:

- He knows Cpl. Peoples and believes that "he is well respected and does a good job."
- He does not coordinate the schedules of CPD officers working at TCM; rather, this is done by the Officer Coordinator, James Sands.
- TCM's policy regarding "Officer Duties and Responsibilities" was authored by Sands. Although the policy is supposed to be communicated to and acknowledged by (via signature) all officers, he admitted that a signed statement was not located for Cpl. Peoples.
- James Sands had direct contact with the officers and was "always recruiting."
- Sands is "probably the best guy to speak with" regarding the officers.
- As a former police officer, he is aware that officers are occasionally released early and receive two-hour minimum overtime slips for court appearances, even if they only last fifteen minutes. He described this as "established practice."
- He considered "off duty" to include an early release or the balance of an overtime slip (that is, difference between actual time and the two-hour minimum).

The state's next witness was the General Manager of TCM, Thomas Bird. During direct examination, Bird testified as follows:

- The payroll records provided to Cpt. Tabaretti were true and accurate copies.
- TCM's policy requires that security officers be "off duty" from CPD.
- He is aware of Cpt. Tabaretti's payroll analysis, which indicates overlapping hours.
- Overlapping is unacceptable because it is a public safety issue—"Police officers need to be where they are supposed to be."
- Cpl. Peoples's employment had been suspended pending the outcome of the investigation.

During cross-examination, Bird testified as follows:

- He knows and respects Cpl. Peoples.
- Prior to this case, he had "little knowledge of the specific policies and procedures" regarding off-duty police officers. This was the task of the Security Director.
- He had "no knowledge of CPD's overtime policy or early releases."
- "Sands managed the off-duty officers . . . and wrote the policy."
- He sees "no problem with clocking in at the mall if released early . . . if not a problem for CPD."
- He "can't verify what hours were worked . . . just what was paid."
- He cannot personally confirm anything because the payroll records "were put together by someone in the payroll department."
- He believes the records are "accurate and complete printouts" of payroll data.
- He told Cpl. Peoples that he was "missed" and "welcome to return" when cleared of the charges. Further, he acknowledged that he trusted Peoples or otherwise "would not have offered him his job back."
- He refused to speak with, and directed other TCM employees not to speak with, defense counsel's forensic accounting expert. When asked why, he responded:
    - It was a "waste of time" because the forensic accountant had already spoken with Cpt. Tabaretti.
    - He didn't want his "words twisted."
    - He did not receive approval from the prosecutor's office.

Two additional witnesses, both TCM employees, were introduced by the state to: (1) verify that the payroll records provided to Cpt. Tabaretti were "accurate copies" and (2) explain the "swipe card" system.

Day 3: Cross-Examination Exposes Weakness in Double-Dipping Case

On day three of the trial (May 20, 2009), the state called its lead investigator, retired Cpt. John Tabaretti, to explain the process and results of the double-dipping investigation. During direct examination, Tabaretti testified as follows:

- He examined the payroll records (time sheets) of Cpl. Keith Peoples for the period Jan. 1, 2001, through Aug. 31, 2004, from both CPD and TCM.
- His analysis (methodology) involved a "massive Excel spreadsheet" for the subject period, providing a day-by-day, hour-by-hour, minute-by-minute comparison of Cpl. Peoples's time sheets for both employers.
- The analysis only considered "overlapping events that exceeded 5 minutes."
- Based on his analysis, Cpl. Peoples had 478 hours of overlapping time between the two employers when "he was on the clock of both employers at the same time."
- He revised (reduced) his original analysis of overlapping hours (478) in response to reasonable explanations (specifically, overtime slips) identified by the defense. He "gave Peoples the benefit of a doubt" and reduced the overlapping hours to "roughly 100."[§]
- The amount of money received by Cpl. Peoples from the alleged fraudulent scheme, using an hourly pay rate of $11.73, was originally estimated at $5,600. With the reduction of overlapping hours, this amount was reduced to $1,173.
- An hourly rate of $11.73 was conservative because it represented the lowest rate of pay received by Cpl. Peoples during the subject period.
- There was no real doubt that the economic loss resulting from Cpl. Peoples's overlapping scheme was substantially more than $1,000.

During cross-examination, Tabaretti testified (or acknowledged) as follows:

- He received his assignment from the CPD Chief.
- The Chief identified Peoples and described the fraudulent scheme.
- Although he had no specialized training in forensic accounting, he was an experienced investigator and was skilled in using Excel spreadsheets.
- He had no working hypothesis but "just followed the evidence." When pressed on this issue, he acknowledged that his assignment was "outlined by the Chief" and limited in scope to Peoples, CPD, and TCM.
- He believed that "verified payroll" meant true and accurate data, not just accurate copies. When challenged regarding the accuracy of the data, he responded, "It doesn't change anything—he got paid what he got paid."
- He is vaguely familiar with the "leads doctrine" and believes it requires investigators to consider and follow up on reasonable leads or tips during an investigation.
- He considered and investigated all reasonable leads received during the subject investigation. However, when challenged, he could not identify any specific leads.
- He conducted interviews of witnesses to gather information. However, when challenged, he acknowledged that he had not interviewed Peoples's supervisors regarding overtime slips and early releases.
- CPD used manual time sheets and not a time clock during the subject period, making the data "not exactly time certain."

[§] The felony charge required a loss of $1,000 or more. Thus, 85.25 hours (@ $11.73 per hour) of overlapping was the minimum necessary to support the allegation.

- The manual time sheets, which were prepared by unit supervisors at the beginning of a pay period, were used both as a "work schedule" and a pay record.
- He did not actually inspect the "source" time sheets but rather the summary (computer) data, because the original time sheets were destroyed by CPD.
- It is possible, although "not likely," that a data-entry error could have been made when entering the time sheet data into the computer. He believes that the City Auditor "double checks" to confirm hours.
- He now understands that "overtime slips from CPD do not necessarily reflect time worked" because officers receive two hours of overtime pay for court appearances even if less time is required.
- He adjusted his original calculation to account for the overtime slips, which reduced the number of overlapping hours from 478 to roughly 100.
- He did not adjust his calculation before the trial because he was unaware that the overtime slips "did not necessarily reflect time actually worked."
- He acknowledged that police officers were occasionally (but "rarely") released early by their supervisors for various reasons; however:
    - He has no knowledge (proof certain) of how early releases were accounted for—the supervisor may have adjusted the time sheets.
    - He has no proof certain of how frequently Cpl. Peoples was released early over the subject period but believes it was "not a hundred hours."
    - He did not adjust his analysis for any early releases because this was speculation on the part of the defense with no supporting evidence.
- He acknowledged his failure to interview Peoples's supervisors regarding the overtime slips and early release issues, because he "thought other officers were doing it." When pressed on this proposition, he could not identify who this might have been.
- He understands the time period is nearly four years ("3 years and 8 months").
- He did "discuss with some folks at CPD" the accounting for early releases. Based on these discussions, he understands that time sheets are "adjusted for early releases."
- He acknowledged that adjusting the time sheets "would make no sense if it were a reward or consideration for working over."
- It would be unreasonable to reduce the overlapping hours for speculation about early releases, defining speculation as "a guess." However, he acknowledged that interviewing witnesses (such as Peoples's supervisors) would have been important.
- He acknowledged that, if a supervisor had confirmed the early releases, it would not be speculation.
- He acknowledged the testimonial evidence from Cpl. Peoples's immediate supervisors confirming early releases. However, he still considers it speculation due to a lack of supporting facts.
- He understands that the state has the burden of proof.
- He asserted that he did consider alternative explanations—the adjustment for overtime hours. However, he acknowledged that alternative explanations were not initially considered.
- He stated, "There is no way Peoples had 100 hours of early releases—it's not reasonable." When asked, "How do you know what's reasonable . . . if you didn't ask," he replied, "I know what's reasonable . . . 100 hours is not believable."

After calling seven witnesses over three days (including Tabaretti), the state rested its case. Peoples's attorney, Dwane Tinsley, then made a Motion for a Directed Verdict,** arguing that the state had failed to meet its burden of proof and failed to present any evidence regarding the requisite element of intent. Tinsley's motion was denied.

** A ruling by the trial judge taking a case from the jury because the evidence will permit only one reasonable verdict.

Day 4: Defense Calls First Witnesses

On day four of the trial (May 21, 2009), the defense called its first witness, former CPD Chief Dallas Staples. During direct examination, Staples testified as follows:

- CPD's time sheets are not time sensitive—that is, do not represent actual hours worked. To suggest otherwise is "disingenuous at best."
- He advised that overtime slips and early releases ("15 to 20 minutes") were very common and could result in the overlapping of time as computed by Tabaretti.
- The time sheets were not adjusted by supervisors for early releases.
- In the case of an early release, "Officers are free to do what they will—go home, go to the gym . . . or go to a second job."
- Overtime slips do not represent actual hours worked; rather they are an "officer incentive."
- All officers are familiar with early releases and minimum overtime for court appearances.

During cross-examination, Staples testified as follows:

- He acknowledged that it is not possible to be in two places at the same time.
- He acknowledged that it is not reasonable for an officer to provide protective services for both CPD and TCM at the same time.
- He had not spoken with Peoples's supervisors regarding early releases or overtime slips.
- He had not conducted an independent investigation.

Attorney Tinsley then requested a re-direct examination, during which Staples testified as follows:

- He had reviewed Tabaretti's analysis—it was not complete.
- Tabaretti's calculation of overlapping hours does not represent the situation described by the state: "You've got to understand that when you're released early you're off duty . . . the same with overtime slips."
- "These overlapping hours do not represent a scheme to cheat anyone . . . this only proves that Peoples used his early release time and excess overtime working at the mall."

The second witness for the defense was retired Cpt. Brad Rinehart, Cpl. Peoples's former shift commander. During direct examination, Rinehart testified as follows:

- Keith Peoples is a "police officer's police officer."
- Early releases were "more common than not, usually 15 to 20 minutes."
- He would not have "adjusted" the time sheets.
- Time sheets are not time clocks and are thus not precise, allowing for "mistakes in hours and dates."
- He recalls occasions when Peoples was released 1–2 hours early for exceptional performance.
- Two-hour minimum overtime is a long-term practice, and these hours do not represent actual hours worked.

During cross-examination, Rinehart testified as follows:

- He considers Peoples a friend and a "great police officer."
- He does not recall the exact number of occasions when Peoples was released early, but it was common.
- He does not consider 100 hours of early releases over a period of three and a half years to be excessive, since it was a very common practice.
- Early releases were considerations or rewards for things such as overtime from a prior day or good work. Thus, "adjusting the time sheets would have made no sense."

The third defense witness was James Sands. During direct examination, Sands testified as follows:

- He is a retired CPD officer currently employed by TCM as Officer Coordinator.
- After his retirement, he entered a plea agreement with the state regarding a double-dipping charge and was ordered to pay back the money he had earned from CPD.
- He had been Keith Peoples's immediate supervisor at TCM.
- He authored TCM's Officer Duties and Responsibility policy.
- The policy was very lax and not enforced, representing "more of a guide than a policy."
- The phrase "off duty" was being taken out of context: "An officer released early is still officially on duty . . . but free to do what he will."
- Overtime slips are used as an incentive and do not necessarily reflect being "on duty."
- He authorized Peoples to leave the mall premises while on the clock if he was called out on an emergency or arrest, with the expectation that Peoples would call to check in.

During cross-examination, Sands testified as follows:

- He had recently entered a felony plea agreement for double-dipping.
- He is not angry with the state because of the felony and early retirement from CPD.
- He considers Peoples a friend.
- Peoples was his "go-to guy" at TCM and was always willing to help.
- He had not reviewed Tabaretti's analysis of overlapping hours and was speaking generally about early releases and overtime slips.
- He has no direct knowledge of Peoples's early releases or overtime slips.

Additional witnesses for the defense (administrative personnel, supervisors, and other police officers) provided testimony supporting Cpl. Peoples and the defense's arguments, specifically minimum overtime hours, frequency of early releases, and unreliability of payroll records.

Day 5: Defense Calls Forensic Accounting Expert

On the fifth and final day of trial (May 22, 2009), the defense called its forensic accounting expert to the stand. During direct examination, the expert testified as follows:

- He was engaged by defense counsel (Attorney Tinsley).
- The engagement had three primary objectives:
  - Evaluate the evidence for certainty
  - Evaluate the data for meaningful conclusions
  - Evaluate the representations made by the state
- For the purpose of the engagement, certainty was measured as the state's burden of proof—beyond a reasonable doubt.
- Reasonable doubt would be defined by the court. However, as a frame for his analysis, it was considered "no real doubt."
- He presented a "probability ladder" to the jury identifying different thresholds—possible, probable, clear and convincing, and beyond a reasonable doubt.
- Probable is measured as "more than 50% likely . . . whereas beyond a reasonable doubt is much, much greater . . . a percentage cannot be assigned because it varies per individual." Research indicates it is most commonly measured as "more than 90% likely."
- A scientific approach was employed in the evaluation process. He explained to the jury each step of the process and each source of evidence considered.
- The state's use of the term "verified payroll" was erroneous and grossly misleading. He explained the limitations and uncertainties of the payroll data to the jury.

- The state (Tabaretti) erroneously accepted and relied on CPD's payroll records as being accurate, time sensitive, and authoritative, although "nothing could be further from the truth."
- The state (Tabaretti) properly calculated overlapping events but failed to refine and confirm the data or to consider alternative explanations.
- The state (Tabaretti) failed to follow-up on leads (per the leads doctrine), specifically with regard to payroll errors, overtime slips, and early releases.
- The state (Tabaretti) failed to conduct interviews of Peoples's supervisors and fellow officers regarding overtime slips and early releases.
- The state (Tabaretti) failed to consider that "permitted" (for example, emergency) exits from TCM would result in an overlapping event.
- The expert's concluding opinions were as follows:
    - The evidence (payroll records analysis) does not provide for certainty.
    - The data presented by the state does not support a meaningful conclusion.
    - The state failed to properly investigate the allegation, including a failure to consider alternative explanations.
    - "Overlapping" is expected and unavoidable.
    - The state's analysis is based on unreliable data, unreliable facts, and a flawed methodology.
    - "The state cannot prove its case to any level of certainty."

There was a limited cross-examination, the highlights of which include the following:

- He acknowledged there was evidence of overlapping.
    - The expert qualified this acknowledgment, stating that overlapping is expected and unavoidable—that is, nothing sinister.
- He acknowledged that the investigative plan outlined by Tabaretti was reasonable.
    - The expert noted that the problem wasn't the plan; it was Tabaretti's failure to follow the plan, including failures to refine and confirm preliminary observations and to consider alternative explanations.
    - The expert opined that Tabaretti ignored evidence that did not support his hypothesis because "he seemed to be on a mission."
- Tabaretti reduced his calculation of overlapping hours from 478 hours to roughly 100 hours.
    - The expert refused to accept the state's proposition that the adjustment was made in response to "new knowledge" regarding overtime slips. He proffered that everyone in CPD knew, or should have known, that overtime slips do not reflect actual time worked.
    - The expert refused to acknowledge any value in Tabaretti's analysis, describing it as "ripe with failure and bias."

There was no re-direct examination. Following the testimony of the forensic accounting expert, the defense rested. Keith Peoples did not take the witness stand.

The Court's Instructions

Before the start of closing arguments, the judge reviewed the jury's instructions and provided legal definitions, specifically those addressing the concepts of evidence, intent, burden of proof, presumption of innocence, and proof beyond a reasonable doubt. Highlights include the following:

- It is the duty of the jury to impartially determine the facts of the case from all the evidence. Your oath requires you to accept and apply the law as stated in these instructions. You must not change the law or apply your own idea of what you think the law should be.
- You are to consider only the evidence presented, and you may not guess or speculate as to the existence of any facts. You must not be influenced in any way by either sympathy or prejudice for or against the defendant or the state.

- You are permitted to draw from facts which you find have been proved and such reasonable inferences as you feel are justified in the light of your own experience, reason, and common sense.
- The burden is always on the state to prove guilt beyond a reasonable doubt . . . the burden never shifts to a defendant.
- If the jury, after careful and impartial consideration of all the evidence in the case, has a reasonable doubt that the defendant is guilty of the charge, it must acquit.
- A reasonable doubt is a doubt based upon reason and common sense, the kind of doubt that would make a reasonable person hesitate to act. Proof beyond a reasonable doubt, therefore, must be proof of such a convincing character that a reasonable person would not hesitate to rely and act upon it.
- The jury will remember that the defendant is never to be convicted on suspicion, conjecture, or speculation.
- A verdict of not guilty does not necessarily mean that the innocence of the defendant has been established. It only means that guilt, beyond a reasonable doubt, has not been proved.
- Nothing said or done by the attorneys who have tried this case is to be considered by you as evidence of any fact.
- Expert testimony was admitted in this case. When scientific, technical, or other specialized knowledge might be helpful in a case, a person who has special training or experience in a particular field is allowed to state an opinion about the matter. That does not mean that you must accept the expert witness's opinion. As with any other witness, you must decide the extent to which, if any, to rely upon the opinion offered.
- You, as the jurors, are the sole judges of the credibility of a witness and the weight of the evidence.
- You may have noticed that the defendant did not testify at this trial. The defendant has an absolute right not to testify, since the entire burden of proof in this case is on the state to prove that the defendant is guilty. It is not up to the defendant to prove that he is innocent. The fact that the defendant did not testify has nothing to do with the question of whether he is guilty or not guilty. You are not to draw any adverse inference against the defendant because he did not testify. You are not to consider it in any way, or even discuss it in your deliberations. You must determine whether the state has proved its case against the defendant based solely on the testimony of the witnesses and the exhibits.

Closing Arguments

The court granted each side 30 minutes for closing arguments. The state advised the court it would use 20 minutes in the opening and 10 minutes for rebuttal.

Reynolds began by reminding the jury that this was a case about fraud—obtaining money by false pretenses. He described Peoples's alleged crime as a common fraud scheme, a case of double dipping where the value of the money is more than $1,000. Reynolds stated, "This case boils down to very simple matters—you can't be in two places at the same time." He told the jury that to be fair, and to remove any doubt, Tabaretti had adjusted his analysis for the overtime slips. Even so, the amount stolen was still more than $1,000. Reynolds acknowledged the possibility of some early releases, but not 100 hours.

Reynolds then moved to the issue of intent, acknowledging that "none of us are mind readers." He reminded the jury of the judge's instructions that intent to commit fraud may be inferred by the facts and circumstances of the case. Further, Reynolds encouraged the jury to remember the facts of the case—that Peoples routinely clocked in at TCM while still on duty with CPD, not once, not a few times, but more than 100 hours' worth.

Reynolds dismissed each of the defense's arguments—two-hour minimum overtime slips, early releases, authorized exits from TCM, and payroll errors. He reminded the jury about TCM's policy mandating that officers be "off duty," the testimony of Thomas Bird regarding his alarm about the overlapping hours and related concern for the public's safety, and, finally, the analysis of retired Captain John Tabaretti.

Reynolds challenged the jury to question whether Peoples knew his actions were wrong. "Sure he did," stated Reynolds, "he most certainly knew. Did we prove it? Yes—remember the evidence." Reynolds concluded by re-emphasizing the importance of common sense: "You simply can't be in two places at the same time."

Tinsley opened by asking the jury to remember his opening questions: Why are we here? Does this makes sense? Tinsley walked the jury through the state's case, first addressing the conflicting testimony of the Auditor, payroll personnel, and Tabaretti regarding the accuracy of the payroll records. He reminded the jury that Tabaretti "thought the data contained in the records was accurate." "Nothing could be further from the truth," stated Tinsley. "Remember these were just accurate copies . . . not accurate data." Tinsley proffered that Tabaretti simply did not understand the "gaps in the data."

Tinsley then turned to the testimony of TCM representatives Dennis Lewis and Thomas Bird. "Remember what they said," prompted Tinsley, "Jim Sands had direct contact with the officers . . . he's the guy to talk to." Tinsley continued, "And what did Jim Sands tell us? That the term of being off duty has been purposely taken out of context by the state . . . that he authorized Peoples to leave the mall premises while on the clock during callout emergencies."

Tinsley argued that Tabaretti was on a mission, stating, "You must ask yourselves, if Tabaretti is a trained investigator, as the state would have you believe, why didn't he investigate?" Tinsley reminded the jury that "Tabaretti got his marching orders from the Chief." He did no investigation but "simply built a spreadsheet . . . and you can't convict someone with a spreadsheet . . . you've got to look beyond the numbers."

After challenging the state's witnesses, Tinsley turned to the testimony of his forensic accounting expert, reminding the jury of the due diligence employed. He stated, "Our expert, the only expert testifying in this case, assessed Tabaretti's work for what it is—a complete investigative failure." Tinsley continued, "The only thing we know for certain from Tabaretti is uncertainty. The state, and its investigator Tabaretti, simply failed to investigate the allegations against Cpl. Peoples. Why? A rush to judgment? A mission? We cannot ascribe a motive, we can't read their minds. We do know, however, that they failed to conduct an investigation . . . and continue to ignore evidence that undermines the charges."

Tinsley's closing argument focused on "two words—intent and burden of proof." He advised the jury, "The state has attempted to confuse you with a spreadsheet—mathematical certainty they cry. Mathematical certainty does not prove intent. The state has presented no evidence of intent—not one piece of evidence." Tinsley reminded the jury that the state has the burden, beyond a reasonable doubt. He questioned, "Has the State met this burden? No! The only thing the state has proven is uncertainty."

Finally, Tinsley encouraged the jury to consider the high stakes of this case—that "Keith Peoples's life, career, reputation, and civil liberties are at stake." He repeated the words of Cpt. Brad Rinehart: "Keith Peoples is a police officer's police officer." Thus, he concluded, "You must acquit."

During his rebuttal arguments, Reynolds advised the jury that the defense "has done a good job of muddying up the water." He stated, "The defense described Cpl. Peoples as a 'police officer's police officer.' And to that, I have no doubt. But even Keith Peoples . . . can't be in two places at the same time. It's simply not possible."

Reynolds continued, "The defense has pulled out all the stops to criticize the work of Cpt. John Tabaretti. What choice did they have? The defense argues that mathematical certainty does not prove intent. We disagree. Think about what they didn't challenge—the certainty of overlapping. The defense argues that 100 hours of early releases is reasonable . . . expected and unavoidable. We disagree. One hundred hours is not expected . . . and certainly not acceptable. This is not a mistake, an oversight."

Reynolds concluded by highlighting the inconsistency of Peoples's alleged actions with the integrity of his office. "The defendant is a sworn police officer . . . sworn to uphold the law. As a police officer, he took an oath to obey the law, to enforce the law—the same body of law he is now accused of breaking. The state has shown, beyond a reasonable doubt, that he has broken the law—intentionally broken the law. Ladies and gentlemen, I've completed my task, and it is now up to you."

The Jury's Verdict

After more than eight hours of deliberation, the jury found Cpl. Peoples not guilty of fraudulent schemes. Upon receiving this news, Charleston Mayor Danny Jones and CPD Chief Brent Webster told the press that Peoples was expected back on the job at the earliest opportunity. They also advised that the verdict signaled an end to the investigation of double dipping within CPD.

Epilogue

On June 1, 2009, Cpl. Keith Peoples was restored to active duty with CPD. Shortly thereafter, on June 15, 2009, he returned to his second job as a TCM security officer. In May 2011, he was promoted to the rank of Sergeant.

On May 21, 2010, nearly two years after his indictment, Keith Peoples sued the City of Charleston in Kanawha County Circuit Court. The lawsuit claims that, as a direct result of the state's unlawful investigation, Peoples was deprived of his liberty, forced to answer criminal charges, forced to endure the mental anguish and strain of a trial, expended large sums of money for legal and expert fees, was subject to personal humiliation and disgrace, and suffered permanent damage to his reputation. In December 2012, the parties entered into a sealed settlement agreement.

Key Terms

Calculus of fraud
Fraud
Fraud triangle
General theory of crime
Neutralization
Opportunity
Organizational misconduct
Pressure
Prosecutorial misconduct
Rational choice theory
Rationalization
White-collar crime

Chapter Questions

6-1. What has caused forensic accounting to become a highly visible component of the accounting profession?

6-2. What unique skills do forensic accountants possess that are useful in the area of fraud investigation?

6-3. Identify and discuss five key aspects of financial crimes.

6-4. What is the difference between robbery and fraud?

6-5. Why is "beyond a reasonable doubt" the applicable standard of proof for a fraud charge?

6-6. Define fraud.

6-7. Identify and discuss the four basic elements of fraud as established by common law.

6-8. Explain why fraud is a crime of intent.

6-9. Define intent.

6-10. Without a confession, how is fraudulent intent established?

6-11. Define circumstantial evidence. In addition to data analysis, what other factors might offer circumstantial evidence of fraudulent intent?

6-12. Define white-collar crime.

6-13. Identify and explain six attributes of white-collar crime.

6-14. Identify several federal agencies that participate in the enforcement of federal white-collar crime.

6-15. Identify the FBI's eight major categories of white-collar crime. Provide one example of each.

6-16. Identify several other categories of white-collar crime that are outside the jurisdiction of the FBI.

6-17. Describe Donald Cressey's seminal research on which fraud theory is founded.

6-18. Identify the three elements of the fraud triangle and provide a short definition of each.

6-19. How does the fraud triangle contribute to a forensic accountant's understanding of why people commit fraud?

6-20. Identify three personal characteristics that might serve as indicators or "red flags" of fraudulent activity. Briefly discuss each.

6-21. Identify three organizational characteristics that might serve as indicators or "red flags" of fraudulent activity. Briefly discuss each.

6-22. How do personal and organizational "red flags" relate to the fraud triangle? Provide an example to support your position.

6-23. What is the most common type of financial statement fraud? What are the two primary motivators of this type of fraud?

6-24. In the fraud diamond, how does capability contribute to the possibility of fraud?

6-25. Explain the knucklehead defense. How is it related to the fraud diamond?

6-26. How does the fraud scale differ from the fraud triangle?

6-27. According to traditional economic theory, what motivates a person to commit fraud?

6-28. Set forth the calculus of fraud equation, and discuss each component.

6-29. Can a simple model fully and accurately explain why a person commits fraud? Explain.

6-30. Define rational choice theory and discuss its two components.

6-31. Define neutralization. How is it related to the fraud triangle?

6-32. Identify three common neutralization techniques and briefly discuss each.

6-33. Discuss three common denial techniques used by fraudsters.

6-34. Define the general theory of crime and discuss its components.

6-35. Compare and contrast high and low self-control. How do these conditions impact a person's propensity to commit fraud?

6-36. What is the relationship between personal misconduct and organizational misconduct?

6-37. How can an organization's "tone at the top" influence the likelihood of organizational misconduct?

6-38. Researchers estimate that 85% of the population would commit fraud given the right stimulus, and 5% would do so regardless of the conditions. Does this statistic surprise you? How might knowledge of this propensity be valuable to organizational leadership?

6-39. Identify several characteristics of a typical white-collar fraudster.

6-40. Explain why the investigation of white-collar crimes is often a low priority for law enforcement agencies.

6-41. Explain why a forensic accountant must understand the perceptions, opportunities, and risk-assessment processes of a fraudster to successfully combat fraud.

Multiple-Choice Questions

Select the best response to the following questions related to fraud and white-collar crime:

6-42. The two methods of illegally obtaining property from others are theft and fraud.

- **a.** True
- **b.** False

6-43. Fraud is:

- **a.** The use of force to obtain property
- **b.** The use of deception to obtain property
- **c.** The use of the law to obtain property
- **d.** The use of political action to obtain property

6-44. Each of the following is a common law element of fraud *except*:

- **a.** A material false statement or omission
- **b.** A fraudster is an expert in the area in which the fraud is committed
- **c.** An intention to induce a victim to rely on false information
- **d.** The fraudster knew the statement was false or information was omitted
- **e.** The victim relied on the statement or omission

6-45. Which of the following best describes fraud?

- **a.** A criminal offense
- **b.** A capital offense
- **c.** A political offense
- **d.** None of the above

6-46. As emphasized in this chapter, fraud is:

- **a.** A crime of passion
- **b.** A crime of force
- **c.** A contest of wills
- **d.** A crime of intent

6-47. If a fraudster does not confess, which of the following is needed in order to establish fraudulent intent?

- **a.** Direct inquiry evidence
- **b.** Negotiation
- **c.** Circumstantial evidence
- **d.** Explicit evidence

6-48. What key factors determine the reliability of circumstantial evidence for the purpose of establishing intent?

- **a.** The degree of impact
- **b.** The nature of the fraud
- **c.** Alternative explanations
- **d.** Both a and b
- **e.** Both a and c

6-49. Under which of the following sets of conditions is circumstantial evidence deemed reliable?

	Alternative Explanations	Degree of Impact
a	Exist	High
b.	None	High
c.	Exist	Low
d.	None	Low

6-50. Which of the following best defines circumstantial evidence?

a. A set of logically obtained facts
b. A collection of fragmented evidence that supports one inference over another
c. Forensic observations and societal models that are developed by a forensic accountant
d. A set of evidence that has been reviewed and approved by a court in an approved jurisdiction

6-51. If properly developed and presented, circumstantial evidence can provide proof certain of fraudulent intent.

a. True
b. False

Select the best response to the following questions related to white-collar crime:

6-52. White-collar crime is a subcategory of theft, but is not considered to be a subcategory of fraud.

a. True
b. False

6-53. There is one specific, comprehensive definition of white-collar crime used by all forensic accountants.

a. True
b. False

6-54 The Commerce Clause of the U.S. Constitution gives the federal government the authority to police white-collar crime.

a. True
b. False

6-55. Each of the following is a type of white-collar crime identified by the FBI *except*:

a. Insurance fraud
b. Health care fraud
c. Securities fraud
d. Social Security fraud
e. All of the above are types of white-collar crime identified by the FBI

6-56. Each of the following is an attribute of white-collar crime *except*:

a. Concealment
b. Intent
c. Adroitness
d. Deceit
e. All of the above are attributes of white-collar crime

Select the best response to the following questions related to fraud theory:

6-57. According to Donald Cressey, fraud results from the convergence of what three factors?

a. Opportunity, preparation, rationalization
b. Rationalization, pressure, opportunity
c. Pressure, preparation, rationalization
d. Opportunity, preparation, pressure

6-58. A nonshareable problem that precedes a criminal violation of financial trust is:

a. Pressure
b. Secrecy
c. Concealment
d. Confidentiality

6-59. An individual who is in a position to manipulate or circumvent controls has:

a. Power
b. Relevance
c. Opportunity
d. Recourse

6-60. When a fraudster concludes that his or her fraudulent act is justified because of some prior action by the victim that caused harm to the fraudster, this is called:

a. Conceptualization
b. Remediation
c. Retribution
d. Rationalization

6-61. All of the following are among the top five personal characteristic "red flags" of fraud *except*:

a. A deep-seeded desire for revenge
b. Feeling of being underpaid
c. Living beyond one's means
d. Undue family and peer pressure

6-62. All of the following are among the top five organizational characteristic "red flags" of fraud *except*:

a. No clear lines of authority
b. No separation of duties between accounting functions
c. Placing too much trust in key employees
d. An autocratic leadership style

6-63. The most common type of financial statement fraud is:

a. Capitalizing expenses
b. Deferring goodwill write-offs
c. Overstatement of revenues
d. Manipulation of ending inventory

6-64. The fraud diamond adds which of the following elements to the fraud triangle?
- **a.** Capability
- **b.** Sensibility
- **c.** Accountability
- **d.** All of the above

6-65. When an attorney argues that "Even if my client was motivated and had the opportunity to commit the crime, he does not have the capability to carry it out," this is known as what type of defense?
- **a.** Rationalization defense
- **b.** Knucklehead defense
- **c.** Appeal to the compassion of the jury
- **d.** None of the above

6-66. In the fraud scale, the fraud triangle is modified by removing rationalization and replacing it with:
- **a.** Balance
- **b.** Behavioral consistency
- **c.** Integrity
- **d.** Mediation

Select the best response to the following questions related to fraud motivation:

6-67. According to economic theory, what motivates an individual to commit fraud?
- **a.** Fear
- **b.** Coercion
- **c.** Peer pressure
- **d.** Self-interest

6-68. Which of the following is *not* a component of the formula for the calculus of fraud?
- **a.** Perceived gravity of the loss
- **b.** Reward
- **c.** Impact on the victim
- **d.** Probability of getting caught

6-69. Human behavior is an exact science that can be predicted with certainty.
- **a.** True
- **b.** False

6-70. Rational choice is considered a crime-specific theory because different crimes meet different needs for the offender and because the context in which the rational choice occurs is unique to each offense.
- **a.** True
- **b.** False

6-71. Neutralization is a sub-theory of rationalization that proposes each of the following as a means that an offender might seek to neutralize his or her role in a crime *except*:
- **a.** Higher loyalty
- **b.** Condemnation
- **c.** Denial
- **d.** Rationale

6-72. Which of the following is *not* a denial technique commonly used by offenders to rationalize their action?
- **a.** Denial of the victim
- **b.** Denial of attribution
- **c.** Denial of responsibility
- **d.** Denial of injury

6-73. An effort to neutralize one's actions by shifting blame to those who are opposed to fraudulent behavior is called:
- **a.** Condemnation
- **b.** Blame shifting
- **c.** Cross blaming
- **d.** Blame denial

6-74. The general theory of crime posits that a crime is a natural consequence of a controlled human desire to seek pleasure and inflict pain.
- **a.** True
- **b.** False

6-75. Criminal motivation, in and of itself, does not produce a crime, because _____ is also necessary.
- **a.** Bravery
- **b.** Poor judgment
- **c.** Opportunity
- **d.** A mean spirit

Workplace Applications

6-76. Please review the *State of West Virginia v. Keith O. Peoples* case and respond to the following challenges:

1. The charge against Peoples was fraud, a criminal offense. Compare and contrast a criminal complaint with a civil complaint. Identify three significant differences.
2. Discuss the requisite standard of proof in a criminal trial—that is, beyond a reasonable doubt. What does this mean? How is it measured?
3. Fraud is an "intent" crime. Absent a confession, the state attempted to establish Peoples's intent via circumstantial evidence. Discuss the concept of intent. Describe the circumstantial evidence compiled by the state's lead investigator to establish intent.
4. Describe the significance of considering alternative explanations when conducting a fraud investigation. Was it important in this case? Explain your response.

5. Discuss the three conditions generally present when fraud occurs (the fraud triangle) in terms of the allegations against Peoples. What conditions can be identified, if any?
6. Review the court's instructions to the jury. Why are such instructions important?
7. What impact, if any, do you think Peoples's failure to testify had on the jury's deliberations?
8. How important were the opening and closing arguments?
9. Research the concepts of adversarial bias and confirmation bias. Was either or both of these biases present in this case? Explain your answer.
10. Based on the case summary, do you think Peoples was guilty of fraud? Explain your position.

6-77. Visit the FBI's web site and review a posting entitled *2009 Financial Crimes Report.* Read the Forensic Accountant Program section and prepare a memo to your instructor summarizing your findings.

Chapter Problems

6-78. Visit the FBI's web site and review a posting entitled *Common Fraud Schemes.* Select one of the fraud schemes and prepare a slide presentation for the class. This presentation should explain how the fraud is conducted and the FBI's tips for avoiding the fraud.

6-79. Visit the FBI's web site and review a posting entitled *2009 Financial Crimes Report.* Read the General Overview, Initiatives, and Significant Cases sections. Using the information in these sections, prepare a memo to your instructor setting forth the key aspects of the material you reviewed.

6-80. Obtain the *2012 ACFE Report to the Nations on Occupational Fraud and Abuse*. Review the sections on Perpetrators of Fraud, Victims of Fraud, and Fraud Detection. Prepare a memo to your instructor summarizing what you learned.

6-81. Obtain the *2007 Oversight Systems Report on Corporate Fraud.* After reviewing this report, respond to the following questions:

a. How has the prevalence of fraud changed since 2005?
b. What are the primary reasons that executive fraud occurs?
c. What measures are considered the most effective in preventing or deterring fraud?

Case

6-82. Mountain Bancorporation (Mountain Bancorp) was a holding company headquartered in Kentucky. The company had assets of just under $1 billion. During the heady days of the early 2000s, inflation was moderate, the economy was growing, and banks were making large real estate loans.

As the economy improved, competition among banks for all types of loans intensified, with commercial loans considered to be the most desirable of all. One specific commercial loan is the focus of this case study.

During this time, a new resort named Sky High was being developed near a major recreation area. This resort was aimed at upscale clients from New York and New Jersey, and it included all the appropriate amenities. The total cost of the development was about $12 million. Mountain Bancorp competed for this loan but lost it to another banking company.

A few years after the project was completed, one of Mountain Bancorp's directors, who also served as legal counsel for Sky High, suggested that the resort might be interested in refinancing with Mountain Bancorp. The lenders began to analyze Sky High's financial statements and perform other diligence work. In the middle of this process, Sky High's management unexpectedly informed Mountain Bancorp that the loan must be completed within two weeks or the resort would stay with its present bank.

The bank officers responsible for authorizing this loan were Terry Randall and Paul Tyre. Randall was the senior lender for Mountain Bancorp's largest bank. He was a 45-year-old college graduate with 20 years of lending experience. Tyre was the president of Mountain Bancorp's largest bank. He was a 43-year-old high school graduate with 18 years of banking experience.

The loan presented several problems for Mountain Bancorp. First, the amount of the loan was $12 million, which was $9 million above Mountain Bancorp's legal lending limit. This meant that $9 million of the loan needed to be shared with a larger banking organization. The organization that Mountain Bancorp normally used for such sharing arrangements was a large regional bank (Correspondent National). Correspondent National's lenders also had to perform financial analysis and other due diligence for the loan, which would take longer than two weeks to complete.

Another problem was created by the abbreviated loan processing period. When it came time to disburse the $12 million, the required financial analysis had not been completed. Moreover, there was only an informal commitment from Correspondent National to participate in the sharing agreement. Even so, Mountain Bancorp's lenders proceeded to close the loan, confident that Correspondent National would eventually underwrite the $9 million.

Correspondent National eventually accepted the $9 million portion of the loan, but with one important caveat. The bank required that the loan participation agreement include a recourse clause that allowed Correspondent National to return the loan to Mountain Bancorp at Correspondent's discretion. The significance of this recourse clause was that, for legal and regulatory purposes, the entire $12 million remained as Mountain Bancorp's credit risk. Thus, a third problem was created—the loan was now in violation of state and federal laws and regulations.

Mountain Bancorp's lenders never informed its board of this recourse provision, and subsequent audits by regulatory examiners, internal auditors, and external auditors never discovered it. The lending-limit violation went undetected until the real estate market crashed. When this happened, Correspondent National experienced significant loan losses. To reduce the risk of further charge-offs, Correspondent returned the Sky High loan to Mountain Bancorp in accordance with the recourse agreement. This required that Mountain Bancorp send $9 million to Correspondent National and that Mountain Bancorp rebook the amount.

To get the $9 million on the books of Mountain Bancorp, its lenders divided the loan into three loans in the amount of $3 million, each with a different name. This made it appear that each subloan was under the bank's legal lending limit. The transaction was not reported to Mountain Bancorp's loan committee or its board, as required by loan policy.

When the economy entered a recession, Sky High could no longer make payments on the $12 million loan. In response, Mountain Bancorp's lenders waived principal payments and capitalized interest, without informing the loan committee or the board. This action was predicated on the belief that the economy would eventually recover, allowing Sky High to resume its full loan payments. However, the situation worsened, and Sky High went into bankruptcy. At this time, it was discovered that Mountain Bancorp held the entire $12 million risk related to this loan. This was the final problem to beset Mountain Bancorp's lenders.

Because of the bankruptcy, a real estate appraisal valued the property at about $3 million, which led to a $9 million charge-off that significantly reduced the bank's capital position. In fact, had Mountain Bancorp not been acquired by another banking organization, it would likely have failed. As a result, jobs were lost, shareholder value was destroyed, and lives were ruined.

These events were discovered by a fraud investigator hired by the bank's board of directors. Following a three-month investigation, the investigator prepared a comprehensive report detailing his findings. This report was used by the local prosecuting attorney to bring charges against several of Mountain Bancorp's officers, including Randall and Tyre.

In their defense, Randall and Tyre argued that they approved the loan because they were under pressure from the board to obtain Sky High as a customer. They further asserted that they were blindsided by Correspondent National's requirement for a recourse agreement and failed to inform the board or the loan committee about it because the funds had already disbursed.

Based on the facts presented in this case, respond to the following questions:

1. Is this a white-collar crime? Explain.
2. Do Randall and Tyre fit the profile of a typical fraudster? Explain.
3. Are the three elements of the fraud triangle present in this case? If so, identify and discuss each.
4. Assuming the role of the fraud investigator, how would you plan your investigation? What evidence would you gather, and how would you analyze it?
5. How might the prosecution attempt to establish fraudulent intent on the part of Randall and Tyre?
6. Can the calculus of fraud be used to explain the actions of Randall and Tyre?
7. Is there an indication that Randall and Tyre used the neutralization techniques described in this chapter?
8. Assuming the role of the defense attorney for Randall or Tyre, what arguments might you present to combat the prosecution's allegation of fraudulent intent?
9. Speculate as to the outcome of the criminal proceeding. Do you think Randall and Tyre were convicted of a crime? As a juror, what evidence would you find the most compelling?

---

1 By permission. From *Merriam-Webster's Collegiate® Dictionary*, 11th Edition ©2013 by Merriam-Webster, Inc. (www.Merriam-Webster.com).

2 From *Black's Law Dictionary* (2009), 9th Edition. Material reprinted with permission of Thomson Reuters.

3 AICPA. (2008). Managing the Business Risk of Fraud: A Practical Guide. Go to www.pearsonhighered.com/rufus for a link to this document.

4 SAS No. 99 / AU §316.05

5 *Johnson v. McDonald.* (1934). OK 743, 170 Okla. 117, 39 P.2d 150.

6 From *Black's Law Dictionary* (2009), 9th Edition. Material reprinted with permission of Thomson Reuters.

7 Eaglesham, J. (May 13, 2012). Missing: Stats on crisis convictions. *The Wall Street Journal.*

8 Collotta, M. A. (1978). The role of circumstantial evidence in proving discriminatory intent: Developments since Washington v. Davis. *Boston College Law Review, 19*(4), 795–812.

9 Williams, H. (2006). *Investigating White-Collar Crime: Embezzlement and Financial Fraud* (2nd Ed.). Charles C. Thomas.

10 Ibid.

11 Ibid.

12 Gottschalk, P. (2010). Categories of financial crime. *Journal of Financial Crime, 17*(4), 441–58.

13 Go to www.pearsonhighered.com/rufus for a link to this document.

14 Go to www.pearsonhighered.com/rufus for a link to this document.

15 Perri, F., & Lichtenwald, T. (2007). A proposed addition to the FBI criminal classification manual: Fraud-detection homicide. *Forensic Examiner, 16*(4), 18–30.

16 Brody, R., & Kiehl, K. (2010). From white-collar crime to red-collar crime. *Journal of Financial Crime, 17*(3), 351–64.

17 Skousen, C., & Wright, C. (2008). Contemporaneous risk factors and the prediction of financial statement fraud. *Journal of Forensic Accounting, 9*, 37–62.

18 Cressey, D. (1953). *Other People's Money: A Sstudy in the Social Psychology of Embezzlement.* Free Press.

19 Dechow, P., Larson, W., & Sloan, R. (2008). Predicting material accounting manipulations. Working paper, University of California, Berkeley.

20 Wolfe, D., & Hermanson, D. (Dec. 2004). The fraud diamond: Considering the four elements of fraud. *The CPA Journal*, 38–42.

21 Dorminey, J., Fleming, A. S., Kranacher, M., & Riley, R. (2012). The evolution of fraud theory. *Issues in Accounting Education, 27*(2), 555–79.

22 Prentice, R. (2003). Enron: A brief behavioral autopsy. *American Business Law Journal, 40*, 427–33.

23 Guerette, R. T., Vanja, M., Stenius, K., & McGloin, J. M. (2005). Understanding offense specialization and versatility: A reapplication of the rational choice perspective. *Journal of Criminal Justice, 33*, 77–87.

Horney, J., & Marshall, I. H. (1992). Risk perceptions among serious offenders: The role of crime and punishment. *Criminology, 30*, 575–594.

Matsueda, R. L., Kreager, D. A., & Huizinga, D. (2006). Deterring delinquents: A rational choice model of theft and violence. *American Sociological Review, 71*, 95–122.

Nagin, D. S., & Patermoster R. (1993). Enduring individual differences and rational choice theories of crime. *Law & Society Review, 2*, 467–96.

Wright, B. R., Caspi, A., Moffitt, T. E., & Paternoster, R. (2004). Does the perceived risk of punishment deter criminally prone individuals? Rational choice, self-control, and crime. *Journal of Research in Crime & Delinquency, 41*, 180–213.

24 Cornish, D. B., & Clark, R. (1986). Crime as a rational choice. In F. Cullen & R. Agnew (Eds.), *Criminological Theory*, 278–83.

25 Ibid.

26 Copes, H. (2003). Society attachments, offending frequency, and techniques of neutralization. *Deviant Behavior, 24*, 101–27.

Evans, R. D., & Porche, D. A. (2005). The nature and frequency of Medicare/Medicaid fraud and neutralization techniques among speech, occupational, and physical therapists. *Deviant Behavior, 26*, 253–70.

Gauthier, D. K. (2001). Professional lapses: Occupational deviance and neutralization techniques in veterinary medicine. *Deviant Behavior, 22*, 467–90.

Piquero, N. L., Tibbetts, S. G., & Blankenship, M. B. (2005). The role of differential association and techniques of neutralization in explaining corporate crime. *Deviant Behavior, 26*,159–88.

27 Gottfredson, M., & Hirschi, T. (1990). *A General Theory of Crime*. Stanford University Press.

28 Spahr, L., & Alison, L. (2004). US savings and loan fraud: Implications for general and criminal culture theories of crime. *Crime, Law and Social Change, 41*, 95–106.

29 Gottfredson, M., & Hirschi, T. (1990). *A General Theory of Crime*. Stanford University Press.

30 Miethe, T. D., & Meier, R. (1994). *Crime and Its Social Context: Toward an Integrated Theory of Offenders, Victims, and Situations*. State University of NY Press.

31 MacLean, T. (2008). Framing and organizational misconduct: A symbolic interactionist study. *Journal of Business Ethics, 78*, 3–16.

32 Lavery, C., Lindberg, D., & Razaki, K. A. (Aug. 2000). Fraud awareness in a small business. *The National Public Accountant,* 40–42.

33 Go to www.pearsonhighered.com/rufus for a link to this study.

34 *Black's Law Dictionary.* (2009). 9th Ed., 1342.

7 Conducting a Fraud Investigation

INTRODUCTION

The objective of a fraud investigation is to gather evidence of a suspected fraud. To that end, forensic accountants might be engaged in a variety of contexts, such as:

- Agent of law enforcement (for example, FBI, IRS, or State Police)
- Member of an audit team (either internal or external)
- Private (external) forensic accountant engaged by the victim or victim's counsel (for example, corporation, audit committee, or board of directors)
- Private (external) forensic accountant engaged by the accused or the accused's counsel

The purpose of this chapter is to employ the many concepts, tools, and techniques previously presented in this text to the challenge of conducting a fraud investigation. In preparation for this challenge, the following cautions and reminders are presented:

- Every fraud investigation is unique and has its own cast of characters, facts, and circumstances.
- Fraud investigations are initiated *after* the fact—that is, in response to an allegation or suspicion of fraud. In other words, once an allegation of fraud is received or a suspicion identified, the company (that is, the victim) is faced with the decision of whether to pursue an investigation. Another necessary decision is who should conduct the investigation—in-house personnel, law enforcement, an external audit team, or a private outside firm.
- Although the initial suspicion of fraud might help frame your case and develop your working hypothesis, it is imperative to remain objective. As discussed in Chapter 1, forensic accountants should operate in a state of disbelief or suspended belief, where information and representations are evaluated in a rational, curious, objective, and systematic manner.
- The scientific process (recall the five steps discussed in Chapter 3) is the most effective and efficient approach to conducting a fraud investigation. Remember, a hypothesis (Step 2) is not a statement of fact; it is simply a tentative explanation based on preliminary observations or suspicions that must be tested. Without a working hypothesis, a fraud investigation is only random data collection.
- As discussed in Chapter 2, evidence is something that tends to prove or disprove the existence of an alleged fact. Forensic accountants gather and analyze both documentary evidence, such as financial data and other business records, and interactive evidence, such as interviews and observations.
- One of the most valuable evidence-gathering techniques forensic accountants use is financial statements analysis. As discussed in Chapter 5, financial statements rarely reflect economic reality and often conceal more than they reveal. Don't forget the importance of context!

Learning Objectives

This chapter presents a case study that challenges you to:

LO1. Evaluate the reasonableness of a suspicion of fraud.

LO2. Create a preliminary fraud hypothesis.

LO3. Test and refine the fraud hypothesis through financial statements analysis and journal entry testing.

LO4. Test and refine the fraud hypothesis by conducting interviews.

LO5. Identify specific schemes used to perpetrate the fraudulent activity.

LO6. Determine the economic loss resulting from the fraudulent activity.

LO7. In response to a finding of fraud, identify potential recommendations for resolution.

- Another widely used investigation tool is the interview, which has two primary advantages: It is a direct means of obtaining evidence, and it provides immediate results. As discussed in Chapter 4, interviewing is much more than just asking questions. It is a systematic process that requires planning, staging, execution, and active listening.
- Fraud is a *crime of intent*. Absent an admission, circumstantial evidence is used to establish or infer fraudulent intent. As discussed in Chapter 6, the reliability of circumstantial evidence for the purpose of establishing intent depends on two key factors: alternative explanations and degree of impact. Because the results of your investigation cannot provide certainty, you should avoid conclusions of guilt or innocence.
- Cressey's fraud triangle suggests that fraud results from the convergence of three conditions: need (pressure), opportunity, and rationalization. As discussed in Chapter 6, research has identified many red flags, or indicators of fraud, that support Cressey's framework. Identifying red flags helps to evaluate the reasonableness of suspicions and allegations of fraud.
- Fraud is not an accounting problem—it is a social phenomenon. Forensic accounting is rooted in law and economics, not psychology or criminology. Thus, our interest in "why" people commit fraud, especially when conducting a fraud investigation, is explanatory (cause and effect), not predictive. Applying traditional economic theory, we propose that people commit fraud when the perceived reward ($) is greater than the probable loss—the calculus of fraud. Because fraud investigators are called in *after* a suspicion of fraud has been identified, the focus is who, when, how, and how much—not why.

Armed with your newly acquired knowledge of the scientific approach, interviewing, financial statements analysis, and fraud concepts, you are equipped to conduct your first fraud investigation—Mountain State Sporting Goods.

Special Note

The case presented in this chapter (*Mountain State Sporting Goods: A Case of Fraud? A Case Study in Fraud Examination*) is derived from an actual fraud occurrence. Written by Robert J. Rufus and William Hahn, the case was published as an instructional resource by the American Accounting Association in *Issues in Accounting Education* (2011, Vol. 26, No. 1, pp. 201–17) and is reprinted with permission. Teaching notes are available to AAA members through its electronic publications system.

SUSPICIONS OF FRAUD

On March 18, 2009, Mountain State Sporting Goods, Inc., held its annual meeting of directors and shareholders at Shawnee Bay Resort located on the shores of Kentucky Lake. The primary purpose of the annual meeting was to review the company's year-end (Dec. 31, 2008) financial statements, specifically its financial condition and annual performance. The company's general manager Thomas Workman and CPA Charles Hess presented the company's financial report and responded to questions regarding the company's failure to meet projections and its current financial instability. Other issues for discussion included a request by the general manager to increase the company's line of credit and enhance employee benefits. Following a heated exchange between the directors and Workman and Hess, both matters were tabled pending an independent assessment of the company's operations. Both Workman and Hess were excused from the remainder of corporate business, including the election of directors and officers.

Immediately following the annual meeting, the company's two shareholders, brothers Robert and Nathaniel Smith, contacted attorney Dwane Peoples, a former federal prosecutor, to discuss their suspicions of fraudulent activity within the company. The shareholders' suspicions were sparked by observations of the general manager's lavish lifestyle, specifically a new home, new cars, and the recent purchase of an exotic vacation home with the company's CPA, Hess. Peoples's staff, including an in-house CPA, developed the following case profile. Information contained in this profile, including historical operations, projections, statements, and Workman's representations, came from a business valuation report as of December 31, 2006, supporting work papers, and interview notes provided by the Certified Valuation Analyst (CVA).

BACKGROUND INFORMATION

Organization and Ownership

Mountain State Sporting Goods is a Kentucky corporation organized by J.D. Smith in 1993. Following J.D.'s death on December 15, 2006, day-to-day management was assigned (via an employment contract, effective January 1, 2007) to Thomas A. Workman, a long-term employee and assistant manager under J.D.

Ownership of the company's stock was inherited equally (50/50) by J.D.'s two children—Robert and Nathaniel, both full-time college students (ages 18 and 19, respectively). During the administration of J.D.'s estate, the business was valued at $350,000* by a CVA, using the capitalization of earnings method. The methodology employed and the value conclusion were considered reasonable by all parties, including the IRS and Workman. The date of valuation was December 31, 2006.

Pursuant to the terms of his employment contract with the company, Workman is required to facilitate the preparation of annual (audited) financial reports with supporting schedules and footnotes. Said financial reports are presented at the company's annual board of directors meeting. The company files its annual federal income tax return as an S corporation via Form 1120S, wherein profits and/or losses flow to its shareholders.

The company has one store located at 33 Park Drive, Beaver Creek, Kentucky. This is the company's second location since its inception. The move to the new location (on March 1, 2006) was managed by J.D. before his death and motivated by the addition of a new profit center—a pawn shop. The facility is leased from Black Oak Realty (an unrelated party), with an option-to-purchase at its appraised value ($240,000) at the end of the first three-year term.

According to J.D.'s projections, the new location and pawn shop activity would complement the company's existing offerings and result in revenue growth of 10% in 2006, 15% in 2007, and 10% in each of the following three years. J.D.'s projections attributed 50% of the increased revenue directly to the pawn component. Importantly, any increase in profits was to be accumulated in a sinking fund to fund a 20% down payment on the building upon exercise of the purchase option. J.D.'s projections and actual results are presented in Table 7-1.

Table 7-1 | Gross Revenues—Projected Versus Actual

Year	Projected Sales*	Actual Sales**	Projected Growth*	Actual Growth
2005	N/a	$2,007,185	N/a	7.72%
2006	$2,210,000	$2,195,901	10%	9.4%
2007	$2,541,500	$2,339,496	15%	6.54%
2008	$2,796,000	$2,513,479	10%	7.44%
2009	$3,075,500	N/a	10%	N/a
2010	$3,383,000	N/a	10%	N/a

* *Source:* J.D.'s business plan and supporting financial forecasts.
** *Source:* Financial statements.

* $518,500 before application of a marketability discount (32.5%).

Products and Services

As of the date of valuation, the company's offerings included a comprehensive selection of high-quality, competitively priced, national and regional brand products. The merchandise mix was comprised of tobacco products, firearms, sporting equipment, and sporting apparel and footwear. As of July 1, 2006, the company also offered short-term secured consumer lending through a pawn shop operation.

According to the valuation report, the company's various product categories were grouped into the five general categories presented in Table 7-2. As illustrated, during the 2006 calendar year, the smallest component (< 1%) of the company's revenues was pawn loans. The company offers 30-day renewable loans at a periodic interest rate of 20%. Borrowers pledge a variety of items as loan collateral, including firearms, tools, and electronics.

The character of items pawned is summarized in Table 7-3. If interest charges are not paid within seven days of the end of each thirty-day period, the collateral is seized and placed in inventory for resale. The company's annual physical inventory *does not include* forfeited pawn items. Advances (pawn loans) are recorded as noninventoried purchases (vs. receivables), and redemptions are recorded as sales (vs. collections). These practices are not in conformity with GAAP, which requires the initial recording of a pawn loan receivable and a subsequent movement of the receivable to inventory when a pawn item is not redeemed.

According to Workman, the company's average loan is $100, with an average redemption rate of approximately 65%. All loans must be repaid with cash, although checks are accepted for interest payments. According to the valuation report, there is no set policy for determining the amount of a pawn loan. However, following J.D.'s death, only Workman is permitted to price and approve a loan. Pricing information sources include Workman's product knowledge, retail prices, and Internet prices. Individual customer history is another factor, with established customers receiving higher loans than new customers.

Customer Service

According to Workman, the company's competitive advantages are its convenient location, unique merchandise selection, and superior customer service, specifically a commitment to identifying and providing merchandise that is relevant to the targeted customer base.

Management

The company was co-managed by Sue Bryant and Workman following J.D.'s death (December 15, 2006) until her retirement on January 6, 2007. Since that time, the company has been managed by Workman pursuant to the terms of his employment contract. Robert

Table 7-2 Product Categories

	2005 Activity		2006 Activity		Avg.	
Department	Sales %	GM	Sales %	GM	Sales %	GM
Tobacco	43.10%	9.61%	40.43%	13.60%	41.76%	11.61%
Footwear	4.12%	44.85%	4.21%	35.77%	4.17%	40.31%
General SG	22.60%	20.15%	23.19%	20.46%	22.89%	20.31%
Guns/Ammo	23.49%	31.14%	22.55%	29.05%	23.02%	30.10%
Licenses	6.69%	4.45%	8.88%	7.74%	7.78%	6.10%
Pawn	N/a	N/a	0.73%	50.00%	N/a	N/a

Source: Valuation report as of Dec. 31, 2006.

Table 7-3 | Pawn Items

Category	% Revenues
Jewelry	<1%
Firearms	80%
Tools	8%
Games & Game Systems	<1%
Electronics	5%
Other	5%

Source: Valuation report as of Dec. 31, 2006.

and Nathaniel do not actively participate in management but attend annual BOD meetings to review financial reports, which are prepared and presented by the company's auditor, Charles Hess, CPA.

Officers' Compensation

According to Workman, his compensation is determined by his employment contract, which specifies a base salary of $50,000 plus 1% of all sales exceeding projections. To date, the company has failed to meet these projections. A comparison of projected sales to reported sales is presented in Table 7-1.

Key Employees, Compensation, and Benefits

The company has an average of eight employees, including Workman's spouse, Anita, and his 17-year-old daughter, Mia. Anita and Mia share in-house accounting duties and responsibilities. Before J.D.'s death, these duties were performed by Sue Bryant, who retired shortly thereafter. No other key employees have been identified. The company offers statutory benefits (Social Security, Workers' Compensation, SUTA, and FUTA) as well as one week of paid vacation. Only Workman receives health insurance benefits.

SIGNIFICANT ACCOUNTING POLICIES

Method of Accounting

The company employs the *accrual method of accounting*. Under the accrual method, income is accounted for (recognized) when earned. It is not the actual receipt, but rather the *right to receive*, that governs. Expenses are recognized as incurred—that is, when all events have occurred that fix the amount of the item and determine the liability to pay. As explained by Hess, the IRS requires taxpayers that maintain inventories to employ the accrual method of accounting.†

Inventory Accounting

Inventory is usually the largest current asset of a business, and its proper measurement is necessary to ensure accurate financial statements. If inventory is not properly measured, expenses and revenues cannot be properly matched. When ending inventory is incorrect, the following balances on the balance sheet are also incorrect as a result: inventory, total assets,

† T. Reg. §1.446-1(c)(2).

and owners' equity. When ending inventory is incorrect, the cost of merchandise sold and net income on the income statement are also incorrect.

The two most common inventory systems are the periodic and perpetual systems. Following J.D.'s death in December 2006, the company abandoned its perpetual system and converted to a *periodic inventory method*. Under this method, a purchases account is used, and the beginning inventory is unchanged during the period (month, quarter, or year). At the end of an accounting period, the inventory account is adjusted by closing out the beginning inventory and recording the ending inventory, as determined by a physical inventory. The company's current practice is to conduct a physical inventory at the end of each year, adjusting cost of goods sold (COGS) and ending inventory accordingly.

As presented by Workman, the perpetual system maintained by J.D. before his death was too complex, too time-consuming, and simply not cost justified. Moreover, the company's auditor did not object and, in fact, encouraged the change.

Method of Valuing Ending Inventory

The valuation of inventory can be a complex process that requires the determination of: (a) the physical goods to be included; (b) the costs to be included; (c) the cost flow assumption to be adopted (that is, cost or lower of cost or market); and (d) the accounting cost flow assumption to be adopted (specific identification, LIFO, FIFO, or moving-average). The company employs the FIFO cost flow assumption.

The company includes in its physical inventory all items on premises (or in transit) for which it has legal title, with the exception of forfeited pawn items. The company employs the lower of cost or market method in valuing its ending inventory, and items identified as unsellable due to obsolescence or condition are valued at bona fide selling prices, as determined by Workman.

Accounting Functions

Effective January 1, 2007, all accounting functions and day-to-day accounting activities have been processed by the company's in-house personnel, Anita and Mia, and supervised by Workman, as the company's manager. Annual financial reports and related income tax returns are prepared by Hess.

THE ENGAGEMENT

You have been contacted by attorney Peoples to discuss this situation. Present at the initial meeting are Robert and Nathanial Smith, Peoples, and the valuation analyst. During the meeting, the background information is confirmed, and all preengagement considerations (see Chapter 3) are evaluated without issue. An engagement letter is executed with the following provisions:

- You are engaged as a consulting expert to assist Peoples in evaluating the Smith brothers' suspicions of fraud. You have confirmed the statutory elements of fraud and the requisite burden and standard of proof. You have also confirmed that statutory interest (7.5%) is to be added to your loss determination, if any.
- Because your investigation will require the cooperation of company personnel, it is agreed that the company's management (Workman) and its CPA (Hess) will be contacted. Specifically, they will be advised that:
    - You have been engaged by the shareholders.
    - The purpose of your engagement is to assess the company's financial viability.
    - They are expected to cooperate fully and provide any requested access to the company's records and employees.
- Throughout the course of your investigation, you will represent to all parties that you have been engaged to independently evaluate the company's operations and financial condition for economic viability. This pretext is required to ensure cooperation and reduce disturbance in the workforce. In this regard, Peoples expressed

specific concerns that Workman and Hess could disrupt the business and/or destroy documents if they suspected the true nature of the engagement.

- The relevant dates for the investigation are identified as December 15, 2006 (date of J.D.'s death) through December 31, 2008.

Given difficulty in predicting the length of time required to complete the investigation and the associated cost, a *phased approach*‡ has been adopted. This approach structures the investigation as a series of steps (a stairstep framework). Each phase has a defined objective and, as completed, results are communicated to the client (attorney). The completion of each phase presents a decision point, at which the client decides to continue, discontinue, or modify the scope of the investigation.

Our experience suggests that a phased approach has several advantages: it enhances client understanding and acceptance through interim (phase) reporting; it enables the management of client expectations for time, cost, and results; it reduces the client's risk by providing periodic options to terminate or adjust the scope of the investigation; and it facilitates a more effective and efficient utilization of investigative resources.

For this engagement, the phases have been outlined as follows:

- Phase I
    a. Confirm the reasonableness of the suspicions of fraud.
    b. If the suspicions of fraud are deemed reasonable, create a fraud hypothesis.
- Phase II
    a. Test and refine your hypothesis via financial statements analysis.
    b. Test and refine your hypothesis via journal entry analysis.
- Phase III
    Test and refine your hypothesis via interactive evidence gathering, such as interviews.
- Phase IV
    Draw your conclusion/s, and communicate your results. This challenge includes a determination of any "misappropriation" and a related discussion of the specific schemes employed.
- Phase V
    Present a discussion of Mr. Hess's role, duties and responsibilities, and professional violations (if any).
- Phase VI
    If fraudulent activity is identified, present your recommendations for resolution and remediation.

Dig Deeper

You are encouraged to research the pawn shop industry to develop an understanding of pawn-related transactions (for example, average loan amounts, finance charges, and redemptions). Other valuable information might include pawnshop accounting, best practices, regulation, and software.

THE INVESTIGATION

Phase I(a): Confirm the Reasonableness of the Suspicions of Fraud

Review the case profile presented previously, and identify ten conditions (red flags)§ that either confirm or fail to confirm the reasonableness of the Smiths' suspicions of fraud.

‡ A common alternative is the holistic approach, that is, no stone unturned.

§ More than twenty such conditions have been identified.

To this end, employ the fraud triangle (need, opportunity, and rationalization) and professional skepticism. As a starting point, consider the following:

Red Flag	Fraud Triangle
• Smiths do not actively participate in management.	Opportunity
• Company abandoned its perpetual inventory system.	Opportunity
• Workman's compensation is in part determined by production.	Need

Phase I(b): Create a Fraud Hypothesis

Having confirmed the reasonableness of the Smiths' suspicions of fraud, you must now develop a fraud hypothesis. Remember, a hypothesis is not a statement of fact—it is simply an educated guess about how something works or an explanation for an event. In this phase, you will exercise your critical thinking and reasoning skills. Brainstorming can also be used. An example of a reasonable fraud hypothesis is presented as follows:

> Workman has systematically eroded the company's internal controls and oversight functions to facilitate fraudulent schemes.

Phase II(a): Test Your Hypothesis via Financial Statements Analysis

As discussed in Chapter 5, financial statements analysis is the examination of financial statements for the purpose of acquiring additional information about the activities of a business. This analysis may reveal unexpected relationships or the absence of expected relationships.

Your next challenge is to use various analytical techniques, such as trend analysis, common-size analysis, ratio analysis, and cash flow analysis, to analyze the company's financial statements (see Exhibits 7A-1, 7A-2, and 7A-3).

Special Note

The data for five years contained in Exhibits 7A-1 and 7A-2 are compiled from the company's income tax returns, whereas the data in 7A-3 come from its annual report. A cash flow statement has not been presented, because this is a component of the student's challenge for this phase.

After completing your analysis, consider the implications of your findings. What questions or concerns have you identified? Does your analysis support your hypothesis? Does your hypothesis need to be refined? Specific questions and observations might include the following:

- Are the company's reported profit margins (gross and net) consistent with prior periods? What do the trends in these margins suggest?
- Do the balance sheet items reconcile with the income statement and your understanding of the business? Consider pawn loans, pawn loan interest, and interest expense.

Exhibit 7A-1 | Mountain State Sporting Goods Operational Analysis

	2003	2004	2005	2006	2007	2008
Gross Receipts	$1,793,346	$1,863,321	$2,007,185	$2,195,901	$2,339,496	$2,513,479
COGS	(1,476,447)	(1,533,750)	(1,642,210)	(1,761,292)	(1,926,462)	(2,080,909)
Gross Profit	316,899	329,571	364,975	434,609	413,034	432,570
Operating Expenses						
Officers' Comp.	60,000	60,000	65,000	65,000	50,000	50,000
Salaries & Wages	68,002	91,927	110,907	139,723	157,320	161,315
Repairs & Maint.	1,177	602	2,620	1,297	1,268	1,769
Rent	12,000	12,000	23,000	24,000	24,000	24,000
Taxes & Licenses	24,065	27,868	43,085	45,711	50,232	54,543
Depreciation	5,407	5,824	11,647	5,860	6,588	6,534
Advertising	1,941	2,658	5,653	4,216	18,778	27,512
Delivery	9,353	10,831	10,337	11,155	12,241	12,669
Insurance	13,121	16,903	19,287	25,089	32,609	38,149
Misc. Expense	1,205	1,839	4,168	3,940	2,736	3,115
Office Exp.	479	357	613	1,040	3,656	4,350
Postage	316	409	847	932	1,082	1,310
Supplies	2,185	2,248	3,320	1,992	1,670	2,021
Telephone	2,372	2,773	3,188	3,374	2,933	3,667
Utilities	5,841	5,467	6,372	7,198	7,144	7,246
Outside Services	1,587	3,097	11,550	24,192	771	698
Travel	2,224	3,319	3,541	3,126	5,217	6,051
Tot. Operating Exp.	211,275	248,122	325,135	367,845	378,245	404,949
Operating Income	**105,624**	**81,449**	**39,840**	**66,764**	**34,789**	**27,621**
Other Income (Exp.)						
Interest Income	-	-	-	6,730	-	-
Interest Expense	(7,928)	(5,789)	(2,731)	(1,648)	-	-
Tot. Other Income (Exp.)	(7,928)	(5,789)	(2,731)	5,082	-	-
Net Income	**$97,696**	**$75,660**	**$37,109**	**$71,846**	**$34,789**	**$27,621**

Source: U.S. Income Tax Return for S Corporation (Form 1120S).

Exhibit 7A-2 Mountain State Sporting Goods Balance Sheet Analysis

	2002	2003	2004	2005	2006	2007	2008
Assets							
Current Assets							
Cash	72,963	60,540	65,057	38,220	54,162	82,803	63,904
Inventory	169,025	204,032	214,046	236,681	264,575	281,147	296,776
Tot. Current Assets	241,988	264,572	279,103	274,901	318,737	363,950	360,680
Fixed Assets							
Equipment	43,996	47,124	49,735	64,642	80,118	83,498	123,498
Accumulated Deprec.	(31,497)	(36,904)	(42,729)	(54,376)	(60,236)	(66,824)	(73,358)
Net Fixed Assets	12,499	10,220	7,006	10,266	19,882	16,674	50,140
Other Assets	1,253	1,253	1,253	1,253	1,253	1,253	1,253
Total Assets	**$255,740**	**$276,045**	**$287,362**	**$286,420**	**$339,872**	**$381,877**	**$412,073**
Liabilities & Equity							
Current Liabilities							
Payroll Taxes Payable		4,879	5,560	15,843	30,190	49,169	51,789
Sales Tax Payable		10,901	12,199	12,456	13,802	16,593	18,410
Other Current Liabilities	12,821						
Tot. Current Liabilities	12,821	15,780	17,759	28,299	43,992	65,762	70,199
Long-Term Debt	110,186	89,690	67,056	24,534	34,441	44,441	42,579
Total Liabilities	123,007	105,470	84,815	52,833	78,433	110,203	112,778
Equity							
Capital Stock	1,000	1,000	1,000	1,000	1,000	1,000	1,000
Retained Earnings	131,733	169,575	201,547	232,587	260,439	270,674	298,295
Total Equity	132,733	170,575	202,547	233,587	261,439	271,674	299,295
Total Liabilities & Equity	**$255,740**	**$276,045**	**$287,362**	**$286,420**	**$339,872**	**$381,877**	**$412,073**

Source: U.S. Income Tax Return for S Corporation (Form 1120S).

Exhibit 7A-3 Mountain State Sporting Goods Annual Report

	Dec 31, 08	Dec 31, 07	$ Change
Assets			
Current Assets			
Checking	63,904.00	82,803.00	(18,899.00)
Inventory	296,776.00	281,147.00	15,629.00
Total Current Assets	360,680.00	363,950.00	(3,270.00)
Fixed Assets			
Furniture and Equipment	123,498.00	83,498.00	40,000.00
Accumulated Depreciation	(73,358.00)	(66,824.00)	(6,534.00)
Net Fixed Assets	50,140.00	16,674.00	33,466.00
Other Assets	1,253.00	1,253.00	0.00
Total Assets	**$412,073.00**	**$381,877.00**	**$30,196.00**
Liabilities & Equity			
Current Liabilities			
Payroll Liabilities Payable	51,789.00	49,169.00	2,620.00
Sales Tax Payable	18,410.00	16,593.00	1,817.00
Total Current Liabilities	70,199.00	65,762.00	4,437.00
Long-Term Debt	42,579.00	44,441.00	(1,862.00)
Total Liabilities	112,778.00	110,203.00	2,575.00
Equity			
Capital Stock	1,000.00	1,000.00	0.00
Dividends	0.00	(9,066.00)	9,066.00
Retained Earnings	270,674.00	244,951.00	25,723.00
Net Income	**27,621.00**	**34,789.00**	**(7,168.00)**
Total Equity	299,295.00	271,674.00	27,621.00
Total Liabilities & Equity	**$412,073.00**	**$381,877.00**	**$30,196.00**

(continued)

Exhibit 7A-3 *(continued)*

	Jan – Dec 08	Jan – Dec 07
Ordinary Income/Expense		
Income		
Sales	2,513,479.00	2,339,496.00
Total Income	2,513,479.00	2,339,496.00
Cost of Goods Sold		
Cost of Goods Sold	2,080,909.00	1,926,462.00
Total COGS	2,080,909.00	1,926,462.00
Gross Profit	432,570.00	413,034.00
Expense		
Advertising and Promotion	27,512.00	18,778.00
Delivery	12,669.00	12,241.00
Depreciation Expense	6,534.00	6,588.00
Insurance Expense	38,149.00	32,609.00
Misc. Expense	3,115.00	2,736.00
Office Supplies	4,350.00	3,656.00
Officer's Compensation	50,000.00	50,000.00
Outside Labor	698.00	771.00
Postage	1,310.00	1,082.00
Rent Expense	24,000.00	24,000.00
Repairs and Maintenance	1,769.00	1,268.00
Salaries & Wages	161,315.00	157,320.00
Supplies	2,021.00	1,670.00
Taxes & Licenses	54,543.00	50,232.00
Telephone Expense	3,667.00	2,933.00
Travel and Entertainment	6,051.00	5,217.00
Utilities	7,246.00	7,144.00
Total Expense	404,949.00	378,245.00
Net Ordinary Income	27,621.00	34,789.00
Net Income	**27,621.00**	**34,789.00**

Phase II(b): Test Your Hypothesis Via Journal Entry Testing

As discussed in Chapter 5, journal entries (JEs) can potentially undermine the validity of financial statements and the financial reporting process. Thus, the importance of JE testing cannot be overstated. The objective of this testing is to identify and assess any inappropriate or unusual activity. This is especially important when, as in this case, there is an ineffective system of internal controls and management has the ability to override the JE process. As outlined in SAS No. 99, fraudulent JEs have several common characteristics:

- JEs made to unrelated, unusual, or seldom-used accounts
- JEs recorded at the end of the period or as post-closing entries with little or no explanation
- JEs containing round numbers or a consistent ending number
- JEs applied to intercompany or related parties

Given your understanding of JE testing, you are now challenged with analyzing the company's adjusting entries for years 2006 through 2008 (see Exhibits B through D). The following example provides a useful approach.

2006	
Adjusting entry at end of year, found on general ledger:	
Sales	$45,000
Line of Credit	20,000
Loans to Employees	$45,000
Payroll Liability	20,000

Again, consider any additional information (questions or concerns) that your analysis identifies. Is your hypothesis supported, or is further refinement necessary?

Exhibit 7B | GL Adjusting Entries 12/31/2006

Type	Date	Entry Date	Split	Debit	Credit	Balance
Checking						38,220
				2,267,631		
					2,251,689	
Total Checking				2,267,631	2,251,689	54,162
Inventory						**236,681**
Adjusting Entry	12/31/2006	02/18/2007	Cost of Goods Sold	27,894	-	-
Total Inventory				27,894	-	264,575
Equipment						**64,642**
				15,476		
Total Equipment				15,476	-	80,118

(continued)

Exhibit 7B | *(continued)*

Type	Date	Entry Date	Split	Debit	Credit	Balance
Accumulated Depreciation						**(54,376)**
Adjusting Entry	12/31/2006	02/18/2007	Depreciation Expense		5,860	
Total Accumulated Depreciation				-	5,860	(60,236)
Leasehold Improvements						-
				15,000		
Adjusting Entry	12/31/2006	08/20/2006	Outside Services		15,000	
Total Leasehold Improvements				15,000	15,000	-
Loan to Employees						-
				45,000		
Adjusting Entry	12/31/2006	03/01/2007	Sales		45,000	
Total Loan to Employees				45,000	45,000	-
Other Assets						**1,253**
Total Other Assets				-	-	1,253
Line of Credit						-
					20,000	
Adjusting Entry	12/31/2006	03/01/2007	Payroll Liability	20,000		
Total Line of Credit				20,000	20,000	-
Payroll Liabilities Payable						**(15,843)**
				15,843		
					10,190	
Adjusting Entry	12/31/2006	03/01/2007	Line of Credit		20,000	
Total Payroll Liabilities Payable				15,843	30,190	(30,190)

Exhibit 7B (continued)

Type	Date	Entry Date	Split	Debit	Credit	Balance
Sales Tax Payable						**(12,456)**
				12,456		
					13,802	
Total Sales Tax Payable				12,456	13,802	(13,802)
Long-Term Debt						**(24,534)**
				3,593		
					13,500	
Total Long-Term Debt				3,593	13,500	(34,441)
Capital Stock						**(1,000)**
Total Capital Stock				-	-	(1,000)
Dividends						**-**
				10,767		
Total Dividends				10,767	-	10,767
Retained Earnings						**(232,587)**
				33,227		
Total Retained Earnings				33,227	-	(199,360)
Sales						**-**
					2,240,901	
Adjusting Entry	12/31/2006	03/01/2007	Loan from Employee	45,000		
Total Sales				45,000	2,240,901	(2,195,901)
Cost of Goods Sold						**-**
				1,789,186		
Adjusting Entry	12/31/2006	02/18/2007	Inventory		27,894	
Total Cost of Goods Sold				1,789,186	27,894	1,761,292

(continued)

Exhibit 7B (continued)

Type	Date	Entry Date	Split	Debit	Credit	Balance
Advertising and Promotion						-
				4,216		
Total Advertising and Promotion				4,216	-	4,216
Delivery						-
				11,155		
Total Delivery				11,155	-	11,155
Depreciation Expense						-
Adjusting Entry	12/31/2006	02/18/2007	Accumulated Depreciation	5,860		
Total Depreciation Expense				5,860	-	5,860
Insurance Expense						-
				25,089		
Total Insurance Expense				25,089	-	25,089
Interest Expense						-
				1,648		
Total Interest Expense				1,648	-	1,648
Misc. Expense						-
				3,940		
Total Misc. Expense				3,940	-	3,940
Office Supplies						-
				1,040		
Total Office Supplies				1,040	-	1,040
Officers Compensation						-
				65,000		
Total Officers Compensation				65,000	-	65,000

Exhibit 7B (continued)

Type	Date	Entry Date	Split	Debit	Credit	Balance
Outside Labor						-
				9,192		
Adjusting Entry	12/31/2006	08/20/2006	Leasehold Improvements	15,000		
Total Outside Labor				24,192	-	24,192
Postage						-
				932		
Total Postage				932	-	932
Rent Expense						-
				24,000		
Total Rent Expense				24,000	-	24,000
Repairs and Maintenance						-
				1,297		
Total Repairs and Maintenance				1,297	-	1,297
Salaries & Wages						-
				139,723		
Total Salaries & Wages				139,723	-	139,723
Supplies						-
				1,992		
Total Supplies				1,992	-	1,992
Taxes & Licenses						-
				45,711		
Total Taxes & Licenses				45,711	-	45,711
Telephone Expense						-
				3,374		
Total Telephone Expense				3,374	-	3,374

(continued)

Exhibit 7B (continued)

Type	Date	Entry Date	Split	Debit	Credit	Balance
Travel and Entertainment						-
				3,126		
Total Travel and Entertainment				3,126	-	3,126
Utilities						-
				7,198		
Total Utilities				7,198	-	7,198
Interest Income						-
					6,730	
Total Interest Income				-	6,730	(6,730)
				4,670,566	**4,670,566**	-

Exhibit 7C GL Adjusting Entries 12/31/2007

Type	Date	Entry Date	Split	Debit	Credit	Balance
Checking						**54,162**
				2,374,496		
					2,345,855	54,162
Total Checking				2,374,496	2,345,855	**82,803**
Inventory						**264,575**
Adjusting Entry	12/31/2007	2/20/2008	Cost of Goods Sold	16,572		281,147
Total Inventory				16,572	-	**281,147**
Equipment						**80,118**
				3,380		83,498
Total Equipment				3,380	-	**83,498**
Accumulated Depreciation						**(60,236)**
Adjusting Entry	12/31/2007	2/20/2008	Depreciation Expense		6,588	(66,824)
Total Accumulated Depreciation				-	6,588	(66,824)

Exhibit 7C | *(continued)*

Type	Date	Entry Date	Split	Debit	Credit	Balance
Other Assets						**1,253**
Total Other Assets				-	-	1,253
Payroll Liabilities Payable						**(30,190)**
				30,190		-
					34,169	(34,169)
Adjusting Entry	12/31/2007	3/7/2008	Sales		15,000	(49,169)
Total Payroll Liabilities Payable				30,190	49,169	(49,169)
Sales Tax Payable						**(13,802)**
				13,802		-
					16,593	(16,593)
Total Sales Tax Payable				13,802	16,593	**(16,593)**
Long-Term Debt						**(34,441)**
Adjusting Entry	12/31/2007	3/7/2008	Sales		10,000	(44,441)
Total Long-Term Debt				-	10,000	**(44,441)**
Capital Stock						**(1,000)**
Total Capital Stock				-	-	**(1,000)**
Dividends						-
				9,066		9,066
Total Dividends				9,066	-	**9,066**
Retained Earnings						**(260,439)**
				15,488		(244,951)
Total Retained Earnings				15,488	-	**(244,951)**

(continued)

Exhibit 7C (continued)

Type	Date	Entry Date	Split	Debit	Credit	Balance
Sales						-
					2,364,496	**(2,364,496)**
Adjusting Entry	12/31/2007	3/7/2008	Split-Payroll Liability Split-Long-Term Debt	25,000		(2,339,496)
Total Sales				25,000	2,364,496	**(2,339,496)**
Cost of Goods Sold						-
				1,937,034		**1,937,034**
Adjusting Entry	12/31/2007	2/20/2008	Inventory		16,572	1,920,462
Adjusting Entry	12/31/2007	3/9/2008	Auto Lease	6,000		1,926,462
Total Cost of Goods Sold				1,943,034	16,572	**1,926,462**
Advertising and Promotion						-
				6,278		**6,278**
Adjusting Entry	12/31/2007	3/9/2008	Travel and Entertainment	12,500		18,778
Total Advertising and Promotion				18,778	-	**18,778**
Auto Lease						-
				6,000		**6,000**
Adjusting Entry	12/31/2007	2/20/2008	Cost of Goods Sold		6,000	-
Total Auto Lease				6,000	6,000	-
Delivery						-
				12,241		12,241
Total Delivery				12,241	-	**12,241**
Depreciation Expense						-
Adjusting Entry	12/31/2007	2/20/2008	Accumulated Depreciation	6,588		6,588
Total Depreciation Expense				6,588	-	6,588

Exhibit 7C (continued)

Type	Date	Entry Date	Split	Debit	Credit	Balance
Insurance Expense						-
				27,609		**27,609**
Adjusting Entry	12/31/2007	3/9/2008	Outside Labor	5,000		32,609
Total Insurance Expense				32,609	-	**32,609**
Misc. Expense						-
				2,736		2,736
Total Misc. Expense				2,736	-	**2,736**
Office Supplies						-
				3,656		3,656
Total Office Supplies				3,656	-	**3,656**
Officers Compensation						-
				50,000		50,000
Total Officers Compensation				50,000	-	**50,000**
Outside Labor						-
				5,771		5,771
Adjusting Entry	12/31/2007	3/9/2008	Insurance		5,000	771
Total Outside Labor				5,771	5,000	**771**
Postage						-
				1,082		1,082
Total Postage				1,082	-	**1,082**
Rent Expense						-
				24,000		24,000
Total Rent Expense				24,000	-	**24,000**

(continued)

Exhibit 7C (continued)

Type	Date	Entry Date	Split	Debit	Credit	Balance
Repairs and Maintenance						-
				1,268		1,268
Total Repairs and Maintenance				1,268	-	**1,268**
Salaries & Wages						-
				157,320		157,320
Total Salaries & Wages				157,320	-	**157,320**
Supplies						-
				1,670		1,670
Total Supplies				1,670	-	**1,670**
Taxes & Licenses						-
				50,232		50,232
Total Taxes & Licenses				50,232	-	**50,232**
Telephone Expense						-
				2,933		2,933
Total Telephone Expense				2,933	-	**2,933**
Travel and Entertainment						-
				17,717		**17,717**
Adjusting Entry	12/31/2007	3/7/2008	Advertising and Promotion		12,500	5,217
Total Travel and Entertainment				17,717	12,500	**5,217**
Utilities						-
				7,144		7,144
Total Utilities				7,144	-	**7,144**
				4,832,773	**4,832,773**	-

Exhibit 7D | GL Adjusting Entries 12/31/2008

Type	Date	Entry Date	Split	Debit	Credit	Balance
Checking						**82,803**
			2,513,479			
					2,532,378	54,162
Total Checking				2,513,479	2,532,378	**63,904**
Inventory						**281,147**
Adjusting Entry	12/31/2008	02/16/2009	Cost of Goods Sold	15,629		296,776
Total Inventory				15,629	-	**296,776**
Equipment						**83,498**
Adjusting Entry	12/31/2008	02/28/2009	Loans to Employees	40,000		123,498
Total Equipment				40,000	-	**123,498**
Accumulated Depreciation						**(66,824)**
Adjusting Entry	12/31/2008	02/16/2009	Depreciation Expense		6,534	(73,358)
Total Accumulated Depreciation				-	6,534	**(73,358)**
Loan to Employees						-
				40,000		40,000
Adjusting Entry	12/31/2008	02/28/2009	Equipment		40,000	-
Total Loan to Employees				40,000	40,000	-
Other Assets						**1,253**
Total Other Assets				-	-	1,253
Payroll Liabilities Payable						**(49,169)**
				34,169		(15,000)
					36,789	(51,789)
Total Payroll Liabilities Payable				34,169	36,789	**(51,789)**

(continued)

Exhibit 7D (continued)

Type	Date	Entry Date	Split	Debit	Credit	Balance
Sales Tax Payable						**(16,593)**
				16,593		-
					(18,410)	18,410
Total Sales Tax Payable				16,593	18,410	**(18,410)**
Long-Term Debt						**(44,441)**
				1,862		(42,579)
Total Long-Term Debt				1,862	-	**(42,579)**
Capital Stock						**(1,000)**
Total Capital Stock				-	-	**(1,000)**
Retained Earnings						**(270,674)**
Total Retained Earnings				-	-	**(270,674)**
Sales						-
					2,513,479	(2,513,479)
Total Sales				-	2,513,479	**(2,513,479)**
Cost of Goods Sold						-
				2,090,538		**2,090,538**
Adjusting Entry	12/31/2008	02/16/2009	Auto Lease	6,000		**2,096,538**
Adjusting Entry	12/31/2008	02/16/2009	Inventory		15,629	2,080,909
Total Cost of Goods Sold				2,096,538	15,629	**2,080,909**
Advertising and Promotion						-
				7,512		**7,512**
Adjusting Entry	12/31/2008	02/28/2009	Travel and Entertainment	20,000		27,512
Total Advertising and Promotion				27,512	-	**27,512**

Exhibit 7D (continued)

Type	Date	Entry Date	Split	Debit	Credit	Balance
Auto Lease						-
				6,000		**6,000**
Adjusting Entry	12/31/2008	02/16/2009	Cost of Goods Sold		6,000	-
Total Auto Lease				6,000	6,000	-
Delivery						-
				12,669		12,669
Total Delivery				12,669	-	**12,669**
Depreciation Expense						-
Adjusting Entry	12/31/2008	02/16/2009	Accumulated Depreciation	6,534		6,534
Total Depreciation Expense				6,534	-	6,534
Insurance Expense						-
				30,149		**30,149**
Adjusting Entry	12/31/2008	02/28/2009	Outside Labor	8,000		38,149
Total Insurance Expense				38,149	-	**38,149**
Interest Expense						-
						-
Total Interest Expense				-	-	-
Misc. Expense						-
				3,115		3,115
Total Misc. Expense				3,115	-	**3,115**
Office Supplies						-
				4,350		4,350
Total Office Supplies				4,350	-	**4,350**

(continued)

Exhibit 7D | *(continued)*

Type	Date	Entry Date	Split	Debit	Credit	Balance
Officers Compensation						-
				50,000		50,000
Total Officers Compensation				50,000	-	**50,000**
Outside Labor						-
				8,698		8,698
Adjusting Entry	12/31/2008	02/28/2009	Insurance		8,000	698
Total Outside Labor				8,698	8,000	**698**
Postage						-
				1,310		1,310
Total Postage				1,310	-	**1,310**
Rent Expense						-
				24,000		24,000
Total Rent Expense				24,000	-	**24,000**
Repairs and Maintenance						-
				1,769		1,769
Total Repairs and Maintenance				1,769	-	**1,769**
Salaries & Wages						-
				161,315		161,315
Total Salaries & Wages				161,315	-	**161,315**
Supplies						-
				2,021		2,021
Total Supplies				2,021	-	**2,021**
Taxes & Licenses						-
				54,543		54,543
Total Taxes & Licenses				54,543	-	**54,543**

Exhibit 7D | *(continued)*

Type	Date	Entry Date	Split	Debit	Credit	Balance
Telephone Expense						-
				3,667		3,667
Total Telephone Expense				3,667	-	**3,667**
Travel and Entertainment						-
				26,051		**26,051**
Adjusting Entry	12/31/2008	02/28/2009	Advertis-ing and Promotion		20,000	6,051
Total Travel and Entertainment				26,051	20,000	**6,051**
Utilities						-
				7,246		7,246
Total Utilities				7,246	-	**7,246**
Interest Income						-
						-
Total Interest Income				-	-	-
				5,197,219	**5,197,219**	**-**

Special Note

Students should carefully examine the JEs (Exhibits 7B through 7D), noting the entry dates, involvement of unrelated accounts (sales and loans to employees), and use of even / round numbers.

Phase III: Refine and Confirm Your Hypothesis via Interviews

As previously discussed (see Chapter 4), an interview is a primary tool used by forensic accountants to gather information and make assessments. At this phase of your investigation, you should have:

1. Developed a working knowledge of the business (including the pawn shop operation).
2. Developed a working knowledge of the company's accounting system, especially the internal controls (or lack thereof).

3. Identified any questionable financial statement (tax return) reporting issues (for example, no pawn receivables, no interest expense, and questionable JEs).
4. Identified the key players to be interviewed and the information sought.

Who should be interviewed? In what order? Should the interviews be formal or informal? To assist you in this phase, we propose the following interview sequence:

1. Neutral third parties (Sue Bryant)
2. Corroborative witnesses and possible co-conspirators (Anita Workman)
3. Suspected co-conspirators (Charles Hess)
4. Target (Thomas Workman)

The previous interviews have been memorialized and are presented as Exhibits 7E through 7H. You must read each one carefully (in sequence) to refine and confirm your hypothesis. All relevant information should be identified and incorporated into your assessment of the case facts and circumstances. At this point, you may be wondering:

- Why did Sue Bryant retire?
- What is the relationship between Hess and Workman?
- Who is responsible for these accounting shenanigans—Anita, Hess, or Workman?
- How might they explain specific questionable transactions?
- Is Anita Workman a corroborative witness or a co-conspirator?
- What about intent? Is this fraud, or do these failures represent innocent errors?
- What role does Hess play? Who relied on whom?

Exhibit 7E | Interview of Sue Bryant

Memo to File

Date: Mar 8, 2009 (transcribed Mar 8)

Re: Meeting with and interview of **Ms. Sue Bryant** (1:00–3:15 pm) Office of Dwane Peoples, Esq.

Subj: Mountain State Sporting Goods

Introduction of self and purpose of visit:

- Advised that I have been engaged by Mr. Peoples, attorney representing shareholders of Mt. State Sporting Goods, to assess the operations of the business, including its books and records.
- Advised that Mr. Peoples was concerned about the viability of the business and the accuracy of the accounting reports.
- Advised that I had previously reviewed the following:
  - The company's income tax returns for years '03–'08;
  - The company's reviewed report for Dec 31, '06 and compilation reports for '07 and '08;
  - The company's valuation report of Dec 31, '06;
  - The company's detailed general ledger and adjusting entries for years '06–'08; and
  - Workman's employment contract

Ms. Bryant freely agreed to be interviewed and provided the following:

1. Personal profile
   - 67 years old
   - Widowed – no children
   - Residence – South Charleston, WV
   - Degree in education – taught high school business math and bookkeeping
   - Helped JD start the business in '93 – his first employee
   - Started out part-time; full-time in '00 or '01
2. Mountain State Sporting Goods
   - '93 through '06
   - Base compensation was $750 per week; also received bonuses (avg about $45k per year)
   - Benefits included health insurance, 3 wks vacation, and IRA contributions
   - Duties included all accounting and payroll
     - ➢ maintained a comprehensive set of books and records
     - ➢ everything was automated
     - ➢ system of checks and balances
     - ➢ generated monthly financial statements
     - ➢ focus was always on cash flow
     - ➢ Tax returns done by H&R Block
   - Pawn shop activity
     - ➢ Thought pawn shop was great idea
     - ➢ Worked hard to develop policies and procedures – controls
     - ➢ JD hired a consulting firm to help set up (purchased specialized software)
     - ➢ Big boost to business – new traffic
     - ➢ Opened in summer of '06 – by year-end about $50k in loans
     - ➢ Interest rate of 20% per month
     - ➢ All principal payments made (and loaned) in cash
     - ➢ Interest payments usually by checks (some cash)
     - ➢ Deposit slips should provide breakdown of deposit source
     - ➢ Default rate about 25–30% (defaults go to inventory – markup of 100%)
     - ➢ Markup is the amount added to a cost price to calculate a selling price
     - ➢ JD's plan was to save pawn revenues for improvements and down payment on building
3. Business After JD's death
   - Total confusion
   - JD had no plan – boys in school; spouse not physically capable
   - Informal agreement with family to *co-manage* with Tom Workman (TW); attempted to split JD's duties
     - ➢ TW was a long-term employee – about 10 years
     - ➢ TW worked as asst. floor mgr – not involved with administrative functions – limited knowledge of overall business; no working knowledge of pawn shop

- First 15 days were hell
    - ➢ Total confusion – TW asserted total control
        - **a.** First problem was bonus – TW insisted that JD had promised; we agreed to complete YE and discuss with family
        - **b.** Second problem was TW's pay and benefits – TW wanted $60k (per advice of Hess); I thought it was excessive – we agreed to discuss with family
        - **c.** Third problem was Hess; I agreed to hire to help with YE – turned into nightmare
            - **i.** First step was to add TW to bank signatory – he started writing checks – big problem
            - **ii.** Second step was to abandon accounting controls, especially over pawn shop
- Met with JD's family on Jan. 3, '07
    - ➢ Advised of problems and decision to retire (too much stress)
    - ➢ Suggested valuation and sale of business
    - ➢ Thought TW could do the job – he is not afraid of work; needed controls
    - ➢ Suggested hiring new in-house accountant and/or different CPA firm for objective review – Hess to close
    - ➢ Suggested employment contract for TW – $50k base plus a percentage of sales (incentive)
    - ➢ Store offered limited benefits – suggested health insurance for TW
    - ➢ Suggested annual audits
    - ➢ Agreed to serve on board
    - ➢ Did not see TW's employment contract
- Limited involvement after Jan 6, 2007
    - ➢ Not invited to attend BOD meetings
    - ➢ Occasional p/conversations with Hess about coding issues
    - ➢ YE adjusting entries made by Hess or staff members
    - ➢ Surprised to hear Anita and Mia were doing day-to-day accounting
    - ➢ Surprised audits not conducted
    - ➢ Have not seen annual reports

Discuss Relationship with Anita and Mia

4. Sue stated as follows:

- Like Anita and Mia
- Anita worked at the store part-time during holidays and for inventory
- Committed to daughter
- Did not want to work full time
- Surprised she was doing accounting work for store
- Calls occasionally to check in
- According to Anita, Hess is running accounting functions
- Mia very sweet – glad she was working at the store – good experience

Discuss Relationship with Hess (CPA)

5. Sue stated as follows:

- Hess involved in negotiations of building lease – worked for landlord
- Hess had visited the store after they moved to offer services

- Hess was a friend of TW's
- Understand Hess has small practice
- Believes Hess saw JD's death as opportunity
- Confused by Hess's suggestions regarding physical inventory and change in accounting software
- Understand that TW hired Hess on full-time basis – took her job
- No direct knowledge – mostly through Anita

Discussion of Specific Transactions

I presented for discussion the following specific transaction; Sue stated as follows:

6. Check for $45,000 on Dec 23, 2006 – initially recorded as employee loan; reclassified (adj) to reduce sales ($45,000); $20k came from company LOC – coded as payroll tax payable **[Copy of $45,000 check presented]**
   - No knowledge
   - Shocked
   - Would not have seen check – would have been included with Dec bank statements – received in mid-Jan

Closing Statements

I concluded my interview and inquired if she had any final statements or information. Sue advised as follows:

7. Very surprised – but not shocked.
8. Understood that TW's lifestyle had changed – house, cars, and trips.
9. Does not believe Anita or Mia aware.
10. Believes bad advice from Hess.

End.

Exhibit 7F | Interview of Anita Workman

Memo to File

Date: Mar 10, 2009 (transcribed Mar 12)

Re: Meeting with and interview of **Ms. Anita Workman** (6:00–7:30 pm) Mt. State Sporting Goods

Subj: Accounting Practices—Duties and responsibilities

Introduction of self and purpose of visit:

- Advised that I have been engaged by Mr. Peoples, attorney representing shareholders of Mt. State Sporting Goods, to assess the operations of the business including its books and records.
- Advised that Mr. Peoples was concerned about the viability of the business and the accuracy of the accounting reports.
- Advised that I had previously reviewed the following;
  - The company's income tax returns for years '03–'08;
  - The company's reviewed report for Dec 31, '06 and compilation reports for '07 and '08;
  - The company's valuation report of Dec 31, '06;
  - The company's detailed general ledger and adjusting entries for years '06–'08; and
  - Her husband's employment contract

- Advised that I had previously interviewed:
  - Ms. Sue Bryant (the company's former bookkeeper); and
  - The company's banking agents.

Anita freely agreed to be interviewed and provided the following:

1. Personal profile:
   - DOB – Jan 26, 1969 (age 40)
   - Married – Thomas Workman (DOM – May 15, 1989)
   - One child – Mia (17)
   - Education – community college – 3 semesters (business classes)
   - Work history:
     i. Jan '07 to current
        Mountain State Sporting Goods – Works as needed; training to be in-house accountant
        - ➢ Training provided by Hess & Associates, CPAs
        - ➢ Attended a QuickBooks workshop at their office
        - ➢ Salary $1,500 per month – salary determined by Charles Hess, CPA
        - ➢ Est. 25 hrs per week – sometimes more – sometimes less
        - ➢ Does some bookkeeping work at home – payables and payroll – takes about hour per week
          - Store purchased computers for use at home
          - Setup by CPA staff
        - ➢ Works at the store as needed – where needed – no set schedule; husband calls when shorthanded – fills in for Mia
        - ➢ Not involved with pawn shop – handled by TW – mostly guns
        - ➢ Does not assist with inventory – done by TW and Hess – not sure how they do it

     ii. 1990 – 2007
        - ➢ Primarily a stay-at-home mom (school volunteer)
        - ➢ Occasionally worked at the store for JD – as needed – register, stocking, or inventory
          a. Assisted Sue Bryant

     iii. 1988 – 1990
        - ➢ Blockbuster
        - ➢ Part-time with H&R Block – personal income tax returns

     iv. 1986 – 1988
        - ➢ Blockbuster
   - No health issues / special needs
2. Spouse's profile – Thomas Workman (TW)
   - DOB – Sept 13, 1967
   - Education – high school graduate
   - Work history
     i. 1995 to current
        Mountain State Sporting Goods
        - ✓ Manager since JD's death in Dec '06
        - ✓ Works all the time if not hunting or fishing
        - ✓ Asst Mgr for about five years

ii. 1990–1995
General Dollar Store, Asst Mgr (store closed)
iii. 1988
Construction work

3. Daughter's profile – Mia Workman
   - DOB – June 20, 1991
   - Education – high school (senior yr)
     i. Already accepted at NC State
   - Work history
     i. June '07 to current
     Mountain State Sporting Goods – as needed – mostly stocking and register
       - $10 per hr.
       - Works full-time in summer; part-time during school

Discussion of Sue Bryant

4. Anita advised as follows:
   - Wonderful person – really knew the business
   - She was always kind and explained things – why or why not
     i. Hess rarely explains why – just do it
   - She offered to train me – TW and Hess said no – they were installing new system
   - Had been with JD from the start – maybe a relative (not sure)
   - College educated – before store she taught high school math
   - Light years ahead on using computers and software – loved them and what they could do
   - Struggled with JD's death – she was like his older sister
   - Initially agreed to co-manage store with TW at family's request
   - Short lived – Sue quit after about 30 days
   - Big blowup over hiring Hess
   - Sue and TW started fighting after JD's death – always fighting about the pawn shop and gun purchases at gun shows
     i. Most guns keep at home in gun safes – 3 safes
   - Sue did not like or trust Hess
   - She suggested other CPAs
   - Sue was not impressed with Hess – did not believe he knew anything about the business – was learning on the store's dollar
   - Sue insisted on audit by outside CPA
   - She decided to retire – not comfortable with changes being proposed
   - Sue is in her late mid-60s – lot of energy
   - Sue very close to JD's kids – also close to Mia

Discuss Relationship with Hess (CPA)

5. Anita stated as follows:
   - Hess a friend of TW's since high school
   - Always together – hunt, fish, poker
   - Trips to Canada (fishing), out west (boar hunting) and Vegas (gambling)

    - Needed special rifles for boar hunting – talking about a trip to Fiji
    - They claim Vegas trips are product shows – all business
- Not sure how trips are paid for
    - TW controls family money
    - TW opened a bank account for paying household bills, groceries, meds, clothing and so forth
- TW hired Hess after JD died
    - TW thinks Hess smartest man alive
    - Hess did not like Sue – thought she was too old and nosey – wanted to know everything
- Hess handles almost all financial affairs – business and personal
    - Knows more about their financial affairs than she does
    - TW hired to negotiate settlement of credit card debt
        - She no longer has a credit card
    - Handles their life insurance and IRAs
    - Does their tax returns
    - Negotiated auto leases and mortgage loans
        - Hess explained car leases better than purchase – tax write-offs
        - Not sure who pays – company or TW
        - Purchased first residence in '07 ($175k)
    - Recent investment in condo
        - Hess convinced TW great investment
        - Condo owned 50/50 – Hess and TW
        - 100% financing
        - Understand note payments made with rental income
- Hess has small practice – secretary and two bookkeepers
- Hess firm reviews all accounting transactions and does payroll reports, W2s, tax returns, etc.
- Her job is to pay the bills – Hess's people set it up
- If she has a question she calls Hess's office
- Does not recall ever writing Hess a check – not sure how he gets paid
- Does not see YE financial statements or company tax returns – prepared by Hess
- Does not attend board meetings

Discussion About Pawn Business

Anita state as follows:

6. Little or no knowledge
    - TW manages
    - Keeps cash on hand – usually $10k
    - TW keeps separate from other transactions
    - TW deposits once a week – ck and cash
    - Interest payments usually by ck
    - Loan payoff by cash – identified on deposit slips
    - No knowledge about forfeited items
    - Not authorized to make loans

Discussion of Specific Transactions

I presented for discussion the following specific transactions; Anita states as follows:

7. Check for $45,000 on Dec 23, 2006 – initially recorded as employee loan; reclassified (adj) to reduce sales ($45,000); $20k came from company LOC – coded as payroll tax payable **[Copy of $45,000 check presented]**
   - Does not recall ever seeing the ck
   - No knowledge
   - Not sure what money was used for
8. Checks payable to Classic Construction – 5 in '07 totaling $5k ($1k each) and 2 in'08 totaling $8k ($3k and $5k)
   - Classic did improvements to house
   - Assumed HW paid with personal funds
   - No reason to be paid by company
9. Checks (3) drawn on Company LOC '07 – Payable to TW – totaling $25,000: Not recorded on books; entry to reduce sales and increase debt. **[Copies of three checks presented - $5,000, $10,000 and $10,000]**
   - No knowledge
   - Entry makes no sense
10. Checks payable to Ford Leasing – $6,000 in '07 and '08
    - Not surprised
    - Adjusting entries make no sense
11. Checks payable to AMX (personal credit card) – 10 cks in '07 totaling $13,212 and 12 cks in '08 totaling $21,409
    - Shocked at amounts and specific charges
    - Adjusting entries make no sense – appears personal not business
12. Check payable to TW May 3, 2008 ($40,000)
    - Initially recorded as loan to employee
      - Adjusting entry on Dec 31 '08 to reclassify to furniture and fixtures
    - No knowledge
    - Acknowledged they invested in property with Hess;
    - Thought down payment was $100k – $50,000 each.
    - Believe TW borrowed from the bank – not the company
13. Checks (3) payable to Fidelity Investment in '08 ($3,000 each)
    - Recalls – IRAs
    - Direction of Hess
    - Entry to COGS makes no sense.

End.

Exhibit 7G | Interview of Charles Hess, CPA

Memo to File

Date: Mar 15, 2009 (transcribed Mar 17)

Re: Meeting with and interview of **Charles Hess** (8:00–11:15 am) Office of Hess & Associates, Charleston, WV

Subj: Mountain State Sporting Goods – Nature of Engagements, Duties, and Responsibilities

Introduction of self and purpose of visit:

- Advised Hess that I have been engaged by Mr. Peoples, attorney representing shareholders of Mt. State Sporting Goods, to assess the operations of the business, including its books and records.
- Advised Hess that Mr. Peoples was concerned about the viability of the business, its current management, and the accuracy of the accounting reports.
- Advised Hess that I had previously reviewed the following:
    - The company's income tax returns for years '03–'08;
    - The company's reviewed report for Dec 31, '06 and compilation reports for '07 and '08;
    - The company's valuation report of Dec 31, '06;
    - The company's detailed general ledger and adjusting entries for years '06–'08; and
    - Workman's employment contract
- Advised Hess that I had previously interviewed:
    - Ms. Sue Bryant (the company's former bookkeeper);
    - Anita Workman; and
    - The company's banking agents.

Hess freely agreed to be interviewed and provided the following:

Personal Background

1. Personal profile:
    - Name – Charles Blevins Hess
    - DOB – June 14, 1965 (age 43)
    - Education – BS in Accounting (1990)
    - CPA – 1994
        - Annual CPE as required
    - No specialized training – valuation, tax, etc.
    - Work history

      1994 to current
      Self Employed – Hess & Associates

      1992 - 1994
      Johnson & Cain, CPAs
      Staff accountant / tax return preparer
      Received limited training or mentoring

      1990 - 1992
      Circuit City
      Asst Mgr
    - Military service
        - None
2. Hess & Associates, CPAs
    - Sole proprietorship
    - Formed after passing the CPA exam
    - Nature of business includes business startup, general ledger accounting, payroll and tax returns
    - Does not do audits – no experience and too risky
    - Always looking for new business
    - Firm growing – recently hired second staff accountant

- Prices determined by size of client and nature of work – usually hourly
- Advertising limited to yellow pages and word of mouth
- Rarely secures engagement letters – sometimes if special engagement – states engagement letters not required
- Member of KY Society and AICPA
- Never been sued – does have malpractice insurance just in case
- Not aware of any ethical complaints

Discuss Relationship with Workman and Mountain State

3. Hess advised as follows:

- Have known TW (Workman) since high school
- TW known as outdoors man – camping, fishing, and hunting
- Occasionally socialize – dinner, fishing, poker
- Acknowledged a couple of trips together – FL and Vegas
- Does accounting work for **Black Oak Realty** (landlord)
    - First met JD in early '06 regarding building
- Visited with JD after he relocated to Black Oak building about his accounting needs – he was happy with in-house bookkeeper and use of H&R Block for taxes
    - Tried to explain benefits of CPA vs. bookkeeper
    - Met and renewed friendship with TW
- TW contacted him after JD died
    - Told me he was taking over the management of the business
    - Needed help getting it organized
    - Wanted me to take over accounting
    - Needed to finish '06 financial reports
- Little or no knowledge about TW's employment contract
    - Not sure who he used to help negotiate
    - May have seen it
    - Recalls general discussions about pay – $50k plus benefits and bonuses
    - Understand that TW has total authority – maybe an option to purchase
- Nature of engagement with Mt. State includes quarterly and annual payroll tax reports, reconciliation of GL, financial statements and annual tax returns.
- **Acknowledged** training of Anita and Mia on accounting system – QuickBooks
    - They usually discuss problems with staff
- Available as needed
- Charge by the hour – rate varies by staff member
    - **Agreed to provide copies of invoices**
- **Does not recall** being paid in cash or property
- Mt. State not largest client – top 50
- Firm also helped purchase and set up computers – allows Anita and Mia to work from home
- Acknowledged helping TW with bank loans and financing arrangements – business and personal
- Acknowledged discussions with TW on inventory; advised him to do YE physical inventory – not aware of change after JD's death – believe physical inventory better then perpetual – less expensive
- Understand store has pawn shop – believe small percentage of overall activity
- Not aware how TW accounts for pawn loans – assumes he runs loans through the books – does not recall discussing

- Understand that checks are cashed to make pawn loans – listing of checks presented memo indicates pawn loans (totals – '07 = $91,230; '08 = $97,315) – surprised at the level
- Understand that all loan payments (except interest) must be cash
- Believe that source of all deposits specified on slip, especially cash deposits
- Believe that interest on pawn loans made by check
- Acknowledged buying a few forfeited items – couple of handguns
- Acknowledged attending annual board meetings and presenting financials – understand JD's kids not happy
- Not aware that annual audits required – seems like a waste of time and money – his firm does not do audits; would be auditing own work – could not do if requested
- *Acknowledged* advising Workman to present compilation reports – little or no added value to reviewed report
- Has no specific expertise in pawn business – not aware how forfeited items booked – not aware how loans booked
- *Acknowledged* helping Anita with adj entries / YE GL; financial statements basis for tax returns.
- Corp is Sub S; K-1s issued to kids (50/50)
- Knows TW is not a shareholder
- No detailed knowledge of TW's specific duties and responsibilities – he's the CEO
- Firm also does TW's personal income tax returns
- Helped TW set up IRAs for '07
- Acknowledged discussing hiring Anita and Mia and acceptable levels of pay

Review of Financial Statements and Tax Returns

Presented Hess with copies of financial statements and related tax returns (and summaries) for inspection and confirmation ('06 –'08). Hess confirmed they were prepared by his firm.

4. Hess advised as follows:
    - Believes financial statements and tax returns are reasonably accurate – not perfect
    - Relied on management – TW and Anita
    - Understands the importance of meaningful financials given nature of TW's responsibility to kids
    - Acknowledges that the kids rely on TW; TW relies on him to some extent
5. Review of income statement summary ('03–'08); Hess states as follows:
    - Profit margins surprising – appear to be going in wrong direction
    - Issue may be inventory – would have to check
    - Have done no analysis
    - Believes interest from pawn loans simply being run through sales
    - No specific knowledge on total pawn loans made – would guess small
    - Assumes all income being reported
    - Acknowledges trends seem misplaced – will investigate if necessary
    - No specific knowledge about car leases
6. Review of balance sheet ('02–'08); Hess states as follows:
    - Not sure what was purchased ($40k) in '08; took IRC 179
    - Agrees money could have been used as down payment on building – not sure how TW made the decision
    - Agrees account balance for payroll tax payable seems high

- Confirms note balances – recalls seeing adj entries
- Not sure where or how payday loans (receivable) accounted for on balance sheet
- Assumes cash on hand for loans included in cash balance
- Inventory value provided by TW – he knows best
- Acknowledges it does not include forfeited pawn items

7. Review of Cash Flow Analysis
    - Cannot explain difference between implied cash balance and reported cash balance – ($33k in '06); must be dividends
    - Bryant processed the '06 GL – relied on her work
8. Discussion of Valuation Report (Dec 31, 2006); Hess states as follows:
    - Aware that one was done – $350K
    - Does not recall seeing
    - Believes valuation completed before his firm was hired
    - Acknowledged doing '06 review
    - Relied on Sue Bryant; long-term in-house accountant
    - Recalls that '06 review requested by valuator
    - Does not recall any discussions with valuator
    - Acknowledged '06 review logically considered in Dec 31, '06 valuation
    - Acknowledged that misstatements or errors in review could result in erroneous value – no specialized training in valuation.
    - Acknowledged that understatement of assets would impact valuation.
9. Sue Bryant; Hess stated as follows:
    - Met once or twice – understands she was a long-term employee – retired after JD's death
    - Recalls she helped with '06 review
    - Understand she could not work with TW, Anita / Mia
    - Understand she resented not being hired as manager – resented TW

Discussion of Specific Transactions

I advised Hess that I had identified specific transactions of concern:

10. Check for $45,000 on Dec 23, 2006 payable to Workman
    - Initially recorded as employee loan
        - Adjusting entry to reclassify
            - Debit to sales ($45,000)
    - Hess stated he had no knowledge – Bryant would have made the '06 YE adjustments
    - Hess stated he had not discussed with Bryant or TW
    - Hess acknowledged reduction of sales might impact valuation – not certain
11. Dec 31 '06 Posting to Payroll Taxes Payable
    - Posting appears erroneous – overstates payroll taxes payable by exactly $20k
        - $20k drawn on LOC on Dec 23 to cover above check to Workman
    - Hess stated he had no knowledge – would have to discuss with TW or Bryant
    - Hess stated he did not review adjusting entries when doing '06 review – relied on Bryant
    - Hess acknowledged that posting might impact valuation – not certain – no specialized training

12. Checks to Cash – Charged to COGS ($91,230 in '07 and $97,315 in '08)
    - Hess stated his understanding that cash needed to make pawn loans
    - Hess stated he has no knowledge of how cash on-hand is reconciled
    - Hess surprised that checks to cash less than pawn sales
13. History of '07 Credit Line
    - 3 checks ($5,000, $10,000, and $10,000) drawn on LOC—Payable to TW—Not recorded on books
    - '07 adjusting entry to reduce sales and increase debt.
    - Hess stated he had no knowledge – '07 adjusting entries made by Anita
    - Hess stated firm did compilation – not audit – would not have detected
14. Checks payable to Classic Construction – 5 in '07 totaling $5k ($1k each) and 2 in'08 totaling $8k ($3k and $5k)
    - Disbursements initially coded as outside labor; adjusting entry to reduce outside labor and increase insurance
    - Hess stated he has no knowledge –YE adjustments made by Anita
15. Checks payable to Ford Leasing – $6,000 in '07 and '08
    - Initially classified as auto lease – adjusting entry each year to reclassify to COGS.
    - Hess stated he was aware they had purchased new cars – had discussed the purchase / lease options
    - Hess stated he was not aware the company was paying leases
    - Hess stated one car might be reasonable – not two
    - Hess advised he had no knowledge of adjusting entries – would talk with Anita
16. Checks payable to AMX (personal credit card) – 10 cks in '07 totaling $13,212 and 12 cks in '08 totaling $21,409
    - Payments made on Workman's personal credit card
    - Payments initially coded as travel – adjusted to advertising, $12,500 and $20,000 respectively
    - Hess stated using personal card and getting reimbursed was ok – IRS did not care
    - Hess advised he had no knowledge of adjusting entries – could not explain why – not sure what difference it makes
17. Check payable to TW May 3, 2008 ($40,000)
    - Initially recorded as loan to employee
        - Adjusting entry on Dec 31 '08 to reclassify to furniture and fixtures
    - Hess stated that he and TW had jointly purchased some rental property in May of '08 – TW's share of the down payment was $50,000 – thought TW had borrowed from the bank – not the company
18. Checks (3) payable to Fidelity Investments on March 3, 2008 ($3,000 each)
    - Disbursements made by company and recorded as COGS.
    - Hess stated payments for company sponsored IRAs – not sure why coded as COGS

Concluding Discussions

I concluded my interview and presented the following summary concerns.

19. Documents indicate a false accounting to the shareholders ($250k to $400k) – maybe even fraud:
    - Hess stated he was surprised
    - Hess stated he thought TW had the authority to made decisions – even make loans to himself – happens every day on Wall Street
    - Hess stated TW worked the business the same way JD did – cannot believe TW knew he was doing something wrong
    - Hess agreed items discussed, if added back, would change the outlook of the company

20. Duty of Hess to the Company and its shareholders vs. relationship with Workman:

- Hess acknowledged other people relied on his compilation reports
- Hess stated his role was after-the-fact – compilations not audits
- Hess stated he did not know company was required to have an annual audit
    - No specific knowledge of TW's employment contract
- Hess stated he was never hired to do analysis – may have uncovered problems – no guarantee
- Hess acknowledged monies take by TW. . . if not properly reported or paid back . . . was a problem
- Hess fears he trained TW and Anita too well
- Hess acknowledged taking trip to Vegas with TW; also acknowledged that TW picked up the tab – they did discuss business
- Hess acknowledged visiting the bank with TW for purposes of borrowing money – business and personal
- Hess stated his role always after-the-fact
- Hess stated he did not notice or think that TW was living beyond his means – that all three worked all the time

I asked if he had any final comments or anything else to add; Hess stated as follows:

- TW and Anita were friends – maybe he should have paid more attention
- Do not believe TW thought about what he was doing – would not steal
- TW loves his job – the business and its customers
- Need to arrive at an agreeable number – maybe buy JD's boys out – $350k
- The family would be devastated
- TW needs a good lawyer

Exhibit 7H | Interview of Thomas Workman

Memo to File

Date: Mar 15, 2009 (transcribed Mar 17)

Re: Meeting with and interview of **Thomas Workman** (1:30–4:15 pm)
Mountain State Sporting Goods, Inc., Charleston, WV

Subj: Assess operations and accounting practices

Introduction of self and purpose of visit:

- Advised Workman that I have been engaged by Mr. Peoples, attorney representing shareholders, to examine the business operations, including but not limited to its books and records.
- Advised Workman that the shareholders (JD's sons) were concerned about the management of the business, i.e., its reduced profitability, cash flow, and failure to fund the down payment for purchase of building.
- Advised Workman that I had previously reviewed the following:
    - The company's income tax returns for years '03–'08;
    - The company's reviewed reports for Dec 31, '06 and compilation reports for '07 and '08;
    - The company's valuation report of Dec 31, '06;
    - The company's detailed general ledger and adjusting entries for years '06–'08; and
    - His employment contract.

- Advised Workman that I had previously interviewed:
  - Mr. Charles Hess (the company's CPA);
  - Ms. Sue Bryant (the company's former bookkeeper);
  - His spouse – Anita Workman; and
  - The company's banking agents.

Mr. Workman freely agreed to be interviewed and provided the following:

Personal Background

1. Personal profile:
   - Name – Thomas Andrew Workman (TW)
   - DOB – Sept 13, 1966
   - Education – high school graduate
   - Work history
     - i. 1995 to current
       Mountain State Sporting Goods
       - ✓ Started out as stocking clerk – asst mgr
         - Avg Comp = $35k including benefits
         - Worked 45–50 hrs per wk
       - ✓ Took over as store manager following Mr. Smith's death in Dec. of '06
         - Comp = $50k plus benefits
           - No bonuses received.
         - Work 50 hrs per wk – always on call
         - Belief he is underpaid – happy to help family
     - ii. 1990 – 1995
       General Dollar Store, Asst Mgr (Comp $25k plus benefits)
       Note: Store Closed.
     - iii. 1985 – 1990
       Construction labor - various
   - Military service
     - None
   - No significant medical issues
2. Spouse's profile – Anita G. Workman
   - DOB – Jan 28, 1967
   - Education – two years of community college (accounting degree)
   - Work history
     - i. Feb '07 to current
       Mountain State Sporting Goods – Secretary and bookkeeper
       - ➢ $500 per week
       - ➢ Works in store 30 to 40 hrs per week – no set schedule
       - ➢ Does a lot of accounting work at home
     - ii. 1990 – 2007
       - ➢ Stay at home mom
       - ➢ Worked part time at the store – as needed
     - iii. 1988 – '89
       - ➢ Tax returns and bookkeeping for H&R Block
3. Daughter's profile – Mia Workman
   - DOB – June 20, 1991 (17 yrs old)
   - Education – high school (senior yr)

i. Active in school functions (band, etc.)
ii. Saving for college

- Work history
  i. Feb '07 to current
  Mountain State Sporting Goods – asst bookkeeper
    - ➢ $250 per week
    - ➢ Works in store 20 to 30 hrs per week – no set schedule
    - ➢ Does a lot of work at home and on weekends
    - ➢ Helps with pawn shop

Discuss Relationship with Hess (CPA)

4. TW advised as follows:
   - Have known Hess since high school
   - Close friends – hunt, fish, vacation together
   - Hess also financial advisor – life insurance, IRAs for self, spouse, and daughter
   - Helped negotiate employment contract
   - Hired by company after J.D.'s death to provide annual reports
   - Hess selected because of friendship
   - Hess was a new CPA – just starting out; hungry for business – low rates; also knew the pawn business
   - Company never pays taxes because of Hess
   - Hess has small practice – secretary and two bookkeepers
   - Hess does quarterly taxes and annual reports – W-2s, tax returns, etc.
   - Hess offers advice as needed
   - Not sure how Hess bills – hourly (bill offset with house account)
   - Allows Hess to charge purchases (at cost) – mostly hunting and fishing gear (guns and ammo) – offset for services at end of year
   - Hess also does personal income tax returns; helped prepare personal financial statements to banks for mortgage loans
   - Hess does not bill for personal work
   - Hess works with spouse and daughter as needed; also helps set up computers
   - Invested with Hess on beach home in '08 – down payment ($50k) borrowed from company – LOC; loan secured by personal note – pays 1% more than company pays – good deal for company.
   - Relies heavily on advice from Hess.
   - Change in inventory accounting (perpetual to periodic) recommended by Hess. No one trained on how to use software – always had problems. Periodic much easier – saves the company time and money
   - Consulted with Hess on pawn business – not recording pawn inventory reduces property taxes, saves on insurance, and eliminates write-offs – saves the company money
   - Annual audits a waste of money – saves the company about $10k per year – the kids wouldn't understand anyway.
   - Hess does year-end accounting – supervises Anita and helps reconciles books – does reports for kids and tax returns.

Review of Management Tasks / Employment Contract

5. TW advised as follows:
   - He understood his contract
   - His job was to do his best – make good decisions

- Job included protecting and growing the company
- Knew JD's kids were not happy – they always wanted more money – they brought nothing to the table
- Not sure about the difference between an audit and compilation – knew an audit costs a lot of money – he was saving the company about $10k a year
- Understood his pay was $50k per year, a percentage of sales plus benefits
- Considered his right to benefits same as JD's – he was running the show
- JD took money when he needed it – he wrote everything off
    - Understood he was the manager not the owner – he was not JD
    - Acknowledged duty to shareholders
- Believed benefits include travel – he was always on duty – 24/7
- Not sure if company pays for IRAs – believed so
- Believed benefits include use of autos, gas, and insurance
- Believed it was ok for him to borrow money from the company – they were in the business of loaning money – pawn business; agreed the loan amounts were different – he always guarantees the loans
- Not sure if he actually signed a note/s – Hess would know
- Smart to hire spouse and daughter – they understand the business and are available as needed
- Hess helped determine their pay

6. Pawn Shop – Operations

- TW advised average loan $100
- TW estimated 20 loans per month
- TW estimated average outstanding loan balance about $50k
- TW estimates redemption rate 60%
- TW acknowledges he makes and collects all pawn loans
- TW states collections treated as sales – processed through register weekly – usually on Sat
- TW states he <u>does not</u> include forfeited pawn items in physical inventory; estimated forfeited pawn items available $40–60k
- Forfeited pawn items sold for loan × 2 (not sure about markup)
- TW states money for loans treated as purchases – COGS
- Cks to cash for pawn loans –cks presented ('07 = $91,230; '08 = $97,315)
- TW estimates cash on hand for loans varies – avg $10k
    - TW acknowledges he has taken forfeited items for family members or for personal use – jewelry, guns, computer – estimate value $500
    - TW acknowledges Hess has taken forfeited items for payment of services – guns and jewelry
    - TW acknowledged accounting for pawn items poor – mostly by hand
    - TW acknowledged trashing paper records (index cards) regarding some pawn transactions – no big deal
    - TW does not send out monthly invoices – keeps index card – figures interest (20%) by hand
    - Average pawn loan balance about $50K
    - Interest rate of 20% per month
    - Default rate about 35–40%
    - All principal payments in cash – identified as such on deposit tickets
    - Pawn collections (cash or check) would be identified on deposit slips

  - Cash deposits identified as pawn payments: '07 = $48,064 and '08 = $52,053 "seems about right"
  - Pawn deposits via check would represent interest payments: '07 = $57,944 and '08 = $61,942, "seems about right"

7. Sue Bryant – TW advised as follows:
   - Decision to retire by mutual agreement (early '07)
   - She could not get over JD's death
   - She thought she knew everything – anal
   - She spent more time hunting for a penny then making dollar
   - She could not work with Hess – refused to follow direction
   - She was too slow – could not adjust to changes
   - She was always questioning his authority and decisions
   - She could not work with Anita / Mia

Discussion of Specific Transactions

I advised TW that I had substantially completed my investigation and would like to discuss some specific transactions.

8. Check for $45,000 on Dec 23, 2006 – initially recorded as employee loan; reclassified (adj) to reduce sales ($45,000); $20k came from company LOC – coded as payroll tax payable **[Copy of $45,000 check presented]**
   - TW requested I discuss with Hess and/or Anita – I advised that I had already discussed it with them and wanted his take
   - TW advised that he had not received his YE bonus promised before JD's death – his work on setting up the pawn business
   - TW stated not sure about his future given JD's death
   - TW not sure if he reported it as income – Hess would know
   - TW discussed with Hess and Bryant
   - Believe it was Bryant's idea – we were acting as co-managers
   - Not sure if she [Sue] took a bonus – does not think so
   - Believe he used bonus to pay off personal debt
   - Not sure if he discussed with or disclosed to JD's family
   - TW did not discuss with valuation guy – Hess handled it

Special Notes:

> ➢ TW stated this was a mistake – he would report as a bonus or pay the money back if necessary

9. Checks to Cash – Charged to COGS **['07 – 19 cks presented totaling $91,230; '08 – 22 cks presented totaling $97,315]**
   - TW advised that cash used to make pawn loans – need ready cash
   - TW states that cash also used for business – out of pocket expenses – gas, employee lunches, supplies
   - TW states it was all business
   - TW advised that average cash on hand for pawns $10k

Special Notes:

> ➢ I advised TW that checks to cash <u>substantially</u> exceeded total pawn sales and interest as reported
> ➢ I advised TW that the cash on hand was only $3,126 vs. $10k
> ➢ I advised TW that total cash deposits were less than checks for cash

10. Checks (3) drawn on Company LOC – Payable to TW – totaling $25,000; Not recorded on books; entry to reduce sales and increase debt. **[Copies of three checks presented – $5,000, $10,000, and $10,000]**
    - TW advised he had to report company debt balances
    - TW acknowledged he had borrowed the money in the Company's name
    - TW stated he thinks he used the money for down payment on residence
    - Not sure if he signed a note or paid it back – thinks so
    - TW states he did not disclose to kids
11. Checks payable to Classic Construction – 5 in '07 totaling $5k ($1k each) and 2 in'08 totaling $8k ($3k and $5k) – disbursements initially coded as outside labor; adj to reduce outside labor and increase insurance
    - TW acknowledged work for contracting done on personal residence
    - Paying the contractors allowed him to continue on the job
12. Checks payable to Ford Leasing - $6,000 in '07 and '08 – initially classified as auto lease; adj entry to reclassify to COGS.
    - TW not sure – does not understand why it matters.
    - TW not sure if they disclosed to family
    - Currently two autos – one for self and one for Anita
        i. Company also pays fuel and insurance
        ii. Leases in Company's name
        iii. Reasonable – always on duty
13. Checks payable to AMX (personal credit card) – 10 cks in '07 totaling $13,212 and 12 cks in '08 totaling $21,409 – payments initially coded as travel – adjusted to advertising, $12,500 and $20,000 respectively:
    - TW states he commonly uses personal cc for business -- no big deal
    - TW acknowledged some charges may have been for clothing or vacations – always on call even when on vacation
    - TW states charges should have been sorted – only business paid by company
    - TW states he discussed with Hess – Hess actually on one fishing trip – all business
    - TW did not disclose to JD's kids
14. Check payable to TW May 3, 2008 – $40,000 – initially recorded as loan to employee; adj Dec 31 '08 to furniture and fixtures **[Copy of $40,000 check presented]**
    - Was saving the money for down payment on building
    - TW states money used for down payment on condo – better investment
    - TW states Hess's idea – great investment
    - TW states condo co-owned with Hess
    - TW states business – allow use by employees and customers
    - TW states not sure why recoded – he needs to talk to Hess
    - TW did not disclose to JD's kids
    - TW thinks he signed a note – Hess would know
    - TW stated he would deed his interest back to the company
15. Checks (3) payable to Fidelity Investment in '08 ($3,000 each) – recorded as COGS.
    - TW advised IRA payments
    - Simply miscoded
16. Checks payable to banks for unauthorized loans '07 ($3,117) and '08 ($3,216).
    - Thought they were appropriate to pay

Representations to Banks

I inquired about alleged representations to the bank that he owned the business.

17. TW advised as follows:
    - He was given the authority to conduct banking business – including borrowing and lending money

- Does not recall representing he owned the business
- Believes he may have told the loan officer he had an option to purchase – he has discussed with both boys
- TW acknowledges an option is not part of employment contract
- Does not believe he provided the bank a copy of his employment contract

Concluding Discussions

I concluded my review of the documents and presented the following summary concerns.

18. I expressed concern that the documents indicate a false accounting to the shareholders – \$250k to \$400k:
   a. TW stated it "was not that much" – the total business was only valued at \$350k
   b. TW agreed to pay back anything in question
   c. TW stated he had "worked his ass off to build the business"
   d. TW stated the best solution is for he and Hess to buy the business – \$350K – the appraised value

19. I expressed concerns regarding the nature and role of Hess as the Company's CPA:
   a. TW stated he relied on Hess
   b. TW stated that Hess made all the accounting decisions – coding of checks and so forth
   c. TW stated Hess was more of a co-manager than an outside CPA

20. I expressed concern regarding the option to buy the building:
   a. TW stated it was not a problem
   b. TW stated that Hess had already worked out a deal to purchase the building from Black Oak and continue the lease with Mt. State – same rent.

21. Inquired how he (TW) saw the problem being resolved:
   a. TW stated that he and Hess had already discussed it – would buy the business – Hess was working on the numbers

22. Inquired if he had any final statements
   a. TW agreed the transactions cast a bad light but he had worked his ass off – built the business up
   b. Neither wife or daughter knew what was going on
   c. TW stated it was just a matter of money – how much?

End.

In addition to considering responses to the questions asked, you should identify any relevant questions that were not asked. Finally, identify any other witnesses you would like to interview and explain why.

Phase IV: Draw Your Conclusions and Communicate Results

This phase of the engagement requires a determination of the amount "misappropriated" and a related discussion of the specific schemes employed. To assist you in this phase, we have identified four different loss components:

- Specific transactions
- Unreported pawn loan interest
- Unreported forfeited pawn sales
- Statutory interest at 7.5%

A ***scheme*** is "an artful plot or plan, usually to deceive others."[1] Examples of fraud schemes experienced in small organizations (such as Mountain State Sporting Goods) are identified in Table 7-4.

Table 7-4 Common Fraud Schemes

Skimming	Stealing cash revenue "off the top," before it is recorded in the accounting system
Cash larceny	Stealing cash revenue after it has been recorded in the accounting system
Register disbursement	Making false entries in a cash register to conceal the fraudulent removal of cash
Less cash scheme	Deducting cash from check deposits
False credits / discounts	Using false credits or discounts to disguise theft of revenue
Diversion of loan proceeds	Diverting proceeds of business loans for personal use
False entries	Falsification of financial information, including false accounting entries and fictitious transactions designed to overstate revenues or understate losses
Unauthorized disbursements	Disbursement of company funds through some trick or device for an unauthorized purpose
Billing scheme	Type of unauthorized disbursement scheme in which a perpetrator submits invoices for fictitious goods and services, inflated invoices, or invoices for personal expenses
Check tampering	Type of unauthorized disbursement scheme in which a perpetrator forges, steals, or alters a company check
Payroll fraud	Type of unauthorized disbursement scheme that involves falsification of payroll records; examples include altering employee time cards and making payments to fictitious (or "ghost") employees
Expense reimbursements	A claim by an employee for reimbursement of fictitious or inflated business expenses
Kickback	Payment back by a seller of a portion of the purchase price to a buyer to induce purchase or influence future purchases
Swap transaction	A scheme in which two conspiring companies exchange payments and services for the sole purpose of inflating revenues

Source: Compiled from AICPA and ACFE definitions.

Specific Transactions

Specific transactions can be been identified in the JEs and confirmed in the interviews. Three examples include:

Transaction	Scheme	2006	2007	2008
12/23/06 check	Unauthorized disbursement; false entries	$45,000		
Draws on LOC (3 checks)	Unauthorized disbursements; false entries		$25,000	
Checks to Classic Construction	Unauthorized disbursements; false entries		$5,000	$8,000

Unreported Pawn Loan Interest and Unreported Forfeited Pawn Sales

Given that J.D. died on December 15, 2006, your challenge is to compute unreported pawn loan interest and forfeited pawn sales for years 2007 and 2008 only. A framework identifying specific variables and reference points is presented Exhibit 7I.

Exhibit 7I | Lost Pawn Revenue Calculation

	Pawn Interest	Pawn Items	Source
07 Loss Projections			
Est. 12/31/06 Pawn Loans	$ 50,000.00		Per S. Bryant interview
07 Pawn Loans	$ 91,230.00		Per check disbursements; confirmed by T. Workman
Expected Defaults @ 35%	$ (49,430.50)	$ 49,430.50	Per T. Workman interview
Available Loan Bal.	$ 91,799.50		
07 Pawn Collections	$ (48,464.00)		Per bank deposits analysis
Calculated 12/31/07 Pawn Loans	$ 43,335.50		
Avg. Loan Bal.	$ 46,667.75		
Interest @ 20% monthly	$ 9,333.55		
Annual Interest	$ 112,002.60		
Interest Paid via Check	$ (57,944.00)		Per bank deposits analysis
Net Estimated Loss	$ 54,058.60		
08 Loss Projections			
Calculated 12/31/07 Pawn Loans	$ 43,335.50		
08 Pawn Loans	$ 97,315.00		Per check disbursements; confirmed by T. Workman
Expected Defaults @ 35%	$ (34,060.25)	$ 34,060.25	
Available Loan Bal.	$ 106,590.25		
08 Pawn Collections	$ (52,053.00)		Per bank deposits analysis
Calculated 12/31/08 Pawn Loans	$ 54,537.25		
Avg. Loan Bal.	$ 48,936.38		
Interest @ 20% monthly	$ 9,787.28		
Annual Interest	$ 117,447.30		
Interest Paid via Check	$ (61,942.86)		Per bank deposits analysis
Net Estimated Loss	$ 55,504.44		
Ending Forfeited Pawn Items		$ (40,000.00)	
Forfeited Pawn Items Sold		$ 43,490.75	
Mark-up @ 100%*		$ 86,980.00	Per T. Workman interview
Total Estimated Loss	$ 109,563.04	$ 86,980.00	
Grand Total	**$196,549.00**		

*Split 50/50 '07 and '08

Calculation of Statutory Interest

Statutory interest is a rate of interest, prescribed by the applicable state (or federal) statute, that is applied to a determined amount of economic loss. For the purpose of your loss calculation, the statutory interest (7.5%) is determined at the end of each year using simple interest.

Phase V: Present a Discussion of Mr. Hess's Roles, Duties, and Responsibilities

The evidence you've collected indicates that Mr. Hess may be a co-conspirator and may have violated the AICPA's ethical and professional standards in his service to Mountain State Sporting Goods. This phase of the engagement requires you to address these concerns with a meaningful discussion of Mr. Hess's activities, including references to Rules 101, 201, and 202. Consider the following questions as a starting point:

- Was Mr. Hess independent with respect to the 2009 meeting with the BOD?
- Did Mr. Hess meet the following requirements:
  - Professional competence
  - Due professional care
  - Planning and supervision
  - Sufficient relevant data

Phase VI: Present Recommendations for Resolution and Remediation

Assuming that fraudulent activity has been identified, present your recommendations for resolution and remediation. Your discussion should consider the following:

- How strong is the evidence?
- Have any alternative explanations been identified?
- Should a criminal complaint be filed? If so, against whom?
- Should a civil complaint be filed? If so, against whom?
- Should alternative dispute resolution (ADR) be considered?

Alternative dispute resolution (ADR) is an alternative to litigation for resolving disputes. ADR strategies generally include mediation, arbitration, or some combination of the two. ***Mediation*** is a confidential and nonbinding structured process. It is generally facilitated by an independent third party (for example, a retired judge), who facilitates the exchange of positions and encourages the identification of common ground. A successful mediation results in a mutually satisfactory resolution. Compared to litigation and arbitration, mediation is generally less expensive and less time-consuming.

Arbitration is a binding process, where both sides present evidence and argue their respective positions to an arbitration panel, which usually includes at least one lawyer. This forum is considerably less formal than a trial and is generally focused on fact finding.

The advantages of ADR versus litigation can be summarized as follows:

- Time (it takes hours or days versus years)
- Cost (hundreds of dollars versus thousands of dollars)
- Flexibility (complete versus limited)
- Privacy (total versus public)
- Formality (low versus high)
- Enforceability (high versus cannot be appealed)

EPILOGUE

You will present your findings at a special meeting of the BOD attended by all concerned parties, including Workman, Hess, and their respective attorneys. Prior to the meeting, a copy of your report will be furnished to both Workman and Hess. Peoples has advised that your report may be the driving force toward a negotiated resolution or, if the case is prosecuted, critical evidence to be presented at trial.

You have also been advised that both Hess and Workman (through their respective attorneys) have advanced various affirmative defenses to explain their behavior. Specifically, Mr. Hess is arguing "frustration" (that is, Workman prevented him from performing his engagement) and negligence on the part of Workman. Workman, on the other hand, is arguing his lack of knowledge and negligence on the part of Hess. In preparation for the BOD meeting, Peoples has requested your assessment of these affirmative defenses, measured against the requisite element of intent.

Key Terms

Alternative dispute resolution

Arbitration

Mediation

Scheme

Statutory interest

---

[1]From *Black's Law Dictionary* (2009), 9th Edition. Material reprinted with permission of Thomson Reuters.

8 Transforming Data into Evidence (Part 1)

INTRODUCTION

Forensic accountants gather evidence in a variety of ways. In previous chapters, we discussed five methods commonly employed for gathering evidence—interviews, observations, public records, social media, and financial statements analysis. In this chapter, we transition from *gathering* evidence to *analyzing* evidence. Analysis, along with interpretation, is necessary for the development of meaningful conclusions.

We first consider the role and purpose of data analysis in a forensic accounting engagement, with an emphasis on *sufficient relevant data*. Next, we frame the data analysis task, focusing on efforts that precede the actual application of analytic methods. Having established the proper framework, we shift to application, introducing versatile tools that can be used in most engagements. The chapter concludes with an explanation of the analytic properties of interview transcription. This broad foundation sets the stage for the following chapter, which presents a variety of methods and techniques that have more specific applications.

THE ROLE OF DATA ANALYSIS

Although described here as a component of the overall investigative process, data analysis should occur throughout the engagement to facilitate hypothesis development and refinement. As illustrated in Chapter 7 (Mountain State Sporting Goods), this iterative process helps to focus the data collection effort (what to look for) and drives reasoned and intellectually honest conclusions. There is, of course, no cookie-cutter recipe, fixed formula, or checklist for analyzing evidence. Instead, much depends on the specifics of the engagement (such as scope limitations and time constraints), the analytic strategy, available resources, and the forensic accountant's experience.

What Is Data Analysis?

Data are simply items of information. Data can include any information about the subject person or organization, whether qualitative or quantitative. Qualitative data cannot be objectively measured, such as observations (sights, sounds, and smells) and words (documents and interviews). In contrast, quantitative data can be measured and expressed numerically, such as profit, weight, time, and age. Although numbers are a comfort zone for traditional accountants, forensic accountants realize that quantitative data alone rarely provide the contextual detail necessary to develop a comprehensive representation of the case evidence. Given this broad definition of data, the scope is seemingly endless. However, forensic accountants are not interested in *any* and *all* data about the subject; rather, we seek to identify data that are *sufficient* to support an expert opinion and *relevant* to the specific objectives of the engagement.

Analysis is defined as "separation of a whole into its component parts."[1] Thus, in ***data analysis***, we take some set of information and break it down into manageable pieces. The purpose of this action is to drill down to the essence or meaning of the information, which may not be apparent when viewed as a whole. This

Learning Objectives

After completing this chapter, you should be able to:

LO1. Describe the role of data analysis in a forensic accounting engagement.

LO2. Identify potential constraints and limitations that frame the data analysis task.

LO3. Compare and contrast four common data sources used by forensic accountants.

LO4. Explain the importance of planning for data analysis.

LO5. Identify ways data can be collected in a forensic accounting engagement.

LO6. Discuss the process of data preparation.

LO7. Identify and describe three data analysis tools: relationship charts, link analysis, and timelines.

LO8. Describe interview transcription as a process of analysis and interpretation.

interpretation highlights an important aspect of data analysis—its *strategic* nature. In a forensic accounting engagement, successful data analysis is not conducted indiscriminately. It requires a well-defined purpose, careful planning, and a systematic process, all aimed at refining the working hypothesis.

Special Note

Although data analysis implies the use of quantitative strategies, the tools introduced in this chapter do not involve numbers. Abstract tools are arguably the most important because they provide a foundation for all subsequent analysis and are revisited regularly to ensure the analysis stays on track. It is important to keep in mind that a more complex approach is not necessarily more effective. In fact, complexity is a challenge that must be overcome when presenting your results, especially to an untrained audience like a jury.

Sufficient Relevant Data

Forensic accounting (expert) opinions must be based on ***sufficient relevant data***. This mandate is found in Rule 702 of the Federal Rules of Evidence (FRE) and Rule 201 of the AICPA's Code of Professional Conduct.

Special Note

Although all forensic accountants are not CPAs, or even members of the AICPA, the AICPA professional standards commonly serve as a benchmark for evaluating forensic accounting services. As discussed in Chapter 10, the AICPA is the foremost source of guidance for accountants in public practice and establishes thresholds for appropriate professional conduct in the industry. Given this widespread influence, failure to comply with the AICPA standards puts the forensic accountant's work and opinion in jeopardy.

FRE Rule 702

As discussed in Chapter 2, FRE 702 allows the testimony of an expert witness if it will help the trier of fact (judge or jury) through the maze of "scientific, technical, or other specialized knowledge." Under this rule, expert testimony is admissible only if it meets three specific criteria:

- The testimony is based upon *sufficient facts or data*.
- The testimony is the product of *reliable principles and methods*.
- The principles and methods have been *applied reliably* to the facts of the case.

Without sufficient facts or data, the application of reliable principles and methods is of little or no consequence and value. In other words, bad data lead to bad results.

AICPA Rule 201

As provided in Rule 201 of the AICPA's Code of Professional Conduct, practitioners must "obtain sufficient relevant data to afford a reasonable basis for conclusions or recommendations in relation to any professional services performed."

What do we mean by sufficient? According to *Black's Law Dictionary*, the term *sufficient,* with regard to data, means "of such quality, number, force, or value as is necessary for a given purpose."[2] In the world of auditing (SAS No. 106, AU Sec. 326), sufficient is connected with appropriateness, with sufficient defined as "the measure of the quantity of the audit evidence" and appropriateness defined as "the measure of the quality of the audit evidence." Extending these definitions, we propose that, in the world of forensic accounting, sufficient data means data of adequate quantity and quality to support the final opinion. Importantly, both quantity and quality are required; a greater quantity of poor data does not compensate for a lack of quality data.

Special Note

According to SEC enforcement actions and Public Company Accounting Oversight Board (PCAOB) observations,[3] the failure of auditors to gather sufficient audit evidence continues to be the number one audit deficiency. We commonly observe this same failure in forensic accounting engagements. Given the adversarial nature of such engagements (involving opposing parties and experts), any weaknesses in supporting data are likely to be discovered and exposed.

What do we mean by relevant? *Black's Law Dictionary* defines relevant data as being "logically connected and tending to prove or disprove a matter in issue; having appreciable probative value."[4] Similarly, FRE 401 states that relevant evidence must have the "tendency to make a fact more or less probable than it would be without the evidence," with the fact being "of consequence in determining the action."

In forensic accounting, relevance is determined by the specific objectives of an engagement (that is, what the expert has been engaged to do). Considering any constraints or limitations that might exist, these objectives drive the formation of working hypotheses, which provide direction for the data analysis task.

Meeting the Thresholds

How do we know when data meet the thresholds of sufficiency and relevance? Like most aspects of forensic accounting, there is no clear-cut answer to this question. This is because both evaluations are *relative* in nature. As previously noted, relevancy depends on the specifics of a given engagement. Data that are relevant in one engagement may not be relevant in another, even among engagements of the same type. For example, in a business valuation, the appropriate universe of data is driven by factors such as the purpose of the valuation and the standard of value.

When evaluating sufficiency, a key consideration is the *availability* of data. If only limited data are available, the relative threshold may be lower. For example, indirect methods for determining unreported income (discussed in Chapter 12) can be used when there is insufficient data to apply a direct method. However, an expert who chooses to ignore available data or fails to exercise due diligence in identifying data does so at his or her own peril.

The threshold of sufficiency is also linked to the standard of proof— either a preponderance of the evidence (in a civil case) or beyond a reasonable doubt (in a criminal case). Recall that, under the preponderance standard, an expert's opinion must be stated within a *reasonable degree of professional certainty* (which implies a probability greater than 50%). Given that all data have some inherent limitations, how can a forensic accountant's testimony ever meet the criminal standard? Importantly, the standard applies to the weight of the evidence as a whole, not to each individual element of evidence.

Although it may be easy to identify grossly insufficient or irrelevant data, there is certainly a gray area where professional judgment is required. Based on the factors discussed previously, the forensic accountant must independently make this determination. Reasonable parties can disagree, which may prompt counsel to file a *Daubert* motion requesting the court's evaluation of the opposing expert's methodology and underlying data. Ultimately, practitioners cannot delegate their responsibility to assess the sufficiency and relevancy of data, as this assessment is critical to the soundness of the ultimate conclusion.

Terminology

The terms *method*, *tool*, and *technique* are often used interchangeably in discussions of data analysis. However, in the context of a forensic accounting engagement, these terms have distinct meanings based on different functions. We describe a ***tool*** as an instrument that creates leverage in processing, understanding, and/or illustrating data. Several tools are introduced in this chapter, including relationship charts, link analysis, and timelines. Perhaps the most versatile tool of data analysis is the computer, which is used in the application of many other tools.

Throughout this chapter, we characterize data analysis as an ongoing and iterative process. The specific nature of the process is defined by the ***methods*** employed. In other words, the method determines *what* data are processed and *how* they are processed. In contrast to tools, which can be applied for a variety of purposes, methods are more targeted in their application. Consider the following examples, which are discussed in later chapters:

- The net worth method examines changes in a taxpayer's net worth over some period to derive an implication of unreported income.
- Descriptive statistics are used to evaluate and describe the distribution of a data set.
- Data mining methods are used to search for patterns in data sets and identify anomalies.
- Digital analysis examines digital frequencies in quantitative data (that is, which numbers are expected to occur in certain digits).

Finally, a ***technique*** is a particular approach for applying a tool or method in a specific situation. Unlike the choice of methodology, which is driven primarily by the nature of the problem, the choice of technique is more subjective in nature. Based on their individual preferences, experiences, and resources, different individuals may reasonably use different techniques for the same task.

FRAMING THE DATA ANALYSIS TASK

Understanding the *purpose* of data analysis, we now shift our attention to the *process*. The process begins before the application of analytic methods, with efforts to properly frame the data analysis task. This includes consideration of various constraints introduced by specific circumstances of the engagement as well as limitations of the data.

Preliminary Considerations

In Chapter 3, we identified certain factors that must be considered before accepting an engagement. Several of these same factors have critical implications for data analysis. At this point in the engagement, the issue is not whether to accept the task but rather how to properly frame it within a given set of operating constraints. Examples of such constraints include the following:

- *Time constraints.* Data analysis is always limited by time constraints, especially when the volume of data is substantial.
- *Access to data.* Data cannot be analyzed unless they are available and can be obtained within the established time frame for the engagement. Although obtaining access usually requires the assistance of the engaging party, it often falls upon the forensic accountant to determine what data are necessary and where they can be obtained.
- *Technological resources.* Technological resources impact a forensic accountant's ability to perform data analysis, as well as the efficiency (time) of the process. Examples of such resources include computers, software, cameras, recording devices, database subscriptions, and presentation aids (such as televisions and projectors).

Special Note

Software is a critical tool in data analysis. A variety of software packages have been developed specifically for auditing and forensic applications, several of which are discussed in Chapter 9. Fortunately, many tasks can be accomplished with basic spreadsheet programs, such as Microsoft Excel and Access.

Data Limitations

Another factor in framing the data analysis task is identifying any limitations inherent in the data. Although the extent of such limitations cannot be fully assessed before the data are collected, potential limitations should be anticipated in advance. Some limitations can be managed (with proper disclosure), but others may render the data unsuitable for the specified objective (that is, unable to meet the threshold of sufficient relevant data). Common examples of data limitations include the following:[5]

- *Missing data.* The analyst must consider whether all relevant data have been disclosed. When reviewing source records, forensic accountants often find that certain types of data are missing altogether (such as bank statements without check copies) or that specific items or time periods have been omitted (such as various missing checks or no checks for a particular month). Some initially undisclosed data may be obtained by alternate means (for example, by revising your request or using another source), while some data may never be obtained. In data analysis, it is not enough to know the data you have—you must also know what data you do *not* have.
- *Altered data.* It some cases, it is possible that the data have been altered. This may occur before the data set leaves the possession of the source, while it is being transported, or while it is in the possession of the analyst. Alterations may be intentional (with the intent to conceal or mislead) or unintentional. In either case, caution must be exercised to avoid not only the actual occurrence, but also the appearance of vulnerability. Especially when the data are sensitive in nature, this requires controlling who has access to the data set and recording all "hands" through which it passes—known in law enforcement as the "chain of custody."
- *Different forms of the same data.* It is possible that the same data are available in more than one form. For example, data may exist in both document and digital form, and certain data may be recorded in several different documents or digital files. To maximize efficiency, the analyst may wish to avoid processing multiple versions of the same data. However, in some cases, it may be useful to review more than one version for the purpose of verification (for example, comparing transactions recorded in a general ledger to actual bank records). Regardless, the analyst should be aware of the various forms in which the data exist and any differences among them.
- *Different definitions of the same data.* As we will explore more thoroughly in the data collection section of this chapter, how one defines data is critical. In response to a data request, you will usually receive only what you *specifically* ask for—nothing more. In addition to willful concealment, the analyst must also consider the possibility of misunderstandings with regard to data definitions. Thus, careful wording of a data request is essential.
- *Nonexistent data.* A final potential limitation is that the data of interest simply do not exist, either now or at any time. Some data are only maintained for a certain period of time. This may be years (for paper records) or only days/hours (for digital data). The analyst should consider whether the life of the data may be limited and, if so, take necessary actions to preserve it. Another possibility is that the data may exist, but not in a usable form for the intended analysis.

DATA SOURCES

Where can forensic accountants obtain sufficient relevant data? Four common data sources, listed in order of preference, are *first-party*, *second-party*, *third-party*, and *fourth-party*. These sources are labeled according to their proximity to the subject— beginning with subject itself and proceeding outward to related and unrelated parties. Each data source has advantages and disadvantages, as well as implications for reliability.

First-Party Data

First-party data are obtained from the subject individual or entity. Examples include the subject company in a business valuation, the plaintiff in an economic damages claim, and the victim of a suspected fraud (or the alleged fraudster, if engaged by the defense). This source is preferable for two primary reasons: it is *direct* and *accessible*. A direct source is often perceived to be the most relevant and comprehensive. With regard to documents and financial data, the subject has the best knowledge of what information is most critical to the activity of interest and the personal incentive to preserve it. For interactive evidence, such as interviews and observations, the subject is usually the most meaningful source and sometimes the only source.

The accessibility of first-party data depends on the forensic accountant's relationship with the subject. If the subject is the engaging party, then direct access (that is, direct communication with the subject) is often possible. However, when working with the party who does have possession of the data (such as the non-asset spouse in a divorce or the defendant in a damages claim), then access usually requires involvement of the attorneys.

Second-Party Data

Second-party data are obtained from individuals or entities that are related (connected) to the subject. The relationship may be personal (such as family or friends) or business (such as co-owners, employees, customers, vendors, or external accountants). Due to their interactions with the subject, these sources may have some firsthand knowledge of the subject's activities. Examples of obtaining data from second-party sources include interviewing a family member or requesting financial data from the subject's CPA.

Third-Party Data

Third-party data are obtained from entities that maintain records regarding the subject, such as financial institutions and government agencies. The primary advantage of this data source is that it is outside the subject's ability to manipulate. For this reason, third-party data can be used to confirm data obtained from other sources. For example, bank statements can be used to confirm components of financial statements and tax returns, such as cash balances, reported expenses, and loan payments. Some third-party data are publicly available, such as organizational data, deeds, liens, and bankruptcy filings (discussed in Chapter 4).

Given the vast number of potential third-party data sources and the amount of data that can be obtained from these sources, consideration of such data may greatly enhance the scope of the analysis. For this reason, a forensic accountant must exercise strategic discretion in selecting specific data sources. In some cases, this decision is facilitated by the availability of the data. Some data (such as bank statements and loan data) are readily available to the subject, whereas others (such as tax records) might require more time to obtain. Even if data can be obtained, there may be an associated cost. For example, banks often charge a fee for producing copies of past bank statements. Such costs must be weighed against the expected benefit—that is, the value of the information to the analysis.

Fourth-Party Data

Fourth-party data are obtained from reference sources, such as news articles, academic journals, trade publications, case law, transaction databases, and government statistics. Unlike the data sources described previously, this information does not reflect the actual activity of the subject. Rather, it is used to gain insight on the environment in which the subject operates, including its local geographic market, its industry, and the broader economy. Thus, it falls within the realm of secondary research rather than primary research (as discussed in Chapter 3). The advantage of fourth-party data is that it can be obtained independently by the forensic accountant, without the assistance of the subject or engaging counsel. Still, secondary research is not without cost. Substantial time and effort can be invested without any guarantee of results, and some reference sources require a fee.

Reliability of Data

Reliability of the data is a key element of sufficiency. Forensic accountants must be able to evaluate the reliability of data and, based on this evaluation, determine its proper use in the engagement. Although a lack of confirmed reliability does not necessarily destroy the data's value, it certainly introduces limitations with regard to analysis and interpretation.

In many cases, the reliability of data is related to its source. As discussed previously, first-party data are obtained directly from the subject, which creates some implication of reliability. However, it is important to recognize that, in certain situations, self-reported data may not be entirely accurate or objective. The purpose for which self-reported data are compiled often provides an indication of potential distortions. For example, financial statements prepared for a loan application are expected to present a positive perspective, whereas personal income data reported in a divorce proceeding may reflect an understatement of reality.

In some cases, second-party data (provided by a related party) may have a higher level of reliability than first-party data. Consider, for example, financial statements prepared by an external CPA. Different types of financial statements (compilations, reviews, or audits) imply different levels of assurance, based on the testing conducted by the preparing CPA. In contrast, the reliability of tax returns (whether internally or externally prepared) is enhanced by the fact that they are submitted to the government *under penalties of perjury,* which means that deliberate misrepresentations are violations of law.

As discussed previously, third-party data such as bank statements are generally considered reliable because they are outside the control of the subject. Finally, the reliability of fourth-party data is highly variable, depending on the quality of the reference source. Because most data are compiled by people, who have various motivations and capabilities, they are inherently vulnerable to manipulation and error. Although it is generally not the forensic accountant's responsibility to independently confirm the reliability of data, there is a duty to disclose any indications of unreliability that may be discovered.

Think About It

Consider how the form in which data are provided may impact reliability. As a rule, original documents are more reliable than photocopies or facsimiles. Why? What about digital data?

PLANNING FOR DATA ANALYSIS

As emphasized throughout this chapter, data analysis is driven by the nature of the engagement (the assigned task) and limited by various constraints, such as time, access to data, technological resources, and inherent limitations of the data. Given this multifaceted framework, it is necessary to begin the data analysis process with proper planning. This involves determining what data will be collected (and from what sources), how the data will be analyzed, and how the results will contribute to refining the working hypothesis.

Although not all practitioners take such a structured approach, a written data analysis plan (document) is commonly developed that outlines specific tasks and expected time requirements. Recording the plan has several benefits: (1) it forces the analyst to explicitly consider the previously noted constraints; (2) it helps the analyst to remain on task, avoiding any unnecessary efforts that consume valuable time and resources; (3) it provides a standard against which to monitor the progress of the data analysis; and (4) it facilitates a detailed description of the analysis, which is a necessary component for communicating results at the completion of the engagement.

Caution

Practitioners must be aware that a written data analysis plan is discoverable. In other words, opposing counsel may use an expert's plan to gain insight into the litigation strategy of the client or to challenge the expert's work process and conclusions. If reduced to writing, a plan must be fully executed with changes and exceptions properly explained.

The Universe of Data

Before data analysis can begin, the proper universe of data must be identified. This is a drill-down process, beginning with a broad assessment of different types of data and data sources and then identifying specific items of interest. In statistics terminology, the ***data universe***, also known as the population, includes all items of interest, whereas a ***sample*** is a subset of these items. In most cases, forensic accountants do not have access to the entire universe of relevant data, nor the time and resources to analyze it all. Thus, we must select a smaller sample to which various analytic methods and tools can be applied. Ideally, the sample should be random, which allows for inferences (or generalizations) from the sample to the larger universe of data, an application of inductive reasoning. However, in some cases, sampling is driven by some specific criteria, such as transactions within a given time period or above a particular dollar value.

Although the entire universe of data usually cannot be analyzed, it is important that it be defined. This involves identifying any relevant data that may exist and disregarding any irrelevant data. Without properly defining the universe, the forensic accountant cannot select a meaningful sample for detailed analysis. Although such an assessment must be performed early in the investigation, maintaining the proper boundaries of the data universe is an ongoing effort. As new information surfaces, the analyst must determine whether and how it should be considered in the analysis.

Case Examples: Data Feast or Famine

Which is more difficult to manage—too much data or not enough? Both situations create challenges for the forensic accountant, as illustrated in the following two cases.

*U.S. v. Rebecca Poe**

On August 3, 2010, Ms. Rebecca Poe was indicted by a federal grand jury for executing a scheme to defraud the N&W Credit Union, a small institution located in Bluefield, West Virginia. The indictment alleged that from 2003 to August 2008, Ms. Poe (while employed by the credit union) created fictitious deposits in her account and the accounts of others, by posting credits to the accounts and making it appear as if the credit union received funds to support the deposits. According to the indictment, Ms. Poe then used these fictitious funds to pay personal expenses. Other components of the alleged scheme included fictitious payments on loan accounts and unauthorized/unrecorded check disbursements.

The indictment alleged that Ms. Poe knowingly attempted to conceal the resulting cash shortages by creating a fictitious investment account. The offense was alleged to have resulted in a loss of $2.4 million and the ultimate liquidation of the credit union due to insolvency.

In August 2008, suspicions of fraud were identified by credit union auditors, and Ms. Poe was placed on administrative leave. In November 2008, a third-party forensic accounting firm was engaged to "supplement a bond claim" filed by the credit union. The auditors identified Ms. Poe as the most likely suspect.

The forensic accountant collected data from January 1, 2003 (six months before Ms. Poe's hire date) through August 31, 2008. Specific items included the following:

- Observations regarding the operating environment at the credit union
- Interviews of all employees, including Ms. Poe
- Interviews of the credit union's directors
- Organizational chart
- Employee personnel files
- The credit union's general ledger and related audit/transaction reports
- All financial statements issued by the credit union during the subject period
- The credit union's daily journal and cash record
- All bank transactions (disbursements and deposits)
- All member deposit account histories and transactions
- All member loan account histories and transactions
- General ledger postings sorted by employee
- Interviews of members regarding specific transactions

The methodology employed by the forensic accountant was "transaction-based," involving a detailed analysis of the credit union's journal and cash record (JCR),† account transactions (deposits and disbursements), general ledger, and automated clearing house (ACH)

* Individual names, aside from the named parties, have been changed to preserve anonymity.

† The JCR is a diary of transactions as they occur. Each day's cash receipts and disbursements are entered into the JCR in chronological order. Thus, a running history of each day's transactions is kept and may be summarized as needed. No entry should be made in the general ledger without first being made in the JCR.

transactions.[‡] The forensic accountant identified five fraudulent schemes that resulted in an estimated loss of $2.5 million, including:

- Fictitious deposits into Ms. Poe's account (and others) by posting credits to the accounts without receipt of funds
- False recording of payments to Ms. Poe's loan accounts (and others) without receipt of funds
- Unrecorded check disbursements to Ms. Poe (and others) for personal expenses
- Failure to post ACH transactions in Ms. Poe's accounts (and others)
- Creation of fictitious loans to conceal funds taken through other schemes

The forensic accountant's findings were presented to the U.S. Attorney's Office for consideration, resulting in Ms. Poe's indictment and subsequent plea agreement.

Think About It

The forensic accountant's data analysis task was driven by the terms of the engagement and the working hypothesis. Where would you have started? Discuss the challenges of identifying the relevant data within this large data set. Also consider the challenges (and value) of developing a data analysis plan.

U.S. v. Diane Shafer

Dr. Diane Shafer was a physician who practiced in the rural town of Williamson, West Virginia. Although Dr. Shafer was trained as an orthopedic surgeon, over the years the focus of her practice shifted to pain management. Given the nature of the local economy—which included industries with a high incidence of workplace injuries—and a shortage of health care providers, there was a high demand for pain management services. Dr. Shafer's office managed a large volume of patients, a fact that was well known in the local area. There was a constant stream of people into and out of the office, and lines sometimes formed at the front door. Observations such as these, along with information obtained from other sources (including a tip from a former employee), prompted a federal criminal investigation of Dr. Shafer. Specifically, the government theorized that Dr. Shafer was violating the law through the following activities:

- Misuse of a DEA number,[§] specifically by allowing prescriptions for controlled substances to be dispensed to patients without evaluation by a physician
- Health care fraud, related to payment by government agencies such as Medicare and Medicaid for unlawful prescriptions.

Essentially, the government accused Dr. Shafer of operating a "pill mill," selling prescriptions for a profit and failing to provide adequate medical care. Dr. Shafer denied the allegations. She attributed her abnormally high patient volume to her long working hours and the fact that most of her appointments were short follow-up visits. Moreover, she explained that many patients brought family members to their appointments, which created the false appearance of even higher traffic.

In the course of the investigation, the government conducted a search and seizure at Dr. Shafer's office. At this time, government agents took all of Dr. Shafer's computers, which contained electronic medical records for her patients. Loss of these records was a major blow to Dr. Shafer's defense, since they were the best evidence regarding the level of care she provided to her patients.

Dr. Shafer's attorney engaged a forensic accountant to assist in building a defense with the limited data that remained. Dr. Shafer had sparse paper copies of records, but the majority of the records were maintained in the computers that were seized by the government. Since the existing data were insufficient, the forensic accountant decided to create new data.

[‡] ACH transactions represent purchases made via debit cards.

[§] DEA registration numbers are assigned to health care providers by the U.S. Drug Enforcement Administration, allowing them to write prescriptions for controlled substances.

Specifically, she conducted a survey of a sample of Dr. Shafer's patients, which was selected from a population of patients the government had identified in relation to the allegation of health care fraud (patients whose prescriptions had been funded by Medicare or Medicaid).

The survey was of critical importance to Dr. Shafer's defense, as the results would be used as a key piece of evidence supporting the adequacy of her patient care. Given the survey's high level of importance, careful planning was required. The forensic accountant invested substantial effort in drafting the survey questions, including consultation with an independent physician. Moreover, a pilot study was conducted before the actual survey, to identify any weaknesses in the survey instrument or process.

Key findings of the survey, all of which reflect an adequate standard of care provided by Dr. Shafer, include:

- Most (99.0%) patients reported they always saw Dr. Shafer at their visits.
- Most (99.5%) patients reported they spent at least five minutes with Dr. Shafer on an average visit.
- Most (99.0%) patients reported they never received a prescription for pain medication without seeing Dr. Shafer.
- Most patients rated the quality of medical care they received from Dr. Shafer as above average (80.7%) or average (18.3%).

Based on these results, the forensic accountant was able to conclude, within a reasonable degree of professional certainty,[**] that the sample responses accurately reflected (via inference) the perceptions of the entire patient population.

Despite the favorable findings of the survey, Dr. Shafer and her attorney determined that the best resolution (given the risk of trial) was a plea agreement. In April 2012, Dr. Shafer entered into a plea agreement with the U.S. Attorney's office, wherein she pled guilty to one count of abuse of her DEA number. She was sentenced in September 2012 to six months in prison. Although the value of the forensic accountant's survey was not "jury tested," it is believed that the effort provided leverage in plea negotiations.

Summary

These cases illustrate two very different universes of data. In *U.S. v. Poe*, the forensic accountant's challenge was to process an abundance of data. In contrast, in *U.S. v. Shafer*, the forensic accountant faced an absence of existing data, which required the creation of new data. Although these challenges call for different strategic approaches to data analysis, proper planning was critical in each case.

DATA COLLECTION

Once a plan has been established, the forensic accountant can begin collecting data. How this is accomplished depends on the type of engagement.

Means for Data Collection

For a corporate investigation, the engaging party may be able to provide any necessary information or provide access to individuals who can assist in obtaining the information. Companies may also have access to personal data for their employees through ***prior consent***, which describes situations in which individuals sign a release allowing specific information to be disclosed for a specific purpose.

In civil cases, the availability of data depends on the engaging party. If the forensic accountant has been engaged by the party who has possession of the data (such as the plaintiff in a personal injury claim or the asset spouse in a divorce), the data may be obtained directly from the client or through the engaging attorney—an example of first-party data.

[**] The sample size was selected to allow for a 95% level of confidence (probability).

In practice, a letter drafted for this purpose is known as a "data request." If the forensic accountant has been engaged by the party who does not have possession of the data, the engaging attorney will use the data request to draft discovery requests (including Interrogatories and Requests for Production, as discussed in Chapter 2).

If the opposing party fails to comply with discovery requests or does not have access to the data, it may be necessary for the attorney to issue a subpoena. A ***subpoena***[††] is a legal notice directing the attendance of a person at a deposition or trial; similarly, a ***subpoena duces tecum*** directs the production of documents or other items. Subpoenas can be issued by a court, a court clerk, or attorneys. They are used in both criminal and civil proceedings.

In criminal cases, data can be obtained by law enforcement through a search warrant. A ***search warrant*** is a court order issued by a judge authorizing a law enforcement agency to perform a search of a person or location and confiscate any evidence that is found. Compared to a subpoena, a search warrant is more specific (with regard to evidence sought and location) and requires more evidentiary basis.

Drafting a Data Request

As previously noted, the engaging party commonly relies on the forensic accountant to identify any data that are necessary for the analysis. To this end, an early task in the engagement is to draft a data request (or "wish list") outlining specific items to obtain. Several suggestions/guidelines for constructing data requests follow.

- *Specificity.* To encourage compliance, a data request should be as specific as possible. Vagueness is a basis for objection (noncompliance) by the opposing party. Although greater specificity requires more initial effort, this effort will reap efficiency gains later in the process. The potential pitfall of specificity is that it requires precise knowledge of the data, so that particular components can be correctly identified and described. With greater specificity, there is a greater risk of accidental exclusions.

Data requests should be specific with regard to several elements:

- ➢ Form of the data—digital or paper
- ➢ Form of paper data—inspection of originals, if available
- ➢ Time periods—duration of the entire period and any specific reporting intervals (for example, monthly financial statements for the years 2008 through 2012)
- ➢ Parties (individuals and/or entities) to which the request applies

- *Supporting documents.* If any schedules, attachments, or other supporting documents are needed, they should be specifically identified.
- *Interviews.* Data requests can include requests for witness interviews or site visits.
- *Alternatives.* Identify any alternative data or forms of data that are acceptable if the requested item does not exist or is unavailable. For example, if you are requesting copies of a company's W-2s for certain years, you may be willing to accept a spreadsheet summary of individual employee wages by year.

DATA PREPARATION

Once the data have been collected, they must be prepared in a form to which analytics can be applied. Data preparation involves processes by which data are gathered from diverse sources, transformed according to specific rules, and staged for later use.[6] As a rule, the preparation task is both time- and labor-intensive. Substantial effort is invested because the task is critical: Data cannot be analyzed unless and until they are properly prepared. Any failures in data preparation will certainly be reflected in the analysis, either through inability to conduct a test or inaccurate results of the test.

[††] Latin for "under penalty."

Maintaining a Data Inventory

The first step of data preparation is to create a ***data inventory*** of all items that have been received, including a list of specific items, sources, and dates requested/received. This inventory can be compared against the data request to determine which requested items are still outstanding. Moreover, maintaining an inventory allows the analyst to note any gaps in the data, which may indicate missing records. The data inventory enhances the efficiency of the analysis process by allowing the analyst to determine which tools or methods can be applied now and which must be delayed until additional data are received. Based on this information, the analyst can refine the data analysis plan to include a specific sequence of tests and an estimated time of completion for each.

In addition to the functions noted previously, which provide value early in the analysis, the data inventory continues to serve a purpose throughout the entire engagement. It is continuously updated as new data are received, acting as a progress meter for the data collection process. Obviously, the larger the volume of data you are working with, the more important the data inventory becomes. As you can imagine, when data (especially documents) are provided on a piecemeal basis or in no apparent order, organizing them can be a monumental effort before the actual analysis even begins. A data inventory can assist in this effort by facilitating a logical organization scheme. For example, data can be organized by category using different worksheets within a single spreadsheet file. Specific locations (such as Box #1, Folder A) can be noted beside each item, so that it can be easily located. Finally, the inventory is used at the conclusion of the engagement, when the report is being prepared. Many reports include a list of items reviewed and/or analyzed as an exhibit or appendix.

Practitioner's Perspective

In litigation, rather than failing to disclose a requested document, a party may choose to disclose it amid a volume of other irrelevant documents. This is a practice known as "document dumping" or "drowning with documents." The purpose is two-fold: (1) it makes the document of interest more difficult to identify (and thus more likely to be overlooked); and (2) it forces the opposing side to expend time and money sorting through the irrelevant documents. This is one reason why small firms are reluctant to take on larger firms in document-intensive cases: They simply do not have the necessary resources to process the data. In situations such as these, proper data management practices, including maintenance of a data inventory, are critical.

Working with Databases

Preparing data often involves the manipulation of one or more databases. A ***database*** is an organized collection of data that has been created for a specific purpose. In a forensic accounting engagement, data compilation efforts are driven by the nature of the data and the anticipated testing procedures. The necessary data may be in one database or may need to be combined from several databases. In many cases, an entirely new database must be created from source records. Key considerations in creating a database include:

- *Data fields.* The relevant data fields (information to be extracted from the source records) must be identified. For bank statements, data fields might include dates of transactions, types of transactions (debit or credit), parties involved (source of deposit or payee), and amounts. *All* relevant data fields must be identified before the extraction process begins. Failure to do so may require the records to be processed more than once, which is a waste of time and resources that can easily be prevented.
- *Accuracy.* Perhaps the most important consideration in data entry is accuracy. As the saying goes, "garbage in, garbage out." To ensure the integrity of the database, any incomplete, erroneous, or irrelevant components must be detected and then corrected (or removed). This process is commonly referred to as "data cleansing."
- *Standardization.* Data recorded in a specific data field must be *standardized*, or presented in a consistent format. This is an important aspect of data quality that is often overlooked. Although a data subset may be valid in its original form, it may

become inconsistent (and thus incorrect) when merged with another database. Consider, for example, different ways of presenting a phone number:

- 5231254
- 523-1254
- (304) 523-1254
- 304-523-1254
- 3045231254

If a data field containing phone numbers is standardized, all entries will be recorded in exactly the same format. This is important because it facilitates sorting and other forms of data mining, which are discussed in Chapter 9. Standardization applies to words as well as numbers. For example, words and phrases can be abbreviated, contracted, or stated as acronyms.

DATA ANALYSIS TOOLS

In this section, we introduce several tools that are commonly used by forensic accountants. A summary overview of these tools is provided in Table 8-1. Because these tools help to create context, they are initially applied early in the engagement. As the engagement progresses, they are continually updated to reflect new information and perspectives. The value of these tools stems from three key advantages:

- They are *widely applicable* because they deal with qualitative data that are present in almost every engagement, such as people, places, times, events, relationships, and communications.
- They are *multifunctional,* serving to record, summarize, analyze, organize, or illustrate information.
- They are *easy* to apply, easy to customize, and easy to understand. As previously noted, a simpler approach is often more effective than a complex approach.

Special Note

This chapter contains visual illustrations of the different tools, which portray information from a case study presented in Appendix 8-A. As you read the explanation of each tool, consider the accompanying illustration in terms of form rather than content.

Relationship Charts

Effective data collection requires the identification of individuals and entities that may provide useful information for the engagement. If the subject has been identified, this process will work from the inside out—identifying individuals of interest based on their relationships with the known subject. However, if the subject is unknown, the process will flow in the

Table 8-1 | Common Forensic Accounting Tools

	Description	Purpose	Form
Relationship Chart	Maps relationships among individuals or entities	Identifies parties of interest, illustrates flows of information or funds	Comprised of shapes that represent individual objects and lines that connect them
Link Analysis	Reveals unapparent relationships (links)	Combines indirect evidence to create a bigger picture	Identifies commonalities among objects, traces from cause to effect
Timeline	Illustrates a sequence of events	Provides visual aid to highlight missing information, suggest causal relationships, validate representations	Arranges events in chronological order along a line

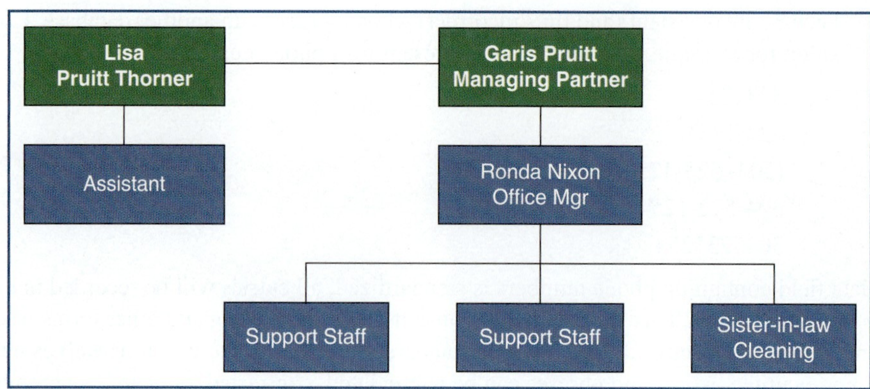

Figure 8-1
Organizational Chart Example

opposite direction—identifying the subject based on information obtained from individuals with some involvement in the activity of interest. In either approach, understanding the present and/or past relationships among the individuals or entities is critical. The nature of the relationships often suggests flows of information or funds that may have occurred.

A visual chart is a useful tool for mapping relationships. The chart usually contains shapes that represent individual objects and lines that connect them. Specific shapes (such as circles, squares, or rectangles) can be used to identify certain classes of individuals/entities, and different types of relationships can be represented by different lines (such as solid or dashed). Moreover, colors can be used to provide additional clarification or detail. Most diagrams of individual relationships fall into one of two categories: ***genograms***, which map family or personal relationships, and ***organizational charts***, which map relationships (based on responsibilities and/or authority) within an organization. Similarly, an ***entity chart*** can be used to illustrate relationships among entities, as well as entity structure and ownership.

In addition to illustrating relationships, charts can also be used to illustrate flows (of information, goods, or money) or the steps in a process. In this case, the chart is called a ***flow chart***. Analyzing flows among objects is often a useful means of identifying additional subjects for investigation. For example, money held by an individual was presumably obtained from some source (or multiple sources) and will eventually be transferred to another party for some purpose. Identifying one element in this chain may logically lead to identifying other elements.

A variety of tools can be used to construct visual charts, ranging from simple (drawing by hand) to sophisticated (specialized software). Microsoft Excel and PowerPoint are usually adequate for basic charts with a limited number of elements. For more complicated charts, specialized software is more efficient and easy to use. Microsoft Visio and SmartDraw are general programs that can be used to illustrate many different types of technical information. Examples of software designed specifically for creating relationship charts include GenoPro and Genogram Analytics.

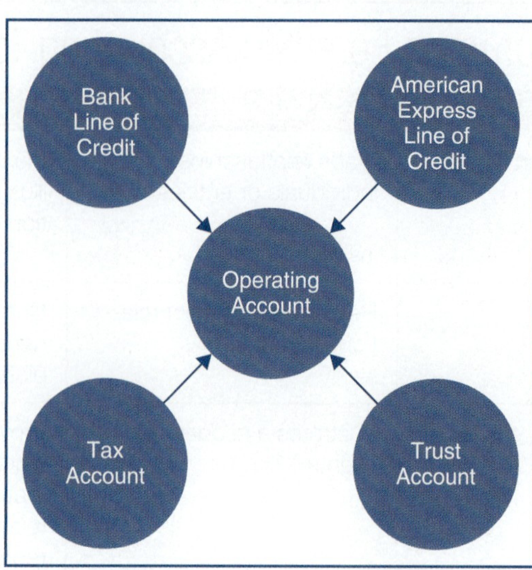

Figure 8-2
Flow Chart Example

Special Note

One might think that forensic accountants use visual charts, such as relationship charts and timelines, solely as a means of presenting the findings of an investigation. While this is true, such tools also serve another purpose—analyzing information. Seeing information in graphical format (as opposed to words) allows the analyst to interpret it differently and to consider alternative explanations. For example, various scenarios can be explicitly evaluated by rearranging the objects in a chart. To serve effectively in this function, charts must be created early in the investigation based on preliminary information and continuously revised as new information is received.

Link Analysis

Forensic accountants often find evidence that, in and of itself, is not directly relevant to the investigation. They must combine such indirect evidence to create a "bigger picture." ***Link analysis***, a method of identifying relationships among objects, is useful in this endeavor. Link analysis can be applied whenever elements are related in some way. Relationship charts, which illustrate relationships and flows, are a form of link analysis. Such charts are useful not only for mapping known relationships, but also for revealing hidden relationships (or links). For example, the observation of flows among a group of entities implies some type of relationship, although the nature of the relationship may not initially be apparent. Further investigation may reveal that the entities share a common owner—the missing link.

Link analysis is an application of ***ripple theory***, which describes the tracing of the incremental effects of some initial stimulus.[7] According to ripple theory, any action has a series of resulting actions or consequences. This proposition is clearly evident in business transactions. Consider, for example, that a person purchases a car from a local dealership. From this one action, several resulting actions ensue:

- The purchase is recorded in the accounting system of the dealership.
- A receipt is issued to the customer.
- A deposit in the amount of the purchase price is reflected in the dealership's bank records.
- If funded with cash, a withdrawal is reflected in the customer's bank records.
- If funded with a loan, a credit application is processed, and loan documents are executed.
- A temporary license tag is issued.
- The customer obtains an insurance policy for the car.

These "ripples" constitute data (specifically, third-party data) that could potentially be collected and analyzed by a forensic accountant. The value of link analysis is that, by discovering any one link in this series of events, the analyst can infer the existence of other links, which ultimately lead back to the action of interest. While typical accountants are trained to look for the usual consequences of transactions, forensic accountants are interested in *unexpected* consequences (or the absence of expected consequences). Continuing with the same example, if there was no evidence that the customer paid for the car with personal funds, this implies the use of some other (perhaps illegitimate) source of funds.

When, you may ask, does an unusual observation warrant suspicion? *Usual* and *unusual* are determined by an individual's behavioral habits or a particular business model, while *suspicious* is a personal judgment of a transaction's legitimacy.[8] Thus, link analysis, like many aspects of forensic accounting, involves some element of subjectivity. Subjective analysis can provide a reasonable basis for an opinion or conclusion if it is based on professional expertise (as established by the expert qualifications identified in Chapter 2).

Special Note

The term *criminal network* reflects the fact that organized crime is often characterized by extensive networking among individuals and entities. Thus, variations of link analysis are commonly utilized to combat money laundering and terrorist activities. For example, researchers were able to map the network of hijackers responsible for the 9/11 terrorist attacks using publicly available data.[9]

A simple form of link analysis can be performed with any database software, such as Microsoft Access or Excel, that allows sorting by data field. Sorting can identify common characteristics among database entries, which may constitute important links. This process is explained in Chapter 9, as a form of data mining. More complex applications of link analysis, such as social network analysis and Bayesian models, require sophisticated software tools and an understanding of statistical methodologies.

Forensic accountants must do more than just identify links—they must also examine the strength of those links and use them to draw conclusions about the greater whole of evidence. The greatest drawback of link analysis, compared with other investigative techniques, is that it can be time-consuming.[10] Substantial time and effort can be wasted following clue after clue in search of a link that turns out to be meaningless. Thus, forensic accountants must develop the ability to distinguish important relationships from those that are simply coincidental. Such filtering is necessary to maintain the proper universe of data for the investigation, which, as previously discussed, is a key component of planning.

Timelines

In almost every forensic accounting engagement, it is useful to create a timeline of key events. A ***timeline*** is a summary of events arranged in chronological order along a line. Suitable material for timelines includes data that have numerous dates/times and activities, such as witness statements (including interviews, depositions, and trial transcripts), organizational records, and communications (such as letters, phone calls, and emails). Even if precise dates or times are not available, a timeline can still be created if the *sequence* of events is known. For example, establishing that event B occurred between events A and C provides useful information by narrowing the time window of interest.

Purposes of Timelines

Timelines can serve a variety of purposes throughout the course of a forensic accounting engagement—from planning to presentation. Common purposes include the following:

- *Defining scope limitations.* Engagements can be limited in scope to certain time periods. When this is the case, a timeline is critical for establishing and maintaining boundaries for the universe of data. To qualify for consideration, data must not only be relevant to the issues in question but also within the established time frame.
- *Visual summary.* A timeline provides a visual summary of key facts and events related to the engagement. Because people have a tendency to think in chronological terms, this is a useful tool for familiarizing various parties with the background of the case. Such parties can include attorneys, corporate boards and committees,

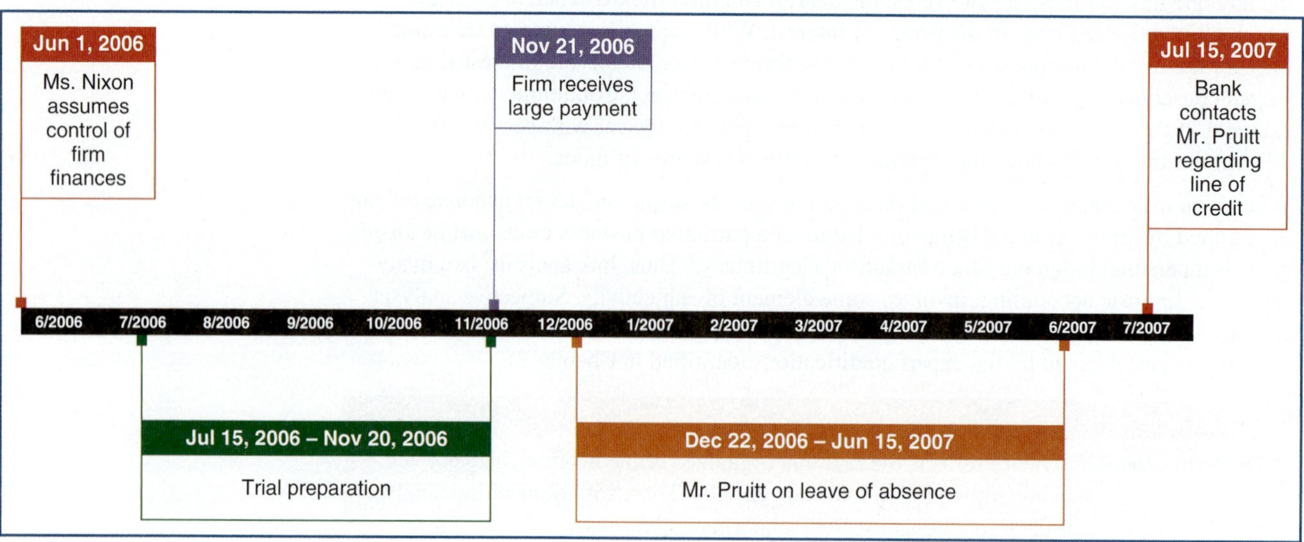

Figure 8-3
Timeline Example

judges, and juries. Moreover, because forensic accountants commonly work multiple cases simultaneously, they often use timelines to stimulate their own recall of individual case facts and players.

- *Analytical tool.* In addition to presenting and summarizing information, timelines can also be used to identify any missing information. Often, clearly delineating what you *do know* highlights what you *do not know*. For example, a large gap in a timeline may indicate the need for further investigation of that specific time interval.

  Given that timelines describe events in sequence, they can offer insight regarding potential causal relationships. To establish a causal relationship, it must be demonstrated that that the alleged cause preceded the effect. Moreover, other factors such as time elapsed between the two events and the presence of any intervening events must be considered. Another analytical use of timelines is to validate representations made by various parties, such as in an interview. Once a valid timeline has been established, it can be used as a benchmark against which any unsubstantiated representations can be evaluated.

  Finally, forensic accountants use timelines to infer meaning from a summary of facts. As emphasized throughout this chapter, to serve as evidence, there must be some *meaning* attached to facts and data. This meaning should be relevant to the issues of concern, as defined by the working hypothesis. In addition to the question of *when*, timelines can offer insight into several other areas of inquiry that serve to establish meaning:

  - *Who* was involved? *Who* was affected?
  - *What* is the significance of each event? *What* are the consequences?
  - *Where* did the events occur?
  - *Why* did the events occur? *Why* did they occur in this particular sequence?

- *Presentation tool.* Perhaps the most obvious use of timelines is as a presentation tool, such as a trial exhibit. In this application, the intent is not just to *summarize* the facts but rather to weave them into a *story*. Based on the same set of facts, it is possible to create multiple stories or explanations. In a legal case, the attorneys will create their own stories, which present the facts in the light most favorable to their respective clients. Given this element of strategy, which implies bias, timelines created for trial cannot be considered objective portrayals. Rather, they are intended to influence the audience—to "tell the story." Due to their simple and straightforward approach, timelines are widely recognized as the most effective means of communicating a story.

Creating a Timeline

As with relationship charts, numerous tools are available for creating timelines. Microsoft Excel and PowerPoint are appropriate for basic purposes, whereas more complicated presentations require programs with additional features, such as Microsoft Visio or SmartDraw. Examples of software designed specifically for timelines include Timeline Maker and TimelineXpress.

Regardless of the tool used, the most difficult aspect of creating a timeline is the choice of what information to include. This depends, in major part, on the purpose of the timeline. For internal use, the forensic accountant might want to include all events that have been recorded. When designed for presentation to a specific audience, the timeline should include only items relevant to the intended message. For example, when presented to a jury, all content of a timeline should contribute to the overall story of the case. Although including more events will convey more information, the *quality* of the information may be compromised: More events means less emphasis on any one individual event.

A final consideration in creating timelines is the choice of scale, which determines how the events are spaced on the line. If the precise timing of events is critical, a constant scale should be used, where equal distances represent equal spans of time. The downside of this approach is that events can be clustered unevenly, which may create challenges with regard to size and placement of graphics. If the sequence of events is more important, a constant scale is not necessary. While this gives the analyst more creative control, it also creates the possibility that viewers will misinterpret the scale (for example, assume a constant scale when one does not exist). This is one of several ways that timelines can display bias in presenting facts.

Reliability of Timeline Data

When timelines are used as evidence, it is necessary that they be reliable. Of course, the reliability of a timeline depends on the reliability of its components—the timing of individual events. Although time is an objective measure, this does not mean that all measurements of time are reliable. As with all forms of data, a primary factor in assessing reliability is the *source*.

Time can be obtained from any device that has a clock, which includes most computerized devices (such as personal computers, cell phones, cash registers, and ATMs). Investigators can also obtain timing information from other documents. For example, checks are dated, receipts are time-stamped, and computers record the time a file was created, accessed, and modified. The investigator must be aware that, while time is objective, the measurement of time is vulnerable to human manipulation and error. Computer clocks can be adjusted, power failures can produce inaccuracies, and people can misdate documents, either intentionally or unintentionally. Thus, it is important to assess the validity of time measurements before relying on them.

INTERVIEW TRANSCRIPTION

Chapter 4 introduced interviewing as a means of data collection. In this discussion, we highlighted the importance of transcribing handwritten interview notes into a memorandum of interview. Although the obvious goal of transcription is to record and preserve the data collected in the interview, the transcription process is a valuable tool that can serve a variety of purposes. As with most forms of qualitative research, interview transcription involves the concurrent activities of data collection, analysis, and interpretation.

Special Note

Applying the terminology introduced earlier in this chapter, interview transcription falls under the category of a method. However, given its qualitative nature, we chose to introduce it following our discussion of tools that utilize qualitative data. In Chapter 9, which describes various other methodologies, we transition from qualitative data to quantitative data.

We have emphasized repeatedly in this text that analysis occurs throughout the entire course of any engagement, from formation of the working hypothesis through the development and presentation of conclusions. Any decision that influences the direction of the investigation is essentially an act of analysis. With interviewing, this includes decisions such as who to interview, what form of interview to utilize, what questions to ask, how to transform spoken words into text, how to organize the interview transcript, and so on. In Chapter 4, we characterized interviews as an *interactive* form of evidence due to the active role played by the forensic accountant. This active role applies not only to the interview itself, but also to the transcription process that follows.

Transcription as an Analytic Process

The *process* of transcribing an interview is equally as important as the end *product*. Recognizing the importance of this process clarifies the value of writing as a method of inquiry, a characterization that is embraced in the qualitative research disciplines. As we write, we must assemble our scattered thoughts about the subject into a coherent structure that facilitates understanding. Moreover, writing is the means by which this analytic process is made apparent and available for review.[11] These propositions highlight two reasons why an interview should be transcribed by the person who conducted the interview. First, it ensures that the record of the conversation is as accurate as possible and allows for the inclusion of contextual elements (such as aspects of the physical setting and sensory observations). Second, it is the forensic accountant's first opportunity to extract meaning from the data—to transform facts into a story.

The story emerges as the forensic accountant organizes the data into a logical structure. Usually, interview notes are transcribed in order (that is, following the actual flow of the interview) and then rearranged into categories based on themes. In qualitative research, this is known as thematic analysis or coding. Identifying key themes and linking the data according to these themes is the primary way that meaning is created.[12] In a fact-finding interview, themes are generally based on facts, but they could also be based on experiences, behaviors, views, or any other factor that becomes apparent. If the interview was semi-structured in nature, then the interview questions are often a good starting point for identifying themes. For less-structured interviews, themes may simply emerge from the flow of conversation. In either case (that is, predetermined or emergent themes), the structure of the transcript should be consistent with the objectives of the engagement.

Active Role of the Transcriber

Interview transcription is not considered creative writing, but there is still a great deal of discretion involved. Although the content is driven by the information that was actually exchanged in the interview, this information can be compiled and presented in any number of ways. Interview transcripts have been characterized as "textual products" that result from a three-part process of construction, each of which is impacted by the active role of the interviewer: (1) the verbal exchanges by which the data are created; (2) collecting the data (through video/audio recording or handwritten notes); and (3) drawing on literary and grammatical conventions to transform verbal accounts into textual accounts.[13] In the third part of this process, the interviewer is challenged with communicating not only *what* was said, but *how* it was said. This allows for the exercise of two key forms of influence—selection and reduction.[14]

- ***Selection*** is determining what information to include in the interview transcript. As with timelines, the goal is to include only relevant information. The challenge is that, early in an engagement, the forensic accountant may not yet have a clear understanding of what is or is not relevant.
- ***Reduction*** is determining how the information obtained in the interview is reduced to words. Examples of specific considerations in this regard include the following:[15]
    - How to reflect pauses, expressions of emotion, tone of voice, or emphasis
    - Where to put punctuation in spoken words
    - How to handle overlapping talk and interruptions
    - Including or ignoring utterances (for example, "uh-huh") and repetition of words

CASE APPLICATION

In Appendix 8-A, we apply the concepts and tools discussed in this chapter to the case *U.S. v. Ronda Nixon.* from Chapter 4. As you may recall, this case involved employee embezzlement at a small law firm (Pruitt & Thorner) in Catlettsburg, Kentucky. A forensic accountant was engaged by the firm's managing partner, Garis Pruitt, to assist the firm in investigating Ms. Nixon's suspected fraudulent activities.

SUMMARY

The development of meaningful conclusions in a forensic accounting engagement requires the analysis and interpretation of various forms of both quantitative and qualitative data. Data analysis involves breaking down a set of information to reveal its essence or meaning, which may not be apparent when viewed as a whole. This process is strategic in nature, with every element evaluated in terms of its contribution toward the goal of refining the working hypothesis. Although data analysis can be considered a component of the overall investigative process, it is more accurately characterized as an iterative process that occurs throughout the entire engagement.

Data analysis must be founded on sufficient relevant data. In the context of a forensic accounting engagement, the meaning of this phrase is derived from the Federal Rules of Evidence and the AICPA Code of Professional Conduct. Because evaluations of sufficiency and relevance are relative in nature, there are no clear-cut thresholds. As with many aspects of forensic accounting, professional judgment is required. This is a critical evaluation, because an opinion that is not based on sufficient relevant data is vulnerable to a *Daubert* challenge.

Several issues must be addressed before proceeding with data analysis, including time constraints, access to data, technological resources, and data limitations. Another key consideration is the reliability of the data, which can be related to the source. Four common data sources are *first-party*, *second-party*, *third-party*, and *fourth-party*. These sources are labeled according to their proximity to the subject, beginning with the subject itself and proceeding outward to related and unrelated parties.

Prior to the actual application of analytic methods, forensic accountants engage in planning, data collection, and data preparation. A key element of planning is determining the proper universe of data, which often involves selecting a sample. Data are collected by various means, depending on the type of engagement. In most cases, a forensic accountant submits a data request outlining specific items to obtain. As data are collected, they are recorded in a data inventory and then compiled into a usable form such as a database. Various tools can then be applied, such as relationship charts, link analysis, and timelines. These tools have the advantages of being widely applicable, multifunctional, and simple. Before proceeding with quantitative methods, forensic accountants often use the qualitative method of interview transcription. In the transcription process, information collected through interviews is organized into a logical structure that creates meaning.

APPENDIX 8-A

Case Application: *U.S. v. Ronda Nixon*

Before proceeding with this exercise, we recommend that you review the summary and epilogue presented in Chapter 4 to refresh your memory of the case facts.

Background

In 2007, Garis Pruitt, the managing partner of Pruitt & Thorner, L.C., a two-partner law firm located in Catlettsburg, Kentucky, was alerted to unauthorized draws on the firm's line of credit by the former bookkeeper, Ronda Nixon, who had resigned her position to attend law school. Following a preliminary review of the firm's accounting records, Pruitt engaged the services of a forensic accountant to assist in evaluating the suspected fraudulent activity.

Preliminary Considerations

Time constraints. During his initial meeting with the forensic accountant, Pruitt communicated his desire to complete the analysis as soon as possible. He advised that the forensic accountant's report would be used to support the filing of an insurance claim for the embezzlement loss.

Scope limitations. Pruitt suspected that the embezzlement occurred primarily during Nixon's last year of employment with the firm, during which she had full control of the firm's accounting functions. Thus, he instructed the forensic accountant to only examine financial records for the period June 1, 2006, to May 31, 2007. He also identified specific accounts to be examined, including three bank accounts, one credit card account, and two lines of credit. Finally, Pruitt requested that the analysis be discontinued when embezzlement losses of $75,000 were identified, the limit of the insurance coverage.

Considering these scope limitations, the forensic accountant determined that the analysis could be completed in a time frame consistent with Pruitt's expectations. In the engagement agreement, the forensic accountant clearly stated both the scope of the records to be examined and the tasks to be completed. These tasks included: (a) identifying any fraudulent schemes employed by Nixon, and (b) determining any losses related thereto.

Access to data. During the initial meeting, Pruitt provided various preliminary records to the forensic accountant and advised that he would assist in obtaining any other data that might be needed. Pruitt also executed an authorization that allowed the forensic accountant to communicate directly with the firm's CPA.

Technological resources. Given the limited time frame and the limited number of accounts, the forensic accountant determined that the volume of financial data to be analyzed was manageable with his existing technological resources. Specifically, he anticipated that the entire analysis could be facilitated with a basic spreadsheet program such as Microsoft Excel.

Data Limitations

This engagement involved multiple types of data: first-party data (provided by Pruitt), second-party data (provided by the firm's CPA), and third-party data (obtained from financial institutions). Because Nixon had been responsible for maintaining the firm's general ledger, there was reason to question the reliability of this data. Given this expectation, the forensic accountant's data analysis plan (presented later in this appendix) included a comparison of the firm's general ledger to actual transactions reflected in the bank and credit card records.

The firm was unable to provide all the requested financial records. Specifically, certain credit card statements and vendor invoices could not be located. The incomplete state of the records was a limiting condition of the analysis that had to be disclosed in the final report (along with the limitations of the time period and the $75,000 loss threshold).

Another data limitation was created by the forensic accountant's reliance on Pruitt to identify the legitimacy or illegitimacy of questionable transactions. While some transactions were clearly manipulated (for example, inconsistencies between payees identified in the general ledger and payees reflected on cancelled checks), the validity of other transactions (such as false loans, false bonuses, and unauthorized credit card charges) could not be independently determined by the forensic accountant.

Planning for Data Analysis

The investigation plan. Based on the specific objectives of the engagement, the forensic accountant prepared an investigation plan. This plan included the following components:

- Identify and request necessary data.
- Conduct a site visit.
- Conduct interviews of firm personnel and external parties, including bank employees and the firm's CPA.
- Review Nixon's personnel file.
- Review communication records, including email and phone.
- Perform analysis of financial records:
    - Track inflows and outflows in the three corporate bank accounts.
    - Compare general ledger entries to cancelled checks to identify potential miscoding or alterations.
    - Review audit logs in the general ledger.
    - Analyze check disbursements to identify illegitimate payments to or on behalf of Nixon.
    - Analyze payroll records to identify illegitimate bonuses paid to Nixon.
    - Analyze credit card transactions to identify payments for Nixon's personal expenses.
    - Analyze bank deposits to identify sources, transfers, and cash withdrawals.
    - Analyze draws against the firm's credit lines.
- Review preliminary findings with Pruitt to confirm the legitimacy of specific transactions.

The universe of data. As previously noted, the relevant time period and accounts were identified by Pruitt. However, the forensic accountant independently determined specific account records to examine and identified additional data sources, such as the general ledger, payroll records, email and phone records, personnel files, and interviews.

Data Collection

Following the initial meeting, the forensic accountant sent a data request to Pruitt, identifying information needed to advance the analysis. Specific items contained in the data request included the following:

- Copies of the firm's income tax returns for years 2005 and 2006
- Forms W-2 and 1099 for years 2005 and 2006
- Bank accounts:
    - Copies of statements, including check copies and deposit tickets, for months June 2006 through May 2007
    - Copies of signature cards
- Credit cards: Copies of statements for months June 2006 through May 2007
- Credit lines:
    - Copies of statements, including check copies, for months June 2006 through May 2007
    - Copies of account applications
- Copy of the general ledger in electronic format
- Copy of Nixon's employee file

The forensic accountant created and maintained a detailed data inventory, which facilitated tracking of received and outstanding items. Because the records were provided on a piecemeal basis, it was necessary to draft a series of follow-up data requests.

Data Preparation

Creation of several databases was necessary to perform the analysis outlined in the investigation plan. As previously noted, the general ledger was requested in electronic format. Because the accounting software (Quickbooks) allowed downloading into a spreadsheet, this eliminated the need for the general ledger data to be manually entered. For the account statements, the forensic accountant identified certain elements of information to extract, which formed the data fields in the databases. The data fields extracted from the bank statements included:

- Date of transaction
- Type of transaction (deposit or disbursement)
- Amount
- For disbursements:
    - Type of disbursement (check, debit card, ATM, or service fee)
    - Payee
    - For checks:
        - Check number
        - Date written
        - Memo
        - Signature
        - Endorsement
- For deposits:
    - Amount of each check deposited
    - Name associated with each check deposit
    - Amount of cash deposited
    - Amount of cash withdrawn

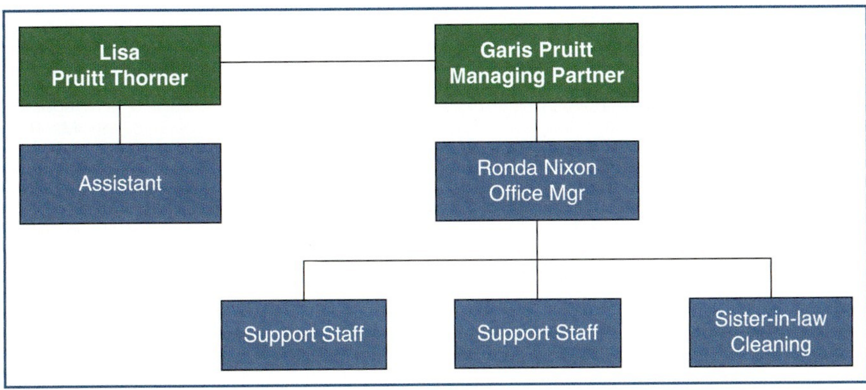

Figure 8A-1
Organizational Chart

Notice that two dates were recorded for check disbursements—date written and date cleared. This distinction was an important consideration in creating the databases, as differences between the two dates could have been significant.

Relationship Analysis

In this case, because the target (Nixon) had already been established, relevant parties were identified from the inside out—based on their relationships with Nixon. After conducting a site visit and interviewing firm personnel, the forensic accountant created the organizational chart depicted in Figure 8A-1. This chart illustrates the delegation of authority within the firm, which highlights the central role played by Nixon and offers an explanation of how she was able to perpetuate her schemes without detection. Moreover, the chart identifies other individuals who worked under Nixon and thus may have been involved, either knowingly or unknowingly, in the embezzlement.

In the personnel interviews, it was revealed that the individual who cleaned the firm's office was a relative of Nixon, her sister-in-law. Discovery of this relationship prompted the forensic accountant to closely examine payments made to this relative. Through this examination, it was found that certain checks written to the sister-in-law were actually cashed by Nixon. If the family relationship had not been identified, these payments would likely have been overlooked.

Another chart prepared by the forensic accountant in this engagement was a flow chart illustrating the flow of funds among the firm's various accounts, depicted in Figure 8A-2. This chart illustrates how Nixon was able to fund her unauthorized disbursements—by drawing on the firm's line of credit. As you recall from the case summary in Chapter 4,

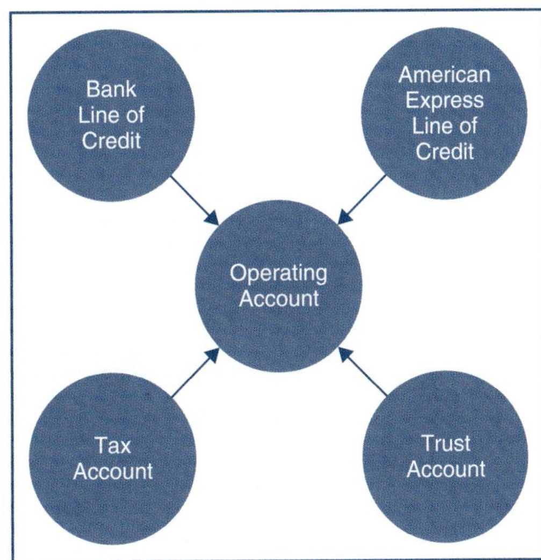

Figure 8A-2
Flow Chart

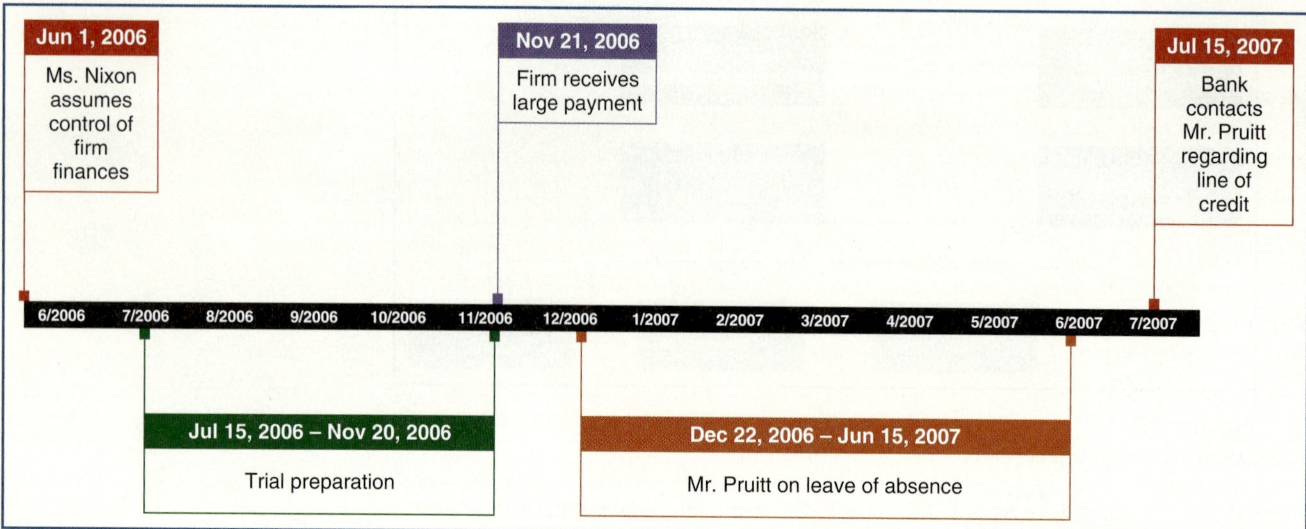

Figure 8A-3
Timeline of Events

Pruitt became aware of the embezzlement due to an inquiry from the bank regarding an outstanding balance on the firm's line of credit.

Because Nixon had already been identified as the target, link analysis was not a critical component of this case. However, given her involvement in all the firm's financial dealings, Nixon could have easily been identified as the common link among the questionable transactions.

Timeline Analysis

A timeline of the embezzlement period is provided in Figure 8A-3. The timeline starts in June 2006, when Nixon assumed control of the firm's finances following the departure of another administrative employee. Shortly thereafter, the firm's two partners became heavily involved in a large case, which consumed their attention for several months. The case was successfully resolved in November 2006, which resulted in the firm receiving a large payment. From

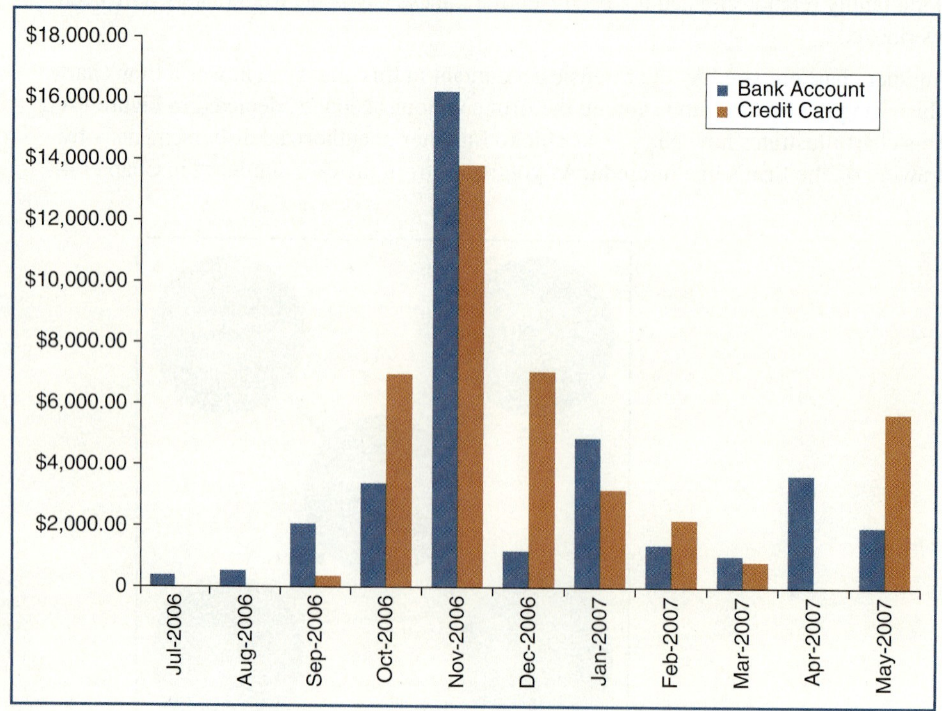

Figure 8A-4
Timeline of Fraudulent Activities

December 2006 through June 2007, Pruitt took a leave of absence from the firm for personal reasons. Soon after his return, he was contacted by the bank regarding the line of credit.

When these events are illustrated on a timeline, the opportunity for Nixon to perpetrate her crime becomes evident. During this period, Nixon had the *ability* to execute unauthorized disbursements and conceal her activities. She was solely responsible for all bookkeeping functions and banking activities, she processed all incoming mail and maintained possession of account statements, she had the authority to sign checks, and she communicated with the external CPA. At this same time, Nixon was operating with little supervision because the partners were consumed with other activities. Finally, a large payment received by the firm provided available funds for the embezzlement, which Nixon supplemented with draws on a line of credit.

A timeline of Nixon's fraudulent transactions, presented in Figure 8A-4, tells a similar story. As with most embezzlements, the magnitude started small and then quickly increased. Nixon initially limited her fraudulent activities to the firm's bank accounts but soon began using the credit card account. The peak occurred in November 2006, when the firm received the large payment.

Interview Transcription

Two key interviews were conducted in this case: Garis Pruitt and Ronda Nixon. For both interviews, the forensic accountant transcribed his handwritten notes into file memos. Through transcribing the interview of Pruitt, the forensic accountant was able to logically structure the facts of the case, which facilitated the identification of other parties to interview and data to collect. The interview transcript for Nixon (provided as an appendix in Chapter 4) was especially critical, given that Nixon offered several admissions in the interview. Moreover, an enlarged version of the transcript was used by the defense as a trial exhibit, serving as the basis for the forensic accountant's cross-examination. The transcript was structured as follows:

- The forensic accountant's introduction of self and explanation of the purpose of the call
- Nixon's free (undirected) representations regarding the allegations
- Nixon's responses to specific inquiries proffered by the forensic accountant:
    - Possible defenses
    - Time frame
    - Specific transactions
    - Specific methods
- Nixon's concluding remarks
- Understanding regarding availability for future contact or follow-up questions

Key Terms

Data
Data analysis
Data inventory
Data universe
Database
Entity chart
First-party data
Flow chart
Fourth-party data
Genogram
Link analysis
Method
Organizational chart
Prior consent
Reduction
Ripple theory
Sample
Search warrant
Second-party data
Selection
Subpoena
Subpoena duces tecum

Sufficient relevant data
Technique
Third-party data
Timeline
Tool

Chapter Questions

8-1. What are data?

8-2. Define qualitative data. Provide examples.

8-3. What are quantitative data? Provide examples.

8-4. What determines the types of data a forensic accountant will decide to analyze?

8-5. What is the purpose of data analysis?

8-6. How does Rule 702 of the Federal Rules of Evidence and Rule 201 of the AICPA's Code of Professional Conduct influence the gathering of sufficient relevant data?

8-7. What is the relationship between the complexity of a forensic accounting tool and its effectiveness?

8-8. What factors determine whether data are sufficient for the requirements of a forensic accounting engagement?

8-9. What makes data relevant to a forensic accounting engagement?

8-10. How does the availability of data impact the evaluation of its sufficiency?

8-11. How does the standard of proof impact the threshold of sufficiency?

8-12. Compare and contrast the terms *tool*, *method*, and *technique* as they apply to forensic accounting.

8-13. Identify and discuss three operating constraints that impact data analysis.

8-14. Identify and discuss three potential data limitations that must be considered by a forensic accountant to determine if available data are useful for a specific engagement.

8-15. Identify and describe first-, second-, third-, and fourth-party data.

8-16. Discuss the reliability of first-, second-, third-, and fourth-party data in the context of a forensic accounting engagement.

8-17. What are the benefits of a written data analysis plan?

8-18. Why is it important to identify the proper universe of data prior to commencing data analysis?

8-19. How do the cases *U.S. v. Poe* and *U.S. v. Shafer* illustrate the value of proper data analysis planning?

8-20. How is the data gathering effort different for a corporate investigation compared to civil litigation?

8-21. If an opposing party fails to comply with discovery requests, what alternative means can be used to obtain necessary data?

8-22. Identify and discuss four things a forensic accountant should consider when drafting a formal request for information.

8-23. Discuss factors that impact the data preparation efforts of a forensic accountant.

8-24. What is the purpose of maintaining an inventory of data collected in a forensic accounting engagement?

8-25. Identify and discuss key considerations in creating a database for data analysis purposes.

8-26. Identify and discuss three types of relationship charts.

8-27. What is a flow chart? How is it useful in a forensic accounting engagement?

8-28. Describe link analysis and discuss its usefulness to a forensic accountant.

8-29. Define ripple theory and explain how understanding this concept might benefit a forensic accountant.

8-30. What is a timeline?

8-31. Identify and discuss four purposes that a timeline might serve during the course of a forensic accounting engagement.

8-32. Describe several factors that should be considered when creating a timeline.

8-33. What factors influence the reliability of timeline data?

8-34. Discuss two reasons why an interview should be transcribed by the person who conducted the interview.

8-35. What is meant by selection and reduction as they relate to the transcription of an interview?

Multiple-Choice Questions

Select the best response to the following questions related to the role of data analysis in a forensic accounting engagement:

8-36. Data analysis always involves the use of quantitative methods.
- **a.** True
- **b.** False

8-37. Quantitative data include the number of interviews conducted and how something looks.
- **a.** True
- **b.** False

8-38. Each of the following is an example of quantitative data *except*:
- **a.** Net income for the period ended 12/31/2013
- **b.** Number of home sales this year in Columbus, Ohio
- **c.** The ages of students in your forensic accounting class
- **d.** The color of the walls in your classroom
- **e.** The speed with which a repetitive task is completed

8-39. Quantitative data are not subject to limitations and always reflect the truth.
- **a.** True
- **b.** False

8-40. The process of taking a set of information and breaking it down into manageable pieces is known as:
- **a.** Data transmutation
- **b.** Parsing the data
- **c.** Data analysis
- **d.** Data manipulation

8-41. Without sufficient facts or data, the application of reliable principles and methods is of little or no value.
- **a.** True
- **b.** False

8-42. The threshold of data sufficiency is related to each of the following *except*:
- **a.** The standard of proof
- **b.** The nature of an engagement
- **c.** The availability of data
- **d.** All of the above are related to the sufficiency of data

8-43. An instrument that creates leverage in processing, understanding, and/or illustrating data is called a:
- **a.** Technique
- **b.** Method
- **c.** Tool
- **d.** Process

8-44. A _____ determines what data are processed and how they are processed:
- **a.** Technique
- **b.** Method
- **c.** Tool
- **d.** Process

8-45. A particular approach for applying a tool or method in a specific situation is called a:
- **a.** Technique
- **b.** Method
- **c.** Tool
- **d.** Process

Select the best response to the following questions related to framing the data analysis task, selecting data sources, and planning for data analysis:

8-46. Each of the following can create an operating constraint that might impact the data analysis task *except*:
- **a.** Technological resources
- **b.** Time needed to complete the analysis
- **c.** Data access
- **d.** All of the above are potential constraints

8-47. Which of the following is not a data limitation?
- **a.** Altered data
- **b.** Coexistent data
- **c.** Different forms of the same data
- **d.** Missing data

8-48. Which of the following types of data are obtained directly from the subject individual or entity?
- **a.** First-party data
- **b.** Second-party data
- **c.** Third-party data
- **d.** Fourth-party data

8-49. Which of the following is an example of second-party data?
- **a.** A conversation with a subject
- **b.** An article in the local newspaper
- **c.** A financial statement prepared by the subject's CPA firm
- **d.** A legal document found on LexisNexis

8-50. The reliability of a tax return is enhanced for data analysis purposes because:
- **a.** It is submitted to the government under penalty of perjury.
- **b.** It is prepared by a professional tax preparer.
- **c.** It is a subject taught in college.
- **d.** None of the above is correct.

8-51. A forensic accountant should request data without consideration of its cost.

a. True

b. False

8-52. When planning for data analysis, each of the following is a consideration *except*:

a. How results will contribute to refining the working hypothesis

b. How the data will be analyzed

c. How the data are viewed by senior management

d. What data will be collected

8-53. In a forensic accounting engagement, a written data analysis plan normally includes how data will be collected, how they will be analyzed, and how results will be communicated.

a. True

b. False

8-54. Benefits of a written data analysis plan include which of the following?

a. It provides a standard against which to monitor progress.

b. It helps a forensic accountant remain on task.

c. It forces a forensic accountant to consider data constraints.

d. All of the above are benefits of a written data analysis plan.

8-55. Which of the following statements best reflects the purpose in this chapter of the illustrative cases *U.S. v. Poe* and *U.S. v. Shafer?*

a. Show how easy it is to obtain and analyze data

b. Provide an example of computer-assisted analysis

c. Illustrate extreme situations where an analyst has too much or too little data

d. Provide examples of mistakes made by forensic accounting practitioners

Select the best response to the following questions related to data collection and data preparation:

8-56. For a corporate investigation, the engaging party often can provide any necessary information or provide access to individuals who can assist in obtaining information.

a. True

b. False

8-57. In a civil litigation engagement, most data are obtained through the engaging attorney.

a. True

b. False

8-58. If an opposing party fails to comply with discovery requests or does not have access to necessary data, it may be necessary for the attorney to seek such data by:

a. Conducting a second request mailing

b. Visiting the opposing party's office

c. Calling the Secretary of State

d. Obtaining a subpoena or a subpoena duces tecum

8-59. In civil cases, a search warrant might be the only way to obtain necessary data.

a. True

b. False

8-60. When drafting a request for data, a forensic accountant should consider each of the following guidelines *except*:

a. Determine whether to use APA style or MLA style

b. Be as specific as possible when identifying the items needed

c. Identify needed supporting materials or attachments

d. Clearly establish the form in which data are needed

8-61. Once the data have been collected, they must be prepared in a form to which analytics can be applied.

a. True

b. False

8-62. The data preparation task should be done early in the analysis process, as it is easy and requires little time and effort.

a. True

b. False

8-63. When data are received, the first thing a forensic accountant should do is:

a. Analyze it

b. Read every word on every item

c. Make an inventory of the item, its source, and the date of receipt

d. Scan it into a data file

8-64. When creating a database, a forensic accountant might consider:

a. What information to extract from a specific source document

b. The type of paper on which the data is presented

c. The size of the font on the source document

d. Each of the above is an important consideration

8-65. It is very important that a data field containing data be standardized, so that all entries are presented in exactly the same manner.

a. True

b. False

Select the best response to the following questions related to data analysis tools:

8-66. Which of the following is not a type of relationship chart?

a. An entity chart
b. Genogram
c. Organizational chart
d. A process flow chart

8-67. Link analysis can be useful whenever elements are related in some way.

a. True
b. False

8-68. The primary thesis of ripple theory is that:

a. Any action has a series of resulting actions or consequences.
b. One finding will lead to another finding, which will lead to the truth.
c. Ripples always move toward the object that caused them.
d. None of the above describes the primary thesis of ripple theory.

8-69. Forensic accountants must do more than identify links, they must also examine the strength of those links and use them to draw conclusions about the evidence.

a. True
b. False

8-70. Timelines can serve a variety of purposes throughout the entire course of a forensic accounting engagement, from planning to presentation.

a. True
b. False

8-71. Each of the following is a purpose of a timeline *except:*

a. It is an analytical tool
b. It is a presentation tool
c. It serves as an engagement sensitivity analysis tool
d. It is useful for defining scope limitations

8-72. Timelines are widely recognized as the most effective way to present evidence at a trial.

a. True
b. False

8-73. Which of the following statements related to the scaling of timelines is correct?

a. The choice of scale is not an important consideration.
b. If the precise timing of events is critical, a constant scale, in which equal distance represents equal spans of time, is appropriate.
c. If the sequence of events is more important, then setting forth the precise time that each event occurred is critical.
d. Placing pictures on the timeline is critical, as doing so will help the trier of fact correctly identify those involved.

8-74. Examples of measuring devices that can help establish the reliability of dates on a timeline include all of the following *except*:

a. A time clock
b. A cell phone
c. The processing date on a check cashed by a bank
d. All of the above are useful sources of event timing

8-75. If time is obtained from a computer data file, it can be considered an infallible indicator of the exact timing of events.

a. True
b. False

Workplace Applications

8-76. One of the textbook authors was born in Defiance, Ohio, in 1946, started grade school in 1952 at Ney Elementary School in Ohio, graduated in 1964 from Fairview High School in Ohio, graduated from Ball State University in 1971 with a B.S. degree (major in accounting), and passed the CPA exam that same year. This author continued his education with an MBA degree (specialty in finance) from the University of Toledo in 1978, earned a DBA (management concentration) from Nova Southeastern University in 1997, and completed post-doctoral studies at Nova Southeastern University (accounting concentration) in 2002.

Using the previous information, develop a timeline using Excel, Word, or PowerPoint. Be prepared to present your timeline to the class.

In addition, respond to the following questions:

1. What did you learn about the progression of educational events by preparing the timeline?
2. What specific data did you include in the timeline? Explain your rationale.
3. Did you omit any events? If so, explain.
4. What scale did you employ in your timeline? Explain.
5. Speculate as to the gaps between educational events. What may have caused them?
6. What was the data source for the information presented in this question?

8-77. Obtain a copy of an article entitled "A CAT Scan of the Madoff Scandal: Diagnosing Fraud Inside the Black Box" by Holtz, Rubenstein, and Reminick, CPAs. Read the article and focus on the organizational charts presented in Figure 2 entitled "Typical Feeder Fund v. Potential Madoff Fund."

1. How could this type of chart make it easier for a forensic accountant to determine how the Madoff organizational structure might have enabled the conduct of Madoff's Ponzi scheme?
2. What type of data source was used to develop this question?

8-78. Revisit the *Mattco Forge, Inc. v. Arthur Young & Co.* case presented in Chapter 3. Using the data provided, develop a timeline for the major events in this case. The purpose of the timeline is to present the key steps in this legal proceeding to the local CPA society. Be prepared to present your timeline in class and to explain:

1. Why you selected the events you included on the timeline.
2. The scale you employed in presenting your data.
3. What you learned (insights you gained) through the development of your timeline.

8-79. Develop an organizational chart for the college or university you attend. This should be limited to the senior management group. Be prepared to present your organizational chart in class and to explain:

1. Where you obtained your data.
2. What you learned about the management structure of the educational institution in terms of relationships and authority.
3. What you learned about the development of an organizational chart.
4. The types of data sources you used to prepare your response to this question.

Chapter Problems

8-80. Go to www.genopro.com. On the home page, perform a search using the term "examples." From the list provided, select "Genogram Examples – GenoPro." Then, select the Tiger Woods example. Study the genogram and prepare for an in-class discussion about how this type of tool might be useful in understanding relationships in a forensic accounting engagement. In your preparation, consider the following:

1. Who are Tiger Wood's mother and father?
2. How many step-brothers does Tiger have?
3. How is Cheyenne Woods related to Tiger?
4. What happened to Earl Wood's first wife?
5. What year did Tiger marry Elin Nordegren?
6. What does the green line that looks like a railroad track between Earl and Tiger signify?
7. How might this type of diagram facilitate expert witness testimony in the courtroom?

8-81. Find a journal or magazine article that includes a timeline. Prepare a short memo that addresses the following:

1. The topic being presented.
2. The story that the timeline tells.
3. The specific information presented for key data points. Explain why this information is important to the story of the timeline.
4. The type of scale used.
5. What you learned about the structure and impact of timeline presentations.

8-82. Find two articles on link analysis. Prepare a short memo to your professor explaining the methods set forth in the articles and how you might use what you learned in a forensic accounting career.

Case

8-83. As part of a forensic accounting engagement, you are asked to determine what factors influence the pricing of homes in the local community. Review the data in the following table that has been collected for sales of homes in Fort Wayne, Indiana, for the period from July 31, 2011, to December 31, 2011. The data were collected for the purpose of determining what factors influence the selling price of homes. Based on your review, respond to the following questions:

1. What specific types of data were collected? Are there other data items you might add?
2. How was the data coded? Is the coding consistent?
3. You need to know which specific factors are most important to a home's value. How might you determine this?
4. What types of data sources do you think were used to obtain the information used in this question?

	Fort Wayne Home Sale Data—July 31 to December 31, 2011			
Price	Square Feet	Age	Extras	Real Est Tax
2,25,500	2,675	5	6	1,793
2,60,200	2,655	10	4	1,315
2,36,500	2,935	3	2	1,790
2,20,000	2,575	6	2	1,905
2,10,000	2,590	6	2	1,688
1,98,000	2,780	2	4	1,940
1,73,000	1,930	15	4	1,282
1,62,000	1,700	20	4	1,111
1,50,000	1,850	16	6	1,310
1,41,000	1,880	20	5	1,013

	Fort Wayne Home Sale Data—July 31 to December 31, 2011 (*continued*)			
Price	**Square Feet**	**Age**	**Extras**	**Real Est Tax**
1,37,000	2,150	17	4	1,092
1,36,000	1,890	15	7	1,213
1,29,000	1,925	8	8	660
1,27,000	1,750	9	5	875
1,20,000	1,650	4	4	963
1,30,000	1,700	11	7	831
1,10,000	1,500	15	6	822
1,08,000	1,400	12	3	805
1,00,000	1,375	26	3	915

---

1 By permission. From *Merriam-Webster's Collegiate® Dictionary,* 11th Edition ©2013 by Merriam-Webster, Inc. (www.Merriam-Webster.com).

2 From *Black's Law Dictionary* (2009), 9th Edition. Material reprinted with permission of Thomson Reuters.

3 Beasley, M. S., Carcello, J. V., & Hermanson, D. R. (2001). Top 10 audit deficiencies. *Journal of Accountancy, 191*(4), 63–66. Public Company Accounting Oversight Board. (Sep. 29, 2010). Release No. 2010-006. Report on observations of PCAOB inspectors related to audit risk areas affected by the economic crisis.

4 *Black's Law Dictionary.* (2009). 9th Ed., 1404.

5 Dorrell, D. D., & Gadawski, G. A. (2012). *Financial Forensics Body of Knowledge*. John Wiley & Sons.

6 Sherman, R. (2005). Set the stage with data preparation. *DM Review, 15*(2), 54–57.

7 Gardner, R. (2008). *Advanced Forensic Techniques for Accountants*. American Institute of Certified Public Accountants.

8 Gao, Z., & Ye, M. (2007). A framework for data mining-based anti-money laundering research. *Journal of Money Laundering Control, 10*(2), 170–79.

9 Krebs, V. E. (2001). Mapping networks of terrorist cells. *Connections, 24*(3), 43–52.

10 Gardner, R. (2008). *Advanced Forensic Techniques for Accountants*. American Institute of Certified Public Accountants.

11 Daly, K. (2007). *Qualitative Methods for Family Studies and Human Development.* Sage Publications.

12 Rowley, J. (2012). Conducting research interviews. *Management Research Review, 35*(3/4), 260–71.

13 Atkinson, P. (1992). The ethnography of a medical setting: Reading, writing, and rhetoric. *Qualitative Health Research, 2*, 451–74.

14 Riessman, C. K. (1993). *Narrative Analysis.* Sage Publications.

15 Daly, K. (2007). *Qualitative Methods for Family Studies and Human Development.* Sage Publications.

9 Transforming Data into Evidence (Part 2)

INTRODUCTION

In Chapter 8, we framed the data analysis task and introduced several versatile tools and techniques applicable to most forensic accounting engagements. In this chapter, we narrow the focus, discussing specific analytic methods that involve *large volumes* of quantitative data. Due to time and resource constraints, it is not feasible for the forensic accountant to individually examine each item in a large data set. Fortunately, technological advances in recent years have produced computer hardware and software tools that can search large databases in a matter of seconds. Although such tools are invaluable, they cannot function independently. More specifically, they cannot determine "what" to look for. This determination must be made by the forensic accountant, based on his or her knowledge and expertise and understanding of the subject case facts and circumstances. As highlighted in previous chapters, these elements facilitate the formation of the working hypothesis, which should guide all components of the analysis, including the data analysis task. This is necessary to ensure that meaningful results are obtained.

In forensic accounting, analysis of large data sets often involves comparison of the subject data to some "normal" or expected profile derived from other similar data. The purpose of the comparison is to identify any deviations or anomalies in the subject data that might signal a problem that warrants further examination. However, some engagements, such as business valuations and economic damages calculations, might not require the analysis of large volumes of case-specific data. Even so, the concepts discussed in this chapter are often still applicable. For example, when forensic accountants rely on data provided by a third party (such as a government agency), they must understand how the data were collected and compiled and be aware of any limitations that can impact the use of the data in the subject engagement.

This chapter begins with a discussion of descriptive statistics, the application of which allows the forensic accountant to become familiar with the data. Next, we evaluate various methods for displaying data in visual form, highlighting ways that such depictions can be manipulated to reflect bias. An introduction to data mining follows, which encompasses numerous methods for identifying individual observations in a large data set. The chapter concludes with a description of tests based on Benford's Law, which have been widely applied in auditing and fraud investigation. In essence, these methods are all examples of inductive reasoning, whereby we reason from the specific to the general or from the symptoms to the cause. Although it is easy to get bogged down in the details of the data analysis process, forensic accountants must not lose sight of its purpose—to derive some meaning that has general implications in the larger context of the engagement.

U.S. v. Khaled and Fatima Saleh

In today's digital age, data are constantly being collected by many types of organizations, including all levels of government. The government uses this data for a variety of enforcement purposes, ranging from tax audits to investigations of violent crimes. One area that has attracted more attention in recent years due to growing concerns about the national debt is the investigation of fraud in government benefit programs, which is estimated to cost billions of dollars each year.

Learning Objectives

After completing this chapter, you should be able to:

LO1. Explain the application of descriptive statistics in forensic accounting engagements.

LO2. Identify and describe various methods for displaying data.

LO3. Explain the purpose and application of data mining in forensic accounting engagements.

LO4. Identify examples of data analysis software, and explain the advantages and disadvantages of each.

LO5. Explain Benford's Law and describe specific digital analysis tests.

The case *U.S. v. Khaled and Fatima Saleh* provides an example of how data analysis is being used to identify fraud in one such program, the federal food stamp program.

The Crime

In June 2011, Khaled and Fatima Saleh were indicted for allegedly defrauding the Supplemental Nutrition Assistance Program (SNAP), formerly known as the Food Stamp Program.[1] At that time, the Salehs owned and operated a small grocery store, known as Sunset Food Market, in Waukegan, Illinois. The store had been authorized to participate in the SNAP program since May 2009. According to the indictment, the Salehs illegally converted more than $500,000 of SNAP funds during the period August 2009 to April 2011. Specifically, it was alleged that the couple redeemed food stamp benefits for approximately 50% of their value in cash. Another component of the alleged conspiracy was the purchase of items from customers who had bought the items at other stores with food stamp benefits, followed by the resale of these items at Sunset Food Market at a higher price.

The charges followed an undercover investigation in which a federal agent, on several occasions, exchanged food stamp benefits for cash and used benefits to purchase infant formula at a WalMart store and then sold the formula for half the retail price to the Salehs.[2] In April 2011, federal agents executed a search warrant at Sunset Food Market and then stopped Mrs. Saleh outside her apartment with a suitcase containing more than $350,000 in cash.

In August 2012, the Salehs entered guilty pleas.[3] The plea agreements specified the loss resulting from their fraudulent activity at $844,629, which exposed the couple to possible prison sentences of 30–37 months.[4] As of the writing of this text, sentencing had not yet occurred.

SNAP

SNAP is a federally funded benefit program that assists low-income individuals and families with purchasing eligible food items. SNAP benefit payments have skyrocketed as the economy faltered in recent years. More than 46.2 million people received a total of $75.3 billion in SNAP benefits in fiscal year 2011, more than double the amount paid in 2008.[5] Nearly half of the beneficiaries are children, and the average monthly benefit is $132 per person.[6]

In 2004, the government replaced paper coupons with plastic cards known as LINK cards, to which benefits are automatically credited each month. Authorized vendors are provided a terminal designed to accept LINK cards. To make a transaction, recipients swipe their cards through the machine and enter a PIN number. The terminal records the LINK card account number, the date and time of the transaction, and the amount of the transaction.

SNAP Fraud

The U.S. Department of Agriculture (USDA) defines SNAP fraud as the exchange of SNAP benefits for cash. This activity, also known as trafficking or discounting, is prohibited by federal law. The USDA reports that, due to increased oversight, the trafficking rate has fallen significantly over the last two decades—from about 4% to 1%.[7] With total annual payments of $75.3 billion, this suggests an annual loss of $753 million to SNAP fraud.[8] Most fraud is attributable to retailers exchanging benefits for cash, but USDA officials are also concerned about people selling or trading their LINK cards in the open market, often through web sites.[9]

About 230,000 retailers nationwide participate in the SNAP program.[10] Although 80% of SNAP funds are spent at large grocery chains, officials report that smaller stores are more likely to participate in fraud.[11] According to the USDA, more than 15,000 stores were investigated for SNAP fraud in 2011.[12] About 2,000 stores were sanctioned for illegal conduct, and 1,200 stores were permanently removed from the program.

The USDA has recently adopted high-tech strategies in its fight against SNAP fraud, including working with social media firms and using data mining techniques. With data mining, officials can analyze the data collected from LINK terminals across the nation to identify suspicious transaction patterns. This is accomplished through the Anti-Fraud Locator using

EBT Retailer Transactions (ALERT) system. The USDA has a team of more than 100 analysts and investigators across the country dedicated to SNAP compliance.[13]

DESCRIPTIVE STATISTICS

Before applying quantitative methods, forensic accountants must first develop a familiarity with the data. This basic understanding not only facilitates the ease and efficiency of the analytic process, but may also determine whether a specific method can be applied (or how the data must be modified to accommodate the method). In most cases, a data set cannot be evaluated in its entirety (that is, observations cannot be individually considered). Thus, it is helpful to create a summary description of the data, which can be accomplished using the tools of descriptive statistics.

What Is Descriptive Statistics?

Although statistics is commonly perceived as a remote and complex science, it is widely applicable in many elements of society, including economics, government, business, and law enforcement. In a general sense, the purpose of ***statistics*** is to "summarize data, analyze them, and draw meaningful inferences that lead to improved decisions."[14] In forensic accounting, such decision making involves the evaluation of a working hypothesis and the development of conclusions/opinions. Throughout this text, we have repeatedly emphasized that expert testimony must be based on *sufficient relevant data* and stated within a *reasonable degree of professional certainty*. Importantly, neither of these concepts requires absolute precision. Even in statistical analysis, there is some degree of imprecision. In fact, a key function of statistics is defining this imprecision, which is represented by terms such as the *error rate*, *significance level*, or *confidence level*.

Special Note

Because it is assumed that you have already been introduced to basic statistics in a previous course, this discussion is not intended to be a comprehensive review. Rather, its purpose is to explain the application of descriptive statistics in forensic accounting engagements and to highlight specific measures that are commonly used. You are encouraged to reference a statistics textbook for more detailed explanations of concepts.

As the name implies, the purpose of ***descriptive statistics*** is to describe data using various numerical measures and graphical depictions. Recall from Chapter 8 that a population is the entire group of observations in which we are interested, whereas a sample is a subset of observations selected from the population. A measure that describes a population is called a *parameter*, and a measure that describes a sample is called a *statistic*. Thus, descriptive statistics are simply measures that describe samples of data.

Statistics and Forensic Accounting

Descriptive statistics can be contrasted with ***inferential statistics***, the purpose of which is to draw conclusions (or inferences) about a population based on information obtained from a sample. Although inference, in general, is often used in forensic accounting engagements, applications of *statistical* inference are much more limited. This is because statistical inference requires that a sample be drawn randomly from a population. Although it is sometimes possible to obtain a random sample, a forensic accountant's data set is usually created based on some specific criteria (such as observations for a specific time period or with a magnitude above or below some threshold) or limited by availability. Unlike inferential statistics, descriptive statistics can be used in any engagement that involves analysis of a numerical data set. The larger the data set, the more valuable these summary measures.

As noted in the introduction to this chapter, a common element among many data analysis methods is the comparison of actual data with expectations. In other words, does the data set look right? To perform such a comparison, we must determine: (a) what the data set *actually* looks like and (b) what it *should* look like. Both of these determinations require the application of descriptive statistics. Just as physical objects can be described in numerous ways, many features of a data set can be measured. The most basic feature is the number of observations. This feature is important because it determines the scope of the analysis, specifically, what methods can be applied to the data, what technological resources (such as computer hardware and software) are necessary, and how long the analysis will take.

Another important feature is the distribution of the data set, which can be described in terms of two dimensions: time and magnitude (or amount). Observations may be compiled at a single point in time (a cross-section) or over some period of time (a time series). This distinction is important because different statistical tests are required for cross-sectional versus time series data. Along the magnitude dimension, an observation may have a negative value, a zero value, or a positive value. Likewise, amounts may be highly positive or highly negative. As with time, the magnitudes of observations in a data set may have implications for the types of analytic methods that can be applied. Moreover, magnitude is an obvious basis of comparison between actual data and expectations. Are the data expected to be mostly high or low in value? Are zero or negative values expected?

Special Note

The application of statistics to forensic accounting is perhaps not as obvious as applications of basic accounting or finance concepts. Still, it is a valuable body of knowledge for the forensic accountant. As emphasized throughout this text, opinions in a forensic accounting engagement must be *evidence-based.* When dealing with large volumes of quantitative data, statistical tools are necessary to derive some meaning that facilitates transformation of the data into evidence.

Common Descriptive Measures

Numerous measures are used to describe a data set, the most common of which are highlighted in this section. Calculation of these measures is a necessary starting point for analyzing any large data set in a forensic accounting engagement. The purpose is to provide a broad overview or "feel" of the data distribution, which serves as a basis for preliminary evaluation. As illustrated in Table 9-1, the various descriptive measures can be divided into two categories: measures of central tendency (where the observations are concentrated) and measures of variability (how the observations are dispersed).

Measures of Central Tendency

Central tendency is the tendency for quantitative data to cluster around certain values.[15] This clustering often (but not always) occurs near the center of the data distribution. The key measures of central tendency are the ***mean***, ***median***, and ***mode***. Of these three measures, the mean is the most commonly recognized. Its advantage is that it considers the magnitude

Table 9-1 | Common Descriptive Measures

Measures of Central Tendency	
Mode	The most frequently occurring value.
Mean	The average value calculated by adding all the observations and dividing by the number of observations.
Median	The center point of the data set, when the observations are ordered by magnitude. This can be a single observation or a point between two observations.
Measures of Variability	
Range	The difference between the values of the largest and smallest observations.
Variance	The average of the squared deviations of the observations from the mean.
Standard deviation	The square root of the variance.

of *all* the observations, representing the point where their mass (or weight) is concentrated. In contrast, the median does not consider the magnitude of each observation, only whether it is located in the upper or lower half of the distribution. For this reason, the median is not affected by extreme observations (outliers).

Measures of Variability

Measures of variability describe how the observations are dispersed around the mean. Low variability indicates that the observations are tightly clustered around the mean, while high variability indicates that the observations are located farther from the mean. Two data sets can have the same number of observations and the same mean, median, and mode but have different variability. Three common measures of variability include the ***range***, ***variance***, and ***standard deviation***. Like the mean, the variance and standard deviation have the advantage of considering all the observations in the data set. Compared to the variance, the standard deviation is more easily interpreted because it is stated in terms of basic units (rather than squared units).

Think About It

Forensic accountants must be familiar with descriptive measures, not only to analyze large case-specific data sets, but also to effectively interpret and apply third-party data. For example, business valuations often involve the comparison of company data, such as financial ratios, to industry benchmarks. In this comparative analysis, several important issues must be addressed:

- What measure of central tendency is provided to represent the industry data set as a whole? If more than one is provided, which one is the best representation? How does the variability of the data set impact this determination?
- How many observations does the industry data set include? How does this impact the usefulness of the descriptive measures?
- Are there any outliers in the industry data set? How are any such outliers reflected in the descriptive measures?

The Shape of the Data Distribution

Suppose we want to know how many observations in the data set are of a certain magnitude—positive or negative, large or small. This question is answered by separating the data into groups or intervals. Once the data are grouped, they can be graphed in a histogram. A ***histogram*** is a bar chart, in which each bar represents a single interval and the height of the bar indicates the number (or frequency) of observations in the interval. The histogram is an important data analysis tool because it illustrates the shape of the data distribution, which is a key determinant of the analytic methods that can be applied.

The first step in creating a histogram is defining the intervals, which is a matter of judgment for the analyst. There is an inverse relationship between the size of the intervals and the number of intervals for a given data set; the smaller the intervals, the larger the number of intervals. Using a larger number of intervals provides a more detailed picture of the data distribution, but it may be misleading if the observations are heavily weighted in only a few intervals. In most cases, between seven and twelve intervals is sufficient. The choice within this range depends on the number of observations in the data set (more intervals for larger data sets). Although there is no prescription for the proper number of intervals, it is necessary that the intervals contain all observations in the data set and do not overlap. In other words, every observation should be included in only one interval.

Although it is common practice to create intervals of equal size, this is usually not appropriate in a forensic accounting engagement. Because financial data sets often contain much larger quantities of small numbers than large numbers (as explained later in this chapter), using equal intervals results in a histogram that has many observations in the first few intervals and very few observations in the remaining intervals. Using an accounts payable data set that contains 352 observations, Figures 9-1 and 9-2 illustrate this point. Figure 9-1 has equal intervals, whereas Figure 9-2 has intervals of various sizes. These two graphs provide

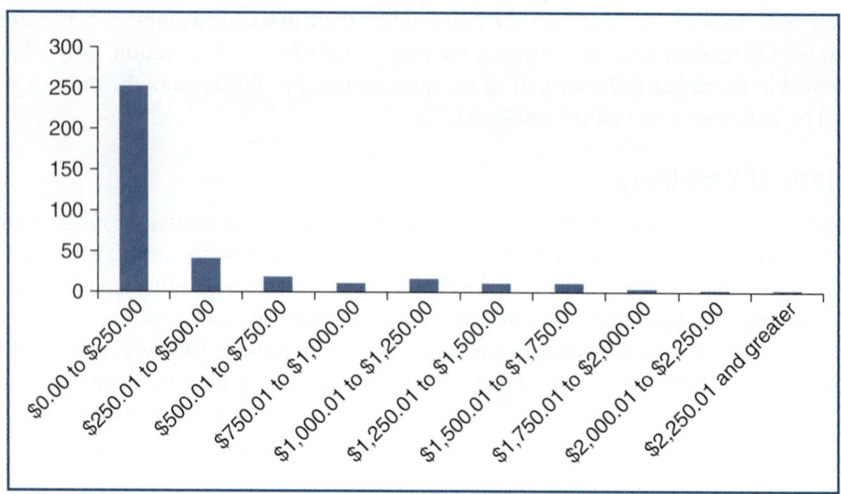

Figure 9-1
Histogram with Equal Intervals: XYZ Company Accounts Payable Transactions, Year 2012

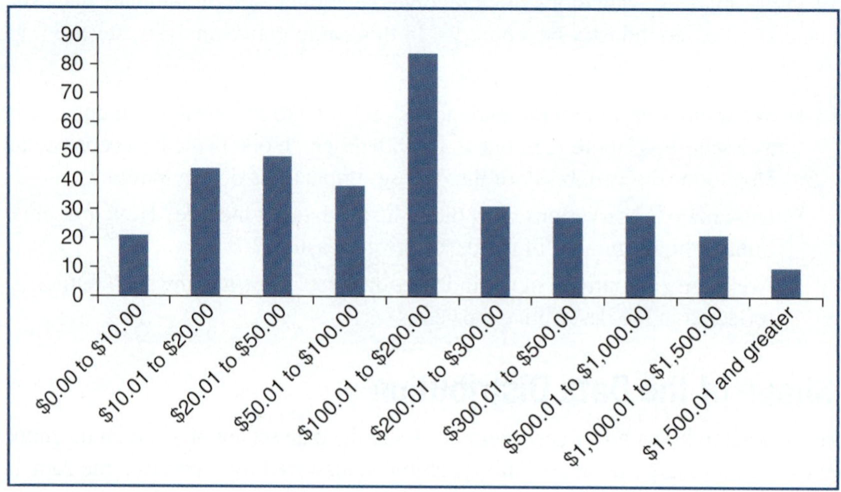

Figure 9-2
Histogram with Non-Equal Intervals: XYZ Company Accounts Payable Transactions, Year 2012

a clear picture of how the definition of intervals can significantly influence the shape of a histogram.

Like many aspects of a forensic accounting engagement, defining the intervals for a histogram is an iterative process, where the analyst considers various alternatives before selecting one that is most appropriate for the specific purpose of the analysis. As previously noted, a primary goal in applying descriptive statistics is for the analyst to develop a feel for the data distribution. Thus, repeated trials in creating a histogram, which allow the analyst to view and consider several different variations of the shape, are actually helpful.

Absolute vs. Relative Frequency

A histogram is simply a graph of the frequencies of grouped data. Frequencies can be represented as absolute frequencies or relative frequencies. ***Absolute frequency*** is the count of observations within an interval, while ***relative frequency*** is the percentage of the total number of observations that fall within an interval. Figures 9-1 and 9-2 are examples of absolute frequency histograms, and Figure 9-3 is an example of a relative frequency histogram.

Notice that the shape of Figure 9-3 is identical to the shape of Figure 9-2. This is because both histograms are created from the same data set and using the same intervals. The only difference between an absolute frequency and relative frequency histogram is the labeling of the vertical axis (number vs. percent).

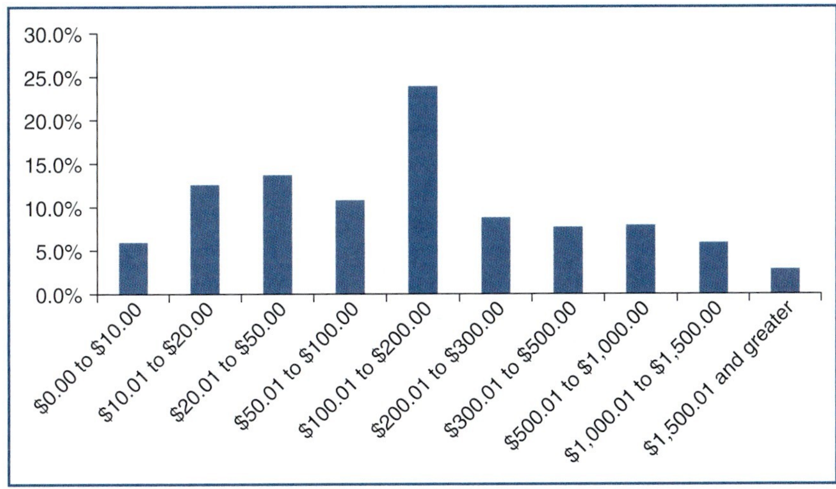

Figure 9-3
Relative Frequency Histogram: XYZ Company Accounts Payable Transactions, Year 2012

The advantage of relative frequencies is that they are standardized, or described relative to a standard quantity—the total number of observations. If created correctly, the relative frequencies of the intervals should total to 1.00, or 100%. Relative frequencies are very useful because they can be interpreted as probabilities. For example, in Figure 9-3, approximately 6% of the observations fall within the interval $0.00 to $10.00. Based on this information, we can say that the probability of selecting one observation from the data set that falls within this interval is approximately 6%.

Special Note

Although it is beyond the scope of this text, probability is another component of statistics that forensic accountants should be familiar with. As you recall from previous chapters, *reasonable degree of professional certainty* is a concept of probability (greater than 50%). Moreover, one of the *Daubert* factors is the *known or potential error rate of the method*, another probability concept. It is not uncommon for experts to be challenged in deposition or cross-examination about probabilities related to their conclusions. An effective response requires knowledge of whether such probabilities can be determined and, if not, the ability to explain why.

Skewness

Another attribute of a data distribution that may be of interest to forensic accountants is its skewness. ***Skewness*** is a measure of the degree of asymmetry of a data distribution around its mean. When a distribution extends farther to the right than to the left, it is considered *positively skewed*, meaning the distribution is more heavily weighted toward smaller numbers. Similarly, when a distribution extends farther to the left than to the right, it is considered *negatively skewed*, meaning the distribution is more heavily weighted toward larger numbers. An important fact to keep in mind is that, for a symmetric distribution (with no skewness), the mean, median, and mode are all equal. For a right-skewed distribution, the mean is greater than the median, which is greater than the mode. The opposite is true for a left-skewed distribution.

The accounts payable data set used for Figures 9-1, 9-2, and 9-3 is positively skewed. This fact is clearly illustrated in Figure 9-1 but less so in Figures 9-2 and 9-3. Again, this shows how the definition of intervals can bias the perceived shape of a data distribution, particularly its skewness (or lack thereof).

Discrete vs. Continuous Distributions

So far, we have been discussing discrete data distributions. In a ***discrete distribution***, the observations are countable, and there is a discrete "jump" between successive values. As we illustrated with accounts payable data, it is not necessary that the values be stated in whole numbers. Since money is measured to the cent, it is considered a discrete variable. In contrast, values in a ***continuous distribution*** can be measured to an infinitesimally small degree of accuracy. In other words, the values are continuous—there is no discrete jump. Examples of continuous variables include time, weight, and distance.

Both discrete and continuous distributions can be graphed as histograms. The difference is that, with a continuous distribution, the measurement scale can be refined (for example, from feet to inches to centimeters, and so on). As the scale of measurement becomes more precise, the width of the intervals (bars) in the histogram decreases until the graph approaches a smooth curve. As noted previously, a frequency distribution can be interpreted as a probability distribution. Thus, the continuous distribution can be interpreted as a probability curve, where probabilities are measured as areas under the curve. As required of all relative frequency distributions (or probability distributions), the total area under the curve is 1.00, or 100%.

The Normal Distribution

The most prominent continuous distribution in statistics is the ***normal distribution***. The value of the normal distribution stems from the fact that many real-world variables roughly follow this distribution. Specifically, if a variable is affected by many independent causes and the effect of each cause is not substantially large compared to the others, then the variable will be approximately normally distributed.[16] Examples include test scores, the amount of oil produced by a well, and the heights of individuals in a group. Important features of the normal distribution include the following:

- It is symmetric around its mean—that is, it has zero skewness.
- Because it is symmetric, its mean, median, and mode are all equal.
- It is completely described by its mean and standard deviation. In other words, graphing the distribution does not require knowledge of the individual data points, just the mean and standard deviation.
- The curve is bell-shaped. For this reason, the normal distribution is often called the "bell curve."

The concept of the normal distribution is particularly important in inferential statistics, where the choice of statistical method depends on whether the distribution is assumed to be normal. As previously noted, most data sets of financial transactions (such as accounts payable, accounts receivable, and sales) are positively skewed and thus not normally distributed. However, many other types of financial data are approximately normally distributed, including stock prices, rates of return (for example, interest rates and stock returns), profits, and commodity or currency prices. Thus, the relevance of the normal distribution to forensic accounting engagements depends on the nature of the data set being examined.

Evaluating the Distribution of a Data Set

After becoming familiar with the data through the application of descriptive statistics, the forensic accountant's next challenge is evaluating the distribution of the data in comparison to previously determined expectations. Such expectations are often based on benchmarks such as past experience for the subject entity or the experience of industry peers. Depending on one's knowledge of the process that generates the data, the comparison between actual and expected values can range from very simple to very complex. As an example of a simple evaluation, assume that you are examining a data set of accounts payable transactions. Based on your knowledge of the company and industry, you might expect the following: (1) only positive values, (2) few round dollar amounts, (3) more small values than large values, and (4) no values above some dollar threshold. In contrast, consider a large corporation that has developed a complex model for projecting sales based on numerous demographic and economic variables. When such a precise definition of expected values is available, the accuracy of the evaluation process is greatly enhanced.

In addition to magnitude, timing is another important dimension for evaluating the distribution of a data set. For example, the distribution of a company's sales for a calendar year may not be comparable to distributions for shorter intervals, such as a quarter or a month. In some industries, sales of higher-priced items may be more frequent at certain times of the year, which would skew the distribution over particular intervals. Similarly, if sales are slow in a particular month, there may not be a sufficient number of transactions to reflect the expected distribution. Finally, it is possible that changes in external variables (such as economic factors, weather, and industry competition) may temporarily or permanently alter the expected distribution. For example, the recent economic crisis has profoundly impacted sales patterns in many industries.

METHODS FOR DISPLAYING DATA

The challenge of how to best display data is of paramount importance to forensic accountants when presenting their ultimate findings to an untrained audience, like a jury. As a result of technological advances in recent years, dynamic visual exhibits (such as PowerPoint presentations) are permitted (and even expected) in most courtrooms. Such tools are utilized for two primary reasons. First, images are more *effective* than words in conveying ideas, especially complex ideas. As the old saying goes, "a picture is worth a thousand words." Second, information can be communicated more *efficiently* in visual form—that is, in less time and with more precision. Although the time permitted for expert witness testimony is technically not limited, brevity is usually the best approach. A long presentation is more likely to exceed the attention span of the judge and jury and less likely to produce memorable highlights.

As discussed in Chapter 8 with regard to timelines and relationship charts, graphical depictions also have analytic value in a forensic accounting engagement. For example, creating a histogram helps the analyst visualize the shape of a data distribution, which is necessary for determining the appropriate analytical methods to apply. Similarly, graphs can be used in business valuations to analyze the composition of revenue and expenses, track trends in profit margins, and facilitate benchmark comparisons.

Quantitative data can be displayed in various ways. The most basic form of presentation is a listing of the value for each individual observation. For large data sets, this strategy is not feasible and does not provide any meaningful information. Thus, it is often useful to summarize the data in some way (such as by value intervals, time intervals, or categories) and present the summary measures in tabular format. Ease of interpretation can be further enhanced by graphing summary data in charts. Two basic charts that can be used for a variety of purposes are pie charts and bar graphs.

Pie Charts

Pie charts are used to display categories of data that sum to a total. The "slices" of the pie represent the percentage of the total contained within each category. For example, if a particular company has several sources of revenue, a pie chart could be used to illustrate these sources. The tabular summary for a convenience store might appear as follows:

Fuel	$ 500,000
Grocery	$ 350,000
Tobacco	$ 125,000
Grill	$ 150,000
Lottery	$ 50,000
	$1,175,000

The pie chart in Figure 9-4 illustrates this same data in a more meaningful format. A person viewing a pie chart does not have to know the specific values but can tell from the sizes of the "slices" what the largest components are. If the slices are labeled with percentages rather than values, it is not necessary to infer the proportions. Depending on the size of the pie graph, both values and percentages may be displayed.

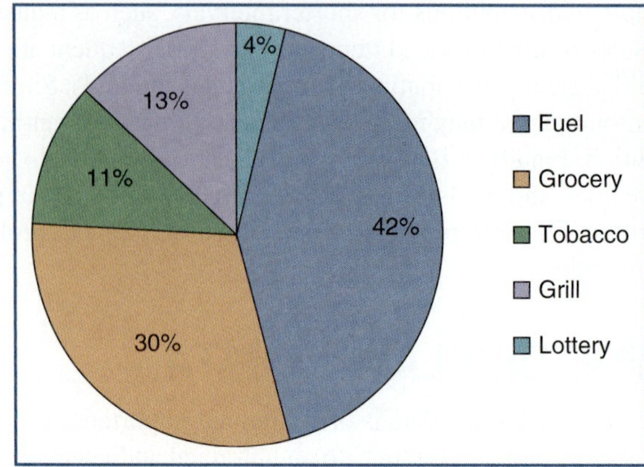

Figure 9-4
Pie Chart: XYZ Company Revenue Categories, Year 2012

Bar and Line Graphs

Like pie charts, bar graphs can also display categorical data. Earlier in this chapter, we discussed how a histogram, a type of bar graph, illustrates the distribution of a data set in terms of absolute or relative frequency. With time series data, the categories are specified as intervals of time (such as a month, quarter, or year). In addition to charting a single time series, a bar graph can be used to chart multiple times series. Graphing more than one time series together provides information about the relationship between the two data sets. The relationship may be positive (moving in the same direction) or negative (moving in the opposite direction), or there may be no identifiable relationship. For example, Figure 9-5 presents the revenue and operating income of a small business for years 2008 through 2012.

Another means for displaying time series data is a line graph. A line graph is similar to a bar graph, but the values on the vertical axis are graphed as points along a line rather than the heights of bars. Figure 9-6 presents the same data as Figure 9-5, in the form of a line graph.

Think About It

Compare the effectiveness of the bar and line graphs (Figures 9-5 and 9-6). Which provides a better representation of the *trend* in each of the two data series? Which provides a better representation of the *relationship* between the two data series? What would be the advantages or disadvantages of graphing the two data series on separate graphs?

Biases in Graphs

Although graphs and charts can enhance the interpretation of data, they can also be misleading. As noted in our discussion of histograms, the definition of intervals is a matter

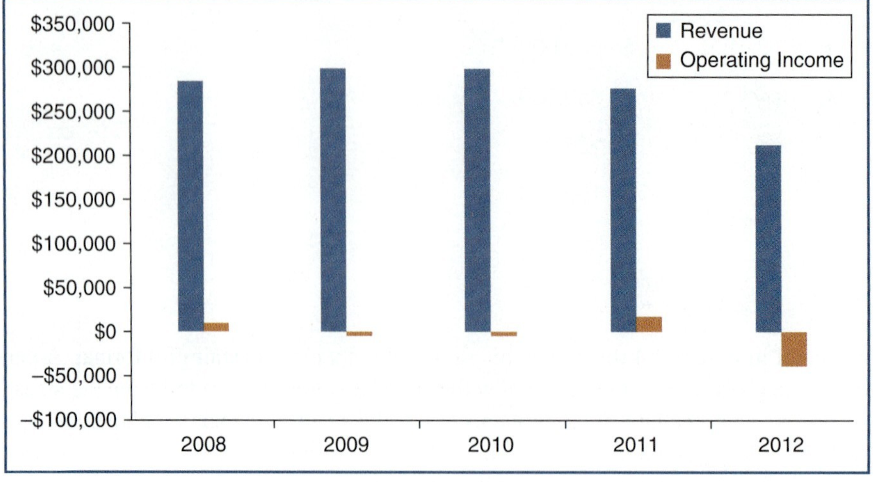

Figure 9-5
Bar Graph: XYZ Company Revenue & Operating Income, Years 2008–2012

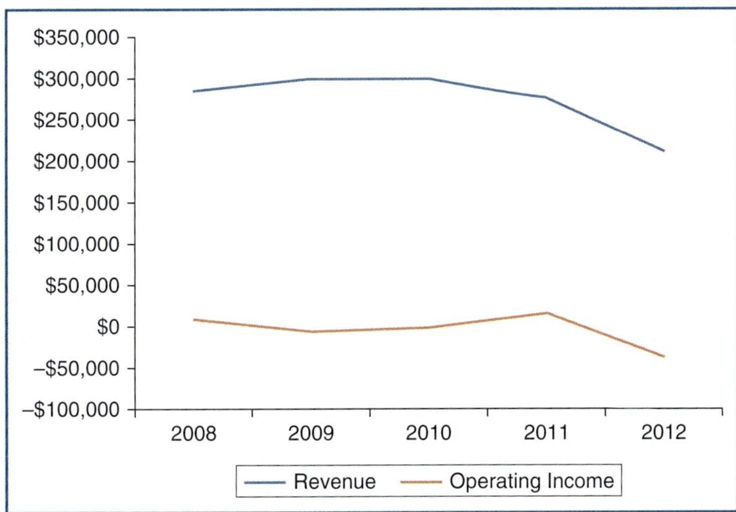

Figure 9-6
Line Graph: XYZ Company Revenue & Operating Income, Years 2008–2012

of judgment for the analyst. A comparison of Figures 9-1 and 9-2 shows how this choice can impact the shape of the histogram, making it appear extremely skewed or only slightly skewed. Any exercise of discretion in creating a graph is an opportunity to introduce bias, whether intentional or unintentional. Perhaps the most common way that graphs are biased is by manipulating the scale.

Figure 9-7 illustrates the same revenue data as Figure 9-6, with a different scale. Although the trend is identical in the two graphs, it appears to be much more drastic in Figure 9-7 due to the scale difference.

Although it is more common to use a scale that includes zero (as in Figure 9-6), this is not necessarily the "right" approach. If the purpose of the graph is to highlight the magnitude of annual changes, then a compressed scale (as in Figure 9-7) may be appropriate. In either case, what is important is that the scale is included in the graph, because failure to do so implies intentional deception.

Another way in which graphs can be manipulated is the inclusion (or lack thereof) of labels, including the title of the graph, labels of the horizontal and vertical axes, and labels of individual data points. A graph should *always* have a title, as this is the first and primary means by which the graph communicates information. Descriptive labels for the two axes may or may not be used, depending on their contribution to the overall clarity of the graph. However, as noted previously, the scale of each axis should always be included. Finally, the choice of whether to include labels for individual data points depends on the purpose of the graph and the available space. If the trend is more important than individual values, then

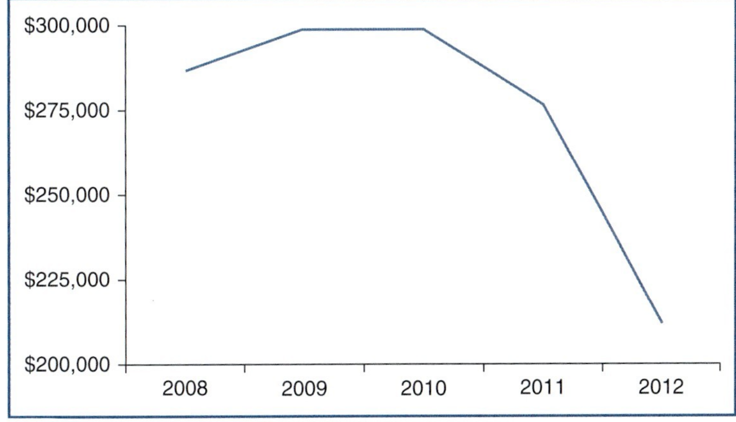

Figure 9-7
Line Graph with Compressed Scale: XYZ Company Revenue Trend, Years 2008–2012

data labels may not be necessary. As with timelines (discussed in Chapter 8), the goal is to achieve a balance—providing enough information to ensure accurate interpretation but not so much that the intended meaning is obscured.

DATA MINING

The forensic accountant uses ***data mining*** to reduce a large number of observations to a smaller number that can be examined more closely. We previously discussed (in Chapter 8) the concept of statistical sampling, wherein a subset of a population is selected for study. Recall that, if the purpose is to infer information obtained from the sample to the entire population, the sample should be selected randomly. In contrast, with data mining, observations are not selected randomly but rather are identified through comparative analysis as being significant for some specific purpose. Through the application of computer processing power, data mining allows the analyst to screen *all* the observations in a data set instead of relying on a sample.

What Is Data Mining?

As the name implies, the goal of data mining is to find individual items of value—in this context, information—in a vast group of items, such as a large data set.[17] This information is valuable because it can be used to identify relationships among factors, known as patterns. If these patterns in existing data reflect expected or normal experience, they can be used to create ***data profiles*** against which new data can be compared. The ultimate goal of this comparative analysis is prediction of the likelihood that a deviant observation is the result of some external influence, such as error or fraud, and not attributable to mere chance.[18]

Data profiles may reflect the past behavior of the system being studied (for example, an individual's history of charges with a particular credit card), may be extrapolated from other similar systems (such as credit card usage among similar demographic groups), or may be the product of complex models that consider multiple factors. Data profiles are often defined in terms of trends over time, which are examined with time series models, and data distributions, which are examined with the methods of descriptive statistics discussed earlier in this chapter. Changes in expected trends or observations that fall outside the expected distribution suggest the need for closer investigation.

A Multidimensional Approach

Data mining allows an observation to be analyzed from multiple perspectives. As discussed in Chapter 8, a single observation, such as a financial transaction, can be comprised of several components, each of which can be recorded in a separate data field. In the case of a payment by check, these components include the source account, the date written, the date cleared, the amount, and the signatory, among others. Each of these components provides a separate dimension along which the transaction can be analyzed to identify trends and changes in trends. For example, in a series of checks written on a single account, we may determine that the frequency or amounts of the checks have increased (or decreased) over time.

Taking the analysis a step further, the relationships among the various factors can be examined. Employing our previous example, we may find that checks are written on a specific day of the week or that certain signatories write checks for certain purposes. Such relationships constitute patterns that can serve as the basis for a data profile. Although this example is simple, actual applications of data mining in the real world are often more complex. With a data set that contains many data fields, particularly numerical data fields, it may be possible to create a multifactor model in which a prediction is based on more than one factor. For example, in an effort to combat money laundering, banks evaluate transactions along five dimensions: customer, account, product, geography, and time. Specialized software is used to develop a large probability matrix that computes the likelihood of each customer's actions based on weighted aggregations of these factors.[19]

Data Mining Applications

As previously noted, the purpose of data mining is to identify patterns and deviations from such patterns that provide information useful for making predictions. Examples of specific applications include the following:

- Marketing research—predicting consumer demand and sales
- Drug research—predicting the effectiveness of drugs and the likelihood of side effects
- Credit scoring—predicting the likelihood of default or bankruptcy
- Operations management—predicting input usage and productive efficiency
- Investment analysis—predicting future changes in asset prices
- Actuarial analysis—predicting life expectancies and probabilities of other insurable events
- Fraud detection—predicting the likelihood that irregular transactions reflect unlawful practices

The list is seemingly endless, as new applications are constantly being developed to address new problems. In forensic accounting, fraud detection is the most widely recognized application of data mining methods. Specific examples include credit card fraud, tax fraud, fraud in government benefit programs, money laundering, embezzlement, and telecommunications fraud.

Although data mining is a valuable fraud detection tool, it cannot detect a fraudulent transaction with certainty. Rather, it is limited to identifying *irregular* transactions that have a *higher likelihood* of being fraudulent. Of course, there may be alternative explanations, such as errors or inefficiencies. Although such findings represent false positives (which are undesirable in statistical testing), they may still have value from a business operations perspective. Moreover, even if a test does not identify fraud, it may identify areas of internal control weakness that may be targets for future fraud. In this way, data mining can serve a preventive, as well as a detective, role in fraud investigation.

Special Note

Not all fraud schemes can be identified with data analysis. To be eligible for data analysis, data must be collected, recorded, stored, and organized. Some frauds, such as bribery, kickbacks, and other forms of corruption, do not create such data.[20] Although a financial transaction may involve a bribe or kickback, the various elements of data that are collected and recorded for the transaction may not reflect the impropriety. Thus, it is necessary for the fraud investigator to develop an understanding of the system—what data it creates and how.

A Closer Look at Credit Card Fraud

A 2012 global study of more than 5,200 consumers found that 27% of respondents have been victims of credit, debit, or prepaid card fraud during the past five years.[21] Of the 17 countries included in the study, the United States had the second-highest rate of fraud, at 42%. The magnitude of the losses from credit card fraud is difficult to determine, due in major part to the aversion of financial institutions to releasing such damaging information. However, loss estimates exceed $10 billion per year, borne partially by card issuers and partially by merchants.[22] Although most cards limit liability for consumers, costs in the form of lost time and privacy can be considerable.

In addition to direct losses from fraudulent transactions, credit card issuers also suffer damage to their reputation, which results in lost revenue. According to the same 2012 study noted previously, attrition rates after experiencing credit card fraud average 21%. Moreover, it was found that cardholders who accepted a replacement card used the new card less than the original. Due to such losses, credit card issuers have a strong incentive to prevent fraud or to detect it as soon as possible. Common types of credit card fraud include the following:

- Stolen card—unauthorized usage of a stolen card
- Counterfeit card—duplicating credit cards for the purpose of fraudulent transactions

- Cardholder-not-present fraud—unauthorized usage of credit card information for transactions via phone, Internet, or mail
- Application fraud—opening a credit account using another person's personal information

Credit card issuers maintain huge databases that contain transactional data such as account number, cardholder name, merchant identification number, amount, date, and location. They use data mining methods to detect potentially fraudulent transactions based on customers' past usage patterns, expected usage patterns, or patterns that are known to be associated with fraud. Examples of such patterns include the following:[23]

- Because slopes of cumulative credit card spending are generally linear, abrupt shifts in these curves or changes of slope may be indicative of fraud.
- Some customers use specific cards for specific types of purchases, which creates a pattern that can be used to identify fraudulent transactions.
- In the case of a stolen card, the fraudster usually spends as much as possible in a short amount of time before the theft is discovered.
- Transactions of first-time credit card users are usually less frequent than usage of long-time cardholders.
- Certain transactional patterns have been identified as red flags of credit card fraud, such as frequent purchases of small electronics or jewelry (which can be readily resold in the black market) and usage across a wide geographic area.

Card issuers monitor their databases in real time for these simple patterns and others based on more complex models. An entire industry has developed that creates software designed specifically for this purpose. In addition to technological systems, substantial human resources are invested in fraud prevention and detection efforts. For example, Chase Card Services reportedly employs more than 1,000 people in this function.[24]

Simple Data Mining Tests

Although data mining in practice often involves complex statistical models and specialized computer software, the basic concept can be illustrated with simple tests.

Sorting

A straightforward form of data mining is sorting. Once the data have been compiled into a spreadsheet with various data fields, they can be sorted by any of the individual data fields. For example, to identify patterns in transaction dates, you would sort by date. Similarly, to identify patterns in transaction amounts, you would sort by amount. Although the concept of sorting is simple, it can become more complex if multiple levels are used for the sort. A sort with two levels sorts first by one factor and then by another factor (such as sorting by date and then by amount). Depending on the number of data fields, multiple sort levels can be used.

Sorting can accomplish several useful tasks, examples of which include the following:

- Identify duplicate entries.
- Identify transactions with round numbers.
- Identify gaps in the data sequence (such as dates, check numbers, or invoice numbers).
- Identify matches in data fields (such as employees and vendors with the same name or contact information).
- Compute category totals (such as total payments made to a specific vendor or employee or total payments for a specific expense category).
- Highlight blanks (or lack of data) in a particular data field (such as employees without a Social Security number or vendors without an address).
- Identify inconsistencies among data fields (such as incompatible telephone numbers and addresses or back-dated checks).

Special Note

For a data set that contains multiple data fields, the meaning of the term "duplicate" must be clarified. The most stringent meaning is that all the data fields match. Such an exact duplicate would almost always constitute a questionable observation. However, a nonexact duplicate may also be of interest in certain contexts. An example would be an observation where some subset of the data fields (perhaps all the fields but one or two) match. Forensic accountants determine the acceptable extent of duplication based on the nature of the data set and the purpose of the test.

Ratio Analysis

Another simple form of data mining is the calculation of ratios for key observations in a data set. For data that have been sorted by amount, the largest value, second-largest value, and smallest value are easily identified. Ratios among these values can be used to identify variation and outliers within a data distribution. Several commonly employed ratios include:

- *Ratio of the largest value to the smallest value.* This is similar in concept to the range, discussed earlier in the descriptive statistics section of this chapter. A larger ratio indicates greater variation in the data set.
- *Ratio of the largest value to the second-largest value.* This ratio is known as the ***relative size factor*** (RSF). A large RSF indicates an outlier in the data set.[25] Although outliers can be identified by other methods discussed in this chapter (such as a histogram or sorting), such methods do not provide a means for assessing the magnitude of the deviation. The value of the RSF is that it provides a numeric measure that can be compared to a benchmark or tracked over time.

Special Note

An outlier identified by a large RSF may be the result of a data entry error (for example, entering $535.31 as $53,531. Another possibility is that the "error" was intentional, because fraudsters may choose strategies that have an innocent explanation.

- *Ratio of the smallest value to the second-smallest value.* Like the RSF, this identifies outliers, but on the opposite side of the distribution.
- *Ratio of the largest (or smallest) value to the mean.* This is another means of identifying outliers, using a different reference point.

Limitations of Data Mining

A key advantage of data mining (the ability to examine all, not just samples, of the data) can also create a potential obstacle. As highlighted in Chapter 3, every engagement is subject to time and budget constraints. Although it may be technically feasible to apply numerous data mining tests, such resource limitations require the forensic accountant to use discretion in identifying the most efficient and effective tests. Throughout this text, we have emphasized that complexity does not equal effectiveness. This is true, even within the realm of quantitative methods. A simple sort can produce valuable information, while an analyst may invest many hours in an unsuccessful attempt to develop a complex multifactor model.

The efficiency of data mining can be evaluated in terms of the true signals it identifies (such as an error or fraud occurrence) relative to false signals, also described as false positives or noise. In statistics, a false positive is called a ***Type I error***, while a miss—that is, failure to identify a true signal—is called a ***Type II error***. There is a trade-off between Type I and Type II errors: Decreasing the occurrence of one increases the occurrence of the other. One might think it best to cast a wide net by designing tests to minimize misses. This is accomplished by increasing the test's ***power***, defined as its discriminatory capability to distinguish a true signal from other unusual variations in the data set.[26] Given the trade-off noted previously, the downside of such an approach is that it increases the number of false positives.

Why are we concerned about false positives? Recall that the goal of data mining is to identify observations *for further examination*. After the observations have been identified, substantial effort is required to examine them individually. In contrast to the data mining process, in which technological tools can be leveraged, examination of individual observations requires the close involvement of the forensic accountant. Specifically, the forensic accountant's task at this juncture is to separate the true signals from the false positives, based on professional knowledge and experience, as well as any preexisting criteria that may be available. Due to this time investment, the examination component of the analysis can be more costly than the data mining component.

Another limitation of data mining is the tendency for forensic accountants to focus on findings that are consistent with the working hypothesis, while ignoring other relevant findings. For example, although preexisting knowledge and data profiles are useful for creating focused tests, they may also hinder the exploratory quality of a comparative analysis. This is why analysts must remain open to the possibility that the wrong (or not the best) data profile has been selected for comparison or that the data profile has changed. With credit cards, for example, people may change their legitimate usage patterns, and fraudsters commonly adapt their behavior in response to advancements in fraud detection methods. Thus, data profiles should be in a constant state of evolution, as information obtained from new data is assimilated.

Finally, the forensic accountant must be mindful of the fact that data mining may identify meaningless relationships and patterns. With large data sets, a comprehensive search will always suggest patterns that are merely the product of random fluctuations.[27] If the pattern is not meaningful, we cannot expect it to be repeated, which means it has no predictive value. As with link analysis (discussed in Chapter 8), the insight of the forensic accountant is necessary to evaluate the meaning (or lack thereof) of data mining results and integrate these results with other relevant evidence.

DATA ANALYSIS SOFTWARE

A variety of software tools can be used to perform data analysis functions. Basic spreadsheet programs, especially newer versions with enhanced capacity, are sufficient for most forensic accounting engagements. However, practitioners who focus on specific types of engagements, such as fraud investigations, may prefer specialized software that offers more user-friendly features. This section briefly describes specific examples of such tools, highlighting their advantages and disadvantages for forensic accounting applications.

Basic Programs

Two basic data analysis programs are Microsoft Excel and Microsoft Access, which are included in the Microsoft Office suite that is distributed with many personal computers. These programs store and display data (numbers, text, or images) in cells, which are arranged in columns and rows.

Advantages

In addition to affordability, the primary advantages of these basic programs are their ease of use and flexibility of application. A variety of functions are available, ranging from simple arithmetic to complex statistical calculations. This multifunctionality, combined with an intuitive user interface, facilitates use across individuals of diverse skill levels. Based on their specific needs, users can combine the individual functions into unique formulas and templates. This flexibility supplies a seemingly endless variety of possible applications.

Excel or Access?

Because Excel and Access have similar capabilities, both are suitable for forensic accounting engagements that require data mining. Excel is more popular among practitioners, probably due to their past experience with the program for general accounting tasks. A key difference between the two programs is that Access forces some structure on the data analysis project, while Excel allows more flexibility.[28] For example, in Excel, either a number or a formula can be entered into a cell. If a number appears in a cell, you will not know whether it is a data point or a calculation (that is, the result of a formula) until you click on the cell. Similarly, column headings can be duplicated, and there is no requirement that consistency be maintained between column headings and the type of data contained in the column.

In contrast, Access has a well-defined structure that includes tables, queries, and reports. Data are stored in tables, which have a layout similar to an Excel spreadsheet. Each row in the table contains data for a single record (such as a transaction), the discrete components of which are stored in fields (columns). Importantly, each field can store only one type of data for all the records. All data-related functions are applied through the creation of queries, the results of which are displayed in reports. Thus, with Access, it is always clear whether you are looking at data (input) or results (output).[29] Finally, Access has a useful feature known as the Database, which creates a complete record of the database contents and allows the user to create explanatory notes regarding tables, queries, and reports. This record facilitates review of the database by another user or by the same user at a later time.

Special Note

Recent capacity enhancements have made Excel suitable for analyzing even large databases. For example, from the 2003 to 2010 versions, the maximum number of rows increased from 65,536 to 1,048,576. Access does not have a maximum number of rows, but rather imposes a total database size limit of 2 gigabytes.

Excel Extensions

The data analysis functions of Excel can be enhanced with add-ins, which are software programs designed to extend or enhance the capabilities of other software programs. Two common Excel add-ins are the Analysis Toolpak and ActiveData for Excel. The purpose of these programs is to increase productivity by streamlining various tasks that can be completed (with more time and effort) using basic Excel functions. Both programs are integrated into Excel, with the tools included in the Excel menu and ribbon bars.

- *Analysis Toolpak.* The Analysis Toolpak is included with Excel and can be accessed through a simple loading process. It includes several basic analysis tools, such as descriptive statistics, histogram, and sampling, as well as more complex statistical tests that are beyond the scope of our discussion. For example, with just one click, the descriptive statistics tool computes all the summary measures discussed in the first section of this chapter, among others.
- *ActiveData for Excel.* Many more tools (more than 100) are available in ActiveData, which must be purchased and installed. It is offered in two versions, a full Professional version and a cheaper Business version that contains limited features.

Disadvantages

The flexibility of Microsoft Excel and Access can also be a disadvantage in certain contexts.[30] These programs allow data to be altered, either intentionally or unintentionally, without record.* Moreover, errors can be easily introduced, commonly through formulas, the copy/paste function, incorrect cell references, or improperly defined cell ranges. Another weakness is that they cannot accommodate data in certain formats, in which case the data must be converted. This conversion process introduces yet another opportunity for the integrity of the data to be compromised.

Specialized Software

Specialized software, known as generalized audit software (GAS), has been developed for use in auditing and fraud investigation engagements. Two common examples of GAS are Audit Command Language (ACL) and Interactive Data Extraction Analysis (IDEA). The

* Both Excel and Access have data protection features, but they must be initiated by the user.

primary advantage of these programs is their user-interface attributes, which are customized for specific tasks. In contrast to the basic programs described previously, which can facilitate data analysis for a variety of purposes but less efficiently, GAS programs are designed to analyze financial data in an auditing environment. For example, these programs have direct commands for processes (such as detecting gaps or duplicates, filtering data, or grouping data) that must be programmed by the user in Excel or Access.

Specialized software programs address the weaknesses of Microsoft Excel and Access that were previously identified.[31] They can process data in a wide variety of formats, which eliminates the need for conversion. Moreover, if the data reside in a database, specialized software can directly access and analyze the data inside the database. This is a read-only operation, in which the data cannot be altered. Such features help ensure the integrity of the data, which is critical in forensic accounting engagements.

A final advantage of specialized software programs is their ability to record the analytics that have been performed, thus creating an audit trail or log.[32] This record is important for a number of reasons. First, it allows the forensic accountant to review the analysis that has already been completed, for the purpose of guiding future efforts and avoiding duplication of past efforts. Next, it facilitates the creation of a template that can be used in future engagements, another productivity-enhancing feature. Finally, a complete record of the data analysis process provides essential context for the results of the analysis. To effectively substantiate any conclusion, the forensic accountant must be able to explain how it was developed.

Major disadvantages of GAS programs are their high cost compared to basic programs and the extensive training required to use them effectively.[33] A single-user license of IDEA or ACL costs several times more than ActiveData for Excel (assuming that one already has Excel). Thus, such programs are usually used in larger firms, where the cost can be shared among multiple users. A large user community also helps to minimize the need for formal training.

DIGITAL ANALYSIS—BENFORD'S LAW

Consider a fraudster who plans to embezzle money from his employer by initiating payments to himself through a fictitious vendor. How should the fraudster determine the amounts of the fictitious payments, so as to give the appearance of valid payments? One might think the digits of the numbers should be random, with each digit having the same probability of occurrence. Unfortunately for the fraudster, numbers selected in this way will *not* blend in with the valid payments data and can easily be detected with digital analysis.

Digital analysis is founded on the counterintuitive observation that individual digits of multidigit numbers are not random, but follow a pattern known as ***Benford's Law***.[34] This pattern describes the expected frequencies of digits in numbers—that is, the probability that any given digit in a number will take a certain value. According to Benford's Law, the distribution of first digits is positively skewed, or more heavily weighted toward smaller numbers. In other words, the first digit (the left-most digit) of numbers is more often low than high— digit 1 appears more frequently than digit 2, which appears more frequently than digit 3, and so on.

History of Benford's Law

Benford's Law is named for Frank Benford, who published the seminal paper on the topic in 1938.[35] While working as a physicist at GE Research Laboratories, Benford made the simple observation that the early pages of his book of logarithm tables were more worn than later pages. From this observation, he concluded that he was reviewing the first pages, which provided the logs of numbers with low digits, more often. Benford hypothesized that he was looking up logs of numbers with low first digits more frequently because more of these numbers exist.[36]

To test his hypothesis, Benford examined the first digits of many different types of data, including random numbers (such as the numbers found in a newspaper), numbers from mathematical tables, population statistics, and geographical measurements. The results of Benford's tests produced the expected digital frequencies in Table 9-2.

Table 9-2 | Benford's Law—Expected Digital Frequencies

Digit	First	Second	Third	Fourth
0		.11968	.10178	.10018
1	.30103	.11389	.10138	.10014
2	.17609	.10882	.10097	.10010
3	.12494	.10433	.10057	.10006
4	.09691	.10031	.10018	.10002
5	.07918	.09668	.09979	.09998
6	.06695	.09337	.09940	.09994
7	.05799	.09035	.09902	.09990
8	.05115	.08757	.09864	.09986
9	.04576	.08500	.09827	.09982

Source: Nigrini, M. J. (1996). A taxpayer compliance application of Benford's Law. *Journal of the American Taxation Association, 18*(1), 72–91. Reprinted with permission of the American Accounting Association. All rights reserved.

As illustrated in this table, the first digit is expected to be 1 about 30% of the time, 2 about 18% of the time, and 9 only 5% of the time. Notice that, as we move across the table to the second, third, and fourth digit, the bias toward lower digits decreases. For large numbers (with three or more digits), the last (right-most) digit is approximately evenly distributed.[37]

Mathematically speaking, Benford's Law is a series of formulas that contain logarithms. The frequencies in the first-digit column of Table 9-2 are calculated as follows:[38]

$$P(d) = \log_{10} [1 + (1/d)]$$

where P represents probability (or frequency) and d is an integer from 1 to 9.

Special Note

Benford's Law can be intuitively understood with a simple example.[39] Suppose that $1,000 is deposited in a savings account that pays 2% annual interest, and $900 is deposited in a different savings account that also pays 2% annual interest. How much time will elapse before the first digit changes in each account? The $1,000 account must double in size before the first digit changes to 2, but the $900 account only needs an 11% return to change its first digit ($900 to $1,000). Accordingly, the number with the lower first digit will exist for a longer period of time than the number with the higher first digit.

Applications of Benford's Law

To conform to Benford's Law, a number series must approximately follow a geometric sequence, in which each successive number is calculated as a fixed percentage increase over the previous number.[40] Almost all natural numbers display such a geometric tendency, including city populations, sizes of geologic objects, and accounting numbers (such as stock prices, company revenues, and trading volume). For each of these data sets, we would expect more small items than large items (for example, more small cities than large cities, more small mountains than large mountains, and more small stocks than large stocks).

Examples of numbers that *do not* follow Benford's Law are data sets with built-in maximums or minimums and assigned numbers (such as Social Security numbers, account numbers, and zip codes).[41] In each of these cases, there is some unnatural (external) influence on the numbers that stifles the development of a geometric pattern.

Many research studies have used Benford's Law to examine various types of accounting data.

- *Net income.* Analyzing net income data for New Zealand companies, Carslaw (1988)[42] found an excess of second-digit 0s and a shortage of second-digit 9s. Based on this evidence, he concluded that companies with income just below certain thresholds have a tendency to round the income number up. Thomas (1989)[43] and Nigrini (2005)[44] found a similar pattern in U.S. net income data.
- *Earnings per share.* Thomas (1989)[45] found that that EPS numbers in the United States displayed unusually high frequencies of 5- and 10-cent multiples, providing additional evidence of deliberate rounding by management.
- *Income tax.* Christian and Gupta (1993)[46] identified a tendency among individuals to claim additional deductions for the purpose of decreasing taxable income to fall within the next-lowest tax bracket. Nigrini (1996)[47] examined interest income and interest expense reported on tax returns, finding evidence of understatement in the former and overstatement in the latter.
- *Fraud detection.* Nigrini (1994)[48] was the first to use digital analysis for fraud detection. Examining numbers from a known instance of a long-term payroll fraud, he compared the actual digital frequencies of the payroll data to the expected frequencies determined by Benford's Law. Consistent with his expectation that invented numbers are unlikely to conform to the expected profile, his comparative analysis identified the fraudulent payroll data and showed that the deviations increased over time.

Basic Tests

Several data analysis tests use Benford's Law to identify irregularities in data sets, which may be indicators of fraud, errors, biases, or processing inefficiencies.[49] As with other data mining methods, the basic concept of these tests is the comparison of actual data to some expected profile. Figure 9-8 illustrates the typical "ski slope" profile for the first digit according to Benford's Law. This is simply a graph of the probabilities contained in the first-digit column of Table 9-2.

Different tests can be applied, based on the expected frequencies of different digits.[50]

First-Digit Test

With the first-digit test, the first-digit profile of a data set is compared to Benford's first-digit profile.

Recall from our earlier example that fraudsters may create fictitious data based on the false premise that the first digit is equally likely to be any number. In this situation, the fictitious data profile would be relatively flat, as illustrated in Figure 9-9.

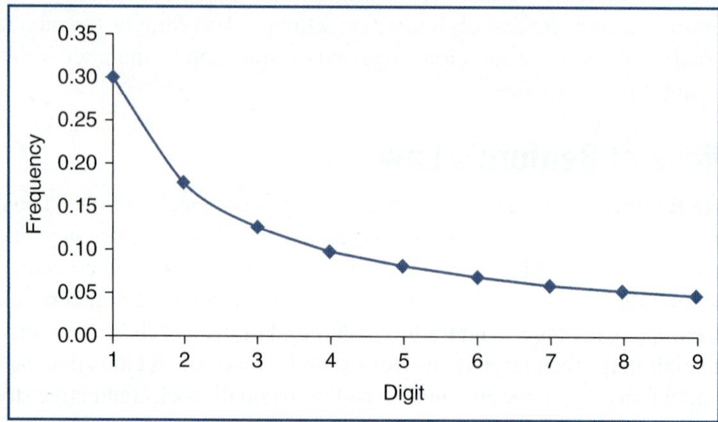

Figure 9-8
Benford's First-Digit Profile

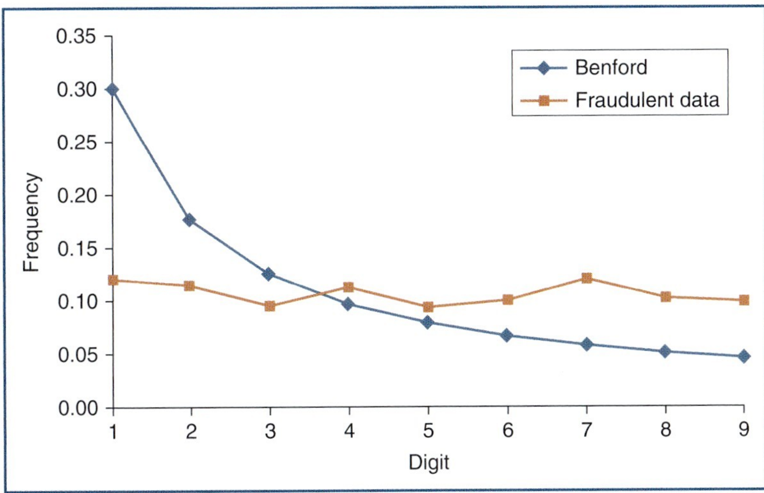

Figure 9-9
Digital Analysis Example—Fictitious Data

In an embezzlement scenario, a fraudster may deliberately issue payments just below some threshold, such as a purchase authorization level. If the threshold is $500, the data profile would display a jump at digit 4, as illustrated in Figure 9-10.

Another common fraud strategy involves the transposition of digits in numbers to make them larger (e.g., $12,313 vs. $21,313). Fraudsters may utilize this strategy because it provides an innocent explanation (error) if the fraud is discovered. If the number of such altered transactions in a data set is large enough, it will reflect the profile illustrated in Figure 9-11.

First-Two-Digits Test

Similar to the first-digit test, the first-two-digits test compares the first two digits of a data set with Benford's profile for the first two digits. Like the first-digit profile, the first-two-digits profile resembles a ski slope (although slightly steeper). With 90 total combinations (10 through 99), this test offers more precision than the first-digit test.

Consider again the embezzlement scenario of fraudulent purchases just below a $500 threshold. With the first-digit test, we were able to identify an above-normal frequency of purchases in amounts beginning with the first digit 4, which could be any amount from $400 to $499. The first-two-digits test would allow us to narrow this range considerably. If the graph showed a spike at 49, we could focus our investigation on purchases from $490 to $499.

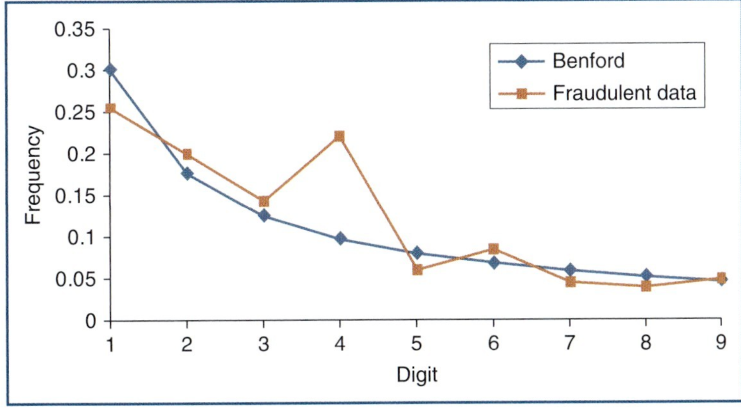

Figure 9-10
Digital Analysis Example—Purchases at $500 Threshold

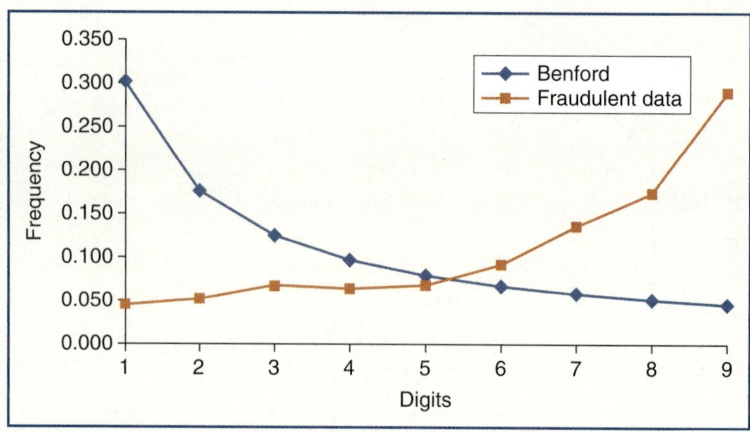

Figure 9-11
Digital Analysis Example—Transposed Digits

Last-Two-Digits Test

The last-two-digits test compares the last two digits of a data set with Benford's profile for the last two digits. There are 100 possible combinations (00 through 99), and each combination has the same probability of occurrence (1%). This test is useful for identifying round or whole numbers, which are red flags for invented numbers.

Special Note

The challenge in applying the last-two-digits test is determining which last-two digits are appropriate for the analysis. For a number such as 215, the last two digits could be 00 (215.00) or 15. For items that are regularly recorded to the decimal (such as currency), it is usually appropriate to consider the decimal places. However, for items that are not recorded in fractional amounts, the decimal places can be ignored.

Size Considerations

Close conformity to Benford's Law requires a large data set, often defined as at least 1,000 observations, with numbers having at least four digits.[51] The size of the data set is important because it is more difficult to identify significant deviations from Benford's profile in small data sets. For example, when performing the first-digit test on a data set with only 100 items, the number of observations with a given first digit must be between 0 and 100. When converted to a proportion, the frequency will have no significant digits beyond the second decimal (hundredths place). These imprecise frequencies are necessarily different from Benford's expected first-digit frequencies, which are much more precise, making it more difficult to identify significant differences.

The relevance of the number of digits is due to the fact that numbers with fewer digits display a slightly higher bias toward lower digits. Because the bias is only slight, it is still acceptable to use a database that contains smaller numbers, as long as the smaller numbers do not dominate.

SUMMARY

Forensic accounting engagements sometimes involve large volumes of data for which items cannot be examined individually. Before applying specific quantitative methods, the analyst must first develop a familiarity with the data using descriptive statistics such as measures of central tendency (including the mean, median, and mode) and measures of variability (including the range, variance, and standard deviation).

The shape of a data distribution can be visually depicted in a histogram, in which the data are separated into groups. Histograms are graphs of the frequencies of grouped data, which can be expressed as absolute or relative frequencies. Relative frequencies are useful because they can be interpreted as probabilities, known as probability distributions. An important attribute of the shape of a data distribution is its skewness, or its asymmetry around the mean. Distributions can be either discrete or continuous, and the most well-known continuous probability distribution is the normal distribution.

Data can be displayed using pie charts, bar graphs, and line graphs. Such visual depictions enhance the interpretation of data, but they can also be misleading. A common way to introduce bias into a graph is to manipulate the scale.

Data mining is used by forensic accountants to reduce a large number of observations to a smaller number that can be examined more closely. Through data mining, analysts can identify relationships or patterns within an existing data set that create a profile against which new data can be compared. The purpose of this comparative analysis to identify any deviations from the profile that may exist in the new data set and determine the likelihood that such deviations are the result of some external influence, such as error or fraud, and not attributable to mere chance. Data mining is facilitated by various computer software programs, ranging from simple spreadsheets to specialized software.

Benford's Law describes the expected frequencies of digits in numbers. According to Benford's Law, the first digit of numbers is more often low than high. Digital analysis is the application of Benford's Law to a series of numbers to determine whether the series reflects the expected digital frequencies. Examples of specific tests include the first-digit test, the first-two-digits test, and the last-digit test. These tests are applied by comparing the actual digital frequencies in a data set to Benford's profile. Digital analysis has been applied to various types of accounting data and is well known for its use in fraud detection.

Key Terms

Absolute frequency
Benford's Law
Continuous distribution
Data mining
Data profile
Descriptive statistics
Digital analysis
Discrete distribution
Histogram
Inferential statistics
Mean
Median
Mode
Normal distribution
Power
Range
Relative frequency
Relative size factor
Skewness
Standard deviation
Statistics
Type I error
Type II error
Variance

Chapter Questions

9-1. What is the general purpose of statistics?

9-2. Does statistical analysis imply absolute precision? Explain.

9-3. What is the purpose of descriptive statistics?

9-4. Explain the difference between a population and a sample.

9-5. What is the purpose of inferential statistics?

9-6. Why are forensic accountants less likely to use inferential statistics to analyze data in an engagement?

9-7. Discuss how the number of observations impacts the application of analytic methods.

9-8. How does understanding the time and magnitude of data impact an analysis?

9-9. Identify three measures of central tendency, and discuss how each is useful to data analysis.

9-10. Explain the concept of variability, and define three measures of variability.

9-11. What is a histogram?

9-12. How might the definition of intervals that are used to construct a histogram impact its shape and explanatory capacity?

9-13. Compare and contrast absolute frequency and relative frequency.

9-14. What advantage does the use of relative frequencies provide to an analyst in the interpretation of data?

9-15. Define *skewness* and discuss its purpose in data analysis.

9-16. What is the difference between a discrete and a continuous distribution?

9-17. Describe a normal distribution. What are its important features?

9-18. Why is timing an important consideration when evaluating the distribution of a data set?

9-19. What is a pie chart, and how is it useful in analyzing and displaying data?

9-20. Compare and contrast a line chart and bar chart. Describe the advantages of each in terms of evaluating trends and relationships.

9-21. Identify and discuss ways in which bias might be incorporated into a graph.

9-22. Define *data mining* and discuss how it is valuable to the data analysis effort.

9-23. Identify and discuss three practical applications of data mining.

9-24. Describe how data can be sorted, and discuss several uses of sorting.

9-25. Define ratio analysis as a form of data mining and describe four specific ratios.

9-26. Explain the difference between a Type I error and a Type II error.

9-27. Why is a forensic accountant concerned with minimizing the risk of identifying false positives?

9-28. What are the advantages of using basic programs, such as Excel and Access, for data analysis?

9-29. Compare and contrast the capabilities of Excel and Access.

9-30. Identify two add-ins that can be acquired to extend the capabilities of Microsoft Excel.

9-31. Discuss the disadvantages of using simple spreadsheet programs in the data analysis process.

9-32. Identify two common specialized software packages that are useful for auditing and fraud investigations, and discuss the merits of each.

9-33. What is the theory underlying digital analysis?

9-34. Define Benford's Law.

9-35. What basic attribute is needed for a data set to conform to Benford's Law?

9-36. Describe four studies that have applied Benford's Law.

9-37. What is a first-digit test, and how is it useful in data analysis?

9-38. Is size a consideration for analytic tests that apply Benford's Law? Explain.

Multiple-Choice Questions

Select the best response to the following questions related to descriptive statistics:

9-39. Descriptive statistics are useful because, in most cases, a large data set cannot be evaluated in its entirety.

a. True
b. False

9-40. Statistics is useful in some cases but is not applicable in many elements of society such as economics, government, and law.

a. True
b. False

9-41. The purpose of statistics includes each of the following *except:*

a. Analyze data
b. Draw meaningful inferences that lead to improved decisions
c. Summarize data
d. All of the above are related to the purpose of statistics

9-42. Statistical analysis is employed to ensure 100% precision in results.

a. True
b. False

9-43. Descriptive statistics are measures that describe:

a. A sample of data
b. A parameter of data
c. A multifaceted data set
d. A single recurring event

9-44. The use of statistical methods to draw conclusions about a population based on information obtained from a sample is called:

a. Descriptive statistics
b. Universal statistics
c. Analytical statistics
d. Inferential statistics

9-45. Descriptive statistics are useful to forensic accountants because:

- **a.** Engagements normally examine data that are accumulated for a specific purpose and are not randomly generated
- **b.** Engagements always use data sets created by random sampling
- **c.** Inferential statistics do not meet the sufficient relevant data criteria
- **d.** None of the above are reasons forensic accountants primarily use descriptive statistics

9-46. The distribution of a data set can be described in two dimensions, which are:

- **a.** Time and series
- **b.** Series and events
- **c.** Time and magnitude
- **d.** Events and populations

9-47. Each of the following is a measure of central tendency *except:*

- **a.** Mode
- **b.** Modularity
- **c.** Median
- **d.** Mean

9-48. Each of the following is a measure of variability *except:*

- **a.** Standard deviation
- **b.** Range
- **c.** Variance
- **d.** Collinearity

Select the best response to the following questions related to the shape of data distributions:

9-49. A histogram is also known as a:

- **a.** Pie chart
- **b.** Line chart
- **c.** Bar chart
- **d.** Distribution chart

9-50. When creating a histogram, a key consideration is the definition of the intervals.

- **a.** True
- **b.** False

9-51. A forensic accountant will normally construct a number of preliminary histograms to determine the appropriate intervals to use for presenting the data to others.

- **a.** True
- **b.** False

9-52. Absolute frequency is defined as:

- **a.** Standard deviation of a population
- **b.** The derivation of all observations within an interval
- **c.** The sum of all observations within an interval
- **d.** The total count of all observations within an interval

9-53. Relative frequency is the percentage of the total number of observations that fall within an interval.

- **a.** True
- **b.** False

9-54. Relative frequencies are useful in statistics because they can be interpreted as:

- **a.** Standard deviations
- **b.** Deductions
- **c.** Inferences
- **d.** Probabilities

9-55. A measure of the degree of asymmetry of a data distribution around its mean is termed:

- **a.** Skewness
- **b.** Robustness
- **c.** Standard deviation
- **d.** None of the above

9-56. A distribution that is more weighted toward smaller numbers is:

- **a.** Incorrectly constructed
- **b.** Positively skewed
- **c.** Negatively skewed
- **d.** Skewered

9-57. Items comprising a discrete distribution are countable and have no discrete separation between successive values.

- **a.** True
- **b.** False

9-58. The most prominent continuous distribution in statistics is:

- **a.** Standard deviation
- **b.** Bayesian distribution
- **c.** Normal distribution
- **d.** Applied distribution

Select the best response to the following questions related to methods of displaying data:

9-59. Large data sets are more effectively analyzed and presented by:

- **a.** Showing each data point
- **b.** Graphing data in a chart
- **c.** Selecting the most important individual items
- **d.** None of the above

9-60. A pie chart is useful for presenting:

a. Hypothetical information
b. Statistical inferences
c. Mathematical formula
d. Categories of data that sum to a total

9-61. A pie chart can be presented in terms of both values and percentages.

a. True
b. False

9-62. When presenting data in a bar chart:

a. Graphing more than one set of data on the same chart provides information about the relationship of the two data sets
b. Only one data set can be presented on a graph
c. Labeling is not important for this type of chart
d. Time is not an important aspect of the presentation

9-63. In a time series graph, time is presented on the horizontal (X) axis, and amounts are presented on the vertical (Y) axis.

a. True
b. False

9-64. Graphs are objective presentations that are always free from bias.

a. True
b. False

9-65. Changing the scale in a graph can have a significant impact that introduces _____ into the presentation:

a. Homogeneity
b. Uniformity
c. Bias
d. Serialization

9-66. It is important to include the scale in a graph to avoid the perception of:

a. Unlawfulness
b. Intuitiveness
c. Counterintuitiveness
d. Intentional deception

9-67. Charts should always have a title.

a. True
b. False

9-68. Descriptive labels for each axis of a graph may or may not be included depending on whether such labels will enhance the overall clarity of the graph.

a. True
b. False

Select the best response to the following questions related to data mining:

9-69. With data mining, observations are selected randomly.

a. True
b. False

9-70. Computer applications allow an analyst to screen all observations in a data set rather than rely on statistical sampling.

a. True
b. False

9-71. A forensic accountant uses data mining to:

a. Select a perfect random sample
b. Avoid making Type IV errors
c. Avoid Type V errors
d. Reduce a large number of items to a smaller number that can be examined more closely

9-72. Data mining often involves the comparison of new data against data profiles for the purpose of identifying:

a. Systematic items
b. Symmetric items
c. Deviant items
d. Regular items

9-73. Data mining is useful in each of the following applications *except:*

a. Investment analysis
b. Credit scoring
c. Fraud detection
d. All of the above are applications of data mining

9-74. Data mining can identify all types of fraud.

a. True
b. False

9-75. Which of the following is a form of data mining?

a. Sorting
b. Accumulating
c. Storing
d. Synthesizing

9-76. Ratio analysis is a form of data mining.

a. True
b. False

9-77. Which of the following is not a commonly used data mining ratio?

a. Ratio of the largest value to the smallest value

b. Ratio of the largest value to the second-largest value

c. Ratio of the smallest value to the second-smallest value

d. The times interest earned ratio

9-78. A Type I error occurs when:

a. An analysis fails to identify a true signal

b. An item is selected for further analysis when it should not be selected

c. An analyst fails to identify the first item that is incorrect in a data set

d. An analyst fails to identify the last item that is incorrect in a data set

Select the best response to the following questions related to Benford's Law:

9-79. The occurrence of different digits in most sets of numbers is random.

a. True

b. False

9-80. _____ is founded on the counterintuitive observation that individual digits of multidigit numbers are not random but follow a pattern known as Benford's Law:

a. Fraud analysis

b. Discrete analysis

c. Open system analysis

d. Digital analysis

9-81. According to Benford's Law, the first digit in a multidigit number is expected to be 1 about:

a. 20% of the time

b. 30% of the time

c. 50% of the time

d. Proportional to the number of digits in a multidigit number

9-82. To conform to Benford's Law, a number series must approximately follow a geometric sequence, where each successive number is calculated as a fixed percentage increase over the previous number.

a. True

b. False

9-83. Data sets that do not follow Benford's Law are data sets:

a. With built-in maximums or minimums and assigned numbers

b. That contain over 10,000 observations

c. That contain economic information

d. None of the above are correctly stated

9-84. Research studies have found Benford's Law to be appropriate for the examination of:

a. Net income

b. Fraud detection

c. Earnings per share

d. Each of the above are correct responses to this question

9-85. A graph of Benford's first-digit frequencies will resemble:

a. A normal curve

b. A positively sloped yield curve

c. A ski slope

d. A U-shaped curve

9-86. If a fraudster is deliberately issuing payments below some policy threshold, such as $9,000, the data profile will show a jump at digit:

a. 1

b. 4

c. 8

d. 9

9-87. Which of the following is not a type of test that looks for deviations from Benford's Law:

a. First-two-digits test

b. Last-two-digits test

c. All digits test

d. First-digit test

9-88. It is easier to identify variations from Benford's law using small, rather than large, data sets.

a. True

b. False

Workplace Applications

9-89. A five-year earnings summary for Hellemn Candy, Inc. is presented in the following table. Using this data, construct a single graph of the three earnings measures, and then prepare a memo to your professor addressing the following items.

1. What type of graph did you create and why? Present your graphs in your memo.
2. Does there appear to be a relationship among the earnings measures? Explain why or why not.
3. Assess your chart's design in terms of presentation bias. If you feel your chart is free from bias, explain why this is so. Then develop a second chart with the data presented in a manner that might be misleading to a viewer.

Hellemn Candy: Earnings Measures, 2008–2011

Year	2012	2011	2010	2009	2008
Income from Operations	5,785	6,450	7,250	6,250	5,975
Net Income	4,385	5,300	5,325	4,737	4,529
Net Cash Flow from Operations	5,050	8,300	7,700	7,530	5,700

9-90. The AICPA provides a free Excel spreadsheet program that can be used to test data for consistency with Benford's Law. A link to this spreadsheet is available at www.pearsonhighered.com/rufus.

Download the spreadsheet and study its structure as well as the manner in which it presents the results of the first-digit and second-digit tests.

1. Once you understand the spreadsheet, perform the following:
   a. Obtain the Excel data file for 1978 taxable income in the Chapter 8 materials via a link at www.pearsonhighered.com/rufus, which will take you to a web site hosted by Dr. Mark Nigrini.
   b. Copy and paste the first 6,000 observations into the data entry tab (Column A) of the Fraud Buster spreadsheet. Remember to clear all existing data prior to performing this step.
   c. Run Fraud Buster.
2. How do the results of the first-digit and second-digit tests compare to Benford's predicted distribution? Are there any digits you might investigate further?

9-91. Refer to question 9-90. Using the Fraud Buster spreadsheet and the 1978 taxable income data obtained from Dr. Nigrini's web site, run a first-digit test on the first 375 observations in the data set. How do the actual digital frequencies for this set of observations compare to Benford's predicted distribution? Are there any digits you might investigate further?

9-92. Obtain the Fraud Buster spreadsheet described in problem 9-90. In the data entry column, use the Excel Rand function to generate random numbers between 1 and 999. Use the formula =RAND()*(1000-1)+1 for this purpose. Once you have the first random number in cell A1, copy the formula so that you have a data set of 1,000 randomly generated observations. Then run the first-digit test in Fraud Buster.

1. What do the results of the first-digit test indicate?
2. Expand the random number list to 25,000 observations by copying the formula. Run the first-digit test for this new set of observations and compare the results to those you obtained for the set of 1,000 observations. Explain the differences.

9-93. You have been hired by the U.S. Department of Education to determine why graduation rates vary from 8% to 100% among U.S. colleges and universities. To facilitate your assignment, you are provided a data set that has been compiled from public sources. The data set can be found at MathForum.org by following these directions:

1. Search using the term "workshops"
2. Select "Math Forum Sponsored Workshops"
3. On the content line, select "Summer"
4. Select "Constructing Mathematics on the Internet 1996"
5. Select "Showcase of Working Group Development"
6. Select "The Data Library"
7. Select "Data Sets"
8. Select "1993 American Colleges and Universities"

The direct link to the data set (compiled by *U.S. News & World Report LP*) is provided with permission from Drexel University (copyright 2013) by The Math Forum @ Drexel. All rights reserved. You may access the link at www.pearsonhighered.com/rufus.

Once you have obtained the data set, perform the following:

1. Sort the file by graduation rate and create a pie chart that displays the following categories: 25%

or less, 26% to 50%, 51% to 75%, and 76% to 100%.

2. Present the pie chart and interpret it.
3. In Step 1, did you encounter any unusable data? Explain.
4. Would further analysis of the data set provide additional insights? Explain why or why not.
5. Are there aspects of the data that might cause the analysis to be misleading or suggest that further investigation is appropriate?
6. Drawing on your prior coursework, what statistical tests might be used to gain additional insight into the relationship of graduation rates to the other information provided in the data set? Explain.

Chapter Problems

9-94. Obtain an article written by Durtschi, Hillison, and Pacini entitled "The Effective Use of Benford's Law to Assist in Detecting Fraud in Accounting Data," published in the *Journal of Forensic Accounting* in 2004 (Volume V, pp. 17–34). Summarize the article in a memo to your professor. At a minimum, you should address:

1. The history of Benford's Law
2. The application of Benford's Law to auditing and accounting
3. When to use digital analysis

9-95. Obtain an article written by Rose and Rose published in the August 2003 edition of *Journal of Accountancy* entitled "Turn Excel into a Financial Sleuth." (You may access the article via a link at www.pearsonhighered.com/rufus.)

1. Read the article and download the Fraud Buster spreadsheet using the link provided by the authors.
2. Analyze the results shown in Fraud Buster for the first-digit and second-digit tests. How are the analysis tables structured, and what do they show?
3. Prepare a memo to your professor explaining what you discovered about the distribution of the data set included in the Fraud Buster spreadsheet and what you learned about digital analysis.

9-96. Perform a Google search using the following search term: "Using Digital Analysis to Enhance Data Integrity." Read the first nine pages of this document, and prepare a memo to your professor summarizing the following three categories covered in the paper:

1. What is Digital Analysis?
2. Uses of Digital Analysis
3. Expected Frequencies of Digits

9-97. Obtain the areas of the 254 counties in Texas via a link to a Texas census report at www.pearsonhighered.com/rufus.

Copy and paste this data into an Excel spreadsheet, then perform the following tasks.

1. Extract the first digit from the data series using the LEFT function.
2. Complete the Absolute Frequency and Relative Frequency columns in the following table: (Note: Use the COUNT IF function for Absolute Frequency.)
3. Graph Relative Frequency and Benford Frequency on a single line graph.
4. Evaluate the graph to determine whether the data set conforms to Benford's Law.
5. Is it not reasonable to expect the areas of the counties in Texas to follow Benford's Law? Why or why not?

Digit	Absolute Frequency	Relative Frequency	Benford Frequency
1			.301
2			.176
3			.125
4			.097
5			.079
6			.067
7			.058
8			.051
9			.046

1 Indictment, *U.S. v. Khaled and Fatima Saleh.* U.S. District Court, Northern District of Illinois, Eastern Division. No. 11 CR 367. Filed June 22, 2011.

2 U.S. Attorney, Northern District of Illinois. Press Release, June 23, 2011. Waukegan grocer and wife indicted for allegedly defrauding U.S. Food Stamp and Nutrition Programs of more than $500,000.

3 Plea Agreement, *U.S. v. Khaled Saleh.* U.S. District Court, Northern District of Illinois, Eastern Division. No. 11 CR 367. Filed August 31, 2012; Plea Declaration, *U.S. v. Fatima Saleh.* U.S. District Court, Northern District of Illinois, Eastern Division. No. 11 CR 367-2. Filed August 31, 2012.

4 Government's Position Paper as to Sentencing Factors, *U.S. v. Khaled Saleh.* U.S. District Court, Northern District of Illinois, Eastern Division. No. 11 CR 367-1. Filed December 5, 2012; Government's Position Paper as to Sentencing Factors, *U.S. v. Fatima Saleh.* U.S. District Court, Northern District of Illinois, Eastern Division. No. 11 CR 367-2. Filed December 6, 2012.

5 O'Keefe, E. (Dec. 6, 2011). Obama administration targeting food stamp fraud as program reaches record highs. *Washington Post.*

6 Hananel. S. (May 24, 2012). Food stamp fraud: Agriculture Department taking new steps to combat selling benefit cards. *Huffington Post.*

7 U.S. Department of Agriculture. Food and Nutrition Service. Fighting Snap Fraud. Go to www .pearsonhighered.com/rufus for a link to this report.

8 Baertlein, L. (Feb. 6, 2012). U.S. targets food stamp fraud as election looms. *Reuters.*

9 Hananel. S. (May 24, 2012). Food stamp fraud: Agriculture Department taking new steps to combat selling benefit cards. *Huffington Post.*

10 O'Keefe, E. (Dec. 6, 2011). Obama administration targeting food stamp fraud as program reaches record highs. *Washington Post.*

11 Ibid.

12 U.S. Department of Agriculture. Food and Nutrition Service. Fighting Snap Fraud. Go to www .pearsonhighered.com/rufus for a link to this report.

13 Ibid.

14 Aczel, A. D., & Sounderpandian, J. (2006). *Complete Business Statistics* (6th Ed.). McGraw Hill.

15 Dodge, Y. (2006) *The Oxford Dictionary of Statistical Terms.* Oxford University Press.

16 Aczel, A. D., & Sounderpandian, J. (2006). *Complete Business Statistics* (6th Ed.). McGraw Hill.

17 Fadairo, S. A., Williams, R., Trotman, R., & Onyekelu-Eze, O. (2008). Using data mining to ensure payment integrity. *The Journal of Government Financial Management, 57,* 22–24.

18 Ibid.

19 Gao, A., & Ye, M. (2007). A framework for data mining-based anti-money laundering research. *Journal of Money Laundering Control, 10*(2), 170–79.

20 Ramamoorti, S. (2003). Procurement fraud and data analytics. *Journal of Government Financial Management.*

21 ACI Worldwide (Oct. 2012). Global consumers react to rising fraud: Beware back of wallet. Go to www .pearsonhighered.com/rufus for a link to this article.

22 *Consumer Reports.* (2012, Jun.). House of cards: Why your accounts are vulnerable to thieves. Go to www .pearsonhighered.com/rufus for a link to this article.

23 Bolton, R. J., & Hand, D. J. (2002). Statistical fraud detection: A review. *Statistical Science, 17*(3), 235–55.

24 *Consumer Reports.* (Jun. 2012). House of cards: Why your accounts are vulnerable to thieves. Go to www .pearsonhighered.com/rufus for a link to this article.

25 Panigrahi, P. K. (Apr. 2006). Discovering fraud in forensic accounting using data mining techniques. *The Chartered Accountant.*

26 Ramamoorti, S. (2003). Procurement fraud and data analytics. *Journal of Government Financial Management.*

27 Gao, A., & Ye, M. (2007). A framework for data mining-based anti-money laundering research. *Journal of Money Laundering Control, 10*(2), 170–79.

28 Nigrini, M. (2011). *Forensic Analytics.* John Wiley & Sons, Inc.

29 Ibid.

30 ACL Whitepaper. Spreadsheets: A high-risk tool for data analysis.

31 Ibid.

32 Ibid.

33 Lanza, R. (Nov./Dec. 2004). Fraud data interrogation tools: Comparing best software for fraud examinations. *Fraud Magazine.*

34 Tackett, J. (2007). Digital analysis: A better way to detect fraud. *Journal of Corporate Accounting & Finance, 18*(4), 27–36.

35 Benford, F. (1938). The law of anomalous numbers. *Proceedings of the American Philosophical Society, 78*(4), 551–72

36 Nigrini, M. (1999). I've got your number. *Journal of Accountancy, 187*(5), 79–83.

37 Nigrini, M. (2011). *Forensic Analytics.* John Wiley & Sons, Inc.

38 Durtschi, C., Hillison, W., & Pacini, C. (2004). The effective use of Benford's Law to assist in detecting fraud in accounting data. *Journal of Forensic Accounting, 5*, 17–34.

39 Tackett, J. (2007). Digital analysis: A better way to detect fraud. *Journal of Corporate Accounting & Finance, 18*(4), 27–36.

40 Nigrini, M. (2011). *Forensic Analytics.* John Wiley & Sons, Inc.

41 Nigrini, M. (1999). I've got your number. *Journal of Accountancy, 187*(5), 79–83.

42 Carslaw, C. (1988). Anomalies in income numbers: Evidence of goal-oriented behavior. *The Accounting Review, 63*, 321–27.

43 Thomas, J. (1989). Unusual patterns in reported earnings. *The Accounting Review, 64*, 773–87.

44 Nigrini, M. (2005). An assessment of the change in the incidence of earnings management around the Enron-Andersen episode. *Review of Accounting and Finance, 4*(1), 92–110.

45 Thomas, J. (1989). Unusual patterns in reported earnings. *The Accounting Review, 64*, 773–87.

46 Christian, C., & Gupta, S. (1993). New evidence on secondary evasion. *Journal of the American Taxation Association, 15*(1), 72–92.

47 Nigrini, M. (1996). A taxpayer compliance application of Benford's Law. *Journal of the American Taxation Association, 18*(1), 72–91.

48 Nigrini, M. (1994). Using digital frequencies to detect fraud. *The White Paper, 8*(2), 3–6

49 Etteridge, M., & Srivastava, R. (1999). Using digital analysis to enhance data integrity. *Issues in Accounting Education, 14*(4), 675–90.

50 Tackett, J. (2007). Digital analysis: A better way to detect fraud. *Journal of Corporate Accounting & Finance, 18*(4), 27–36.

51 Nigrini, M. (2011). *Forensic Analytics.* John Wiley & Sons, Inc.

10 Professional Responsibilities

INTRODUCTION

Although professional responsibilities have been highlighted throughout the text, our conversation would not be complete without a focused discussion on this important subject. Thus, the purpose of this chapter is to consider the forensic accountant's specific professional responsibilities—to the client, the court, the profession, and the public.

We recognize that not all forensic accountants are CPAs, or even members of the AICPA. Moreover, forensic accountants commonly belong to multiple professional organizations, such as the AICPA, the Association of Certified Fraud Examiners (ACFE), and the National Association of Certified Valuators and Analysts (NACVA), each with its own set of professional standards. Although practitioners must comply with the standards of all professional organizations to which they belong, our discussion is focused on the AICPA's Code of Professional Conduct, which is considered the foremost source of guidance for accountants in public practice. Even so, given the relevance of ACFE and NACVA in forensic accounting, their professional standards will also be considered.

Specifics topics to be discussed (or revisited) include:

- AICPA Code of Conduct[1]
- AICPA Statement on Standards for Consulting Services No. 1
- AICPA Statement on Standards for Valuation Services No. 1
- ACFE Code of Professional Standards[2]
- NACVA Professional Standards[3]
- Rules of evidence applicable to experts (FRE 702–705)
- Rules of civil procedure (FRCP 26)
- Practitioner's Perspective

An understanding of the requisite professional standards is a *must* for forensic accountants. As discussed in Chapter 3, this is an important preengagement consideration that plays a role in framing your case. Moreover, testifying experts are commonly challenged on their knowledge of the professional standards—both the underlying reasoning and proper application. Failure to adhere to the standards will likely be recognized and exposed, thereby undermining the validity of the expert's opinion. When considering the importance of professional responsibility, it is important to keep in mind that, unlike accounting-related engagements (for example, tax or auditing), forensic accounting engagements are adversarial in nature. This means that opposing experts are engaged to evaluate you and your work, including your compliance with the requisite professional standards.

Following an overview of professional responsibilities and the applicable standards and rules, we next consider how this knowledge can be integrated into the practice of forensic accounting. In other words, how are problems identified and how should they be addressed? To assist in this challenge, we introduce the ***threats and safeguards approach*** for evaluating professional responsibility issues. This approach is used by the AICPA's Professional Ethics Executive Committee (PEEC) to develop ethics interpretations and rulings. Our discussion concludes

Learning Objectives

After completing this chapter, you should be able to:

LO1. Define professional responsibility and understand how it impacts a forensic accounting engagement.

LO2. Understand the AICPA Code of Professional Conduct, including its principles and rules.

LO3. Describe how the AICPA's Statement on Standards for Consulting Services No. 1 impacts the work of a forensic accountant.

LO4. Compare and contrast the professional standards of the AICPA with other accounting-related professional organizations.

LO5. Explain the adversary-advocacy nature of forensic accounting.

LO6. Describe the threats and safeguards approach and how it is useful to a forensic accountant.

with cautions and concerns related to the adversary-advocacy nature of forensic accounting engagements and practice tips for addressing conflicts among different sets of standards.

PROFESSIONAL RESPONSIBILITY

To help us understand the concept of "professional responsibility," let's deconstruct it. A ***profession*** is an occupation that requires advanced education and training. Examples of well-known professions include law, medicine, and accounting. By extension, a ***professional*** is a person who practices a profession, such as a lawyer, doctor, or CPA. Characteristics of a profession include, but are not limited to, the following:

- It is organized into associations, such as the American Institute of Certified Public Accountants (AICPA), American Medical Association (AMA), and American Bar Association (ABA). There are specific requirements for admission into such associations and maintenance of membership. For example, CPAs must pass the CPA exam, complete two years of work experience, pay periodic dues, and maintain competence through continuing professional education.
- There are published authoritative performance and ethical standards, such as the AICPA's Code of Professional Conduct and the AMA's Code of Medical Ethics.
- Violations of the profession's performance and ethical standards may be cause for disciplinary action, such as censure, suspension, or expulsion from membership.
- It enjoys a high level of public trust and confidence.
- It is legalized by a regulatory body, such as a state board of accountancy.

Building on our understanding of the terms profession and professional, let's now consider the concept of ***responsibility***. According to Webster's dictionary, responsibility involves a condition of accountability, obligation, or duty.[4] Similarly, *Black's Law Dictionary* defines responsibility as being held accountable for one's duty, action/inaction, or obligation.[5]

Consolidating these concepts, we can reason that ***professional responsibility*** includes the following obligations:

- To employ the degree of knowledge, skill, and judgment ordinarily possessed by members of the profession
- To follow the highest standards of conduct prescribed by each of the organizations to which the professional (or firm) belongs
- To adhere to the provisions of any regulatory or licensing authority

To put this discussion into context, let's consider the 2010 case of *Dock's Creek Land Company, LLC v. Tolliver Engineers and Architects, Inc.,*[*] a real-world experience.

Dock's Creek Land Company

Dock's Creek Land Company (Dock's Creek) is an Ohio limited liability company (LLC) managed by H.B. Wiseman, a solo-practicing CPA with an office in Honeywell, Ohio. Members of the LLC include Wiseman (a 30% owner) and two physician clients (owning 35% each). The purpose of the LLC is real estate development.

Background

In May 2008, Dock's Creek purchased a 2.5-acre tract located 15 miles outside Cleveland's city limits for $500,000. Wiseman advised his two partners that the property was a "solid investment" given its proximity to downtown Cleveland, particularly Newhaven Hospital and Cleveland State University.

In November 2008, Newhaven Hospital announced an expansion of its services and a renewed relationship with Cleveland State's School of Medicine, creating a variety of new medical internships, fellowships, and other opportunities for advanced medical education.

[*] Names and locations have been changed to protect the privacy of the parties.

Following this announcement, Wiseman approached his partners about developing the newly acquired tract to accommodate an expected surge in short-term housing demand. With his partners' approval, Wiseman discussed the project with Robert Tolliver. Tolliver, also one of Wiseman's accounting clients, is the senior partner of Tolliver Engineers and Architects, Inc., also located in Honeywell, Ohio.

On or about February 10, 2009, Wiseman (on behalf of Dock's Creek) entered into an agreement to pay $1.5 million to Classic Custom Homes, Inc., of Brentwood, Indiana, to construct thirty prefabricated efficiency apartments on the 2.5-acre tract. An initial payment of $250,000 was made upon the execution of the agreement, with subsequent payments to be made based on percentage of completion. The entire project was to be completed on or before June 15, 2009.

On April 20, 2009, following total payments to Classic of $750,000, Wiseman was advised by the County Zoning Board that it would not issue a building permit as requested. He was also advised that he could request a variance and, if denied, could appeal the Zoning Board's decision. Wiseman was personally contacted because he was listed as the owner, applicant, and contractor of record.

Wiseman failed to persuade the Board at the variance hearing and subsequently opted to abort the project. On May 29, 2009, in an effort to mitigate Dock's Creek's financial exposure, Wiseman advised Classic to stop construction. On September 15, 2009, Dock's Creek and Classic entered into a settlement agreement requiring a final payment by Dock's Creek of $250,000. Thus, payments to Classic totaled $1 million, although no product was ever delivered.

The Complaint

In January 2010, Wiseman (on behalf of Dock's Creek) filed a lawsuit against Tolliver Engineers and Architects, Inc., claiming professional negligence, breach of contract, restitution, and reliance. The complaint alleged that Tolliver had been contracted to conduct a "feasibility study" of the project, including architectural design and zoning ordinances. The complaint also alleged that the decision to sign the contract with Classic Custom Homes was driven by Tolliver's confirmation that, with regard to zoning, "anything goes" outside the city limits.

Tolliver denied the allegations and filed a counterclaim, alleging breach of contract and abuse of process.[†] Specifically, Tolliver alleged that the "oral" contract between the parties was limited to architectural design and property placement. The counterclaim further stated that code compliance was the duty of the contractor (that is, Wiseman), unless specifically assigned via an owner-architect agreement.

Following the initial pleadings (complaint and answer), Dock's Creek submitted the expert report of T. R. Robertson, MBA, CPA, CVA, a forensic accountant and seasoned expert witness. Robertson's report opined that the damages suffered by Dock's Creek ranged "from a low of $1.25 million to a high of $2 million, depending upon two discounting and occupancy assumptions."

Robertson's Deposition

The following are excerpts from Robertson's deposition.

Defense Attorney: Who is your client in this matter?

Robertson: Dock's Creek Land Company, LLC

Defense Attorney: Did you secure an engagement letter that outlines the specifics of your engagement?

[†] Abuse of process is the "improper and tortious use of a legitimately issued court process to obtain a result that is either unlawful or beyond the process' scope"—also known as abuse of legal process and malicious prosecution. From *Black's Law Dictionary* (2009), 9th Edition. Material reprinted with permission of Thomson Reuters.

Robertson: No. Engagement letters are not mandatory. I've known Mr. Wiseman for several years and did not think it was necessary.

Defense Attorney: Specifically, what were you engaged to do?

Robertson: Calculate the economic damages resulting from the failure of the project.

Defense Attorney: Identify all the facts and data you considered in calculating the economic damages.

Robertson: The primary predicate was a compilation[‡] of revenue and expenses associated with an investment holding period of ten years. Based on my conversations with Mr. Wiseman, this was a relatively risk-free endeavor and thus risk-free rates were used in calculating the present value of the damages. Moreover, the material risks were captured in the modeling of revenues and expenses.

Defense Attorney: So the compilation is the foundation of your report?

Robertson: Yes.

Defense Attorney: What other facts or data did you consider?

Robertson: I also considered RealtyRates.com to test the expense functions.

Defense Attorney: Who prepared the compilation you relied on?

Robertson: It's my understanding that it was prepared by Mr. Wiseman.

Defense Attorney: Did you have discussions with Mr. Wiseman regarding the compilation—how it was developed?

Robertson: Yes, several.

Defense Attorney: Do you have any memoranda of your discussions with Mr. Wiseman?

Roberson: No. I didn't think it was necessary.

Defense Attorney: Was the compilation you relied on prepared before or after the filing of the complaint?

Robertson: I don't know for sure. I suspect it was prepared before the project was undertaken.

Defense Attorney: What makes you suspect that?

Robertson: Such compilations are commonly prepared in the decision making stage for project assessment. They are also used to help secure financing.

Defense Attorney: Would it make a difference, in your opinion, if the compilation was prepared by Mr. Wiseman after the complaint was filed?

Robertson: It might. However, what's important is not when it was prepared but how it was prepared. As long as it was reliably prepared and based on sufficient data. Projections are fluid—always changing.

[‡] Prepared by Wiseman in his capacity as a CPA.

Defense Attorney: Do you know what information Mr. Wiseman relied on to prepare the compilation of revenues and expenses?

Robertson: Not specifically. It's my belief that he conducted market research regarding fair rental values and unit demand.

Defense Attorney: What is your belief based on? Did you see his work papers or his market research? Is this what he told you?

Robertson: I don't recall specifically how my understanding was developed. As I stated, we had several conversations. I know Mr. Wiseman is a CPA and understands the process.

Defense Attorney: In what capacity was Mr. Wiseman serving when he prepared the compilation? In other words, was he acting as a member of Dock's Creek or in his capacity as a CPA?

Robertson: I'm frankly not sure. That said, I don't think it matters. The members of Dock's Creek certainly benefited from Mr. Wiseman's education and training.

Defense Attorney: Was Dock's Creek one of Mr. Wiseman's clients?

Robertson: Certainly. He would not have outsourced the accounting and tax work.

Defense Attorney: Tell me everything you know about Mr. Wiseman's education and work experience.

Robertson: He graduated from Cleveland State and is a CPA. Before starting his own CPA firm he worked in auto manufacturing as an internal auditor. He is a member of the AICPA and licensed to practice in Ohio. The nature of the Dock's Creek complaint would suggest he has experience in the real estate development business.

Defense Attorney: Describe your knowledge of Mr. Wiseman's experience in the real estate development business.

Robertson: As I previously stated, I've known Mr. Wiseman for several years. It's my understanding that, in the normal course of his practice, he provides management consulting and tax services to clients invested in various types of real estate ventures.

Defense Attorney: Describe any and all professional dealings you've had with Mr. Wiseman.

Robertson: None.

Defense Attorney: Has Mr. Wiseman ever referred any business to you or other members of your firm?

Robertson: He may have. I don't recall. We get referrals from many CPAs.

Defense Attorney: Please describe the methodology you used to calculate the damages in this case.

Robertson: I used the present value of cash flows method. I also considered the terminal value of the project.

Defense Attorney: How was the terminal value determined?

Robertson: The predicates were provided by Mr. Wiseman, and I did the computations.

Defense Attorney:	You do understand that Mr. Wiseman is a plaintiff in this matter?
Robertson:	Indirectly, yes. He's one of the owners of Dock's Creek.
Defense Attorney:	Mr. Robertson, did you exercise any professional skepticism in the course of this engagement?
Robertson:	Of course. That said, I relied on the information provided. As you know, Mr. Wiseman is a CPA. It's reasonable for me, as an expert, to rely on other experts in developing my opinion. Mr. Wiseman's education, training, and experience in the real estate business certainly make him an expert.
Defense Attorney:	Mr. Robertson, did you consider any qualitative issues or pressures during your engagement in this case?
Robertson:	I am unaware of any qualitative issues that would impact my opinion.
Defense Attorney:	Did you interview the other members (partners) in Dock's Creek?
Robertson:	No—it was not necessary. Mr. Wiseman was the LLC's managing principal.
Defense Attorney:	Did you do any research regarding compliance (zoning) responsibility?
Robertson:	No. That issue is outside the scope of my engagement.

Subsequent Discovery

In subsequent discovery, it was found that the compilation had, in fact, been prepared by Wiseman *after* the complaint had been filed. Moreover, it was determined that Wiseman had no previous experience in real estate development and had exercised little or no due diligence in evaluating the feasibility of the real estate project. It was also discovered that Mr. Wiseman had billed Dock's Creek for all services provided, including the preparation of the compilation. Finally, discovery revealed that Wiseman had been contacted by his partners in Dock's Creek (*before* the filing of the complaint against Tolliver) regarding their intent to sue him for professional malpractice.

Motion to Exclude Expert's Testimony

In November 2010, a motion was granted to exclude Robertson's testimony because his opinion was speculative and not based on sufficient facts or data, as mandated by Rules 701–705 of the Ohio Rules of Evidence.[6] The Court provided the following notes:

- Consistent with the generally inclusionary and expansive thrust of the Rules of Evidence, the rule on expert testimony is notably liberal. Absent strong factors favoring exclusion, doubts regarding whether an expert's testimony will be useful should generally be resolved in favor of admissibility.
- Courts are not allowed to take on faith whatever a paid expert claims, no matter how distinguished his credentials.
- Trial judges have an independent obligation—a screening function—to ensure that proffered expert testimony is grounded on reliable facts and data.
- Like all evidence, expert testimony must be relevant to be admissible.
- Hypothesis is not proof, nor is speculation.
- Generally, lost profit damages can be established with the aid of expert testimony, economic and financial data, market surveys and analyses, and business records of similar activities. However, evidence considered by the plaintiff's expert in this case falls far

below the threshold of reasonable certainty. An expert's opinion cannot be based on self-serving estimates prepared by the plaintiff which amount to little more than hopeful speculation and conjecture. Experts must protect the integrity of their work, maintain objectivity, and avoid any subordination of their judgment.

Settlement Agreement

Following the exclusion of Robertson's testimony, the parties entered into a settlement agreement favoring Tolliver's counterclaims.

Special Note

The epilogue for this case is presented at the conclusion of the chapter. It describes a subsequent lawsuit filed by Dock's Creek and its majority members against Robertson alleging professional malpractice. Although a separate claim was also filed against Wiseman, its consideration is beyond the scope of our discussion.

AICPA CODE OF PROFESSIONAL CONDUCT

As previously noted, our discussion is focused on the AICPA's Code of Professional Conduct, considered the foremost source of guidance for accountants in public practice. Although AICPA membership is voluntary, membership mandates compliance with the Code.

The purpose of the Code is to influence the behavior of AICPA members through guidance, rules, interpretations, and rulings. Simply stated, it helps members monitor their own behavior and provides a program for resolving disputes. The Code has two sections: principles and rules. The principles provide a framework for the rules, which govern the performance of all professional services provided by members.

Notable Quote

"Rules are not necessarily sacred; principles are." *Franklin D. Roosevelt*

What's the difference between a principle and a rule? Moreover, how do principles provide a framework for rules? A ***principle***, although conceptual in nature (and thus not enforceable), is a value-based (internal) force for behavioral action, such as honesty and integrity. A ***rule***, on the other hand, is an authoritative (external) regulatory force for behavioral action. Because principles define the spirit, reasoning, and meaning (the framework) underlying rules, principles must be considered when resolving disputes related to rule violations.

Special Note

To illustrate the difference between a principle and a rule, consider a person's tendency to speed while driving. Suppose you are driving in a residential community where children are known to play near the street. Because you value the safety of children, you will probably reduce your speed, regardless of the actual speed limit. Now, suppose you are driving on the interstate. If you do not feel that moderate speeding significantly threatens safety, you are more likely to exceed the speed limit. In this example, the driver is more influenced by the principle (perception of safety) than by the rule (the speed limit).

Principles of Professional Conduct

Six principles are identified in the Code. They call for a commitment to moral behavior and an emphasis on maintaining the public's trust. Individual principles and related explanations are provided in Table 10-1.

Table 10-1 AICPA Principles of Professional Conduct

Code Reference	Principle	Explanation
ET Sec. 52, Article I	Responsibilities	Members have responsibilities to all those who use their professional services. They also have a responsibility to cooperate with each other to improve the art of accounting, maintain the public's confidence, and carry out the profession's special responsibilities for self-governance.
ET Sec. 53, Article II	The public trust	Members are expected to discharge their responsibilities with integrity, objectivity, due professional care, and a genuine interest in serving the public.
ET Sec. 54, Article III	Integrity	Integrity requires a member to be honest and candid within the constraints of client confidentiality. Service and the public trust should not be subordinated to personal gain and advantage. Integrity also requires a member to observe the principles of objectivity, independence, and due care.
ET Sec. 55, Article IV	Objectivity and independence	The principle of objectivity imposes the obligation to be impartial, intellectually honest, and free of conflicts of interest. Independence precludes relationships that may appear to impair a member's objectivity in rendering attestation services.

Code Reference	Principle	Explanation
ET Sec. 56, Article V	Due care	Due care requires a member to discharge professional responsibilities with competence and diligence. Competence is derived from a synthesis of education and experience. Diligence imposes the responsibility to render services promptly and carefully, to be thorough, and to observe applicable technical and ethical standards.
ET Sec. 57, Article VI	Scope and nature of services	Each of these principles should be considered by members in determining whether to provide specific services in individual circumstances.

Source: Adapted from the AICPA Code of Professional Conduct, revised through Aug. 31, 2012.

Rules of Professional Conduct

Unlike the principles discussed previously, the Rules of Conduct are *specific* and *enforceable*. Although a comprehensive discussion of the rules and their interpretation is beyond the scope of this chapter, an overview is presented in Table 10-2. Students are urged to visit the AICPA's web site for detailed discussions and updates.

Table 10-2 | AICPA Rules of Professional Conduct

Code Reference	Rule	Explanation
ET Sec. 101, Rule 101	Independence	Members shall be independent in the performance of professional services.
ET Sec. 102, Rule 102	Integrity and objectivity	Members shall maintain objectivity and integrity, shall be free of conflicts of interest, and shall not knowingly misrepresent facts or subordinate their judgment to others.
ET Sec. 200, Rule 201	General standards	Members shall comply with the following standards: • ***Professional competence***: Undertake only those professional services that the member or the member's firm can reasonably expect to be completed with professional competence. • ***Due professional care***: Exercise due professional care in the performance of professional services. • ***Planning and supervision***: Adequately plan and supervise the performance of professional services. • ***Sufficient relevant data***: Obtain sufficient relevant data to afford a reasonable basis for conclusions or recommendations in relation to any professional services performed.
ET Sec. 200, Rule 202	Compliance	Members shall comply with standards promulgated by bodies designated by Council.

(continued)

Table 10-2 | *(continued)*

Code Reference	Rule	Explanation
ET Sec. 200, Rule 203	Accounting principles	A member shall not (1) express an opinion or state affirmatively that the financial statements of any entity are presented in conformity with GAAP or (2) state that he or she is not aware of any material modifications that should be made to such statements if they contain any departure from accounting principles that has a material effect.
ET Sec. 300, Rule 301	Responsibilities to clients	Members shall not disclose any confidential client information without the specific consent of the client.
ET Sec. 500, Rules 501-503	Other	Other considerations include discreditable acts, advertising, commissions and referral fees, form of organization, and name.

Source: Adapted from the AICPA Code of Professional Conduct, revised through Aug. 31, 2012.

Special Note

A historical version (rather than the current version) of the Code may be applicable in an engagement, depending on the time period of the subject professional activity. A member's past services are evaluated against the Code *as it existed at that time.* Historical versions of the Code are available at the AICPA's web site.

What do these rules mean in practice? Let's operationalize them by considering the following situations.

1. You are a CPA employed by a national CPA firm that markets itself as a "one-stop shop." The firm has recently been engaged by a new client to provide forensic accounting (expert witness) services, specifically the computation of economic damages resulting from the wrongful act of a competitor. The case has been assigned to you with a note that "time is of the essence," specifically that your report is due within thirty days. Although you are a CPA and a member of the firm's litigation support group, you have had no forensic accounting training or experience in litigation matters and know little or nothing about the industry. *Focus your discussion on the General Standards—Rule 201.*
2. You are a sole practitioner (CPA) offering forensic accounting and income tax services. You have recently been engaged by a tax client (a dental partnership) to assist in the determination of a withdrawing partner's entitlement. The withdrawing partner is also a tax client. This matter has created contention between the partners, with threats of litigation. *Focus your discussion on Rule 102.*
3. You have been engaged by counsel to assist a fellow CPA (and former member of your firm) in an accounting malpractice action. She has agreed to do most (if not all) of the grunt work and provide you with summary data, research findings, and report drafts. *Focus your discussion on Rules 102 and 201.*

STATEMENT ON STANDARDS FOR CONSULTING SERVICES NO. 1

As provided by Rule 202 of the Code (see Table 10-2), member CPAs must also comply with standards promulgated by bodies designated by Council. In the context of forensic accounting, these include the Statement on Standards for Consulting Services (SSCS) No. 1 and the Statement on Standards for Valuation Services (SSVS) No. 1.

Consulting services, as defined by SSCS No. 1 (para. 5), include all "professional services that employ the practitioner's technical skills, education, observations, experience, and knowledge of the consulting process." Forensic accounting services are more specifically defined in SSCS No. 1 (para. 5d) as "transaction services, in which the practitioner's function is to provide services related to a specific client transaction," such as business valuations and litigation services.

Seven consulting service standards are contained in SSCS No. 1, including the four general standards provided by Rule 201 of the Rules of Professional Conduct: professional competence, due professional care, planning and supervision, and sufficient relevant data (see Table 10-2). Three additional standards are specified, including:

- *Client interest.* Requires the member to serve the client while maintaining integrity and objectivity. As previously discussed, integrity requires a member to be honest and candid within the constraints of client confidentiality, while objectivity requires the member to be impartial, intellectually honest, and free of conflicts of interest.
- *Understanding with the client.* Requires an understanding with the client (written or oral) about each party's respective responsibilities and the nature, scope, and limitations of the engagement.
- *Communication with the client.* Requires the member to inform the client of conflicts of interest (reference to Rule 102), significant reservations regarding the scope and benefits of the engagement, and significant findings.

Special Note

SSVS No. 1, which applies to valuation engagements, will be discussed in Chapter 11.

In addition to the previous standards, we encourage forensic accountants to understand and operationalize Rule 301 (client confidentiality), Rule 302 (contingent fees), and Rule 503 (commissions and referral fees).

ACFE CODE OF PROFESSIONAL STANDARDS

ACFE is generally acknowledged as the world's largest antifraud organization, with more than 65,000 members. ACFE's Code of Professional Standards requires its members to comply with six fundamental principles (not rules) identified in Table 10-3.

Table 10-3 | ACFE Standards of Professional Conduct

A	Integrity and objectivity • Members shall conduct themselves with integrity. • Prior to accepting an engagement, members shall investigate for potential conflicts of interest and disclose any potential conflicts to prospective clients. • Members shall maintain objectivity in discharging their professional responsibilities within the scope of the engagement. • Members shall not commit discreditable acts and shall always conduct themselves in the best interests of the profession. • Members shall not knowingly make a false statement when testifying in a court of law or other dispute resolution forum.
B	Professional competence • Members shall not accept assignments where competence is lacking. • Members shall maintain the minimum program for continuing professional education.

(continued)

Table 10-3 *(continued)*

C	Due professional care • Members shall exercise due professional care in the performance of their services, which requires diligence, critical analysis, and professional skepticism. • Conclusions shall be supported with evidence that is relevant, competent, and sufficient. • Members' professional services shall be adequately planned and supervised.
D	Understanding with client or employer • Members shall reach an understanding with the client regarding the scope and limitations of the engagement. • Members shall qualify this understanding for any significant changes.
E	Communication with client or employer • Members shall communicate significant findings made during the course of the engagement.
F	Confidentiality • Members shall not disclose confidential or privileged information obtained during the course of an engagement without the express consent of the client or order of a court.

Source: Adapted from the ACFE Code of Professional Standards, adopted Feb. 22, 2001. Copyright © 2013, Association of Certified Fraud Examiners, Inc., www.acfe.com.

NACVA PROFESSIONAL STANDARDS

As discussed in Chapter 1, NACVA is a prominent force in forensic accounting by virtue of its influence in the business valuation industry. NACVA's Professional Standards, which are applicable to its members when providing valuation services, require compliance with the ten fundamental principles (not rules) identified in Table 10-4.

Table 10-4 NACVA General and Ethical Standards

A	Integrity and objectivity • Members shall remain objective and maintain professional integrity. • Members shall not knowingly misrepresent facts. • Members shall not subrogate judgment to others. • Members shall not act in a manner that is misleading or fraudulent.
B	Professional competence • Members shall accept only assignments that can reasonably be completed with a high degree of professional competence.
C	Due professional care • Members must exercise due professional care in performance of their services, including completing sufficient research and obtaining adequate documentation.
D	Understandings and communications with clients • Members must establish an understanding with the client regarding the scope and limitations of the assignment and responsibilities of the parties.
E	Planning and supervision • Members shall adequately plan and supervise the performance of services.

F	Sufficient relevant data • Members shall obtain sufficient relevant data to afford a reasonable basis for their opinions.
G	Confidentiality • Unless required to do so by a competent legal authority, members shall not disclose any confidential client information without the express consent of the client.
H	Discreditable acts • Members shall not commit any act discreditable to the profession.
I	Client interest • Members shall serve the client's interest by seeking to accomplish the objectives established with the client, while maintaining integrity and objectivity.
J	Financial interest • Members shall not express an opinion without qualification that the member (or firm) has no financial interest or contemplated interest in the subject business.

Source: Adapted from the NACVA Professional Standards, effective June 1, 2011.

SIX ESSENTIAL QUALITIES

In the preceding summaries of the professional standards of the AICPA, ACFE, and NACVA, you may have noticed several commonalities. From a practical standpoint, this reflects the fact that many professionals are members of multiple organizations, which creates a need for some level of consistency among the various standards. More importantly, however, these commonalities represent qualities that are widely recognized as being most essential to the practice of forensic accounting. These essential qualities include integrity, objectivity, competence, due professional care, sufficient data, and professional behavior.

Each of the six essential qualities facilitates the establishment and maintenance of *trust*. Trust is important in any professional relationship, but especially so for forensic accountants given the *adversary-advocacy* nature of their work (explained in a later section of this chapter). Trust plays a role not only in the development of a forensic accountant's opinions, but also in the communication of those opinions, especially in a trial setting. As emphasized throughout this text, the outcome of a case is ultimately decided by the *trier of fact* (for example, the jury in a jury trial). In this role, the trier of fact must assess the credibility of witnesses, including expert witnesses. To be deemed credible and thus facilitate a connection with the jury, forensic accountants must display the attribute of trustworthiness.

REVISITING THE RULES OF EVIDENCE AND DISCOVERY

Several concepts covered previously in the text are applicable to the discussion of professional responsibility, thus warranting further consideration.

Special Note

As noted in Chapter 2, although states determine their own rules and procedures, most have adopted rules and procedures modeled after the FRE and FRCP.

Rules of Evidence

As discussed in Chapters 2 and 8, specific rules of evidence apply to forensic accountants, most notably Rules 702 and 703. Rule 702 addresses the admissibility of expert testimony and allows such *only* if it will assist the trier of fact in understanding the evidence and meets three specific criteria: sufficient facts or data, reliable principles and methods, and case-specific application. Rule 703 governs the sources (information reasonably relied upon by experts in the specific field) on which experts may base their testimony.

As discussed in Chapter 2, testifying experts can expect their opinions and any supporting data to be thoroughly challenged by opposing counsel. Remember the perils illustrated by *Mattco*!

Rules of Civil Procedure

Chapter 2 highlighted discovery rules of special interest to forensic accountants. Relevant to our immediate discussion is Rule 26(a)(2), which requires the disclosure of all experts and their respective reports. Moreover, this rule mandates that expert reports contain the following elements:

- A complete statement of all opinions and the basis for those opinions
- The facts or data considered
- Any exhibits to be used to summarize the opinions
- The expert's qualifications
- A list of all cases where sworn testimony has been given (last four years) and all publications (last ten years)
- Statement of compensation

In summary, clearly stated opinions supported by sufficient relevant data are a must. Remember the matter of *U.S. v. Bonnie Bain* from Chapter 2?

OTHER STANDARDS AND REGULATORY AGENCIES

In addition to professional standards and the rules of evidence and discovery, licensed CPAs are also subject to regulation by their respective states and state boards of accountancy. State boards serve to enforce state accounting regulations, including licensure and licensure maintenance. Although most states have adopted the AICPA's provisions, forensic accountants must have a working knowledge of any differences.

Special Note

In 1984, the AICPA and the National Association of State Boards of Accountancy (NASBA) developed and published a model bill to regulate the practice of public accounting—the Uniform Accountancy Act (UAA). The objective was to provide a uniform approach to licensing and regulating the accounting profession, thereby safeguarding the public. In July 2011, the Sixth Edition was published. The major provisions of the UAA have been adopted in 49 states. Students are encouraged to review the accounting rules codified by their respective states and compare them to the UAA Model Rules.

Finally, forensic accountants must be aware of other professional standards and regulatory guidance that may be engagement-specific, such as the AICPA's Statement on Standards for Tax Services (for tax-related engagements), IRS Circular 230 (also for tax-related engagements), and Revenue Ruling 59–60 (for tax-related business valuations).

PROFESSIONAL RESPONSIBILITIES AND THE EXPERT

Let's operationalize the preceding discussion by evaluating the professional responsibilities of T. R. Robertson in our case study for this chapter.

- How does Robertson's role differ from Wiseman's?
  - Are the professional standards applied differently?
- What professional responsibility guidance (rules) apply to Robertson?
- Was Robertson independent in the performance of the engagement?
- Did Robertson maintain his objectivity and integrity in the performance of the engagement?
- Did Robertson misrepresent facts?

- Can Robertson, as an expert, rely on other experts to develop his opinion?
    - Can Robertson rely on Wiseman as an expert in this case?
- Did Robertson subordinate his judgment to Wiseman?
- Did Robertson exercise due professional care in the performance of the engagement?
- Did Robertson obtain sufficient relevant data to afford a reasonable basis for his opinion?
- Did Robertson place service to the client above service to the court?
    - The profession?
    - The public?
- Was Robertson being intellectually honest?
- What specific duty does Robertson have to the court?
- Explain the court's statement that "Like all evidence, expert testimony must be relevant to be admissible."
- Explain the court's statement that "Hypothesis is not proof, nor is speculation."
- Did Robertson exercise professional skepticism in the course of the engagement?
- How might qualitative issues (such as pending claims against Wiseman by his partners in Dock's Creek) impact Robertson's reliance on Wiseman?
- In summary, where did Robertson go wrong?

Special Note

These same questions are revisited as a Workplace Application at the end of the chapter.

RECONCILING CONFLICTS

Although professional standards generally serve to improve the consistency and quality of practice, there are some areas of inconsistency in the organizational standards (such as AICPA v. NACVA) that must be reconciled. To assist practitioners in this challenge, we suggest the following sequence of actions:

1. Contact each organization, *in writing*, regarding the perceived conflict. If this fails to provide a resolution, proceed to Step 2.
2. Follow the most rigorous standard that serves the client and the public good.
3. Inform the client which professional standards were applied and why.
4. Qualify the adopted standard in your report as an assumption or limiting condition.

THE ADVERSARY-ADVOCACY NATURE OF FORENSIC ACCOUNTING

Despite the professional guidance described previously, ethical challenges are commonly encountered in forensic accounting engagements. These challenges are attributable in major part to the *adversary-advocacy* nature of the field. This term reflects the facts that: (a) litigation is inherently an adversarial situation; and (b) expert witnesses face constant pressure to assume the role of an advocate rather than an objective party. When expert witnesses yield to this pressure, a condition known as *expert witness partisanship* (bias) develops. This condition is openly recognized throughout the legal community—by judges, lawyers, and even experts themselves.[7] For example, in a 1998 study, judges ranked expert partisanship as the most prevalent problem with expert testimony in civil cases.[8] Why? Consider the following propositions:

- Expert testimony can literally make or break a case.[9]
- Expert testimony is prevalent in tort cases.[10]
- Experts are handpicked by the opposing parties and thus expected (pressured) to support the engaging party's cause.
- There is an inherent conflict between attorneys, as consumers of forensic accounting services who advocate for their clients, and testifying experts, who advocate for truthful and accurate opinions.

- Our judicial system is adversarial, not scientific. The objective is to win, not to reach a greater understanding or advance the science.

Adversarial Bias

Adversarial bias, as the name implies, refers to a testifying expert who works, consciously or unconsciously, as the client's advocate, offering a biased opinion. Adversarial bias has at least three sources:[11]

- Conscious bias (a "hired gun")
- Unconscious bias (extremely prevalent among law enforcement and government witnesses)
- Selection bias (implying that the expert was specifically hired to represent the engaging attorney's theory)

Identifying and eliminating, or at least neutralizing, adversarial bias is no small task. The first opportunity falls to the expert. As emphasized throughout this text, testifying experts have a duty to the court, the public, and the profession to offer objective and independent opinions that will assist the trier of fact. The second opportunity falls to the trial judge, serving as the gatekeeper, who is tasked with excluding unreliable testimony under FRE 702. The third opportunity falls to opposing counsel, who can attempt to expose any bias during cross-examination of the expert. The final opportunity, of course, falls to the trier of fact.

Special Note

An expert's opinion flows from professional judgment and probability rather than certainty. Ethical problems surface when an expert becomes an advocate for the client rather than an advocate for an objective and independent opinion. As discussed previously, the AICPA Code of Professional Conduct is clear: "In the performance of any professional service, a member shall maintain objectivity and integrity, shall be free of conflicts of interest, and shall not knowingly misrepresent facts or subordinate his or her judgment to others" (Rule 102).

Let's reconsider the expert opinion of T. R. Robertson. Did he subordinate his judgment to Wiseman? Was he an advocate for an objectively developed opinion or an advocate for Wiseman?

MAKING GOOD DECISIONS

Regardless of the pressures discussed previously, professionals are capable of making and acting on informed ethical decisions. To assist practitioners in this decision-making process, the AICPA issued *A Guide for Complying with Rules 102–505* (2008). The Guide provides an approach, known as the *threats and safeguard approach*, for evaluating situations and circumstances not explicitly addressed in the Code or its interpretations and rulings. Although not authoritative, we advise that using the Guide is a wise compliance effort.[§]

The threats and safeguard approach is a three-step process, including (1) identifying threats to compliance with the Code, (2) evaluating the significance of any threats identified, and (3) determining whether safeguards are available to eliminate the threats or reduce them to an acceptable level.

Let's first consider operative definitions provided by the Guide.

- ***Threats***. The risk that the situation or circumstances could compromise a member's compliance with the rules.
- ***Safeguards***. Actions or other measures that eliminate threats or reduce them to an acceptable level.

[§] The Guide applies to all rules except Rule 101 (Independence), which is covered by the *Conceptual Framework for AICPA Independence Standards* (2006, AICPA, *Professional Standards*, Vol. 2, ET Sec. 100.01).

- ***Acceptable level***. A level at which a reasonable and informed third party would be likely to conclude, weighing all the specific facts and circumstances, that compliance with the rules is not compromised.

Step 1: Identification

Identifying the threat is the first step. To that end, the Guide identifies six types of threats:

- *Self-review threat.* The threat that a member will not appropriately evaluate the results of a service performed by the member or by an individual in the member's firm as part of providing another service.
- *Advocacy threat.* The threat that a member will promote a client or employer's position to the point that his or her objectivity is compromised.
- *Adverse interest threat.* The threat that a member will not be objective because his or her interests are in opposition to those of a client or employer.
- *Familiarity threat.* The threat that, because of a long or close relationship with a client or employer, a member will become too sympathetic to that entity's interests or too accepting of its work.
- *Undue influence threat.* The threat that a member will subordinate his or her judgment to that of an individual associated with a client, employer, or other relevant third party because of the individual's (1) reputation or expertise, (2) aggressive or dominant personality, or (3) attempts to coerce or exercise excessive influence over the member.
- *Self-interest threat.* The threat that a member will act in a manner that is adverse to the interests of his or her firm, employer, client, or the public, as a result of the member or his or her close family member's financial interest in or other relationship with a client or the employer.

Were any of these threats present in Robertson's engagement with Dock's Creek?

Step 2: Evaluation

Having identified any threats, the next step is to evaluate their significance. This evaluation process is driven by the benchmark of "whether a reasonable and informed third party, weighing all the specific facts and circumstances, would be likely to conclude that the threat would compromise the member's compliance with the rules" (Guide, p. 3).

Although no specific factors are identified in the Guide, all relevant quantitative and qualitative factors should be considered. This constitutes a matter of professional judgment.

Step 3: Action

If a member evaluates a threat as being acceptable, no further action is required. However, if the threat is evaluated as significant (unacceptable), safeguards must be applied. The type of safeguard is a matter of professional judgment and is evaluated against the benchmark of a third-party perspective.

As discussed in the Guide (p. 5), safeguards generally fall into two broad categories:

- Professional, legislation, or regulation (such as the Code)
- Workplace (such as internal controls)

If, in the member's professional judgment, the employment of safeguards reduces the threat(s) to an acceptable level, compliance with the rules is not compromised. However, if a significant threat cannot be eliminated or reduced to an acceptable level, the member is not in compliance with the rules and should withdraw from the engagement.

Caution

Despite its systematic nature, application of the threats and safeguards approach is driven by professional judgment. In addition to employing this strategy, we recommend that, when in doubt, members obtain written advice from the appropriate professional body (for example, the AICPA) or legal counsel.

COMMON PROFESSIONAL RESPONSIBILITY FAILURES

This chapter has discussed the myriad of professional standards to which forensic accountants are subject. Given this complex operating environment, practitioners must be attentive and cautious in developing and offering opinions. Our experience suggests that the primary drivers of professional responsibility failure include:

- *Lack of knowledge.* Simply stated, practitioners do not have an adequate working knowledge of the applicable professional standards.
- *Pressure.* Relational dynamics of the subject engagement and prospects of future work drive a desire to please, which leads to undue influence and/or subordination of judgment.
- *Objectivity.* Practitioners are not objective regarding engagements and simply fail to recognize and evaluate threats.
- *Training.* Practitioners overestimate their respective skill sets. In other words, they don't know how much they don't know—until it's too late.
- *Conflicts of interest.* Practitioners inaccurately measure a suspected conflict (threat) in terms of audit materiality or economic magnitude. In forensic accounting engagements, the level of compensation received from a client (relative to total revenue) does not determine the existence of a conflict. Depending on the circumstances of the engagement, a conflict may exist even if the related compensation is economically insignificant.

EPILOGUE: *DOCK'S CREEK LAND COMPANY, LLC V. T. R. ROBERTSON, CPA*

Lawsuits against CPAs are generally based on one of three causes of action or theories of liability: breach of contract, negligence, and fraud. As discussed in Chapter 2, the plaintiff has the burden of proof. The complaint against Robertson (filed by Dock's Creek and its majority members) alleged breach of contract and negligence.

The breach of contract claim asserted that:

1. There was a contract with Robertson.
2. The contract was breached.
3. The plaintiffs suffered damages.
4. Those damages were directly caused by Robertson's breach of contract.

The plaintiffs had no difficulty sustaining the burden to prove that a contract existed. The challenge was establishing the terms of the "oral" contract and the failures related thereto. Interestingly, their allegations as to the level of work to be performed and failures by Robertson were supported by Wiseman.

The negligence claim asserted that:

1. Robertson owed them a duty to perform in a professional manner.
2. Robertson failed to perform in accordance with the applicable professional standards.
3. The plaintiffs suffered damages.
4. Their damages were directly caused by Robertson's negligence.

In a negligence case, the principal point of contention is generally the applicable professional standards. As you might expect, the professional standards and the defendant's compliance therewith are presented to the trier of fact through expert testimony. In this case, it was alleged that Robertson failed to comply with the following professional standards:

- AICPA Code of Professional Conduct (Rules 102 and 201)
- AICPA SSCS No. 1
- FRE 702

Robertson's deposition and the exclusion of his testimony in the underlying case drove a quick resolution. The only issue in dispute was the amount of damages caused by his negligence. The case was ultimately settled for $125,000. Interestingly, the fee charged by Robertson in the underlying case was $5,000, which was never paid.

Key Terms

Acceptable level
Due professional care
Planning and supervision
Principle
Profession
Professional
Professional competence
Professional responsibility
Responsibility
Rule
Safeguards
Sufficient relevant data
Threats
Threats and safeguards approach

Chapter Questions

10-1. What is the difference between a profession and a professional?

10-2. Identify and discuss five characteristics of a profession.

10-3. Identify three obligations that relate to professional responsibility.

10-4. What is the purpose of the AICPA's Code of Professional Conduct?

10-5. What is the difference between a principle and a rule?

10-6. Identify the six principles of professional conduct and provide an explanation of each.

10-7. Describe each of the six primary rules of professional conduct.

10-8. Identify and discuss the four general standards included in the Rules of Professional Conduct.

10-9. How does the Statement on Standards for Consulting Services No. 1 define consulting services?

10-10. Identify and discuss three additional standards (other than the general standards) set forth in SSCS No. 1.

10-11. Identify and discuss six fundamental principles set forth in the ACFE Standards of Professional Conduct.

10-12. Identify and discuss five of the ten general and ethical standards established by NACVA.

10-13. Compare the principles, standards, and rules set forth by the AICPA, ACFE, and NACVA, and identify five areas of commonality.

10-14. What are the primary purposes of Rules 702 and 703 of the Federal Rules of Evidence?

10-15. Explain the six elements that must be included in an expert report according to Rule 26 of the Federal Rules of Civil Procedure.

10-16. Must a CPA practicing as a forensic accountant comply with state regulations? Explain.

10-17. What is meant by the adversary-advocacy nature of forensic accounting?

10-18. What is expert witness partisanship? Explain.

10-19. Identify and discuss three sources of adversarial bias.

10-20. Discuss three ways that adversarial bias might be identified and eliminated.

10-21. What is the purpose of the threats and safeguard approach set forth in the AICPA's Guide for Complying with Rules 102–505?

10-22. What are the three steps in the threats and safeguard approach?

10-23. Identify and discuss six types of threats that should be assessed in the ethical consideration of an engagement.

10-24. Discuss the benchmark that a forensic accountant should use when evaluating the significance of a threat.

10-25. What are the two broad categories of safeguards set forth in the Guide for Complying with Rules 102–505?

10-26. Identify and discuss five drivers of professional responsibility failure.

Multiple-Choice Questions

Select the best response to the following questions related to professional responsibility and the AICPA Code of Professional Conduct:

10-27. Which of the following is not a characteristic of a profession?

a. It enjoys a high level of public trust and confidence.
b. It is organized into associations.
c. There are published authoritative performance and ethical standards.
d. It is legalized by a regulatory body.
e. All of the above are characteristics of a profession.

10-28. Professional responsibility includes each of the following obligations *except*:

a. To follow the highest standards of conduct
b. To adhere to the provisions of a licensing authority
c. To always do exactly what a client wants no matter what the circumstances
d. To employ the degree of knowledge, skill, and judgment ordinarily possessed by members of the profession

10-29. A professional does not need advanced training in order to become licensed.

a. True
b. False

10-30. To practice as a forensic accountant, a person must be a member of the AICPA.

a. True
b. False

10-31. The AICPA's Code of Professional Conduct provides useful information, but it is not the foremost source of guidance for accountants in public practice.

a. True
b. False

10-32. Which of the following is a correct description of a principle and a rule?

	Principle	Rule
a.	Conceptual	Pragmatic
b.	Pragmatic	Internal force
c.	Internal force	External force
d.	External force	Pragmatic

10-33. Which of the following is a principle of professional conduct?

a. Be independent in the performance of professional services.
b. Exercise due care by performing in a competent and diligent manner.
c. Be in compliance with professional standards.
d. Do not disclose confidential client information.

10-34. Which of the following is not a general standard under the Rules of Professional Conduct?

a. Obtain sufficient relevant data.
b. Exercise due professional care.
c. Adequately plan and supervise all professional services.
d. Perform duties with a high level of professional skepticism.

10-35. If a forensic accountant is not a CPA, he or she must still comply with the AICPA's Code of Professional Conduct.

a. True
b. False

10-36. A forensic accountant conducting a fraud examination must follow GAAP when presenting the subject's financial data.

a. True
b. False

Workplace Applications

10-37. Answer the following questions related to the Dock's Creek Land Company case presented in the chapter:

1. How does Robertson's role differ from Wiseman's?
2. Are the professional standards applied differently to Robertson and Wiseman?
3. What professional responsibility guidance applies to Robertson?
4. Was Robertson independent in the performance of the engagement?
5. Did Robertson maintain his objectivity and integrity in the performance of the engagement?
6. Did Robertson misrepresent facts?
7. Can Robertson, as an expert, rely on other experts to develop his opinion?
8. Can Robertson rely on Wiseman as an expert in this case?
9. Did Robertson subordinate his judgment to Wiseman?
10. Did Robertson exercise due professional care in the performance of the engagement?
11. Did Robertson obtain sufficient relevant data to afford a reasonable basis for his opinion?

12. Did Robertson place service to the client above service to the court? To the profession? To the public?
13. Was Robertson being intellectually honest?
14. What specific duty does Robertson have to the court?
15. Explain the court's statement that "Like all evidence, expert testimony must be relevant to be admissible."
16. Explain the court's statement that "Hypothesis is not proof, nor is speculation."
17. Did Robertson exercise professional skepticism in the course of the engagement?
18. How might qualitative issues (such as pending claims against Wiseman by his partners in Dock's Creek) impact Robertson's reliance on Wiseman?
19. Finally, where did Robertson go wrong?

Chapter Problems

10-38. Visit the AICPA's web site and read Sections ET 50 to 57 of the Code of Professional Conduct and Bylaws. Prepare a memo to your professor setting forth the important professional guidelines incorporated in the Code. For each principle you identify, provide an example of how that principle might impact you in your career as a forensic accountant.

10-39. Visit the AICPA's web site and read Section ET 100, paragraphs .06 to .26 of the Code of Professional Conduct and Bylaws. Prepare a memo to your professor providing:

1. The definition of independence
2. Types of threats a CPA might encounter
3. The effectiveness of a safeguard
4. The broad categories of safeguards
5. One example of a safeguard suggested by this section of the Code

In your conclusion, discuss the value of understanding each of these rules.

10-40. Visit the AICPA's web site and read the Statement on Standards for Consulting Services No. 1. Prepare a memo to your professor addressing each of the following:

1. The definition of consulting services
2. The general standards; in particular, establish which apply to CPAs generally and which apply only to CPAs conducting consulting services
3. The impact of the specific consulting standards in a forensic accountant's determination of whether to accept a consulting engagement

10-41. Visit the AICPA's web site and read the Guide for Complying with Rules 102–505, paragraphs .08 to .18. Study the threats and safeguard approach; then prepare a memo to your professor explaining this concept and how the guidance is useful to a forensic accountant.

10-42. Visit the AICPA's web site and read the Guide for Complying with Rules 102–505, paragraphs .19 to .23. Study the guidance on ethical conflict resolution; then prepare a memo to your professor explaining this concept and how the guidance is useful to a forensic accountant.

---

1 Go to www.pearsonhighered.com/rufus for a link to this document.

2 Go to www.pearsonhighered.com/rufus for a link to this document.

3 Go to www.pearsonhighered.com/rufus for a link to this document.

4 Agnes, M. (Ed.). (1999). *Webster's New World College Dictionary*, 4th Ed., 1221.

5 *Black's Law Dictionary* (2009). 9th Ed., 1427.

6 Go to www.pearsonhighered.com/rufus for a link to this document.

7 Murphy, J. (2000). Expert witnesses at trial: Where are the ethics? *Georgetown Journal of Legal Ethics, 14,* 217–40; Masterson, L. (1998). Witness immunity or malpractice liability for professionals hired as experts? *The Review of Litigation, 17,* 393-414; Hagen, M. (1997). *Whores of the Court.* HarperCollins.

8 Hill, J. W., Hogan, P., Karam, Y., & Langvardt, A. (2009). Increasing complexity and partisanship in business damages expert testimony: The need for a modified trial regime in quantification of damages. *University of Pennsylvania Journal of Business Law, 11,* 297.

9 Ibid.

10 Krafka, C., Dunn, M. A., Johnson, M. T., Cecil, J. S., & Miletich, D. (2002). Judge and attorney experiences, practices, and concerns regarding expert testimony in federal civil trials. *Psychology, Public Policy, and Law 2002, 8*(3), 309–22.

11 Bernstein, D. (2008). Expert witness, adversarial bias and the (partial) failure of the Daubert revolution. *Iowa Law Review, 93,* 451–89.

11 Fundamentals of Business Valuation

INTRODUCTION

As discussed in Chapter 1, business valuations (BVs) account for about half of all forensic accounting engagements. BVs are most commonly driven by one of three situations:

- Litigation, such as divorce, shareholder dispute, economic damages, or bankruptcy
- Transactions, such as buy-sell agreements,* acquisitions, or mergers
- Tax, such as gift or estate tax

Like a fraud investigation (Chapter 7) or an economic damages engagement (Chapter 12), performing a BV requires *specialized knowledge*. As the name implies, business valuation is the process of determining the value of a business. As you may have previously studied in accounting, economics, and finance courses, the value of a publicly traded company is determined in the capital markets via competitive bidding among buyers and sellers. In a public market, data (such as earnings announcements, earnings forecasts, and various economic variables) are readily available to all market participants. Although the veracity of the data may be uncertain, the market is considered efficient because everyone has equal access and thus no advantage (as least theoretically, according to the efficient markets hypothesis). Without an open and competitive market, how is the value of a private (or closely held) company determined?

The purpose of this chapter is to frame the challenge of valuing closely held companies. To that end, we operationalize the concept of "business value" and provide an overview of the fundamentals of business valuations. Although the science (what and why) of BV is relatively straightforward, the practice (how) is substantially more complex, including many gray areas that are largely influenced by professional judgment. Given this breadth of scope, a single chapter in a book (or even an entire book) cannot prepare you to perform a business valuation. Rather, our goal is to lay the theoretical foundation necessary for future development of practical knowledge.

Special Note

Although BV engagements are common, they are not performed by all forensic accountants, such as fraud investigators. Moreover, it must be emphasized that performing a BV requires specialized knowledge that is developed over time through experience and advanced training and education.

We start our discussion with a review of the underlying theory of BV—the time value of money—and the concept of value, followed by an outline of the basic business valuation process. Our discussion considers a number of variables (both internal and external) that impact value, common valuation approaches, and underlying methods. We conclude the chapter with a discussion of the controlling professional standards and regulations.

Learning Objectives

After completing this chapter, you should be able to:

LO1. Recognize various purposes for which a business valuation may be performed, and identify the types of information that are generally necessary in a valuation engagement.

LO2. Explain valuation theory in terms of the time value of money, distinguishing between the concepts of discounting and capitalization.

LO3. Identify the five basic steps in the business valuation process.

LO4. Identify four standards of value that may be used in a business valuation engagement, and explain how this factor impacts the valuation process.

LO5. Describe the three valuation approaches, and identify a common method under each approach.

LO6. Understand how professional standards and regulatory requirements impact the business valuation process.

---

* A buy-sell agreement is an agreement among the owners of a company that governs the surrender of an owner's interest upon certain triggering events, including a determination of the compensation paid for the interest.

Special Note

The bedrock for any discussion of BV is IRS Revenue Ruling 59–60, issued in January 1959.[1] Revenue rulings are official IRS pronouncements that serve to operationalize the Internal Revenue Code and related regulations regarding specific issues. Although more than fifty years old, Rev. Rul. 59–60 continues to be recognized as the single most important piece of BV literature and is generally adopted for both tax and nontax purposes.[2] It provides an overview of the approaches, methods, and factors to be considered in performing a BV. You are encouraged to visit the IRS web site (www.irs.gov) to review the ruling and related valuation pronouncements.

HOW MUCH IS THE BUSINESS WORTH?

The operative question throughout this chapter is "How much is the business worth?" In other words, what is its *value*? As a backdrop for our discussion, we consider The Diamond Ridge Golf Course, located in Asheville, North Carolina.

The Diamond Ridge Golf Course[†]

1. Organization/Activity/Ownership

The Diamond Ridge Golf Course is a closely held North Carolina S-corporation[‡] formed in November 1996. The business activity of the company includes the operation of a "public" 18-hole golf course in Wilshire Park, Buncombe County, North Carolina, five miles off I-26, Exit 185.

Ownership of The Diamond Ridge is shared equally (one-third each) by brothers Barry, John, and Robert Means. The corporation was formed to purchase the golf course out of bankruptcy in November 1996. The purchase price of $1.5 million was funded via a mix of debt and equity. Each of the brothers contributed $250,000, of which $15,000 (or $5,000 each) was classified as common stock and $735,000 ($245,000 each) was classified as loans from shareholders.

2. Location

The Diamond Ridge is located at 200 Fairway Drive, Wilshire Park, Buncombe County, North Carolina. The golf course comprises approximately 157 acres. Located immediately outside Asheville's city limits, the course is surrounded by the Blue Ridge Mountains and offers lush fairways, cool breezes, scenic beauty, and four very distinct seasons of golf.

3. Target Market and Competition

The Diamond Ridge has identified its primary target market as the Asheville metropolitan area, including Buncombe, Haywood, Henderson, Madison, and Brevard counties in North Carolina, which have a combined population of 508,415 (as estimated by the 2010 census). Select demographic data for these counties are presented in Table 11-1.

The Diamond Ridge considers all public and semi-public golf courses within a 30-mile radius to be competition. Competing golf courses, locations, and 2012 prices are presented in Table 11-2.

The Diamond Ridge is one of 22 area golf courses listed in a 25-page "Great Smoky Mountain Golf Trails Guide" available at the Asheville Visitor Center.

[†] The name, location, and other identifying information of the business have been changed to protect the privacy of the parties.

[‡] S corporations are conduit entities, meaning that profits and losses are passed through to shareholders on a pro-rata (% of ownership) basis. The shareholders must report the income (loss) on their individual income tax returns.

Table 11-1 | Market Demographics§

County	Population	Median Income	Male (%)	Age 25–44	Age 45–64
Buncombe	139,603	$42,749	49.0%	28.7%	25.6%
Haywood	106,761	$42,142	48.1%	26.8%	25.4%
Henderson	85,784	$31,610	49.3%	28.7%	24.8%
Madison	92,172	$39,127	48.0%	28.0%	24.5%
Brevard	84,095	$37,352	48.9%	27.7%	25.3%

§Demographic data are presented for illustration purposes only and do not represent actual census data.

Table 11-2 | Local Golf Courses

Name	Location (Dist. from Asheville)	2012 Prices (18-hole WD/WE)
Diamond Ridge	13 miles	$ 39.00/48.00
Asheville Municipal	12 miles	$ 35.00/45.00
Deer Creek	18 miles	$ 44.00/50.00
Mountain Park	22 miles	$ 53.00/58.50
Berry Mountain	29 miles	$ 47.95/47.95
Blue Ridge Valley	25 miles	$ 64.00/76.00
Sugarwood	30 miles	$ 58.62/62.33
Esquire	31 miles	$ 60.00/64.00

4. Tourism Statistics and Implications

Tourism is big business in the Asheville area. It is estimated that overnight leisure visitation in Buncombe County accounts for an economic impact of $2 billion each year. According to the Asheville Visitor Center, Buncombe County hosted 120,000 visitors in 2012. The profile of a typical visitor is described as follows:

- Age: 50s
- Household income: approx. $100,000/yr.
- No children in the home (empty nesters)
- More than half employed full-time, more than a third retired
- Married and traveling as a couple
- Have Internet access
- Avg. party size: 2.6 people
- Avg. length of stay: 2.8 days

Based on surveys conducted by The Diamond Ridge, an estimated 25% of the company's revenue is directly related to tourism.

Table 11-3 | Officers and Key Employees

Name	Title/Compensation	Responsibility/Function
Barry Means	VP/General Manager Shareholder (1/3 interest) Member of BOD Compensation = $65,000/yr.	• Clubhouse operations • Clubhouse staffing • Customer development • Administrative/accounting
Robert Means	VP/Course Superintendent Shareholder (1/3 interest) Member of BOD Compensation = $65,000/yr.	• Grounds maintenance • Outside labor, time, materials, and financial resources needed to manage the grounds • Director of Safety
John Means	VP/Equipment Manager Shareholder (1/3 interest) Member of BOD Compensation = $65,000/yr.	• Implement and manage preventive maintenance programs • Assist the Superintendent in developing training programs for equipment use • Maintain equipment records • Capable of managing grounds operations and staff in absence of the Superintendent
Thomas Halloran	Director of Golf/PGA Pro Compensation = $47,500/yr.	• Assist GM regarding golf operations, tournaments, marketing, and communications with members
Scott Miller	Assistant Superintendent Compensation = $42,000/yr.	• Greenskeeper • Capable of managing grounds operations and staff in absence of the Superintendent

5. Officers, Management, and Compensation

The daily affairs of the company are segregated by function and managed by the designated officer. Corporate officers and other key employees, along with their respective duties and compensation as of Dec. 31, 2012, are presented in Table 11-3.

Table 11-3 includes all key employees identified by management. Compensation for key employees was determined by competitive market surveys. The average employee count (excluding those listed in Table 11-3) is ten, including both inside and outside workers. These employees work an average of 1,800 hours per year and earn an average of $12 per hour.

6. Financing

Operations have historically been self-funded. However, a $250,000 revolving line of credit is in place, which is collateralized by a second deed of trust on the company's real property.

7. Competitive Advantages and Disadvantages

The Diamond Ridge, working under the premise that price is the primary consideration for golfers, has promoted value (price) as its primary competitive advantage. Development of new courses over the last ten years has been driven by housing demand (golf communities) rather than golf demand, resulting in excess supply and competitive pressure. Competition has intensified following the downturn in the housing market. Table 11-4 identifies the principal competitive advantages and disadvantages of The Diamond Ridge.

Table 11-4 Competitive Analysis

Rank	Advantage	Disadvantage
1	Price	Competition
2	Course condition	Lack of resort referrals
3	Staff	Population
4	Extended season	Off-season pricing
5	Access (I-26)	Marketing

8. Revenue Base and Rounds Played

During the last two seasons, The Diamond Ridge witnessed a greater than industry average erosion of its revenue base (core, occasional, and alternative golfers) and by-product kitchen and pro shop revenues. Total revenue and rounds played from 2008 through 2012 are detailed in Table 11-5.

9. S-Corporation Dividend Distributions

An S-corporation is a pass-through entity whose income is taxed at one level—the shareholder level—rather than taxed at both the corporate and shareholder levels, as with C-corporations.** The accumulated adjustments account (AAA) of an S-corporation reflects its accumulated, undistributed net taxable income. The AAA is increased when earnings exceed distributions or decreased when distributions exceed earnings in any year. Restricted only by its policy of maintaining a minimum cash balance of $100,000, The Diamond Ridge distributes all earnings every year. The company's earnings and distributions for years 2008 through 2012 are presented in Table 11-6.

10. Golf Industry

Although the consequences of the 2008 financial crisis continued to have a negative impact on the golf industry through 2012, a 1% annual growth rate in demand (rounds played) is predicted through 2020. Even so, increasing costs such as fuel, labor, chemical supplies, and equipment maintenance have intensified competitive pressures. Oversupply also creates a need for development of competitive strategies.

Table 11-5 Revenue/Rounds Played

Year	Golf Revenue	Kitchen Revenue	Pro Shop Revenue	Total Revenue	% Change	Rounds Played*	% Change
2012	$847,182	$92,934	$44,561	$984,677	−11.79%	19,320	−10.96%
2011	$956,925	$107,654	$51,681	$1,116,260	−14.13%	21,699	−13.96%
2010	$1,108,375	$137,438	$54,201	$1,300,014	+11.21%	25,219	+6.36%
2009	$1,011,316	$105,682	$52,021	$1,169,019	+9.52%	23,712	+7.76%
2008	$917,168	$99,966	$50,235	$1,067,369	+5.02%	22,005	+4.20%

*Equivalent 18-hole paid rounds.

** A corporation and its shareholders can elect to be taxed as an S-corporation by filing Form 2553 with the IRS. A corporation that does not make such an election is known as a C-corporation.

Table 11-6 Company Earnings/Distributions

Year	Net Income	S-Corp. Distributions
2012	$91,288	$17,370
2011	$107,217	$124,000
2010	$217,406	$261,850
2009	$134,286	$180,200
2008	$106,126	$110,000

According to research conducted by the National Golf Foundation, the top five reasons for decreasing (slowing) growth in golf demand are:

1. Economy
2. Weather
3. Competition
4. Oversupply
5. Course conditions

The following U.S. golf industry quick facts are presented for your consideration:

- Although the immediate past pattern in golf demand is negative, a 1% annual growth rate is projected through 2020.
- Although the number of reported rounds played across the country in 2012 was up 7.4% from 2011, overall gross revenue decreased 2%. This follows a 5% reduction in gross revenues from 2010 to 2011.
- Private courses saw revenue from membership dues decline by 5% from 2011 to 2012.
- 8% to 12% of the U.S. population plays golf.
- 28% of the golfing population is over age 50.
- Avid golfers (25+ rounds per year) account for 68% of all rounds played.
- 80% of golfers play the majority of their rounds (90%) at public courses.
- 22% of the golfing population is female.
- Price is the major barrier to current golfers and the major reason why former golfers quit.

11. The Economic Outlook

Gross Domestic Product

Gross domestic product (GDP), which measures the value of a nation's output of goods and services, is generally considered the most comprehensive measure of economic activity. Estimates released by the U.S. Bureau of Economic Analysis on October 26, 2012, showed that inflation-adjusted GDP grew at an annualized rate of 2% in the third quarter of 2012. This growth is higher than the previous quarter's growth (1.3%) and higher than the average growth over the past two years (1.7%).

Interest Rates

According to the Federal Reserve's Statistical Release of Selected Interest Rates, the three-month T-bill rate as of Dec. 1, 2012, was 0.09%, and the ten-year T-note rate was 1.75%. These rates are different than those reported one year earlier, at which time the rates were 0.01% and 1.98%, respectively.

Unemployment

The Employment Situation Summary for December 2012, published by the Bureau of Labor Statistics (BLS), states that nonfarm payroll employment stayed relatively flat while the unemployment rate remained at 7.9%. Unemployment has fallen from the 8.3% annual rate for 2011. According to the BLS, the current unemployment rate in North Carolina is higher than the national average, at 9.6%.

Inflation

The December 2012 Livingston Survey predicts an inflation rate of 2% in 2013, up from the 1.7% forecast in the June 2012 survey. Inflation is expected to reach 2.3% in 2013, which is also higher than the June forecast.

12. Company Financial Summary

Condensed financial information for the company is presented in Exhibits 11-A through 11-C at the end of the chapter. This information was extracted from unaudited financial summaries and tax returns, without any adjustments.

So, how much is The Diamond Ridge Golf Course worth? What is its value? As critical thinkers, your immediate questions might include:

- What do we mean by *value*? How is this term defined?
- Value *to whom*?
- Value *under what conditions*?
- Value *for what purpose*?
- Value *for what interest*—33%, 50%, 100%?
- Value *as of what date*?
- How do the underlying assets (land, equipment, etc.) contribute to this value?

To illustrate how these factors interact, we present three hypothetical valuation scenarios (or circumstances) for The Diamond Ridge Golf Course.

Litigation

Robert Means has recently filed for divorce. In North Carolina, like most states, all property acquired during the marriage (such as the golf course) and owned on the date of separation[††] is marital property, subject to equitable (generally 50/50) distribution. The parties (Robert and Martha) bear no ill will and have agreed on all matters except the value of their one-third (1/3) interest in the company.

Transaction

At the encouragement of their insurance agent (and their respective spouses), the Means brothers have finally agreed to execute a buy-sell agreement. The agreement restricts the transfer or sale of the company's stock to the company and/or its existing shareholders. As a funding strategy in the event of death, the company will purchase term life insurance policies on each of the shareholders. Consistent with the advice of their CPA, the brothers have agreed to use the fair value standard (discussed later).

Tax

Barry Means and his spouse Mary want to transfer their one-third (1/3) stock interest in the company to a trust for the benefit of their two children. The couple's CPA has advised that such a "gift" is a taxable event, the tax consequence of which can only be determined by valuing the company and their one-third (1/3) stock interest therein. The CPA further advised that the valuation must comply with IRS regulations (Rev. Rul. 59–60).

Although the same company is being valued in these three scenarios, each represents a unique valuation engagement. The specifics of the engagement will drive the valuation

[††] Date the parties last lived together as husband and wife.

process, as outlined later in the chapter. However, before considering the process, we must establish the underlying theory.

VALUATION THEORY (THE TIME VALUE OF MONEY)

Theoretically, the value of a business (or an interest therein) is the present value (PV) of its expected future benefits. Recall that present value reflects the relationship between $1 today and $1 in the future. Key factors in this relationship are the forces of inflation, opportunity costs, and risk. What would you pay *today* for a business with prospective future benefits of $100,000 per year for the next five years, which would then be shut down with a residual (or terminal) value of $1.5 million? Would you pay $2 million, the total of the expected future benefits, or something less? This relationship, illustrated in Figure 11-1, is known as the ***time value of money*** and is the heart of BV theory.

In Table 11-7, we apply the time value of money to evaluate the hypothetical transaction proposed previously. The expected stream of future benefits ($2 million total), discounted at a rate of 10%, has a present value of $1,310,460.

This example illustrates the point that BV theory boils down to two primary issues:

- The expected stream of future benefits
- The appropriate discount rate

Although this proposition seems simple, its application in valuation engagements is often fiercely contested. Why? Consider the challenge of getting two or more interested parties (buyers and sellers), with different (or rival) economic and business expectations, to agree on the many factors that impact value, specifically:

- Facts and assumptions used to develop the expected stream of future benefits
- Facts and assumptions used to determine the required rate of return, which reflects the risk that the expected stream of future benefits will (or will not) be realized.[‡‡]

Expected Future Benefits

Accepting the proposition that the value of a business is the PV of its expected future benefits, an immediate consideration is the determination of the expected future benefits. Consider three potential data sources for this determination: forecasted data, projected data, or historical data. Although the terms *forecast* and *projection* are frequently used

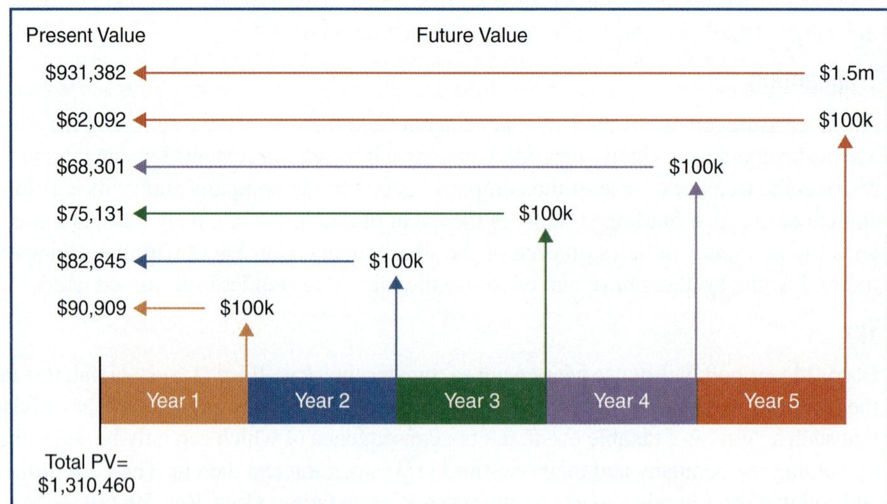

Figure 11-1
Time Value of Money Illustration

[‡‡] The required rate of return is the sum of a risk-free rate plus various risk premiums. It functions as the discount rate, converting a stream of expected future benefits to a single present value.

Table 11-7 | Present Value Illustration

Year	Expected Future Benefit	Discount Factor (10%)	PV of Future Benefit
1	$100k	0.90909	$90,909
2	$100k	0.82645	$82,645
3	$100k	0.75131	$75,131
4	$100k	0.68301	$68,301
5	$100k	0.62092	$62,092
Terminal Value	$1.5m	0.62092	$931,382
Value Today (PV)			**$1,310,460**

interchangeably, there is an important difference. A ***forecast*** reflects *expected* conditions, based on current knowledge of trends in relevant factors. Because current knowledge is short-lived in today's business environment, forecast periods are typically short (less than 2 years). In contrast, a ***projection*** reflects conditions that *may* occur, given the realization of one or more hypothetical assumptions regarding certain factors. Given their hypothetical nature, projections can be made several years into the future.

Figure 11-2 illustrates how historical and prospective (forecasted and projected) data relate to present value. In practice, prospective data are rarely used to value closely held companies. Why? First, such data are seldom developed (or fully developed) for these companies and, if so, not likely to be shared, especially during litigation. Moreover, prospective data are by definition subjective, which invites rebuttal arguments of speculation and bias. Given this subjective nature, it is important that prospective data (if considered) be communicated to, not developed by, the valuation expert.

As an alternative to prospective data, several valuation methods (discussed later in this chapter) have been developed using historical data. Although historical conditions are not necessarily an accurate indicator of future conditions, they do have the advantage of known feasibility. In other words, we don't have to wonder whether past events could occur, because they actually did occur. Due to this apparent credibility, historical data are more readily accepted by fact finders (judges and juries). For the purposes of our discussion, historical data, as opposed to forecasted or projected data, are deemed to be the most appropriate indicator of expected future benefits.

Think About It

Consider the respective merits of using historical versus prospective data. Why might history tell us something about the future? Why might it *not*? Does the use of historical data provide a false sense of accuracy? How far back should we look? What if there is no history, as with a start-up company? Can prospective data support the reasonable degree of professional certainty (more likely than not) threshold required in an expert's opinion?

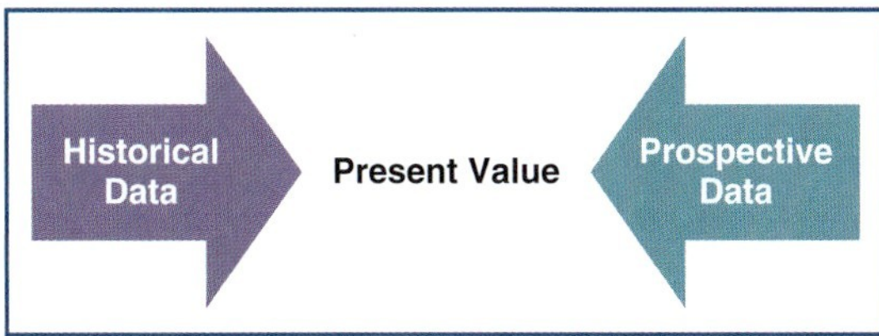

Figure 11-2
Historical vs. Prospective Data

Discounting

As illustrated in Figure 11-1, the process of ***discounting*** converts future benefits to an implied present value. In the context of BVs, the discount rate is known as the ***required rate of return*** (ROR). This return is required by investors to compensate for two factors: delay of receipt of the benefits and the risk inherent in the specific business being valued, specifically the risk that the expected benefits will not be realized. How is an appropriate ROR determined?

Although several methods are employed in practice,[§§] we limit our discussion to the buildup method. As the name implies, the ***buildup method*** is an additive process where specific components are identified and added to arrive at an appropriate ROR. Five common components are identified in Table 11-8.

In Table 11-9, these components are used to develop a required ROR for The Diamond Ridge Golf Course.

Table 11-8 | ROR—Buildup Method

Component	Definition
Risk-free rate	The risk-free rate is the starting point in our computation. It includes compensation for the real cost of borrowing (delay of consumption) and the loss of purchasing power due to inflation. This rate represents the interest rate being paid on riskless investments, most commonly proxied by U.S. Treasury securities. In the context of BVs (specifically going concerns), the appropriate proxy is a long-term Treasury bond.
+ Equity risk premium	The equity risk premium is the additional return required to compensate investors for investing in equity securities instead of risk-free investments. In practice, forensic accountants use authoritative third-party data sources (such as *Ibbotson SBBI*) to determine equity risk premiums. Said premiums are generally calculated as the excess of stock market returns over government bond returns.
+ Firm size premium	The firm size premium is the additional return required to compensate investors for investing in small companies instead of large companies. Research indicates that small companies (measured by market capitalization) have greater risk than large companies. As above, forensic accountants use authoritative third-party data sources to determine firm size premiums.
+ Industry risk premium	The industry risk premium is the additional return required to compensate investors for investing in a particular industry. This premium reflects the risk of an industry relative to the risk of the market as a whole. As above, forensic accountants use authoritative third-party data sources to determine industry risk premiums.
+ Specific company risk premium	The specific company risk premium is the additional return required to compensate investors for investing in the specific company. This factor reflects the risk of a company relative to other companies in the same industry, due to issues such as depth of management, customer concentration, financial strength, labor constraints, and pending litigation. Although forensic accountants can use market research to evaluate these factors, their quantification is largely based on professional judgment.

[§§] Others include the capital asset pricing model (CAPM) and the weighted average cost of capital (WACC).

Table 11-9 ROR for The Diamond Ridge Golf Course Buildup Method

Component	Rate	Reference
Risk-free rate	4.10%	U.S. Treasury Bond Rate
Equity risk premium	6.70%	*Ibbotson SBBI*
Firm size premium	6.36%	*Ibbotson SBBI*
Industry risk premium	2.73%	*Ibbotson SBBI*
Specific company risk premium • Limited customer base • Price competition • Key-man dependence	5.00%	Professional judgment
Required ROR	24.89%	

With discounting in a BV context, the critical point to grasp is the fundamental relationship that exists between the required ROR and the risk of the business—the greater the risk, the greater the required ROR. Although methods such as the buildup method provide a guiding framework for quantifying this risk, it is by no means an automatic process. Professional judgment is necessary to ensure that the resulting discount rate accurately reflects the risk of the *specific* business, accounting for any intangible factors that cannot be captured in quantitative data.

Capitalization

How do we convert historical data (our recommended data set) into an implied PV? This is accomplished with capitalization. Capitalization is similar to discounting, in that both processes serve to convert prospective future benefits into a present value. However, unlike discounting, which is applied to a finite *series* of future benefits ending with a terminal value, capitalization is applied to a *single* benefit stream. We call this single benefit stream, which represents expected future benefits into perpetuity, the ***proxy benefit***. Although the proxy benefit can be derived from prospective data, capitalization is more commonly used with historical data. Capitalization is the process of converting the proxy benefit to a present value by dividing by a capitalization rate.

Special Note

A capitalization rate can function as either a divisor or a multiplier. For example, a capitalization rate (divisor) of 25% is equivalent to a multiplier of 4 times (calculated as 1 divided by 0.25).

The Capitalization Rate

The ***capitalization rate*** is equal to the discount rate minus the expected long-term sustainable growth rate in the proxy benefit. If the growth rate is zero, the discount and capitalization rates are equal. Both rates reflect the same level of risk, and the difference is purely functional. With a discount rate, the growth rate is incorporated into the benefit stream, while, with a capitalization rate, it is incorporated in the capitalization rate itself. To illustrate this difference, consider a discount rate of 20% and a growth rate of 3%, which implies a capitalization rate of 17%. Over many periods, the same present value can be computed by either (a) discounting at 20% a series of benefits that begins with the proxy benefit and grows each period at 3% or (b) capitalizing the single proxy benefit at 17%.

Like the discounting process, we have only two real issues in capitalization:

- The proxy benefit, which is a single compressed value that represents expected future benefits into perpetuity
- The appropriate capitalization rate

Determining the Proxy Benefit

Let's now consider the determination of the proxy benefit. For illustration purposes, the historical earnings data of The Diamond Ridge Golf Course are presented in Table 11-10.

Four "types" of earnings are presented in Table 11-10. Which of these best represents benefits to an investor? Although each type has its respective merits and may be used in specific circumstances (a discussion that is beyond the scope of this chapter), in practice, cash flow is most commonly used. This is because cash is what investors ultimately expect to receive from their investment. The appropriate level of cash flow (for example, net cash flow or cash flow from operations) depends on the subject industry and company.

Accepting "net cash flow from operations" as the appropriate earnings measure for our valuation of The Diamond Ridge, we must now determine the proxy benefit based on historical data. This raises two questions: (1) how many historical years to consider, and (2) what averaging method to use. Common practice is to consider five years of historical data, a period that is expected to capture an entire business cycle. Although it may be appropriate to consider fewer years in certain circumstances, there must be a defensible reason for doing so, such as a significant change in business strategy or the operating environment. With regard to averaging, two methods are commonly employed: weighted average and simple average. The weighted average method is used when the forensic accountant determines that one or more of the historical years under consideration is more, or less, indicative of future expectations. For example, if the historical data reflect a trend that is expected to continue in the future, recent years are better indicators and thus should receive greater weight. The simple average method is used when there is no discernible pattern or trend.

For the purposes of our illustration, we employ the simple average method, the application of which is illustrated in Table 11-11. A simple average is appropriate since the company's net cash flow from operations does not display a consistent trend for years 2008 through 2012.

Bringing It All Together

Our next challenge is to convert our discount rate (24.9%) into a capitalization rate. As previously explained, this is accomplished by subtracting the expected long-term sustainable growth rate (if any). Given that a 1% growth rate has been projected for the golf industry, our capitalization rate is 23.9% (24.9% – 1% = 23.9%).

Table 11-10 The Diamond Ridge Golf Course Earnings Summary (2008–2012)

	2008	2009	2010	2011	2012
Income from Operations	$154,673	$180,583	$261,569	$144,420	$45,467
Net Income	106,126	134,286	217,406	107,217	91,288
Net Cash Flow from Operations	250,095	274,301	376,233	205,074	108,762
S-Corp. Distributions	110,000	180,200	261,850	124,000	17,370

See Exhibits 11-A through 11-C.

Table 11-11 The Diamond Ridge Golf Course Simple Average Earnings (2008–2012)

	NCF from Operations
2008	$250,095
2009	$274,301
2010	$376,233
2011	$205,074
2012	$108,762
Total	$1,214,465
Average	$242,893

Having selected the appropriate type of earnings (net cash flow from operations), determined a single proxy benefit ($242,893), and determined an appropriate capitalization rate (23.9%), we can now compute an implied value for The Diamond Ridge Golf Course:

Indicated Value = $242,893/.239 = **$1,016,289**

Dig Deeper

As highlighted throughout this text, forensic accountants can expect their opinions and supporting propositions to be challenged by opposing experts and the court. A recent illustration involving a business valuation is the 2013 case *U.S. Bank National Association v. Verizon Communications Inc.* (Civil Action No. 3:10-CV-1842-G, U.S. District Court, Northern District of Texas). In this case, U.S. Bancorp alleged that Verizon loaded a subsidiary entity (Idearc, Inc.) with debt prior to its spinoff, which drove the spinoff entity into bankruptcy only 28 months later. At the time of the spinoff, Idearc, Inc. had a market value of $12 billion. Both sides offered expert valuation opinions ($4.5 million apart) that were rejected by the court as self-serving and unreliable. The court ultimately found that Idearc was worth "no less than" $12 billion on the spinoff date, based on its publicly traded price. You are encouraged to research this case to identify the valuation approaches that were utilized by the opposing experts and how they were challenged.

Armed with an understanding of the underlying theory of BV (time value of money), discounting, and capitalization, we now consider the business valuation process.

BUSINESS VALUATION PROCESS

This text advocates a systematic (scientific) approach to forensic accounting engagements. In the context of BVs, we propose five basic steps:[3]

1. Define the engagement.
2. Gather the necessary information.
3. Analyze the information gathered.
4. Estimate the value of the business.
5. Issue the valuation report.

As previously discussed (Chapter 3), a systematic process provides order, reasoning, and direction to an assignment. Given the many factors at play, clarity of purpose and direction are especially critical in BV engagements.

Step 1: Define the Engagement

This first step in the valuation process includes qualifying the purpose, type of engagement, standard of value, premise of value, valuation date, and the ownership interest to be considered. These specifics create the frame of the engagement, which influences the remainder of the valuation process.

Purpose

Purpose, simply stated, is the "why" or the objective. As illustrated in the three hypothetical scenarios proposed earlier in the chapter, the same business can be valued for a variety of purposes. Why is the purpose important? Let's consider the following:

- Purpose helps identify the specific levels of competence, due care, scope (time and data collection/analysis), communication, and compensation.
- Purpose determines the type of engagement, specifically whether the engagement provides for a conclusion of value or a calculation of value (discussed later).
- Purpose may introduce different controlling factors such as applicable regulatory/professional guidelines (for example, Rev. Rul. 59–60).
- Purpose may mandate specific standards of value (discussed later).
- Purpose may identify assumptions and limiting conditions.
- Purpose may determine a responsibility to update the valuation (to account for subsequent events).
- Purpose may determine specific development or reporting criteria, including the consideration of different valuation approaches and methods.
- Purpose helps to identify the specific level of risk associated with the engagement (as discussed in Chapter 10).

Type of Engagement

There are two types of business valuation engagements: valuation and calculation. A ***valuation engagement*** is a comprehensive effort wherein the forensic accountant is responsible for a full development of the case facts and is free to apply any approaches and methods deemed appropriate, resulting in a *conclusion of value*. A ***calculation engagement***, on the other hand, is limited in scope to specific approaches and methods determined by agreement with the client, resulting in a *calculated value*. Simply stated, a calculation engagement does not include all the procedures required for a valuation engagement.[4]

Standard of Value

Defining the engagement also involves determination of the appropriate ***standard of value***, which may be fair market value, fair value, book value, or investment value.

- ***Fair Market Value (FMV)***. The most widely recognized standard of value is fair market value (FMV), which is mandated for all federal tax matters. As defined by the IRS (Rev. Rul. 59–60), FMV is:

  The price at which the property would change hands between a willing buyer and a willing seller, when the former is not under any compulsion to buy and the latter is not under any compulsion to sell, both parties having reasonable knowledge of relevant facts.

  FMV proposes a "hypothetical" sale price for cash. Logically, an actual (arm's-length) sale would be the best indicator of value. Absent an actual sale, a hypothetical sale is proposed. Willingness on the part of the buyer and seller suggests a positive state of mind—the participants want (but are not compelled) to enter into the transaction. Moreover, both parties hold an equal amount of knowledge of the relevant facts and valuation factors. Finally, this hypothetical sale takes place in an open and unrestricted marketplace.
- ***Fair Value (FV)***. The second most widely recognized standard of value is fair value (FV), which is often used in dissenting minority interest (or oppression) litigation.

Because FV is statutorily or judicially defined, its operational meaning varies from state to state (and even court to court).[***] Nonetheless, a common working definition is the pro-rata value of a business, as a going concern, without consideration of any valuation discounts (discussed later in the chapter).

Importantly, FV *does not* propose a hypothetical sale in an open and unrestricted market. Dissenting shareholder litigation generally involves a willing buyer but not a willing seller. Moreover, the buyer—the controlling shareholder(s)—generally has more "inside" information than the seller. In such a context, it is argued that excluding valuation discounts allows for a more equitable determination of value.

Special Note

Another context in which the FV standard may be used is divorce, although the majority of states have adopted the FMV standard. Those who promote the FV standard liken divorce to dissenting shareholder litigation, where the nonowner spouse is in the position of the dissenting shareholder and the owner spouse is in the position of the controlling shareholder.[5]

- ***Book Value***. A less common standard of value is book value (BV).[†††] Simply stated, the book value of a business is cost-based and represents owners' equity, the difference between the total assets (at cost and net of depreciation, amortization, and depletion) and total liabilities as they appear on the balance sheet. The book value of a business rarely represents its fair market value. Nonetheless, many buy-sell agreements use net book value as the applicable measure of value.
- ***Investment Value***. The final standard of value for consideration is investment (or strategic) value (IV). IV is the value to a *specific* buyer based on unique investment requirements and expectations.[6] If an investor's requirements and expectations are representative of the market, IV will approximate FMV. However, if an investor's requirements and expectations are different than the market, the two standards may diverge. Our experience suggests that IV is usually greater than FMV (and thus greater than FV), because it is driven by strategic or synergistic considerations that create intangible value.

Think About It

A potential example of IV is when a buyer is employed by (or plans to be employed by) the business. Why would this buyer be willing to pay more than another buyer? What other examples can you think of?

Premise of Value

After defining the purpose and the appropriate standard of value, the next step is to confirm the ***premise of value***. This is an assumption of the most likely set of *transactional circumstances* applicable to the subject engagement.[7] Two premises of value apply to most business valuations: going concern or liquidation.

- ***Going concern***. As the name implies, going concern is the premise that the business will continue to operate into the future.[‡‡‡] In other words, it is assumed that the requisite policies, procedures, and resources (plant, equipment, workforce, and so forth) are in place and will continue to function in an orderly and productive fashion.[8]
- ***Liquidation***. Liquidation, on the other hand, is the premise that the business will be terminated and its assets sold.[9] Liquidation can be orderly or forced. As a general rule, an orderly liquidation results in a greater value than a forced (or fire sale) liquidation.

[***] It should be noted that the definition (and context) of FV presented herein is different than that used for financial reporting purposes (FASB Statement No. 157).

[†††] Although book value is often considered a premise of value, we classify it as a standard of value because of its common use in buy-sell agreements as the applicable measure of value.

[‡‡‡] As provided by AU Section 341.02, an entity's ability to continue as a going concern is measured using a reasonable period of time, generally not exceeding one year beyond the date of the financial statements being audited.

Importantly, the premise of value is communicated to the forensic accountant. Thus, forensic accountants, unlike auditors, have no specific responsibility to evaluate an entity's ability to continue as a going concern. Most business valuations are performed under the going concern premise.

Valuation Date

The ***valuation date*** is the date to which the estimate of value applies, such as May 15, 2011, or December 31, 2012. It is a specific point in time that limits (or stops) the information being considered. In other words, although BVs are forward-looking (considering expected future benefits), they are based on facts available (either known or knowable) *on the valuation date*. Because BVs are performed after the valuation date (usually several months but sometimes even years), the forensic accountant must properly manage an element of hindsight.

Special Note

Unlike most situations, in which hindsight is considered an advantage, it creates a potential obstacle in a BV engagement. This is because the forensic accountant's knowledge of any information that was not available on the valuation date may create a bias, known as the hindsight bias. Avoiding such a bias may require that the forensic accountant ignore relevant information, if such information was not known or knowable on the valuation date.

Ownership Interest

Identification of the ***ownership interest*** to be valued—either controlling or minority—is important because it determines the subject's ability to affect decisions. For example, a controlling interest can make a decision to sell or liquidate the business, while a minority interest cannot. Importantly, control rights are not determined solely by the percentage ownership (for example, 51% or 49%). Other factors, such as the company's dispersion of ownership and provisions contained in organizational documents (such as the corporate charter or an operating agreement) must be considered. For example, in a company with widely dispersed ownership, an interest below 50% may have the ability to exercise substantial powers of control. Moreover, for some companies, percentage ownership above 50% (a supermajority) is required for certain decisions or actions.

Application

In Table 11-12, we apply these factors to define the three valuations engagements (scenarios) previously proposed for The Diamond Ridge Golf Course.

Step 2: Gather the Necessary Information

What information is logically required to perform a business valuation? Although each valuation engagement involves a unique set of source data, a common "wish list" submitted to engaging counsel may contain the following items:

- Financial information (five years), such as financial statements, income tax returns, and property tax returns
- Fixed assets (depreciation) schedule
- Current appraisals of fixed assets, such as real property or equipment
- Organizational information, such as articles of incorporation, corporate minute book, stock ledger, and buy-sell agreement
- Management, such as key persons, tenure, experience, and employment contracts
- Competition, such as competitive strengths and weaknesses, the target market, advertising, and market demographics
- Staffing, such as an organizational chart, roles and responsibilities, and benefits
- Customer base, such as tenure, relationships, and significance of relationships

Table 11-12 Defining the Engagement

Scenario	Litigation	Transaction	Tax
Client	Robert Means	Company and Means brothers	Barry Means
Purpose	Divorce	Buy-sell agreement	Gift tax
Valuation Date	Date of separation	Defined by agreement – triggering event	Date of gift
Standard of Value	FMV	FV	FMV
Premise of Value	Going concern	Going concern	Going concern
Ownership Interest	33% minority interest	100% controlling interest	33% minority interest
Impact of Defining Factors	Selection of valuation method/s depends on statutory definition of value and related case law in NC	FV generally excludes the consideration of discounts for control and marketability	Provisions of Rev. Rul. 59–60 are mandated
Depth of Analysis 1 (Low) to 5 (High)	3	2	5

Following a preliminary analysis of the financial data (strengths, weaknesses, trends, and so forth), the forensic accountant generally tours the subject facilities and gathers additional information via interviews and observations. What information would a tour of The Diamond Ridge Golf Course provide?

In addition to the *internal* factors previously noted—that is, attributes of the subject company—forensic accountants must also evaluate *external* factors that define the environment in which the company operates. This usually entails researching the subject industry and any relevant economic variables (local and national) that may impact the company's future expectations.

Rev. Rul. 59–60

Consistent with the preceding discussion, Rev. Rul. 59–60 (Sec. 4) identifies eight valuation factors, although not all-inclusive, that should be considered:

- The nature of the business and the history of the enterprise from its inception
- The economic outlook in general and the condition and outlook of the specific industry in particular
- The book value of the stock and the financial condition of the business
- The earning capacity of the company
- The dividend-paying capacity
- Whether or not the enterprise has goodwill or other intangible value
- Sales of the stock and the size of the block of stock to be valued
- The market price of stocks of corporations engaged in the same or a similar line of business having their stocks actively traded in a free and open market, either on an exchange or over-the-counter

Dig Deeper

You are encouraged to review Rev. Rul. 59–60 (Sec. 4) for a discussion of each of the factors listed here. Why are these factors important? Consider the information provided for The Diamond Ridge Golf Course. What relevant factors, if any, are missing?

The necessary information will, of course, vary from case to case. Moreover, the specifics of the valuation engagement (for example, calculation vs. valuation engagement or tax vs. divorce purpose) may dictate a greater or lesser information requirement. Still, in any case, the objective is to gather sufficient relevant data that enables you to quantify and qualify: (1) the ability of the business to produce future earnings, and (2) the risk associated with the production of such earnings. As previously discussed, the forensic accountant's assessment of risk is reflected in the discount or capitalization rate.

Step 3: Analyze the Information Gathered

This third step is best demonstrated by doing, so let's continue with our example of The Diamond Ridge Golf Course. Suppose your valuation engagement has been defined as follows:

Purpose:	To support the company's buy-sell agreement
Standard of value:	Fair value
Premise of value:	Going concern
Type of engagement:	Valuation (vs. calculation)
Valuation date:	December 31, 2012
Interest being valued:	100% controlling interest

Our analysis can be broken down into two phases:

Phase I

The first phase should be the analysis of the company's financial statements (Exihibits 11-A through 11-C), employing the many methods discussed in Chapter 5. After completing the financial statements analysis, your next challenge is to identify and evaluate the company's current state of operations and financial condition, including any strengths, weaknesses, and trends. Remember, your objective is to develop a basis for estimating the company's future expected earnings and assessing the risks associated therewith.

Phase II

The second phase of your analysis includes the identification of other significant relevant factors that might impact the value of The Diamond Ridge Golf Course. This can be facilitated by considering the eight factors identified in Rev. Rul. 59–60. Although most of this information is provided in the case profile, you are challenged to reconcile it with the financial statements analysis and employ it in the development of a meaningful discount rate.

Step 4: Estimate the Value of the Company

This fourth step involves estimating the value of the company by selecting and applying both a valuation approach and a specific valuation method under that approach. There are three common valuation approaches: asset, income, and market.

- ***Asset approach.*** With the asset approach, a company's value is based on its assets rather than its income. The most common valuation method under the asset approach is the ***Net Asset Value (NAV) method***, which determines a company's value as the difference between the fair market value of its assets and the fair market value of its liabilities. Simply stated, this method requires the forensic accountant to adjust the company's balance sheet from book value to fair market value, thus arriving at an adjusted equity position. The process commonly requires the assistance of other professionals (such as real estate and equipment appraisers) to provide fair market value assessments.

The NAV method is a logical selection when engaged to value a nonoperating company or a company pending liquidation. Its most common use, however, is to establish a "floor" value for a company. In other words, a company should be worth no less than the value of its net assets.

For the purposes of discussion, we submit that the fixed assets (excluding cash and inventory) of The Diamond Ridge Golf Course have been appraised (FMV) at $2 million and that all liabilities have been recorded. Given this information, what is The Diamond Ridge's NAV?

- ***Income approach.*** As the name implies, the income approach is an income-oriented process with a focus on future expected earnings, discounted (or capitalized) to provide an indicated value. As previously discussed, this approach employs the time value of money.

  In practice, the most common method under the income approach is the ***capitalization of earnings (COE) method,***[§§§] which involves the development of a proxy benefit and the capitalization of this benefit to provide an indicated business value. In the case of The Diamond Ridge Golf Course, recall that our proxy benefit is $242,893 and our capitalization rate is 23.9%, providing an indicated value of $1,016,289. How does this compare with the NAV you determined?
- ***Market approach.*** Under the market approach, a company's value is determined relative to market comparisons (or comps). Two methods that are commonly considered under this approach are the ***dividend payout method*** (which must be considered under Rev. Rul. 59–60) and the ***guideline transaction method***. The dividend payout method is similar to the COE method, except dividends are capitalized instead of earnings and the capitalization rate is derived from dividend yields of publicly traded companies (thus, the market aspect).

  Guideline transactions may be previous transactions in the subject company's stock or sales of ownership interests in similar companies. Although various databases are available that collect and report transactions data for closely held companies, these databases may not offer the level of detail necessary to determine whether the transaction is indeed comparable. Due to difficulty in identifying valid comps, market methods are considered (perhaps for purposes of a "sanity check") but rarely employed as the primary indicator of value.

The Selection Process

Selection of the most appropriate approach and method requires the consideration of several factors, including (but not limited to) the requirements of the engagement, regulatory requirements, and data availability. In practice, absent valid market comps, forensic accountants most commonly use the NAV method (which establishes a floor) in combination with the COE method.

Regardless of the method selected, the forensic accountant's report (or testimony) must be based on sufficient facts and data, reliable principles and methods, and reliable application of the selected methods to the facts of the case (as mandated by FRE 702).

Step 5: Issue the Valuation Report

A ***valuation report*** is an oral or written communication to the client containing the conclusion or calculation of value. Oral submissions should be clear and concise, providing all information necessary to avoid any misunderstandings. In practice, oral submissions are documented in the forensic accountant's work papers or memorialized in a file note.

[§§§] The discounted earnings method also falls under the income approach. Application of this method would require prospective earnings data, as discussed previously in the chapter.

There are three types of written reports—two types in valuation engagements (detailed or summary) and one type in calculation engagements (calculation report):

- ***Detailed report.*** As the name implies, a detailed report is a structured and comprehensive submission designed to provide the reader with a sufficient understanding of the data, reasoning, and analysis underlying the conclusion of value.[10]
- ***Summary report.*** A summary report offers an abbreviated version of the information contained in a detailed report, including certain minimum elements.[11]
- ***Calculation report.*** A calculation report communicates the results of a calculation engagement. This is a limited scope report and should thus be explicitly identified as a "calculation report." The report should identify the procedures and scope of work performed.

An important note: A valuation performed in litigation is exempt from the reporting provisions of professional standards. Why do you think this is so?

OTHER VALUATION ISSUES

Our discussion has focused on the underlying theory of BV (time value of money) and served to introduce you to the fundamentals of this specialized area of practice. Although this is a valuable foundation, you must be aware that many issues exist beyond the scope of our discussion, including but not limited to the following:

- *Assumptions and limiting conditions.* All BVs are subject to certain assumptions and limiting conditions that must be explicitly disclosed. Some of these are common to all engagements, while others are engagement-specific. Examples include reliance on third-party information (such as information provided by management or property appraisers) and any identified insufficiencies in source data (such as information requested but not provided).
- *Normalizing adjustments.* In an actual valuation engagement, as part of the analysis step, the forensic accountant would consider potential ***normalizing adjustments*** that may be necessary to reflect ***economic reality***. Normalizing adjustments can be made to both the income statement and the balance sheet. Because the owners and managers of closely held businesses are often one and the same, operating decisions may deviate from the standard of what a normal investor (or hypothetical buyer) would require. Common examples of income adjustments include excessive (or deficient) owners' compensation, wages or rent paid to related parties, and payment of personal expenses through the business. Adjustments may also be necessary to normalize extraordinary revenues or expenses in a given year that are not expected to continue. For the balance sheet, adjustments are often necessary to convert from the cash basis to the accrual basis.
- *Adjustments for control.* As previously discussed, an investor with a control position can influence management decisions that affect the future benefit stream. Thus, controlling interests are considered more valuable than similar minority interests. An ***adjustment for control*** (either a premium or a discount) considers the powers of control, or lack thereof, associated with the subject ownership interest.
- *Discount for lack of marketability.* Ownership interests in closely held businesses are illiquid compared to many other types of investments, such as publicly traded securities. This is primarily because the pool of potential buyers for closely held business interests is a small fraction of the pool of potential buyers for publicly traded securities. All else equal, an ownership interest in a business, whether controlling or minority, is worth less if it is not readily marketable. The ***discount for lack of marketability*** is "an amount or percentage deducted from the value of an ownership interest to reflect the relative absence of marketability."[12]
- *Subsequent events.* As previously discussed, a BV can only consider information available as of the valuation date. Events that occur after this date are known as ***subsequent events***. If there has been a significant subsequent event, it is appropriate to explicitly disclose (as a limiting condition) that the event has not been considered.

- *Partial-year data.* When the valuation date is not the company's year-end, the proper treatment of partial-year income data becomes an issue. If the valuation date falls shortly after a year-end, it is usually reasonable to exclude the partial-year data from calculations under the income approach. Otherwise, the forensic accountant must exercise professional judgment in making this determination, based on whether the data would have any meaning to a hypothetical buyer.
- *Income tax adjustment.* The future benefit stream must be adjusted for income taxes, either by deducting estimated taxes from the proxy benefit *before* applying the capitalization rate, or by adjusting (increasing) the capitalization rate itself. The more common approach is deducting estimated taxes before capitalization. For C-corporations, the appropriate tax rate to apply is clearly the corporate income tax rate. However, for S-corporations, there is disagreement in the BV community about whether the corporate rate or some personal rate should be applied.
- *Consequence of nonoperating assets.* Businesses may hold ***nonoperating assets***, which, as the name implies, are not necessary for operations. In the context of BV, nonoperating assets are not required to produce the expected future benefit stream. These assets should be *excluded* from the valuation, regardless of which valuation approach and method is used. Examples of common nonoperating assets are excess cash and marketable securities.
- *Documentation.* Forensic accountants are required to disclose all information upon which they relied to produce a conclusion or calculation of value. It is common to include a list of this information in the valuation report.
- *Goodwill.* The common definition of ***goodwill*** is "that intangible asset arising as a result of name, reputation, customer loyalty, location, products, and similar factors not separately identified."[13] In divorce valuations, it may be necessary to distinguish between enterprise goodwill, which is tied to the business entity, and personal goodwill, which is tied to a particular individual. This distinction is important because, in many states, enterprise goodwill is considered a marital asset while personal goodwill is not. The total amount of goodwill is simply the excess value of a company (as determined under the market approach or income approach) above its NAV. Bifurcation of this total amount between enterprise and personal goodwill is determined by the forensic accountant based on various attributes of the business. Although systematic approaches have been developed for this bifurcation process, it is ultimately a matter of professional judgment.

PROFESSIONAL STANDARDS

As discussed in Chapter 10, the AICPA's Code of Professional Conduct is the foremost source of guidance for accountants in public practice. In addition to the Code, forensic accountants performing BVs must also comply with the specific standards established by the AICPA's Statement on Standards for Consulting Services (SSCS) No. 1 (discussed in Chapter 10) and Statement on Standards for Valuation Services (SSVS) No. 1.

SSVS No. 1

In June 2007, the AICPA introduced SSVS No. 1, its newly developed standards for BV. Specifically, the standards govern engagements to estimate the value of businesses, business ownership interests, securities, and intangible assets. SSVS No. 1 provides overall BV engagement considerations, along with specific development and reporting guidelines that address many of the issues covered in this chapter. This comprehensive pronouncement includes a sample list of assumptions and limiting conditions, a glossary of valuation terms, and interpretations of the standards.

Other Professional Standards

As highlighted in Chapter 1, aside from the AICPA, the National Association of Certified Valuators and Analysts (NACVA) is the foremost professional organization for the BV discipline. According to NACVA's web site, it has more active credential holders (Certified

Valuation Analysts) than all other valuation credentials combined. Other BV organizations include the Institute of Business Appraisers (IBA), which merged with NACVA in 2012, and the American Society of Appraisers (ASA).

Although each of the professional valuation associations has its own set of professional standards, most are substantially equivalent to SSVS No. 1. That said, you are reminded that practitioners must comply with the standards of all professional organizations to which they belong. Finally, BV practitioners must be cognizant of any applicable governmental regulations such as Rev. Rul. 59–60.

Special Note

Complete copies of the Code, SSCS No. 1, and SSVS No. 1 can be easily obtained at the AICPA's web site. Likewise, a complete copy of NACVA's Professional Standards is available at that association's web site.

CONCLUDING TRUTHS

In conclusion, we propose five basic truths about the practice of business valuations:

- Every valuation engagement is unique because no two sets of facts and circumstances are the same.
- There are no absolutes, only general guidelines that must be supplemented with professional judgment. As provided by SSVS No. 1, "the use of professional judgment is an essential component of estimating value."[14]
- Given the important role of professional judgment, business valuation can be considered part science and part art.
- There is no irrefutable "right" answer, and experts will—and should—disagree. Experts may reasonably choose different approaches and methods that result in different values. Moreover, two experts using the same method will probably not reach the same conclusion.
- Despite this diversity, a reliable conclusion must be based on correct application of theory, followed by logical identification of relevant factors and justification of assumptions.[15]

Exhibit 11-A | The Diamond Ridge Golf Course Income Statement Analysis

	2008	2009	2010	2011	2012
Revenue					
Green Fees & Cart Fees	917,168	1,011,316	1,108,375	956,925	847,182
Kitchen	99,966	105,682	137,438	107,654	92,934
Pro Shop	50,235	52,021	54,201	51,681	44,561
Total Revenue	1,067,369	1,169,019	1,300,014	1,116,260	984,677
Operating Expenses					
Salaries - Officer	195,000	195,000	195,000	195,000	195,000
Salaries - Course	147,070	171,264	175,867	170,216	159,375
Salaries - Clubhouse	165,345	173,090	165,715	163,785	155,635

Exhibit 11-A | *(continued)*

	2008	2009	2010	2011	2012
Employee Taxes	69,262	73,622	73,243	72,209	69,616
Office Supplies	12,573	19,761	16,155	13,572	16,859
Service Fees	4,797	6,063	6,408	5,925	5,580
Pro Shop	41,182	43,714	44,819	40,941	33,031
Uniforms	5,078	6,115	6,011	4,915	4,456
Kitchen	44,486	49,914	61,411	55,753	41,497
Dues & Subscriptions	1,602	1,175	1,120	1,334	1,660
Advertising	42,744	45,135	42,608	43,475	46,270
Clubhouse Maintenance	12,335	17,209	14,468	11,250	12,719
Utilities	12,659	11,547	12,661	11,765	11,144
Telephone	3,591	3,945	4,587	3,887	3,810
Course Supplies	27,792	23,306	25,145	26,013	20,874
Seed & Fertilizer	10,624	7,553	12,342	10,815	16,977
Stone & Soil	7,851	6,839	8,556	9,574	12,787
Equipment Rental	2,601	1,106	3,251		
Equipment Repair	11,567	14,449	22,982	23,938	21,973
Fuel	27,563	35,422	39,002	38,865	37,949
Depreciation Exp.	60,307	75,540	100,427	61,774	64,908
Bad Debts				167	423
Amortization Exp.	6,667	6,667	6,667	6,667	6,667
Total Operating Expenses	912,696	988,436	1,038,445	971,840	939,210
Operating Income	**$154,673**	**$180,583**	**$261,569**	**$144,420**	**$45,467**
Other Income (Expense)					
Sign Income	27,000	27,000	27,000	27,000	27,000
Gain on Sale of Equipment					75,704
Tax Credit			1,991	2,165	1,662
Interest Expense	(75,547)	(73,297)	(73,154)	(66,368)	(58,545)
Total Other Income (Expense)	(48,547)	(46,297)	(44,163)	(37,203)	45,821
Net Income	**$106,126**	**$134,286**	**$217,406**	**$107,217**	**$91,288**

Source: Financial Statements / Tax Returns.

Exhibit 11-B | The Diamond Ridge Golf Course Balance Sheet Analysis

	2008	2009	2010	2011	2012
Assets					
Current Assets					
Cash	121,996	127,703	112,817	105,707	148,268
Inventory	22,615	31,904	37,510	29,423	22,091
Total Current Assets	144,611	159,607	150,327	135,130	170,359
Fixed Assets					
Furniture & Fixtures	62,163	63,063	67,520	67,520	72,288
Golf Carts	159,380	159,380	159,380	159,380	-
Equipment	442,921	450,019	471,828	474,505	489,535
Buildings & Improvements	494,331	543,433	549,090	558,299	584,299
Automobiles	48,700	48,700	52,700	52,700	52,700
Accumulated Depreciation	(305,934)	(305,699)	(406,126)	(467,900)	(399,550)
Land	500,000	500,000	500,000	500,000	500,000
Going Concern	100,000	100,000	100,000	100,000	100,000
Amortization	(34,168)	(40,835)	(47,502)	(54,169)	(60,836)
Net Fixed Assets	1,467,393	1,518,061	1,446,890	1,390,335	1,338,436
Total Assets	**$1,612,004**	**$1,677,668**	**$1,597,217**	**$1,525,465**	**$1,508,795**
Liabilities & Shareholders' Equity					
Current Liabilities					
Accounts Payable	21,103	14,789	19,777	17,896	13,788
Payroll Taxes Payable	3,423	5,645	7,635	7,909	6,961
Line of Credit				15,000	40,000
Total Current Liabilities	24,526	20,434	27,412	40,805	60,749
Long-Term Liabilities					
N/P - Shareholders	735,000	735,000	720,000	645,000	645,000
Long-Term Debt	812,892	854,027	823,391	811,292	784,667
Total Long-Term Liabilities	1,547,892	1,589,027	1,543,391	1,456,292	1,429,667
Equity					
Capital Stock	15,000	15,000	15,000	15,000	15,000

Exhibit 11-B (continued)

	2008	2009	2010	2011	2012
Retained Earnings	24,586	53,207	11,414	13,368	3,379
Total Equity	39,586	68,207	26,414	28,368	18,379
Total Liabilities & Shareholders' Equity	**$1,612,004**	**$1,677,668**	**$1,597,217**	**$1,525,465**	**$1,508,795**

Source: Financial Statements / Tax Returns.

Exhibit 11-C The Diamond Ridge Golf Course Cash Flow Analysis

Operating Activities	2009	2010	2011	2012
Operating Income	180,583	261,569	144,420	45,467
Depreciation	75,540	100,427	61,774	64,908
Amortization	6,667	6,667	6,667	6,667
Change in Inventory	(9,289)	(5,606)	8,087	7,332
Change in Payroll Taxes Payable	2,222	1,990	274	(948)
Change in Accounts Payable	(6,314)	4,988	(1,881)	(4,108)
Net Cash from Operations	249,409	370,035	219,342	119,317
Investing Activities				
Purchase of Furniture & Fixtures	(900)	(4,457)	-	(4,768)
Purchase of Equipment	(7,098)	(21,809)	(2,677)	(15,030)
Building Improvements	(49,102)	(5,657)	(9,209)	(26,000)
Purchase of Automobiles	-	(4,000)	-	-
Proceeds from Sale of Equipment				101,826
Net Cash from Investing Activities	(57,100)	(35,923)	(11,886)	56,028
Financing Activities				
Change in LOC	-	-	15,000	25,000
Change in N/P - Shareholders	-	(15,000)	(75,000)	-
Change in Long-Term Debt	41,135	(30,636)	(12,099)	(26,625)
Interest Expense	(73,297)	(73,154)	(66,368)	(58,545)
Sign Income	27,000	27,000	27,000	27,000

Exhibit 11-C | *(continued)*

Operating Activities	2009	2010	2011	2012
Tax Credits	-	1,991	2,165	1,662
S-Corp. Distributions to Shareholders	(181,440)	(259,199)	(105,263)	(101,277)
Net Cash from Financing Activities	(186,602)	(348,998)	(214,566)	(132,784)
Net Cash Flow	**$5,707**	**($14,886)**	**($7,110)**	**$42,561**
Cash Reconciliation				
Beginning Cash	121,996	127,703	112,817	105,707
Ending Cash	127,703	112,817	105,707	148,268
Implied Change in Cash	(5,707)	14,886	7,110	(42,561)

Source: Financial Statements / Tax Returns.

Key Terms

Adjustment for control
Asset approach
Book value (BV)
Buildup method
Calculation engagement
Calculation report
Capitalization of earnings (COE) method
Capitalization rate
Detailed report
Discount for lack of marketability
Discounting
Dividend payout method
Economic reality
Fair market value (FMV)
Fair value (FV)
Forecast
Going concern premise
Goodwill
Guideline transaction method
Income approach
Investment value (IV)
Liquidation premise
Market approach
Net asset value (NAV) method
Nonoperating assets
Normalizing adjustments
Ownership interest
Premise of value
Projection
Proxy benefit
Required rate of return
Standard of value
Subsequent events
Summary report
Time value of money
Valuation date
Valuation engagement
Valuation report

Chapter Questions

11-1. Identify three different situations that commonly drive business valuations.

11-2. Define business valuation and discuss the challenge of valuing private or closely held companies.

11-3. Business valuation theory boils down to what two primary issues?

11-4. Describe the time value of money, and explain how it applies to business valuation.

11-5. Assuming a 10% annual interest rate, what is the present value of $1 to be received at the end of five years?

11-6. What two items are required to calculate the present value of a future benefit stream?

11-7. What is a discount rate?

11-8. Why are different parties likely to disagree on the factors that impact value?

11-9. Compare and contrast the terms *forecast* and *projection*.

11-10. Identify and discuss three reasons that prospective data are rarely used to value closely held companies.

11-11. In the context of a business valuation engagement, what are the advantages of historical data relative to prospective data?

11-12. Does the use of historical data as a proxy for expected future benefits make sense? Explain.

11-13. Does the use of historical data provide a false sense of accuracy?

11-14. Can prospective data support the reasonable degree of professional certainty (more likely than not) threshold required in an expert's opinion? Why or why not?

11-15. What is the appropriate discount rate for a business valuation?

11-16. When using the buildup method for determining a required rate of return, what five components are commonly included? Discuss each.

11-17. What is the relationship between the value of a business and the required rate of return?

11-18. Define *capitalization* and explain its two components.

11-19. Why is cash flow commonly used as the proxy benefit in capitalization?

11-20. Compare and contrast the weighted average and simple average methods of converting historical earnings data to a single proxy benefit.

11-21. How is a discount rate converted into a capitalization rate?

11-22. Identify the five basic steps in a systematic approach to a business valuation.

11-23. In defining a business valuation engagement, what are the six specific factors that must be considered?

11-24. Why is the purpose of the valuation important?

11-25. Compare and contrast a valuation engagement with a calculation engagement.

11-26. What is meant by a standard of value? Describe the four standards of value commonly used in business valuation engagements.

11-27. Define *premise of value* and discuss two common premises of value used in business valuation engagements.

11-28. How does the valuation date impact a business valuation?

11-29. What are the two types of ownership interests that a forensic accountant might be engaged to value?

11-30. What types of information might a forensic accountant need to perform a business valuation?

11-31. Identify and discuss the eight valuation factors set forth in Rev. Rul. 59–60 (Sec. 4).

11-32. What is the objective of the data gathering process in a business valuation engagement?

11-33. What are the two phases that must be accomplished in the data analysis step of a business valuation? Describe how the analysis conducted in each phase is useful to the business valuation effort.

11-34. What are the three common valuation approaches?

11-35. Describe the asset approach and explain when it is an appropriate selection.

11-36. Describe the income approach and compare it to the asset approach.

11-37. Describe the market approach and discuss two methods under this approach.

11-38. What factors are considered in selecting the appropriate valuation approaches and methods in a business valuation engagement?

11-39. Identify three types of reports a forensic accountant might prepare. Describe each.

11-40. Comment on the following statement: After completing this chapter, a student has all the necessary knowledge and skill to prepare a business valuation for a client.

Multiple-Choice Questions

Provide the best response to each of the following multiple-choice and true-false questions relating to business valuation theory, part 1:

11-41. Each of the following is a situation that may drive a business valuation engagement *except*:

a. An estate or gift tax matter
b. Divorce, economic damages, or other litigation
c. A financial statement fraud
d. Acquisitions and buy-sell transactions

11-42. Publicly traded companies are valued in the marketplace through:

a. Competitive bidding
b. Analyst recommendations
c. Strategic efforts
d. All of the above

11-43. Determining a value for a private company is easier than determining a value for a public company.

a. True
b. False

11-44. The Revenue Ruling that remains the single most important piece of business valuation literature is:

a. 54–1040
b. 69–1120
c. 92–32
d. 59–60

11-45. In theory, the value of a business is the total of its estimated future cash flows.

a. True
b. False

11-46. In a positive interest rate environment, the concept that a dollar today is more valuable than a dollar in the future is known as:

a. Value added
b. Time value of money
c. Risk-reward theory
d. The efficient markets hypothesis

11-47. In computing present value, the two primary components are:

a. The expected stream of future benefits and today's asset value
b. Residual asset value and the appropriate discount rate
c. The expected stream of future benefits and the appropriate discount rate
d. The market value of assets and the book value of liabilities

11-48. Forensic accountants usually agree on the facts and assumptions used to develop the expected stream of future benefits.

a. True
b. False

11-49. A projection and a forecast are different terms for the same set of cash flow assumptions.

a. True
b. False

11-50. Each of the following is a reason prospective data are seldom used to value a closely held business *except*:

a. Such data are seldom developed by closely held companies.
b. Prospective data cannot be developed in a form that can be discounted to a present value.
c. Prospective data are subjective, which invites rebuttal arguments of speculation and bias.
d. All of the above are reasons.

Provide the best response to each of the following multiple-choice and true-false questions relating to business valuation theory, part 2:

11-51. If prospective data are not provided by the management of a company being valued, such data should be estimated by the forensic accountant.

a. True
b. False

11-52. Historical data are preferable to prospective data for each of the following reasons *except*:

a. They are based on actual events
b. They are more accepted or meaningful to fact finders
c. There is less likelihood of challenge in an adversarial litigation setting
d. Use of such data is mandated by the IRS

11-53. In the context of business valuation, the discount rate is known as:

a. The risk-free rate of return
b. The required rate of return
c. The actual rate of return
d. The accounting rate of return

11-54. How is an appropriate discount rate commonly determined?

a. Using ROE as a proxy
b. Using the firm's current bank borrowing rate
c. Using the buildup method
d. Using the forensic accountant's best estimate based on his or her experience

11-55. When employing the buildup method, each of the following is a consideration *except*:

a. An industry risk premium
b. Risk-free rate
c. The firm's size
d. A premium for specific-company risk
e. All of the above are considerations in the buildup method

11-56. Which of the following is considered an objective source of information for use in building a required rate of return?

- **a.** The IRS interest rate database
- **b.** The Chicago Board of Trade
- **c.** The Treasury Database
- **d.** Ibbotson SBBI

11-57. Capitalization is a method in which expected future benefits are compressed into a single value, which is then divided by the capitalization rate.

- **a.** True
- **b.** False

11-58. When using the capitalization of earnings method, the two primary issues are:

- **a.** A single proxy benefit and a discount rate
- **b.** An estimated stream of future benefits and a capitalization rate
- **c.** A single proxy benefit and a capitalization rate
- **d.** An asset base and a capitalization rate

11-59. Which of the following earnings streams is most commonly used in business valuations?

- **a.** Net income
- **b.** Net cash flow from investing activities
- **c.** Net cash flow from operations
- **d.** Net income plus depreciation

11-60. Which of the following correctly sets forth the process of converting a discount rate to a capitalization rate?

- **a.** The discount rate minus the expected growth rate of the proxy benefit
- **b.** The discount rate minus the expected growth rate of sales
- **c.** The discount rate plus an inflation premium
- **d.** The discount rate minus the prime lending rate

11-61. When developing a single proxy benefit, prior years' cash flows should be weighted if the earnings stream displays a consistent trend and unweighted if there is no identifiable pattern.

- **a.** True
- **b.** False

11-62. To determine an indicated value using the capitalization of earnings method:

- **a.** The proxy benefit is divided by an appropriate capitalization rate
- **b.** A stream of future benefits is discounted using the capitalization rate
- **c.** A stream of future benefits is discounted using the discount rate
- **d.** None of the above are correctly stated

Provide the best response to each of the following multiple-choice and true-false questions relating to the business valuation process, part 1:

11-63. Which of the following is not a basic step in the business valuation process?

- **a.** Analyze the information gathered
- **b.** Estimate the value of the business
- **c.** Present the valuation report to the IRS
- **d.** Define the engagement

11-64. The use of a systematic business valuation process provides order, reasoning, and direction to an engagement.

- **a.** True
- **b.** False

11-65. It is important to clearly establish the purpose of a valuation engagement because:

- **a.** The court's rules require it
- **b.** It is the only way to ensure a forensic accountant is paid for his or her efforts
- **c.** It is impossible to perform a valuation without it
- **d.** Professionalism requires it, as purpose clearly establishes the objective of the engagement

11-66. The two types of business valuation engagements are:

- **a.** Valuation and calculation
- **b.** Valuation and financial statement presentation
- **c.** Calculation and financial statement presentation
- **d.** Valuation and fair value determination

11-67. A valuation engagement is a comprehensive effort wherein the forensic accountant is responsible for a full development of the case facts and is free to apply the approaches and methods deemed appropriate to arrive at a conclusion of value.

- **a.** True
- **b.** False

11-68. Which of the following best describes fair market value?

- **a.** The exact selling price of the item being valued
- **b.** A hypothetical sales price for cash of the item being valued
- **c.** An amount agreeable to the seller
- **d.** An amount acceptable to the IRS

11-69. The fair market value standard assumes that both parties are hypothetical and hold an equal measure of knowledge of the relevant facts and valuation variables.

- **a.** True
- **b.** False

11-70. Fair value is normally used in dissenting minority interest litigation and is identically defined in all fifty states.

- **a.** True
- **b.** False

11-71. The book value method of determining value:

a. Subtracts the market value of assets from the market value of liabilities

b. Is the most commonly used valuation approach

c. Subtracts the book value of liabilities from the book value of assets, arriving at net book value

d. Arrives at the fairest fair market value determination

11-72. Investment value is the value to a specific investor based on his or her respective investment requirements and expectations.

a. True

b. False

11-73. A going concern premise of value:

a. Assumes that a business will never fail

b. Assumes that a business is making a profit

c. Assumes that a business has free cash flow

d. Assumes that a business will continue to operate into the future

11-74. A liquidation premise of value:

a. Ensures that a firm's assets are worth more in liquidation than as a going concern

b. Assumes that a business will be terminated and sold

c. Can only be employed if a court directs it

d. Is not a method acceptable under GAAP

11-75. The date of valuation is not an important consideration in a valuation engagement.

a. True

b. False

11-76. What are the two types of ownership interest?

a. Individual and goodwill

b. Controlling and investment

c. Minority and controlling

d. None of the above are correctly stated

11-77. The ability to affect decisions is an important aspect of determining the type of ownership interest to be valued.

a. True

b. False

Provide the best response to each of the following multiple-choice and true-false questions relating to the business valuation process, part 2:

11-78. Which of the following sources of information would not be useful to a forensic accountant performing a business valuation?

a. Financial statements, income tax returns, property tax returns

b. Articles of incorporation, corporate minute book

c. Organizational chart, benefits

d. Genogram of the president's family

11-79. Once financial data are reviewed and analyzed, a forensic accountant:

a. Files his or her valuation report

b. Discloses the information to interested parties

c. Tours the client's facilities to gather additional information

d. None of the above are undertaken in a business valuation engagement

11-80. It is important for a forensic accountant to understand the client firm's industry as well as local and national economic conditions.

a. True

b. False

11-81. A forensic accountant need not consider the factors set forth in Rev. Rul. 59–60.

a. True

b. False

11-82. The objective of the data gathering effort is to obtain sufficient data to quantify and qualify:

a. The ability of the business to produce future earnings

b. The risk associated with the production of future earnings

c. Both a and b

d. Neither a nor b

11-83. Each of the following is an acceptable valuation approach *except*:

a. Asset approach

b. Market approach

c. Income approach

d. Owner valuation approach

11-84. The asset valuation approach often requires a forensic accountant to rely on assistance from other professionals, such as real estate and equipment appraisers.

a. True

b. False

11-85. The net asset value method is most commonly used in valuations of:

a. A company pending liquidation

b. A company with over $1 billion in total assets

c. A company with net earnings below $100 million

d. Both b and c are correct responses to this question

11-86. When using the income approach, a forensic accountant employs:

a. A future value of prior year earnings concept

b. Time value of money techniques

c. Residual value analysis techniques

d. IRS approved procedures

11-87. The market approach is used by forensic accountants to value a business when it is easy to obtain data on comparable companies in the client's industry.

a. True

b. False

11-88. Once a forensic accountant has completed his or her valuation analysis, each of the following report types might be issued *except*:

a. Calculation report

b. Detailed report

c. Summary report

d. Explanatory report

Workplace Applications

11-89. Review the calculations for The Diamond Ridge Golf Course example discussed in the chapter.

1. Based on these calculations, is there any goodwill value? If so, how much?
2. How did you make this determination?
3. Considering the factual background provided in the chapter, what are possible drivers of this goodwill value?

11-90. Reconsider the following engagement assumptions for The Diamond Ridge Golf Course, as outlined in the chapter:

- Purpose: To support the company's buy-sell agreement
- Standard of value: Fair value
- Premise of value: Going concern
- Type of engagement: Valuation (vs. calculation)
- Valuation date: December 31, 2012
- Interest being valued: 100% controlling interest

In addition, assume that in January 2013 there was a public announcement that Jack Nicklaus was designing a new 18-hole championship course about 20 miles from The Diamond Ridge Golf Course. This course will have a full practice facility and a clubhouse that provides dining to both members and the public. Fees for an 18-hole round are expected to range from $60 to $75. This announcement took the local golfing community by surprise, and the new course is expected to impact the competitive environment once completed. You have not yet issued your valuation report to the owners of The Diamond Ridge Golf Course. How will this new information impact your conclusion of value?

11-91. Barry Means and his spouse Mary want to transfer their one-third (1/3) stock interest in The Diamond Ridge Golf Course to a trust for the benefit of their two children. The couple's CPA has advised that such a "gift" is a taxable event, the tax consequence of which can only be determined by valuing the company and their one-third (1/3) stock interest therein. You have been engaged to value the Meanses' stock interest for the purpose of filing a gift tax return. Assume that the date of the gift is December 31, 2012.

Since this valuation is for tax purposes, the factors outlined in Rev. Rul. 59–60 apply. Identify these factors and discuss each within the context of this engagement scenario, using the factual information for The Diamond Ridge Golf Course provided in the chapter.

11-92. Suppose you have been engaged to value a retail clothing chain as of December 31, 2012. You have selected the capitalization of earnings method and determined that net cash flow is the appropriate measure for expected future benefits. The company's income data for years 2008 through 2012 are presented in the table below ($ in thousands).

Year	Net Cash Flow
2008	$109,627
2009	$162,196
2010	$199,462
2011	$210,767
2012	$236,320

In order to complete your engagement, you must consider the following:

1. What is the purpose of the valuation? Create a plausible valuation scenario.
2. Given this scenario, what is the appropriate standard of value?
3. Your selection of the income approach implies what premise of value?
4. The income data in the above table would be sufficient to estimate a value as of what date (the valuation date)?
5. What percentage ownership interest are you valuing? Is this a controlling or a minority interest?
6. Will you use a weighted or a simple average to determine the proxy benefit? Explain your rationale.
7. Using your chosen averaging method, what is the proxy benefit?
8. What expected growth rate will you use and how did you determine that rate? Assume the expected industry growth rate is 6%.

9. If you have determined a 21% required rate of return, what is the capitalization rate?
10. Using the determined proxy benefit and capitalization rate, what is the indicated value for the entire business? For the specific ownership interest you are valuing?
11. Would an adjustment for control or a discount for marketability be applicable to this ownership interest?
12. Suppose that, three months after the valuation date, the company learned that leases for several of its stores would not be renewed. How would this impact your valuation analysis?

11-93. Reconsider the valuation of the retail clothing chain presented in the previous problem. Use the following benefit stream information for this purpose. You have selected the capitalization of earnings method and determined that net cash flow is the appropriate measure for expected future benefits. The company's income data for years 2008 through 2012 are presented in the following table ($ in thousands).

Year	Net Cash Flow
2008	$109,627
2009	$110,321
2010	$112,576
2011	$115,877
2012	$120,320
Total	$568,721

1. Given the benefit stream set forth in the table, how would you determine the proxy benefit?
2. If you have determined a 21% required rate of return, what is the capitalization rate? Assume the expected industry growth rate is 3%.
3. Using the determined proxy benefit and capitalization rate, what is the indicated value for the entire business? For the specific ownership interest you are valuing?
4. How does your conclusion of value compare to the one developed in the previous problem?

Chapter Problems

11-94. At the end of 2012, Tootsie Roll had a price-earnings ratio of 30.7, and Hershey had a price-earnings ratio of 25.3. These convert to capitalization rates of 3.25% for Tootsie Roll and 3.95% for Hershey. Given that the 30-year bond rate at the end of 2012 was about 3.0%, how might you explain the difference between the capitalization rates of these two companies in terms of the buildup criteria set forth in the chapter?

11-95. Obtain IRS Revenue Ruling 59–60 through the IRS web site. Read this Ruling and prepare a memo to your professor explaining how each of its eight valuation factors fits into the theory of business valuation as discussed in this chapter.

11-96. Perform a Google search on the following: "Discount for Lack of Marketability: Job Aid for IRS Valuation Professionals." After reading pages 7 through 11 of this document, choose any seven of the factors that are identified as influencing marketability. Prepare a memo to your professor explaining, in your own words, why each of these seven factors would influence the marketability of a closely held business.

Case

11-97. Hellemn Candy is a small candy manufacturer located in Defiance, Ohio. Founded in 1912, the company offers a full line of candy products to the marketplace, including its popular HoHo lollipops, Christmas candy canes, and various chocolate treats.

Company Background

Operating from state-of-the-art manufacturing facilities, Hellemn employs 275 full-time associates. The company pays competitive wages and is noted for its employee-focused approach to daily operations. Its motto is, "If our employees are happy, our customers will be happy." Because of this, the company has never experienced an effort to unionize.

Competitive advantages for Hellemn include its brand name products, state-of-the-art manufacturing facilities, highly liquid balance sheet, a proven management team, an abundant supply of nonunion labor, and its loyal customer base. Disadvantages are its size (Hellemn's total assets are about 8% of Tootsie Roll's and 2% of Hershey's), its limited presence in certain candy product lines, and fewer available dollars to devote to research and development. Due to its relatively small size compared to competitors, the company also has low buyer power and cannot achieve significant economies of scale.

Major customers include all the major retail chains. While these are important customers, Hellemn's sales are not concentrated with any one retailer. Indeed, the company works hard to maintain excellent working relationships with each of its suppliers and customers. Sales are seasonal, with about 75% of sales occurring around Halloween, Christmas, and Easter. Throughout the remainder of the year, sales are fairly consistent from month to month. Hellemn is able to adjust its payroll according to operational needs. Manufacturing lead time is four months, and most of the company's products have an average shelf life of about six months.

Hellemn Candy is a family business. President Dale Hellemn is a fourth-generation descandant of the founder, and the chief financial officer, Vicki Hiler, is a third-generation descandant. Dale Hellemn owns 52% of the company's common stock, and six other family members each own 8% as shown in the following table.

Compensation for key employees (as shown in the previous table) was determined by competitive market surveys.

Officers/Key Employees	Title/Compensation	Responsibility/Function
Dale Hellemn	President and CEO Shareholder (52% interest) Member Board of Directors Annual Comp. = $250,000	Responsible for all company operations and is Chairman of the Board of Directors
Donald Hellemn	VP in charge of Operations Shareholder (8% interest) Member Board of Directors Annual Comp. = $165,000	Responsible for all manufacturing operations
Letha Hellemn	VP/Human Resources Shareholder (8% interest) Member Board of Directors Annual Comp. = $100,000	Responsible for all human resource functions
Vicki Hiler	Controller/Treasurer Shareholder (8% interest) Member Board of Directors Annual Comp. = $125,000	Responsible for accounting and financial management
Jason Hiler	Marketing Director Husband of Vicki Hiler Annual Comp. = $105,000	Responsible for all marketing functions
Other Hellemn family members	Three other family members own 8% interest	They do not participate actively in company management but serve as board members.

Financial Data

Financial information for Hellemn Candy is set forth in the following tables.

Income Statements Hellemn Candy	For the years ended December 31 ($000 omitted)		
	2012	2011	2010
Sales	$53,250	$52,150	$49,900
Cost of Goods Sold	$36,625	$35,050	$32,050
Gross Profit	$16,625	$17,100	$17,850
Operating Expenses	$10,840	$10,650	$10,600
Operating Income	$5,785	$6,450	$7,250
Other Income (Expense)	$300	$900	$175
Income Before Income Taxes	$6,085	$7,350	$7,425
Provision for Income Taxes	$1,700	$2,050	$2,100
Net Income	$4,385	$5,300	$5,325

Balance Sheets Hellemn Candy	As of December 31 ($000 omitted)		
	2012	2011	2010
Current Assets:			
Cash and Equivalents	$7,875	$11,600	$9,099
Accounts Receivable, net	4,190	3,750	4,600
Inventory	7,170	5,670	5,650
Investments	1,100	800	850
Other Current	560	720	901
Total Current Assets	20,895	22,540	21,100
Property, Plant, Equipment, net	21,300	21,600	22,100
Other	1,605	2,660	2,600
Total Assets	$43,800	$46,800	$45,800
Current Liabilities:			
Accounts Payable	$1,100	$1,000	$900
Other Current	4,770	4,850	4,700
Total Current Liabilities	5,870	5,850	5,600
Long-Term Debt	8,500	8,200	8,000

Balance Sheets Hellemn Candy	As of December 31 ($000 omitted)		
	2012	2011	2010
Stockholders' Equity	29,430	32,750	32,200
Total Liabilities and Equity	$43,800	$46,800	$45,800
Additional Information:			
Dividends Paid	$1,850	$1,810	$1,800
Shares Outstanding	6,000	6,000	6,000
Depreciation and Amortization	$2,050	$1,910	$1,800

The Industry

The industry is dominated by several large manufacturers, such as Barry Callebaut and Nestlé in Europe; Hershey, Mars, and Tootsie Roll in the United States; and Ferrero in Italy. These companies, as well as their smaller counterparts, operate in three segments: (1) those that manufacture chocolate from beans, (2) those that use manufactured chocolate to make candy, and (3) those that manufacture nonchocolate candy.

Demand for candy products is primarily driven by consumer tastes and preferences and population growth. Candy manufacturers reinvest about 5% of sales in research and development in an effort to meet both changing customer preferences and to provide healthier products to customers. Similar to many industries, profitability is driven by manufacturing capability, the ability to maintain supply chain efficiency, and branding and other marketing considerations. The industry is concentrated, and economies of scale exist for large companies. Smaller firms compete by offering specialized products in niche markets. Analysts estimate that U.S. consumers eat about 25 pounds of candy per capita per year.

Annual global industry sales exceed $150 billion, with U.S. sales comprising about $9 billion of that amount. Since this is a mature industry, sales are expected to grow at about 3% per year into the foreseeable future. Revenue components include the following: 50% from purchased chocolate, 30% from nonchocolate candy, and 20% from chocolate candy. The nonchocolate candy segment includes products such as hard candies, marshmallow products, and gum, to name a few.

The Economy

The economy is growing slowly. Gross domestic product (GDP) in 2012 grew at an annualized rate of 2%. This growth is slightly higher than the average growth over the previous two years (1.7%). Interest rates remain at historically low levels. The December 2012 three-month T-bill rate was .09%, while the 30-year T-bond rate was 3.00%. The inflation rate was 1.75% in 2012 and is expected to reach 2.3% in 2013. The specific risk premium is 1.00%.

The Assignment

Hellemn Candy is considering a sale to a major candy manufacturer. In order to negotiate a sales price, Hellemn Candy wants to estimate its fair market value. As a forensic accountant, you have been retained to perform a valuation of Hellemn Candy as of December 31, 2012.

Your engagement is defined as follows:

1. Engagement Purpose: Prospective sale
2. Standard of Value: Fair Market Value (but Hellemn understands that Investment Value may be relevant to the buyer)
3. Interest Being Valued: 100%
4. Type of Engagement: Valuation
5. Premise of Value: Going Concern
6. Valuation Date: December 31, 2012

To assist you with this effort, the following earnings data are provided:

Hellemn Candy Earnings Analysis (2008–2012), $000 omitted					
Year	2012	2011	2010	2009	2008
Income from Operations	$5,785	$6,450	$7,250	$6,250	$5,975
Net Income	$4,385	$5,300	$5,325	$4,737	$4,529
Net Cash Flow from Operations	$5,050	$8,300	$7,700	$7,530	$5,700

Using Ibbotson SBBI, you have determined that an appropriate equity risk premium is 5.00%, the firm size premium is 4.00%, and the industry risk premium is 1.75%.

To complete your assignment, you will need to perform the following phases of analysis:

Phase One:	Analyze Hellemn Candy's financial statements
Phase Two:	Determine a capitalization rate
Phase Three:	Determine a proxy benefit
Phase Four:	Calculate an indication of value

---

1 26 CFR 20.2031-2: Valuation of stocks and bonds. (1959-1 C.B. 237; 1959).

2 NACVA. (2012). *Business Valuations: Fundamentals, Techniques and Theory.*

3 Ibid.

4 AICPA. (June 2007). Statement on Standards for Valuation Services No. 1, p. 13.

5 Stockdale, J. (2008). The State of the Fair Value Standard in Divorce. *Business Valuation Update,* Vol. 14, No. 8.

6 *International Glossary of Business Valuation Terms.*

7 Ibid.

8 Ibid.

9 Ibid.

10 AICPA. (June 2007). Statement on Standards for Valuation Services No. 1, p. 23.

11 Ibid., p. 31.

12 Pratt, S. (2008). *Valuing a Business: The Analysis and Appraisal of Closely Held Companies.* 5th Ed. New York: McGraw Hill.

13 From the *International Glossary of Business Valuation Terms.* Reprinted by permission of the American Institute of CPA's.

14 AICPA. (June 2007). Statement on Standards for Valuation Services No. 1, p. 8.

15 Atyeh, M. H. (2012). Business Valuation Process Review. *The Business Review, Cambridge, 20*(1), 166–171.

12 Special Topics

This chapter introduces four special topics (specialized content) that have been previously mentioned in the text but not yet discussed in detail. The topics are presented in four sections as follows:

12.1 Methods of Proof (Direct vs. Indirect)

12.2 Economic Damages

12.3 Computer Forensics

12.4 Reporting Results

Although a comprehensive discussion of these specialized subjects is beyond the scope of this text, a basic understanding of each is important to your overall forensic accounting education. These topics have been selected based on their significance in our practitioner experience and prevalence in forensic accounting engagements. An overview of each topic is provided, including identification, explanation, and application of key concepts.

Learning Objectives

After completing this chapter, you should be able to:

LO1. Explain the concept of method of proof.

LO2. Compare and contrast direct and indirect methods of proof.

LO3. Describe the three basic approaches and underlying indirect methods of proof used by forensic accountants, circumstances when used, and their respective strengths and weaknesses.

LO4. Explain the concept of economic damages.

LO5. Understand the role of the forensic accountant among other damages experts.

LO6. Describe different types of economic damages a forensic accountant may be asked to calculate.

LO7. Identify the key factors in an economic damages calculation, and explain the significance of each.

LO8. Understand the relevance of computer forensics to forensic accounting.

LO9. Identify various storage devices where digital evidence may be located.

L10. Explain the importance of legal parameters and scope parameters in a computer forensics engagement.

L11. Identify key considerations in collecting and storing digital data.

L12. Provide examples of the types of information that can be obtained from analyzing digital data.

(continued)

12.1 Methods of Proof (Direct vs. Indirect)

INTRODUCTION

In the world of forensic accounting, *method of proof* is a term of art with special meaning. For the purpose of clarity, let's deconstruct the concept. A method, simply stated, is a procedure or way of doing something.[1] Proof, as discussed in Chapter 2, is the consequence of evidence. Proof (or lack thereof) is the basis for accepting (or rejecting) allegations or facts at issue, such as embezzlement, tax fraud, economic damages, malpractice, or business value. Thus, ***method of proof*** can be defined as the means by which evidence is developed and presented to establish (or not) the requisite degree of belief or standard of proof, either a preponderance of the evidence or beyond a reasonable doubt. Methods of proof employed by forensic accountants can be direct, indirect, or a combination of the two.

DIRECT METHOD OF PROOF

As the name implies, a ***direct method of proof*** is a clear-cut or definite means of conclusively establishing a fact at issue (such as a false expense or unreported income) *without* inference or presumption. In practice, a direct method of proof is always preferable to an indirect method (discussed in the following section) because it: (a) provides a greater level of certainty, (b) is more easily understood, (c) is harder to refute, and (d) is generally more persuasive.

Direct methods of proof typically rely on documentary evidence (such as tax returns, books and records, bank statements, invoices, cancelled checks, and contracts) and the testimony of witnesses with firsthand knowledge (such as bookkeepers, tax return preparers, employees, bankers, or real estate agents) to establish—or prove—what someone did or didn't do. Thus, employing a direct method of proof requires access to a meaningful set of books and records and the willingness of individuals with firsthand knowledge to testify. Although both paper and witness testimony can serve as evidence, our experience suggests that paper is the more critical of the two in a direct method case. This is because paper

Learning Objectives *(continued)*

After completing this chapter, you should be able to:

L13. Understand the expert reporting mandates of Rule 26.

L14. Recognize the challenges of presenting an oral report.

L15. Identify and describe three types of written reports.

evidence tends to be persuasive—it speaks for itself, it is not self-serving, and it doesn't forget or change its mind. Moreover, it doesn't break down under cross-examination.

To illustrate a direct method of proof, let's consider the case of Dr. X.

The Case of Dr. X*

Dr. X was a dentist doing business as a sole practitioner. In response to a Currency Transaction Report (CTR),† the IRS initiated a criminal investigation that led to an indictment for tax evasion. Specifically, Dr. X was charged with willfully failing to deposit and report cash payments received from patients. During the investigation, it was determined that only checks (no cash) were deposited into the business bank account.

Case for the Prosecution

The first five witnesses were a sample of Dr. X's patients, who testified that they had paid Dr. X in cash and received a "cash receipt" as evidence of the transaction.

The sixth witness was the office manager of Dr. X's practice, who testified that patients routinely made payments in cash. She further testified that a "cash receipts book" was maintained for each of the three years in question (2010 to 2012) and that all cash payments received were recorded in this book. The office manager examined the cash receipts books and confirmed the amount of cash received in each year ($216,050 in 2010, $234,507 in 2011, and $241,745 in 2012). She also identified a sample of "daily reconciliation sheets" in which all receipts (cash and check) were reconciled daily with patient activity (number of visits) and testified that these sheets were given to Dr. X (with both cash and checks) at the day's end for the preparation of bank deposits.

The seventh witness was a representative from Dr. X's bank, who identified Dr. X's "deposit tickets" and testified that Dr. X routinely made bank deposits on behalf of the practice. Based on his review of the practice's deposits for the three years in question, this witness also testified that Dr. X made no cash deposits into the business bank account but did make cash deposits (evidenced by deposit tickets in Dr. X's handwriting) into Dr. X's son's account ($51,175 in 2010, $46,315 in 2011, and $63,742 in 2012).

The eighth witness was Dr. X's tax return preparer, who identified Dr. X's tax returns for the three years in question and confirmed that she had prepared the returns using information provided by Dr. X. The tax return preparer testified that reported gross receipts were determined via bank deposits; thus, if receipts were not deposited into the business bank account, they were not reported as income. She also testified that: (a) the tax returns were carefully reviewed with Dr. X to confirm their accuracy and his understanding, and (b) Dr. X never said anything about depositing receipts into his son's account. Finally, the tax return preparer testified about Dr. X's knowledge and understanding of the accounting and tax reporting process.

The ninth witness for the prosecution was the IRS criminal investigator (Special Agent), who testified about his efforts to investigate the case, including the investigative process (the steps), witnesses interviewed, and records collected.

The final witness for the prosecution was a Revenue Agent (RA) from the IRS Special Enforcement Group, who was present throughout the trial. Based on the file data and evidence presented, the RA computed the amount of tax due and owing.

Direct Method Summary

The government applied a direct method of proof, including both documentary and testimonial evidence, to support its criminal allegations against Dr. X. A summary of the government's case presentation follows.

---

*This illustration is based on an actual engagement. Names, locations, and other identifying information have been changed to protect the privacy of the parties.

† Financial institutions are required to file CTRs with the IRS for currency transactions valued at more than $10,000. CTRs can be accessed by federal, state, and local law enforcement agencies and are commonly used as an investigative source.

- Patients confirm (via cash receipts) that cash payments were made.
- The office manager confirms (via the cash receipts book and daily reconciliation sheets) that cash payments were received, recorded, and given to Dr. X.
- The banker confirms (via bank deposit tickets) that cash was not deposited into the business account but was deposited into Dr. X's son's account.
- The tax return preparer confirms (via tax returns and related work papers) that the cash revenue was not reported and that the returns were reviewed with Dr. X to confirm completeness and accuracy. The return preparer also confirms (via work papers) Dr. X's level of knowledge and understanding.
- The Special Agent confirms the investigative process, the specific return failure (unreported income), and Dr. X's efforts to conceal.
- The Revenue Agent computes and confirms the additional tax due.

Conviction and Sentencing

Dr. X was convicted of tax evasion and subsequently sentenced to a year and a day in prison, with no chance of probation. In addition, he was fined $40,000 and ordered to cooperate with the IRS in the amendment of his tax returns and payment of all income taxes due for the subject periods (approx. $550,000).

INDIRECT METHOD OF PROOF

An ***indirect method of proof*** is not straightforward (or direct) but is instead built on circumstantial evidence. As discussed in Chapter 2, circumstantial evidence is based on inference rather than personal knowledge or direct observation. Indirect methods are most commonly employed in the absence of reliable books and records. Other examples of facts and circumstances that support the consideration of indirect methods include the following:

- Inconsistent or unreliable method of accounting
- Significant increase in net worth unsupported by reported income
- Inconsistency in gross profit percentages across time or in comparison with industry averages
- Unexplained bank deposits
- Atypical uses of cash (such as equipment purchases, wages, or rents)
- Lifestyle (spending) in excess of reported income

Indirect methods of proof are founded on logic, common sense, critical thinking, and deductive reasoning, all of which are necessary skills of the forensic accountant discussed in Chapter 1. Remember Al Capone!

There are three basic indirect approaches: cash flow, asset accumulation, and ratios. As illustrated in Table 12-1, under each of these approaches are several indirect methods. Moreover, some indirect methods are based on a combination of approaches. Selection and application of the various methods are dictated by the case facts and circumstances.

Dig Deeper

Forensic accountants are commonly engaged by defense counsel and tax return preparers to assist in federal and state tax examinations or investigations. Such engagements require a working knowledge of the various indirect methods of proof used by the IRS and state agencies. Although developed for use in tax matters, the indirect methods discussed in this chapter are applicable to other forensic accounting engagements as both primary and secondary methods of proof. For additional information, visit the IRS web site and access the Internal Revenue Manual (IRM), Part 9.5.9, which addresses IRS criminal investigation and methods of proof. Another valuable resource is the IRS Audit Techniques Guide (Chapter 5) for cash intensive businesses.

Table 12-1 Indirect Methods of Proof

Approach	Methods	Reasoning
Cash Flow	Source and Application of Funds (or Expenditures) Method	The source and application of funds method is based on the general proposition that you can't spend what you don't have. Thus, if consumption exceeds identified sources, unreported income is inferred.
	Bank Deposits Method	The bank deposits method employs bank account records (specifically deposits) to reconcile reported income. Excess (or unidentified) deposits may indicate unreported income or unknown sources.
	Cash Method	The cash method, which is a variation of the expenditures method, focuses on expenditures made in currency (cash only).
Asset Accumulation	Net Worth Method	The net worth method extends the concept of application of funds to include the accumulation of assets. It employs a balance sheet formula: Assets – Liabilities = Net Worth. If the increase in net worth (plus consumption) during some period exceeds identified sources, unreported income is inferred.
Ratio	Percentage Markup (or Gross Margin) Method	The percentage markup method is generally limited to retail establishments (rather than illegal businesses), because it requires reliable information regarding opening and closing inventories and the appropriate percentage markup (or gross margin).
	Unit and Volume Method	The unit and volume method, which has limited application, is feasible only when the number of units and price can be determined.

Source: Internal Revenue Manual Part 9, Chapter 5, Section 9.

Net Worth Method

The net worth method is most commonly used when there is an accumulation of assets without a corresponding source of funds. For illustration purposes, let's revisit the case of Al Capone.

Indictment

In March 1931, Capone was indicted for five counts of tax evasion (years 1924 to 1928). The IRS estimated his annual gross earnings during this period (from gambling, prostitution, and bootlegging) at more than $100 million. Capone maintained no bank accounts, kept no activity records, bought no property in his own name, and conducted all his financial transactions in cash.

Method of Proof

Absent direct evidence of Capone's income, specifically paper evidence, IRS Special Agent Frank Wilson developed and employed the net worth and expenditures method (a combined method). The underlying theory of this method is quite simple—you can't spend what you don't have. Wilson's analysis is illustrated in Table 12-2.

Wilson's analysis was supported by witness testimony regarding Capone's lifestyle (expenditures) and accumulation of assets (nominee[‡] ownership of businesses and

[‡] A nominee is an owner in name only. Capone would remain anonymous by purchasing property using nominees such as brokers, attorneys, corporations, friends, and relatives (many of which were deceased).

Table 12-2 | Net Worth Calculation

Step	Action	Example Calculation*
1	Determine ending net worth.	$2.5m
2	Determine beginning net worth.	$1.125m
3	Calculate the change in net worth during the period.	$1.375m
4	Determine expenditures (consumption) during the period.	$.500m
5	Calculate the sum of funds used for asset acquisitions and consumption.	$1.875m
6	Calculate the sum of reported income and other legitimate sources of funds. (Remember, Capone never filed tax returns.)	0
7	Calculate the difference between legitimate sources and uses of funds, which indicates (infers) unreported income.	$1.875m

*Numbers are for illustration purposes only.

property). As discussed in Chapter 1, this indirect method of proof allowed the government to explain to the jury the complexities of accounting and tax in a manner that was not only persuasive, but also defensible.

The principal strength of the net worth method is its intuitive appeal—it makes good sense. Although the underlying theory is straightforward, its application in practice—specifically, the challenge of gathering supporting evidence—is no simple task. Successful use of the net worth method requires a complete reconstruction of the subject's financial history, including all assets, liabilities, expenditures, and sources of funds. Of critical importance is a credible (firm) beginning net worth, which provides the starting point for identifying an increase in net worth.

Dig Deeper

You are challenged to step into the shoes of Special Agent Frank Wilson and review the records[§] related to the Capone investigation. What evidence (paper and people) did Wilson use to support his analysis? How did Capone's lawyers challenge the net worth method? What weaknesses (if any) were identified?

Source and Application of Funds Method

Another indirect method of proof is the source and application of funds (or expenditures) method, which is used when the subject (individual or business) consumes income rather than accumulates assets. Simply stated, the process involves determining total expenditures (cash outflows) during a specific period and deducting known and legitimate sources (cash available). Excess expenditures infer unreported income.

Effective use of this method requires the forensic accountant to qualify, or confirm, all beginning and ending asset and liability accounts, which serves to identify both sources and applications of funds. Most critical is beginning cash-on-hand, which defends against the argument that excess expenditures were funded with cash accumulated in prior years. In practice, this method is most commonly employed in a preliminary analysis or in conjunction with the net worth method.

[§] Can be accessed via a link at www.pearsonhighered.com/rufus.

Table 12-3 | Source and Application of Funds Analysis

Source of Funds		Application of Funds	
Beginning cash-on-hand	$50,000	Ending cash-on-hand	$65,000
Reported (net) income	$25,000	Increase in assets	$20,000
Noncash expense	$5,000	Personal living (consumption)	$25,000
Increase in debt/payables	$10,000	Increase in savings	$5,000
Total sources	$90,000	Total applications	$115,000
Excess Applications over Sources = Inferred Unreported Income			$25,000

An example calculation using the source and application of funds method is provided in Table 12-3.

Like the net worth method, the strength of the source and application of funds method is its commonsense appeal. Also like the net worth method, it has the disadvantage of being fraught with peril and time-consuming. A specific challenge is its requirement of a defensible (certain) beginning cash-on-hand (vs. a beginning net worth). As illustrated in the Capone case, the source and application of funds method is commonly combined with the net worth method.

Percentage Markup Method

A third indirect method for consideration is the percentage markup (or gross margin) method. This method identifies and employs a relationship of relative values (ratios) to infer income. It is most effectively used with retail establishments such as restaurants, bars, and gas stations where a "per-unit" sales price and cost (relative value) can be established with reasonable certainty or where the gross margin (percentage markup) is fairly constant within the industry.

The percentage markup method employs elementary algebra and the relative accounting expression (Sales – Cost of Sales = Gross Margin) to infer income. An item's ***percentage markup*** is the difference between the per-unit cost and the per-unit sales price (the dollar markup), stated as a percentage of the cost. For example, if the cost is $5 and the price is $7.50, the dollar markup is $2.50 and the percentage markup is 50% (calculated as $2.50/$5.00). A similar concept is the ***gross margin percentage***, which is the dollar markup stated as a percentage of the sales price, rather than the cost. To clarify these concepts, consider the following simple example: If the cost per unit is $5 and the gross margin percentage is 34%, what is the sales price?

$$\text{Sales Price} = \text{Cost} + \text{Gross Margin}$$
$$1 = (\$5 / \text{Sales Price}) + 0.34$$
$$0.66 = \$5 / \text{Sales Price}$$
$$0.66(\text{Sales Price}) = \$5$$
$$\text{Sales Price} = \$5 / 0.66 = \$7.58$$

The activity of Stats Bar & Grill, discussed in the following section, provides a real-world scenario.

Stats Bar & Grill

Stats Bar & Grill (SBG) is a local sports bar owned and operated by Tom and Stacey Settle. You have been engaged by Ted Jones, a prospective buyer, to evaluate the activity of SBG and the credibility of the representations made by its owners, specifically that the bar generates substantial profits, a significant portion (estimated at 25%) of which is not reflected in the books and records. In other words, the Settles are skimming cash prior to its entry into the accounting system. This means that the books will reconcile to the tax returns and bank deposits, but income (cash) will be understated. The owners have provided this sensitive information (skimming) to support their asking price for the business. The value of the information can best be tested by applying markup percentages.**

Following a preliminary analysis of SBG's financial statements and a tour of its facilities, you conduct a comprehensive interview with the Settles and determine the following:

- Detailed purchase, inventory, and sale records have not been maintained.
- Beverage products are purchased from only a few suppliers (confirmed via invoices and cancelled checks).
- Revenue components include:
    - Beer – Bottle / Can
      Estimated at 50%–55% of revenue
      Cost = $25 per case / 24 cans per case = $1.04 per can
      Avg. sales price = $2.50 per can
      Spoilage or waste = 2%
      Primary supplier = Eagle Distributing (80%)
    - Beer – Draft
      Estimated at 5% of revenue
      Cost = $125 per keg (1,984 oz.)
      Avg. sales price = $1.75 per 16 oz. serving
      15% spillage = 1,686 oz. per keg = 105 servings = $184.45 sales value
      Profit margin = 32%
      Primary supplier = same as above
    - Liquor
      Estimated at 30%–35% of revenue
      20 drinks per bottle (net of spillage)
      Cost = $20 per bottle
      Avg. sales price = $2.50 per drink
      Primary suppliers = Liquor Plus, Classic Liquor (90%)
    - Wine
      Estimated at 2.5% of revenue
      Cost = $9 per bottle
      5 glasses per bottle
      Avg. sales price = $2.75 per glass
    - Food
      Estimated at 2%–3% of revenue
      Breakeven (0% profit margin)

Unit sales prices were confirmed against SBG's menu, and purchases were confirmed with reasonable certainty by contacting suppliers. The next step, summarized in Table 12-4, is to do the math and compare the results with the reported income.

As illustrated, the percentage markup method suggests (or infers) that SBG's income was understated by $41,412, roughly 9%. A 25% understatement, as proposed by the Settles, would have totaled roughly $116,000. How would these observations impact your recommendation(s) to Mr. Jones?

** The percentage markup method is commonly used by state agencies in sales tax audits.

Table 12-4 Stats Bar & Grill Calculation of Revenue by Percentage Markup Method, Jan. 1–Dec. 31, 2012

Product	Purchases	Cost Extension	Sales Value	Profit Margin	% of Revenue
Beer – Bottle/Can	5,830 cases	$145,750	$349,800	58.3%	75.3%
Beer – Draft	52.5 kegs	$6,562	$9,684	32.2%	2.1%
Liquor	1,860 bottles	$37,200	$93,000	60.0%	20.0%
Wine	417 bottles	$3,753	$5,734	34.5%	1.2%
Total Beverages		$193,265	$458,218	57.8%	
Total Food		$6,412	$6,412	0.0%	1.4%
Inferred Income		$199,677	$464,630	57.0%	100%
Reported Income			$423,218		
Inferred Skimming			$41,412		8.9%

Special Note

Another current example of an indirect method is the 2009 case *U.S. v. Abdul Karim Khanu*. Khanu, a nightclub operator in Washington, D.C., was indicted on twenty-two counts, including tax evasion, conspiracy, and false returns. To prove its case, the IRS employed the cash method, an indirect method of proof that focuses on expenditures made in currency (cash only). A comprehensive case narrative, including opening statements, witness testimony, closing arguments, and jury instructions, is presented in Appendix 12-A.

METHOD OF PROOF SELECTION

In selecting a method of proof, the objective is to develop a presentation of the evidence that is best suited to the facts and circumstances of the case. Notwithstanding this general proposition, the direct method of proof is always preferable to an indirect method. As previously noted, the direct method is (or should be) simpler, more accurate, more easily understood by jurors, and more defensible. Thus, indirect methods are generally used only when the direct method is not viable. Because the various indirect methods are closely related and complementary, combinations (such as net worth and expenditures in the Capone case) are common. Several factors should be considered in selecting indirect methods:

- Availability of records
- The subject industry (availability of average profit margins)
- Significance of inventory
- Significance of cash revenue
- Number of suppliers (ability to establish a reliable cost)
- Ability to establish reliable prices
- Banking practices
- Volume and mix of products or services offered
- Expenditures/lifestyle
- Changes in net worth

- Ability to establish beginning cash-on-hand
- Ability to establish beginning net worth
- Duration of the period under consideration (three years, five years, ten years, and so forth)

INDIRECT METHODS AND THE COURTS

As emphasized throughout this text, an expert's opinion must be based on sufficient, reliable facts and data and be the product of applicable, reliable methodology (FRE 702). Given this requirement, a pertinent question is how indirect methods (which imply data limitations) are viewed by the courts—the gatekeepers of evidence. The courts have upheld the use of the net worth, expenditures, bank deposits, and cash methods to establish *prima facie* evidence of unreported income, which creates a logical inference that must be overcome by the defendant.[2] However, the courts have established several defenses to protect against abuse, such as the following:

- *Net worth method.* The user must establish a beginning net worth with reasonable certainty, consider all relevant leads (alternative explanations), and establish a likely source of funding for the increase in net worth.[3] Moreover, the defense is given wide latitude in presenting evidence of beginning net worth.[4]
- *Source and application of funds.* The user must establish beginning cash-on-hand with reasonable certainty, and expenditures cannot be speculative or arbitrary.[5]
- *Percentage markup.* The use of reliable percentages (ratios) and a supportable base are required.[6] Even so, the IRS cautions against the use of this method,[7] and no judicial precedent has been identified or cited.[8]

Although practitioners must recognize these limitations, our experience suggests that challenges of indirect methods should be focused on application (errors) rather than theory. Moreover, all methods of proof are only a means of establishing a proposition (such as unreported income)—not intent, which is an essential element in a criminal case.

Think About It

As noted on numerous occasions in previous chapters, the burden of proof in a criminal case is on the prosecution (the government), and the standard of proof is beyond a reasonable doubt. Given this high threshold, how can indirect methods of proof, which are based exclusively on circumstantial evidence, be used in criminal cases? This chapter explains that, under the net worth method, an increase in net worth provides an inference of unreported income. But when does an inference become a presumption? What is the difference (if any) between the two concepts?

12.2 Economic Damages

INTRODUCTION

This section introduces the concept of economic damages, types of damages, the roles of damages experts, and common methodologies employed in damages calculations. In an economic damages claim, the forensic accountant's assignment is usually the determination (calculation) and presentation of the *present value* of alleged damages. As with all forensic accounting engagements, this analysis must use reliable data and appropriate methodology. Economic damages calculations, like business valuations, boil down to a handful of factors that are based on various facts and assumptions. The concept—replacing lost value due to some economic injury[††]—is simple, and the methodological approach—loss equals the

[††] We use the term "economic injury" to generally represent an adverse economic impact due to the alleged cause of action, which is not limited to a physical injury.

difference between pre-injury value and post-injury value—is straightforward. However, the challenge of identifying suitable measures for the various factors is considerably more complex.

WHAT ARE ECONOMIC DAMAGES?

We have all heard tales in the news of large damage awards in lawsuits. In such cases, it is easy to embrace the proposition that the defendant did something "wrong" that resulted in some harm to the plaintiff. But how, you may wonder, was the *amount* of damages determined? How much money is required to compensate for the loss of a job, or a limb, or even a life? How are future losses valued today? Issues such as these are resolved with the assistance of forensic accountants or forensic economists.

Special Note

Economic damages experts are sometimes referred to as *forensic economists* rather than forensic accountants, because the required expertise involves more economics than accounting. Although it is common for forensic accountants to perform several different types of engagements, those who call themselves forensic economists often work exclusively in the realm of economic damages.

Concept of Economic Damages

In Chapter 11, we defined the value of a business as the present value of its expected future benefit stream—that is, its ability to generate income. A business generates income by using its assets to produce some product or service. Although we generally think of tangible assets such as property and equipment, an important intangible asset of a business is its workforce, known as human capital. In addition to any income they generate for their employers, people also have an individual productive capacity—they are "assets" who can generate income for personal use. Similar to equipment, people require repairs and maintenance to keep them operational.[9] Damage to a machine may put it out of service either temporarily or permanently, and the same is true of people.

Economic damages are the monetary compensation that is awarded in civil litigation, such as a tort or breach of contract claim. In a previous business law course, you learned that a *tort* is a civil action where one party (the plaintiff) alleges injury, damage, or loss due to the negligent or intentional acts of another party (the defendant).[10] Common tort actions include personal injury or wrongful death claims (such as auto accidents), medical and professional malpractice claims, product liability claims (such as tobacco or asbestos), and employment actions (such as discrimination or wrongful termination). *Contract disputes*, also civil actions, involve allegations of nonperformance that give rise to a claim for damages.[11]

Special Note

As reported by the Bureau of Justice Statistics (2009),[12] tort actions account for about 60% of the civil cases decided by bench or jury trial. Interestingly, the vast majority (96%) of such actions are settled before trial. Research indicates that expert witness testimony is critical to a successful pretrial resolution.[13]

Businesses as well as individuals can suffer economic damages. A common example is lost profits resulting from some act or failure by the defendant, such as when a fire caused by a faulty piece of kitchen equipment forces a restaurant to close for some period of time. A wrongful act may also cause the permanent impairment or complete destruction of a business, in which case the economic damage would be lost business value. Another type of economic damages claim, mostly involving large corporations, is infringement of intellectual property rights such as patents, copyrights, or trademarks. In such a claim, the plaintiff alleges lost income due to the defendant's unauthorized use of the intellectual property, such as using the plaintiff's patented design to produce a competing product.

Compensatory vs. Punitive Damages

So far, we have discussed ***compensatory damages***, the purpose of which is to make the plaintiff whole—that is, to put the individual or entity in the economic position that would have occurred if not for the defendant's wrongful conduct. Compensatory damages are meant to compensate for a loss—not to reward a plaintiff or punish a defendant. This is in contrast to another component of economic damages, ***punitive damages***, which are awarded by a court to punish a defendant's intentional or reckless behavior and/or deter similar misconduct by the same defendant or other parties in the future.

Although punitive damages can be large, often several times the magnitude of compensatory damages, they are determined separately from compensatory damages and are thus outside the scope of this introductory discussion. For the remainder of this chapter, we focus on compensatory damages related to personal injury and wrongful death actions, which we refer to as "personal damages." This involves the measurement of people's ability to produce income and the costs to return to them to their pre-injury condition.

Special Note

You may be wondering, in a wrongful death claim, who is being compensated? Obviously, a deceased individual cannot be restored to any type of position, economic or otherwise. In these situations, the economic loss is suffered by those people who benefited from the plaintiff's earnings or household services, such as family members. Thus, for a wrongful death involving a person who lived alone with no dependents, there may be no economic damages.

Noneconomic Damages

Economic damages, which are monetary in nature, can be contrasted with ***noneconomic damages***, which refer to nonmonetary losses such as pain, suffering, emotional distress, loss of companionship, and loss of enjoyment of life.[14] While economic damages can, in theory, be objectively verified and measured, noneconomic damages are inherently subjective in nature. For this reason, noneconomic damages, or "intangibles," are generally considered outside the realm of expert witness testimony. Few economic experts are willing to present such testimony, and most courts deny its admission based on findings that either (a) experts may not testify about intangible values, or (b) the scientific basis for the testimony is unreliable under FRE 702, as interpreted by *Daubert*.[15]

Roles of Damages Experts

The primary role of the economic expert in a damages claim is to place a dollar value on the various damages components that have been identified. Because these losses have been incurred in the past or will be incurred in the future, the expert's calculations must include a conversion to present value. Like business valuations, economic damages calculations have a valuation date—the date at which present value is determined. In a litigation context, this may be the date the report is issued or the date of a future arbitration, settlement conference, or trial. The actual damages components may be identified by the engaging attorney or independently by the expert. For example, the attorney might ask you to consider any and all economic damages or might instruct you to exclude a certain component based on some strategic consideration. In either case, this should be disclosed in the expert report, along with a number of other facts and assumptions discussed later in this section.

Special Note

Although liability for the alleged injury is an important part of the overall claim, it is not a matter of concern for economic experts. Experts engaged by the plaintiff's counsel are often asked to assume the causation of the subject injury. Although this, like all assumptions, should be disclosed in the expert's report, it has no bearing on the calculation of damages. Knowledge of why an injury occurred or who is at fault is not necessary to evaluate its economic impact.

Engaging Counsel

An economic expert can be engaged by counsel for either the plaintiff or the defendant. An expert's estimate of damages can be used by the plaintiff's counsel to support a damages award or by the defendant's counsel to discredit the plaintiff's request for such an award. As we have repeatedly emphasized in this text, expert witnesses must be *independent* and *objective* in developing and presenting their opinions. Given this requirement, an expert's analysis should be the same, whether he or she has been engaged by the plaintiff or defendant. Even so, the expert's role in the case may be different. When engaged by the plaintiff's counsel, the expert will usually prepare a report that sets forth his or her opinion of damages. When engaged by the defendant's counsel, the expert may be asked not to prepare a report, but to review and critique the opposing expert's report and to assist in preparing deposition or cross-examination questions for the opposing expert.

Think About It

Why do you think the defendant's counsel would not want to present an expert report with a specific dollar value of economic damages? What would this imply about the defendant's liability for the alleged injury?

Other Damages Experts

The economic expert is often not the only damages expert that is involved in a personal injury or wrongful death claim. Depending on the specific circumstances, there may be three different categories of damages experts:[16]

- Those who establish the *facts* of the damages claim. This would include physicians, physical therapists, or psychologists who define the nature and extent of the injury. For example, a physician might determine that the plaintiff has a spinal injury that prevents him from walking or standing for extended periods of time.
- Those who establish the *parameters* of the damages.[‡‡] This would include vocational experts, who determine the impact of the injury on the plaintiff's ability to work, and life care planners, who identify any medical provisions the plaintiff may require in the future.
- The economic expert, who estimates the *dollar value* of the damages.

Each successive link in this "chain" of experts relies on the previous link. The economic expert relies on the opinions of the vocational expert, who relies on the opinions of the physician. On the side of either the plaintiff or the defendant, the economic expert is often the last witness to testify. This is because his or her task is to summarize all the preceding testimony into a single total dollar value of economic damages.

Given this buildup approach, the strength of the economic expert's opinion is contingent on the validity of the assumptions provided by other experts. Even if the economic methodology is sound, unreliable facts and assumptions will lead to an unreliable conclusion of damages. Thus, although it is not necessary for the economic expert to understand the process used by other experts to arrive at their opinions, he or she must understand the opinions. For example, if a vocational expert determines that the plaintiff will be limited in the future to an "entry-level job," the economic expert must understand exactly what this means. Does it mean minimum wage? Some level above minimum wage? Is this limitation permanent or temporary?

TYPES OF COMPENSATORY DAMAGES

Before an economic expert can place a total dollar value on the damages resulting from an injury, the relevant damage categories must be identified. For compensatory damages, this includes damages that are (1) *compensable* by law, and (2) *measurable* within the realm of economics.[17] The first factor depends on the jurisdiction where the claim is filed.

[‡‡] Obviously, in a wrongful death claim, the extent of the injury and its residual impact are quite clear.

As previously noted, some jurisdictions exclude consideration of certain intangible damages, while others do not. The second factor reflects the requirement of a market basis for the specific type of damage. Simply stated, the loss must have some economic value that can be measured in terms of market equivalents. In personal damages claims, three broad categories of damages meet these two requirements: lost earnings, lost household services, and medical expenses.

Lost Earnings

As previously noted, people can use their physical and mental resources to produce income for their own benefit and the benefit of others, such as family members or other dependents. If the subject injury impairs (or, in a wrongful death case, eliminates) this ability to earn income, then the plaintiff is entitled to recover ***lost earnings***. This category of damages can be segregated into two subcategories: *past lost earnings*, which are measured from the date of injury to the valuation date, and *future lost earnings*, which are measured from the date of valuation forward.

Although we commonly think of earnings in terms of cash earnings (wages or salary), it also includes noncash earnings like fringe benefits. Examples of fringe benefits that are commonly considered in personal damages claims include various types of insurance (for example, health, life, or disability), retirement benefits (pension or defined contribution), and paid leave (such as vacation pay and holiday pay).

Lost wages and fringe benefits have market equivalents, because there are generally prevailing (or standard) wages for different types of work, based on the necessary skill, education, and experience, as well as supply/demand factors. For people with an employment history, a good measure is their past earnings—what they were actually paid for their services in the labor market. For people with no employment history in the subject occupation (such as children, college students, or someone in transition between occupations), the expert considers wages paid to others in the same occupation with similar qualifications.

Lost Household Services

People have the ability to produce income by providing services not only in the labor market, but also in their own homes. Such services, known as ***household services***, include tasks such as cooking, cleaning, shopping, repairs, yard work, and management of household finances, to name just a few. Although people generally receive no payment for this work (since this would essentially be paying oneself), it still has economic value. When a person cannot perform some household service, he or she may need to hire someone else to do the job. Thus, the economic value of the ability to perform household services is the money saved by doing the work yourself rather than hiring it out. As with a person's occupation, market wages for different types of household services can be used as measures of damages.

Medical Expenses

Personal injury and wrongful death claims often involve medical expenses such as hospitalization, surgery, physician care, medications, and medical equipment or supplies. Even with wrongful death cases, there can be medical expenses preceding the person's death, such as the cost of ambulance transportation and emergency room treatment. As with lost earnings, medical expenses can be measured as either past or future relative to the valuation date. Almost all personal damages claims involve past medical expenses, which are the costs of the actual medical care rendered to the injured person.

For injuries that are more severe in nature, medical care may be required into the future, sometimes for the duration of the person's life. Unlike past medical expenses, which are actual in nature, future medical expenses are projected. Because an economic expert is not qualified to make such a projection, this is typically done by a life care planner. A life care planner is a medical professional, often a registered nurse, who projects the specific items of medical care that will be needed by the plaintiff, when (or how often) the care will be needed, and approximately how much it will cost. These projections are outlined in a ***life care plan***, which is a document that provides an "organized, concise plan for current and future needs, with associated costs, for individuals who have experienced catastrophic injury or have chronic health care needs."[18]

Application to a Specific Case

Although lost earnings and medical expenses are common types of compensatory damages, the relevant damages for any specific engagement will be determined by the unique facts and circumstances of the case, such as the person's age, education, employment history, past earnings, medical history, and household setting, among many others. If the person was retired at the time of the injury and had no expectations of returning to work, then there would be no lost earnings. Similarly, if the person worked (and was expected to continue working) in an entry-level position that would not typically have fringe benefits, then there would be no lost benefits. Remember, the purpose of compensatory damages is to restore the plaintiff to his or her pre-injury economic position. This cannot be accomplished without first determining what the pre-injury position was, considering both the present state and expectations for the future.

Of course, the inclusion or exclusion of damage components in a specific case is also subject to the direction of engaging counsel. Suppose the plaintiff's attorney is seeking an award of a certain dollar amount, and a specific damages component, such as lost household services, is not necessary to reach this amount. In this situation, the attorney may ask the expert to ignore household services, even if it constitutes a compensable loss based on the case facts. Such an attorney directive should be disclosed in the expert's report, so that the exclusion of household services from the analysis does not suggest the nonexistence of the loss. This allows the expert an opportunity to address the component at a later time if necessary.

CALCULATING ECONOMIC DAMAGES

Understanding the concept of economic damages, you are now prepared for a discussion of how an expert calculates such damages, including necessary data and sources for that data, the use of facts and assumptions, and key methodological factors. Given the limited scope of this chapter, we will focus on the most basic component of damages, lost wages. Although calculations for different types of damages have some unique aspects, there is a common framework:

1. Define the benefit stream the plaintiff would have received if not for the injury.
2. Define the benefit stream the plaintiff will receive (for future damages) or has already received (for past damages), given the injury.
3. Calculate the difference between the two benefit streams, which is the economic loss in terms of past or future values.
4. Convert the loss to present value.

Facts and Assumptions

Calculations of economic damages, regardless of type, are based on a set of foundational facts and assumptions. A fact is something that can be objectively verified, such as the plaintiff's demographic attributes (for example, age, gender, race, and marital status), educational attainment, and employment history. Assumptions, in contrast, are subjective, which leaves room for reasonable disagreement. As previously noted, the economic expert is provided various assumptions by other experts such as physicians (who determine the lasting physical consequences of the injury), vocational experts (who evaluate how any physical impairments will impact the plaintiff's ability to earn income), and life care planners (who specify the required medical care and related costs). Other important assumptions, discussed later, are independently determined by the economic expert.

Special Note

Although facts can be independently verified, it is not necessary for the economic expert to perform such verification. In other words, you don't need to view the plaintiff's birth certificate or driver's license to confirm the date of birth. Thus, it can be said that you are *assuming* a given proposition is a *fact*. This statement illustrates the importance of semantics in economic damages, which can create a potential stumbling block in a deposition or on the witness stand.

Table 12-5 | Sources of Information

• Filings
  ◦ Complaint
  ◦ Answer
  ◦ Discovery responses
  ◦ Deposition transcripts
• Earnings data
  ◦ Tax returns
  ◦ W-2s
  ◦ Pay stubs
  ◦ Social Security earnings statements
• Education and employment data
  ◦ Resume
  ◦ Employment application
  ◦ College transcripts
  ◦ Certificates and licenses
	• Physician evaluation
	• Vocational evaluation
	• Life care plan
	• Interviews of the plaintiff and/or family members
	• Statistical sources
	  ◦ Market wage rates
	  ◦ Life expectancy tables
	  ◦ Worklife expectancy tables
	  ◦ Interest rates
	  ◦ Inflation rates
	  ◦ Unemployment rates
	  ◦ Wage growth trends
	  ◦ Fringe benefits costs

Facts and assumptions are derived from various sources of information, as illustrated in Table 12-5. Different items of information are necessary, depending on the type of case (personal injury vs. wrongful death), the relevant components of damages, and the unique attributes of the specific case. As emphasized throughout this text, there is no checklist of information that can be universally applied. Rather, it is the expert's responsibility (part of his or her expertise) to identify any relevant information and where it might be obtained. Although experts might create a basic list to use as a starting point for a data request, it will almost always need to be supplemented. Remember the threshold—*sufficient relevant data*.

Projected Earnings

Calculating lost wages requires the projection of two separate earnings streams: ***pre-injury earnings***, what the plaintiff would have earned if not for the injury, and ***post-injury earnings***, what the plaintiff will earn, given the injury. The difference between these two streams constitutes lost earnings. As previously noted, lost earnings include both past and future lost earnings, measured in relation to the valuation date. The same measure of loss (pre- vs. post-injury streams of income and expenses) applies to other types of damages as well, including fringe benefits (a component of earnings), household services, and medical expenses.

Base Earnings

Any projection must be based on a starting point. For estimations of lost earnings, the starting points are the initial streams of both pre- and post-injury earnings, known as ***base earnings***. The determination of base earnings is critical because all calculations, such as growth and discounting, can be considered an adjustment to the base.[19]

Pre-injury base earnings are often derived from actual past earnings. This can be either the most recent year or some average of multiple years. Similar to calculating the proxy benefit in a business valuation, the goal is to determine the single value that provides the best indication of future earnings. If a person's past earnings have increased each year, it may be appropriate to use a weighted average or even the single most recent year. In contrast, if there is substantial variation in past earnings, a simple average may be more appropriate.

Importantly, when earnings change significantly from year to year, the economic expert should attempt to determine the reasons. Possible explanations include a pay raise, a promotion, overtime hours, or an absence from work due to illness or some other reason. Identifying explanatory factors is necessary to determine whether they are expected to continue into the future and thus how they should be reflected in base earnings. Another issue in the determination of pre-injury base earnings is the treatment of partial-year earnings in the year of injury. For partial-year earnings to be included, they must be annualized. This may or may not be appropriate, depending on the specific circumstances, specifically whether earnings are expected to be distributed evenly throughout the year.

Special Note

In situations when there is no earnings history, pre-injury base earnings can be estimated using statistical resources, such as data compiled by the Bureau of Labor Statistics (BLS). The BLS compiles historical average earnings for various demographic categories, such as gender, age, ethnicity, and education.

In contrast to pre-injury base earnings, which is usually an assumption determined by the economic expert, the assumption of post-injury base earning is often provided by the vocational expert. Or, if the injured person has already returned to work, actual post-injury earnings can be used as a basis for future projections.

Earnings Growth

Historical evidence clearly shows that wages generally increase over extended periods of time. Thus, base earnings streams must be adjusted over time to account for expected future growth. Two factors may contribute to this expected growth:

- *Inflation.* The purchasing power of a dollar falls as prices rise due to inflation. Thus, to preserve purchasing power, wages must increase at a rate commensurate with inflation.
- *Productivity.* Productivity is generally defined as the rate of output for a given level of inputs. It can be measured at various levels: the national economy, the industry, the firm, or the individual.

For individuals with an extended work history, actual past earnings growth can be used as a proxy for future growth. When a sufficient work history is not available, the economic expert must rely on statistical data, such as historical averages or future forecasts. For example, historical wage growth for various classes of workers is tracked by changes in the Employment Cost Index (ECI), compiled by the BLS. A forecast of future long-term wage growth is provided in the annual OASDI Trustees Report, which describes the financial outlook for Social Security. Projections for shorter periods can be obtained from the Congressional Budget Office (CBO), which prepares a ten-year forecast of several economic variables. Based on these statistics, it is widely agreed among economic experts that a reasonable range for nominal wage growth is 3% to 5%.

Special Note

Wage growth can be expressed in either nominal or real terms. Nominal wage growth is total wage growth, including both the inflation and productivity components. In real wage growth, the inflation component is subtracted out, leaving only the productivity component.

Worklife Expectancy

Most people are familiar with concept of life expectancy, or how many years a person is expected to live. A similar concept is ***worklife expectancy***, which is the period of time a person is expected to work. In a lost earnings calculation, this is the period over which lost earnings are projected into the future. A simple approach would be to assume a retirement age, such as 65, and project continuous lost earnings through that date. However, several uncertain factors challenge the reasonableness of this assumption. Specifically, there is some chance that the person would have died before reaching age 65. Moreover, it is possible that the person would have been absent from the workforce or unable to find a job (unemployed) for some periods of time before reaching age 65. Economic experts can address such uncertainties related to worklife expectancy by using either statistical worklife tables or the LPE (Life, Participation, and Employment) method.

Special Note

Although there remains some academic debate regarding the relative strengths and weaknesses of the two methods, the preference of practitioners is clear. A 2011 practitioner survey found that 67.5% of respondents use worklife tables, compared to only 3% for the LPE method.[20] Recall from Chapter 2 that one of the *Daubert* factors is the degree of acceptance within the professional community. The low rate of acceptance for the LPE method is certainly a deterrent to its use. Thus, we will discuss only worklife tables in this section. For an explanation of the LPE method and comparative evaluations of the two methods (worklife tables vs. LPE), you are encouraged to review past articles published in the *Journal of Legal Economics* and the *Journal of Forensic Economics*.

Worklife Tables

Worklife tables define worklife expectancy as the "average number of years that a person will spend either working or actively looking for work during the remainder of his or her life."[21] Specifically, these tables display lifetime labor force activity of a cohort of 100,000 newborns, by age, gender, labor force status, and an additional variable—either education or race. They are built on the assumption that the numbers of individuals in these cohorts who enter and exit the labor force reflect the probabilities of making these transitions. Using these tables, an economic expert can estimate the number of years that an average person in a specific peer group is expected to participate in the labor force. For example, if a 42-year-old female has a worklife expectancy of 19 years, this does not mean she is expected to exit the labor force (retire) at age 62. Rather, she is expected to participate in the labor force for a compressed period of 19 years, which may occur over some longer period.

Worklife tables were formerly published by the BLS, based on data collected in the Current Population Survey (CPS).[§§] The last BLS worklife tables were created in 1986, using 1979–1980 data. For many years, these tables were used by economists to estimate worklife expectancy. Since the 1990s, economists have taken on the task of periodically updating the tables, using underlying data provided by the BLS. The most recent example is a 2011 study by Skoog, Ciecka, and Krueger, which provides worklife tables based on 2005–2009 data.[22]

Special Note

It may seem unreasonable for an economic expert to estimate worklife expectancy based on data collected years earlier. While this might be true for many types of economic variables, research has shown that labor force participation rates change slowly over time. In the three decades since the BLS tables were first created, worklife estimates have remained fairly stable for males and increased slightly for females.[23]

It is important to keep in mind that worklife tables apply averages derived from large populations. Whether such an average is appropriate depends on the unique characteristics of the plaintiff. If a particular person has displayed a tendency to be either above or below average with regard to a specific factor, it is reasonable to present an alternative scenario. Consider a person with a long history of consistent employment (that is, no periods of unemployment or absences from the workforce). For this individual, in addition to estimating worklife expectancy using statistical tables, an economic expert may also use an assumption of uninterrupted employment until some retirement age (for example, Social Security retirement age).

Discount Rate

All future economic damages must be reduced to present value, which requires the application of a discount rate. This is one of the most controversial issues in economic damages calculations, due in part to a lack of agreement among experts and in part to a lack of

[§§] A nationwide monthly survey of households conducted by the Bureau of the Census. A variety of data are collected, including whether individuals in the household are active or inactive in the workforce.

understanding among attorneys. As accounting students, you know that a higher discount rate means a lower present value. Moreover, you know that even a very small change in the discount rate can result in a large change in present value, especially for projections over long periods of time.

Risk-Free Rate

As discussed in Chapter 11, a discount rate can be considered a summation of several components, including the real cost of borrowing, inflation, term to maturity, and the risk of default. In business valuations, a key challenge is to determine the proper risk component—risk that expected future earnings will not be realized. In economic damages calculations, risk is not an issue, since the discount rate is supposed to represent a risk-free rate. Application of a risk-free rate allows the plaintiff to replicate the lost earnings stream by reinvesting the damages award in safe investments.[24]

Special Note

The requirement of a risk-free rate was introduced in *Jones & Laughlin Steel Co. v. Pfeifer*, a 1983 U.S. Supreme Court case. This is considered the foremost legal decision governing projections of economic damages at the federal level.[25]

Areas of Disagreement

In business valuations, the risk-free rate is almost a given, and all the disagreement surrounds the components that are added to the risk-free rate. In economic damages calculations, where the risk-free rate is the only component to consider, there is still much debate. What, you may be asking, is there to argue about? Why not use a long-term government bond yield, as we did in Chapter 11 for business valuations? The issue of a risk-free rate is a bit more complex in economic damages calculations, as highlighted by the following three primary areas of disagreement:[26]

- *Choice of the type of asset.* Although Treasury bonds are the most common proxy for a risk-free rate, high-quality municipal bonds are another alternative.
- *Choice of maturity.* U.S. government debt is issued in three maturities: short-term (called *bills*), intermediate-term (called *notes*), and long-term (called *bonds*). Because the projection periods for economic damages calculations are often long, it seems reasonable to use a long-term rate. However, one must keep in mind that long-term securities are not really "risk-free," as they contain an element of maturity risk. Bond prices move inversely with interest rates (that is, as rates increase, bond prices decrease), and long-term bonds experience greater price fluctuations than short-term bonds.
- *Choice of current rates, historical averages, or forecasts.* Interest rates are essentially market prices, and, like other financial market prices (for example, stock, commodity, and currency prices), they change frequently. Given this fluctuation, the application of an interest rate on any particular day to discount a long-term future benefit stream may not be appropriate. A reasonable alternative is to take an average of past rates. However, as discussed in Chapter 11, the past is not necessarily indicative of the future. Moreover, this raises the question of how long the look-back period should be.

Some economic experts take the position that the look-back period should exactly match the projection period. In other words, if the projection period is 23 years, the look-back period should also be 23 years. Other experts take a similar but less precise approach, choosing to generally match the duration of the two streams. Although the matching approach seems intuitive, there is no economic basis for the expectation that a historical average of a particular duration is a more accurate predictor of the future than any other.

As an alternative to using a current interest rate or a historical average, another approach is to use a forecasted interest rate. Various government agencies and independent organizations provide short- and long-term forecasts of several economic variables, including interest rates. Examples of these sources are identified in Table 12-6.

Table 12-6 Data Sources for Discount Rates

Current and historical interest rates • Federal Reserve Economic Data (FRED)—Federal Reserve Bank of St. Louis
Interest rate forecasts • OASDI Trustees Report • CBO Baseline Economic Forecast • Livingston Survey—Federal Reserve Bank of Philadelphia • The Economic Report of the President

Interest on Past Damages

In addition to discounting future losses to present value, the economic expert must also convert past losses to present value. As previously noted, present values are determined on the specified valuation date, with past losses occurring before this date and future losses occurring after this date. Unlike the discount rate, which is determined by the economic expert, the applicable interest rate for past damages is jurisdiction-specific. Thus, it is common for economic experts to simply exclude any past interest from their calculations, leaving this component to the court's determination. What remains then is not truly a present value calculation, but rather the present value of future damages and the nominal value of past damages.

CONCLUDING COMMENTS

The "science" of economic damages is rather old, as most of the research and publications occurred in the 1980s and 1990s. Although some level of consensus has been reached regarding the necessary elements of damages calculations (subject, of course, to the unique case facts and legal jurisdiction), there remains much honest disagreement about specific methodological issues. As with most facets of forensic accounting, uniformity of opinions among damages experts is not to be expected for three primary reasons:

- Economic damages calculations require the application of logic, which allows for multiple interpretations (there is more than one way to solve a problem).
- Damages are calculated for specific individuals or entities, with many unique attributes that may not be universally perceived or evaluated.
- A large component of economic damages is future damages, the calculation of which relies on projections of inherently uncertain future events.

Thus, it appears that economic damages calculations involve elements of both science and art. Forensic accountants gather as much factual information as possible, which they supplement with reasonable assumptions and valid statistical data. From this foundation, they make projections of the most likely course of future events had the subject injury not occurred. In sum, by "combining the best of scientific methods with the best logical interpretations,"[27] damages experts can develop and present opinions that meet the threshold of a reasonable degree of professional certainty.

12.3 Computer Forensics

INTRODUCTION

Just as forensic accounting is the application of accounting principles in a legal action, ***computer forensics*** is the application of computer technology in a legal action. Like forensic accounting, the goal of computer forensics is to gather and interpret evidence that can be presented in a court of law. A difference, however, is its more narrow focus. While forensic accounting may involve the consideration of many different forms and sources of evidence, computer forensics is focused on evidence contained in computer equipment and various related storage devices.

Given the growth of the Internet, the widespread adoption of personal computers, and the increasing complexity of technological environments, there is a need across many fields for professionals skilled in computer forensics. We live in a digital age, where many types of information are available in digital form (and sometimes only in digital form). Because such information may constitute evidence relevant to a forensic accounting engagement, forensic accountants must have at least a basic understanding of computer forensics. This need is becoming increasingly apparent to the professional community, as shown by a 2011 AICPA survey of forensic accounting practitioners.[28] Approximately 83% of the survey's respondents anticipated greater demand for computer forensic investigations in the next several years, and more than half reported intentions to hire more staff in this area.

Although a basic understanding will not prepare you to perform a computer investigation, it will allow you to recognize situations in which such expertise is needed and take preliminary actions (or precautions) to facilitate the investigation. Specifically, it will help you identify data that may exist in digital form and the types of information that can be produced by analyzing the data. In cases where a computer expert is needed, the forensic accountant may assist in selecting the expert and may need to rely on the expert's opinions in forming his or her own opinions. Although forensic accountants are not expected to evaluate a supporting expert's analysis, they should have sufficient knowledge of the subject matter to identify any gross errors or failures. Moreover, they must understand the meaning and applicability of the supporting expert's findings in relation to issues within the realm of forensic accounting expertise.

In Chapter 9, we discussed data analysis in the context of financial or other quantitative data, which can be analyzed with various mathematical procedures. Although we noted certain technical challenges, such as data extraction (from source databases) and conversion (to alternative file formats), our focus was the application of quantitative methods and tools. In this chapter, we broaden the scope of our attention to include other types of digital evidence that fall farther outside the realm of general accounting.

Applications to Forensic Accounting

Computer forensics is widely applicable to forensic accounting engagements, in both criminal and civil contexts. Digital evidence may be the primary focus of the engagement or only one of many different components of evidence.

Cybercrime

Perhaps the most obvious application of computer forensics is the investigation of cybercrime, which is a significant threat to almost all individuals and organizations. Although digital information is useful for many constructive purposes, it can also be used to facilitate illegal activity, including various forms of financial fraud and even terrorism. Computer technology plays a role in most fraudulent activity—as the tool of the crime, the target of the crime, or a potential source of evidence about the crime.

Although much cybercrime goes unreported, statistics of reported incidents reflect a widespread impact. In the United States, complaints of cybercrime against individuals are fielded by the Internet Crime Complaint Center[***] (IC3). In 2011, IC3 received 314,246 complaints with a total dollar loss of $485.3 million.[29] The most common victim complaints included FBI impersonation scams, identify theft, and advance fee fraud. For corporations, data breaches (theft of corporate information) are the primary area of concern. Sources of attack can be either external, ranging from individual hackers to organized criminal networks, or internal, perpetrated by company employees. A 2010 study of 454 U.S. organizations found that cybercrime costs individual organizations an average of $3.8 million per year, including both direct costs (information loss, business disruption, and property destruction) and indirect costs (internal mitigation activities, such as detection and investigation).[30] Key characteristics of corporate data breaches, based on a 2011 study, are highlighted in Table 12-7.

*** A partnership among the National White Collar Crime Center, the Bureau of Justice Assistance, and the FBI.

Table 12-7 | Characteristics of Corporate Data Breaches

Who is behind data breaches?	What commonalities exist?
• 98% stem from external agents • 4% implicate internal employees • 58% are tied to activist groups	• 79% of victims are targets of opportunity • 96% are not highly difficult to execute • 94% of all data compromised involved servers • 85% of breaches took several weeks or longer to discover • 92% of incidents were discovered by a third party • 97% of breaches were avoidable through simple or intermediate controls
How do breaches occur? • 81% use some form of hacking • 69% incorporate malware • 10% involve physical attacks • 7% employ social tactics • 5% result from privilege misuse	

Source: Compiled from Verizon 2012 Data Breach Investigations Report.

Other Engagements

In addition to illegal activity (criminal cases), computer investigations can also detect violations of government regulations and company policies (civil cases). Litigation engagements (such as bankruptcy, divorce, and economic damages) may also require the identification and evaluation of digital evidence. In these cases, various issues in dispute can be confirmed or discounted by such evidence. Examples include various types of files (such as documents, photographs, and spreadsheets) or features of those files (for example, when the files were created or modified and by whom). In sum, there is a growing demand for computer forensics experts among law enforcement, corporate management, audit teams, attorneys, and even individuals.

Although forensic accountants involved in these engagements may not play the role of the computer forensics expert, they must have an understanding of computer hardware and software systems and investigative and evidence-gathering protocols. The importance of this knowledge base is underscored by its inclusion in the bodies of the knowledge for the following credentials:

- AICPA's Certified in Financial Forensics (CFF)
- AICPA's Certified Information Technology Professional (CITP)
- ACFE's Certified Fraud Examiner (CFE)

Additional information regarding the application of computer forensics to forensic accounting can be obtained from publications and other resources provided by these organizations.

Speaking the Language

A basic understanding of computer forensics requires familiarity with the technical language used in the field. Although a comprehensive list is beyond the scope of our discussion, select key terms are identified in the following abbreviated list. These concepts may seem self-evident, but forensic accountants should be aware of their precise meanings within the context of computer investigations.

- A ***computer system*** is comprised of hardware and software that process data.[31] Specific hardware components of the system may include:
    - A case that contains circuit boards, microprocessors, a hard drive, memory, and interface connections
    - A monitor, keyboard, and mouse
    - Various peripheral (externally connected) drives and devices

Computer systems can take a variety of forms, such as laptops, desktops, tower computers, minicomputers, and mainframe computers.

- A ***computer network*** consists of two or more computers, connected by a data cable or a wireless connection, that share resources and data.[32]
- ***Electronically stored information*** (ESI) is information created, manipulated, and stored in electronic form. Examples include email messages, Internet browsing history, Internet chat logs and contact lists, photos, image files, document files, and databases. ESI differs from paper information in several ways:[33]
    - The volume of ESI is usually much greater than paper information. It is easy to see how communication records, such as emails and text messages, can quickly accumulate. Moreover, ESI can be stored in multiple locations, which enhances its volume by virtue of duplication. For example, a document or spreadsheet file can be stored in an employee's work computer, his or her home computer, and in the computers of any co-workers or other individuals with whom the file was shared, as well as on the organization's back-up tapes.
    - Unlike paper information, ESI can be easily altered or damaged. Implications of this fact for a computer investigation are discussed later in this section.
    - Some features of ESI have no counterpart in paper form. Specifically, electronic files contain both visible data and embedded data, known as metadata. ***Metadata***, often called "data about data," describe, explain, locate, or otherwise facilitate the retrieval, use, or management of an information resource.[34] Examples include information about a file's author, when it was created, when and by whom it was edited, and what edits were made.
    - Deleting ESI does not destroy it, as burning or shredding a paper document would. In many cases, a deleted file can be recovered if it has not been overwritten and may be found on the computers of other people or on back-up tapes.

Special Note

The existence of ESI creates challenges in the discovery phase of litigation. Such challenges of "e-discovery" include: (a) the scope of discovery, (b) the form in which ESI is produced, (c) the question of whether inadvertent production of ESI results in a waiver of attorney-client privilege or work product protection, (d) allocation of costs, and (e) the preservation of ESI and related spoilage considerations.[35] Amendments to the Federal Rules of Civil Procedure that specifically address the discovery of ESI became effective Dec. 1, 2006. With these amendments, ESI was identified as a distinct category of information subject to discovery alongside "documents" and "things."

Storage Devices

Before digital evidence can be obtained and analyzed, it must be located. In other words, the analyst must identify where it is stored. Digital evidence can be stored in a variety of storage devices (or media), which vary in capacity and in the manner in which they store information. Specific types of digital storage media and examples of each are identified in the following list:[36]

- ***Flash memory media***. Data are stored in memory chips that are modified electronically. The absence of moving parts or sensitive surfaces makes this type of media relatively less vulnerable to damage. Common examples include USB flash drives (also known as "thumb drives"), memory cards (often used in digital cameras), and external solid-state disk (SSD) drives.
- ***Writable optical media***. Data are recorded by a laser that alters light-sensitive dyes within the disk. Once data are written to a disk, it usually cannot be modified (with the exception of rewritable disks). Because the layers of the disk (the dye layer where data are recorded and the metallic layer that reflects laser light) can be easily damaged by exposure to light, humidity, or heat, this is a vulnerable type of digital media. Common examples include CDs, DVDs, and Blu-ray disks.

- ***Magnetic media***. Data are stored by altering the magnetic polarity of disks or tapes. The recording process requires rotation of the disk or tape (moving parts), which introduces the possibility of mechanical failure. Common forms include hard disk drives (internal and external) and tape cartridges (which are used almost exclusively for archival purposes).

These storage devices are housed in a number of locations, including computer workstations, personal digital devices (such as cell phones and tablets), and removable media (such as CDs, DVDs, external hard drives, thumb drives, and back-up tapes). Analysts must also be aware that individuals can store data in "the cloud"—that is, on devices maintained by others that can be accessed through the Internet. Examples include third-party storage hubs (such as Google Docs and Microsoft SkyDrive), email hosts (such as Gmail and Hotmail) and social networking sites (such as Facebook, Twitter, and YouTube).

COMPUTER FORENSICS IN CONTEXT

Armed with an understanding of the basic computer environment (the "what"), we now turn our attention to the "why" of computer forensics—the purpose or goal. According to the AICPA, its purpose is to determine what activity took place on a specific device by a specific user or to restore deleted, corrupted, or encrypted data.[37] User activity can include dates and times a computer was in use and what web sites were visited, as well as dates and times that actions were taken with specific files, such as creation or revision. Challenges of a computer forensics investigation include identifying where the relevant data are located, how they can be accessed, and how they can be converted to a format that can be processed by a data analysis tool.

Computer forensics differs from simple data recovery, which involves recovering lost information from a computer (for example, accidentally deleted or lost during a power surge or server crash).[38] In data recovery, you usually know what you're looking for. Computer forensics, in contrast, seeks to uncover data that have been intentionally hidden or deleted, with the goal of securing the data for use as evidence.

A Systematic Approach

As with all forensic accounting engagements, a computer forensics investigation should be systematic in nature. Given the fragile and dynamic nature of digital evidence, a structured approach is necessary to ensure the data are collected, preserved, and analyzed without damage or alteration. In this text, we have repeatedly emphasized that (given the unique aspects of each engagement) the work of a forensic accountant cannot be simplified into a series of checklists. Perhaps one exception to this general proposition is computer forensics, where protocols are quite common. Examples include protocols for evaluating and documenting a scene; collecting evidence; and packaging, transporting, and storing the evidence. Especially in law enforcement, where preliminary tasks are performed by officers without extensive training and expertise, such guidelines are essential.

Throughout the investigation process, there are numerous opportunities for the data to be compromised (either intentionally or unintentionally). To withstand challenges in this regard, it is important that the results of the investigation be reproducible—that is, able to be repeated and confirmed by others. This requires that the process be planned and executed in a logical manner, with comprehensive supporting documentation. Documentation is especially critical in relation to evidence custody practices. The ***chain of custody*** describes the route evidence takes from the time it is collected until the investigation is completed and identifies everyone that had access to it along the way.

Legal Parameters

Computer forensics investigations are subject to unique legal considerations.[39] To whom does the data belong? Does the forensic accountant or client have legal authority to collect the data? Such authority can be granted by a subpoena in civil cases or a search warrant in criminal cases. For corporate investigations, corporate policies must be considered (for example, policies concerning usage of company-owned equipment such as computers and cell phones). Privacy rights related to confidential personal information must also be observed, because improperly accessing data stored on electronic devices may constitute a violation of federal laws.[†††] Finally, the analyst must be aware of any expectation that data located on the target devices may require reporting to law enforcement authorities (for example, related to child pornography or national security threats).

Scope Parameters

In our discussion of preengagement considerations in Chapter 3, we highlighted the importance of defining the scope of the assignment. Given the volume of data involved, this is an especially critical consideration in computer investigations. First, the subject storage devices must be *specifically* identified. Broad parameters, such as any devices found in an organization's office, are insufficient. This gives the analyst no indication of the number, types, and storage capacities of the devices that may be involved—information that is necessary for proper planning and staging. Obviously, the number of devices is a primary factor in estimating the time necessary to complete the analysis. Even more important, however, is total storage capacity of the devices to be analyzed. The devices described in the preceding section range in capacity from megabytes (CDs) to terabytes (hard disk drives).[‡‡‡]

Special Note

Digital storage capacity is measured in bytes. Common storage units listed from smallest to largest include: kilobyte (KB), megabyte (MB), gigabyte (GB), and terabyte (TB). The prefixes in these terms represent powers of 1,000: 1 KB equals 1,000 bytes, 1MB equals 1,000 KB, 1 GB equals 1,000 MB, and 1 TB equals 1,000 GB. To help you put these measurements in perspective, consider the following examples:[40]

- Sizes of newer laptop hard drives are measured in hundreds of gigabytes; 100 GB of data is equivalent to 50,000 trees converted to printed pages.
- External hard drives can hold several TB of data. One TB of data is equivalent to an entire academic research library, and the print collection of the U.S. Library of Congress is estimated to total only 2 TB.

The type (make/model) of the subject storage devices must also be identified, because this may impact the selection of tools used to extract the data. Moreover, the analyst must have a clear definition of the investigation's target—what he or she is looking for. This may be specific occurrences, such as key words or names, or exceptions to some established pattern, such as unexpected user activity or file transfers. In either context, the investigation may be limited in scope to certain users, certain types of files, or specific time periods. Finally, the location of the subject devices must be determined. This is important because the devices may not be readily visible (perhaps stored out of sight) or may be portable (able to be removed from the premises). All of these issues impact the necessary resources (tools, time, and budget) for the engagement.

THE PROCESS OF A COMPUTER FORENSICS INVESTIGATION

In this section, we provide a brief overview of the computer forensics investigation process, including basic components and key considerations. This discussion does not contain the level of detail necessary to offer meaningful guidance for an actual investigation. Rather, our goal is convey the complexity of the process and identify various challenges and risks that are involved.

[†††] Including the Electronic Communications Privacy Act of 1986 and the Cable Communications Policy Act (both as amended by the USA Patriot Act of 2001) and the Privacy Protection Act of 1980.

Gathering Preliminary Information

Before attempting to collect and analyze ESI, the analyst should gather as much information as possible about the environment in which the target devices are located. The most direct means of gathering this information is through interviews. In an organizational environment, potential interview prospects include management, who can describe the key players and explain the general operating environment, and IT personnel, who can provide more detail about user access and specific systems and policies. Although residential settings are relatively less complex, interviews of household members may still provide useful information. In either situation, the goal is to determine how technology is being used and by whom.

It is important to distinguish interviews related specifically to a computer investigation from the more comprehensive interviews discussed earlier in the text (Chapter 4). With computer forensics, because the role of the analyst is limited, the information sought is limited. Employing the concepts you learned in Chapter 4, these interviews tend to be formal in nature, including mostly informational questions. Another difference is the number and order of witnesses. While forensic accountants often interview many people, beginning with neutral third parties and ending with the target, a computer analyst will focus on a smaller group (people who are expected to have specific information) that might not include the target.

Examples of interview questions that can be used by a computer analyst include:

- What devices did the target user have knowledge of and access to?
- What is the skill level of the target user?
- What is the security of the subject devices, including both physical security (for example, located in a locked facility or room) and data security (such as a password protection)?
- Is there a computer network? If so, is a map of the network available?
- What user accounts (log-ins and passwords) are on the device or system?
- Are any activity logs (physical or electronic) available?
- How were the devices used (for example, processing, storage, or communication)?
- How frequently were the devices used?
- Is there remote access to the devices?
- What operating systems, email systems, and software applications are used?
- Are any encryption tools used?
- Is there offsite storage (for example, back-up tapes at another location or Internet storage)?
- Who is the system administrator? Does anyone else have administrative privileges?
- What are the relevant corporate policies (such as confidentiality, privacy, IT security, and usage)?

Collecting and Storing Digital Evidence

Because digital evidence is easily altered or damaged, it must be collected, transported, and stored with extreme care. The goal is to ensure that, throughout the entirety of the investigation, the evidence is not changed. Key considerations include the following:

- Digital evidence is vulnerable to extreme temperatures, humidity, physical trauma, static electricity, and magnetic fields.
- Digital evidence can be time sensitive, because some data are intended for only temporary storage and may be overwritten on a regular basis.
- Digital evidence may be lost if the device loses power.
- Data on some devices, such as mobile phones, can be overwritten or deleted even after the device is seized, if it remains in the range of a communication signal. Specifically, software exists for mobile phones that can be remotely activated to render

the phone unusable if it is lost or stolen. For this reason, all such devices should be transported and stored in signal-blocking material, such as aluminum foil or a faraday isolation bag.

- After collection, digital evidence should be inventoried and stored in a secure and climate-controlled environment. Any subsequent access to the evidence should be documented with a chain of custody form.

Special Note

The National Institute of Justice (NIJ), the research, development, and evaluation agency of the U.S. Department of Justice, has created a flow chart for collecting digital evidence. It appears in a special report titled *Electronic Crime Scene Investigation: A Guide for First Responders* (2nd Ed., April 2008), which is available in print form and at NIJ's web site (www.nij.gov/nij/publications/).

Analyzing Digital Evidence

In a computer forensics context, *analysis* means interpreting recovered data and compiling the data in a logical and useful format.[41] Before data can be analyzed, they must be extracted or recovered from the source media. Depending on the circumstances of the engagement, this can be accomplished through either static forensics or live forensics.[42] As the name implies, ***static forensics*** is the analysis of static data. This involves creating a copy of all the data stored on the subject device and analyzing the copy in a secure environment. In contrast, with ***live forensics***, extraction processes are performed against live (or dynamic) data rather than a copy. This may be necessary if, for example, a server is critical to an organization's operating environment and thus cannot be shut down.

Another important categorization is the types of data than can be analyzed, including active data, archival data, and latent data.[43]

- ***Active data*** can be seen, such as data files, program files, and files used by the operating system.
- ***Archival data*** have been backed up and stored, such as back-up tapes or entire hard drives.
- ***Latent data*** have been deleted or partially overwritten.

Although the importance of the different types of data depends on the specific purpose of the engagement, latent data is often a primary focus, especially when deception or other wrongdoing is suspected. Because latent data are not intended to be viewed, their recovery requires expertise and specialized tools.

As noted previously, it is common for a computer analyst to conduct his or her analysis on a forensic copy of the data. A forensic copy is a ***bit-stream copy***, which is a bit-by-bit copy of the original drive, or an exact duplicate.[§§§] This is different from a simple back-up copy, because all the data (every single bit) is copied. Back-up software can only copy or compress files that are stored in a folder or are of a known file type, not deleted files or file fragments.[44] A bit-stream copy can be created with forensic imaging software or a hardware forensic disk copier.

After a forensic copy has been created, the analyst begins the most time-consuming task of the investigation—the actual application of analytical tools and methods. As noted previously, analysis involves interpreting and making use of the data. The relevant questions, then, are what types of analysis can be applied and what useful information do they produce? Three common types of analysis are timeframe analysis, hidden data analysis, and file analysis.[45]

- ***Time frame analysis*** is useful for determining when specific events occurred on a computer system. This may include reviewing the time and date stamps contained in the metadata (for example, date created, last modified, or last accessed) to link certain

[§§§] A bit (a contraction of the term "binary digit") is the basic unit of information in computing. It is a binary variable that can take two values: either 1 or 0. A byte consists of eight bits.

files to the relevant time frame of the investigation. Another example is the review of system and application logs, such as error logs, installation logs, and security logs.

- The purpose of ***hidden data analysis*** is to detect and recover data that have been concealed on a computer system. For example, file names can be evaluated against their file extensions to identify any inconsistencies that may indicate intentional deception, such as labeling a spreadsheet file as a photo. This type of analysis also includes the recovery of deleted, password-protected, or encrypted files.

Special Note

Deleted files remain on a storage device until a new file is saved to the same physical location, overwriting the original file. In the meantime, those files can still be retrieved using ***data carving*** techniques. The larger the storage capacity of the device, the higher the likelihood that deleted files can be retrieved.[46] The disk space will be considered "available," but it could be a long time (possibly even years) before the space is overwritten.

- ***File analysis*** may offer insight into the capability of the system and the knowledge of the user. Examples include the following:
    - Key word searches or graphic searches
    - Reviewing file names for patterns
    - Examining file content
    - Correlating the files to the installed applications
    - Evaluating the file structure to determine if files have been stored in their default or alternate locations
    - Examining user-configuration settings

TRENDS IN COMPUTER FORENSICS

We end this section by highlighting current trends in computer forensics that are impacting the work of forensic accountants. The previously cited 2011 survey of forensic accounting practitioners identified the following issues as the greatest technology-related threats to organizations in coming years:[47]

- *Use of mobile phone devices.* Today's smartphones are essentially miniature computers that contain a wealth of personal information (such as passwords, financial information, contacts, and email or text messages). Although a few applications (or "apps") attempt to protect this sensitive data, none are comparable to the antivirus software available for computers.
- *Malicious insiders.* Threats from insiders increase in a deteriorating economy, due to financial pressures that contribute to the motivation element of the fraud triangle. Such threats may include the theft of intellectual property, such as trade secrets, proprietary product designs, and marketing plans, or fraudulent transactions, such as payments to fake vendors or employees.
- *Remote access.* As the workforce becomes more mobile, employees are increasingly requiring access to systems at any time and from any location. New technology has enabled remote access capabilities, but security features have not kept pace, leaving organizations vulnerable to unauthorized access to key systems and data.
- *Social networking.* Social networking sites, including Facebook, YouTube, Twitter, and Instagram, have become valuable sources of evidence. Their content might be useful for a variety of purposes, such as conducting a background investigation, impeaching a witness, establishing relationships among individuals, and confirming dates and locations of activities.
- *Malware.* The development and dissemination of malware has become a significant challenge for computer analysts. Malware can be used to eavesdrop on communications, extract credit card information from transaction systems, and cause damage to targeted systems (such as web site crashes and data wiping).

A FINAL CAUTION

As provided by Rule 201 of the AICPA's General Standards, acceptance of an assignment "implies" that the forensic accountant has or can obtain the necessary competence to complete the assignment. Competence, as previously discussed, involves the technical subject matter and the aptitude to exercise sound, professional judgment. We submit that, although a basic understanding of computer forensics (as presented herein) should be a component of the forensic accountant's knowledge base, it does not constitute the level of competence necessary to independently conduct a computer investigation. Thus, we caution that digital evidence should be collected and analyzed only by professionals trained specifically for this purpose. Because many forensic accountants do not have this specialized training, it may be necessary to outsource the computer forensics component of an engagement. Of course, such an arrangement requires clear delineation of each expert's role and responsibilities.

12.4 Reporting Results

INTRODUCTION

The final stage of a forensic accounting engagement is the communication of results and opinions in a report. This is perhaps the most critical element of the engagement process, representing the culmination of all preceding efforts. Although the form and content of any report is determined by the nature, scope, purpose, and terms of the specific engagement, practitioners must adhere to applicable judicial mandates (Rule 26[****]) and professional guidelines (such as AICPA, NACVA, and ACFE). In this section, we introduce these mandates and guidelines, highlighting key elements that reflect the rigor of the reporting task.

Special Note

It is understood that not all forensic accountants are CPAs or even members of the AICPA. Moreover, forensic accountants are often members of more than one professional association. Although practitioners must comply with the standards of all professional associations to which they belong, the AICPA is considered the leading practice authority, and its guidelines are commonly embraced as practice benchmarks. Thus, the AICPA guidelines are emphasized in this chapter.

To illustrate the potentially severe consequences of a forensic accountant's failure to meet applicable reporting requirements, let's consider the matter of *Walter International Products, Inc., et al. v. Walter Mercado-Salinas, et al.*[††††]

The Complaint

This case involves a contract dispute between the parties over rights to market and exploit the name, image, persona, and work product of television psychic Walter Mercado-Salinas. The parties amicably did business together under the contract for about eleven years. The plaintiffs ("Bart Group") alleged that the defendants ("Mercado") breached the contract in November 2006 by not attending scheduled appearances, failing to provide required materials (such as accounting reports), and improperly attempting to terminate the contract. Mercado countered that, because the Bart Group failed to remit payments pursuant to the terms of the contract, he terminated it "with cause" in a letter dated Nov. 22, 2006.[‡‡‡‡]

**** As discussed in Chapter 2, the Federal Rules of Civil Procedure (FRCP) govern civil procedure in the federal courts. Although states may determine their own rules, most have adopted rules based on the FRCP.

†††† U.S. Court of Appeals, 11th Circuit, Civil Action No. 09-15971, 2011. Opinion available via a link at www.pearsonhighered.com/rufus.

‡‡‡‡ *With cause* in this instance means breach of obligations under the contract.

The Forensic Accounting Expert

To support its claim for damages (Sec 12.2), the Bart Group engaged Leonard M. Cusano, CPA. The purpose of Cusano's assignment was to calculate the present value of the damages suffered by the Bart Group as a result of Mercado's actions. On the deadline for expert witness reports (Nov. 20, 2008), the Bart Group faxed a letter to Mercado identifying Cusano's engagement as follows:

- Provide a net present value calculation of future damages as of the date of trial.
- Provide a calculation of prejudgment interest on the monetary stream of claimed past damages.
- Offer rebuttal testimony in response to any opinions of opposing experts regarding damage calculations.

Attachments to the facsimile included "formulas" used by Cusano, his engagement letter, and an unsigned chart titled "Damages Summary," denoting total damages of $14,727,177. There was no explanation for how the total was calculated (the methodology), no disclosure of the underlying facts and assumptions considered, and no disclosure of Cusano's qualifications.

Motion to Strike the Expert's Testimony

On Dec. 5, 2008, the district court conducted a hearing on Mercado's motion to strike Cusano's testimony. During the hearing, Mercado argued that Cusano (specifically, the materials faxed on Nov. 20, 2008) failed to comply with the reporting mandates of Rule 26(a). In an order issued on Dec. 10, 2008, the court granted Mercado's motion. Moreover, the court rejected the Bart Group's motion to use Cusano as a rebuttal witness. The Bart Group was then limited to the factual testimony of its bookkeeper and the company's president regarding the Mercado contract, historical data, and damage claims.

Trial and Jury Verdict

The case was tried in January 2009 in two phases. In Phase I, which lasted eight days, the jury considered the breach of contract arguments and found in favor of the Bart Group. In Phase II, which lasted two days, the jury considered the matter of damages and found that the Bart Group had not been damaged by the actions of Mercado. Thus, no damages were awarded, and the court entered a final judgment on Feb. 4, 2009.

The Appeal

The Bart Group filed an appeal, requesting a new trial on the matter of damages. Specifically, the Bart Group argued that the district court abused its discretion by striking the testimony of the forensic accountant.[§§§§] On Aug. 23, 2011, the appeals court affirmed the district court's decision, finding no abuse of discretion. Moreover, the appeals court embraced the denial of the forensic accountant's testimony due to failure of the Bart Group (and the expert) to comply with the disclosures required under Rule 26(a). The appeals court did not find this failure to be justified or harmless, factors that must be demonstrated to preclude exclusion of the evidence.

JUDICIAL MANDATE—RULE 26

Rule 26 of the Federal Rules of Civil Procedure (introduced in Chapter 2) governs the disclosure of expert testimony. Specifically, Rule 26(a)(2)(B) states that "except as otherwise stipulated or directed by the court, this disclosure shall . . . be accompanied by a written report prepared and signed by the witness." Moreover, the report *must* contain the following components:

- A complete statement of all opinions to be expressed and the basis and reason for them
- The facts and data considered by the witness in forming the opinions
- Any exhibits to be used as a summary of, or support for, the opinions

[§§§§] In addition to the forensic accountant, five other proposed experts were not allowed to testify due to failure to comply with Rule 26.

- The qualifications of the witness (for example, his or her CV)
- A list of all publications authored by the witness within the proceeding ten years
- The compensation to be paid for the study and testimony
- A list of all cases in which the witness has testified as an expert at trial or by deposition within the preceding four years

As illustrated in the case example, failure to comply with the mandates of Rule 26 exposes an expert witness to challenge and possible exclusion.

Rule 26 limits discovery to "nonprivileged" information, which includes expert testimony. However, in December 2010, Rule 26 was amended to impose new limits on expert discovery. A notable provision is the protection from discovery of an expert's draft report and related disclosures. Before the amendment, such materials were considered discoverable. They now fall under work product protection, with the following three exceptions:

- Communications regarding the expert's compensation
- Communications regarding the facts and data to be relied on by the expert in forming his or her opinions
- Communications regarding the assumptions to be relied on by the expert in forming his or her opinions

Although draft reports and related disclosures are clearly protected as attorney work product, there remains uncertainty regarding disclosures of other attorney-expert communications. Because the courts can broadly view the exceptions previously noted, both attorneys and experts should always be mindful of the potential for disclosure, especially when communicating in writing (including email correspondence).

Think About It

Before the 2010 amendment to Rule 26, it was common practice for experts to avoid draft reports and other written communications with engaging attorneys. A popular strategy was to begin the engagement with the expert acting as a consultant, thereby allowing a free discussion of ideas and theories, and later change the expert's status to that of a testifying expert. What concerns or issues do you think may have prompted the amendments to Rule 26? What is the practical impact, if any, on the work of a forensic accountant?

PROFESSIONAL GUIDELINES

As a rule, forensic accounting reports prepared in the course of litigation[*****] are exempt from professional report writing standards, such as those promulgated by AICPA and NACVA for business valuations. The rationale for this is twofold. First and foremost, published judicial or governmental authority (such as Rule 26 or Rev. Rul. 59–60) must take priority over professional guidelines. Second, this allows experts to exercise discretion in how they present their opinions, which are subject to cross-examination by the opposing party.

Special Note

No specific report writing standards have been established by the AICPA for submissions within the context of litigation, aside from the standards contained in *Statement on Standards for Consulting Services No. 1* (discussed in Chapter 10) for written communications with clients.

Even outside litigation, there are no established reporting standards for forensic accounting engagements, other than those applicable to business valuations (discussed in Chapter 11). Such a generic set of standards would be difficult to create, given the unique attributes of

***** Includes all matters before a court, arbitration panel, mediation, or a matter in a governmental or administrative proceeding.

the different types of engagements. As would be expected, the form of a fraud investigation report is different from a business valuation report or an economic damages report. Even so, most reports share some common elements and fall within a few basic categories.

Chapter 11 identified three types of business valuation reports: summary, detailed, and calculation.[†††††] We apply this same terminology to describe reports more generally (that is, reports other than business valuations), along with the addition of a new category—the oral report. Thus, we propose that a forensic accounting report can be either written or oral and, within these categories, either a summary, detailed, or calculation report.

Oral Report

Forensic accountants are often asked to relay their findings via an ***oral report***. As the name implies, an oral report is verbal in form with no written documentation. While this may be desirable from the engaging attorney's perspective (given the discovery issues previously noted), it creates several potential pitfalls for the forensic accountant. For example, the information relayed in the oral report may be misunderstood by the recipient and later misrepresented to others, either intentionally or unintentionally. Without documentation, there is no way to confirm the essence of the communication—what was (or was not) actually said.

Think About It

When an oral report is requested, it is important to consider possible reasons why, such as cost, secrecy, confidentiality, or competitive advantage. An understanding of the client's motivation is necessary to manage expectations without putting yourself at risk. How might an oral report put a forensic accountant at risk?

To avoid such challenges, we recommend that forensic accountants prepare a written prereport outline, followed by a memo-to-file[‡‡‡‡‡] documenting the substance of the oral report. The prereport outline should contain all necessary information about the engagement, including the scope, assumptions, limitations, and results. Moreover, there must be consistency between the memo-to-file and the prereport outline, as both are subject to discovery. In addition to this specific guidance, we offer the following general cautions and recommendations for oral reports:

- The presenter must understand that speech differs from writing in both function and style.
- The length of an oral report is generally short (15–30 min.).
- The focus of an oral report is usually the results (findings), which are presented concurrently with analysis and discussion.
- The presenter is responsible for selecting the necessary information to be communicated and ensuring that it is relayed successfully.

Practitioner's Perspective

Engaging attorneys will often ask forensic accountants to provide "preliminary numbers" or a "rough estimate" in oral form. Our experience suggests that compliance with such a request creates the potential for at least two pitfalls. First, false expectations may be created, as the attorney will likely embrace the estimate (especially if it is favorable to his or her position) and resist later revisions. Another more damaging possibility is that the attorney may represent the communication as an oral report without the forensic accountant's knowledge. If this occurs, the forensic accountant is put in the precarious position of trying to support an opinion that he or she never intended to give. To prevent this situation, we recommended that preliminary estimates be avoided when possible, and offered only in writing with explicit labeling as a "draft."

[†††††] As identified in the AICPA's SSVS No. 1 and consistent with NACVA's reporting standards.

[‡‡‡‡‡] A memo that is written for documentation purposes and retained in the file.

Written Report

Written reports are more consistent with the common perception of what a "report" should be. Although documentation avoids many of the pitfalls previously noted for oral reports, written reports introduce their own challenges. Most notably, any representation that is put in writing can be reviewed, parsed, and analyzed in any number of ways to challenge the credibility of its source. Thus, the threshold for quality and accuracy is much higher.

Although written reports share the same basic form, they differ in other aspects of structure, such as content, organization, and level of detail. In the following sections, we describe three types of written reports—summary, detailed, and calculation.

Summary Report

A summary report is a brief narrative used to communicate the main points at issue, which create an adequate context for presenting results of the engagement. The decision to issue a summary report (vs. a detailed report, discussed in the following section) depends on the level of reporting detail agreed to by the forensic accountant and the client. Oftentimes, this agreement is based on time and cost limitations imposed by the unique circumstances of the engagement.

As noted in the introduction to this section, all reports will have engagement-specific elements. That said, some basic parameters comprise a minimum threshold. Specifically, a summary report should be addressed to the engaging party and contain *at least* the following information:

- Purpose of the assignment
- Intended use of the report
- Scope limitations
- Report limitations
- Facts, data, and assumptions relied upon
- Sources of information
- Methodology employed
- Summary opinions
- Signature of forensic accountant
- Exhibits

The challenge of a summary report is to satisfy the information requirements of the reader, providing just enough information—not too much or too little. More importantly, the forensic accountant's objective is to provide a credible and legally sufficient communication. This requires adherence to judicial mandates (such as Rule 26 and FRE 702) and professional guidance (such as the AICPA's SSVS No. 1 and SSCS No. 1).

Detailed Report

As the name implies, a detailed report communicates the same meaning as a summary report, but in greater detail. It is structured to provide a comprehensive discussion of the assignment, allowing the reader to develop a greater understanding of the data, reasoning, and analyses leading to the opinions (conclusions) stated. In addition to the items noted for a summary report, we suggest that a detailed report contain (at a minimum) the following information:

- Letter of transmittal
- Table of contents
- Methodologies considered but not used
- Explanation of application of methodology
- Qualifications of the expert

Calculation Report

The work product of a calculation engagement is a calculation report. As discussed in Chapter 11 with regard to business valuations, a calculation engagement is limited in scope to a specific methodology determined by agreement with the client. A calculation report presents a calculated value (or range of values), given certain facts and assumptions. Although calculation reports are most common in business valuation and economic damages engagements, they can be used in any type of engagement where the scope of analysis is limited.

The content of a calculation report is similar to that of a summary report, with the addition of necessary disclosures regarding the scope limitations that define the engagement. For example, the engagement should be explicitly identified as a *calculation engagement* and the result as a *calculated value*. For business valuations, other specific language is mandated by the professional reporting standards (AICPA's SSVS No. 1 and NACVA's reporting standards). Thus, while a calculation engagement is simplified in some respects, care must be exercised in properly drafting the report to qualify the scope.

TIPS FOR EFFECTIVE REPORTS

Effective report writing is a skill that is developed over time with experience, training, and education. No book or course could possibly cover everything you need to know to prepare a quality report. However, we can offer the following "top ten" tips, assembled from our experience as practitioners, that will help you recognize strengths and weaknesses in your own writing and that of others.

1. Be clear.
2. Be concise but comprehensive.
3. Focus on the purpose (why you are writing).
4. Be mindful of your audience.
5. Use correct grammar.
6. Maintain a professional tone.
7. Avoid redundant statements.
8. Proof, proof, and proof again.
9. Expect your report, and every word contained therein, to be closely examined and challenged.
10. Read others' work.

In conclusion, we must direct our discussion of reporting results back to its primary purpose. As highlighted throughout this text, the responsibility of a testifying expert is to render an opinion that will assist the trier of fact (judge or jury) in understanding the evidence. To that end, an expert's opinion (written and oral) must be stated in a legally sufficient manner and must be based on reliable facts, data, and methodology.

APPENDIX 12-A

*U.S. v. Abdul Karim Khanu**

The Indictment

On April 1, 2009, a federal grand jury returned a 22-count indictment against Abdul K. Khanu (age 41), a nightclub operator in Washington, D.C. The charges included one count of conspiracy, three counts of tax evasion, four counts of filing false corporate income tax returns, and 14 counts of filing false employment tax returns. The indictment alleged that, from 1999 through December 2003, Khanu and three unindicted co-conspirators, all co-owners of a corporation called TAF, Inc. ("TAF"), unlawfully, voluntarily, intentionally, and knowingly conspired and agreed together to defraud the United States for the purpose of impeding, impairing, obstructing, and defeating the lawful government functions of the IRS in the ascertainment, computation, assessment, and collection of income and employment taxes.

---

* United States of America, Appellee, v. Abdul Karim Khanu, Appellant. No. 10-3039, United States Court of Appeals for the District of Columbia Circuit. Argued Apr. 4, 2011 to Oct. 7, 2011. This narrative is paraphrased from the trial transcripts, which can be accessed via a link at www.pearsonhighered.com/rufus.

The alleged object of the conspiracy was to skim cash from TAF's gross receipts so the conspirators could pay wages to the corporation's employees in cash, thereby evading the payment of both employment and income taxes. It was also alleged that this cash skimming enabled TAF's owners (including Khanu) to conceal their true income and evade the payment of income taxes. Methods allegedly employed in the conspiracy included payment of wages in cash, failing to report cash wages paid, filing of false employment tax returns (Form 941), filing of false corporate income tax returns (Form 1120), and filing of false individual income tax returns (Form 1040). Alleged overt acts included diverting cash receipts, creating false corporate books and records, false entries, presenting false books and records to the tax preparer, signing and filing false employment and income tax returns, and using cash extensively for personal expenditures.

Special Note

Recall from Chapter 2 that an *indictment* is the formal manner of charging a person (or company) with a crime in order to bring that person to trial. It puts the person on notice and identifies what the charges (alleged offenses) are. An indictment is not evidence or proof of wrongdoing but is simply an allegation. As you consider this case, keep in mind that Khanu is presumed to be innocent. The presumption of innocence remains with Khanu throughout the trial, unless and until he is proven guilty beyond a reasonable doubt. The burden is on the government to prove Khanu's guilt, and this burden never shifts throughout the trial. Finally, it is important to remember that the law does not require Khanu to prove his innocence, produce evidence, or testify.

The Trial[†]

Following is a summary of the trial proceedings from opening to closing arguments, including paraphrased excerpts of actual trial testimony.

Opening Statement by Michael Vasiliadis, U.S. Department of Justice

This is a case about cash . . . where it came from, where it went, and where it didn't go. In this case, you'll hear about how the defendant, Abdul Khanu, owned and operated two successful nightclubs . . . which took in lots of cash. Some of the cash was accounted for the right way—it was deposited and properly reported on the business tax returns, the way the business accountant had advised. But a lot of the cash, several million dollars, was not reported. Mr. Khanu skimmed off part of the cash to pay employees under the table, off the books. He also took some of the money for himself, again off the books.

In this case, you'll hear evidence about three ways Mr. Khanu cheated on taxes. First, he tried to get out of paying taxes for himself personally. Second, he was responsible for false business tax returns filed by the nightclubs, because those returns did not include the cash he took and did not include the cash he paid to employees. And, third, this case is about how Mr. Khanu agreed with others to cheat the IRS by paying employees under the table.

The evidence in this case will show that, from 1999 through 2003, Mr. Khanu skimmed millions of dollars of cash from the nightclubs to pay employees, himself, and others. The cash skimmed was not reported—not by the nightclubs, not by Mr. Khanu, and not by the employee recipients. This case is framed by two dates: April 12, 1999 and October 28, 2003. On April 12, 1999, Mr. Khanu presented a personal financial statement for the purposes of leasing property for one of the nightclubs. This document, signed by Mr. Khanu, reports that he had $700,000 cash-on-hand and in bank accounts on April 12, 1999. Now, fast forward roughly five years to October 28, 2003. On that day, Mr. Khanu was caught, in the course of a search warrant, with $1.9 million cash at his home. These dates and respective cash balances are critical pieces of evidence. Where did the increase in cash ($1.2 million) come from? Mr. Khanu's lifestyle and expenditures will be fully explained by IRS Agent Fred Lewis.

[†] This narrative is paraphrased from the trial transcripts, which can be accessed via a link at www.pearsonhighered.com/rufus.

Mr. Lewis will testify how he examined the financial records in this case, including Mr. Khanu's personal and business bank accounts. Agent Lewis will talk about the records that show all of Mr. Khanu's sources of cash, and he'll talk about the records that show how Mr. Khanu used millions of dollars more in cash, far more than those sources. The evidence will show that the cash was income to Mr. Khanu, that it came from the nightclubs, and that he did not pay taxes on that income. Finally, Agent Lewis will explain how Mr. Khanu cheated on his personal taxes as a result of that skimmed cash by not paying hundreds of thousands of dollars in taxes owed.

The evidence will show, beyond a reasonable doubt, that Mr. Khanu agreed with others to cheat on taxes, that he attempted to cheat on his own personal taxes, and that he was responsible for false business returns filed by the nightclubs. The evidence in this case will show where the cash came from (the nightclubs), where the cash went (to Mr. Khanu), and where it did not (on his tax returns).

Opening Statement by Mr. Martin on Behalf of Mr. Khanu

We are here because the IRS and the government have alleged that Mr. Khanu committed a crime. They have alleged that he was in charge of two nightclubs over a five-year period and during this time knowingly and intentionally, two very important concepts in this case, skimmed millions of dollars in cash to evade employment and income taxes. But there are two sides to this story. You've heard the government's side. We completely disagree. And unless they can prove Mr. Khanu guilty, beyond a reasonable doubt, he is innocent.

Contrary to the government's side of the story, we submit there was no skimmed cash. Skimming involves removing cash receipts without recording it—off the books. We've never denied that the nightclubs generated millions of dollars in cash receipts—it was a thriving cash business. Where did the cash go? Much of it was deposited into corporate bank accounts and thus reported. Some of the cash, specifically the $1.9 million that was seized by the IRS in October of 2003, was corporate cash-on-hand pending deposit. The balance of the cash was paid to promoters, who in turn paid their expenses, including cash to contract laborers. Please listen to the evidence about the promoters. Listen to the evidence about the business model used by Mr. Khanu involving the use of promoters.

You will hear testimony regarding the clubs' business activities immediately preceding the search and seizure of October 23, 2003, particularly the Howard University Homecoming. The nightclub, through a special permit, hosted one of the biggest 5-day block parties in D.C. history. Depending on the night and time of night, the cover charge ranged from $10 to $100. Once admitted, you were serviced by an array of inside and/or outside alcohol stations. The records confirm that, on Saturday night alone, the nightclubs reported close to a million dollars in revenue. Although this information has been shared with the government, they refuse to accept that during the festival the business earned close to $1.9 million. Why? Because it provides an explanation that doesn't fit their theory of the case.

And where did the money go? You will hear testimony confirming the clubs' policy regarding daily cash proceeds, specifically that they are bagged and taken to Mr. Khanu's home pending deposit. No cash is left on premises. Is this a crime? No, this is simply good business practice. Was it reported as income? Yes, every penny! Interestingly, the government forgot to mention that, after seizing the $1.9 million from Mr. Khanu's home, it was applied to the nightclubs' tax accounts, and they were subsequently issued refund checks.

You will also hear testimony regarding Mr. Khanu's 1999 personal financial statement and the $700,000 cash-on-hand. This is a critical component of the government's case and the starting point for the IRS's calculation. The IRS attempts to use the cash method of proof to determine Mr. Khanu's unreported income. This method, simply stated, compares how much money Mr. Khanu had available with how much he spent. In other words, you can't spend or save what you don't have. Thus, the IRS must establish with certainty Mr. Khanu's beginning cash balance. We submit that this is a major failure in the government's case. Importantly, Mr. Khanu's 1999 financial statement was not an audited financial statement certified by a CPA or submitted under oath. This was a quickly prepared statement presented at the request of a landlord to determine a security deposit. What if the real cash-on-hand balance was $1.2 million? Or $1 million? The government refuses to consider the evidence. Why? It destroys their case.

A trial is a search for the truth. And the truth in this case is that there may be a civil dispute between the government and Mr. Khanu about his income, his personal tax returns, and the status of some of the workers at the nightclubs. The truth in this case is that the government is attached to a flawed criminal theory and refuses to consider any evidence that doesn't support it. There are two sides to this story. We submit that the government's side of the story, their evidence, is not sufficient to find, beyond a reasonable doubt, that Mr. Khanu conspired with anyone to cheat the IRS, attempted to file fraudulent tax returns, or caused fraudulent tax returns to be filed. Abdul Khanu is not guilty. The evidence in this case will not support the government's allegations. If there is a dispute on these taxes, send it to tax court.

Government's Case-in-Chief

The government presented its case-in-chief over the course of six days, the events of which are described in the following sections.

Days 3–4

The presentation of evidence to the jury began on day three of the trial. The government's first four witnesses were IRS investigators (Special Agents), who explained the events of October 28, 2003, specifically the seizure of $1.9 million from Mr. Khanu's residence. The next five witnesses were former employees who testified about the level and cash nature of Mr. Khanu's business activities (a lot of cash). They also testified that they were paid in cash and never received a W-2 or 1099 evidencing the monies earned.

Days 5–6

On day five of the trial, the government's witnesses included three bank representatives, who verified the records presented to the IRS and testified about their communications with Mr. Khanu. On day six, the government's first witness was a representative of Intuit, who testified about a contract with Mr. Khanu's company to prepare payroll and discussions regarding employees receiving cash, specifically tips. The government closed the day with testimony from three IRS investigators, who testified about records seized.

Day 7

On day seven, the government's first witness was Khanu's former bookkeeper, who testified about the company's accounting system and reporting process, specifically the "cash deposit process." She also testified about Mr. Khanu's control over the process, specifically his control of cash receipts. The government's next witness was Mr. Khanu's business and personal CPA (Craig White), who testified about the nature of services provided to Mr. Khanu. He also testified that he met with Mr. Khanu on a quarterly basis to review the financial condition of the nightclubs and on an annual basis to review the company's corporate income tax returns.

On cross-examination, Mr. White testified that the $1.9 million was reported as income on the company's income tax returns and that the seized funds were claimed as tax payments, resulting in substantial refunds. He further testified that door revenue collected belonged to the promoter/s and should not have been reported by the company. He also testified that the company was not responsible for employment taxes regarding individuals employed by the promoters (for example, security). Moreover, he testified that he had advised Mr. Khanu that the door revenue wasn't income to the company and should not have been reported. Finally, Mr. White testified that Mr. Khanu had reasonably relied on him regarding the employment and income tax issues.

Day 8

Day eight of the trial was filled with the testimony of the government's summary witness, IRS Revenue Agent Fred Lewis. Mr. Lewis, a 28-year IRS veteran working with the Special Enforcement Group, explained his assignment in the Khanu case, specifically to examine Mr. Khanu's personal income taxes for years 2001 through 2003. Mr. Lewis testified that, given the cash involved and the questionable condition of Mr. Khanu's business records, he employed an indirect method of analysis—the cash method of proof. Mr. Lewis testified that, with the cash method of proof, the focus is on cash. Thus, you must consider all sources of cash, as well as cash expenditures—just cash, no checks. Mr. Lewis testified that spending more cash than you should have is an indication of unreported income.

Excerpts of Mr. Lewis's examination (direct and cross) are presented below.‡

Direct Examination

Mr. Vasiliadis: Agent Lewis, please describe your education, occupation, and work history.

Mr. Lewis: I'm an IRS Revenue Agent currently assigned to the Special Enforcement Group. Special Enforcement's primary focus is the development of fraud cases. I've been employed with the IRS for over 28 years and have held various positions, including field agent, management, and quality review staff. I have a B.S. in Accounting and an M.S. in Tax Law. I've also received extensive IRS training over the last 28 years in tax law, evidence gathering, investigative techniques, and work as an expert witness.

Mr. Vasiliadis: What was your assignment in this case?

Mr. Lewis: To conduct an examination of Mr. Khanu's income tax returns for years 2001 through 2003 and to compute the amount of any tax due and owing.

Mr. Vasiliadis: What information did you consider?

Mr. Lewis: Everything available—Mr. Khanu's personal income tax returns; his personal bank records, including deposits and cancelled checks; his corporate books and records, including tax returns and bank records; and interviews conducted of various witnesses.

Mr. Vasiliadis: Explain to the jury the methodology you employed, why you employed it, and how it works.

Mr. Lewis: Given the facts and circumstances of the case, specifically the cash nature of Mr. Khanu's business activities, I decided the most appropriate method to determine Mr. Khanu's taxable income was the cash method of proof.

The cash method of proof is a means of determining undeclared income by focusing exclusively on expenditures made in cash. In this case, I considered the extent to which Mr. Khanu's cash expenditures exceeded his known cash sources. I determined that Mr. Khanu used more cash than he could account for (non-taxable and declared cash sources). I classified the excess—unexplained cash—as taxable unreported income.

Mr. Vasiliadis: Is the cash method of proof commonly used and recognized by the IRS in conducting investigations?

Mr. Lewis: Yes. It's most commonly used when a taxpayer's unreported income comes entirely in the form of cash. The cash method is most appropriate in investigations involving drug dealing or cash skimming from businesses.

Mr. Vasiliadis: Agent Lewis, to ensure the jury understands, can you provide an illustration?

Mr. Lewis: Gladly. Let's say your beginning cash balance is $100, and during the course of the year you have additional cash sources of $50. We add these together to arrive at your total cash available for spending—$150. Let's now pretend that during the same year you spent $400 on a big screen TV. Using the cash method of proof, we've just determined your unreported income as $250 ($150 – $400 = −$250).

Mr. Vasiliadis: Agent Lewis, just to confirm our understanding . . . only cash transactions were considered—just cash, no checks.

‡ These excerpts have been taken from trial transcripts and have been paraphrased for clarity.

Mr. Lewis: That's correct; that's the essence of the cash method of proof—only cash.

Mr. Vasiliadis: Agent Lewis, during the course of your examination, what sources of cash were identified?

Mr. Lewis: I identified twenty-one (21) sources of cash during the periods under consideration (2001 to 2003), including taxable and non-taxable sources. Sources identified included cashed payroll checks, cash returned on deposits, checks written to cash, cash withdrawn from financial accounts and credit cards, cash loans, cash contents of a safe deposit box, and cash-on-hand. Importantly, anything in doubt, for example missing checks, were considered sources.

Mr. Vasiliadis: Agent Lewis, what types of expenditures were identified during your examination?

Mr. Lewis: Anything that Mr. Khanu would have used cash for—cash deposits, loans paid in cash, and cash expenditures. Examples of cash expenditures identified included purchases of furniture, cashier's checks, housing repairs, landscaping, fencing, and gifts.

Mr. Vasiliadis: Agent Lewis, how important is the beginning cash balance to your analysis?

Mr. Lewis: It's critical. The integrity of the cash method requires a reliable beginning cash balance. The beginning balance serves as the base or starting point of the analysis.

Mr. Vasiliadis: Agent Lewis, please explain how you used the cash method of proof in this case.

Mr. Lewis: I first determined Mr. Khanu's beginning cash-on-hand. Moving forward year by year, I added sources and subtracted expenditures. In the three years under consideration (2001 to 2003), I found more expenditures than sources, confirming unreported income.

Mr. Vasiliadis: And you did this analysis year by year, is that correct?

Mr. Lewis: Yes. Tax liabilities are determined on an annual basis.

Mr. Vasiliadis: Agent Lewis, how did you determine Mr. Khanu's beginning cash-on-hand balance?

Mr. Lewis: It was determined from a financial statement presented by Mr. Khanu to a prospective landlord. The statement, dated April 12, 1999, stated Mr. Khanu's cash balance was $700,000. I subtracted the money Mr. Khanu had in his bank accounts on April 12, 1999 to determine his cash-on-hand balance—$698,886.

Mr. Vasiliadis: And you worked forward, using April 12, 1999 as your starting date, is that correct?

Mr. Lewis: Yes.

Mr. Vasiliadis: Agent Lewis, did you consider where the beginning cash balance ($700,000) came from?

Mr. Lewis: Certainly, as an IRS Agent I was curious. However, the source of the beginning balance was not relevant. I accepted it at face value, as legitimate.

Mr. Vasiliadis: Agent Lewis, at issue in this case is the $1.9 million seized from Mr. Khanu's residence on October 28, 2003. Please explain to the jury how these funds were classified in your analysis.

Mr. Lewis: I classified the seizure of the funds as an expenditure. The funds were in Mr. Khanu's possession and under his control. There was no evidence that the funds belonged to his company and were simply in his possession for safekeeping.

Mr. Vasiliadis: Did you consider this as a possible explanation?

Mr. Lewis: Absolutely. To support the integrity of my analysis, three factors were critical: (1) a reliable beginning cash-on-hand; (2) a likely source of the unreported income; and (3) the consideration of all potentially nontaxable sources of income. In other words, all reasonable leads must be considered.

Mr. Vasiliadis: Agent Lewis, did you consider the argument that the $1.9 million seized on October 28, 2003 actually belonged to Mr. Khanu's company and was simply being held by him for safekeeping to be a reasonable lead?

Mr. Lewis: It was considered and rejected. I never considered it a reasonable proposition. Importantly, the company had no record of the funds in Mr. Khanu's possession on October 28, 2003.

Mr. Vasiliadis: Agent Lewis, did you complete a summary chart summarizing all the uses and sources of cash for Mr. Khanu from April 12, 1999 through the end of 2003?

Mr. Lewis: Yes. *Exhibit 900 was introduced into evidence.*

U.S. v. Khanu Cash Method of Proof Exhibit 900

	1999	2000	2001	2002	2003
Beginning Cash Balance	$698,886	$559,554	$371,652	$65,035	-0-
Additional Sources	$15,158	$82,323	$82,225	$91,021	$65,378
Total Sources	$714,044	$641,877	$453,877	$156,056	$65,378
Cash Expenditures	($154,490)	($270,225)	($388,842)	($609,151)	($385,164)
Cash Seized					($1,907,904)
Ending Cash-on-Hand	$559,554	$371,652	$65,035	($453,095)	($2,227,690)
Taxable Income Reported	$35,000	$68,033	$197,599	$129,060	$315,186
Unreported Taxable Income	-0-	-0-	-0-	$453,095	$2,227,690
Corrected Taxable Income				$582,155	$2,542,876
Additional Tax Due				$217,818	$790,204
Cumulative Tax Due					$1,008,022

Source: Created from trial transcripts of United States of America, Appellee, v. Abdul Karim Khanu, Appellant. No. 10-3039, United States Court of Appeals for the District of Columbia Circuit. Argued Apr. 4, 2011 to Oct. 7, 2011. Transcripts are available via a link at www.pearsonhighered.com/rufus.

Mr. Vasiliadis: Agent Lewis, based on your analysis, education, and 28 years of experience as an IRS agent, please summarize your findings regarding Mr. Khanu's unreported income and resulting tax due.

Mr. Lewis: That Mr. Khanu's personal income tax returns (Form 1040) substantially understated his taxable income—$453,000 in 2002 and $2.2 million in 2003—resulting in additional income tax due of $217,000 and $790,000, respectively.

Cross-Examination

Mr. Martin: You've previously testified that Mr. Khanu's beginning cash balance is critical in your calculations, is that correct?

Mr. Lewis: Yes.

Mr. Martin: You've told this jury that you calculated Mr. Khanu's beginning cash balance to be $698,886, is that correct?

Mr. Lewis: Yes.

Mr. Martin: How exactly how did you make this determination?

Mr. Lewis: I determined the amount of money in Mr. Khanu's bank accounts as of April 12, 1999 and subtracted this amount from $700,000, providing a cash-on-hand balance of $698,886.

Mr. Martin: And where or how did you determine the $700,000 amount?

Mr. Lewis: The $700,000 was provided by Mr. Khanu. It was listed on his financial statement dated April 12, 1999, which was presented to a prospective landlord.

Mr. Martin: So the reliability of your analysis starts with the financial statement presented to a prospective landlord in April of 1999, is that correct?

Mr. Lewis: Yes.

Mr. Martin: How did you determine the reliability of the April 12, 1999 financial statement, which served as your starting point?

Mr. Lewis: I confirmed that it was presented to the prospective landlord by Mr. Khanu on or about April 12, 1999. I also confirmed that it was prepared by a real estate agent based on information provided by Mr. Khanu. I then confirmed Mr. Khanu's bank account balances for that same day. This allowed me to compute cash-on-hand.

Mr. Martin: Was this financial statement presented to the landlord under penalties of perjury?

Mr. Lewis: No.

Mr. Martin: Was this an audited financial statement?

Mr. Lewis: No.

Mr. Martin: Please explain to the jury what an audited financial statement is, if you know.

Mr. Lewis: The information contained in the financial statement has been audited, confirmed, or tested by an independent CPA.

Mr. Martin: So no one tested or confirmed the information on the financial statement?

Mr. Lewis: Not to my knowledge.

Mr. Martin: That includes you, doesn't it? You didn't test or confirm the information on the statement, did you?

Mr. Lewis: No.

Mr. Martin: Why not? You've got 28 years of experience with the IRS and access to their data.

Mr. Lewis: I accepted it as the best evidence available regarding the amount of cash-on-hand held by Mr. Khanu. Moreover, it would have been impossible to go back in time and count the cash-on-hand held by Mr. Khanu.

Mr. Martin: Did you attempt to verify or audit any of the information on the financial statement?

Mr. Lewis: Yes. As I've previously testified, I confirmed when it was presented, to whom it was presented, by whom it was presented, and why it was presented.

Mr. Martin: Mr. Lewis, would you agree with me that the use of even numbers, for example $700,000, most likely represents an estimate or guess? In other words, no precision?

Mr. Lewis: Yes, most likely.

Mr. Martin: So, if Mr. Khanu's cash-on-hand balance, as of April 12, 1999, was actually $1.3 million instead of $700,000, your analysis would be incorrect, is that right?

Mr. Lewis: Yes. However, a review of Mr. Khanu's past tax returns would not support such an accumulation of cash. In fact, they don't support the $700,000 claimed.

Mr. Martin: Mr. Lewis, have you determined if Mr. Khanu's corporations reported as income the $1.9 million that was seized from Mr. Khanu's home?

Mr. Lewis: No.

Mr. Martin: Why not? The IRS certainly doesn't plan to tax Mr. Khanu's corporations and Mr. Khanu, does it?

Mr. Lewis: How it was accounted for after the fact is not relevant to my analysis. I've confirmed that it was not reported on the corporate books before it was seized. It was in Mr. Khanu's possession and control.

Mr. Martin: Mr. Lewis, you witnessed the testimony of Mr. Khanu's corporate accountant (Craig White), is that correct?

Mr. Lewis: Yes.

Mr. Martin: So, you know that the $1.9 million seized from Mr. Khanu's home has in fact been reported by the corporations as both income and assets, is that correct?

Mr. Lewis: Yes. But, as I just stated, how it was accounted for after the fact is not relevant.

Motion for Acquittal

At the conclusion of the government's case, Mr. Khanu's attorneys moved for judgment of acquittal. They argued that the government's evidence was insufficient to permit a rational trier of fact to find all the essential elements of the crimes alleged beyond a reasonable doubt. In response, the court found that sufficient evidence for each of the essential elements of the crimes charged had been presented and thus denied the motion.

Defense's Case-in-Chief

The Defense presented its case-in-chief on days 9–10 of the trial. Primary fact witnesses included the following individuals:

- Tarek Stevens, a booking agent who testified about the activity of the business preceding the raid of October 28, 2003, specifically the Howard University Homecoming and the reasonableness of having earned $1.9 million during the week-long celebration.
- Terry Young, the former director of security at the nightclubs, who testified about prior robberies at the club and the reasonableness of removing the money from the clubs at night.
- Peter Mallios, a real estate broker who handled the April 1999 transaction, specifically the April 12, 1999 financial statement, and testified that it was common practice to limit the amount of cash listed to amounts required to secure the deal.
- Edward Federico, a retired IRS Special Agent, who questioned the reasonableness of the beginning cash balance ($700,000) used by Agent Lewis and the inclusion of the $1.9 million seized by the IRS on October 28, 2003.

Closing Arguments

The trial ended with closing arguments, wherein each attorney summarized his case and made a final attempt to persuade the jury.

Closing by Mr. Roth, U.S. Attorney's Office

When we first started this case, we told you it was about cash—where it went and where it didn't go. Over the last two weeks, we've heard undisputed testimony about the millions of dollars in cash generated by Mr. Khanu's nightclubs. The question is where did the cash go? The undisputed evidence is that some of it was used to pay employees—cash wages. Some of it was used to pay for security, promoters, vendors, and loans to Mr. Khanu and others. Some of it was deposited into the nightclub's bank accounts, and some of it was dropped into a safe located at the club. Some of it was deposited into Mr. Khanu's personal bank account. Some of it was used by Mr. Khanu to buy cashier's checks. Also undisputed is that some of it ($1.9 million) was taken by Mr. Khanu and was seized by the IRS at his home on October 28, 2003.

Agent Lewis, an IRS agent with 28 years' experience, carefully and honestly illustrated where the cash went and where it didn't go. Using the cash method of proof, Agent Lewis determined that Mr. Khanu was using more cash than he had legitimate sources for and rightfully classified the excess cash as unreported income, having been skimmed from his nightclubs. Agent Lewis told us you need a solid starting point—remember, he used $700,000, which was taken from Mr. Khanu's financial statement. Agent Lewis didn't make the number up; he wondered about where the $700k had come from, but he accepted it as being legit. Agent Lewis used the same process year after year in determining that Mr. Khanu had under-reported his income by more than $2.5 million, resulting in tax due and owing of more than $1 million.

The Defense has argued the $700,000 was an estimate based on what Mr. Khanu needed to report to secure a lease. They've suggested it could have been $1.2 million or $1.3 million. What proof was offered to support these numbers? Absolutely nothing! Maybe it was more, and maybe it was less. All we know for a fact is what Mr. Khanu reported on the financial statement—$700,000. Remember what Agent Lewis told us—Mr. Khanu's tax returns do not support that level of accumulation.

The Defense has argued that the $1.9 million was being held by Mr. Khanu for safekeeping pending deposit into the club's bank accounts. They've argued that it was earned during the Howard University Homecoming festivities, which ended on October 12, 2003. They've argued that it was reported by the corporations and cannot be taxed twice. Remember what Agent Lewis told us—on October 28, 2003 there was no record of this cash belonging to the corporations and what Mr. Khanu did after the seizure is not relevant. It was in Mr. Khanu's possession and control.

So what does the evidence tell us? That Mr. Khanu ran two very successful nightclubs that generated millions of dollars in cash. That Mr. Khanu used the cash to pay employees under the table. That Mr. Khanu used the cash to make unreported loans to his partners. That Mr. Khanu skimmed more than $2.5 million for his own personal use.

Closing by Mr. Martin on Behalf of Mr. Khanu

As Judge Kotelly has explained to you, the government has the burden, and it's a very high burden. They have to prove the guilt of Mr. Khanu beyond a reasonable doubt. And because of this challenge, they get a second chance to speak with you. This, however, is my last chance, and I don't want to blow it. The stakes are too high. Mr. Khanu's freedom is at stake.

During opening arguments, I told you that every story has two sides. You've certainly witnessed that in this case. We agree that there are disputes between Mr. Khanu and the IRS regarding the classification of employees, corporate automobiles, and loans to officers. But when does a dispute with the IRS become criminal? Your taxes become a criminal issue when you willfully, with criminal intent, try to defraud, evade, and defeat the tax laws. That did not happen in this case.

This case got off to an ugly start more than six years ago (October 28, 2003), when the IRS broke down the front door of Mr. Khanu's home and terrorized his family for more than eight hours while they searched for business records. Business records—not cash, drugs, or weapons. They were looking for general ledgers, receipt books, vendor invoices, and bank records. Recall the testimony of the agent—that Mr. Khanu was very cooperative. Why? Because he had nothing to hide.

I caution you that the government has played fast and loose with the evidence in this case. First, let's consider the $1.9 million seized from Mr. Khanu's home. The government would have you believe that it should have been deposited into the corporate bank accounts. Who says? There is no law that requires a company to deposit its revenue. Given the robberies experienced at the nightclubs, it made perfectly good sense for Mr. Khanu to take the cash home where he had an enhanced security system. Was the $1.9 million reported as income by the corporations? Yes. And how does the government respond? They say, "So what—it was reported after the fact." What they're not telling you is that the company was not required to report the cash until September 31, 2004. Importantly, the government doesn't dispute that the clubs may have earned the $1.9 million during the Howard University Homecoming. Their argument is that Mr. Khanu didn't deposit it. There is no law that requires a taxpayer to put his money in the bank.

What about Mr. Lewis' use of $700,000 as the starting point in his analysis? Remember the testimony of Peter Mallios, who told you that the industry standard was to report only enough cash to secure the lease—in this case $700,000. So what did the government do to verify the information? Nothing, absolutely nothing! However, they do acknowledge that the statement was not audited or presented under oath. These are important considerations when considering the reliability of the financial statement.

Let's discuss the testimony of Mr. Lewis. Please remember that Mr. Lewis was not here as an expert witness offering objective testimony—he was here as a summary fact witness. He's an IRS agent and has been for 28 years. He was not here as an objective third party. He was here as an advocate for the government's side of the story. Remember what he told us about his work—its integrity mandates a reliable beginning cash balance and the consideration of all reasonable leads. We submit he failed on both fronts. We submit that he adopted an IRS best-case scenario regarding the $700,000 and again regarding the $1.9 million. Alternative explanations were not considered or investigated.

A most important consideration is this case is Mr. Khanu's reliance on his CPA, Craig White. Remember Mr. White's testimony—he advised Mr. Khanu not to report the cash paid to the promoters, he advised Mr. Khanu that the cash wages were the responsibility of the promoters, he told us there was nothing wrong with Mr. Khanu's possession of the $1.9 million belonging to the corporations, and, most importantly, he told us that the corporations had in fact reported the $1.9 million as income. Mr. Khanu relied on his CPA and followed his advice. Is this a crime? Absolutely not! And don't forget that Mr. White was the government's witness. Mr. Khanu's reliance on his CPA creates reasonable doubt. If he followed the advice of his CPA, he is not guilty.

The court will remind you that, to find Mr. Khanu guilty of these alleged tax crimes, you must find that he acted willfully, with criminal intent, to defraud, evade, and defeat the tax laws. The evidence in this case does not support these charges. If the income tax returns are wrong, the IRS can deal with that. But Mr. Khanu's income tax returns, business and personal, are not criminally and willfully wrong. What about the employment tax returns? Mr. Khanu relied on his accountant.

Ladies and gentlemen, my time is up. On the evidence in this case, there is only one true and just verdict, one verdict that brings justice to this courtroom. That verdict is not guilty. Thank you.

Closing Argument by Mr. Roth on Behalf of the Government

I have just a few final comments. First is the use of $700,000 as a starting number for Agent Lewis' analysis. This number was provided by Mr. Khanu on his personal financial statement—we didn't make it up. The court will tell you that the proof need not show the exact amount of cash-on-hand, as long as it's been established as reasonably accurate. Did we investigate all reasonable leads? Yes—that was the government's obligation, and that's what we did. Remember the testimony of the many IRS agents who worked on this case.

It's very important to remember what was undisputed by Mr. Khanu, specifically the amount of cash he spent. Aside from arguments regarding the beginning cash balance and the $1.9 million, Mr. Khanu has not disputed Agent Lewis' analysis regarding cash expenditures. Even if you ignore the $1.9 million, Mr. Khanu still spent $500,000 more than he can account for. This is unreported income, and this is tax fraud.

Now, with regard to the $1.9 million, one of the virtues of a jury system is that you get to use your common sense, and you are the sole judges of the facts here. What Mr. Khanu would have you believe is that he took that money for safekeeping and kept it in his home for 13 days, if in fact that money was made during the Howard Homecoming. Ladies and gentlemen, that's simply not reasonable. And exactly how would it work? Would he take three huge duffle bags full of cash to the bank, haul it in the back seat, in the truck? That's not how business works. Was there a record of the cash belonging to the corporations before the seizure? No.

The government has shown in the course of this trial that the defendant, Abdul Khanu, is guilty of tax evasion, filing false tax returns, and conspiracy to defraud the IRS. Actions have consequences. We ask you to fairly evaluate the evidence, look at the exhibits, and come back with a verdict that Mr. Khanu is guilty on all charges. Thank you.

The Verdict

On December 1, 2009, following five days of deliberations, the jury found Mr. Khanu guilty of two counts of tax evasion for the years 2002 and 2003 and not guilty of 20 charges including conspiracy, tax evasion for 2001, aiding and abetting the filing of false corporate returns, and aiding and abetting the filing of false employment tax returns.

Following the jury verdict, Mr. Khanu was taken into custody and held without bail.

Sentencing

On May 11, 2010, Mr. Khanu was sentenced to 38 months in prison and ordered to pay more than $950,000 in restitution to the IRS for underreporting his annual income. The Judge also ordered that, after his release from prison, he must pay no less than $1,000 a month toward $951,520 in restitution to the IRS. The Judge imposed a three-year term of supervised release on Mr. Khanu after he serves his prison sentence. She also ordered that he undergo alcohol counseling. Mr. Khanu was released on August 31, 2012.

The Appeal

In April of 2011, Mr. Khanu appealed his conviction and sentence on two counts of attempted tax evasion. He argued that the government had failed to prove the element of tax loss because it relied on a flawed calculation under the "cash method of proof," wherein $1.9 million of alleged income was attributed to Mr. Khanu, when those funds, as a matter of law, belonged to his two corporations.

On October 7, 2011, the judgment of the district court was affirmed.

Key Terms

Active data
Archival data
Base earnings
Bit-stream copy
Chain of custody
Compensatory damages
Computer forensics
Computer network
Computer system
Data carving
Direct method of proof
Economic damages
Electronically stored information
File analysis
Flash memory media
Gross margin percentage
Hidden data analysis
Household services
Indirect method of proof
Latent data
Life care plan
Live forensics
Lost earnings
Magnetic media
Metadata
Method of proof

Noneconomic damages
Oral report
Percentage markup
Post-injury earnings
Pre-injury earnings
Punitive damages
Static forensics
Timeframe analysis
Worklife expectancy
Writable optical media

Chapter Questions

12-1. What is a method of proof?

12-2. What is the difference between a direct and an indirect method of proof? When is each used? Explain.

12-3. Identify six facts and circumstances that support the use of an indirect method of proof.

12-4. Identify and discuss three commonly employed indirect methods under the cash flow approach.

12-5. Explain when the net worth method is appropriate and how it works.

12-6. When is the source and application of funds method employed? Explain how it works.

12-7. Describe how the percentage markup method works. What must be present for this method to be effective?

12-8. What is the primary objective when selecting an appropriate method of proof?

12-9. Identify five factors that should be considered when selecting an indirect method of proof.

12-10. What defenses have the courts established to protect against abuse when an indirect method of proof is employed?

12-11. What are economic damages?

12-12. What is the difference between compensatory and punitive damages?

12-13. What are noneconomic damages?

12-14. What is the primary role of an economic expert in a damages claim?

12-15. Identify and discuss three different types of damages that experts might evaluate in an economic damages engagement.

12-16. For compensatory damages, what is the significance of the phrases "compensable by law" and "measurable within the realm of economics"?

12-17. Identify two subcategories of lost earnings and describe each.

12-18. Do uncompensated household services have value? Explain.

12-19. How are medical expenses considered in personal injury and wrongful death claims?

12-20. Identify four components that comprise a common framework for calculating economic damages.

12-21. Identify five sources of information that are useful to a forensic accountant in an economic damages calculation.

12-22. Compare and contrast pre-injury and post-injury earnings.

12-23. Why is the determination of base earnings important for projecting lost earnings?

12-24. Identify and discuss two factors that might contribute to earnings growth.

12-25. What is worklife expectancy?

12-26. What is the appropriate discount rate used in economic damages calculations?

12-27. Identify and discuss three areas of disagreement related to the selection of a risk-free rate.

12-28. What is computer forensics?

12-29. What is cybercrime, and how prevalent is it in the United States?

12-30. What are corporate data breaches? How do these breaches occur?

12-31. Identify three types of storage devices and discuss how each stores data.

12-32. As defined by the AICPA, what is the purpose of a computer forensics engagement?

12-33. Discuss legal and scope parameters that might impact a computer forensics engagement.

12-34. What are the three primary components of the process of a computer forensics investigation?

12-35. What are the five greatest technology threats organizations will face in the future, as perceived by practicing forensic accountants?

12-36. What is the final stage of a forensic accounting engagement? Discuss.

12-37. As required by the Federal Rules of Civil Procedure, specifically Rule 26(a)(2)(B), what elements must be included in a report submitted by an expert witness? Explain.

12-38. What three types of communications between the expert and engaging counsel are discoverable by opposing counsel?

12-39. What are some pitfalls of oral reports, and how can these pitfalls be overcome?

12-40. Compare and contrast summary, detailed, and calculation reports.

Multiple-Choice Questions

Select the best response to the following questions related to methods of proof:

12-41. Methods of proof used to develop evidence can be any of the following *except:*
- **a.** Indirect methods
- **b.** Direct methods
- **c.** Straightforward
- **d.** A combination of direct and indirect

12-42. Which of these statements is *not* a reason why a direct method of proof is preferable to other methods?
- **a.** It is generally more persuasive.
- **b.** It provides a greater level of certainty.
- **c.** It is more easily understood.
- **d.** It is harder to refute.
- **e.** All of the above are reasons why a direct method is preferable.

12-43. Indirect methods are most often used when a firm's books and records are complete and accurate.
- **a.** True
- **b.** False

12-44. Which of the following is *not* an indirect method employed by forensic accountants?
- **a.** Source and application of funds method
- **b.** Net worth method
- **c.** Accounting equation transcription method
- **d.** Percentage markup method

12-45. The indirect method that is most commonly used in situations where there is an accumulation of assets without a corresponding source of funds is the:
- **a.** Net worth method
- **b.** Gross profit method
- **c.** Cash account method
- **d.** None of the above

12-46. An indirect method that is used when a subject consumes income rather than accumulates assets is the:
- **a.** Net worth method
- **b.** Cash account method
- **c.** Gross profit method
- **d.** Source and application of funds method

12-47. For a forensic accountant to effectively employ the percentage markup method:
- **a.** Unit sales prices and costs must be able to be established with reasonable certainty.
- **b.** The number of customers must be known.
- **c.** Administrative costs must be known.
- **d.** None of the above is correct.

12-48. The primary driver for the selection of a method of proof is:
- **a.** To employ a method that is sure to win
- **b.** To develop evidence that is best suited to the facts and circumstances of the case
- **c.** To ensure all revenue is accounted for
- **d.** To ensure all assets are correctly valued

12-49. An expert's opinion must be based on sufficient, reliable facts and data and be the product of applicable, reliable methodology.
- **a.** True
- **b.** False

12-50. Methods of proof can establish:
- **a.** Intent to commit a crime
- **b.** A proposition, such as unreported income
- **c.** Both a and b are correct responses
- **d.** Neither a nor b is a correct response

Select the best response to the following questions related to economic damages:

12-51. Economic damages are the monetary compensation that is awarded in civil litigation, such as a breach of contract claim.
- **a.** True
- **b.** False

12-52. The purpose of _____ is to put an individual or entity in the economic position that would have occurred if not for a defendant's wrongful conduct.
- **a.** Punitive damages
- **b.** Fiduciary damages
- **c.** Restoration damages
- **d.** Compensatory damages

12-53. Awards by a court to punish a defendant's intentional or reckless behavior are:
- **a.** Punitive damages
- **b.** Fiduciary damages
- **c.** Restoration damages
- **d.** Compensatory damages

12-54. Which of the following are noneconomic damages?
- **a.** Pain and suffering
- **b.** Loss of companionship
- **c.** Emotional distress
- **d.** Loss of enjoyment of life
- **e.** All of the above are noneconomic damages

12-55. The primary role of a forensic accountant engaged as an expert in a damages claim is to place a dollar value on the various damage components that have been identified.

a. True

b. False

12-56. An expert's analysis of economic damages should be the same, whether he or she has been engaged by the plaintiff or defendant.

a. True

b. False

12-57. Determining the dollar value of compensatory damages requires that the damages be:

a. Identified and calculated

b. The result of an event that has economic implications

c. Compensable by law and measurable within the realm of economics

d. Attributable to something and have an economic half-life

12-58. Lost earnings have two components, including:

a. Past lost earnings and current lost earnings

b. Past lost earnings and future lost earnings

c. Current lost earnings and recoverable lost earnings

d. None of the above

12-59. Household services such as cooking, cleaning, shopping, repairs, yard work, and management of household finances have economic value.

a. True

b. False

12-60. The difference between pre-injury earnings and post-injury earnings is:

a. Based on the nature of the work involved

b. Not an economic concept used by forensic accountants

c. The basis for lost earnings

d. The basis for seeking a new college degree

12-61. The measurement of earnings growth can be related to all of the following factors *except:*

a. Inflation

b. Consistency of effort

c. Productivity

d. All of the above

12-62. Worklife expectancy is the period of time a person is expected to live past retirement.

a. True

b. False

12-63. In economic damages calculations, risk is not a factor considered in the discount rate.

a. True

b. False

12-64. There are no disagreements among economic damages experts relating to the selection of a discount rate.

a. True

b. False

12-65. Interest on past damages is never calculated by a forensic accountant.

a. True

b. False

Select the best response to the following questions related to computer forensics:

12-66. The application of computer technology in a legal action is called:

a. Data analysis

b. Data mining

c. Computer forensics

d. Technology forensics

12-67. The demand for computer forensics services over the next several years is expected to:

a. Stay the same

b. Slow down

c. Speed up

d. Speed up sharply then decline quickly

12-68. Cybercrime is a threat to almost all individuals and organizations.

a. True

b. False

12-69. Over half of all corporate data breaches involve internal employees.

a. True

b. False

12-70. Information created, manipulated, and stored in electronic form is known as:

a. Data processing

b. A computer network

c. A computer system

d. Electronically stored information

12-71. Each of the following is a type of data storage media *except:*

a. Flash memory media

b. Magnetic media

c. Writable optical media

d. Data mining media

12-72. The route evidence takes from the time it is collected until the investigation is completed is known as:

a. Data chain

b. Data flow

c. Chain of custody

d. Data responsibility

12-73. The process of a computer forensics investigation includes each of the following components *except:*

a. Gathering preliminary information

b. Analyzing digital data

c. Collecting and storing digital data

d. Staking out suspects using electronic devices

12-74. In a computer forensics context, _____ means interpreting recovered data and compiling it in a logical and useful format:

a. Compilation

b. Analysis

c. Scrubbing

d. Collating

12-75. The most time-consuming task of a computer forensics investigation is the actual application of analytical tools and methods.

a. True

b. False

Select the best response to the following questions related to report writing:

12-76. The final stage of a forensic accounting engagement is the communication of results and opinions in a report.

a. True

b. False

12-77. Rule 26 of the Federal Rules of Civil Procedure identifies specific components that an expert report must contain.

a. True

b. False

12-78. An expert's draft reports are discoverable.

a. True

b. False

12-79. Each of the following is discoverable *except:*

a. Communications regarding the expert's compensation

b. Notes related to conversations with the engaging attorney

c. Communications regarding the assumptions to be relied on by the expert in forming his or her opinions

d. Communications regarding the facts and data to be relied on by the expert in forming his or her opinions

12-80. Reports prepared in the course of litigation must follow strict guidelines set forth by the AICPA.

a. True

b. False

12-81. It is better to render an oral report to eliminate all possibility that the report will be misunderstood.

a. True

b. False

12-82. Each of the following is a type of report a forensic accountant might issue *except:*

a. Certified report

b. Calculation report

c. Detailed report

d. Summary report

12-83. Regardless of the form of a report, the report must be stated in a legally sufficient manner and must be based on reliable facts, data, and methodology.

a. True

b. False

Workplace Applications

12-84. Charles Choi was the owner/operator of a grocery store in California called Gene's Modern Market. In addition to the sale of normal grocery items, the store cashed payroll, personal, and third-party checks for a fee. The fee was 1% of the face amount of the check. From 1991 to 1993, the store used two cash registers, but the cash register tapes were not used to make entries into the accounting system. Rather, all entries were made based on cash payments and receipts. While monies were held in bank accounts, these accounts were not reconciled and the sales activity that Mr. Choi provided to the company's accountant were lower than the amounts that appeared on daily cash register tapes. In addition, inventory records were not maintained.

The Chois challenged an IRS audit determination that contained the following findings: (1) failure to report income for two years; (2) incidence of fraud, resulting in assessment of a fraud penalty; (3) liability for self-employment taxes; and (4) denial of a dependency deduction. The matter was considered by the United States Tax court in 2002.

The tax court memorandum is available at www.ustaxcourt.gov. At the homepage for this site, select the "Opinions Search" tab. Then use the case keywords feature and enter: "Choi." A case with the name *Charles Y. and Jin Y. Choi* will be among the cases listed. Select this case for further use.

After reading the case, respond to the following questions.

1. How did Mr. Choi obtain the funds he used to cash checks?
2. How were gross receipts fabricated?
3. How did Mr. Choi provide accounting information to the store's accountant, Mr. Kim? How did this facilitate the fraud?
4. Did Mr. Choi admit to understating gross receipts for Gene's Modern Market?
5. How did Mr. Choi account for cash receipts from Gene's?

6. What method did the IRS examiner use to determine the amount of unreported cash receipts? Why did the IRS examiner select this as an appropriate method for this case?
7. Using the data presented in the case, recreate in an Excel spreadsheet the indirect deposits and cash expenditures worksheet for 1991 and 1992. Then provide an explanation of how each component of the spreadsheet contributes to the reconstruction of taxable income. In other words, explain the methodology employed by the IRS examiner.
8. How did the tax court view the methodology developed in question 7?
9. In his defense, what method of determining revenues did Mr. Choi attempt to use as an alternative to the indirect approach employed by the IRS examiner? How did the tax court consider this alternative approach?
10. How was intent proven in this case?
11. How was fraud defined (considered) in this case?
12. What was the court's ruling, and what was the standard of proof employed by the tax court?
13. Why was this case tried in the U.S. Tax court rather than U.S. District court? What is the difference? Who decides?
14. What is the difference between civil fraud and criminal fraud?

12-85. Glen and Diane Flood owned and operated Flood's Auto Parts and Glenwood Wrecker Service in Chatsworth, Georgia. The companies' offerings to the local market included the sale of wholesale and retail auto parts, a wrecker service, and the sale of wrecked autos. Mr. Flood did not consistently prepare invoices for customers and had no other way to determine total sales for his businesses. Although Mr. Flood deposited some of the cash revenue into the company's bank accounts, he stored some of it in a safe at his home.

Over several years, Mr. Flood purchased multiple businesses and sold all or parts of others. The terms of payment were not always recorded in written form, and not all of them were reported on Schedule C of Mr. Flood's individual tax returns.

Through a routine examination of the company's tax returns, an IRS examiner discovered that Mr. Flood had not reported all of the sales generated by his businesses. Specifically, the examiner determined that Mr. Flood had understated taxable income for 1991, 1992, and 1993 by $28,195, $22,695, and $74,013, respectively.

The Floods challenged the IRS audit findings, specifically that: (1) Mr. Flood failed to maintain adequate books and records; (2) sales were routinely omitted from the recordkeeping process; (3) employees may have forgotten to record sales; (4) not all cash revenue was deposited in the bank; and (5) Mr. Flood was aware of these failures and chose to withhold this information from the tax preparer.

The tax court's memorandum is available at www.ustaxcourt.gov. At the homepage of this site, select the "Opinions Search" tab. Then, use the case keywords feature and enter: "Flood." A case with the name *Glenn H. and Diane J. Flood* will be among the cases listed. Select this case for further use.

After reading the case, respond to the following questions.

1. What method did the IRS examiner use to determine the amount of unreported income? Why did the IRS examiner select this as an appropriate method for this case?
2. Explain how the source and application of funds method works.
3. Using the data presented in the case, recreate in an Excel spreadsheet the source and application of funds worksheets for 1991, 1992, and 1993. Then provide an explanation of how each component of the spreadsheet contributes to the reconstruction of taxable income. In other words, explain the methodology employed by the IRS examiner.
4. In what specific area did the Floods disagree with the IRS examiner's findings? If the Floods are correct, what impact would it have on the amounts calculated as unreported income? How did the tax court rule on this matter?
5. How did the tax court view the indirect methodology used by the IRS examiner to develop unreported income?
6. How did the tax court determine whether a loan from Mr. Flood to his father was in fact a loan that became worthless in 1992? How did the tax court rule?
7. The IRS examiner determined that a 20% accuracy penalty on the unreported amounts was appropriate. What was the basis for this determination? How did the court rule, and why?
8. Why was this case tried in the U.S. Tax court rather than U.S. District court? What is the difference? Who decides?

12-86. Using an Internet search engine or a library database, enter the search term "McDonald's coffee verdict" to research the case *Liebeck v. McDonald's Restaurants* (1994). Based on your research, prepare a memo to your professor that answers the following questions:

1. How did the injury occur?
2. In what state was this case decided?
3. How old was the plaintiff at the time of the injury? Based on this fact, would you expect economic damages to include lost earnings? Why or why not?

4. How much did the jury award the plaintiff in compensatory damages?
5. What types of damages were included in compensatory damages? Were these damages economic or noneconomic?
6. How much did the jury award the plaintiff in punitive damages? How was this amount determined?
7. Did the trial judge adjust the jury's punitive damage award? If so, by how much and for what reason?
8. Based on your research, do you agree with the common perception of this case as a "poster child" for frivolous lawsuits? Why or why not?

12-87. Martin Myers was injured in an automobile accident and is suing for lost wages. Facts relating to this personal injury scenario are outlined in the following table. Assume you have been engaged by the plaintiff's attorney to evaluate economic damages, limited to lost wages.

Case Facts	
Plaintiff	Martin Myers
Gender	Male
Ethnicity	African American
Date of Birth (DOB)	Jan. 15, 1984
Date of Injury (DOI)	Feb. 21, 2013
Nature of Injury	Head injury from motor vehicle accident
Household Setting	Married with two children, ages 2 and 4
Educational Attainment	Bachelor's degree in Business Administration
Employment History	Employed by Fifth Third Bank as a branch manager

According to Mr. Myers's physicians, the subject injury has permanently damaged his cognitive functioning, specifically with regard to verbal communication and short-term memory. Based on these physical limitations, a vocational expert has presented the following opinions:

- Mr. Myers is incapable of returning to employment as a banking manager.
- He will be permanently limited to entry-level positions earning at or near minimum wage.

As part of your data collection effort, you have asked to review Mr. Myers's personnel file at Fifth Third and to interview the bank's Human Resources Director. From the personnel file, you learned that Mr. Myers was paid an annual salary of $49,000 at the time of the injury. You also learned that his current position of branch manager was obtained on Jan. 1, 2012, the latest in a series of promotions since his initial hire as a part-time teller in 2003. Finally, you obtained the five-year wage history presented in the following table.

Wage History of Martin Myers	
Year	**Gross Wages**
2008	$32,965
2009	$37,250
2010	$37,250
2011	$38,368
2012	$51,500

Highlights of your interview with the Human Resources Director include the following:

- All bank employees received 3% raises in 2008 and 2011. Although such across-the-board raises have historically occurred at Fifth Third every few years, they are not guaranteed.
- Mr. Myers's 2012 wages include a $2,500 bonus, which he was awarded because his branch achieved certain performance targets for the year.
- Mr. Myers's ultimate career goal at Fifth Third was to become Vice President of Branch Operations, a position that currently pays $75,000 per year. He could reasonably have achieved this goal within five years.

To complete your assignment, perform the following tasks:

1. Determine a reasonable assumption for Mr. Myers's pre-injury base earnings. Explain your rationale for this determination.
2. Use the current federal minimum wage (at 2,080 hours per year) to determine Mr. Myers's post-injury base earnings.
3. For years 2008 through 2012, calculate the annual growth rate for each year and the cumulative average growth rate for the entire period.
4. From the BLS web site (www.bls.gov), obtain the average annual percentage change in the Employment Cost Index (all civilian workers, total compensation, not seasonally adjusted) for the ten-year period 2003 to 2012.
5. According to the 2012 OASDI Trustees Report, what level of average annual wage growth is predicted for the period 2021 to 2086?
6. From your responses to items 3 through 5, determine a reasonable assumption for Mr. Myers's future wage growth (to be applied to both pre- and post-injury base earnings). Explain your rationale for this determination.
7. Determine Mr. Myers's normal Social Security retirement age at the date of injury, and use this as his worklife expectancy.

8. Using the FRED database available at the St. Louis Federal Reserve web site (www.stlouisfed.org), determine the average 10-year Treasury constant maturity rate for years 1993 through 2012. Use this as your discount rate.
9. Using Dec. 31, 2013 as the valuation date, calculate the present value of Mr. Myers's future lost wages. Note: Wage growth should be applied only to future lost earnings (after the valuation date).
10. Based on the information provided, do you think it would be reasonable to consider an alternative scenario that assumes Mr. Myers would have achieved the contemplated promotion? Why or why not?

Chapter Problems

12-88. Obtain the following article: DiGabriele, J. A. (2012). A case study on the determination of lost profits for the forensic accountant. *Issues in Accounting Education, 27*(3), 751–59. This case study challenges students to determine economic damages in a business interruption case. The instructor will distribute specific assignments related to the solutions required in this case.

12-89. Obtain a forensic accountant's report issued to Representative Ann Rivers in the State of Washington. The report can be accessed via a link at www.pearsonhighered.com/rufus.

The report can also be located by performing a Google search using "forensic accountant slams high costs, low competition" as a search term. A link to the white paper is available at the bottom of the couv.com article.

a. As described in the chapter, is this a summary, detailed, or calculation report?

b. Assess the quality of this report using the following ten tips for effective report writing presented in the chapter:

1. Be clear.
2. Be concise but comprehensive.
3. Focus on the purpose (why you are writing).
4. Be mindful of your audience.
5. Use correct grammar.
6. Maintain a professional tone.
7. Avoid redundant statements.
8. Proof, proof, and proof again.
9. Expect your report, and every word contained therein, to be closely examined and challenged.
10. Read others' work.

---

1 *Webster's New World College Dictionary.* (1999). 4th Ed., 906.

2 Internal Revenue Manual (IRM), Part 9. Chapter 5, Section 9.2.2.

3 Holland v. U.S. 75 S.Ct. 127 (1954).

4 U.S. v. Keller, 523 F2d 1009 (9th Cir. 1975).

5 U.S. v. Johnson, 319 U.S. 503 (1943) 63 SCt 1233; Taglianetti v. U.S., 398 F2d 558 (1st Cir 1968); Oxford Associates, 209 F Supp 242 (DNJ 1962).

6 IRM, 9.5.9.9.1-10.

7 Ibid.

8 IRM, 9.5.9.2.2.5 (11-05-2004).

9 Martin, G. D. (2011). *Determining Economic Damages.* James Publishing.

10 *Black's Law Dictionary.* (2009). 9th Ed., 1626.

11 *Black's Law Dictionary.* (2009). 9th Ed., 213.

12 Cohen, T. (2009). Tort bench and jury trials in state courts, 2005. *Bureau of Justice Statistics Bulletin,* NCJ 228129.

13 Androgue, S., & Baker, C. (2011). Litigation in the 21st century: The jury trial, the training, & the experts. *The Advocate—State Bar of Texas Litigation Section Report, 56,* 8–19.

14 Martin, G. D. (2011). *Determining Economic Damages.* James Publishing.

15 Ireland, T. R. (2004). The Role of a Forensic Economist in a Damage Assessment for Personal Injuries. Working paper, University of Missouri at St. Louis.

16 Brookshire, M. L., Slesnick, F., & Ward, J. O. (2003). *The Plaintiff and Defense Attorney's Guide to Understanding Economic Damages.* Lawyers & Judges Publishing Company, Inc.

17 Ireland, T. R. (2004). The Role of a Forensic Economist in a Damage Assessment for Personal Injuries. Working paper, University of Missouri at St. Louis.

18 Definition from the Standards of Practice for the International Association of Rehabilitation Professionals, IALP Section.

19 Brookshire, M. L., Slesnick, F., & Ward, J. O. *The Plaintiff and Defense Attorney's Guide to Understanding Economic Damages*. Lawyers & Judges Publishing Company, Inc.

20 Brookshire, M. L., Luthy, M. R., & Slesnick, F. L. (2009). A 2009 survey of forensic economists: Their methods, estimates, and perspectives. *Journal of Forensic Economics, 21*(1), 5–34.

21 Foster, E. M., & Skoog, G. R. (2004). The Markov assumption for worklife expectancy. *Journal of Forensic Economics, 17*(2), 167–83.

22 Skoog, G. R., Ciecka, J. E., & Krueger, K. V. (2011). The Markov process model of labor force activity: Extended tables of central tendency, shape, percentile points, and bootstrap standard errors. *Journal of Forensic Economics, 22*(2), 165–229.

23 Skoog, G. R., & Ciecka, J. E. (2001). The Markov (increment-decrement) model of labor force activity: Extended tables of central tendency, variation, and probability intervals. *Journal of Forensic Economics, 11*(1), 1–21.

24 AICPA. (2012). Discount rates, risk, and uncertainty in economic damages calculations. AICPA Forensic and Valuation Services Practice Aid.

25 Ireland, T. R. (2004). The Role of a Forensic Economist in a Damage Assessment for Personal Injuries. Working paper, University of Missouri at St. Louis.

26 Ibid.

27 Martin, G. D. (2011). *Determining Economic Damages.* James Publishing.

28 AICPA. (2011). The 2011 Forensic and Valuation Services Trend Survey.

29 Internet Crime Complaint Center. (2011). 2011 Internet Crime Report.

30 Moscaritolo, A. (Jul. 26, 2010). Cybercrime costs businesses $3.8 million per year. *SC Magazine*.

31 National Institute of Justice. (2008). *Electronic Crime Scene Investigation: A Guide for First Responders*, 2nd Ed., NIJ Special Report.

32 Ibid.

33 Rothstein, B. J., Hedges, R. J., & Wiggins, E. C. (2007). *Managing the Discovery of Electronic Information: A Pocket Guide for Judges.* Federal Judicial Center.

34 AICPA. (2012). Computer and Forensic Services and the CPA Practitioner. Forensic and Valuation Services Section, 2010–2012 Forensic Technology Task Force.

35 Rothstein, B. J., Hedges, R. J., & Wiggins, E. C. (2007). *Managing the Discovery of Electronic Information: A Pocket Guide for Judges.* Federal Judicial Center.

36 National Park Service. (2010). Digital Storage Media. *Conserve O Gram, 22*(5).

37 AICPA. (2012). Computer and Forensic Services and the CPA Practitioner. Forensic and Valuation Services Section, 2010–2012 Forensic Technology Task Force.

38 Nelson, B., & Phillips, A. (2008). *Guide to Computer Forensics and Investigations,* 3rd Ed. Course Technology, Cengage Learning.

39 AICPA. (2012). Computer and Forensic Services and the CPA Practitioner. Forensic and Valuation Services Section, 2010–2012 Forensic Technology Task Force.

40 Ibid.

41 National Institute of Justice. (2004). Forensic Examination of Digital Evidence: A Guide for Law Enforcement. NIJ Special Report.

42 AICPA. (2012). Computer and Forensic Services and the CPA Practitioner. Forensic and Valuation Services Section, 2010–2012 Forensic Technology Task Force.

43 Pachghare, V. K. (2010). *Cryptography and Information Security.* PHI Learning Private Limited.

44 Nelson, B., & Phillips, A. (2008). *Guide to Computer Forensics and Investigations,* 3rd Ed. Course Technology, Cengage Learning.

45 National Institute of Justice. (2004). Forensic Examination of Digital Evidence: A Guide for Law Enforcement. NIJ Special Report.

46 Beek, C. (2011). Introduction to File Carving. McAfee White Paper.

47 AICPA. (2011). The 2011 Forensic and Valuation Services Trend Survey.

Glindex (A Combined Glossary and Subject Index)

A

B

C

D

E

F

G

H

I

J

K

L

M

Measures of central tendency, 262–263
Measures of variability, 262, 263
Median. The center point of a data set, 262–263
Mediation. A nonbinding informal process wherein a mediator evaluates the arguments of both sides and helps the parties reach common ground, 30, 224–225
Medical expenses, compensatory damages for, 361
Memorandum of interview. The final document resulting from the memorialization of interview notes, 77
Memorializing. The process of transcribing interview notes into a permanent document for file, 77
Message during the communication process, 72
Meta model of white-collar crime, 151, 152
Metadata. Describe, explain, locate, or otherwise facilitate the retrieval, use, or management of an information resource, 370
Method. A regular, systematic way of doing something, 230
Method of proof. The means by which evidence is developed and presented to establish (or not) the requisite degree of belief or standard of proof, 349–357
  direct method of proof, 349–351
  indirect method of proof, 351–356, 357
  indirect methods and the courts, 357
  net worth method of proof, 351
  selection of, 356–357
Micro Strategy, 103
Microsoft Access, 242, 274–275, 276
Microsoft Excel, 240, 242, 274–275, 276
Microsoft PowerPoint, 240
Microsoft SmartDraw, 240
Microsoft Visio, 240
Mindset. A mental state that evolves from education, experience, prejudices, and other life experiences, 3–4
Minkow, Barry, 95–97
Mobile phone trends, 375
Mode. The most frequently occurring value in a data set, 262–263
Money laundering, 147
Mortgage fraud, 147
Mountain State Sporting Goods, Inc., 176–225
  accounting policies, 179–180
  customer service, 178
  engagement, 180–181
  fraud investigation, 181–225
  key employees, compensation, and benefits, 179
  management, 178–179
  officers' compensation, 179
  organization and ownership, 177
  pawn items, 178, 179, 223–224
  products and services, 178
  suspicions of fraud, 176

N

NACVA. *See* National Association of Certified Valuators and Analysts
NASBA. *See* National Association of State Boards of Accountancy
National Association of Certified Valuators and Analysts (NACVA)
  AICPA standards vs., 305
  forensic accounting credentials, 14
  professional standards, 302–303, 333–334, 381
National Association of State Boards of Accountancy (NASBA), 101, 304
National Institute of Justice (NIJ), 374
Nature of the assignment, preengagement considerations, 51
Nature of the engagement, 54, 299
Negatively skewed, 265
Net asset value (NAV) method. Determines a company's value as the difference between the fair market value of its assets and the fair market value of its liabilities, 330–331
Net income, research studies applying Benford's Law, 278
Net worth calculation, 353
Net worth method of proof
  Capone case, 2, 352–353
  courts and, 357
Neutral third parties. Those having some knowledge but no involvement in an event, 78
Neutralization. A type of rationalization that proposes denial, condemnation, and higher loyalty as means by which offenders neutralize their role in a crime, 155
NLRB v. Weingarten, 79
Noise in the communication process, 72
Noneconomic damages. Nonmonetary losses such as pain, suffering, emotional distress, loss of companionship, and loss of enjoyment life, 359
Nonfinancial measures, 104
Nonoperating assets. Assets not regularly employed in business operations, 333
Normal distribution. A symmetric data distribution in which the mean, median, and mode are all equal, 266
Normalizing adjustments. Adjustments to historical income statements or balance sheets that are necessary to reflect economic reality, 332

O

OASDI Trustees Report, 364
Objectivity. A mindset in which an accountant is neutral (unbiased) and intellectually honest, 50
  ACFE Code of Professional Standards, 301
  AICPA Principles of Professional Conduct, 298
  AICPA Rules of Professional Conduct, 299
  NACVA Professional Standards, 302
  professional responsibility failures, 308
Objectivity principle. Requirement that accounting transactions be supported by objective (arm's-length transaction) evidence, 100
Observations, 80–82
  auditory, 81
  legal, 80–81
  pretexts, 81–82
  public records, 81
  questioned documents, 82
  value of, 80
  visual, 80–81
Ohio Rules of Evidence, 296–297
Online research, 59

P

Q

R

S

Credits

Chapter 1: page 1, © Everett Collection Historical/Alamy; page 2, © Bettmann/CORBIS; page 10, Sean Nel/Shutterstock

Chapter 2: page 24, © klikk-Fotolia.com; page 25, © Image Source Plus/Alamy; page 28, © OJO Images Ltd/Alamy

Chapter 5: page 95, Denis Poroy/AP Images

Chapter 6: page 152, © Sergey Ilin/Fotolia